Learning and Memory

Second Edition

John F. Hall
The Pennsylvania State University

Allyn and Bacon

Boston London Sydney Toronto

Series Editor: John-Paul Lenney
Series Editorial Assistant: Susan S. Brody
Production Administrator: Annette Joseph
Production Coordinator: Susan Freese
Editorial-Production Service: TKM Productions
Cover Administrator: Linda K. Dickinson
Cover Designer: Richard Hannus

Library of Congress Cataloging-in-Publication Data

Hall, John Fry
  Learning and memory / John F. Hall.—2nd ed.
    p. cm.
  Rev. ed. of: An invitation to learning and memory. c1982.
  Bibliography: p.
  Includes index.
  ISBN 0-205-11712-0
  1. Learning, Psychology of. 2. Memory. 3. Conditioned response.
4. Psychology, Comparative. I. Hall, John Fry Invitation
to learning and memory. II. Title.
BF318.H35 1988
153.1--dc19   88-18688
                                                          CIP

Printed in the United States of America

10 9 8 7 6 5 4 3 2 1   93 92 91 90 89 88

Brief Contents

Contents

chapter three ▶

chapter four ▶

chapter five ▶

chapter six ►

Instrumental Conditioning: Acquisition and Extinction of Positive and Negative Reinforcement Tasks   137

chapter seven ►

Punishment and Avoidance Conditioning Tasks   165

chapter eight ►

Stimulus Generalization and Discrimination   191

chapter nine ►

Discrimination Learning: General Considerations   209

Preface

The learning and memory literature is so extensive that many authors of learning texts have made the decision to limit their coverage to a single area (e.g., classical conditioning, animal learning, human memory, etc.). I believe, however, that students, particularly those who are unable to take additional learning and memory courses, should have the opportunity to become acquainted with as many of the basic learning and memory topics as possible. Therefore, my objective in writing this text is to provide as wide a coverage as possible, consonant with appropriate depth, that can be covered in a single semester.

Some time ago, I was convinced that learning and memory principles were basically the same, regardless of the type of task employed by the investigator. Now I am not as sanguine that such is the case. In keeping with this point of view, I believe the most appropriate organization has been to examine separately the varying paradigms or procedures that have been traditionally included in the study of learning and memory.

The conceptual framework I have adopted in the examination of learning and memory can be described as functional. This position emphasizes the identification of empirical relationships that exist between an independent variable that has been manipulated by an investigator and the dependent variable—the behavior of the experimental subject from which a specific learning or memory process is inferred. Such an approach means that environmental (or stimulus) and internal variables (or motivational and/or cognitive processes) be identified (or hypothesized) in order to determine their contribution to learning and memory processes, and ultimately to performance.

This approach does not ignore the role of cognitive processes since I believe that they have made an immeasurable contribution to a better understanding of learning and memory processes. But like other central-state constructs, I believe it is important to conceptualize cognitive processes, at least for the most part, as intervening variables, with their measurement tied to specific antecedent and consequent observables. In certain instances, cognitive processes have been treated by some investigators as metaphors—as representations of what theorists assume is taking place when material is placed in memory and later remembered.

Plan for the Text

Chapter One of *Learning and Memory* describes early experimental learning and memory studies. In addition, appropriate definitions of the constructs of learning, retention, and memory are provided. The next three chapters cover classical conditioning. Chapter Two examines the Pavlovian procedure as well as extensions, including second-order conditioning and autoshaping (or sign tracking). Chapter Three considers how classical conditioning takes place as a function of the contribution of stimulus and cognitive variables, and Chapter Four provides a discussion of a variety of theoretical issues. In each of these chapters, human conditioning studies are presented along with animal experiments in order to provide a more complete picture of the conditioning process.

Chapters Five, Six, and Seven cover the varying instrumental and/or operant conditioning paradigms that have been employed in laboratory studies. Stimulus, motivational, and cognitive variables, all related to both the acquisition and extinction of such conditioning, have been identified. Chapter Eight is concerned with the process of stimulus generalization and how it influences instrumental conditioning.

Chapters Nine and Ten are devoted to discrimination learning. Chapter Nine considers such learning as a function of stimulus and motivational variables; Chapter Ten emphasizes the role of cognitive processes, as well as provides an examination of the concept of choice. The application and generalization of instrumental and operant conditioning principles are discussed in Chapter Eleven.

Chapters Twelve and Thirteen present the functional approach to the study of verbal learning, retention, and forgetting. Chapter Fourteen describes the nature and function of memory as viewed from an information processing position, with discussion centering on the concepts of encoding, storage, and retrieval. Chapter Fifteen considers memory for prose in which the information processing position also plays an important role. Chapter Sixteen covers the learning and retention of motor skills.

Features of This New Edition

Inasmuch as this book is a revision of a previous one, it is appropriate to identify similarities and differences between the two editions. My goal in writing and my conceptual approach to the study of learning and memory remain the same as presented in my first edition. But substantial differences between the two editions can be found, particularly in the organization of the first eleven chapters.

In the first chapter, the student is introduced not only to Ebbinghaus and Pavlov as pioneers in the study of learning and memory but also to the works of Thorndike and Watson and the later contributions of Tolman, Hull, and Skinner.

Classical conditioning is considered as a separate paradigm from instrumental and operant conditioning; three chapters are devoted to the former and four chapters to the latter. A notable feature of the classical conditioning chapters is the consideration of a variety of theoretical issues not covered in the first edition. I discuss such topics as the kind of association that is formed, the selective character of the associative relationship, the nature of the conditioned response, and the role of pairing or contingency in the establishment of a conditioned response. Two classical conditioning models—the established Wagner-Rescorla model and the more recent formulation proposed by Prokasy—are also presented.

Four chapters are devoted to an examination of instrumental and operant conditioning. The organization of this material centers around five paradigms: (1) positive reinforcement, (2) negative reinforcement, (3) punishment, (4) avoidance, and (5) omission training.

This edition devotes two chapters to discrimination learning, since current research reveals a great deal of interest by experimenters with the discrimination process. Experiments employing the delayed matching to sample task (DMTS) and the radial maze from which the operation of a memorial process has been inferred are discussed. The application and generalization of instrumental and operant conditioning principles are considered in Chapter Eleven, with the revised organization of this chapter centering on answers to three questions: (1) Do learning and memory processes play as important a role in determining behavior as learning theorists have believed? (2) Can laboratory findings be generalized to the nonlaboratory environment? and (3) Can the experimental results obtained with animals be generalized to humans?

The chapters on verbal learning and memory and motor skills remain similar to those found in the first edition, although one chapter has been devoted solely to memory for prose.

Overall, this edition provides a more complete historical account of the development of constructs that are of basic importance in the study of learning and memory. Cognitive processes have been given due consideration, although not to the exclusion of stimulus and motivational variables. Finally, consideration has been given to the experimental findings and theoretical positions that have appeared in the learning and memory literature after the first edition was published.

Acknowledgments

I am indebted to many individuals for their help with this edition. In particular, I would like to thank Stephen R. Coleman (Cleveland State University), Kenneth L. Leicht (Illinois State University), Gayle A. Olson (University of New Orleans), Michael J. Scavio (California State University, Fullerton), and Arno F. Wittig (Ball State University) for their many constructive comments which helped to make this a better text. Very special thanks must be given to my wife, Jean. Without her patience and help, beginning with the typing of the first rough draft, and continuing through the compilation of the indexes, all of this would not have been possible.

chapter one

▶

Introduction

In the fall of 1980, a young woman was found in a city park in Florida, nude, emaciated, and near death. She was taken to a state hospital and over a period of several months was gradually nursed back to health. The discovery of the woman in the park produced only a short story in the local newspaper, but after her physical rehabilitation she obtained national attention when her story was picked up by the wire services. Appearances on national television networks followed. Why? Because she had lost her memory. She could not remember a single thing that had taken place prior to her being discovered in the park; she had no recollection of who she was, where she lived, her schooling, work, or anything about her earlier personal life. The psychiatrist who was working with her stated that she had total amnesia, which is an infrequently found occurrence.

During the past decade, numerous newspaper and magazine articles, television reports, and books have described Alzheimer's disease, an affliction that has been described as the disease of the century. Perhaps its most debilitating effect is the gradual loss of memory. Minor lapses—an individual forgets where she left her glasses, or where he placed his car keys—represent the disease's first stage. But these minor lapses blend into more serious ones—an expert carpenter may not be able to construct a simple wooden box or a grandmother who once baked hundreds of cookies over the Christmas holidays cannot remember how to begin. As the disease progresses, individuals forget where they live, the schools they attended, the names of their grandchildren; even one's spouse is considered a stranger. Eventually, their memory loss progresses to the point where almost everything they have learned has been forgotten so that they cannot perform even the simplest of activities. Remaining in the home becomes impossible and as a result these individuals must be placed in an institution for their care.

Cases such as these have resulted in many of us having a greater appreciation of the role that learning and memory processes play in our lives. From an evolutionary point of view, it is likely that the emergence of human beings as the most complex organisms on this planet has stemmed from the superior development of learning and memory processes. Certainly the emphasis on education and schooling found in the Western culture is testimony to the importance that society places on these processes. But the role of learning and memory extends far beyond formal educational experiences. Books on improving memory often make the best-seller list. Procedures have been developed to teach people how to learn to control their physiological responses (e.g., blood pressure and heart rate) as well as emotional responses. And it has been generally accepted that many of our anxieties, fears, and phobias have been learned. The medical community has become increasingly aware that learned behaviors contribute to many of our illnesses and has urged investigators to increase their efforts in their search for ways of teaching people how to modify their behavior so as to produce sound health habits—not smoking, abstaining from drugs, limiting alcohol intake, eating properly, and engaging in appropriate exercise patterns.[1]

The comprehension and appreciation of learning and memory processes has been explicitly accepted as a major objective in the development of a better society. As a first step in the understanding of this topic, let us trace the development of our interest in learning and memory.

Some Landmarks in the Study of Learning and Memory ►

Interest in learning and memory can be traced to the Greeks' concern with memory focused on the study of mnemonics. (A *mnemonic* is a technique used to improve memory.) In an age before printing, when the spoken word was the basic form of communication, it was necessary for Greek orators to memorize their material. What could be more helpful than methods that would assist in this demanding endeavor, particularly since one's speech might last for hours? The mnemonic techniques used by the Greeks have been passed on and even now continue to be employed as the foundation for many current memory systems.

One system, identified as the *method of loci*, has the individual associate terms or ideas with discrete geographical locations, preferably familiar places. For example, each item in a list of groceries to be purchased might be associated with the various rooms in your house. First, entering the kitchen, you might visualize a loaf of bread placed in the middle of the floor, while a bottle of milk dangles from the ceiling. Moving to the dining room, you would see a bottle of mustard had been spilled on the dining room table. Proceeding to the living room, you might envision a large light bulb protruding from one of chairs, and so on. At the supermarket, you would visually "walk" through your house, recalling the items associated with each of the rooms.

---

[1] For example, the Centers of Disease Control have estimated that about half the mortality arising from the leading causes of death in the United States can be strongly linked to long-term, learned patterns of behavior.

Early Experimental Studies

The study of mnemonics, however, did not play a role on the early *experimental* examination of learning and memory. Rather, the antecedents for such an examination are found in the works of Gustav Fechner, a German physiologist and physicist who published the *Elements of Psychophysics* in 1860.

Fechner's general objective was to work out the precise relationship between mind and body (matter), a problem that occupied the attention of many philosophers. Fechner believed that a relationship could be demonstrated between the physical characteristics of a stimulus (matter) and the sensations produced by the stimulus and received by the individual (mind). But it was necessary for him to place this point of view in such concrete form that it would persuade those who were wrestling with the problem. In an effort to do this, he embarked on a series of studies in which he demonstrated how the intensity of a visual stimulus (or the weight of an object) was related to the sensations the stimulus produced in an experimental subject.

Fechner's work did not provide philosophers with their long-sought solution to the problem of mind and body; however, it was the first successful instance of an individual being able to quantify a mental phenomenon (sensation). His investigations are noteworthy since they inspired Hermann Ebbinghaus, another German scientist, to extend the examination of mental processes to the areas of learning and memory.

The foundation for Ebbinghaus's work was the *philosophy of associationism*, as expressed by the nineteenth-century British philosophers. One of these was Thomas Brown, who in 1820 proposed twelve laws of mental association, three of which were considered as primary or basic and nine considered as secondary. The three primary laws of association were (1) contiguity, (2) similarity, and (3) contrast. These primary laws indicated that the association of any two items or elements would take place if they (a) occur together in time or space (contiguity), (b) resemble each other (similarity), or (c) are so juxtaposed as to emphasize their differences (contrast).

In the years 1879 to 1880 and 1883 to 1884, Ebbinghaus undertook an extensive series of experiments designed to measure the mental processes involved in human learning and memory. Before commencing, however, he had to solve several problems: deciding what kind of material to be learned, determining the type of learning task, and resolving how learning and memory should be measured. His answers to the first two questions were to invent the nonsense syllable, employing a number of them to form a list, thus making up the learning task.[2] The measurement problem was solved by Ebbinghaus counting the number of repetitions necessary (or the amount of time required) to learn a list. Following the original learning, Ebbinghaus measured memory for the list items by comparing the number of repetitions required to relearn the list with the number originally required to learn it. Ebbinghaus's experimental studies culminated in the publication of his classic monograph *Memory* (1885), which was translated into English in 1913. In the sections that follow we shall be primarily

---

[2] The nonsense syllable, invented by Ebbinghaus, has been generally accepted by current investigators to consist of two consonants separated by a vowel; words formed by this procedure are excluded from consideration.

concerned with the area of animal learning, encompassing classical and instrumental conditioning. Further discussion of the experimental work in verbal learning will be covered in Chapters Twelve through Fourteen.

Not all of the early experimental investigations of learning and memory were directed toward determining how humans learn and remember lists of nonsense syllables. A little more than a decade after Ebbinghaus's work, the studies of Ivan Pavlov and Vladimir Bechterev, using animals as experimental subjects, also made substantial contributions to an understanding of learning and memory processes.

Ivan Pavlov was a Russian physiologist who was awarded the Nobel prize for his studies in the physiology of digestion. While examining the contribution of salivation to the digestive process, Pavlov noted that as he walked across the laboratory floor the sound of his footsteps would elicit salivation in those dogs who had frequently served as his experimental subjects. Pavlov believed that salivation in response to such a stimulus was a "psychic secretion," so designated to differentiate it from salivation elicited by traditionally used stimuli (e.g., meat powder or a weak solution of acid placed on the animal's tongue).

The discovery that salivation could be elicited by a so-called neutral stimulus so aroused Pavlov's interest that he devoted the remainder of his life studying this phenomenon. Basic to such study was the establishment of an experimental methodology designed to examine how such learned responding took place. The general procedure he devised was to present his animals with a tone (produced by a tuning fork) and, a few seconds later, a small quantity of meat powder. After presenting both stimuli in this sequence for a number of trials, Pavlov found that the presentation of the tone alone would elicit salivation—a response that he identified as a *conditioned reflex*.

Pavlov believed that the onset of the tone had to precede presentation of the meat powder in order for conditioning to take place. In order to demonstrate that such was the case, a control group was presented with a backward pairing of the stimuli (i.e., the meat powder was presented ten, five, or only a single second before the onset of the tone). Using this procedure, conditioning was found not to take place; thus Pavlov found that the temporal relationship between the two stimuli was important in establishing a conditioned reflex, or a conditioned response as it has now been identified. In summary, the capacity of the tone to elicit the conditioned response was used to infer the presence of a learning process since the organism after training responded to a stimulus that previously was ineffective in eliciting that response.[3]

Working at about the same time as Pavlov was another Russian investigator, Vladimir Bechterev, whose methodology was similar to that used by Pavlov. Bechterev noted that if a cold stimulus was suddenly applied to the skin of a dog, the animal would catch its breath, which is a familiar reflex. It was then noted that if another stimulus was repeatedly applied at the same time as the cold, the other stimulus would serve as a substitute for the natural stimulus in eliciting the reflex. Another series of experiments followed, in which shock was used as the natural stimulus; the response elicited was voluntary—foot withdrawal. Bechterev found that if a neutral stimulus,

---

[3] We shall discuss Pavlov's procedures and the terminology that is employed in conditioning studies in Chapter Two.

such as a bell, was presented just prior to the onset of shock, the response of withdrawing the limb in order to avoid the painful stimulus was rapidly acquired. Bechterev's finding indicated that the learning of skeletal responses could be also investigated— responses of a voluntary nature in contrast to salivation, an involuntary response. Bechterev's work also represented an early examination of *avoidance learning*, a paradigm that many subsequent experimenters have used.

By the 1900s, investigators in the United States became interested in examining the nature of the learning process, but their experimental procedures differed markedly from those of their European counterparts; the studies of Ebbinghaus, Pavlov, and Bechterev had not been translated into English, so few details of their work were known. Let us briefly examine the contributions of some of the more prominent U.S. experimenters.

E. L. Thorndike

E. L. Thorndike was the most prominent of early American investigators, publishing his monograph *Animal Intelligence* in 1898. Like Pavlov, Thorndike conducted a large number of experiments with animals; unlike Pavlov, Thorndike frequently used cats as his subjects. The task Thorndike utilized was a puzzle box (see Figure 1–1), a specially designed wooden cage with a latched door that could be opened from the inside if the animal pulled on a loop of string hanging from the top. (Other mechanisms to open the

Figure 1–1
Thorndike's puzzle box for studying trial and error behavior of cats. Escape from the box was made contingent on various responses.

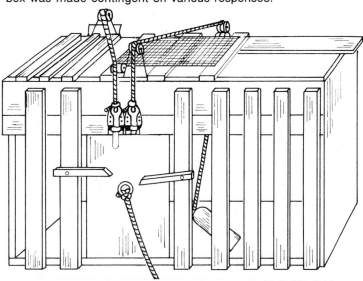

door were also used in some of his experiments.) Hungry cats were placed inside the box and were motivated to get out when the experimenter placed a piece of fish in full view just outside the door. The cats initially responded with a variety of behaviors but eventually would come to pull the looped string that would release the door. On subsequent trials the cats would confine their responses to the general location of the string; thus the pulling of the loop and the opening of the door took place in progressively shorter periods of time.

In the early 1900s, *psychology* was defined as the study of consciousness. In keeping with this definition, Thorndike's (1898) early concern was with "what is in an animal's mind, when, having profited by numerous experiences, he had formed the association and does the proper act when put in a certain box" (pp.98–99). Thorndike believed that those attributes that are part of human consciousness, such as memory and judgment, were derived from the associative processes observed in lower animals, and he engaged in some interesting speculations on the differences existing between animal and human consciousness.

Soon thereafter, as evidenced in his revision of *Animal Intelligence* (1911), Thorndike's interest in the mental activity and consciousness of animals declined; in keeping with the behavioristic movement led by John B. Watson (discussed in the next section), Thorndike focused his interest on analyzing the organism's learned behavior. Thorndike described what was taking place in his puzzle box studies (as well as in other learning experiments he conducted) as *trial and error behavior*, believing, in contrast to Pavlov's emphasis on conditioned response learning, that it represented the most frequently observed type of learning in animals. More generally, Thorndike proposed that learning involved the establishment of connections between situations, or stimuli (S) and responses (R). Such associations between the S and R took place according to certain principles or laws, the most important of these being the law of effect. In this law, Thorndike maintained that the connection (or association) between the S and R would be strengthened if the response had the effect of producing a satisfying state of affairs for the animal. In contrast, the connection would be weakened if the response had the effect of producing an annoying state of affairs.

The Rise of Behaviorism ►

In the early 1900s, the dominant school of psychology was structuralism, led by E. B. Titchener. Psychologists of this school believed that the subject matter of psychology was the mind or conscious content. Their approach was to examine conscious content as the chemist would analyze a compound—by breaking it down into its elements. Using this mental chemistry approach, three components of the mind were identified: (1) sensations, (2) images, and (3) feelings or affect. These components, or elements, made up the basic structure of consciousness, and different combinations of these elements were believed to be responsible for making up all of an individual's experiences. The method of investigating conscious content was introspection—the procedure whereby any experience could be analyzed and separated into its respective elements.[4]

John B. Watson

Structuralism soon came under attack by investigators who believed that conscious content could not be used as a subject matter upon which to base a science. Even if one accepted its reality, experimenters pointed out that it was subject only to private inspection, and science demanded public verification. Moreover, applying the introspective method to experiments conducted with animals was a hazardous undertaking since it was necessary for experimenters to try to determine the animal's introspective experience. (We have already noted Thorndike's turning away from the study of an animal's associations to the examination of its behavior.)

John B. Watson, like Thorndike, was also interested in animal behavior; in fact, his book *Behavior: An Introduction to Comparative Psychology* (1914) has been regarded as the most influential book in bringing about the rapid growth of animal psychology. This volume redirected psychology's interest from conscious experience to *behavior*. Watson wrote that "on account of its bearing upon human training, learning in animals is probably the most important topic in the whole study of behavior" (p. 45).

Thorndike, as well as others, was interested in studying behavior during this time, but it was Watson's constant and strident criticism of the structuralists approach and his total rejection of the introspective method that ultimately resulted in the redefinition of psychology as the science of behavior. Two basic tenets emerged from Watson's position. First, he stated that investigators should begin with what they can observe and postulate as little as possible beyond that. Thus introspection was rejected as an appropriate method for psychologists to use, and the employment of mentalistic and/ or subjective constructs was abandoned. Watson argued that no one can "see" the thoughts and feelings of another person; therefore, these processes, which are available only to the individual, cannot be used as a subject matter for science. Such constructs as images, feelings, and memory were all considered private and unsuitable for use in a science of behavior.

Second, Watson proposed that the scientific investigation of behavior be conducted by analyzing any act, whether learned or innate, in terms of a stimulus and a response. The environment provided a stimulus that elicited a response in the organism; a *response* was defined as some movement of a muscle or secretion of a gland. The task of

---

[4] We should point out that Titchener cautioned that the use of introspection by the trained structuralist should not be confused with the personal thoughts and feelings that were frequently associated with the usual use of the term. Rather, the introspective method was concerned with the observer attending to and analyzing the stimulus in terms of only those elements of which it was comprised. Thus an individual who reported that her conscious content of a four-legged piece of furniture to be a *table* was failing to distinguish what she as an individual knew about the stimulus from her immediate introspective experience, which provided her with only the color, brightness, and particular spatial pattern of the object.

the psychologist was to (1) determine the stimulus that was responsible for eliciting a response and (2) predict the response from one's knowledge of the nature of the stimulus.

Watson's early work suggested that the conditioning experiments of Pavlov and Bechterev were examples of objective methods that should be used by investigators to examine learned behavior. Later, Watson (1924) regarded conditioning as not only the simplest form of learning but also as the basic process to which all learned responding was reducible. Thus the skills that characterized typewriting, piano playing, and so on were nothing more than a chaining together or concatenation of conditioned responses.

It is difficult to convey the importance that Watson's work held not only for psychologists but for the public as well. When Watson's book *Behaviorism* (1924) was reviewed, the *New York Tribune* indicated it to be perhaps the most important book ever written, and the *New York Times* reported that the book marked an epoch in the intellectual history of humanity.

The Post-Watson Era

During the 1930s and into the late 1950s, most learning and memory research was conducted within Watson's stimulus-response framework and could be divided into two major areas. First, some investigators preferred to follow the work of Ebbinghaus, studying verbal learning and memory by using lists of nonsense syllables or words as the experimental material to be learned. These experimenters have often been identified as functionalists since their major concern was to examine the functional relationship between the learning of the list and the type of material utilized or the conditions of practice. Inasmuch as we shall discuss the area of verbal learning and memory in later chapters, we shall delay further consideration of this topic until that time.

The second area was that a number of experimenters chose to continue to work in the tradition of Pavlov, Thorndike, and Watson, using animals as their experimental subjects and employing relatively simple learning tasks that they believed would best illustrate the nature of the learning process. Their interest was not in animal learning per se; rather, their objective was in finding laws or principles of learning and memory that presumably had relevance for all organisms, including humans. This period began in the early thirties, reaching its zenith during the next decade but continuing to exert some, albeit declining, influence in the years that followed.

The three men who were the most influential during these years, often identified as the neobehavioristic era, were E. C. Tolman, B. F. Skinner, and C. L. Hull, with all three writing landmark texts.

E. C. Tolman

In 1932, Tolman published *Purposive Behavior in Animals and Men*. The proper subject matter for psychology, Tolman wrote, was behavior; however, such behavior was molar as well as purposive. By *molar*, Tolman meant that behavior should be described in terms of acts—behavior in which the organism was engaging, as well as the goal object sought (e.g., an author writes a novel in order to earn money and acclaim). Tolman rejected Watson's emphasis on the action of specific muscles and glands as psychology's subject matter. Such responses, Tolman believed, were more the concern of the physiologist.

Molar behavior was also *purposive*. This meant that the organism was interested in achieving some goal or end and that such behavior generally persisted until the goal object was reached. Such persistence usually meant that an organism's behavior was variable as well as teachable, or, as Tolman described, docile. He believed that Thorndike's cats had purpose since they persisted in their activity until one of their responses released the latch that opened the cage door, thus enabling them to secure food. In summary, the concept of purpose involved both persistence and docility.

Tolman assumed that any complete *act* was initiated by an environmental stimulus as well as the organism's existing physiological state. Certain processes were then set in motion, with behavior being the end result. But what was the nature of these processes? Tolman defined them as *intervening variables*—processes that intervened between the antecedent (or stimulus) conditions and the resulting consequences (behavior). Two such intervening variables that were basic to his system were expectancy and demand. *Demand* was identified or inferred from the change in behavior that arose as a result of changing the deprivation state of the animal. Thus the demand for the goal object (e.g., food) would be expected to increase as the animal experienced a greater and greater number of hours of food deprivation.

Tolman inferred that learning consisted of the development of expectancies—what leads to what. But how was an expectancy transformed into behavior? Tolman believed that when there was a demand to be met or a motive to be satisfied, the organism would use its expectancies in order to behave appropriately. Such a position meant that it was necessary to distinguish between the presence of learning (or an expectancy) and the subsequent behavior (or performance) that was related to it. To illustrate the distinction, consider a student who had diligently studied for an examination. Upon entering the room where the test is to be given, the student becomes so nervous and anxious that she is unable to remember any of the material that had been learned the evening before. At the end of the class period, after walking out of the examination room, the student recalls many of the answers to the questions that were asked—answers that she could not remember only a few minutes earlier. It is obvious that the student had learned the material, although it was not evident from her performance in the classroom. It was only later that the student's performance was in keeping with what had been learned.

Tolman's theoretical position, which was not given precise formulation, was overshadowed by Skinner's descriptive system and Hull's detailed S-R theory (described in the next sections). However, the learning-performance distinction, which was a basic tenet in Tolman's system, has been an integral aspect of virtually all learning theories that have followed. And many current psychologists have been inclined to believe that Tolman's emphasis on the role of cognitive processes represented a major contribution to a better understanding of the learning process. Such an emphasis on cognition has raised the question of why Tolman should be considered a behaviorist. The answer is that Tolman insisted that any inference about the presence or operation of cognitive processes be based on behavioral observations.

B. F. Skinner

Like other neobehaviorists, Skinner (1938) was interested in providing a descriptive and systematic account of those variables that controlled behavior. The variables he considered important were those found in the organism's environment; his system had no place either for mental states or for speculation about those physiological processes that many psychologists considered to provide a foundation for the organism's behavior.

Skinner felt that Pavlovian conditioning was of little importance in understanding the role of learning in behavior. He reasoned that only simple responses could be conditioned, and these represented only a small fraction of responses in the organism's behavioral repertoire.

Skinner believed that the kind of operation utilized by Thorndike in which the experimental subject was reinforced or rewarded for making a particular response was of far greater importance in understanding how adaptive behavior took place. Skinner identified such behavior as *operant* since the organism "operated" on its environment in order to secure reinforcement. (Others have termed this type of learning task *instrumental* since the organism's response is instrumental in securing reward.)

In analyzing the learning process, Thorndike and other learning investigators used puzzle boxes and mazes of varying complexity in order to observe how such learned responding took place. Skinner deemed that these kinds of apparatus were too complex to be of much value and as a result, invented the operant conditioning chamber, or *Skinner Box*. This was a very small experimental chamber in which a lever or stirrup was placed on one wall; beneath it was a food cup. When combined with a food delivery system, the apparatus could be programmed so that a depression of the lever would result in a food pellet falling into the cup. When Skinner began to use pigeons rather than rats as his experimental subjects, the apparatus was modified by replacing the lever with a plastic disk; pecking at the disk by the birds would result in a hopper of grain being made available for a fixed amount of time (e.g., ten seconds).

Inasmuch as it was possible for an experimental subject to press the bar (or peck at the disk) hundreds of times during a thirty-minute experimental session, Skinner devised a recording system that produced a tracing of the number of lever presses plotted against the length of time that the animal was in the experimental chamber. Such records are obtained with the use of a cumulative recorder. Figure 1–2 illustrates a Skinner Box used for rats.

In his analysis of the operant, Skinner believed that external stimuli did not elicit such responding. This position was consistent with the then current conceptualization of behavior in which psychologists assumed that all learned behavior could be analyzed into stimulus-response relationships. Rather than placing emphasis on the stimulus in his analysis of operant behavior, Skinner called attention to the role of reinforcement as being responsible for the strengthening of the response. Over the years, Skinner and his students have had much more to say about the varying conditions that influence operant responding, and we shall discuss these in subsequent chapters.

Figure 1-2
A close-up of the experimental chamber used with a rat or small squirrel monkey. Courtesy of Gerbrands Corporation, Arlington, Massachusetts.

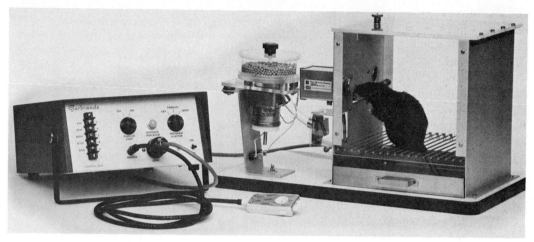

C. L. Hull

Like Watson, Hull was interested in examining behavior, and he studiously avoided any reference to the organism's conscious content. He was impressed with Pavlov's *Conditioned Reflexes*, which was translated into English in 1927. Hull's early papers were attempts to demonstrate that such mentalistic terms as *purpose,* which were used in describing everyday behavior, could be explained by using conditioning principles.

The nature of the Hullian system is found in his *Principles of Behavior* (1943). First, as the title indicates, Hull believed that he was providing a set of principles that generalized to humans even though the bulk of the research that was used to generate these principles was conducted with rats. Second, he assumed that learning, identified as *habit* in his system, consisted of the establishment of stimulus and response relationships. The organism's conscious content did not play any role in Hull's analysis of behavior. However, his system did emphasize the role of intervening variables and/or hypothetical constructs. Hull pointed out that physical and biological scientists frequently used intervening variables to represent entities that could not be physically seen or directly measured; nonetheless, such variables could be hypothesized to account for certain processes or entities (e.g., electrons and genes). Like Tolman (1932), Hull emphasized that behavioral scientists should do the same. He recognized that when such constructs were posited, they had to be anchored to some antecedent (stimulus) condition that could be measured, as well as to a consequent condition, namely, the organism's response, which was also measurable.

Finally, Hull provided a set of sixteen postulates that formed the basic structure of his theory. Some of the most important of these will be discussed in later sections of this book.[5]

Hull's *Principles* had a fundamental impact on the theoretical and experimental activity of investigators working in the area of learning. It is a tribute to Hull that from the time his *Principles* appeared until more than a decade later, his theory of learning literally dominated the scene, either as the focus of controversy or as a source of hypotheses for further experimental elaboration or evaluation.

Challenges to Neobehaviorism

All psychologists were not convinced that neobehaviorism in general, or Hull's *Principles* in particular, could explain how the learning process and its related construct, performance, operated. Shortly after Hull's volume was published and continuing for the next several decades, a host of theoretical arguments along with a variety of empirical findings appeared, which resulted in the steady decline of Hull's influence. Let us examine the nature of some of the arguments that were raised.

Many investigators, particularly the European ethologists, were critical of the laboratory setting that Hull and other U.S. investigators used to elucidate learning principles. Ethologists believed that learning was most adequately studied and accurately portrayed when animals were observed in their natural habitat. It was argued that the types of experimental apparatus and laboratory procedures were, because of their artificiality, inappropriate to use in any examination of the animal's learning process.

A more basic criticism was that associative mechanisms, presumably arising from the learning process, were unable to account for the learning of many complex types of tasks that were found in higher organisms, particularly in humans. It was pointed out that the learning of a language, for example, could not be viewed in terms of the establishment of associations—associations between what? Rather, such learning was conceptualized as a dynamic process that interacted with the organism's innate capacities, its previous experiences, and the present environment to produce behavior appropriate for the situation in which the organism found itself.

With regard to more specific objections, Hull assumed that associations could be established only between a stimulus and a response and that any stimulus could be attached to any response. Vigorous objections were raised to both assumptions. It was argued that if associations were established, they could be established between any two events—between one stimulus and another, between a response and a stimulus, or between two responses. Moreover, it was found that it was not always possible to attach any response to any stimulus; in many instances, there was a selectivity of stimuli and responses that could enter into an associative relationship.

In contrast to the neobehaviorists' framework utilized by many psychologists in the fifties and sixties, currently no single theoretical position can be said to dominate

---

[5] Hull published a brief revision of his behavior principles in *The Essentials of Behavior* (1951); another volume, *A Behavior System*, was published in 1952. It was Hull's *Principles of Behavior* (1943), however, that provided the foundation of his system.

the learning area. It is not surprising that Jenkins (1979), in commenting on contemporary research, wrote that "the specialization in research and theory makes it difficult to present a coherent picture of the whole enterprise" (p. 203).

At the risk of oversimplifying the current state of affairs, it is possible to provide a general description of several different approaches adopted by current experimenters. One group, as Dickinson (1980) has indicated, can be identified as behavior analysts; their objective is to formulate behavioral laws and principles that transcend the confines of the laboratory and the species of animal whose behavior is investigated. These analysts see their task as specifying the relationship between some physical event in the environment (the stimulus) and some acquired behavioral pattern (the response) without reference to mental processes.

A second group of investigators has rejected this approach since it is believed that the most interesting types of behavior are not susceptible to this type of analysis. Rather, learned behavior, at least the more complex type, is seen as a reflection of events operating at some other level, with cognitive processes (e.g., expectancy, surprise, etc.) making a basic contribution to the behavior under scrutiny. Moreover, it is recognized that learning may occur in the absence of any change in behavior, thus acknowledging the distinction between learning and performance that was originally posited by Tolman (1932). In fact, some investigators have shifted their basic objective from an examination of learned performance to one in which there is an attempt to understand the nature of the learning process itself. A related approach has been to consider stimuli as information and to examine how the organism goes about processing it. The information-processing position, broadly conceptualized, probably represents the most frequently adopted approach to the current study of learning and memory.

Finally, many experimenters have forsaken any attempt to identify and describe the operation of learning principles and have concentrated their efforts on relatively specific performance areas that appear to involve the learning process. Language performance in animals, the search and procuring of food (foraging), and taste aversion are examples of this circumscribed research effort.

Definitions of Learning, Retention, and Memory ▶

Although we have provided a brief historical summary of the study of learning and memory, we have not as yet defined these processes.

Learning

Learning, like respiration or digestion, is a biological process, undoubtedly of a neurological nature, the operation of which is inferred from changes taking place in the organism's behavior. All changes, however, cannot be used to infer the learning process.

For example, a behavior change may arise from maturation (defined as the growth and development of the nervous system), yet this process is basically different from learning. We shall not discuss in detail the various criteria used by investigators to differentiate learning from maturation, but certainly one factor has to do with the fact that learning involves the subject having some experience or interaction with the task to be learned. Thus it was necessary for Ebbinghaus to recite to himself the list of nonsense syllables several times prior to mastering the list; similarly, Pavlov's dogs required pairings of the tone and meat powder before they would salivate to the tone.

In our examination of the learning experiments, we shall note that experience (often identified as repetition or practice and appearing as learning trials) is a basic condition necessary for learning to take place. However, practice does not encompass all of the events or operations that result in learning. For example, one experimental subject may simply observe another subject making a learned response. Rats, cats, and monkeys, in addition to humans, all have been able to learn when their only practice consisted of watching or observing another organism successfully perform the act. As a result, it seems more appropriate to suggest that learning is dependent on experience, which includes but is not limited to practice. (See Box 1–1.)

In summary, we would define learning as a neurological process that arises from experience and is inferred from changes in the organism's behavior.[6] Such a definition is admittedly imprecise. It does not say anything about the nature of the neurological process, it does not define the specific characteristics of the experience that will result in learning, nor does it specify the kind of behavior change from which the learning process is inferred. These are questions that current investigators have been attempting to answer, and it is likely that their findings will eventually contribute to a more adequate definition of learning. However, as Hilgard (1951) wrote some years ago, "A precise definition of learning is not necessary so long as we agree that the inference to learning is made from changes in performance that are a result of training [experience] . . . the experiments themselves define the field" (p. 518).

Retention

Retention is intimately related to learning. The neurological process arising from the learning process persists in the organism for some period of time. When the subject is able to recognize, recall, or reproduce a response that had been learned at an earlier time, the process of retention is inferred from such behavior.

We should recognize that it is not possible to make any absolute distinction between the constructs of learning and retention. Performance of any learning or

---

[6] Material or skills that are learned are often retained for relatively long periods of time; thus some investigators have suggested that all definitions of learning should include some reference to the permanence of the process. However, there are a sufficient number of instances where the material learned has been retained for only a short period of time. For example, remembering a telephone number only long enough to permit the dialing of the digits suggests that the telephone number was learned but the forgetting took place quite rapidly. As a result, we believe that a definition of learning should not include any reference to the permanence of the process.

box 1-1

Thorndike (1898) was interested in determining if cats and chickens could learn to escape from a puzzle box or a confined area by observing a previously trained subject perform an appropriate escape response. He was unable to determine that any of his animals had learned by observing the responses of others. However, other experimenters have reported positive findings. Kinnaman (1902) provided one monkey with a box that could be opened by pulling out a plug that secured the lid. His subject failed to work the mechanism and gave up in despair. A second monkey was able to open the box by seizing the end of the plug with his teeth and pulling it out. The first monkey, after observing the action of the second, immediately solved the problem when given a second try. Over the years, experimenters have confirmed Kinnaman's findings that animals can learn by observation. (See Warden and Jackson, 1935; Herbert and Harsh, 1944; Corson, 1967; Jacoby and Dawson, 1969; and Menzel, 1978.)

Observational learning, or what Kling (1971) has described as *exposure learning*, never entered the mainstream of learning theory. One reason was the difficulty in assimilating observing behavior into the familiar stimulus-response paradigm, which emphasizes the importance of reinforcement for the acquisition of S-R relationships.

acquisition trial reflects not only the operation of a learning process on that trial but also involves the retention of material from earlier trials. But in spite of this difficulty in separating learning and retention, a distinction has been made between these constructs, which is related to the experimental operations that have been used. Investigators interested in examining the learning process provide their subjects with multiple trials and assume that the performance increments taking place over these trials reveal the learning process. In contrast, when examining retention, a number of trials are provided, followed by a time interval, usually measured in minutes, hours, or even days. This is followed by a trial (or trials) in which the subject's performance reflects the retention of the original material.

Memory

Ebbinghaus's (1885/1913) classic monograph was entitled *Memory*. For some years after its publication, the concept of memory was recognized as a basic construct in psychology and was generally used as a synonym of retention. But with the advent of behaviorism, Watson (1924) believed that the term *memory* was too closely associated with conscious content to be of value. He wrote that psychologists did not need the term *memory* variegated as it was with all kinds of philosophical and subjective connotations; he advocated the use of the term *retention*. The result was that the concept of memory disappeared from the literature for several decades. With the introduction of cognitive constructs in the psychological literature, *memory* again made its way into the psychologist's lexicon.

Some contemporary investigators have provided idiosyncratic definitions of memory, which we shall not discuss here but refer the reader to Tulving and Madigan (1970) and Howe (1970). Most generally, however, *memory* has been used as a synonym for retention and has been defined as the persistence of learned responding, with a retention test being used to measure such persistence.

Learning, Memory, and Performance

It has been readily apparent to many investigators that a change in the organism's behavior cannot be used to infer that learning has taken place. An individual may be unable to recall a name or a place immediately only to find that a few minutes later it comes to mind. The material had been learned but it was not immediately evident from the individual's performance. We may note, then, that there is not always an identity between learning and performance; as we indicated earlier, psychologists have been indebted to Tolman for calling attention to this distinction between the two constructs.

An experimental example of the learning-performance distinction is provided by an early revealing study conducted by Blodgett (1929). Blodgett gave three groups of rats one trial a day on a six-unit multiple T-maze. One group (control) was run for seven days; each animal was permitted to eat food in the goal box for three minutes on each trial. A second group (Experimental Group I) was also run for seven days; for the first two days this group did not find food in the goal box, but on the third day and each day thereafter, food was present. A third group (Experimental Group II) was treated similarly to Experimental Group I, except that reward was omitted for the first six days and introduced on the seventh. These animals were then run two additional days, with food in the goal box each day. Results are illustrated in Figure 1-3.

It may be noted that the discovery of food by Experimental Group I at the end of Trial 3 resulted in reduction in the error score on Trial 4, not unlike that found for the control group for Trial 4. This change in performance as a function of finding reward on a single trial is even more dramatically revealed by the reduction of error scores made by Experimental Group II on Trial 8. Since the control group's gradual reduction in errors gives rise to the inference that the learning process does not take place rapidly, the results of Blodgett's study have been used to distinguish between learning and performance. Learning was obviously taking place for all animals; changes in performance were related to the presence or absence of reward.

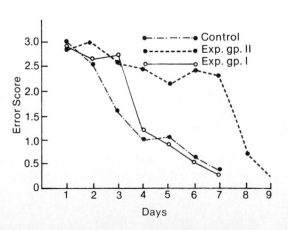

Figure 1-3
The influence of reward on maze learning. The control group has been reinforced on every trial. Experimental Group I had reward introduced on Trial 3, whereas Experimental Group II had reward introduced on Trial 7. Adapted from H. C. Blodgett, "The effect of the introduction of reward upon the maze performance of rats," *University of California Publications in Psychology*, 1929, 4, (8), 113-134. Reprinted by permission of the University of California Press.

An example of the distinction between performance and memory is found in the study of Tranel and Damasio (1985) in their work with patients who have prosopagnosis—the inability to recognize the faces of familiar persons. One of their subjects was a sixty-two-year-old woman who suffered a stroke and as a result could not recognize the faces of individuals she knew. In fact, she could not recognize even her own face. She had normal vision, with average reading and language abilities; she was also aware that a face was a face and could name its parts and distinguish differences among faces. But it was only through the use of other cues—hearing the individual's voice or remembering a specific feature of the face such as the presence of a mustache—that she was able to correctly identify the individual. In the authors' study, fifty black-and-white photographs were presented to the subject; eight represented faces of individuals with whom the patient was well acquainted (target faces) and the other forty-two were unfamiliar. In keeping with her disability, the patient was unable to recognize, by her oral response, any of the target faces. However, when the experimenters replaced the verbal response with a physiological one—the electrodermal response (EDR)—recognition of the target faces was observed. The authors had previously demonstrated that when the EDR was used as a response measure in neurologically sound subjects, familiar faces resulted in significantly elevated positive responses. If the EDR is accepted as a valid measure of memory, it appears that the visual memory of this woman was intact but that she was unable to perform, at least as far as providing appropriate verbal responses. The study of a second female patient, twenty years of age and suffering from the same disability, revealed similar findings. (See Box 1–2.)

box 1–2

An interesting everyday example of the distinction between learning and memory processes and performance can be noted in the newspaper account of a mentally retarded ten-year-old boy who spoke mostly in isolated words but began to converse in complete sentences after he encountered a talking Christmas tree. The tree, on display at a department store in Fargo, North Dakota, was wired with a microphone and speakers so that employees who were hidden from view could chat with shoppers.

"Duane usually talks with just a single word, usually not a lot of sentences," his teacher said in an interview. "But he saw the tree and really got excited about it. For a long time, we've told Duane that trees, motorcycles, lawnmowers—those things he takes an interest in—don't talk. But this time, the tree talked back to him and he really got excited and he's been talking in whole sentences ever since. He's done it before, but it hasn't been a constant thing."

Duane's teacher said the tree struck a responsive chord in Duane when he noted that another little boy was talking to it. Duane listened briefly and then said, "Hey tree." The tree asked, "Who are you?" and Duane answered with his name. He then asked, "What are you doing here, tree?" and the tree said, "Talking to you." An animated five-minute conversation followed, the teacher indicated. "Duane just responded to the tree. I've worked with him for four months. It was real spontaneous. He just kept on talking."

In this encounter, it is obvious that although the child had learned to speak in complete sentences, his performance did not so indicate until his interest or motivation stimulated him to do so. (From the *Tampa Tribune*, 12/16/1981.)

Performance: Acquisition and Maintenance

Having distinguished among the concepts of learning, memory, and performance, we should note several aspects of performance that have interested investigators, namely, *acquisition* and *maintenance*.

A look at a hypothetical performance curve reveals two phases, as shown in Figure 1-4. The first (A) has been designated as acquisition and consists of the organism gradually approaching a performance asymptote. Experimenters interested in the learning process have generally concentrated their attention on the acquisition phase since it is there that the change in the organism's performance over trials has been used to infer the operation of the learning process. Referring to Figure 1-3, the control group's reduction in errors over trials was used by Blodgett (1929) to make the inference that these animals were learning to make the correct response at each choice point in the maze.

The second phase (B), maintenance or steady state responding, consists of the subject's performance after nearing asymptote, continuing to remain at approximately this level. Most human responding is maintenance behavior. Such behavior generally exhibits little variability—a condition that enables individuals to operate successfully in their environment.

A Current Point of View ▶

In view of the behavioristic tradition involved in the study of learning and memory, as well as the challenges provided to neobehaviorism, what is the nature of the conceptual framework that we shall use on our study of learning and memory?

One obvious task for the investigator is to identify those conditions and/or variables that make a contribution to the learning process as well as to performance. These two objectives acknowledge the distinction between learning and performance, which we have previously discussed, as well as suggest the possibility that the some variables may contribute to performance but not necessarily to learning.

Regardless of the nature of the investigator's objectives, we must take our cues

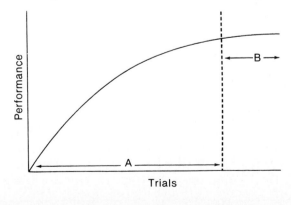

Figure 1-4
Hypothetical learning curve revealing acquisition phase (A) and maintenance phase (B).

about the nature of learning from the responses of the organism. Such responding takes place in a particular environmental setting—a stimulus situation. The behavior of the organism, as well as the characteristics of the stimulus situation within which the behavior is expressed, thus represent the foundation upon which the study of learning and memory must rest. In addition to the concepts of stimulus and response, we can add a third construct—the organism's central or organismic state. The organism's motivation, strategies, ideas, and so on are of fundamental importance in our understanding how and why learning takes place. The role of stimulus variables has been accepted since Pavlov's early work; however, the importance of recognizing the contribution of organismic or central state variables is a more recent development. Woodworth and Schlosberg (1954) wrote that the aim of the experimenter is to discover what goes on within the organism between the stimulus and the response. Many current experimenters have been interested in identifying central-state processes, which they have identified as cognitive. Regardless of how described, the specification of these processes (or variables) represents an integral aspect of our approach to the study of learning and memory.

In summary, three components provide a conceptual framework for examining the learning process: (1) the task, or stimulus situation; (2) the organismic, or central state, of the organism; and (3) the response. Let us look at these in greater detail.

The Task, or Stimulus Situation

The learning task can be described as an event or stimulus that is presented to the subject within an environmental context. Early investigators directed their attention primarily to examining some aspect of the task in an effort to determine its effect on learning and memory. For example, Ebbinghaus was interested in determining how learning was related to the length of the list he used, whereas Pavlov was concerned with how the intensity of a tone or the amount of meat powder contributed to the strength of a conditioned response.

When we examine the stimuli that make up the task, it is now apparent that the subject responds to only a few of the many stimuli that are present. Since there is a difference between the stimuli that make up the task and the specific stimuli to which the organism responds, many psychologists have distinguished between them. The stimuli provided to the subject by the experimenter have been designated as *nominal stimuli*, whereas *functional stimuli* are the stimuli as perceived and responded to by the subject. Each investigator hopes that there is an identity between the nominal and functional stimuli, but such is not always the case. One example of this disparity is found in a verbal-learning study reported by Underwood (1963). The task consisted of subjects learning to associate a trigram (three unrelated letters, such as *xft*) with a three-lettered word (e.g., *gas*). Eight of these trigram-word combinations made up the list. There was no physical similarity among the trigrams, since twenty-four different letters were used in constructing them. Following the completion of the task, the subjects were questioned as to how they had formed associations between each pair of items on the list. Underwood reported that a majority of the subjects stated they had used only the first letter of the trigram as the stimulus to cue the response. Although the nominal stimulus consisted of three letters, the functional stimulus for most subjects was only the initial one.

Experimenters have become increasingly aware of the importance of contextual stimuli in learning and memory experiments. Such stimuli refer to those aspects of the experimental environment that are present along with the stimuli that make up the learning task. A list of common nouns to be remembered may represent the learning task, whereas the contextual stimuli would include the type of apparatus that exposes the material to the subject, the nature of the room in which the experiment is conducted, the characteristics of the experimenter, and so on. All of these conditions make up the contextual stimuli, and recent experimental studies have demonstrated their contribution to influencing performance. One example of the role of context in the area of verbal learning has been that if a subject is asked to recall a list of words in a room that is substantially different from the room in which the material was originally learned, a marked reduction in retention can be noted. Quite obviously, the change in contextual stimuli has resulted in a performance decrement.

The Organism's Central, or Organismic, State

Many experimenters now believe that they must examine the organism's central state if an adequate understanding of the learning and memory process is to be achieved. It is obvious that experiments that deal with the analysis of only external stimuli—overt response relationships—are too limited in their approach to adequately understand what is going on when the organism learns. But if one acknowledges Watson's early concern about working with only those events that are observable, how does one go about investigating those constructs that are inaccessible to the experimenter?

One answer to this problem stems from the work of Hull (1943), who, as we have earlier noted, stressed the role of intervening variables or hypothetical constructs in behavior theory. Such posited constructs must be anchored or related to some antecedent (stimulus) condition that can be measured, as well as to a consequent condition, namely, the organism's response.

The use of an intervening variable approach has been of inestimable value in the psychologist's attempt to work with central-state variables or processes, particularly those that have been designated as cognitive and motivational. Let us examine one example.

Intuitively, most people acknowledge that motivation makes an important contribution to behavior—the success that individuals have in school, in athletics, or on the job is frequently attributed to motivation. *Webster's* defines a *motive* as "a need or desire which prompts an organism to act in a certain way." Since needs and desires are not subject to direct observation and measurement, the psychologist's approach has been to conceptualize motivation as an intervening variable, anchored to both specific antecedent and consequent conditions.

Since organisms need nourishment to survive, depriving an organism of food for a specific number of hours (the antecedent condition) and then measuring some resultant behavior (the consequent condition) represented a first step in studying motivation. An early experiment of this type was conducted by Richter (1922), who found that the activity of the rat, as measured in an exercise or activity wheel, could be related to the length of time it was deprived of food.

Many psychologists adopted Richter's approach in studying motivation (or *drive*, as they frequently have termed this motivational construct). The word *drive* was used to emphasize the fact that biological needs appeared to prompt the organism to activity. Since motivation or drive was grounded in specific deprivation and behavioral measurements, it is not surprising that motivation, at least as related to the organism's biological need states, was acknowledged to be an appropriate construct in the behaviorist's analysis of behavior.

The problem of analyzing motivation grows more complex when attempts are made to identify and measure constructs that do not appear to be tied to the biological requirements of the organism. However, this discussion is not meant to provide a systematic examination of motivation, but only to demonstrate how it is possible to study central-state or organismic processes or variables that influence behavior.

Cognitive processes represent a second central-state construct that demand consideration if one is to understand the nature of learning. A *cognitive process* is defined as a subject's ideas, images, expectancies, hypotheses, strategies, and the like.

Watson and the early behaviorists did not believe that cognitive variables should be included in the study of behavior, but many current investigators believe that excluding the contribution of cognitive processes may do irreparable harm to the understanding of the learning process. Razran (1971), for example, has written that recourse to cognitive variables is essential to the meaningful comprehension of the principles of learning. He suggested that, at a minimum, awareness, affect, images, and meanings must be studied for such comprehension. His twenty-five years of experimental work in conditioning human subjects has suggested the importance of identifying such processes in order to understand even this simple type of learning task. Many psychologists would not agree on the importance of the specific cognitive constructs that Razran has delineated, but they would acknowledge that the identification of cognitive variables is necessary for an adequate examination and understanding of the learning process.[7]

Since cognitive processes are private events, there is a problem in identifying and measuring them. Like motivational variables, however, they can be conceptualized as intervening constructs, tying their measurement to specific antecedent conditions and consequent behavior. The search for appropriate consequent behavior or public indicators of these cognitive processes has been an active one, and an early study by Tinklepaugh (1928) using monkeys as experimental subjects illustrates this approach.

---

[7] There have been some dissenters to this point of view. Skinner (1986) has written, "I think the experimental analysis of behavior, an analysis based on an appropriate knowledge of the stimulus conditions, can best proceed as it started, until the control of the behavior is very near total. A science of behavior will then have given neurology its clearest assignment, will have left nothing for cognitive science to explain with its mental operations, and will lead most rapidly to an effective technology of behavior in the world at large" (p. 235).

(See Box 1–3.) When humans are used as subjects, verbal behavior becomes one such indicator. The use of this type of overt responding is not without its problems, but it can provide the experimenter with some valuable insights about the role of cognitive processing in human learning.

In summary, we have indicated that stimulus as well as central-state variables contribute to the learning process. However, in the final analysis, we believe that our understanding of learning and memory processes and correlated performance must ultimately be tied to the operation of central-state processes that are inferred from the organism's behavior. For example, it has been found that if a temporal delay is placed between the making of a response and the securing of reward, the acquisition of the learned response is a function of the length of the delay period. Traditionally, the delay period has been related to the role of reward—a motivational construct. Some investigators have argued that it is not the delay period per se that contributes to performance decrement; rather, they have attributed such decremental responding to the operation of specific memorial processes taking place during the delay. And by manipulating the nature of the activity demanded of the subject during the delay interval, it should be possible to manipulate the hypothesized memorial process, which in turn should be reflected in variations of performance decrement.

The Response

As we discussed earlier, the psychologist must use changes in the organism's response from which to infer the presence of the learning process. The responses from which such an inference is made will vary markedly in complexity and kind. In some studies, the response may be quite complex; for instance, a college student solving a difficult

box 1–3

An early experiment conducted by Tinklepaugh (1928) illustrates his inference about the presence of a cognitive construct—expectancy—operating in a delayed response experiment. In this study, a monkey observed a piece of banana being placed under one of two cups. The animal was prevented from responding immediately by a restraining board placed in front of the container. After a few seconds' delay, the board was removed and the monkey was permitted to make a choice; responding to the baited cup was readily noted.

In what Tinklepaugh has described as a substitution test, the experimenter, without being observed by the monkey, substituted for the banana a piece of lettuce—a much less preferred food. Tinklepaugh reported what happened when the monkey lifted the correct cup and found the lettuce: "She looks at the lettuce but . . . does not touch it. She looks around the cup and behind the board. She stands up and looks under and around her. She picks up the cup and examines it thoroughly inside and out. She has on occasion turned toward the observers present in the room and shrieked at them in apparent anger" (p. 224). Tinklepaugh's explanation for such responding was that the animal *expected* to find food; her searching clearly revealed the operation of this cognitive variable.

mathematical problem. In other instances, the response may be as simple as a rat pressing a bar or a student closing his eye. Learning and memory studies have also utilized physiological responses. Earlier we noted that Tranel and Damasio (1985), unable to obtain a verbal response (recognition) from their subject, employed the electrodermal response (EDR) from which to infer the presence of facial memory.

In addition to complexity, responses differ as to kind. Responses have been differentiated on the basis of whether they are controlled by the central nervous system or the autonomic nervous system. The autonomic nervous system exercises control over the functioning of glands and smooth muscles (e.g., salivation, dilation or constriction of the pupil, etc.), whereas the central nervous system controls responses involving our striped musculature. Although subjects can exercise direct control over the striped muscles, it has been accepted by most experimenters that control over autonomic responses is not possible, at least without a period of training, which suggests some central nervous system contribution.

Some learning theorists have not been concerned by the distinctions we have enumerated. That is, they have assumed that the principles governing the learning process and the modification of behavior are quite general and may be inferred from either simple or complex responses and without regard to the specific nervous system involved. Other theorists, however, have assumed that the nature of the learning principle depends on whether the learned response is controlled by the central or autonomic nervous system. It is not our intent to discuss these theoretical considerations, since this is an issue that transcends any discussion of response measures. However, it should be pointed out that the theoretical predilection of the investigator may play an important role in determining the kind of response used to infer the learning process.

Summary ▶

Learning occupies a central place in the lives of most individuals; its contribution extends far beyond the role it plays in our formal educational experiences. The experimental investigation of learning began with the work of a German scientist, Hermann Ebbinghaus, who was inspired by the work of an earlier German philosopher and physicist, Gustav Fechner. Fechner developed a method for measuring the mental process of sensation; Ebbinghaus was interested in determining how another mental process, learning, could be examined. For his experimental work, Ebbinghaus invented the nonsense syllable. The task he set for himself was to learn varying lists of these units and then examine how a number of conditions (e.g., length of the list) contributed to such learning. List learning thus became a basic task in the study of verbal learning.

A decade after Ebbinghaus began his experimental studies, Russian physiologist Ivan Pavlov, while examining the digestive process, found that one of the elements of digestion, salivation, could be elicited in dogs by the footsteps of the caretaker walking across the floor. The capacity of such neutral stimuli to elicit salivation aroused Pavlov's interest. He identified the response elicited by such neutral stimuli as being conditioned, and devoted the remainder of his life to studying this phenomenon. American investigators became interested in animal learning around the turn of the century, the most prominent of these being E. L. Thorndike. As a result of his extensive experimental work, Thorndike proposed that all learning involved the establishment of connections between stimuli and responses, with such associations being formed according to certain principles. The most important of these is the law of effect.

Under the leadership of John B. Watson, psychology was redefined as the study of behavior. Following Watson, the work of E. C. Tolman, B. F. Skinner, and C. L. Hull during the 1930s and 1940s all provided theoretical approaches to the study of learning and memory processes. Current approaches to the study of these processes have been diverse, although an information-processing position has attracted more interest than any other.

There has been some controversy regarding an acceptable definition of learning; and many investigators define learning as a neurological process that arises from experience and is inferred from changes in the organism's behavior. Such a definition acknowledges the distinction between the concepts of learning and performance. Both retention and memory refer to neurological processes that are responsible for the persistence of such changes over time.

The conceptual framework for the study of learning and memory adopted by this book involves an examination of (1) the stimulus situation; (2) the organismic, or central state, of the organism; and (3) the response. These conditions must be scrutinized to study learning and memory processes.

chapter two

▶

Classical Conditioning: General Considerations

Pavlov's work, which was described briefly in Chapter One, was the first *experimental* investigation of classical conditioning. Note that we emphasize the word *experimental*, since many individuals were aware of this phenomenon long before Pavlov conducted his experiments. For example, Bernard, in his lecture series in Paris, circa 1885, described the salivary conditioning of a horse. (See Rosenzweig, 1959 and Box 2–1.)

The Pavlovian Procedure ▶

Pavlov's procedure consisted of surgically transplanting the opening of a dog's salivary ducts from inside the mouth to outside. Such an operation permitted the animal's salivation to be measured more easily. After the effect of the surgery wore off, Pavlov trained his animals to stand quietly in a loose harness on a table in a sound-deadened room. Seven or eight seconds after the sounding of a metronome or tuning fork, a small quantity of meat powder was moved within reach of the animal's mouth. The first presentation of the sound did not elicit salivation, but after a number of pairings of the two stimuli, Pavlov noted that salivation was elicited by the tone. A conditioned response had been established.

Pavlov's experiments were of basic importance since they enabled him to study a higher nervous system activity, learning, by purely objective means, and without speculation about the conscious experience of his animals. Salivation, which he described as a rather inconsequential response, served only as an objective measure from which the properties of the nervous system could be inferred. Pavlov's emphasis on objectivity was not unique but in keeping with the position of many other scientists of

box 2–1

Some secondary sources have given credit for the discovery of the conditioned response to an American, E. B. Twitmyer. Twitmyer (1902), a graduate student at the University of Pennsylvania, published a Ph.D. dissertation describing his accidental discovery of the conditioned response. Twitmyer was interested in investigating the nature of the knee jerk. He used the ringing bell to prepare his subjects to receive simultaneous blows on each patellar tendon, which in turn elicited this response in both legs. Twitmyer described his discovery as follows:

> *During the adjustment of the apparatus for an earlier group of experiments with one subject (Subject A) a decided kick of both legs was observed to follow a tap of the signal bell occurring without the usual blow of the hammers on the tendons. It was at first believed that the subject had merely voluntarily kicked out the legs, but upon being questioned, he stated that although quite conscious of the movement as it was taking place, it had not been caused by a volitional effort, and further, that the subjective feeling accompanying the movement was similar to the feeling of the movement following the blow on the tendons with the exception that he was quite conscious that the tendons had not been struck. Two alternatives presented themselves. Either (1) the subject was in error in his introspective observation and had voluntarily moved his legs, or (2) the true knee jerk (or a movement resembling it in appearance) had been produced by a stimulus other than the usual one (p. 1059).*

Twitmyer found that many of his other subjects responded similarly and concluded that "the occurrence of the kick without the blow on the tendons cannot be explained as a mere accidental movement on the part of the subjects. On the contrary, the phenomenon occurs with sufficient frequency and regularity to demand an inquiry as to its nature" (p. 1061). Unfortunately, American investigators were not sufficiently curious to further examine this phenomenon.

However, Pavlov had been examining salivary conditioning for some time prior to Twitmyer's accidental discovery of the conditioned knee jerk response. Pavlov's discussion of a variety of conditioning phenomena, given to the plenary session of the International Medical Congress in Madrid in 1903, would indicate that his experimental investigations undoubtedly commenced prior to 1900. Windholz's (1986) in-depth examination of this issue has indicated that Pavlov's research preceded Twitmyer's work by three or four years.

his time (e.g., Beer, Bethe, and von Uexkull), all of whom had called for the use of completely objective methods in studying animal behavior.

Terminology

Pavlov believed that it was important to provide specific designations for the stimuli and responses used in his procedure, and subsequent experimenters have continued to employ his terminology. In the experiment cited, the two stimuli Pavlov utilized were designated as the unconditioned stimulus (US) and the conditioned stimulus (CS). The unconditioned stimulus was the meat powder; more generally, an *unconditioned stimulus* is defined as a stimulus that will elicit a regular and measurable response over an extended series of presentations. The conditioned stimulus that Pavlov paired with the

US was the tone. By definition, a *conditioned stimulus* is initially neutral; that is, it is not capable at the beginning of the experiment of eliciting the response that is elicited by the unconditioned stimulus.

Pavlov observed three different responses in his conditioning experiments. First, he noted that his animals frequently turned their heads to look at the tuning fork or metronome (which produced the CS), a response that he termed *investigatory*, or "What is it?" In fact, Pavlov found that even slight alterations in the experimental environment—a slight sound or a faint odor—would elicit these investigatory responses. Pavlov concluded from his early studies that these responses provided an obstacle to conditioning and that it was necessary to eliminate them in order to permit the establishment of the CR. Subsequently, he suggested that conditioning proceeded best to CSs that elicited investigatory responses of medium intensity; those that were too strong or too weak appeared to interfere with the conditioning process.

Current experimenters have used the term *orienting response* (OR) rather than *investigatory*, recognizing that all of the varying skeletal and autonomic responses elicited by the CS (as well as extraneous stimuli) may be so categorized. The analysis of the OR has not, however, generated a great deal of experimental interest. Vinogradova (1965) has suggested that a stimulus must be capable of eliciting an orienting response if that stimulus is to serve later as a successful CS—a CS which, after pairing with a US, will have the capacity to elicit a CR. Öhman's (1974, 1979, 1983) experimental and theoretical examination of the OR, particularly as it relates to the conditioned electrodermal response in human subjects, merits attention.

Kaye and Pearce (1984) have also exhibited interest in examining the nature of the orienting response. These investigators have viewed the OR as providing a behavioral index of a type of control activity engaged in by the experimental subject, with such activity being of basic importance in the establishment of an associative relationship between the CS and US. Their work has suggested that experimental subjects will learn most rapidly about a stimulus that elicits a strong orienting response.

Pavlov termed the response elicited by the US as the *unconditioned response* (UR). In his experiments, the salivation and all of the other responses elicited by the meat powder (e.g., tongue and jaw movements, chewing) were identified as unconditioned responses.

The third response is the *conditioned response* (CR), which in Pavlov's study consisted of the dog salivating to the tone. Early investigators made the assumption that the CR was either the same as the UR or was a component of it. This resulted in some experimenters believing that conditioning trials resulted in the CS becoming a substitute for the US. This stimulus substitution position was deemed to be in error by many subsequent writers (e.g., Zener, 1937; Kimble, 1961) athough as late as the mid-seventies some writers continued to view a stimulus substitution position as viable. Thus, Mackintosh (1974) concluded that "the evidence against stimulus-substitution theory is surprisingly sparse" and that "there is often a close similarity between the CR and UR" (p. 104). Figure 2–1, a diagram frequently used in introductory texts, illustrates this point of view, since both the CS and US appear to be eliciting the same response.

Many current investigators have chosen not to address the stimulus substitution controversy. Their position has been to consider classical conditioning only as an

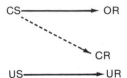

Figure 2-1
Typical diagram depicting the
classical conditioning procedure.

operation in which the pairing of the CS and US results in the CS eliciting a response different from that which the CS could elicit prior to the pairing operation. Such a consideration does not require that there be an identity or similarity between the CR and UR, although frequently this is the case. Further consideration of this issue will be found in Chapter Four.

Differential Conditioning

Pavlov's experimental work that we have just described involved the presentation of only a single CS being paired with the US. Another type of classical conditioning task investigated by Pavlov is differential conditioning, or *conditioned discrimination.* The procedure consists of the experimenter employing two CSs; on some trials one CS is presented and is always followed by the US, whereas on other trials the second CS is presented but never followed by the US. These two stimuli have been designated as the CS+ and CS−. This type of conditioning task demands that on each trial only one of these CSs be presented, with random presentation of each stimulus being provided.

An example of a conditioned discrimination experiment employing the random presentation of the CS+ and CS− is found in a human conditioned eyeblink study by Hartman and Grant (1962). Their apparatus consisted of two 10 cm. circular milk-glass disks with their centers approximately 15 cm. apart. The illumination of one disk was always followed by the US (a puff of air to the cornea of the eye). The illumination of the adjacent disk was never followed by the US. Subjects were given 44 reinforced trials and 44 nonreinforced trials; these trials were assigned randomly. Figure 2-2 illustrates responding to the CS+ and CS− where it may be observed how responding to the CS+ has increased over trials whereas responding to the CS− has declined.

Experimental Extinction and Spontaneous Recovery

Pavlov's experimental investigations continued for more than two decades. One basic problem that concerned him was how conditioned responses could be eliminated. He found that following the establishment of a conditioned response, the repeated presentation of the tone without the meat powder led to a decrease in conditioned responding. After a number of CS alone trials, the CR could no longer be elicited by presenting the CS. Pavlov termed this decline in responding *experimental extinction.* The term is now used not only to describe the operation (presenting the CS without pairing it with the US), but also to indicate the decrement in responding that takes place as a function of the CS alone trials. An example of the extinction of a conditioned salivary response, as reported by Pavlov, is found in Figure 2-3.

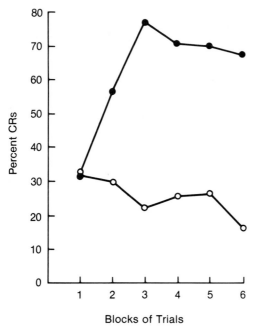

Figure 2-2
Percentage frequency of anticipatory responses to the positive and negative stimuli during successive blocks of acquisition trials. Block 1 consisted of 4 trials; all other blocks consisted of 8 trials. Adapted from T. F. Hartman and D. A. Grant, "Differential eyelid conditioning as a function of the CS-UCS interval," *Journal of Experimental Psychology,* 1962, *64,* 131–136. Copyright © 1962 by the American Psychological Association. Reprinted by permission.

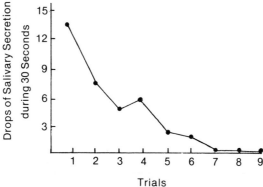

Figure 2-3
The conditioned stimulus (CS) was presented once every three minutes without the unconditioned stimulus. Plotted from data provided by Pavlov (1927).

Pavlov also found that if his subjects were provided with a rest period following the response decrement which arose from the extinction operation, the presentation of the CS would once again result in the conditioned response being elicited. The strength of this response was somewhat diminished. This recovery of an extinguished response after an interval of rest was termed *spontaneous recovery.*

Methodological Considerations ▶

In our examination of classical conditioning, three methodological issues should be considered. These have to do with (1) the nature of the CS-US presentations, (2) the measurement of the conditioned response, and (3) the definition and characteristics of a control group.

The Nature of the CS–US Presentation

Pavlov's conditioning procedure consisted of presenting the CS a few seconds prior to the presentation of the US. He became interested, as have subsequent investigators, in examining the role that this CS-US sequence played in the establishment of the conditioned response. The three basic sequences have been identified as (1) forward, (2) simultaneous, and (3) backward.

Forward conditioning is a procedure in which the onset of the CS occurs prior to the onset of the US. Simultaneous conditioning refers to simultaneous onset of the CS and the US. Backward conditioning refers to the onset of the US occurring prior to the onset of the CS; many investigators demand also that US offset take place prior to the onset of the CS.

With the forward conditioning paradigm, the termination of the CS can be manipulated, resulting in either a delayed or a trace procedure. Delayed conditioning, which is the most frequently employed, consists of the CS continuing until the US is presented, at which time it may either be continued or terminated.

The trace procedure consists of presenting and terminating the CS prior to the onset of the US. With this procedure, an interval of time occurs between the termination of the CS and the onset of the US. The term trace arises from the assumption that it is the neural trace left by the presentation of the CS that actually serves as the CS. Figure 2–4 illustrates these varying CS-US relationships.

Studies examining the simultaneous procedure (e.g., Smith, Coleman, and Gormezano, 1969) have indicated that this procedure does not result in conditioning. Findings obtained from backward conditioning studies have been controversial, with some investigators reporting positive findings but others unable to demonstrate conditioning with this procedure. Hall's (1984) review of the literature has suggested that US-CS trials employed with most classical conditioning paradigms will not result in acquisition of a CR. But some recent investigators have demonstrated backward conditioning, and a lively debate concerning the status of backward conditioning has ensued. We shall discuss this issue in greater detail in Chapter Four.

When a forward conditioning experiment is undertaken, it is necessary to decide whether to use a delayed or a trace procedure. Manning, Schneiderman, and Lordahl (1969) found that delayed conditioning was superior to trace when conditioning the heart rate of the rabbit. The length of the trace was either 2, 9, or 26 seconds. On the other hand, Ross, Ross, and Werden (1974) examined trace and delayed procedures with human eyelid conditioning and found no difference in conditioned responding between the two procedures. The length of the trace interval used by these investigators was quite short, ranging from 0.75 to 1.35 seconds.

These studies suggest that the critical feature contributing to differences in performance when using either delay or trace procedures may be the length of the trace. Thus, in the studies cited, if a long trace was used, delayed conditioning was superior; if the

Figure 2-4

Forward, simultaneous, and backward conditioning paradigms, with the delayed and trace conditions illustrated. The upward deflection of the line denotes stimulus onset, whereas a downward deflection denotes offset.

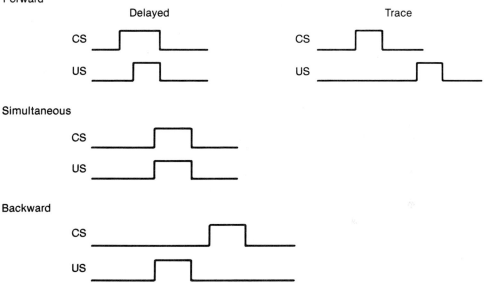

trace was short, little difference in performance was observed. It is readily apparent, however, that studies using the same CS, US, and UR must be conducted before arriving at any firm conclusion regarding performance differences taking place as a function of delay or trace procedures.

Response Measurement

The second methodological issue is how the CR should be measured. Generally, CRs are measured during acquisition trials, with measures of (1) frequency, (2) latency, and (3) amplitude of the response being obtained. *Frequency* refers to the number, or percentage of times, that the CS is able to elicit the CR over the course of the CS-US presentations. *Latency* is the length of time it takes the CR to appear, as measured from the onset of the CS to the onset of the CR. *Amplitude* refers to the amount or size of the CR.

Some investigators have also considered the subject's resistance to experimental extinction as a measure from which to infer the strength of the previously established conditioned response. With this measure, an extinction criterion is established (e.g., two successive trials in which the CS does not elicit the CR). The number of CS alone trials that is required for the subject to reach the criterion is used as a measure of the strength of the previously established CR.

The use of the extinction measure from which to infer CR strength has declined markedly since correlational studies have revealed little relationship between the strength of conditioning as measured by resistance to extinction and those response measures obtained during acquisition trials. An increasing number of experimenters have concluded that resistance to extinction appears to be a measure of persistence and not an indicator of CR strength.

Measurement of More Than a Single Response   It has been a common practice of experimenters to use only a single response measure in their conditioning experiments. One development in classical conditioning has been the simultaneous measurement of two or more responses.[1] Such a practice demands that the same US be capable of eliciting all URs, in order for the accompanying CRs to be recorded.

A study by Yehle (1968) illustrates multiple response recording. Yehle had his experimental subjects, rabbits, learn a classically conditioned discrimination task. It will be recalled that with this procedure the presentation of one CS (CS+) is followed by the US, whereas the presentation of a different CS (CS−) is never followed by the US. Different frequencies of a tone served as the CS+ and the CS−, with shock employed as the US to elicit (1) the nictitating membrane response, (2) changes in the heart rate, and (3) changes in respiration rate.

The percentage of conditioned responses to presentation of the CS+ are presented in Figure 2–5. As can be observed, heart rate responses appeared at full strength on the first day of training, whereas nictitating membrane responses increased from almost 0 percent frequency on Day 1 of training to more than 80 percent on Day 8. Respiration rate responding rose to a maximum on Day 2 and then exhibited a slow decline.

What is the value of multiple response recording? One contribution is in the further elucidation of the distinction between learning and performance. Thus, the rapid conditioning of heart rate and respiration rate in Yehle's study suggests that an associative relationship had been established between the tone and the shock in the organism's nervous system. The fact that the nictitating membrane response did not reveal conditioning taking place during the early trials suggests that although learning had occurred (as evidenced by heart rate and respiration rate CRs) performance indicators of the nictitating membrane response were absent.

The Use of Control Groups

The last methodology issue relates to the use of control groups. It will be recalled from Chapter One that Pavlov (1927) assumed it was necessary for the onset of the tone to precede presentation of the meat powder by a few seconds (forward conditioning) in order to establish a conditioned response. His use of a control group, which received a backward pairing of stimuli (US-CS presentation) and did not exhibit conditioned

---

[1] The procedure of making multiple response measurements has been in use for some time (e.g., Davis, 1939), but as McGuigan (1987) has indicated, such methodology has been employed infrequently.

Figure 2-5

Responses to the CS+ for each of three response systems. Adapted from A. L. Yehle, "Divergencies among rabbit response systems during three-tone classical discrimination conditioning," *Journal of Experimental Psychology,* 1968, *77,* 468–473. Copyright © 1968 by the American Psychological Association. Reprinted by permission.

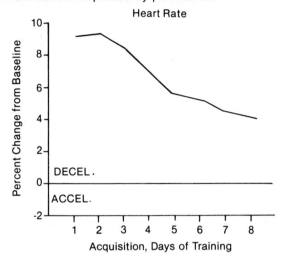

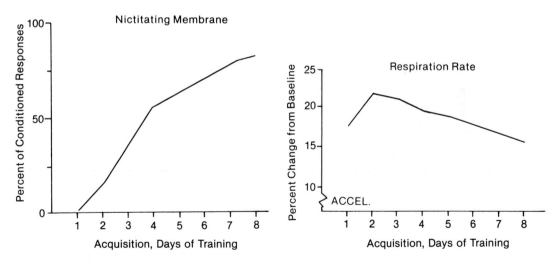

responding, clearly established the necessity of CS-US presentations if conditioning was to take place.

Many investigators following Pavlov also assumed that the establishment of a conditioned response resulted from a double stimulation procedure—the pairing of the CS with the US. But how can we be sure that such is the case? Is it not possible that the CR may arise as a result of some particular experimental condition other than the pairing of stimuli?

In order to guard against this possibility, experimenters have compared the performance of the experimental group, the group receiving the CS-US pairings, with a control group. Traditionally, the control group has received unpaired presentations of both the CS and the US, with these single presentations of stimuli occurring randomly. Thus, this procedure provides control subjects with the opportunity to experience both the CS and US but omits the pairing operation that has been assumed to be necessary for conditioning to take place. If the experimenter finds that the "conditioned" responses resulting from the paired presentation of stimuli cannot be distinguished from those responses arising from an unpaired presentation, these latter responses are identified as *pseudoconditioned.*

A provocative paper by Rescorla (1967) rejected the traditional assumption that the CR arises from the association occurring from the paired presentation of the CS and US. Rescorla proposed that a CR was established because the experimental subject learned a contingency between the CS and US. (A contingency differs from an association in that it is an association with a probability attached to it.) The establishment of an association indicates that the US will invariably follow the CS; the establishment of a contingency states that it is possible to assign some probability to the occurrence of the US following the CS.

The nature of the control group that an experimenter utilizes is related to the assumptions that are made about the conditioning process. Since Rescorla rejected the pairing operation as a necessary condition for the establishment of a conditioned response, he also rejected the use of the traditional control procedure described earlier. This procedure was methodologically inadequate, he pointed out, since the unpaired presentation of the CS and US provided control subjects with the opportunity to learn the contingency that the presentation of the CS would *not* be followed by the US. The learning of this contingency would produce an inhibitory state, resulting in a suppression of the response and thus depressing the control's performance. Such learning would be a confounding variable in any comparison of the experimental group's and control group's performance.

In place of the traditional control group, Rescorla (1967) suggested the use of the so-called *truly random control*. With this procedure "both the CS and the US are presented to S [subject] but there is no contingency whatsoever between them. That is, the two events are programmed entirely randomly and independently in such a way that some 'pairings' of the CS and US may occur by chance alone" (p. 74).[2]

More than a dozen investigators examining a variety of conditioned responses have been unable to find a difference in responding between the traditional control group and the truly random control group, thus suggesting that no methodological advantage is obtained when the latter type of control group is employed. In fact, Wasserman, Deich, Hunter, and Nagamatsu (1977) have indicated that the truly random control procedure may establish excitatory or inhibitory effects in the control group, thus

---

[2] Our discussion of Rescorla's contingency position has centered only on its relationship to the use of appropriate control group procedures. A more detailed account of the contingency position is presented in Chapter Four.

nullifying its value as a control. One example is found in a study by Benedict and Ayres (1972) who found that if the truly random control procedure fortuitously resulted in CS-US pairings early in the experimental session, some conditioning occurred.

Because many investigators have been unable to find any differences in performance between the traditional control group and the truly random control, the superiority of the latter type of control procedure remains to be established. Rescorla's contingency position, however, has continued to serve as an important alternative to the association position held by many traditional investigators.

What Responses Can Be Conditioned? ▶

The years following Pavlov's experimental demonstration that the salivary response could be conditioned revealed a host of experimenters demonstrating that many other responses could be conditioned. The responses most frequently employed by investigators in the United States have been the following:

1. Galvanic skin or electrodermal response (EDR)
2. Eyeblink
3. Heart rate
4. Nictitating membrane
5. Conditioned emotional response (CER)
6. Taste aversion

Recently, there has been a lively experimental interest in conditioning physiological responses, as reflected in changes in blood glucose level and immune response processes.

The Galvanic Skin or Electrodermal Response

The galvanic skin response (GSR), or electrodermal response (EDR), is measured by placing two electrodes on the surface of the skin. When a direct current is provided, a voltage develops across these electrodes and it is possible to measure the skin's apparent resistance or conductance. It is a response measure often used in lie detection, since lying can be an effective stimulus for its elicitation.

The EDR has two well-defined characteristics. First, it has a relatively long latency, ranging from three to five seconds, as measured from the onset of an eliciting stimulus. Second, the response is of long duration, requiring another three to five seconds in order to reach maximum amplitude.

An examination of the topography of the EDR, as found in classical conditioning experiments that have used long CS presentations, reveals that the EDR generally consists of three humps (or components), as illustrated in Figure 2-6. The first component has been identified as an orientation response made to the presentation of the CS, whereas the third component is elicited by the US. It is the second hump, often

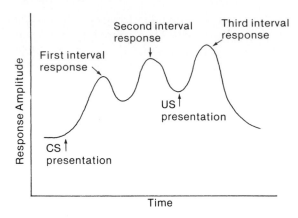

Figure 2-6
Electrodermal skin responses to the conditioned and unconditioned stimuli.

described as an anticipatory or second interval response, that has been acknowledged by many to reflect the "conditioned" response.[3] Many of the findings obtained in the early EDR conditioning studies are suspect, since these experimenters did not differentiate among the varying components.

The Eyeblink

A second conditioned response frequently examined by investigators in the United States is the human eyeblink. Usually the CS is a tone or a change in the illumination of a small glass window that is placed in front of the subject; the US is a puff of compressed air or nitrogen delivered to the cornea of the eye, which produces the blink. Early investigators measured this response by using a photochronograph, which simultaneously controlled the presentation of the CS and US and photographically recorded the movement of the eyelid. Current experimenters measure the blink by lightly cementing a thin wire to the subject's eyelid so that movement of the lid moves the wire which in turn rotates the shaft of a microtorque potentiometer. The resistance changes obtained from the potentiometer are amplified and recorded.

One problem that has concerned some investigators has been that the response to the CS results in the air puff falling upon the closed lid, which largely, if not totally, eliminates the aversive characteristics of the air puff. Thus, in many instances the conditioned eyeblink response has the characteristics of an instrumental response since the blink is instrumental in reducing the aversiveness of the unconditioned stimulus. An alternative has been to use shock (US) delivered to the paraorbital region of one eye that elicits eye closure; thus, the subject's response does not eliminate the aversiveness of the US. Results from both procedures, however, have yielded similar findings.

---

[3] There is not complete agreement on the identification of the *conditioned* EDR. Some experimenters believe that first interval responses can also be conditioned, whereas others have assumed that the conditioned EDR is nothing more than the reappearance of an orienting response to the CS. See Prokasy (1977), Furedy and Poulos (1977), Grings (1977), Stern and Walrath (1977), and Öhman (1983) for a discussion of this issue.

Heart Rate

The unusual aspect of heart rate conditioning is that the CR is represented by a change in rate. Watson (1916) made an early attempt to condition the heart rate in humans, but contemporary interest in conditioning this response began with a study by Notterman, Schoenfeld, and Bersh (1952), who used college students as subjects. The CS was a 750 Hz tone, with shock serving as the US. These experimenters found that after 11 CS-US pairings, they obtained a CR in the form of a reduction in the number of beats per minute. Many subsequent investigators working with animals as well as humans have reported successful attempts to condition heart rate. A puzzling aspect of these studies is that some experimenters have reported heart beat acceleration whereas others have found deceleration. Still others have reported a biphasic cardiac response pattern. Here, during the initial seconds of the CS presentation, there is heart rate acceleration followed by deceleration during the terminal portion of CS presentation and prior to US onset.

An interesting area of investigation has been the conditioning of heart rate when electrical stimulation to the brain is used as the US. Malmo (1964) has demonstrated that such stimulation to the lateral septal area of the rat's brain resulted in a slowing of the animal's heart rate. By pairing a tone with this kind of US, Malmo (1965) was able to demonstrate a conditioned response consisting of deceleration.

The Nictitating Membrane (NMR)

In an effort to overcome certain methodological difficulties found in the human conditioning of the EDR and eyeblink, Gormezano and his associates have found the albino rabbit's eyeblink and nictitating membrane response (NMR) to be ideally suited for conditioning studies. The US consists of either a puff of air to the cornea or a weak electric shock to the paraorbital region, with such stimulation accompanied by a closure of the eyelid as well as a sweeping of the animal's nictitating membrane across the surface of its cornea. Although early interest was centered on the conditioning of the animal's eyeblink, subsequent work has focused on the nictitating membrane response, beginning with an early study by Schneiderman, Fuentes, and Gormezano (1962). An important reason for the interest in this response was that when the membrane was activated, it rarely extended past the midline of the pupil, always leaving a portion of the cornea exposed. Inasmuch as the eyelid was held open by a suture, it was not possible for the animal to eliminate the sensory consequences of the US. A review provided by Gormezano, Kehoe, and Marshall (1983) and a more recently edited volume by Gormezano, Prokasy, and Thompson (1987) reveal this preparation to be a powerful tool in the examination of classical conditioning.

Conditioned Emotional Response (CER)

The classical conditioning of an emotional response is found in the pioneer study of Watson and Rayner (1920). Their single subject, Albert, an 11-month-old child, was not afraid of animals but had a distinct fear of loud noises. The experimental procedure consisted of placing Albert on a table and presenting him with a white rat, which served as a CS. A loud sound, produced by striking a steel bar with a hammer, served as the US. After just five presentations of the white rat and loud sound, the sight of the rat resulted in Albert's withdrawing and beginning to whimper. After two additional paired presentations, the authors report that the "instant the rat was shown alone, the baby began to cry. Almost instantly he turned sharply to the left, fell over on his left side, raised himself on all fours and began to crawl away so rapidly that he was caught with difficulty before reaching the edge of the table" (p. 5). It was evident that a conditioned emotional response had been established by using a classical conditioning procedure.

The difficulties in obtaining human subjects to serve in emotional conditioning experiments of the type just described are obvious. In fact, current psychologists would not undertake this type of study because of ethical considerations. One alternative has been to use animals as subjects but the question that immediately arises is how do you measure their emotionality?

Estes and Skinner (1941) and Hunt and Brady (1951) have developed such a procedure, now widely used, for doing this, with the conditioned response being identified as the *conditioned emotional response* (CER).

Rats were first trained in a Skinner Box to press a bar for food. Once the animals were bar pressing at a steady rate, the emotional conditioning stage of the experiment was instituted. The animals were placed in a different type of apparatus and a tone (CS) was paired with the presentation of shock (US). The experimenters assumed that shock elicited an emotional response, so after the animals had been given a number of tone-shock pairings, the tone was expected to be capable of eliciting this response. Note, however, that no direct measurement of the emotional response was made. Following the conditioning trials, the animals were returned to the Skinner Box, where they resumed pressing the bar for food. The tone (CS) was presented from time to time, with the experimenter noting how the rate of bar pressing changed as a function of the presentation of the tone. A comparison of the rate of bar pressing prior to the presentation revealed a marked decline in the rate of responding during presentation of the tone. This decrement in responding has been termed *response suppression*. In summary, the rationale for classifying this procedure as classical conditioning is that a double stimulation procedure, the presentation of a tone and shock, is assumed to result in the tone being able to elicit an emotional response.

It is important to keep in mind that the presence and strength of the classically conditioned emotional response is inferred from the reduction or suppression of the previously learned instrumental response. In contrast to the direct conditioned stimulus-conditioned response (CS-CR) paradigm noted in EDR, eyeblink, and heart rate studies, the CER involves a conditioned stimulus-conditioned response-instrumental response (CS-CR-IR) relationship.[4]

---

[4] In spite of its widespread use, there is some evidence to indicate that there are methodological and statistical problems with the use of the CER. In addition, the empirical results obtained with CER studies have not always mirrored the findings obtained with the CS-CR experiments. (See Hall, 1986.)

Taste Aversion

Our experience with food and illness is such that we sometimes avoid eating a particular type of food because an earlier experience suggested that ingestion of that food was the cause of the illness. This avoidance of food, or taste aversion, is undoubtedly learned, with classical conditioning being the paradigm that accounts for this change in behavior.

In an early taste aversion study, Smith and Roll (1967) deprived rats of liquid for 24 hours and then gave them access to a saccharin solution for 20 minutes. Following this period, and after either 0, .5, 1, 2, 3, 6, 12, or 24 hours, the experimental animals were irradiated, which produces nausea. Control subjects were given sham exposure for 200 seconds. Twenty-four hours later, each animal was given access to the saccharin solution and a bottle of plain water. The amount consumed from each bottle over a 48-hour period (expressed as a preference score) indicated that very little of the saccharin solution was consumed by those animals that were irradiated up to six hours after the original ingestion of the saccharin solution. This finding is in marked contrast to the drinking behavior of the control subjects who preferred to drink the saccharin solution almost exclusively. (See Figure 2–7.)

Current investigators have considered taste aversion studies to be examples of classical conditioning since there is the presentation of a CS (saccharin or other foodstuff) and a US (irradiation or the injection of a poison that produces illness), which is independent of any response made by the subject. The instrumental response

Figure 2–7
The median preference score for each delay condition for the experimental and control subjects. Adapted from J. C. Smith and D. L. Roll, "Trace conditioning with X-rays as an aversive stimulus," *Psychonomic Science,* 1967, *9,* 11–12. Reprinted by permission of the Psychonomic Society.

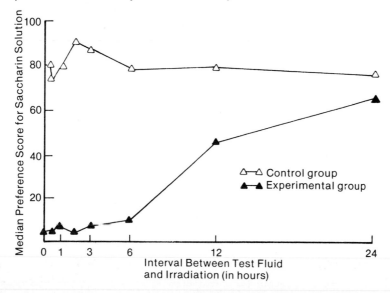

box 2-2

Most of us have experienced taste aversion, but only a few investigators have used human subjects in experimentally validating this effect. Bernstein (1978) is one of these. In this study, a population of 41 children, ages 2 to 16, served as subjects, all of them being treated as outpatients in a hospital and clinic. Twenty-six of these children were receiving intravenous doses of chemotherapeutic drugs that produce gastrointestinal upset. Fourteen of these 26 subjects were given Mapletoff (an unusual ice cream prepared with maple and black walnut flavor extracts) to eat prior to their receiving the chemotherapeutic drug; the other 12 served as Control Group 1 and did not receive the ice cream. Control Group 2 consisted of 15 children who were receiving a drug that was nontoxic to the GI tract; these children were also given Mapletoff ice cream. Two to four weeks later, the acceptance (or rejection) of Mapletoff ice cream was measured by offering all 41 children a choice of either eating the ice cream or playing with a game. Results indicated that only 21% of the children receiving chemotherapeutic drugs chose the ice cream, in contrast to 67% for Control Group 1 and 73% for Control Group 2. Approximately 4$^{1}/_{2}$ months after this first preference test was provided, the subjects were given a second preference test. Here, patients were given a choice of either Mapletoff ice cream or another relatively novel ice cream, Hawaiian Delight. During this second testing, patients were asked to taste both ice cream flavors, indicate which they preferred, and eat as much as they wished. Results indicated that Mapletoff ice cream was preferred by 25% of the experimental group, in contrast to 66% and 50% of Control Groups 1 and 2. Aversion to the Mapletoff ice cream appeared to be a specific learned response. As Bernstein has noted, the demonstration of taste aversions in humans receiving chemotherapy treatments may be of importance to physicians who administer treatments that induce nausea. Such aversions may be one factor contributing to the anorexia and weight loss seen in patients with cancer.

of avoiding the specific foodstuff associated with the illness is used from which to measure the strength of the CS (taste of food)–US (illness) relationship that has been established. In this regard, we may note that taste aversion is similar to the CER since with both paradigms the conditioned response is not measured directly but inferred from the strength of an instrumental response. Thus, the CS-CR-IR sequence that is found with the CER is also observed with taste aversion studies. (See Box 2-2.)

Conditioned Physiological Responses ►

As we noted in our introduction to this section, investigators have become increasingly interested in the conditioning of physiological responses.

Blood Glucose Level

A review of the conditioning of endocrine response by Woods and Burchfield (1980) has indicated that changes in blood glucose level can be conditioned in humans, dogs, and rats, as revealed in the experimental studies of Lichko (1959), Alvarez-Buylla and Carrasco-Zanini (1960), and Woods, Makous, and Hutton (1968).

Woods, Makous, and Hutton's (1968) procedure consisted of first obtaining a blood sample to measure the glucose level of both experimental and control animals, following which experimental subjects were injected with insulin.[5] Control animals were injected with physiological saline. Twenty minutes later, a second blood sample was obtained in order to measure any change in glucose level. Fifteen such conditioning trials were distributed over 33 days. On the first test day, two days following the last conditioning trial, the same procedure was followed except that the experimental subjects were injected with physiological saline, as were the control subjects.

The experimental findings were as follows: No difference in blood glucose level was noted between experimental and control animals prior to the experimental subjects receiving the first injection of insulin. For each of the 15 conditioning trials, the injection of insulin in the experimental animals resulted in a decrease in the glucose level (hypoglycemia) ranging from 14 to 50%; the injection of saline in the control animals was followed by an increase in the blood glucose in almost every instance. On the test day, the injection of saline in the experimental group resulted in a decrease in glucose level, whereas an increase was noted with the control animals. The difference between the groups was statistically significant.

Conceptually, Woods, Makous, and Hutton (1968) assumed that their US was the insulin that produced the UR—the lowering of blood glucose level in the animal. The CS was the injection of the drug, whereas the response that was conditioned mirrored the UR—a lowering of blood glucose level. In a second study by Woods, Makous, and Hutton (1969) these findings were replicated. In addition, it was noted that if the CS was made more distinctive by introducing the odor of menthol within the experimental chamber, experimental-control differences were accentuated.[6]

Immunosuppressive Responses

The discovery of cyclophosphamide, a drug that inhibits the body's immune system from rejecting the organ of a donor, has resulted in a major breakthrough in transplant surgery. A question that interested investigators since the mid-1920s was whether or not it was possible to condition immunosuppressive responses. Studies of the condition-

---

[5] The principal function of insulin released by the pancreas is to aid in removing glucose (sugar) from the blood. If insulin is injected, its effect is to remove glucose from the blood. Diabetics who use insulin injections do so because their own production of insulin is too low, which results in their blood sugar levels being too high. The injection of insulin aids in the restoration of blood glucose to a normal level.

[6] We should note that studies by Siegel (1972, 1975a) revealed findings opposite to those obtained by the investigators cited by Woods and Burchfield (1980). Siegel has reported the conditioning of an elevation in blood level (hyperglycemia) rather than a decrease (hypoglycemia). Flaherty, Uzwiak, Levine, Smith, Hall, and Schuler (1980) have noted that whether a conditioned increase or decrease in blood glucose level was obtained appeared to be dependent on the environment in which the experimental subjects were placed. These investigators were not able to provide any explanation as to why the different environments produced different results. It is obvious that more research is needed in order to arrive at a firm conclusion regarding the conditioning of blood glucose level.

ing of such responses were initiated in the United States in the mid-seventies, with early experiments conducted by Ader and Cohen (1975). Their experimental design was quite complex so we shall provide only a general description of their study.

Rats were trained to drink their daily requirement of water over a single 15-minute period. The conditioning procedure consisted of the experimental animals receiving a 0.1% saccharin solution during their drinking period, with the saccharin identified as the CS. This was followed 30 minutes later by an injection of cyclophosphamide, which served as the US and has the property of suppressing the body's immune system. Most of the experimental animals received only a single conditioning trial. Following this trial, these animals were injected with a 1% suspension of sheep red blood cells—an antigen that stimulates the production of antibodies in the blood. Thirty minutes later, the animals received only the CS—the ingestion of saccharin. A few days later, the subjects were sacrificed in order to make an analysis of the level of antibodies in their blood. Results indicated that the experimental animals, in contrast to the controls, had undergone a significant lowering of their antibody response. This lowered response was attributed to the presentation of the CS, which the authors believed elicited an immunosuppressive response similar to that produced by the cyclophosphamide. In an extensive series of experiments following their early study, Ader and Cohen (1981) reported that they were able to condition the immunosuppressive response, but that the difference in criteria measures was very small. They were not able to increase the magnitude of the difference, in spite of their manipulation of a host of variables, all of which have been found to increase the strength of the conditioned response.

Other studies, however, have successfully demonstrated the conditioning of immunosuppression (e.g., Rogers, Reich, Strom, and Carpenter, 1976; Wayner, Flannery, and Singer, 1978; Ader and Cohen, 1982; Klosterhalfen and Klosterhalfen, 1983). Ader and Cohen (1982), using cyclophosphamide as the US and a saccharin solution as the CS, were able to condition immunosuppression, noting that the mortality of conditioned New Zealand hybrid mice that had developed lupus erythematosus was significantly retarded relative to appropriate control groups. And Klosterhalfen and Klosterhalfen (1983), also using cyclophosphamide as the US and a saccharin solution as the CS, have found conditioned immunosuppression to have applicability in arresting inflammatory joint disease (e.g., adjuvant arthritis).

Histamine release, another example of the conditioning of an immune response, has been reported by Russell, Dark, Cummins, Ellman, Callaway, and Peeke (1984). In a conditioned discrimination study, either a sulfur or fish odor served as the CS+ and CS−; the US was an injection of a 5% solution of bovine serum albumin, which elicited a histamine release. Presentation of the CS− was accompanied by an injection of a saline solution. Random presentation of five CS+ and five CS− trials were provided, with trials given one week apart to permit the animal to recover from any allergic reaction. Test trials administered after training revealed a significant increase in plasma histamine when the CS+ alone was presented. The authors concluded that "associative learning should be included in understanding the development and treatment of allergies" (p. 734).

A Methodological Note

One methodological problem that must be addressed when physiological responses are conditioned has to do with an appropriate determination of the US. A provocative article by Eikelboom and Stewart (1982) has suggested that in the conditioning of some physiological responses, the US in not the injection of the drug. (The authors assumed that the central nervous system [CNS] is not involved in these drug-produced responses and an appropriate definition of conditioning includes CNS activity.) In such instances, the functional US is the physiological change that is produced by the drug, which in turn results in feedback to the subject's nervous system. Thus, the UR resulting from the direct action of the drug injection will often be different than a UR that is elicited by the physiological change produced by the drug. For example, Eikelboom and Stewart have indicated that the manner in which glucose change is produced by insulin injection in glucose conditioning studies, is critical in determining the nature of the UR, as well as the CR. The well-known mechanism by which insulin produces hypoglycemia (lowering of glucose level in the blood) is direct cellular action. Since this is a direct action of the insulin on an effector mechanism, insulin injection should not be identified as the US. The authors have suggested that it is the observed hypoglycemia itself that acts as the US. The UR is acknowledged to be the activation of effectors that increase blood glucose, with hyperglycemia being the predicted CR.

Such an analysis cannot account for findings obtained by Flaherty, Uzwiak, Levine, Smith, Hall, and Schuler (1980) who noted that although their experimental procedure remained the same, obtaining hypoglycemia or hyperglycemia was depen-dent on the environment in which the subjects were placed. Nonetheless, it becomes important for investigators to determine whether the assumed UR arises from the direct action of the US.

The Conditioning of Other
Organisms and Other Responses ▶

In the previous section, our examination of conditioning was limited to those organ-isms and responses that have been frequently employed in laboratory investigations or that are of current concern. However, readers should be aware of the generality of conditioned response learning, with experimenters demonstrating conditioning in a diversity of subjects, using a wide range of responses. For example, Thompson and McConnell (1955) have been able to condition the head movement of planaria; Walters, Carew, and Kandel (1981) have conditioned head and siphon withdrawal and the secretion of inking in the amplysia.

The conditioning of unborn subjects has been also obtained. In an early study, Spelt (1938) appears to have established conditioned movement in the intact human fetus, ages $6^{1}/_{2}$ to $8^{1}/_{2}$ months. In this study, an auditory stimulus was used as the US and a tactile vibration of the mother's abdomen served as the CS. The position of the fetus was determined by X-rays; movement was measured by tambours placed on the stomach. Some years later, Hunt (1949) was able to condition gross bodily movement in chick embryos.

Conditioning has been also found to occur in less than the intact organism. The conditioning of gross efferent volleys from the motor nerve has been obtained with spinal animals, as revealed in the work of Buerger and Dawson (1968, 1969), Patterson, Cegavske, and Thompson (1973), and Durkovic (1975). In the Patterson, Cegavske, and Thompson study, adult cats were each given a spinal transection with artificial respiration being instituted in order to keep them alive. Animals were classically conditioned by pairing stimulation of an exposed sensory nerve (CS) with cutaneous shock to the ankle of the same limb (US). The unconditioned response was the efferent volley from the motor nerve, with the acquisition of the CR reaching asymptote in approximately 20 trials.

More recently, Lukowiak and Sahley (1981) have been able to demonstrate in vitro conditioning of gill withdrawal in the amplysia. In this study, the in vitro preparation consisted of the organism's siphon, mantle, gill, and abdominal ganglion with only the siphon, branchial, ctenidial, and pericardial nerves left intact. The CS was a light and the US consisted of a train of tactile stimuli applied to the gill which elicited gill withdrawal (UR); conditioned responding took place after a number of CS-US presentations.

These examples are only a sampling of the variety of organisms and types of responses that have been conditioned. Evidence suggests that some responses in almost all living organisms can be conditioned.

The Concepts of Excitation and Inhibition ►

Pavlov was a physiologist, so it is not surprising that he was interested in speculating about those neurological processes that could be related to classical conditioning phenomena. The process that he believed was responsible for acquisition was *excitation;* for extinction, it was *inhibition.*[7] Contemporary investigators have continued to be interested in relating the functioning of these inferred neurological processes to a variety of conditioning phenomena.

Pavlov assumed that during the presentation of the CS and US—a conditioning trial—there was the growth of excitation and that such excitation was responsible for the establishment of responses of a positive character. In his examination of inhibition, Pavlov (1927) hypothesized two types: (1) external inhibition and (2) internal inhibition.

External inhibition arose as a result of the introduction in the conditioning experi-

---

[7] We have introduced the concepts of *excitation* and *inhibition* because many investigators believe that any theoretical examination of classical conditioning must include these constructs; thus, the reader should have some familiarity with them.

ment of an external stimulus. Pavlov's description of the circumstances leading to the postulation of external inhibition was as follows:

> The dog and the experimenter would be isolated in the experimental room, all the conditioning remaining for a while constant. Suddenly some disturbing factor would arise—a sound would penetrate into the room: some quick change in illumination would occur, the sun going behind a cloud.... If any one of these extra stimuli happened to be introduced just at the time of application of the conditioned stimulus, it would inevitably bring about a more or less pronounced weakening or even a complete disappearance of the reflex response, depending on the strength of the extra stimulus (p. 44).

In summary, external inhibition was posited to arise from the introduction of some unexpected stimulus into the conditioning experiment, which resulted in a decline in the strength of the CR. Because external inhibition generally had a transient effect on conditioned responding, as well as the assumption that such inhibition was not a learned phenomenon, it has not been extensively researched by U.S. investigators.

Internal inhibition, in contrast to external inhibition, arose from several different conditioning operations. The most prevalent of these was the presentation of the CS without the US—experimental extinction. Extinction trials did not result in Pavlov's dogs "forgetting" to make the CR; rather, the extinction operation was assumed to result in the accumulation of internal inhibition that temporarily prevented or blocked the conditioned response from being elicited by the CS. Rest or the presentation of an unexpected stimulus (e.g., loud noise) would result in the CS again becoming capable of eliciting the CR. Inhibition arising from the omission of the US was also demonstrated in a compound-conditioning task described as *summation.* Here, Pavlov (1927) noted:

> A positive conditioned stimulus [CS$_1$] is firmly established in a dog by means of the usual repetitions with reinforcement [US]. A new stimulus [CS$_2$] is now occasionally added, and whenever the combination [CS$_1$ + CS$_2$] is applied, which may be at intervals sometimes extending to hours or days, it is never accompanied by the unconditioned stimulus. In this way the [CS$_1$ + CS$_2$] combination is gradually rendered ineffective, ... although when applied singly and with constant reinforcement [CS$_1$] retains its full powers (p. 69).

Internal inhibition is now identified as conditioned inhibition since many current investigators assume that the presentation of the CS without the US is responsible for the growth and development of the inhibitory state. The examination of inhibition was neglected for many years and it was not until about two decades ago that investigators once again became interested in this construct.

Measurement

Conditioned responding and the inferred construct of excitation arises from a pairing of the CS and US, followed by a change in the behavior of the experimental subject. However, if the pairing operation does not result in a behavior change, it has been assumed that conditioning has not taken place, hence an absence of excitation. But the defining operations for the establishment of conditioned inhibition are not as explicit.

It has been generally held that a stimulus, which through learning comes to control a tendency that is opposite to that produced by conditioned excitation, is a conditioned inhibitor. But there is a problem in defining *opposite.* Although there are a few conditioned responses that are bidirectional (or opposite) in nature (e.g., heart rate) that could be used in the examination of conditioned inhibition, most conditioned responses examined by experimenters do not have this characteristic. As a result, current investigators regard a decrement in responding (or not responding) as the criterion for determining the presence of conditioned inhibition. Such criteria, at least from a causal viewing, provides problems since it may be difficult to determine if such decremental responding arises from the contribution of conditioned inhibition or from some other process (e.g., lack of motivation) or even the absence of excitatory strength.

In an effort to solve this difficulty, varying procedures for measuring conditioned inhibition have been proposed. Two of the most frequently used have been (1) summation and (2) retardation of acquisition.

In our discussion of Pavlov's identification of conditioned inhibition we have already described the summation test: a more recent example is found in a study by Szwejkowski and Konorski (1959). Using dogs as experimental subjects, positive salivary conditioning was established to each of two stimuli: a bell (S_1) and bubbling water (S_2). Then two new stimuli, a metronome (S_3) and whistle (S_4), were separately introduced, each of which was never paired with reinforcement. This procedure was assumed to result in each new stimulus acquiring inhibitory strength. Approximately 1,500 positive trial presentations of S_1 were provided along with 425 negative S_3 or S_4 trials. The testing phase of the study consisted of pairing two stimuli, one positive and one negative, providing four possible combinations of stimuli (e.g., $S_1 + S_3$, $S_1 + S_4$, $S_2 + S_3$, $S_2 + S_4$). Each combination of stimuli was presented once in about 250 trials; the other trials consisted of continuing to present either S_1 or S_2 with the US, and the S_3 or S_4 without the US. Results on test trials revealed that the effect of the positive conditioned stimulus was, on average, diminished to about 50% of its normal positive value, a finding attributed to the inhibitory strength of S_3 or S_4.

The second method for measuring conditioned inhibition, retardation of acquisition, rests on the assumption that if a conditioned stimulus inhibits a response, it should be more difficult to condition that stimulus to elicit responding than if a stimulus did not have such inhibitory properties. In an experimental examination of this method of measuring conditioned inhibition, Marchant and Moore (1973) used the conditioned nictitating membrane response of the rabbit. During Stage 1, training consisted of 50 reinforced presentations of an increase in illumination (L), with the US being a slight shock to the animal's intraorbital region of the right eye. The CS-US trials were interspersed with 50 nonreinforced presentations of a compound stimulus—the increase in illumination (L) plus a 1,200 Hz tone (T). Such training was assumed to result in the tone becoming an inhibitory stimulus since it had never been associated with the US. Preliminary findings revealed that acquisition of the CR took place when only the light was presented; presentation of the light and tone did not result in acquisition. In order to demonstrate that the tone had acquired inhibitory properties, the investigators then used the tone as a CS, followed by orbital shock as a US. Findings revealed that excitatory conditioning took place more slowly then the conditioning exhibited by subjects who had no previous experience with the tone.

Extensions of the Pavlovian Procedure ▶

Some psychologists believe that classical conditioning plays a very minor role in the organism's repertoire of learned behavior. It has been argued that the unconditioned responses that can be elicited by stimuli are relatively few; moreover, these responses are quite simple and frequently reflexive. Although it cannot be posited that classical conditioning is capable of accounting for many of the complex behaviors that characterize human behavior, there has been the discovery of several procedures that extend the generality of this type of learning.

Second-Order Conditioning

One procedure that broadens the scope of stimuli capable of eliciting the conditioned response was demonstrated by Pavlov (1927), who identified it as *higher-order conditioning*. The procedure is as follows: After establishing a conditioned response, the experimenter provides the subject with additional trials in which a new CS (CS_2) is paired with the previously employed CS (CS_1). In effect, the original CS appears to serve as a US. After a number of pairings of CS_2-CS_1, the CS_2 becomes capable of eliciting the CR.

An illustration of such conditioning is found in one of Pavlov's early experiments. The ticking of a metronome (CS) followed by the presentation of meat powder (US) resulted in the metronome eliciting salivation. Following such training, a visual stimulus in the form of a black square (CS_2) was paired with the metronome (CS). By the tenth pairing, presentation of the black square elicited salivation, although the response was only half as strong as that elicited by the original CS.

The capacity of a CS_2 to elicit the CR has been identified by current investigators as *second-order conditioning*. Third-order conditioning procedures would involve the presentation of a CS_3 paired with the CS_2, which in turn had been previously paired with a CS_1.

Inasmuch as Pavlov's investigations suggested that second-order conditioning was quite fragile, this paradigm generated little attention among experimenters in the United States. In the 1970s, however, studies by Rizley and Rescorla (1972) and Holland and Rescorla (1975), using both aversive and appetitive unconditioned stimuli, indicated second-order conditioning to be a robust phenomenon.

In the first experiment, Rizley and Rescorla (1972) used the conditioned emotional response in order to examine such conditioned responding. Rats were trained to press a lever in order to secure food. After this response had stabilized, the emotional response was conditioned by pairing a light (or tone), serving as the CS with shock (US). The second phase of the study consisted of providing pairings of the CS_2 tone (or light) with the original CS. Phase three consisted of presenting the CS_2 during lever pressing, with a significant amount of response suppression being noted. Such depressed responding could be contrasted with the performance of two control groups in which the presentation of the CS_2 had no influence in suppressing the response.

In the Holland and Rescorla (1975a) study, first-order conditioning was established by presenting hungry rats with a light flashing off and on for 12 seconds. Ten seconds after the light onset, two food pellets were presented. The animal's response to the delivery of food in the experimental cage was increased activity; such activity, the CR, was measured as the animal moved around in the cage.

Following a training period in which the experimental animals received 84 light-food presentations over a period of 11 days, second-order conditioning was undertaken. The animals received a total of 16 presentations of 10 seconds of a clicker (CS_2) followed by 10 seconds of the flashing light.

The number of movement responses/minute elicited by the clicker increased steadily over the 16 trials, clearly demonstrating second-order conditioning. Appropriate control groups, on the other hand, revealed a decline in responding.

The reported studies involve the second-order conditioning of excitatory tendencies, but Rescorla (1976) has also shown that such conditioning can be extended to conditioned inhibition. We shall not provide the details of his study, other than to point out that Rescorla was able to demonstrate second-order inhibition by using the conditioned emotional response paradigm. Thus, a neutral stimulus, by being repeatedly paired with a previously conditioned inhibitor, was observed also to produce inhibition during the test phase of the study.

Rescorla's work has generated considerable interest in second-order conditioning, with a variety of stimuli, experimental subjects, and conditioning paradigms being examined, a sampling of which includes odor aversion in the neonatal rat (Cheatle and Rudy, 1978), eyelid conditioning in the rabbit (Sears, Baker, and Frey, 1979), and appetitive conditioning in goldfish (Amiro and Bitterman, 1980).

A basic question that has interested investigators is whether the learning principles observed to operate with first-order conditioning operate similarly with second order. We shall not delve into this issue other than to point out that the evidence is mixed; some investigators report a similarity of principles whereas others have been unable to support this finding. One interesting operation arising from this question has been to examine how extinguishing the CR to the CS_1 influences the capacity of the CS_2 to elicit the CR. Holland and Rescorla (1975a) have shown that extinguishing the CR to the CS_1 did not influence the capacity of the CS_2 to elicit the CR. This finding suggested to Rescorla (1980) that the association that is established in second-order conditioning is between the CS_2 and the CR. However, other investigators (e.g., Rashotte, Griffin, and Sisk, 1977) have been unable to find support for this suggestion. Inasmuch as different conditioning paradigms have been used in these conflicting studies, it is not clear how they have influenced the findings.

Interest during the past decade in second-order conditioning has centered on laboratory experiments examining its general operation and similarity to first-order conditioning. Unfortunately, such concern may have obscured how second-order conditioning can extend the generality of Pavlovian conditioning to everyday experiences. But consider the hypothetical situation in which a traumatic event takes place when an individual is riding in an elevator. The elevator may serve as a CS to elicit fear responses (with the resultant avoidance of elevators); since elevators have been associated with tall buildings, this latter stimulus situation may also serve to elicit fear and subsequent avoidance behavior. It would appear that fear as well as other emotional responses are the kinds of conditioned responses that are likely to be elicited by second- and third-order CSs.

Stimulus Generalization

A second phenomenon that enables stimuli not present in the basic conditioning operation to elicit responding has been identified as *stimulus generalization*.

Earlier we discussed Watson and Rayner's (1920) study of conditioning Albert, an 11-month-old child, to be afraid of a white rat. In a second part of this study, Watson and Rayner found that five days after such conditioning had taken place, a rabbit, a dog, a fur coat, cotton wool, and a Santa Claus mask were also capable of eliciting the conditioned fear response. Thirty days later, the presentation of these stimuli continued to elicit fear. This finding that a classical conditioning response can be elicited by stimuli other than the conditioned stimulus, has been defined as stimulus generalization.

The fact that Albert was afraid of a variety of objects or stimuli to which he had not been originally conditioned is not surprising. We are all aware that behavior may be controlled by stimuli that differ from those originally encountered. Such a process makes good adaptive sense, since it is obvious that the stimulus found in one situation is never precisely duplicated in a second, yet survival may depend on appropriate responding. This point was recognized by Pavlov (1927) who wrote:

> Natural stimuli are in most cases not rigidly constant but range around a particular strength and quality of stimulus in a common group. For example, the hostile sound of any beast of prey serves as a conditioned stimulus to a defence reflex in the animal which it hunts. The defence reflex is brought about independently of variations in pitch, strength and timbre of the sound produced by the animal according to its distance, and tension of its vocal cords and similar factors (p. 113).

The first *experimental* demonstration of stimulus generalization was conducted in Pavlov's laboratory. One of Pavlov's associates, Petrova, conditioned a dog to salivate whenever tactile stimulation, which had been used as the CS, was applied to a point on one of its hind paws. The US was an acid solution placed in the mouth. Four other points were plotted equal distances apart and up from the paw along the hind leg. Petrova found that stimulation at these points also elicited salivation.

In the United States, early stimulus generalization studies using classical conditioning operations were performed by Bass and Hull (1934) and Hovland (1937a, 1937b, 1937c, 1937d). Hovland planned to condition the electrodermal response (EDR) to one tone and then use other tones to test for generalization. But how was he to select the tones to be used? His answer was to use tones that were equally discriminable from each other. Thus, he would not be subject to the criticism that the test stimuli he used were not discriminable from the conditioned stimulus or from one another.

In order to obtain equally discriminable tones, he used a psychophysical procedure that scales or arrays tones along the dimension of a just noticeable difference (JND). This operation resulted in Hovland selecting four tones—namely, 153, 468, 1,000, and

1,967 Hz—each of which was 25 JNDs from the adjacent tone. Note that Hovland's scale was based not on physical differences among tones (frequency), but on the psychological dimension of discriminability. His experiments consisted of conditioning one group of subjects to the highest tone (1,967 Hz) and a second group to the lowest tone (153 Hz). Following 16 conditioning trials, extinction trials were provided. Each subject was presented with the original CS and the three test tones on each of four separate occasions, thus providing 16 extinction trials in all. The extinction data were combined for both groups of subjects to form the generalization curve found in Figure 2-8.

For some time, Hovland's finding of a smooth, downward concave gradient was considered to reflect the basic feature of stimulus generalization—maximum responding being made to the original CS followed by smaller values of response strength as the generalized stimuli became more discriminatable from the original CS. But many later investigators have been unable to replicate the smooth course of decremental responding as noted by Hovland. It is now apparent that Hovland's experimental procedure contained several methodological difficulties that make some of his results suspect. Nonetheless, Hovland's findings that revealed response strength weaker to generalized stimuli than to the CS, have for the most part, continued to be found. Most current stimulus generalization studies have been conducted, however, using instrumental and/or operant procedures, a topic discussed in Chapter Four.

Secondary, or Learned, Stimulus Generalization

In many generalization studies, experimenters have used auditory stimuli varying in pitch or loudness, or visual stimuli varying in hue or brightness. When such sensory stimuli are used, it has been often assumed (Hull, 1943) that the connection existing between the stimulus used in training and the test stimulus has been innately determined. These innately determined connections, presumed to exist among sensory

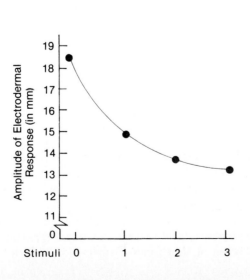

Figure 2-8
Composite curve showing responses to the CS (Stimulus 0) and to the three test tones (Stimuli 1, 2, and 3), which were 25, 50, and 75 JNDs removed from the CS. Adapted from C. I. Hovland, "The generalization of conditioned responses: I. The sensory generalization of conditioned responses with varying frequencies of tone," *Journal of General Psychology*, 1937, *17*, 125-148. Reprinted by permission of the Helen Dwight Reid Educational Foundation. Published by Heldref Publications, 4000 Albemarle St., NW, Washington, DC 20016. Copyright © 1937.

stimuli and hypothesized to play an important role in generalization findings, have been the defining characteristic in the concept of *primary* stimulus generalization.

It is possible, however, that the connections existing among the stimuli used in a generalization experiment have been established through learning; when such stimuli are used, the generalization process has been designated as *secondary*, or *learned*. For example, when an experimental subject has been conditioned to respond to the word *frigid*, using the word *cold* as a test stimulus may also elicit a response. Undoubtedly, the synonymous relationship between the two words has been established through learning.

An early study by Razran (1939) utilizing synonyms and homophones as test stimuli illustrates secondary generalization. A salivary CR was established in college students by using words such as *style* or *urn* as conditioned stimuli; pretzels or candy served as the US to elicit the salivary response. This response was measured by placing a roll of dental cotton under the tongue of the subject and removing it after a specified length of time (usually a minute). The amount of salivation was measured by comparing the weight of the cotton before and after it was placed in the subject's mouth. After the CR had been established, test stimuli consisting of synonyms such as *fashion* or *vase* and homophones such as *stile* or *earn* were presented. Razran's findings indicate that it is possible to obtain conditioned responses to both synonyms and homophones, with the synonyms providing the greater response strength. Secondary stimulus generalization experiments such as Razran's using verbal stimuli or units of language as the conditioned and test stimuli, have been identified as *semantic generalization* studies.

Intuitively, it would appear that stimulus generalization operating in everyday situations is more likely to be secondary than primary. In spite of its much greater frequency or occurrence, secondary stimulus generalization has been only infrequently studied.

Autoshaping, or Sign Tracking

A third extension of the traditional Pavlovian paradigm is found in the investigations of a phenomenon identified as *autoshaping*, or *sign tracking*. As we noted in Chapter One, Skinner (1938) and others believed conditioned response learning was a relatively unimportant phenomenon and that its study could make only a limited contribution to our understanding of the learning process. It will be recalled that the reasoning behind this belief was that only simple responses could be conditioned and these represented only a small number of the responses in the organism's response repertoire.

It is within this context that an important development took place in the 1960s—a finding that suggested that the Pavlovian procedure could be broadened to include a range of behavior much more extensive than had been previously assumed could take place. More specifically, an experiment by Brown and Jenkins (1968) suggested that the Pavlovian procedure was not just a matter of conditioning simple, discrete responses such as salivation or the eyeblink, but that this procedure could modify more extensive responding (e.g., locomotion) as well as significantly influence the organism's contact with reinforcing events.

The experimental procedure employed by Brown and Jenkins (1968) was to place pigeons in a Skinner Box and to repeatedly pair an eight-second white key light with food presented at the offset of key illumination. Although the subjects were not required to respond in order to secure food, the experimenters were surprised to find that repeated pairings of the two stimuli resulted in the reliable emergence of pecking at the lighted key. A comparison of this group's responding with that of an appropriate control group indicated that the acquisition of the response was dependent on the light-food pairing in that order. Traditionally, it was necessary to "shape" the pigeon's response in order to get it to peck at the illuminated key.[8]

Brown and Jenkins coined the term *autoshaping* since they discovered that pigeons could be trained without going through the time-consuming task of shaping. Thus, after placing a pigeon in the experimental chamber, it was necessary to provide only trials in which the response key was illuminated for a few seconds followed by the presentation of food. Such food delivery was, of course, independent of any response made by the subjects.

Although some investigators have argued that the strengthened pecking response occurred as a result of the accidental association of a key peck with the delivery of food, thus placing it within the instrumental learning or operant response classification, most experimenters believe that autoshaping reflects a classical conditioning operation. Experimental evidence has accumulated to indicate that there is an impressive similarity between the findings obtained utilizing the traditional classical conditioning paradigm and results obtained using an autoshaping procedure.

In the Brown and Jenkins study, the kind of pecking response made by the pigeon to the lighted key can be viewed as a part of its consummatory response to food.[9] If such is the case, one would predict that the response to the key would change if the reward (US) were changed. Moore (1973) has provided experimental support for the correctness of this prediction. Moore found that if the pigeon was made thirsty and water was used as a reward, a different type of pecking response to the lighted key was observed. When the lighted key was presented with food, the pecking response was short and forceful, with the beak open. When the key signaled water, the pigeon moved its head laterally across the key, with a slight opening and closing of the beak. In effect, the key was "eaten" or "drunk," depending on the kind of reward associated with it. In summary, the pigeon's autoconditioned response bears a marked similarity to the response made to the reward (or unconditioned stimulus), thus suggesting autoshaping to be a type of classical conditioning task.

The skeptic might argue that the pecking response varies little from the Pavlovian conditioned eyeblink (or other conditioned skeletal responses) in complexity, thus denying a wider role in behavior for conditioned responses. But what is of basic

---

[8] Shaping involves the operation of rewarding successive approximations of the instrumental response. In training pigeons to peck at a key, shaping would consist of rewarding the birds whenever they were standing near the key, then whenever they oriented themselves toward the key, then when they pecked near the key, and, finally, when they actually pecked at the key.

[9] Consummatory responses are those that terminate or conclude a period of goal-directed activity.

importance in that locomotion was also a part of the response noted in the Brown and Jenkins (1968) study, since it is obvious that their pigeons must have approached or locomoted toward the key prior to pecking at it. Hearst and Jenkins (1974) have experimentally demonstrated such to be the case. In their study, the Brown and Jenkins apparatus was modified from the one-foot square chamber to one that was three feet long. In addition, the response key was placed at one end of the wall and the food delivery system was placed at the other end. The procedure of pairing the key light with the presentation of food was continued, and results revealed that the birds continued to peck at the light, even though the pecking response took the birds away from the end of the chamber that resulted in food delivery. The implication of Hearst and Jenkins's finding was that an animal's locomotion in its environment, toward stimuli or places associated with appetitive events such as the presence of food, can be changed by Pavlovian procedures. This phenomenon has also been termed *sign tracking*, since experiments of the Hearst and Jenkins type suggest that organisms will approach and track or come in contact with a sign or stimulus that signals the presence of a reinforcing event.[10]

Mackintosh (1983) has written that the results from these types of experiments:

require a drastic reappraisal of the importance of classical conditioning, for much of the behavior studied in the psychologist's laboratory, perhaps much of the behavior of animals in the real world, can be thought of as approaching or avoiding places where benefit or harm will come to them, and much of what an animal must learn in order to survive both in the psychological laboratory and in the real world is to recognize the signs of impending events of consequence, so that appropriate approach or withdrawal can occur in anticipation of them (p. 7).

Summary ▶

Classical conditioning, considered to be one of the simplest types of associative learning, was demonstrated by Pavlov, who presented a tone and meat powder to his experimental subjects (dogs) and found that after several trials, presentation of the tone would elicit salivation. Pavlov designated the stimuli and responses in his experiment as follows: The unconditioned stimulus (US) was the meat powder, more generally defined as a stimulus that will elicit a regular and measurable response. The tone was the

---

[10] It appears that some of the experimental findings obtained with sign tracking experiments have applicability only for the pigeon. Sidman and Fletcher (1968) have found that the topography of the monkey's key-pressing response, obtained by the repeated pairings of a lighted key and the presentation of food, is much different from its consummatory response, a finding that would be expected if an instrumental conditioning procedure was used. Gamzu and Schwam (1974), also using monkeys as experimental subjects, were unable to confirm the Williams and Williams (1969) finding that omission training did not eliminate responding. Gamzu and Schwam found that the introduction of a negative contingency between the presentation of an illuminated key and reward markedly reduced responding. It is suggested that not all of the demonstrations of sign tracking can be considered to be under the control of those processes that are primarily responsible for the phenomena obtained in pigeons.

conditioned stimulus (CS). Conditioned stimuli are neutral in that they are not capable at the beginning of the experiment of eliciting the response that arises from CS-US presentations.

The responses that Pavlov observed in his study were:

1. The orienting response (OR), which consisted of head turning and other investigatory responses.
2. The unconditioned response (UR), which consisted of salivation as well as eating and chewing movements.
3. The conditioned response (CR), which consisted of salivation and was made to the presentation of the CS.

After a CR has been established, Pavlov noted that the repeated presentation of the CS without the US resulted in experimental extinction—cessation of the CR. If a rest period was placed between the last extinction trial and a subsequent presentation of the CS, the conditioned response reappeared, although not with the same strength as previously observed. The reappearance of the CR after extinction has been indentified as *spontaneous recovery.*

Several methodological issues are involved in classical conditioning studies. They include (1) the nature of the CS-US presentations, (2) how the CR is measured, and (3) the characteristics of the control group that is used.

Presentation of the CS prior to the US has been designated as *forward conditioning* and represents the basic classical conditioning procedure. The simultaneous presentation of the CS and US defines *simultaneous conditioning,* whereas presentation of the US prior to the CS is known as *backward conditioning.* There is some question as to whether either simultaneous or backward conditioning will result in the establishment of a CR. The measurement of the CR during acquisition takes the form of examining the frequency or percentage of CRs that are exhibited, as well as the CR's latency and/or amplitude.

It has been generally assumed that CRs are established as a result of the pairing operation (e.g., CS-US), so that the traditional control group consists of the random and single presentation of the CS and the US. Some investigators have assumed that the CR does not develop from the pairing operation but arises from the subject learning a contingency between the CS and US. These investigators have argued that the traditional control group that receives unpaired presentation of the CS and US also learns a contingency—that the US will not follow the CS. As a result, it has been argued that any comparison between the experimental group and the traditional control group's performance is flawed. The alternative has been to use a control group in which the subject cannot learn any contingency between the CS and US, with the basic operation being the random presentation of the CS and US, which on occasion may result in a CS-US pairing.

Many different responses have been conditioned. The most frequently examined in the laboratory include:

1. The galvanic skin or electrodermal response (EDR)
2. The eyeblink

3. The nictitating membrane of the rabbit
4. Emotional responses
5. Taste aversion

Recent interest has centered on the conditioning of a variety of physiological responses, including blood glucose level and immunosuppressive responses.

Pavlov speculated that the physiological processes that were responsible for the acquisition and extinction of conditioned responses were excitation and inhibition. Inhibition has provided some problems with its measurement, although summation and retardation of CR of acquisition have been used.

Extension of the Pavlovian procedure has been acknowledged to take place through several processes, namely, (1) higher-order conditioning, (2) stimulus generalization, and (3) autoshaping, or sign tracking. *Higher-order conditioning* refers to the elicitation of the CR by stimuli that have not been paired with the US but with the original CS. *Stimulus generalization* refers to the elicitation of conditioned responding by stimuli that bear some similarity to the original CS but which have never been paired with the US. Finally, *autoshaping,* or *sign tracking,* represents an operation in which the presentation of a CS and US will result in a type of responding that bears a marked similarity to instrumental responding.

chapter three

▶

Classical Conditioning: Stimulus Variables and Cognitive Processes in Acquisition and Extinction

In this chapter we shall describe how the manipulation of stimulus variables and hypothesized cognitive processes influence the acquisition and extinction of conditioned responses. This kind of research is not very exciting; in fact, some investigators have viewed it as quite tedious. It is an important endeavor, however, since it provides experimenters with basic information that identifies and describes the conditions that influence the growth and decline of conditioned responding. Such research is also significant because the data provide a body of knowledge for which any theoretical analysis of classical conditioning must account.

Acquisition ▶

In keeping with the organization that we believed is most satisfactory for the study of learning, and which we outlined in Chapter One, we shall examine how stimulus variables and cognitive processes each contribute to the strength of the classically conditioned response.

Stimulus Variables

Investigators examining stimulus variables have concentrated their efforts on four areas of inquiry: (1) the frequency of CS-US pairings; (2) the intensity and characteristics of the CS, including the contribution of compound and contextual stimuli; (3) the intensity and nature of the US; and (4) the interstimulus interval (ISI)—the length of time placed between the onset of the CS and the US.

Frequency of CS-US Pairings   An examination of many classical conditioning experiments reveals that the strength of the conditioned response is a function of the number of the CS-US pairings, with a negatively accelerated performance curve often being found.[1] However, as Hall's (1987) review has indicated, there are major differences among species and responses in the number of trials needed to reach asymptote. The conditioning of the eyeblink in humans takes place very gradually, with at least 40 CS-US pairings usually being necessary for near asymptotic responding to be observed. The acquisition of the conditioned eyeblink and nictitating membrane in rabbits also takes place quite gradually. But the conditioning of taste aversion in both animals and humans often takes place with only a single CS-US presentation. Similarly, as Silver's (1977) review has indicated, near asymptotic responding of the conditioned electrodermal response (EDR) also takes place in just one or two trials. Conditioning of the heart rate, however, has been obtained in 10 to 15 trials, whereas conditioned salivation takes place quite slowly. For example, Fitzgerald (1963) reported that near asymptotic responding in dogs was not achieved until after more than 200 trials had been provided.

It would be unusual if these conditioning trial disparities in acquisition that we have delineated were not found since different species (and different responses) have been examined. But it must also be kept in mind that any comparison that is made is between measures of performance and not the underlying neurological process. In this regard, Prokasy (1984) has suggested that the learning of the CS-US relationship in most instances occurs very rapidly, although performance differences may not reflect the presence of the learning process until a substantial number of conditioning trials have been provided. Support for Prokasy's position can be found in the work of a number of physiological investigators. When conditioning the nictitating membrane of the rabbit, these investigators found that certain neurological changes that have been associated with the conditioning of this response take place prior to the animal actually exhibiting a CR. To illustrate, Thompson, Berger, Cegavske, Patterson, Rosemer, Teylor, and Young (1976) have found that increments in dorsal hippocampus multiple unit responding could be observed with as few as eight CS-US presentations, although many more trials were necessary before conditioned responding was observed.[2]

Conditioned Stimulus Intensity   How does the intensity of the conditioned stimulus influence the conditioning process? Most current experimenters have found that

---

[1] Many current investigators reject the traditional position that the establishment of a CR is related to the number of paired presentations of the CS and US. It is their position that the learning of a CR is dependent on the subject learning a CS-US contingency—the probability that the US will follow the presentation of the CS. See the discussion in Chapter Four.

[2] We do not want to give the impression that hippocampal activity is the only neurological event with which the learning process is associated. Lesions of the hippocampus or the septum do not prevent conditioning from taking place, thus indicating that other structures are involved.

increasing the intensity of the CS results in more rapid conditioning. Such findings have been reported for the flexion response in the dog (Walker, 1960), respiration response in the fish (Woodward, 1971), heart rate in the pigeon (Cohen, 1974), eyeblink in the rabbit (Scavio and Gormezano, 1974), and conditioned emotional response in the rat (Kamin and Schaub, 1963; Jakubowski and Zielinski, 1978).[3]

Investigators have found that the intensity effect will be accentuated if the experimental design provides for each subject to experience more than a single level of stimulus intensity. The procedure used to demonstrate this is a within-subjects design. It can be compared with the more frequently used between-subjects design, in which different intensity levels of the CS are presented to different groups of subjects. In a study by Grice and Hunter (1964) employing both of the experimental designs, the eyeblink response was conditioned for 100 trials to a tone (CS); an airpuff served as the US. A within-subjects group received 50 trials with a soft tone and 50 trials with a loud tone. Two between-subjects groups were used; one group conditioned to the loud tone and the other group conditioned to the soft. The findings for the last 60 trials to the loud and soft tones for the within- and between-subjects groups are presented in Figure 3–1. The presentation of two intensities of the CS to the same subject substantially increased the effect of the intensity variable.

Pavlov explained stimulus intensity effects by assuming that the presentation of an intense stimulus resulted in greater neural activity, which in turn resulted in more rapid conditioning. A similar approach was suggested by Hull's (1949) dynamism theory,

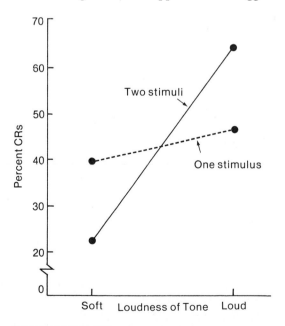

Figure 3-1
Percentage of conditioned responses during last 60 trials to the loud and soft tones under the one- and two-stimulus conditions. Adapted from G. R. Grice and J. J. Hunter, "Stimulus intensity effects depend upon the type of experimental design," *Psychological Review,* 1964, *71,* 247–256. Copyright © 1964 by the American Psychological Association. Reprinted by permission.

[3] Grant and Schneider (1948), Prokasy and Ebel (1967), and Orlebeke and van Olst (1968), all examining the conditioned EDR, and Grant and Schneider (1949), conditioning the eyeblink, were unable to demonstrate a CS intensity effect. There is the suggestion from these studies that CS intensity plays only a minor role in contributing to the strength of a CR.

which proposed that a basic property of the nervous system was to produce more vigorous responding with increased stimulus intensity.

Tangential support for Hull's position can be found in reaction time experiments. Grice and Hunter (1964) found that reaction time to a weak stimulus was significantly slower than reaction time to a more intense stimulus. But Hull's theory cannot adequately explain why the intensity effect is accentuated when using a within-subject, as contrasted with a between-subjects design as demonstrated by Grice and Hunter (1964).

Kamin (1965) has shown that a large decrease in stimulus intensity will result in more rapid conditioning than a small decrease, a finding also not in keeping with Hull's theoretical analysis. In Kamin's (1965) experiment, a conditioned emotional response (CER) task was used, with an 80 db sound serving as background noise in the experimental chamber. Kamin used a reduction of the noise level from the 80 db level to either 70, 60, 50, 45, or 0 db as his CS. Five groups of rats received a different reduction in noise level. Conditioned suppression was obtained in all groups, but it was largest for the two groups in which the CS was represented by a reduction in noise level from 80 to 45 db or from 80 to 0 db. The largest decrease in noise intensity was accompanied by the most rapid conditioning. Kamin's findings suggest that intensity effects be viewed within a context of stimulus change rather than intensity per se.

Conditioned Stimulus Compounds   Most experimenters in their examination of classical conditioning use only a single CS (e.g., tone, light, etc.). Laboratory experiments are different from those found in everyday situations where there are many stimuli constantly impinging on the organism. The acknowledgment that multiple stimuli are present in any conditioning situation raises the question of how the varying combinations of stimuli serving as CSs, as well as the procedures used in this examination, influence responding. An early study by Grings and O'Donnell (1956) illustrates one type of experimental design used to examine the contribution of stimulus compounding. The CSs employed by these investigators consisted of small colored dots, (red, green, blue, and yellow) projected on a ground glass screen. Shock served as the US, which elicited the EDR. Conditioning trials consisted of the single presentation of each of three stimuli; two of these were associated with the US, whereas the third stimulus was presented with the US omitted. Following 10 reinforced or nonreinforced trials to each stimulus, test trials consisted of simultaneously presenting two lights in the following combinations: (1) two previously reinforced lights, (2) one reinforced and one nonreinforced light, and (3) one reinforced light and one light not previously presented. Results indicated that the response to the stimulus compound composed of the two reinforced lights was significantly greater than the response to any other compound. The magnitude of the response to the stimulus compound, which combined the reinforced stimulus and a stimulus that had not been previously presented, was greater than that to the combination of the reinforced and nonreinforced stimulus. These findings support the position that a response to a compound stimulus reflects not only the presence of excitatory tendencies developed as a result of reinforcing specific stimulus elements, but also inhibitory tendencies produced by the association of a stimulus element without reinforcement.

The Grings and O'Donnell (1956) experiment is just one of many studies that have examined how classical conditioning is related to compound stimuli serving as the CS. We cannot review all of these, but would like to examine several compounding operations that result in the following conditioning phenomena: (1) overshadowing, (2) blocking, and (3) potentiation.

Overshadowing   Pavlov (1927) noted that if two stimuli of the same modality and equal in intensity were presented together, thus forming a compound CS, each stimulus when tested alone would elicit a CR of equal strength. However, when such stimuli were of different intensities, the high-intensity CS elicited a strong CS; in contrast, the weak-intensity CS evoked only a minimal CR. Pavlov wrote, "A compound stimulus was established, made up of the same sound of the whistle plus the tone a' of a tuning fork of weaker intensity. When tested separately the whistle in this case elicited a secretion of seven drops of saliva during thirty seconds, and the tone only one drop" (p. 142).

If the compound stimulus was composed of stimuli of different modalities, different findings were reported. Here it was noted that after conditioning trials with a tactile and thermal stimulus serving as the compound CS, testing with the tactile stimulus produced a salivary secretion almost as large as that obtained with the compound stimulus; when the thermal stimulus was presented alone, however, no salivation was obtained. This obscuring of a less intense stimulus by a more intense one was termed *overshadowing*. Pavlov (1927) wrote that the stronger of the two component stimuli would overshadow the weaker to a greater or lesser extent, depending on the relative intensities of the two stimuli.

Current experimenters have been interested in the phenomena of overshadowing and Pavlov's findings have been confirmed by a variety of experimenters (e.g., Kamin, 1969; Mackintosh, 1976; and Kehoe, 1982).

Kehoe's (1982) study (Exp. I) illustrates the overshadowing effect in conditioning the nictitating membrane of the rabbit. Six days of acquisition training were provided to three groups being trained with a compound stimulus consisting of light and tone. For all groups, light intensity was constant; however, each group received a different intensity of tone, the values being 85, 89, or 93 db. Groups received 54 reinforced trials per day interspersed with three nonreinforced test trials each to the light and tone. Four single CS control groups were used. One was trained with the light and the others with the 85, 89, and 93 db tones, respectively. Results are presented in Figure 3–2, revealing clear evidence of overshadowing in that the acquisition of the conditioned response to the light was impaired by training in compound with the more intense tones. Across the three compound stimulus groups, the rate and level of acquisition of responding to the light decreased as tone intensity increased.

Blocking   A phenomenon related to overshadowing has been identified by Kamin (1969) as *blocking*. Kamin has found that conditioning a response to stimulus A prior to later conditioning with the compound stimulus A-B may result in virtually no conditioning to stimulus B when B was presented singly on subsequent test trials. Using the conditioned emotional response (CER) paradigm, Kamin first trained rats to bar press for food. Next, 16 noise-shock conditioning trials were provided. This was then followed by eight compound stimulus (light and noise) and shock trials. When the light

Figure 3-2

Mean percentage of conditioned responses (CRs) plotted as a function of 2-day blocks. (Panels A, B, and C depict CR acquisition to the compound and its components for Groups LT85, LT89, and LT93, respectively. Panel D shows the CR acquisition curves for Groups T85, T89, T93, and L.) Adapted from E. J. Kehoe, "Overshadowing and summation in compound stimulus conditioning of the rabbit's nictitating membrane response," *Journal of Experimental Psychology: Animal Behavior Processes,* 1982, *8,* 313–328. Copyright © 1982 by the American Psychological Association. Reprinted by permission.

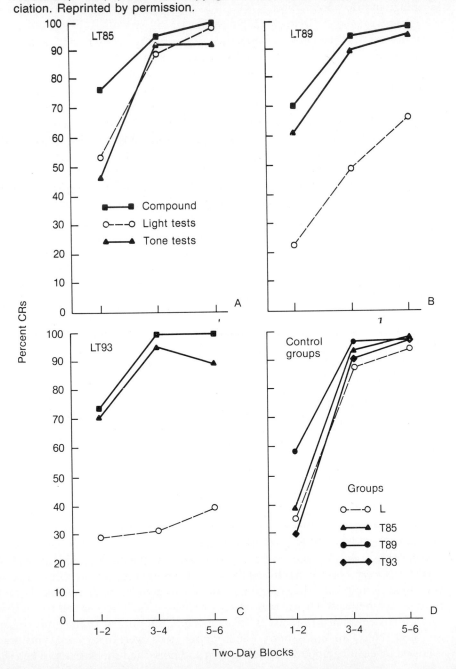

was presented alone after these trials, Kamin noted that virtually no conditioning to the light had taken place. This finding was in contrast to a control group that did not receive the early conditioning trials with noise as the CS, and revealed substantial conditioning. If the conditions were changed so that the light became the early training stimulus followed by the light and noise compound CS, and then tested with noise as the CS, no CRs were observed to the noise.

As a result of a host of replications, the blocking effect has been found to be a robust and readily reproducible phenomenon. It has been confirmed by investigators who have used experimental subjects other than rats and conditioned responses other than the CER (e.g., Marchant and Moore, 1973; Maleske and Frey, 1979).[4]

Using the CER, Kamin (1969) has demonstrated that blocking continues to be exhibited under a variety of experimental conditions. These conditions have included shortening the typically used three-minute CS to one minute, increasing the intensity of the US from 1 ma to 3 ma, and increasing the number of compound conditioning trials. Gaioni (1982) has also shown that if the second stimulus is not presented simultaneously with the first stimulus during compound stimulus conditioning trials, as has been traditionally done, but is presented only during the last 30 seconds of first stimulus presentation (first stimulus presentations of 0.5, 1.5, 3.0 and 5.0 minutes having been used), the blocking effect continues to be demonstrated.

Kamin's explanation of the blocking effect was that the added stimulus could not serve as an effective CS because it was redundant; the first stimulus already predicted the occurrence of the US. In Kamin's experiments, the noise predicted the onset of the shock—the added light that served as the second CS was thus redundant as a predictor of the US.

A correlate of Kamin's hypothesis has been that the US must be surprising to the subject if conditioning is to take place. If the US is already predicted by the first component of the compound stimulus, the added component is not surprising, which in turn limits its capacity to become associated with the response.

A host of other studies have been conducted examining Kamin's position that the redundancy and lack of surprise of the added stimulus to the compound is responsible for the blocking effect. The approach adopted by many investigators has been to change the nature of the US at the same time that the second stimulus becomes a part of the CS. Presumably, the new US reduces the added stimulus's redundancy as well as providing the factor of surprise. In one experiment, Kamin (1969) increased the intensity of the US from 1 to 4 ma when the compound stimulus was introduced. The second stimulus was thus made more informative and less redundant by being associated with a US of increased intensity. When this was done, results indicated that conditioning using the added stimulus as a CS was readily accomplished, with the blocking effect being eliminated. In a second experiment, Kamin (1969) programmed a second (and presumably surprising) shock five seconds after each compound stimulus conditioning trial had been completed. Results similar to those obtained in the first experiment were noted—the blocking effect was not obtained.

---

[4] Blocking has been also found using inhibitory conditioning, as Suiter and LoLordo (1971) using the CER have demonstrated.

Subsequent studies conducted by Dickinson, Hall, and Mackintosh (1976) and Mackintosh, Dickinson, and Cotton (1980) consisted of introducing a variety of changes during the compound conditioning trials each of which attenuated the blocking effect. These experimenters have indicated that it is not necessary that the surprise be a second shock since either the temporary postponement of an expected second shock or its complete omission was as effective as the addition of an unexpected shock in eliminating blocking. Moreover, it has been demonstrated by Gray and Appignanesi (1973) that the surprising effect need not be limited to the role of the US since these investigators found that a 30-second combination of a light flash and a white burst of noise, presented either three or five seconds after the presentation of the CS during the compound conditioning trials, also eliminated the blocking effect. (It should be noted that if the light and noise were presented ten seconds following the presentation, the blocking effect was obtained.)

In summary, Kamin's hypothesis attributing the attenuation of blocking to a surprise process operating during the compound conditioning trials has had experimental support from a variety of studies. A basic problem, of course, is in providing an appropriate definition of *surprise,* as well as identifying how the surprise mechanism operates.[5]

Potentiation   As we have noted with overshadowing, when two CSs making up a compound stimulus are reinforced, the presentation of only the weaker CS in a subsequent test situation will result in little or no conditioned responding. A somewhat similar effect is obtained in blocking—conditioning a response to one CS which is subsequently paired with a new CS in order to form a compound stimulus. This results in the new CS being unable to elicit the CR when presented alone. Both the overshadowing and blocking operations involve the weakening of one CS (in its capacity to elicit the CR) by associating it with another CS.

One exception to this result is noted with some taste aversion studies that have employed compound conditioning stimuli. The early experiments of Hankins, Garcia, and Rusiniak (1973), Rusiniak, Hankins, Garcia, and Brett (1979), and Palmerino, Rusiniak, and Garcia (1980) have indicated that odor serving as a single CS for taste aversion is a weak cue, whereas taste is quite strong. But when both cues are combined into a compound CS and followed by lithium-induced illness, odor as a single stimulus becomes a very strong cue. In effect, taste *potentiates,* or augments, the effectiveness of odor in inducing avoidance of the solution.

Current investigators of taste aversion have been interested in examining the varying stimuli that can be potentiated. Galef and Osborne (1978) were able to demonstrate that the association of a visual cue with toxicosis could be augmented or potentiated if the illness was induced immediately after the ingestion of a distinctively marked food capsule. Experiments conducted by Best, Batson, Meachum, Brown, and Ringer (1985) have demonstrated that the environment in which the illness has been experienced can also serve as a potentiated stimulus. Thus, when rats drink a novel

---

[5] Other explanations for the blocking effect have been proposed. Mackintosh (1975) has explained blocking on the basis of the organism's limited capacity for attending to stimuli.

flavor in a distinctive environment and are then injected with lithium, potentiated aversions are established to that environment, as indicated by the animal's unwillingness to consume a familiar nonaversive solution in the environment that had been associated with the novel flavor and illness.

Contextual Stimuli   When describing the stimuli used in their classical conditioning studies, most traditional investigators focused their attention on the nature and characteristics of the CS and US. The contextual stimuli that were inherent parts of the experiment were only briefly mentioned; in addition, there was the implicit assumption that such stimuli did not make any contribution to the experimental findings. This assumption is now being challenged. During the past decade, the role of context is being reevaluated and there has been considerable interest in determining how contextual stimuli influence a variety of phenomena found in classical conditioning tasks. The thrust of many of these studies has been to demonstrate that contextual stimuli can serve or function as any traditional CS. The previously cited study by Best and colleagues (1985) in our examination of potentiation is such an example.

Balsam (1985) has described a variety of experimental procedures that investigators have employed in examining the contribution of contextual stimuli to learning and memory processes. In this introductory presentation, we shall describe only the most frequently employed of these—a procedure that has been described as the *context-shift test*. This procedure provides experimental animals with training on a task in one environmental context, followed by examining task retention (or extinction) in a different environment. Control animals receive all training and retention trials in the same environment. Most generally, it has been found that a context change results in poorer performance than if the environmental context remains the same. Archer, Sjoden, Nilsson, and Carter (1979) have demonstrated this decremental effect arising from context in a taste aversion study. Saccharin and lithium chloride served as the CS and US; rats received their conditioning trial in a context consisting of specific visual, auditory, tactile, and olfactory cues. Results indicated that the contextual cues present in the conditioning trial controlled the amount of saccharin drunk on the extinction trials. As the context was changed, extinction took place more rapidly.

Inasmuch as contextual stimuli are always a part of the experimental situation, it is important that we examine how such stimuli interact with other experimental variables in contributing to a variety of conditioning phenomena. As Balsam's (1985) volume attests, substantial progress is being made. One illustration is found in relating contextual stimuli to the phenomenon of pseudoconditioning. In Chapter Two we indicated that control subjects serving in a classical conditioning experiment will occasionally appear to have been "conditioned" since the presentation of the CS (without this stimulus ever having been paired with the US) will result in the CR. Such responses were identified as being *pseudoconditioned*. Sheafor and Gormezano (1972) and Sheafor (1975) have suggested that such responding, at least as observed with the conditioning of the rabbit's jaw movement, has arisen from contextual cues serving as CSs.

These investigators have found that presentations of only the US (intraoral water) is sufficient to enable a subsequently presented CS (tone) to elicit conditioned response levels significantly above those produced by appropriate control treatments. Sheafor

(1975) has noted that such responding is retained and gradually extinguished over a thirty-day period in which no further USs are presented. Moreover, this extinction effect does not demand the normal extinction procedure (e.g., presentation of the CS alone); rather, Sheafor has found that simple confinement of the animals in the experimental situation in the absence of further US presentations was sufficient to extinguish the response. Sheafor's (1975) experiments have further indicated that US alone presentations appear sufficient to produce pseudoconditioning responding, thus suggesting that contextual background cues arising in the experimental situation can serve as CSs in the subsequent elicitation of CRs.

Unconditioned Stimulus Intensity   Pavlov's (1927) early experiments indicate that the strength of a conditioned response was related to the intensity of the unconditioned stimulus used, and many later investigators have confirmed Pavlov's findings.[6] Razran's (1957) review indicated that Soviet investigators have found CR latency and magnitude to vary directly with the magnitude of the US employed; many American investigators have obtained similar findings. For example, Wagner, Siegel, Thomas, and Ellison (1964) conditioned the salivary response of two groups of dogs using either one or six food pellets as the US. After 11 days of eight training trials per day, they found that the six-pellet group reached a higher level of conditioned responding than the group receiving one pellet.

A second method of manipulating US intensity has been to vary the intensity of shock, with a positive monotonic relationship to the strength of the CR being revealed over a wide range of preparations. The conditioned leg flexion in dogs (Ost and Lauer, 1965), heart rate and nictitating membrane in the rabbit (Sideroff, Schneiderman, and Powell, 1971; Smith, 1968), the eyeblink and EDR in humans (Prokasy and Harsanyi, 1968; Harvey and Wickens, 1973), and the CER in rats (Annau and Kamin, 1961; Kamin and Brimer, 1963) are only a few of the many responses that have reflected different CR strength as a function of US intensity.

To illustrate, in the Annau and Kamin (1961) study, four CS-US pairings per day for ten days were provided. The CS was white noise and the US was either a 0.28, 0.49, 0.85, 1.55, or 2.91 ma shock. The suppression of bar pressing that took place in each test session following the CS-US trials is presented in Figure 3–3 and clearly reveals the role of US intensity.

The acquisition of a conditioned discrimination task has also been found to be a function of US intensity. In an experiment by Kehoe, Poulos, and Gormezano (1985) utilizing three groups of subjects, differential conditioning of the rabbit's jaw movement response was examined. A tone of 600 Hz served as the CS+ and 2,100 Hz as the CS−; the US was either 1 ml, 3 ml, or 9 ml of water delivered into the animal's mouth. Phase I consisted of providing the CS+ with 60 reinforced trials, thus stabilizing this response; during Phase II, discrimination training was instituted, which consisted of providing four reinforced (CS-US) and four nonreinforced (CS only) trials each day for

---

[6]US duration is frequently considered along with intensity. However, the experimental evidence relating the duration of the US to the strength of the CR is so controversial that we have decided to omit consideration of this aspect of the US.

Figure 3-3

Median suppression ratio as a function of day of acquisition training. Adapted from Z. Annau and L. J. Kamin, "The conditioned emotional response as a function of intensity of the US," *Journal of Comparative and Physiological Psychology*, 1961, *54*, 428–432. Copyright © 1961 by the American Psychological Association. Reprinted by permission.

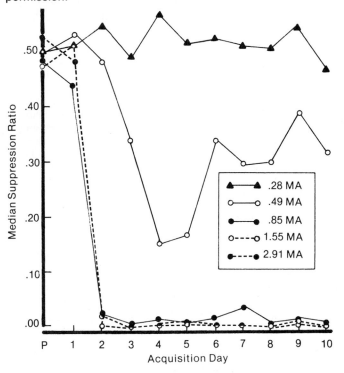

24 days. Figure 3–4 supports the findings of other investigators in demonstrating that conditioned discrimination also is a function of the intensity of the US.

What is the nature of the process whereby the US influences classical conditioned responding? One suggestion comes from the theoretical positions of Hull (1943), Prokasy (1972), and Rescorla and Wagner (1972) who have posited that the US is a motivational variable that determines the limit of asymptote or conditioning. A weak US will result in a lower asymptote than a strong US. It is assumed that each CS-US trial results in a performance increment, with the amount of the increment being determined, at least in part, by asymptotic strength. Thus, a weak US produces a low asymptote, which in turn results in a smaller performance increment than if a strong US is employed, which provides a higher asymptote and larger increments in performance.

Some support for this theoretical position can be found by noting that investigators who have shown conditioned responding to be a function of US intensity, have demonstrated that different US intensities also produce different performance asymptotes. One example can be noted in a study by Prokasy and Harsanyi (1968) who found that when three intensities (weak, medium, strong) of an air puff were used as the US in

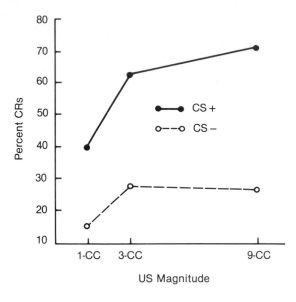

Figure 3-4
Conditioned responding as a function of the magnitude of the US. Adapted from E. J. Kehoe, C. X. Poulos, and I. Gormezano, "Appetitive differential conditioning of the rabbit's jaw movement response," *The Pavlovian Journal of Biological Science*, 1985, *20*, 29–38. Copyright © 1985 by J. B. Lippincott. Reprinted by permission.

a conditioned eyeblink experiment, different terminal levels of responding were obtained, with the strong US producing the highest level and the weak US producing the lowest level of responding. Additional research needs to be undertaken in order to determine if US intensity serves as a motivational variable in that it influences only the organism's performance, or that it contributes also to strengthening the learning process.

The CS-US Interval   Another variable related to the strength of the conditioned response is the interval of time separating the onset of the CS from the onset of the US, called the *interstimulus interval* (ISI). Early studies conducted by Wolfle (1930, 1932) and Kappauf and Schlosberg (1937) resulted in these investigators finding that optimal conditioning took place when a 0.5 second interstimulus interval was used. Using these findings, as well as neurological information related to the strength of the afferent impulse produced by the action of the CS, Hull (1943) assumed that the optimal interval for all conditioning tasks was 0.5 second. This conclusion was echoed by many psychologists for the next decade.

An examination of the findings of many later ISI studies—using both humans and animals and employing a variety of response measures—reveals that Hull was in error; optimal conditioning may take place with intervals that differ markedly from 0.5 second.

Using fish as their experimental subjects, Noble, Gruender, and Meyer (1959) and Noble and Adams (1963) found that the frequency of conditioned responding increased as the ISI was lengthened from 0.5 to 2.0 seconds, while further increases in the ISI resulted in a declining response frequency. Ost and Lauer (1965), examining ISIs of 2, 5, 10, and 15 seconds in their study of salivary conditioning in dogs, reported that "the highest response rates appear in the 5 and 15 second groups" (p. 203).

These studies suggest that the optimal ISI will vary as a function of the type of response conditioned. If further evidence is needed, Vandercar and Schneiderman's (1967) findings in their classically conditioned discrimination study are most revealing. The rabbit's nictitating membrane and heart rate were simultaneously conditioned, with a 550 Hz tone serving as the CS + and a 2,400 Hz tone as the CS −. Shock, as the US, elicited both responses. Four groups of subjects received ISIs of either (a) 0.25, (b) 0.75, (c) 2.25, or (d) 6.75 seconds. Seven days of training, with 80 trials per day, were provided. Results revealed that the optimal interval for the nictitating membrane was an ISI of 0.75 second, whereas the optimal ISI for conditioning heart rate was 2.25. These findings provide compelling evidence that no single interval is optimal for conditioning of all responses.

An examination of the optimal ISI employed in establishing the conditioned response, although variable, is rarely longer than several seconds and the ISI function is curvilinear. An ISI either shorter or longer than the optimal interval will result in poorer conditioning. The use of very long ISI intervals will result in no conditioning at all.

A good example of the curvilinear relationship—actually an inverted U-shaped function—is found in a study by Smith, Coleman, and Gormezano (1969) who examined a variety of ISI functions using the rabbit's nictitating membrane response. Subjects trained with a backward ISI function (− 50 ms), as well as with very short ISIs, revealed no CR acquisition. When ISIs of 100, 200, 400, and 800 ms were employed, CRs were acquired, with the rate of acquisition being most rapid at 200 and 400 ms, moderate at 800 ms, and slowest at 100 ms.

No satisfactory reason has been provided for why different response systems require different ISIs for optimal conditioning, although a number of investigators have grappled with the problem (e.g., Gormezano, 1972; and Mackintosh, 1974). The response latency of the effector system examined plays an obvious role but since little relationship between the reaction time of the response and the length of the inter-stimulus interval leading to optimal conditioning can be discerned, other unidentified variables must make a contribution. The search for these variables has been a continuing one.

Our discussion of the ISI function has omitted consideration of the role of this variable with CER and taste aversion studies. It will be recalled that both of these paradigms utilize instrumental response measures from which the strength of the CR is inferred. When the ISI with the CER is examined, investigators have found that ISIs may vary from a few seconds to three minutes with no optimal interval noted—all ISIs produce about the same level of conditioning.

When the taste aversion procedure is examined, the findings have been even more unusual. In the Smith and Roll (1967) study discussed in Chapter Two, it will be recalled that ISIs were used that ranged in time from 0.5 to 24 hours, with little difference in conditioning being observed among those intervals ranging from 0.5 to 6 hours. These unusual findings have resulted in some experimenters believing that the conditioning of taste aversion is qualitatively different from traditional conditioning studies employing the eyeblink, salivary response, and so on. In her review of the taste aversion literature, Logue (1979) has acknowledged that the difference in an optimal ISI "between taste aversion and traditional learning appears to be an instance of such a large quantitative difference that simply calling it a quantitative, and not a qualitative difference seems inappropriate" (p. 286). She has continued to maintain, however, "that at the present time it is not necessary to dispense with the notion of general laws of learning" (p. 276).

An Examination of Other Stimulus Conditions

Conditioning experimenters over the years have expanded their search of variables influencing acquisition to include a wide variety of stimulus conditions. We will examine those that appear to be of major significance.

The Role of CS Alone Trials – Partial Reinforcement   In their examination of classical conditioning, early investigators used trials that invariably consisted of pairing the CS and US. In the late 1930s, Humphreys (1939) employed a procedure which at that time was most unusual—interspersed among 48 CS-US trials were placed 48 presentations of the CS alone. This procedure omitted the US on some trials and has been identified as intermittent or *partial reinforcement.*

Let us examine Humphreys' study in greater detail in order to determine the effect of omitting the US on half of the training trials. Three groups of college students were given the following training trials: (1) 96 trials with 100% reinforcement; (2) 96 trials with 50% reinforcement—here the CS was presented alone on half of the training trials; and (3) 48 trials with 100% reinforcement, with rest intervals substituted for the nonrewarded trials. Surprisingly, Humphreys found no significant differences among the groups with regard to the frequency of conditioned responding. This finding led Humphreys to write that "the lack of effect from reinforcement . . . is indeed paradoxical" (p. 146). An inspection of Humphreys' data reveals, however, that after the first few trials, the frequency of CRs obtained with the partial reinforcement group never attained the performance level of the continuously reinforced groups at any point throughout the remaining acquisition trials.

This latter finding that a partial reinforcement schedule results in poorer acquisition has been confirmed by many investigators employing many different species and a variety of conditioned responses. Gibbon, Farrell, Locurto, Duncan, and Terrace's (1980) survey of continuous versus partial reinforcement studies conducted in the 1960s and 1970s with animals indicates that a preponderance of them revealed that a partial reinforcement schedule retarded acquisition.

Moreover, it has been demonstrated that when the percentage of reinforced trials is systematically varied, the frequency of conditioned responding is a function of the percentage of reinforced trials. In a conditioned eyelid response experiment conducted by Grant and Schipper (1952), 60 training trials were provided on day 1, and 32 trials on day 2. Using light as the CS and an air puff as the US, the following percentages of US presentations were provided: 0, 25, 50, 75, or 100. Results revealed that the probability of conditioned responding was an increasing function of percentage of US presentations.

The superiority of continuously reinforced trials has also been reported when the autoshaping or sign tracking paradigm is employed. Gonzalez (1973) has noted that there is a slower approach to asymptotic response levels under 25%, as opposed to 100% reinforcement. Wasserman, Hunter, Gutowski, and Bader (1975) have also reported that when heat reinforcement was employed with baby chicks, the number of trials to the first pecking response was a decreasing function of the percentage of reinforced trials with 0, 33%, 67%, and 100% schedules being utilized. (See Box 3–1.)

US Alone Trials Presented Among CS-US Pairings   It has been found that the partial reinforcement operation, which consists of interspersing CS alone trials among CS-US presentations, results in slowing the acquisition process. A related operation used by some investigators has been to intersperse US alone trials among CS-US presentations, with the usual finding also being retarded acquisition. Hupka, Kwaterski, and Moore (1970) and Leonard, Fishbein, and Monteau (1972) have found that when the number of CS-US presentations has been held constant, the presentation of additional US alone trials will delay acquisition. In the latter study, the nictitating membrane response of rabbits was classically conditioned using a tone (CS) paired with shock (US). A continuous reinforcement group received 100 paired CS-US trials; two additional groups also received 100 CS-US trials but in addition to 100 US alone trials. For one group, these trials were presented midway between a 60-second intertrial interval, whereas the second group received the US alone trial midway between a 120-second intertrial interval. Results indicated that the continuous reinforcement group conditioned significantly more rapidly than either of the other groups, reaching asymptote by about the 80th trial. In contrast, the groups receiving US alone trials required 100 CS-US presentations to approximate the same level of responding.[7]

Preexposure of the Conditioned Stimulus   In an early study by Lubow and Moore (1959), goats received 10 reinforced presentations of one of two stimuli, either a flashing light or a turning rotor. Following these 10 CS preexposure trials, a classical conditioning procedure was instituted, with the animals being presented with either the pretest stimulus or a new stimulus as the CS; shock served as the US, which elicited leg flexion. Both CSs were presented during the course of conditioning trials. Results indicated that when conditioned responding to the preexposed stimulus and the new stimulus were compared, conditioning to the preexposed stimulus was significantly lower. The mean number of trials to reach the learning criteria (10 CRs) was 19.75 for the new stimulus and 37.38 for the preexposed stimulus. Since this early study, and as Lubow's (1973) review and later studies have indicated, many investigators have replicated these findings using a variety of experimental organisms (e.g., goldfish [Braud, 1971], sheep [Lubow, 1965], rabbits [Lubow, Markham, and Allen, 1968], and rats [Chacto and Lubow, 1967]). Lubow and Moore (1959) identified their finding as a *latent inhibition*

---

[7] This decremental effect on conditioning that is provided by using US alone trials along with CS-US presentations has been cited to support Rescorla's (1967) position that classical conditioning arises from the learning of a contingency. We shall discuss this issue in Chapter Four.

box 3-1

When examining autoshaping in pigeons, Gibbon, Farrell, LoCurto, Duncan, and Terrace (1980) obtained some interesting findings in relating partial and continuous reinforcement schedules to acquisition of responding. Their procedure consisted of projecting a green light on the response key for 10 seconds; the subjects had access to a food hopper for 3.5 seconds on all reinforced trials. The probability of the subjects receiving reinforcement following presentation of the green light was 0.0, 0.2, 0.4, 0.6, 0.8, or 1.00. Each group was subdivided with five different intertrial intervals: 15, 30, 50, 100, or 250 seconds. The acquisition criterion was pecking at the response key within the 10-second presentation period on three of four successive trials.

One part of their experimental findings was in keeping with the results previously reported; as the panel of Box Figure 3-1 indicates, the log median number of trials to reach the acquisition criterion decreased as a function of the probability of reinforcement. But the interesting part of their study can be noted from the right panel of the figure, which reveals the number of reinforcers required to reach the criterion. Note that when acquisition was measured as a function of this variable, the effect of reinforcement probability virtually disappeared, with a regression analysis of the logged median indicating that the slopes did not differ.

The investigators have written, "The data seems quite clear that, at best, there is no discernible effect of intermittent reinforcement on the speed of acquisition when acquisition is accessed per reinforced trial and trial spacing is held constant" (p. 52). The significance of this finding is that with virtually all theories of conditioning, unreinforced trials that make up part of the partial reinforcement regimen are assumed to make an important contribution to what is learned. The failure to find partial reinforcement effects when performance is assessed per scheduled reinforcer poses a problem for these theoretical positions. It is important that this general finding be replicated with other classical conditioning preparations as well as with other types of experimental subjects.

Box Figure 3-1
Log median number of trials (left panel) and reinforcements (right panel) to satisfy the acquisition criterion as a function of probability of reinforcement. The linear functions are least-squares regressions, and the parameter is ITI duration. Adapted from J. Gibbon, L. Farrell, C. M. Locurto, H. J. Duncan, and H. S. Terrace, "Partial reinforcement in autoshaping with pigeons," *Animal Learning & Behavior,* 1980, *8,* 45–59. Copyright © 1980 by the Psychonomic Society, Inc. Reprinted by permission.

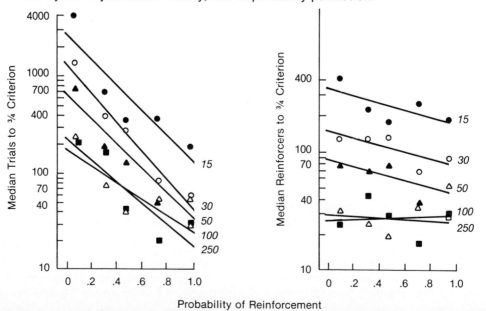

effect, but most current investigators have preferred to use a more neutral term—*CS preexposure*—to describe the operation and experimental findings. One of the reasons for not using the term *inhibition* has been that many investigators assume that for a stimulus to become a conditioned inhibitor, it must signal the omission of the US. The presentation of one CS prior to the subject being exposed to the US in the experimental situation would not satisfy this condition, so it would not be expected that such preexposure would turn the CS into a conditioned inhibitor.

Preexposure of the Unconditioned Stimulus   A similar effect identified as US preexposure has been observed when the US is presented for a number of trials prior to being paired with the CS in a conditioning study. In an early conditioned eyeblink experiment conducted by Kimble and Dufort (1956), one group of subjects was preexposed to the US, receiving 20 presentations of the air puff prior to receiving 60 CS-US trials. Results indicated that the US preexposure group conditioned less rapidly than a control group that was not given the US preexposures. Mis and Moore (1973) have also obtained the US preexposure effect using the conditioned nictitating membrane of the rabbit. The CER and taste aversion paradigms have been also frequently used in examining US preexposure effects, with virtually all such studies revealing positive findings (e.g., Kamin, 1961; and Elkins, 1974).

One area of concern for investigators of the US preexposure effect has been to determine if such US preexposure influences inhibitory conditioning. We shall not provide a detailed description of Saladin and Tait's (1986) study, but in their examination of the differential conditioning of the nictitating membrane response, they found that US preexposure resulted in retarding excitatory conditioning, thus extending the US preexposure effect to differential conditioning. In addition, they found that inhibitory conditioning was facilitated. As a result, they suggested that a common process was acting to produce both effects.

A second and more general concern of investigators has been to examine the varying characteristics of the US preexposed stimulus in order to determine their contribution to the retardation effect. We shall briefly summarize the results of some of these studies.

Several studies have demonstrated that the retardation of conditioning is an inverse function of the number of preexposed US presentations (e.g., Hobson [1986] conditioning the human eyeblink; Mis and Moore [1973] the nictitating membrane response of the rabbit; and Elkins [1974] and Cannon, Berman, Baker, and Atkinson [1975] employing the taste aversion paradigm with rats). Elkins (1974) preexposed groups of rats to injections of cyclophosphamide for either 0, 1, 3, or 6 days over the course of a two-week period, following which an aversion to saccharin was produced by pairing the drinking of a saccharin solution (CS) with another injection of cyclophosphamide (US). On the day following the single CS-US presentation, and for 60 days following, each subject was given free access to both a saccharin solution and tap water presented in separate bottles. Results indicated that the decline of the aversion to saccharin to be a direct function of the number of US preexposures. In addition, Mis and Moore (1973) and Cannon and associates (1975) have found that the amount of CR retardation decreases as the amount of time between the last US preexposure and the beginning of CS-US pairings increases.

The contribution of the intensity of the preexposed US has also interested experimenters but different findings, dependent on the kind of conditioning paradigm employed, have been obtained. To illustrate, the results of Kamin (1961) and Rescorla (1974) employing the CER have suggested to Randich and LoLordo (1979a) that when preexposure and US conditioning intensities are the same, response suppression will be maximized by such an identity of stimuli; as the two intensities grow more disparate, response suppression will grow progressively less. This means, as Randich and LoLordo (1979a) have suggested, and as Randich and LoLordo (1979b) have experimentally demonstrated, if groups of subjects are preexposed to a wide range of US intensities and all are conditioned at an intermediate US intensity, the retardation of conditioned responding is represented by an inverted U-shaped function.

When the results from taste aversion experiments are examined, it may be noted that they differ from those obtained with the CER. For example, the findings obtained from a recent taste aversion study by Klein, Mikulka, and Lucci (1986) suggest that the role of the intensity of the preexposed stimulus is quite complex and appears to be dependent on whether the US alone dose was either below or above the conditioning US dose. In any event, it is clear that the relationship existing between the intensity of the preexposed US and the intensity of the US employed in the conditioning paradigm plays an important role in determining the extent of the retardation effect.

Explanations for the US preexposure effect, for which we shall provide only brief summaries, have occupied the attention of a host of investigators. Such explanations can be identified as nonassociative or associative. The most widely accepted nonassociative explanation of the preexposure effect is that some central habituation process takes place in response to repeated presentations of the US during the preexposure phase of the study, thus reducing the organism's responsiveness to the US. Thus, the conditioning phase of the study results in the habituated US having a diminished capacity to elicit the UR, which in turn results in CR retardation. If drugs are used as unconditioned stimuli, it has been suggested that a tolerance for the drug taking place during the US preexposure period develops, which also diminishes the capacity of the drug when serving as the US to elicit the UR.

Probably the most frequently adopted associative explanation for the US preexposure effect is blocking. Here, it is suggested that some stimulus, perhaps of an environmental or contextual nature, serves as a CS during the US preexposure period, and thus becomes capable of eliciting a CR. When the conditioning phase of the study begins, the environmental or contextual stimulus continues to be present in the experimental situation and thus blocks the conditioning of the response to the CS provided by the experimenter.

A variety of experiments have been conducted to support one or the other explanation of the preexposure effect, but there has been little success in providing a viable explanation that can handle all of the experimental findings that have been obtained. As Randich and LoLordo's (1979a) review of the US preexposure phenomenon suggests, both "associative and nonassociative factors may both play a role in any given situation, and indeed, the relative importance of the two may vary across conditioning paradigms" (p. 545).

Cognitive Processes

Cognitive processes presumably arising from the manipulation of stimulus variables and inferred from the subject's responding represent a class of organismic or central state conditions that may contribute to the acquisition of a classically conditioned response. As we noted in Chapter One, Watson's position that cognitive processes were private events, and therefore not appropriate for scientific investigations, effectively prevented many early psychologists from studying such processes. Nonetheless, a few experimenters did examine several experimental conditions from which cognitive processes can be inferred.

The Role of Verbal Instructions   Some psychologists became interested in determining how the kinds of instructions given to subjects influenced the acquisition of the conditioned response. Since giving such instructions can be viewed as a procedure for manipulating a cognitive process, these studies can be considered as precursors to the examination of cognitive processes.

Cook and Harris (1937) demonstrated that a conditioned EDR could be obtained merely by instructing the subject that shock would follow the presentation of a green light. Their experimental findings revealed that the presentation of 15 or 30 CS-US trials following such instructions did not increase the strength of the conditioned response beyond the strength obtained when only a single conditioning trial plus instructions was used. While conditioning heart rate, Deane (1961) noted that "verbal instructions regarding when to expect shock were apparently more effective in bringing about the deceleration than actually receiving the shock itself" (p. 492).

The contribution of instructions has also been examined with the classical conditioning of skeletal responses. Unlike the autonomic conditioning studies of Cook and Harris (1937) and Deane (1961), in which their subjects were told when to expect the presentation of the US, skeletal conditioning studies have used more indirect instructions, as illustrated in an eyelid conditioning study conducted by Nicholls and Kimble (1964). Here, two groups of subjects were provided with 40 conditioning trials. One group received facilitative instructions: "Relax and let your eye reactions take care of themselves. If you feel your eye close or about to close, do nothing to stop it." The second group received inhibitory instructions: The subject was asked to "concentrate on not blinking until you feel the puff of air. That is, try not to blink after the light comes on until you feel the air puff." The percentages of CRs for the two groups, presented in Figure 3–5, clearly reveal the role of instructions in facilitating or inhibiting responding.

The facilitating and inhibiting effect of instructions to the subject in the conditioning of both autonomic and skeletal responses has been confirmed in more recent experiments (see Hill, 1967; Swenson and Hill, 1970; and Harvey and Wickens, 1971, 1973). In summary, there seems to be little doubt that the strength of a human classically conditioned response can be manipulated by the kinds of instructions provided. It is reasonable to assume that such instructions are responsible for providing some change in the subjects' cognitive structure, which in turn is responsible for determining the strength of the conditioned response.

Figure 3-5

Mean percentage of conditioned responses for subjects conditioned with facilitative and inhibitory instructions. Adapted from M. F. Nicholls and G. A. Kimble, "Effect of instruction upon eyelid conditioning," *Journal of Experimental Psychology,* 1964, *67,* 400–402. Copyright © 1964 by the American Psychological Association. Reprinted by permission.

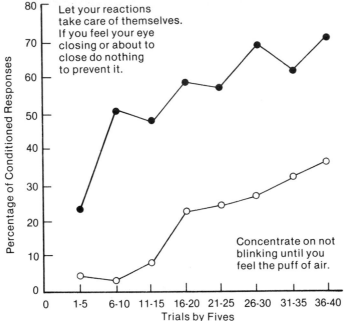

Awareness of the CS-US Contingency   In the studies that we have just reviewed, it is obvious that the experimental instructions given to subjects provided them with an awareness of the relationship existing between the CS and US. But what contribution does awareness make in the establishment of a conditioned response? In an effort to examine the role of awareness, many investigators have employed procedures that mask or conceal the relationship between the CS and US. Experimental subjects are provided instructions that mislead them about the purpose of the study. This has been the objective of obscuring the CS-US relationship; control subjects, however, are informed about the CS-US relationship.

A study by Dawson (1970) that examined the conditioning of the EDR illustrates the method and experimental findings. In Dawson's study (Experiment 2), subjects were given 60 trials, with six tones presented on each trial. The first tone was either 950, 1,000, or 1,050 Hz. The other five tones were 800, 950, 1,000, 1,050, and 1,200 Hz, presented in random order. Subjects were instructed to perform three tasks following the presentation of the last tone: (1) determine which of the last five tones had the same pitch as the first tone, (2) determine which of the last five tones had the highest pitch, and (3) determine which of the last five tones had the lowest pitch. The 1,200 and 800 Hz tones served as CS+ and CS−; the CS+ followed by the US (shock) 75% of the time. An aware group was instructed that the shock would usually but not always follow the highest (or the lowest) tone, but would never follow any other tone. An unaware group was told that shock would be presented periodically, since the experimenter was interested in determining whether such stimulation would facilitate the subject's ability to respond correctly. At the end of 60 trials, all subjects were administered a questionnaire, which included the multiple-choice item "Shock usually followed (a) the highest tone, (b) the middle tone, (c) the lowest tone, (d) it was not systematic, (e) I couldn't tell."

The findings obtained from this study, as revealed by the mean EDR discrimination scores for the aware and unaware groups, are presented in Figure 3–6. The unaware group failed to condition, whereas conditioning was observed with the group made aware of the CS-US contingency. These findings confirm the results of earlier experiments conducted by Dawson and Grings (1968) and Dawson and Satterfield (1969), and are in keeping with subsequent studies of Dawson and Biferno (1973) and Dawson, Schell, and Banis (1986). All of these studies have indicated that for unaware subjects, CS-US pairings that were embedded in a masking task were not sufficient to establish EDR conditioning. When an identical number of CS-US pairings was provided on the same task and the subject was told of the nature of the CS-US contingency, a conditioned response was readily established.

The results of the findings provided by Dawson and his associates have been used to support the position that an awareness of the CS-US contingency should be considered as a condition that must be present if a CR is to be established in the human subject, thus supporting a cognitive explanation of human classical conditioning.

But not all psychologists have agreed with Dawson's position that in order for a conditioned EDR to be established, the subject must be aware of the CS-US contingency.

First, some investigators examining this position (e.g., Fuhrer and Baer, 1969) have found that some experimental subjects have been unable to verbalize the CS-US

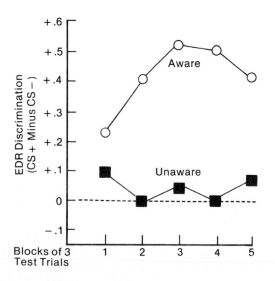

Figure 3-6
Mean discrimination scores on blocks of test trials. Adapted from M. E. Dawson, "Cognition and conditioning: Effects of masking the CS-UCS contingency on human GSR classical conditioning," *Journal of Experimental Psychology*, 1970, *85*, 389–396. Copyright © 1970 by the American Psychological Association. Reprinted by permission.

contingency, and yet have revealed conditioned responding. Other experimenters (e.g., Furedy, Riley, and Fredrikson, 1983), although not disputing the position that a subject's awareness or cognitive state *may* make a contribution to conditioned EDR responding, have argued against the hypothesis that all EDR conditioning can be attributed to awareness of the CS-US contingency. Rather, the position has been advanced that the available experimental evidence demands an explanation based on the operation of several processes rather than just one. But what is the nature of this experimental evidence?

A series of studies has been conducted by Furedy and his associates which reveals a basic limitation on the role of awareness. In one of these experiments conducted by Schiffman and Furedy (1977) a delayed EDR conditioning experiment was conducted using a five-second interstimulus interval, with tone and shock serving as the CS and US. The unusual feature of this study was the obtaining of a continuous measurement of the subject's awareness (or unawareness) of the CS-US contingency. The measurement operation consisted of subjects being asked to indicate their belief that the US would follow the CS, using a specially designed apparatus to do so. This consisted of an adjustable pointer that could be moved by the subject around a 180° dial. The vertical position of the pointer indicated Uncertainty (on the subjects' part); the positions of 90° to the left and 90° to the right of the vertical position were identified as Marked Certainty and Zero Probability (that the US would follow the CS). The subjects were asked to respond continuously with the pointer beginning with CS onset and continuing until 10 seconds after CS onset, thus providing a subject contingency score on each trial. Three groups of subjects participated:

1. An experimental group, which received 15 CS-US trials
2. A traditional control group, which received a similar number of single and random presentations of the CS and US, with the constraint provided that the US would never follow the CS within a 29-second period
3. A truly random control group, which received 15 presentations of the CS randomly distributed over the conditioning session with such presentations being independent of 15 presentations of the US

Measurement operations consisted of sampling the subject's subjective contingency score at one-second intervals and measuring conditioned responding as reflected by EDR conductance changes.

Results obtained from the subject's contingency scores for the last five trials revealed highly reliable and statistically different CS-US contingency discriminations made by the three experimental groups. Subject contingency (SC) values for the experimental group reflected Marked Certainty that the US would be presented; SC values obtained by the traditional control group (where the US never followed the CS) was reflected in primarily Zero Probability ratings, whereas Uncertainty described the score value for the truly random control group.

Conductance changes revealed the conditioning of the EDR for the experimental group; however, such changes as measured for the two control groups did not reveal any differences between them. Thus, although the subject contingency values for the truly random control group indicated the awareness that the US would never follow the CS, such awareness was never reflected in EDR conductance changes. In addition, an overall examination of the correlation between the subject's contingency values and EDR scores revealed no relationship among these measures.

The experiments of Öhman (1979) and Fredrikson and Öhman (1979) were also cited by Furedy, Riley, and Fredrikson (1983) to support the position that there could be some disassociation between awareness and the conditioned EDR. Fredrikson and Öhman (1979) have found that it is possible to use laboratory procedures to mimic the responding of phobic subjects in nonfearful subjects by using aversive classical conditioning of autonomic responses to phobogenic stimuli. Such conditioning typically takes place in a single trial, reveals minimal extinction, and resists cognitive manipulations once the CR has been acquired. The experimental findings of these investigators have revealed that although subjects were aware that the US would no longer be presented, they continued to show substantial EDR responding to the CS, a result that also supports the existence of a disparity between the subject's awareness of the contingency and related autonomic responding. Although Öhman (1979) is supportive of a cognitive explanation of classical conditioning, he wrote that there is a body of experimental data, however, which poses problems for the cognitive approach.

Additional support for the disassociation between the subject's awareness of the CS-US contingency and appropriate responding is found in a study by Campbell, Sanderson, and Laverty (1964). In this experiment, a conditioned EDR was established in five subjects. A tone served as the CS and the administration of the drug succinylcholine chloride dihydrate (scoline) was the US. The effect of this drug, which produces total paralysis of all muscular activity, lasted for about 100 seconds. The sudden termination of respiration was terrifying—the subjects later expressed the belief that they thought they were going to die. Only a single CS-US trial was presented, followed by presentation of only the CS (extinction trials) over a period of three weeks. Results indicated that the EDR during these trials appeared to become stronger over time. And yet all subjects were aware that after the first conditioning trial they would never again receive the US. It seems reasonable to assume, as is found in the case of phobias or other irrational fears, that one's knowledge of a contingency (or absence of such a contingency) does not necessarily result in behavior that is in keeping with such awareness.[8]

The evidence that we have reviewed has led Furedy and associates (1983) to posit that the autonomic nervous system is relatively insensitive to CS-US contingencies. These investigators point out discrimination along the negative contingency dimension is poor and contingency variations especially in a negative direction, as in the case of extinction following acquisition, are not readily processed.

The general problem of relating awareness to EDR conditioned responding sug-

---

[8] The five experimental subjects were male alcoholic patients who volunteered for the experiment. All of them had long histories of drinking and had been in the hospital for several weeks. The use of such a procedure without informing the subjects about the action of the drug prior to conducting the experiment poses a serious ethical problem and would not be employed by current investigators.

gests that experiments should be conducted with other conditioning paradigms. Nelson and Ross (1974) have examined the differential conditioning of the eyeblink using (1) a masking task, (2) a modified masking task, and (3) no masking task, along with their subjects either (a) looking at or (b) not looking at a movie. An awareness of the tone-air puff (CS-US) contingency was not manipulated as it was in many studies but was assessed by using a postexperimental questionnaire.

The masking task used by Nelson and Ross required subjects to estimate the length of two- and five-second intervals of time, with the explanation that the purpose of the study was to examine time estimation during distraction. The subjects not given the masking task were informed that the experimenters were interested in measuring their reactions to "certain events." During this time, subjects were (or were not) looking at the film. One hundred conditioning trials were provided, with conditioned responding measures by a CS+/CS− difference score. The postexperimental questionnaire identified those subjects who became aware of the CS-US contingency during the experiment and those who did not. Results indicated that engaging in the masking task or viewing the film resulted in much poorer differential conditioning than if no masking task or film viewing was provided. In keeping with Dawson's (1970) earlier findings, unaware subjects (as measured by the questionnaire) performed more poorly than aware subjects across all conditions. But contrary to Dawson's results, Nelson and Ross (1974) found that some unaware subjects did reveal conditioning. Moreover, subjects who were aware of the CS-US contingency but did not view the film performed better than aware subjects who did view the film. As Nelson and Ross point out, some factor other than the knowledge of the relationship among the stimuli, at least defined by the postexperimental interviews, would appear to operate to reduce differential responding in such instances.

The findings by Nelson and Ross (1974) are in keeping with Grant's (1973) examination of the role of awareness in eyelid conditioning studies, which resulted in his concluding that the relationship between awareness and conditioning is tenuous at best. He wrote: "The poor correlation between reported awareness of CS-US contingencies and conditioning performance strongly suggests that this cognitive activity, at least as presently assessed, is not sufficient and may not be necessary to produce eyelid conditioning or differential eyelid conditioning" (p. 80).

Grant's conclusion has had the support of a clinical study by Weiskrantz and Warrington (1979) who examined eyelid conditioning in patients, one a postencephalitic case and the other an alcoholic Korsakoff patient. With both subjects, conditioning occurred in the apparent absence of any recall of the situation. After many learning trials and clear evidence of conditioning, neither patient could remember anything about the conditioning procedure.

In their examination of the role of awareness on conditioning, Frcka, Beyts, Levey, and Martin (1983) found that there are different types of awareness that may influence responding. This finding is not always recognized by other investigators. One type of awareness, manipulated by some of the investigators previously cited, has to do with the awareness of stimulus contingencies. Here, the subject becomes aware that the US will (or will not) follow the CS. Frcka and colleagues have also pointed out that there is "demand awareness," which has to do with the subject being aware of the purpose of the experiment and complying with the experimenter's expectations by providing appropriate responses.

In two experiments conducted by Frcka and associates, the eyeblink served as the response to be conditioned, a tone was used as the CS, and an air puff (Experiment 1) or shock (Experiment 2) served as the US. In each study 50 acquisition and 10 extinction trials were provided. Subjects, recruited from newspaper advertisements, ranged in ages from 16 to 58 years. A major reason for obtaining subjects in this manner was to preclude their being aware of the nature of conditioning. Moreover, a masking task was used; the subjects were informed that the purpose of the experiment was to measure reaction time in the presence of distracting stimuli.

Following the conditioning and extinction trials, a postexperimental questionnaire was provided, which included questions related to the subjects' awareness of the CS-US contingency as well as questions related to demand awareness. Other questions on the questionnaire were concerned with the subjects' awareness of their own responding and with the issue of voluntary responding—whether subjects deliberately closed their eyes at the onset of the CS to avoid the shock or air puff.

We shall not detail the experimental findings other than to indicate that the results revealed no relationship between level of conditioning and either contingency awareness or demand awareness. Thus, subjects who were unaware of the CS-US contingency revealed a level of conditioning that was similar to that exhibited by those subjects who were aware of the contingency; similarly, demand-unaware subjects conditioned as well as demand-aware subjects. Findings by Frcka and associates have provided additional support for Grant's (1973) conclusion, which indicated the tenuousness of any relationship between awareness and conditioning; perhaps more important, these investigators have pointed to the complexity of the awareness issue with the need for experimenters to familiarize themselves with the varying facets or dimensions of the concept of awareness.

Extinction ▶

The presentation of the US is a basic operation in the establishment of a classically conditioned response. But what if the US is no longer presented following the acquisition of a response? Under such circumstances, there is a gradual cessation of responding. As we noted earlier, both the operation of omitting the US and the ensuing decrement in responding have both been defined as *experimental extinction*. But such cessation of responding arising from an extinction operation should not be confused with a loss of responding due to forgetting. The basic experimental operation for producing forgetting is to place a time interval between the original learning and the test for retention. Within this time interval, some type of intervening event is usually presented to the subject in order to determine how this event influences the forgetting of the original learning. In Chapter Thirteen we shall examine the forgetting process.

What Does Extinction Measure?

Prior to 1940 a common practice among experimenters was to infer from an extinction measure the amount or degree of learning that had taken place during acquisition. In his *Principles of Behavior,* Hull (1943) lent support to this practice by considering experimental extinction to be one of the four basic response measures from which the strength of the conditioning process could be inferred. But as we pointed out in Chapter Two, experimenters are now recognizing that using extinction to measure the strength of a previously conditioned response is undoubtedly in error.

Although investigators are virtually certain that experimental extinction is an inappropriate measure from which to infer the strength of a previously established conditioned response, they are unsure as to what extinction does measure. Most classical conditioning investigators probably consider extinction to be only a particular kind of response decrement, with their major objective to determine how certain variables influence such behavior. Far and away, the variable that has provided experimenters with the greatest interest has been a partial reinforcement schedule that has been provided during acquisition.

Partial Reinforcement Schedules

The effect of partial reinforcement on experimental extinction has been extensively examined. Humphreys (1939), in his classically conditioned eyeblink study that we described earlier in the chapter, obtained a most unusual extinction effect (or so it was regarded at that time) with a partial reinforcement schedule. In this study, it will be recalled that three groups of college students were given one of the following training schedules: (1) 96 CS-US trials; (2) 48 CS-US trials and 48 CS alone trials (the partial reinforcement group); and (3) 48 CS-US trials. Humphreys reported that the group given 96 trials with 50% reinforcement took significantly longer to reach extinction than either of the two continuously reinforced groups. See Figure 3–7 for these results. The superiority of a partial reinforcement schedule in producing resistance to extinction has been designated as a *partial reinforcement effect* (PRE).

When animals have been used as experimental subjects in classical conditioning experiments, the partial reinforcement effect has not been always obtained (see Wagner, Siegel, Thomas, and Ellison, 1964; Berger, Yarczower, and Bitterman, 1965; Wagner, Siegel, and Fein, 1967). Mackintosh's (1974) careful examination of these animal studies has led him to conclude that "although it is clear that partial reinforcement may increase resistance to extinction of a classically conditioned response, the generality of the effect leaves much to be desired and even when an effect does occur, it is often relatively small" (p. 74).

An obvious next step, after Humphreys (1939) found that a 50% reinforcement schedule increased resistance to extinction, was to vary the percentage of trials reinforced during the acquisition series. In their examination of the classically conditioned eyelid response, Grant and Schipper (1952) varied the percentage of US presentations. The US was programmed to follow the CS on 0, 25, 50, 75, or 100% of 60 training trials

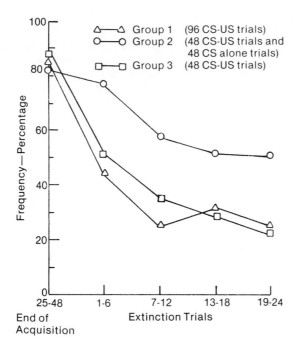

Group 1 (96 CS-US trials)
Group 2 (48 CS-US trials and 48 CS alone trials)
Group 3 (48 CS-US trials)

Figure 3-7
Course of extinction frequency.
The 24 extinction trials are divided
into four groups of 6 trials each.
An average for the preceding 24
acquisition trials (labeled 25–48) is
plotted to serve as a reference
point for the extinction results.
Adapted from L. G. Humphreys,
"The effect of random alternation
of reinforcement on the acquisition and extinction of conditioned
eyelid reactions," *Journal of Experimental Psychology,* 1939, *25,*
141–158. Copyright © 1939 by
the American Psychological Association. Reprinted by permission.

provided on Day 1 and of 32 trials on Day 2. Performance on the 25 extinction trials, which immediately followed Day 2's training trials, revealed a U-shaped function, with the 0, 25, and 100% reinforcement groups showing the least resistance to extinction and the 50 and 75% groups indicating the greatest.

It is important to examine these findings somewhat more analytically. At the end of the acquisition trials, there were substantial differences among the varying groups in the percentage of conditioned responses: the 75 and 100% groups had the largest number of CRs, whereas the 0 and 25% groups had the fewest. Grant and Schipper (1952) hypothesized that two factors appeared to be responsible for the U-shaped function they obtained: (1) the organism's terminal level of acquisition performance, resulting from differing numbers of reinforcements or CS-US trials; and (2) the organism's ease of discriminating the acquisition effects from extinction trials.

When the partial reinforcement has been obtained with animals, Gibbs, Latham, and Gormezano (1978) obtained a similar functional relationship between extinction performance and the percentage of CS-US trials. In their study examining the classically conditioned nictitating membrane response of the rabbit, 600 acquisition trials were provided, with 0, 15, 25, 50 or 100% of these trials being reinforced. Three hundred extinction trials were provided after acquisition. Figure 3–8 presents the percentage of conditioned responses made during the extinction trials for each of these reinforcement schedules.

It must be concluded, however, that instrumental conditioning investigators have been much more interested in the role of partial reinforcement and experimental extinction than their classical conditioning counterparts. As a result, we shall delay discussion of their contributions until Chapter Six.

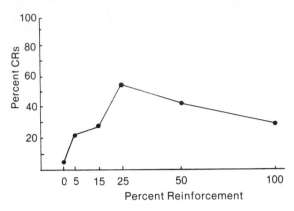

Figure 3-8
Percentage of CRs made during 300 extinction trials for each of the varying reinforcement schedules provided during acquisition. Adapted from C. M. Gibbs, S. B. Latham, and I. Gormezano, "Classical conditioning of the rabbit membrane response," *Animal Learning and Behavior,* 1978, *6,* 209–215. Copyright © 1978 by the Psychonomic Society, Inc. Reprinted by permission.

Silent Extinction

We should like to examine one additional extinction phenomenon: silent extinction. Pavlov (1927) found that when a conditioned response had been extinguished so that a response could no longer be elicited by the conditioned stimulus, further nonreinforced presentations of the CS would serve to strengthen the extinction effect as measured by a decrement in spontaneous recovery or slower reconditioning. A study by Brogden, Lipman, and Culler (1938) has provided support for Pavlov's findings. In this study, four dogs were conditioned to flex their forelimb when a 1,000 Hz tone (serving as a CS) was presented. Shock was used as the US. Following acquisition trials, extinction trials were provided until the CR could not be elicited by the presentation of the CS. Two dogs were then reconditioned but 400 additional extinction trials were provided the other two animals prior to their being reconditioned. Reconditioning was much more readily obtained with the two animals that had not received the 400 additional extinction trials. The results of this study suggest the need to make a distinction between not responding and its neural correlate, inhibition. It is obvious that inhibition continued to increase with additional extinction trials although it was not revealed in the organism's performance.

Summary ►

Much research in classical conditioning has been related to how stimulus variables and cognitive processes contribute to the acquisition and extinction of the CR.

Stimulus variables that have been examined include (1) frequency of CS-US pairings, (2) the intensity of the CS as well as the role of compound and contextual stimuli, (3) US intensity, and (4) the interstimulus interval (ISI). The strength of the CR appears to be a function of the number of CS-US pairings. Conditioned responding has been found also to be a function of the intensity of the CS. It has been noted that the intensity effect will be accentuated if the experimental design provides for each subject to experience more than a single level of stimulus intensity.

The role of stimulus compounds (e.g., $S_1 + S_2$) has been examined with several different procedures being used to demonstrate (1) overshadowing, (2) blocking, and (3) potentiation. Overshadowing has been demonstrated to take place when a compound CS consists of a weak and strong CS first used to obtain a CR, following which each CS is presented singly. Such tests reveal that, in contrast to the strong CS, the weak CS has very little strength in eliciting the CR; the strong CS appears to overshadow the weak CS during the original conditioning trials. Blocking is found when a single CS, *A*, is first used to establish a CR, following which a compound stimulus consisting of the old CS plus a new CS, *A + B*, is presented for additional conditioning trials. When the new CS, *B*, is then presented alone, it cannot elicit the CR. Presumably the early conditioning of the response to *A* has blocked stimulus *B*'s capacity to elicit the CR. Potentiation, frequently found in the conditioning of a taste aversion, refers to the increased capacity of a weak CS to elicit a response after it has been paired with a strong CS.

When US intensity has been manipulated, the strength of the CR is a function of the intensity of the US. Other stimulus variables that have been examined include providing CS alone and US alone trials within CS-US pairings, with both procedures resulting in poorer conditioning when compared with groups not provided either of these additional presentations. Two other stimulus conditions that have been investigated include the exposure of the CS prior to CS-US pairings, often identified as a *latent inhibition operation*, as well as exposure of the US prior to CS-US pairings, identified as the *preexposure procedure*. Both of these operations produce poorer conditioning than appropriate control groups.

Interest in cognitive processes has centered around the role of awareness by the subject of the CS-US contingency. Although Dawson and his colleagues have found strong support for the position that awareness of the CS-US contingency is a necessary condition for conditioning to take place, other investigators have not been able to replicate these findings; the suggestion has been that awareness may contribute to conditioning but it is not a necessary condition for a CR to be established.

The extinction operation and related experimental findings have been of interest to some investigators. The variable that has been manipulated most frequently with extinction has been the percentage of reinforced trials. Investigators have generally reported the relationship between resistance to extinction and percentage of partially reinforced trials to be U-shaped. Extinction is maximized when the partial reinforcement schedule approximates 50 to 75% of the trials.

chapter four

▶

Classical Conditioning:
Issues and Application

Our approach to the study of classical conditioning, as can be noted from the two previous chapters, can be described as functional. That is, we have been interested in identifying the major features of the classical conditioning experiment, as well as discussing some basic methodological problems involved in such experimentation. In addition, we were interested in examining how the strength of a conditioned response was related to a number of experimental variables. In this chapter we will discuss some of the theoretical issues that have been raised concerning the nature of conditioning, as well as take a brief look at the application of the conditioning paradigm to everyday situations.

Must the US Have Motivational Significance? ▶

It will be recalled that we defined the US as a stimulus that has the capacity to elicit a regular and measurable response. Meat powder eliciting salivation in a hungry dog, shock producing withdrawal of a limb, or a puff of air that will produce closure of the eyelid are examples of unconditioned stimuli used by investigators in classical conditioning experiments. Such stimuli as these have been identified as being motivational. Some investigators have raised the question, If a stimulus is to serve as an adequate US, must it have motivational characteristics?[1]

---

[1] There has been some disagreement among investigators in defining the concept of motivation. We would suggest that motivation, which should include the construct of reinforcement, should be defined functionally as a stimulus that elicits responding as well as increases the probability of specific responses. In classical conditioning experiments, such stimuli have generally been considered to have appetitive or aversive characteristics.

Early studies that were brought to bear on this question were conducted by Cason (1922), Hudgins (1933), and Baker (1938), all of whom reported positive findings in their attempt to classically condition pupillary dilation using a bright light as the US. Light readily elicits pupil dilation but its aversive characteristics (at least with the intensities used by these investigators) appear to be minimal. But a lively controversy ensued when Steckle and Renshaw (1934) and Steckle (1936), also using an increase in illumination as their US, were unable to obtain any evidence for conditioning. Negative findings were also reported by Hilgard, Miller, and Ohlson (1941), and Young (1954).[2] In summary, the early evidence suggested that a stimulus, although having the capacity to elicit a regular and measurable response, also had to have motivational characteristics in order to serve as an effective US.

A different approach in the examination of a motivational role of the US has been the attempt to condition so-called spinal animals. This consists of transecting the spinal cord of the experimental subject and then attempting to condition a response below the transection. Stimulation received below the transection cannot be transmitted to the brain so that shock, which has been typically used to elicit a response, could not be perceived by the subject as painful (e.g., nonmotivational).

As with the pupillary conditioning studies, early investigation provided conflicting findings. Shurrager and Culler 1940; and Shurrager and Shurrager (1946) reported that they were unable to condition dogs whose spinal cords were severed at the level of the third lumbar spinal root. Two weak shocks applied to the tip of the tail served as the CS; the US was a much stronger shock to the paw, which elicited a full contraction of the whole semitendinous muscle that had been previously exposed and excised, with movement of the muscle observed through a microscope. Gradual acquisition of the CR, which appeared as a contraction of a small group of muscle fibers, was observed as a function of conditioning trials. Extinction of the response, following acquisition, was noted when the CS was presented alone.

Subsequent experiments resulted in the confirmation of the findings of these early studies (e.g., Shurrager and Culler, 1940; and Dykman and Shurrager, 1956) but have provided a host of failures to replicate as well (e.g., Kellogg, Pronko, and Deese, 1946; Deese and Kellogg, 1949; Pinto and Bromiley, 1950). In summary, the controversy regarding the conditioning of spinal dogs as experimental subjects was not resolved.

More recently, Fitzgerald and Thompson (1967) and Buerger and Dawson (1968, 1969) were able to obtain spinal conditioning using kittens. And a series of experiments by Patterson and associates (e.g., Patterson, Cegavske, and Thompson, 1973; Patterson, 1975; and Beggs, Steinmetz, Romano, and Patterson, 1983) have replicated the findings using adult cats.

The general procedure employed in the experiments of Patterson and colleagues (1973) was to transect the spinal column of adult cats, then inject them with Flaxedil (a curare derivative that produces paralysis). Artificial respiration was used in order to keep the animals alive. The superficial sensory and deep peroneal motor nerves below

---

[2] We do not want to give the impression that pupillary conditioning cannot be obtained. Gerall, Sampson, and Boslov (1957) employed shock as the US and were readily able to condition this response.

the transection were each dissected from each animal's lower left leg, and electrodes were attached to each of the nerves. Experimental animals were classically conditioned by pairing stimulation of the exposed sensory nerve (CS), with cutaneous shock to the ankle of the same limb (US). The UR was a gross efferent volley from the motor nerve. Control groups received either unpaired presentations of the CS and US, or only CS presentations. Results clearly revealed the development of a conditioned response rising to asymptote by about 20 CS-US presentations.

Patterson, Cegavske, and Thompson (1973) concluded:

> There is no a priori reason why polysynaptic reflexes of the neurally isolated vertebrate spinal cord ought not to exhibit conditioning-like phenomena. Anatomically it is not a simple neuronal structure but contains a complex 'isodendritic core' of interneurons analogous to that of the brain structures. The spinal flexion reflex is primitive, generalized and defensive in character and can be expected to show some adaptive plasticity even in the absence of control from higher brain regions (pp. 94–95).

The experimental studies of Patterson and colleagues (1973) indicate that the classical conditioning of a very simple response in the cat can take place without the US having motivational significance. The results of Ince, Brucker, and Alba (1978), who were able to condition urination in a human subject who sustained a complete lesion of the spinal cord, would indicate that the studies of Patterson and his associates have generality for human subjects, and would suggest that a stimulus, at least in certain situations, need not have motivational significance in order to serve as a US. (See Box 4–1.)

The Nature of the Association ▶

The diagram found in Figure 2–1, a figure that is frequently found in elementary psychology texts, suggests that the association established in the classical conditioning experiment is between the CS and the CR. This position can be traced to Watson's (1919) dictum that learned behavior consisted of the establishment of stimulus-response relationships—a position accepted by many later investigators. But almost all current experimenters have rejected this point of view. Thompson (1972) has written, "The assumption that behavioral responses must occur to mediate learning . . . is an obsolete inheritance from early behaviorism. The evidence from many sources is now over-whelming that behavioral responses are not necessary for learning" (p. 123). Thompson suggested that any two events—stimuli, responses, or reinforcement—could be associated one with the other.

Experimental support for the position that it was possible for two stimuli to be associated, one with the other, was demonstrated in an early study conducted by Brogden (1939b), with his procedure (and outcome) now being identified as *sensory preconditioning*. In this experiment, dogs were given 200 pairings of a light and a bell presented simultaneously. A conditioning phase of the experiment was then conducted in which one of these stimuli was used as the CS; a shock, which elicited foot withdrawal, served as the US. A criterion of 10 consecutive CRs was established.

box 4–1

An interesting extension of the work of Patterson and his associates in the spinal conditioning of kittens and cats is found in a study by Ince, Brucker, and Alba (1978) who were able to establish spinal conditioning in a human subject. A 40-year-old male had sustained a complete lesion of the spinal cord at the level of the eighth thoracic vertebra; a neurological examination revealed a complete cord transection with the absence of sensation and motor ability from the lesion down. One result was that the subject was incontinent of urine since the time of his injury. The experimental procedure employed by the investigators consisted of providing a US in the form of electric shock to the lower abdomen which produced visible contractions of the abdominal musculature and an unconditioned response of urination. The CS was a mild electrical stimulus provided by a small, hand-held, battery-powered device with a circular plate that acted as an electrode when in contact with the skin. It was activated by depression of a small button on top of the unit.

Inasmuch as the reflex involved in urination is found in the sacral portion of the spinal cord, below the site of the subject's lesion, the CS was administered below the lesion, and applied to the right thigh between the knee and groin. The initiation and duration of the CS was cued by signal lights. Several preliminary sessions were conducted in which the experimenters observed that the presentation of the CS did not result in any urination, but that the application of the US did produce a reliable voiding response. Fifty-four CS-US trials were then provided over seven sessions. The duration of the CS was 3 seconds; the US was presented 0.5 second after CS onset, with both CS and US terminating together. Results revealed that after less than 100 CS-US trials, a reliable CR of urination was elicited by the CS alone. Subsequent training resulted in the subject being able to provide self-stimulation outside the laboratory, which resulted in a satisfactory urine output. As the authors have written, the conditioning procedure provides "the potential for conditioning techniques such as those employed . . . to become sufficiently refined as to be of treatment value in cases of spastic neurogenic bladder secondary to spinal cord injury" (p. 801).

Following such training, a transfer test was provided in which the other stimulus was presented to the subjects. A control group of animals was given similar conditioning and transfer trials; however, the preconditioning session of presentations of the light and bell was omitted. Results indicated that animals in the experimental group produced 78 conditioned responses during the transfer test, whereas only 4 conditioned responses were made by the control animals. These findings resulted in Brogden concluding that the subjects had established an association between the two stimuli, the bell and the light, which were presented during the preconditioning session. A large number of sensory preconditioning studies have all confirmed Brogden's findings as well as identifying many variables that contribute to this phenomenon (see Wickens and Briggs, 1951; Silver and Meyer, 1954; Hoffeld, Thompson, and Brogden, 1958; and Adamic and Melzack, 1970).

Contemporary experimenters assume that the classical conditioning operation results in the CS becoming associated with the US. Such an association has been demonstrated by the findings obtained in those experimental studies that indicated that the US did not need to elicit an overt response in order for a CR to be established. Light and Gantt (1936) crushed the motor nerves of the rear leg of a dog and then conditioned the animal by using a buzzer as the CS. The US was a shock administered to the foot of the same leg. It was observed during the training trials that a UR could not be elicited by the US. However, after recovery of the damaged motor nerve, the animals were tested with the CS and the conditioned response of leg lifting was observed.[3]

Some investigators have taken the CS-US association position one step farther, hypothesizing that an association that was established was not between CS and US sensations, but rather, the association was between the memorial (or cognitive) representations of these stimuli. Presumably, an effective CS retrieved or aroused the representation of the US, which in turn resulted in a response identified as the CR. One approach designed to examine this memorial representation position has been to change the nature (devalue) of the US after conditioning had taken place. The purpose of this procedure has been to determine if such a manipulation would influence the experimental subject's response to the CS following such devaluation. In one such study, conducted by Holland and Rescorla (1975b), rats were presented with a tone or light (CS) followed by food (US). The UR elicited by the US was general activity. Following the establishment of a CR, experimental animals received pairings of food with high-speed rotation (e.g., the animals were rotated at 125 rpm on a phonograph which in turn produced nausea). The last phase of the study consisted of again presenting the CS which resulted in a significant decline in conditioned responding.

Such a change in the CR, the authors reasoned, must have meant that the CS was originally associated with some central representation of the US (food), and argued against the position that the conditioning trials established any *direct* connection between the CS and the US. Thus, if the new association that was established between the food and nausea was to influence the old tendency of the CS to elicit the CR, the path from the CS to the CR must be routed through some central representation of the US.

The Selective Character of
Associative Relationships ►

Pavlov (1927) assumed that the choice of the response in the conditioning experiment was a matter of experimenter indifference. He wrote, "It is obvious that the reflex activity of any effector organ can be chosen for the purpose of investigation, since signalling stimuli can be linked up with any of the inborn reflexes" (p. 17). A similar position was taken by many traditional investigators who believed that any CS could be associated equally well with any US.

But this point of view has been replaced by current investigators' acknowledgment that one stimulus may have a unique relationship with another stimulus as well as with

---

[3] A more frequently used (as well as more humane) technique has been to prevent responding during training trials by injecting the subject with curare. Artificial respiration is then used to keep the animal alive. Experiments conducted by Solomon and Turner (1962) and Leaf (1964) have confirmed the findings of Light and Gantt (1936): Overt responding is not a necessary condition for learning to take place.

the response. Naturalistic observation has resulted in ethologists being long aware that a particular species could quite easily associate a particular response with one environmental event but had great difficulty in attaching that response to another stimulus situation. Garcia and Koelling (1966) demonstrated a similar finding in an early classical conditioning study of taste aversion.

In their experiment, rats were first trained to drink water with two characteristics: (1) the water was sweetened with saccharin (gustatory stimulus) and (2) flashes of light and a clicking noise (audiovisual stimuli) were produced whenever the animal made contact with the drinking tube. For one group of animals, the drinking of the sweet, bright-noisy water was accompanied by shock to the feet. For a second group of animals, the sweet bright-noisy water was mixed with lithium chloride or was followed by irradiation; either treatment subsequently produced nausea.

In a second phase of the experiment, the experimenters were interested in determining if avoidance conditioning to the audiovisual and/or gustatory characteristics of the stimuli had taken place. The group of animals that had been made sick was provided with the opportunity to drink sweetened water unaccompanied by the light and click or to drink unsweetened water in the presence of the light and click. Animals that had been shocked were given the opportunity to drink under either of these same conditions. Results indicated the selective character of the associative relationship that had been established. Rats that had been made sick after drinking sweetened water avoided drinking it but did not show an aversion to regular water accompanied by audiovisual stimuli. Rats that had been shocked did not avoid the sweetened water. Revusky and Garcia (1970) have commented on these findings:

> If an animal wants to decide what made it sick, it will tend to ignore external events and carefully consider the flavors of previously consumed substances; if it wants to decide what produced an external event, it will tend to ignore flavor and will carefully consider the preceding exteroceptive stimuli (p. 22).[4]

Garcia and Koelling's result, along with similar findings obtained by a variety of investigators, resulted in an area of experimental studies that is now identified as *selective association, stimulus-reinforcer interaction,* or *biological constraint.* All of these studies have indicated that some stimulus selectivity is exercised by the organism in the acquisition of associative relationships. When the classical conditioning paradigm is used to examine selective associations, it involves a comparison of the relative ease with which different types of conditioned stimuli can be associated with different kinds of unconditioned stimuli. The findings from such a comparison are interpreted to indicate that a selective association has been established if the association of one stimulus, CS-1, occurs more rapidly with US-1 than with US-2, and when CS-2 is more readily conditioned employing US-2 than with US-1.

---

[4] Rats do not always ignore external events as a cause of illness, as the experimental study of Best, Best, and Mickley (1973) has demonstrated. In their experiment, they found that rats subjected to apomorphine-induced illness following a two-minute placement in a black compartment avoided this compartment significantly more frequently than control subjects when given a choice of entering either a black or white compartment.

Domjan's (1983) review of the area has indicated that selective association has been demonstrated with many species involving a variety of stimuli. For example, Wilcoxin, Dragoin, and Kral (1971) have noted that birds learn to avoid eating toxic monarch butterflies by sight, suggesting that birds, in contrast to rats, may be more disposed to associate nausea with visual cues than with gustatory ones. These investigators have also experimentally demonstrated that quail readily learned to avoid blue water when this visual stimulus had been previously associated with illness; however, these birds did not learn to avoid sour water, a gustatory stimulus, although it also had been associated with illness. Rats, on the other hand, revealed an aversion to sour water but not colored water, after both types of water had been associated with nausea.

Selective associations, or what they termed a *stimulus-reinforcer interaction*, has been also revealed in a study by Shapiro, Jacobs, and LoLordo (1980) who used pigeons as their experimental subjects. A classical conditioning paradigm was used in which a compound CS (e.g., tone and red light) was paired with a US consisting of either a brief shock or access to food. Five daily conditioning sessions consisting of 90 trials/session were provided, followed by a testing session in which there were seven presentations each of the (1) red light, (2) tone, and (3) no signal, interspersed among 49 presentations of the compound CS. The result obtained from this experiment, along with similar findings obtained from a second study, indicated that the red light CS was dominant in appetitive conditioning, reliably eliciting the pecking response; in contrast, the tone was more reliable in eliciting head raising and a prancing response, originally elicited by the shock. As the authors have indicated, their experiments demonstrated a stimulus-reinforcer (CS-US) interaction with strong visual dominance observed when food was used as the US, whereas strong auditory dominance was noted when the US was shock.

The experimental findings that we have reviewed, along with a host of confirming studies, make it clear that the selective association between and among stimuli is a frequently found phenomenon. What is not apparent, however, is the process or mechanism responsible for such selectivity. Probably one part of the answer lies in the fact that certain species are more sensitive to one type of stimulus than another—an innate characteristic of the species. But it seems likely that other factors, which at this time have not been identified, are also operative.

Backward Conditioning ▶

In Chapter Two we indicated that there had been some controversy regarding the outcome of backward conditioning. We will now discuss this issue in greater detail. As a result of his early experimental work, Pavlov (1927) believed that US-CS trials would not result in the establishment of a CR; subsequently, he revised his position, believing that such conditioning was possible, although unstable.

The early American backward conditioning studies conducted by Switzer (1930) and Wolfle (1932) revealed excitatory conditioning of the eyeblink and finger withdrawal, thus supporting Pavlov's revised position. The experimental findings obtained over the next forty years yielded some support for these studies (e.g., Spooner and

Kellogg, 1947: Champion and Jones, 1961), but at the same time, many investigators were unable to provide either confirmation of the early studies or to demonstrate backward conditioning with other conditioning paradigms (e.g., Bernstein, 1934; Harris, 1941; and Fitzwater and Reisman, 1952). The result was that most texts, pointing to a variety of methodological flaws present in studies reporting positive findings, indicated that excitatory conditioning arising from US-CS trials was not possible (e.g., Kimble, 1961; Mackintosh, 1974; and Hall, 1984).[5]

Beginning in the late 1960s, two developments emerged. One, stemming from Rescorla's (1967) contingency anlaysis of conditioning, was that inhibitory conditioning was a likely outcome of US-CS trials, since presentation of the CS indicated that the US would not be forthcoming. The experimental findings of Siegel and Domjan (1971, 1974) and Plotkin and Oakley (1975), using the retardation of acquisition test to measure inhibition, supported Rescorla's inhibition position. Plotkin and Oakley (1975) employed two backward conditioning groups using a trace conditioning procedure in which the length of the trace (termination of the US to the onset of CS) was 200 msec for one group and 500 msec for the other. Four control groups were used. One group received only the same restraint and exposure to the conditioning chamber as the backward conditioning groups; no stimuli were presented. A second control group received presentations of only the CS. The third group received the US 55 seconds after the CS, a period that was used to match the post-CS safe period received by the backward conditioning groups. Finally, a fourth group was provided forward conditioning trials. After 125 trials, a forward conditioning phase involving a delay rather than a trace procedure was instituted with 80 CS-US trials provided. Results indicated that when compared with the control group, the 2 US-CS groups were significantly retarded in their acquisition performance, although the length of the trace did not result in producing differences between them.

The second development was the experimental finding that US-CS pairings provided in the CER paradigm would yield excitatory responding (e.g., Heth and Rescorla 1973; Mahoney and Ayres, 1976; Burkhardt, 1980; Shurtleff and Ayres, 1981; Gordon, McGinnis, and Weaver, 1985; van Willigen, Emmett, Cote, and Ayres, 1987; and Ayres, Haddad, and Albert, 1987).

Reconciliation of the diverse findings has been proposed by both Hall (1984, 1986) and Cautela (1965, 1987). Hall has suggested that the CER, which provides the bulk of the support for the existence of US-CS excitatory conditioning, may not be a suitable paradigm with which to examine this type of classical conditioning functioning.[6]

A different explanation has been put forth by Cautela (1965, 1987), who has

---

[5] One notable exception was Razran (1971) who, citing primarily the experimental findings of Russian investigators, wrote that backward conditioning was a genuine CR associative manifestation.

[6] Several difficulties with the use of the CER as a model for classical conditioning have been discussed by Hall (1986). Methodological as well as statistical problems have been identified by a number of investigators (e.g., Blackman, 1968, 1977; and Hurwitz and Davis, 1983). In addition, the empirical findings obtained from CER studies are sufficiently disparate from the results noted with direct CS-CR classical conditioning paradigms that some question can be raised about the equivalence of the two different types of paradigms.

indicated that all experiments reporting backward conditioning have employed a noxious stimulus as the US. One characteristic of such stimuli is that the perception of pain arising from such stimulation continues for some time after the noxious stimulus is removed. Cautela (1987) has indicated support for this position by citing the reporting of subjects who perceive pain for as long as a minute after shock has been terminated. Physiological evidence is also provided with Cautela citing Fulton (1946) and Gardner (1952), who have indicated that the larger myelinated nerve fibers conduct rapidly the intense, sharp pain followed a second or two later by a delayed pain, conducted by small unmyelinated fibers that is most unpleasant. Such pain can last a matter of minutes after the noxious stimulus is removed. Thus, Cautela has proposed that the perception of pain arising from the US may continue until the onset of the CS which results functionally in a simultaneous conditioning procedure.[7]

It may be possible that all instances of backward conditioning cannot be explained by one or the other of these proposals but that both explanations have relevance in different situations.

The Nature of the Conditioned Response ►

The traditional view of the nature of the CR has been that the CR closely resembles the recorded UR. This position was in keeping with the stimulus substitution theory of classical conditioning proposed by Pavlov (1927)—the CS served as a substitute for the US and was capable of eliciting the response originally evoked by only the US. Similarities between the conditioned and unconditioned eyeblink, and the conditioned and unconditioned leg flexion have been also noted by investigators. Thus, Culler, Finch, Girden, and Brogden (1935) in conditioning leg flexion in dogs have written that a dog reveals precisely the same signs of disturbance when the tone (CS) begins as when the animal actually feels the shock (US).

In their examination of autoshaping, Jenkins and Moore (1973) have also noted a similarity between the CR and UR. It will be recalled that we discussed their study in Chapter Two in which they were interested in examining the characteristics of the pigeon's autoshaped response when food and water served as the US. Their experimental findings revealed that the CR that developed to the CS that signaled food was a brief, forceful peck that was characteristic of the response to food; in contrast, the CR made to the CS that signaled water was similar to that made when water served as the US.

But it has also been evident, even to some of the early experimenters, that the CR and UR were not always identical. Zener's (1937) observations of the conditioned salivary response in dogs resulted in his writing that except for the component of salivary secretion, the CR and UR were quite different. Recently, Holland (1977) has demonstrated that such disparities between the CR and UR may arise as a function of the characteristics of the CS that is used. He conducted a series of experiments using rats

---

[7] Cautela (1987) believes that US-CS presentations that result in inhibition is an example of forward conditioning since the CS is followed by the nonappearance of the US, which in turn results in inhibition.

as subjects and employing either a light or tone as the CS. Presentation of food, which served as the US, elicited general activity (UR) in the animals as measured in the stabilimetric cage. Six different conditioned response categories were recorded during conditioning trials when different CSs were employed. Results indicated that light serving as a CS elicited a substantially different form of the CR than did the tone. To illustrate, rats standing on their hind legs was a fairly frequent response made to the light; in contrast, presentation of the tone serving as a CS produced a short, rapid horizontal and/or vertical movement of the head.

As a result of his examination of much of the experimental evidence bearing on the CR-UR similarity issue, Mackintosh (1983) concluded:

> Given that the responses directly elicited by the presentation of a reinforcer depend both upon the precise sensory properties of the reinforcer and on the context in which it is delivered, it is hardly surprising that the responses elicited by a CS signalling the occurrence of that reinforcer should both depend on the sensory properties of the CS and differ in some respects from those elicited by the reinforcer itself (p. 71).

In summary, Mackintosh (1983) and Holland (1977) are proposing that the nature of the specific CS that is used can contribute, along with the US, to determine the characteristics of the CR.

Finally, some investigators have suggested that the examination of the relationship existing between the CR and UR is of little significance. Their position has been to define classical conditioning as a set of experimenter operations that exposes a subject to the presentation of a CS and US. The CR is defined as a response, which as a result of these paired presentations, can be elicited by the CS; but whether or not the CR is similar or identical to the US is of little importance since these experimenters are not interested in the analysis of the observed behavior as an end in itself. Rather, interest is placed on understanding the inferred processes that yield that behavior.

It is obvious that the relevance of this operational position, in contrast to the interest of relating the form of the CR to the UR, rests on what the experimenter deems to be important in the study of classical conditioning. Mackintosh (1983) indicated:

> It is reasonable to suppose that one of the tasks of a theory of classical conditioning is to explain the form taken by the change in behavior recorded during conditioning. Thus, it is a matter of some importance to know whether CRs generally resemble URs, and if they do not, to try to understand the nature of the divergence (p. 68).

In contrast, to the extent that the nature of the modified behavior, the CR, is believed to be of little importance in understanding the associative process, any examination of CR-UR similarity or identity is peripheral to the experimenter's basic objective.

Pairing versus Contingency Views of Classical Conditioning ▶

Of the varying issues that we have discussed in this chapter, undoubtedly the most important is the issue of whether classical conditioning should be viewed as (1) dependent on the pairing of the CS and US, and often identified as a contiguity position, or (2) dependent on the establishment of a contingency. Beginning with Pavlov (1927) and continuing until the middle 1960s, most investigators believed that the CS-US pairing was the basic operation necessary for the establishment of a CR. But Prokasy's (1965) analysis of experimenter operations and Rescorla's (1967) theoretical paper both suggested that the traditional position was in error. Rescorla pointed out that the acquisition of the CR was related not to the CS-US pairings, but rather to the establishment of a contingency between the CS and US, a position that we briefly described in Chapter Two. As Rescorla (1967) has written:

> *An alternative theoretical view of Pavlovian conditioning . . . is that the temporal* contingency *between CS and US is the relevant condition. The notion of* contingency *differs from that of* pairings *in that the former includes not only what* is *paired with the CS but also what* is not *paired with the CS (p. 76).*

During the past decade, some investigators have recast the contingency position in the form that the CS should be informative—the CS must be a useful predictor of the occurrence of the US.

Several different experimental approaches have been taken in examining the contingency explanation for conditioning. One has been to degrade the CS-US contingency with the prediction that such degradation would result in poorer conditioning.

One method of manipulating degradation is to provide a partial reinforcement regimen in which the CS is presented but not followed by the US. We examined the influence of partial reinforcement on the acquisition of a conditioned response in Chapter Three. It will be recalled that Gibbon, Farrell, Locurto, Duncan, and Terrace's (1980) survey of continuous versus partial reinforcement studies indicated that a partial reinforcement schedule retarded acquisition—a finding in keeping with the contingency prediction.

Many investigators, however, have considered that it is the presence of the US that determines the level of CR responding, so that the degradation procedure they have employed has been one in which the US is presented singly—it is not preceded by the CS. Figure 4–1 examines the manipulation of the CS and US in which (1) the CS and US are presented together (the probability of the US following the CS is indicated as $p(US|CS)$ and (2) the US is presented without the prior presentation of the CS (identified as $p(US|\overline{CS})$).

Studies by Rescorla (1966, 1968) and Leonard, Fishbein, and Monteau (1972) have provided findings supporting the contingency position. Let us examine one part of Rescorla's (1968) study in which the conditioned emotional response paradigm was employed, with the suppression of the bar-pressing response being the dependent variable. Rats were first trained to press the bar using a one-minute VI schedule. Four groups of rats were then provided five daily two-hour conditioning sessions consisting of tone-shock pairings with the probability of the US following the CS being 0.40. Thus, on four of every ten occurrences of the CS, the US was presented. The four groups were different, however, in terms of the likelihood that they would experience the US in the absence of the CS. One group of animals never experienced the US alone; for the second, third, and fourth groups, the probability of shock occurring in the absence of the CS was 0.1, 0.2 or 0.4. Following such training, six test sessions were

Figure 4–1

Let us assume that our experiment consists of eight one-minute sessions. During each session one of the following events will take place: (1) the CS will precede the US by 0.5 second, (2) the US may occur alone, and (3) neither stimulus will be presented.

Two-Minute Sessions

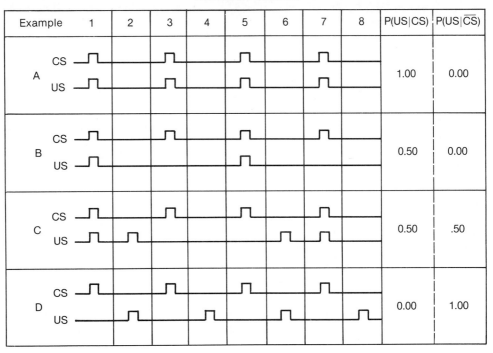

Example	1	2	3	4	5	6	7	8	P(US|CS)	P(US|C̄S̄)
A									1.00	0.00
B									0.50	0.00
C									0.50	.50
D									0.00	1.00

In Example A, the CS and US are always presented together, thus the probability that the US will follow the CS is 1.00, whereas the probability that the US will be presented without having been preceded by the CS is .00.

In Example B, the CS precedes the US only 50% of the time. As with Example A, the probability that the US will be presented without having been preceded by the CS is .00.

In Example C, the CS and US are presented together on half of the four CS presentations; thus p(US|CS) is .50. On two other occasions, the presentation of the US is not preceded by the CS, hence, p(US|CS) is also .50.

In Example D, the CS and US are never presented together, thus the probability of the US being preceded by the CS is .00. The US is presented alone on four occasions, thus providing a p value of 1.00. It may be noted that although this procedure has been typically used as a control group by traditional investigators, Rescorla (1967) has indicated that this contingency of the CS never being followed by the US should result in the CS developing inhibitory strength.

provided in order to examine the amount of response suppression taking place when the CS was presented on four occasions during each session.

Figure 4–2 reveals the suppression ratios over the test sessions for the four groups. It is clear that these groups ordered themselves in keeping with the probability of shock, which was received in the absence of the CS. When shock was not experienced

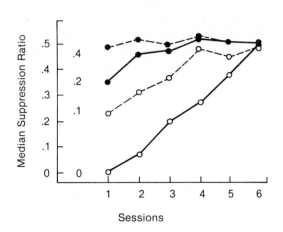

Sessions

Figure 4-2
Median suppression ratio over the six test sessions. All groups had a .4 probability of receiving the US during presentation of the CS. The value attached to each curve reflects the probability of presentation of the US in the absence of the CS. Adapted from R. A. Rescorla, "Probability of shock in the presence and absence of CS in fear conditioning," *Journal of Comparative and Physiological Psychology*, 1968, *66*, 1–5. Copyright © 1968 by the American Psychological Association. Reprinted by permission.

alone, suppression of the bar-pressing response was maximized. As the probability of receiving shock alone increased, the tendency for the CS to elicit response suppression decreased, so that when the US was experienced alone as frequently as it was paired with the CS, conditioning did not occur.

Conditioning the nictitating membrane of the rabbit, Leonard, Fishbein, and Monteau (1972) degraded the CS-US contingency by interpolating US alone trials among CS-US presentations for two experimental groups, which differed only in the length of the intertrial interval that was employed. A control group did not receive any interpolated presentations of the US. The number of CS-US pairings remained the same for all groups. The findings, in keeping with the results of Rescorla's (1968) study, indicated that the US alone groups revealed poorer acquisition than the controls. Other studies by Hupka, Kwaterski, and Moore (1970) and Gamzu and Williams (1973) using an autoshaping paradigm have also supported the contingency position.

A compound conditioning procedure has been used in a somewhat different examination of the information versus contiguity position. Here, a compound stimulus consisting of two stimuli are both presented at the same time followed by the US. One stimulus, however, has a history of being previously correlated or associated with the US whereas the other has not. What happens when each stimulus is then presented alone? It will be recalled from Chapter Three that this experimental design is one that has resulted in the phenomenon of blocking. Thus, if stimulus A has had a prior history of being followed by shock, following which a compound stimulus AX is also associated with shock, subsequent testing with stimulus X will reveal that this CS had acquired very little excitatory strength, whereas stimulus A will reveal a great deal. In such instances, when stimulus A is presented alone it is highly predictive of shock. When stimulus X is then added, forming the compound stimulus AX, and the US continues to be presented, stimulus X provides no new information; when stimulus X is subsequently presented it will not elicit a CR although it had been paired with the US.

Our last examination of Rescorla's (1967) position has to do with the outcome of US-CS or backward conditioning trials. The contingency position would predict that US-CS trials should result in inhibitory conditioning since the organism learns the contingency that the CS is not followed by the US. The contiguity position would predict that conditioned responding should not take place. As Hall (1984) has suggested, there has been a problem in detecting the presence of inhibition in many backward conditioning studies since not responding to the CS by the backward conditioning group might simply reflect a lack of excitatory strength. The presence of inhibition has been revealed, however, when a retardation of acquisition procedure has been used, as we have noted in the earlier cited studies of Siegel and Domjan (1971, 1974) and Plotkin and Oakley (1975).

Inasmuch as our review of the varying examinations of the contingency position has yielded positive findings, it is not surprising that this position has been widely adopted. Schwartz (1984) has written:

> It seems clear that our understanding of Pavlovian conditioning requires a fundamental change. Up until 1967 it was believed that presentation of CS and US contiguous in time would result in conditioning. However, Rescorla's experiments demonstrated that the organism is sensitive to the degree to which one stimulus provides information about the other. In some way the organism computes probabilities . . . and the outcome of this computation determines whether a potential CS will actually be an effective CS (pp. 96–97).

But it must be recognized that the information or contingency position does have some difficulties. For example, there is a methodological flaw in the studies of Rescorla (1966, 1968), Leonard, Fishbein, and Monteau (1972), and others in which these investigators have degraded the CS-US contingency by interspersing US alone presentations among the conditioning trials. Jenkins and Shattuck (1981) have pointed out that before attributing poorer conditioning to unsignaled USs, it is necessary to demonstrate that the addition of an unsignaled US is more damaging to acquisition than is the addition of a signaled US. The CER paradigm was used to examine this possibility. We shall not detail their experimental procedure but will indicate that these investigators found that lowering the percentage of USs that were signaled did not reduce the level of conditioning—a finding not in keeping with the contingency position.

A second problem has been identified by Damianopoulos (1982), who has indicated that contingency cannot be considered to be a *necessary* condition for the establishment of a conditioned response—a position taken by contingency theorists.

First, let us consider what is meant by a *necessary* condition. A factor is considered necessary in the context of an experiment when its removal, keeping other factors constant, results in the absence of the phenomenon. Thus, the experimental test for pairing or contiguity as a necessary condition in classical conditioning would be one in which the pairing condition is excluded in the environmental manipulation while contingency continues to be present; the test for contingency would be to exclude contingency in the experimental manipulation while pairing continues to be present.

It is readily apparent that in typical conditioning operations, both pairings and contingency are present. Damianopoulos (1982) has pointed out, however, that conceptually, pairing and contingency can be distinguished as being logically independent if the pairing operation is defined in terms of time and more specifically in terms of an interstimulus interval (ISI) that will support conditioning. (Very long ISIs will not result in the establishment of a CR; thus, the presentation of such stimuli would not be considered to represent a pairing operation.) On the other hand, Rescorla's (1967) concept of contingency, as Gormezano and Kehoe (1975) have indicated, has been formulated in time-free fashion, referencing only the relative probabilities of US occurrence in the presence and absence of the CS, and without reference to any temporal relationship existing between CS and US presentations.

Damianopoulos has indicated that the role of the ISI in conditioning can be most informative in examining the pairing versus contingency hypothesis since the use of a very long ISI will effectively eliminate pairing as an experimental condition; at the same time, contingency would continue to be present since the termination of the CS is followed by US onset. Two ISI studies have been used to examine the controversy. One was a conditioned eyeblink experiment conducted by McAllister (1954) who, using college students as subjects, examined five ISIs, namely, 100, 250, 450, 700, and 2,500 msec. Results indicated that conditioned responding was obtained in all but the 2,500 msec. condition. A second study was conducted by Schneiderman and Gormezano (1964) conditioning the nictitating membrane of the rabbit, with 250, 500, 1,000, 2,000, and 4,000 msec. ISIs being used. These investigators reported that conditioned responding with the 4,000 msec. ISI resulted in only a 20% level of conditioned responding after more than 500 CS-US trials had been provided. In contrast, the use of the other ISIs resulted in substantial amounts of conditioned responding.

In analyzing the very poor conditioning obtained in both studies when long ISIs were used, it will be noted that the pairing operation was experimentally excluded, but contingency continued to be present. In contrast, when shorter ISIs were used, conditioned responding climbed to above 80%. The very limited contribution made by contingency to conditioned responding when long ISIs were employed can be contrasted to the substantial increase in conditioning when a short ISI (from which the pairing condition was inferred) was utilized. This anlaysis, along with other supportive arguments, resulted in Damianopoulos (1982) concluding that the pairing of stimuli is a necessary factor since its exclusion led to little or no conditioning, whereas contingency was conceptualized as a modulating factor that controlled minimum and maximum effects of the pairing operation.[8]

---

[8] It should be noted that Rescorla (1978) has revised his contingency hypothesis to include a time factor: "One feature which contiguity and contingency share is that they may be described in purely temporal terms, without reference to the quatitative properties of the events involved" (p. 17). Damianopoulos (1982) has pointed out that Rescorla's inclusion of a temporal factor in the contingency concept makes the issue between pairing and contingency untestable since "for a testable difference, the contingency concept must be restricted to a logical . . . relation between CS and US and the contiguity concept to a temporal one" (p. 220).

Two Theories of Classical Conditioning ▶

We have reviewed a number of issues that have arisen in classical conditioning but have not as yet discussed any of the formal models that have appeared in the literature. A number of models have been proposed over the years but we shall limit our presentation to just two of these. Such a presentation, although limited in scope, will give the reader some appreciation of the kinds of models that are being proposed by current investigators. The first, and perhaps most widely accepted, was formulated by Rescorla and Wagner (1972); the second is a more recent and much different model provided by Prokasy (1984, 1987).

Rescorla and Wagner Model

Rescorla and Wagner (1972) have proposed that the basic foundation for conditioned response learning is the establishment of a contingency between the CS and US, the end result being that the CS is a signal or a stimulus that provides information about the occurrence of the US. The learning of the contingency is expressed in terms of excitatory strength arising from the CS-US trials, and is inferred from the performance of the subject. The presentation of the CS without being paired with the US—experimental extinction—results in the formation of a contingency in which the CS indicates that the US will not occur, and which in turn is reflected in inhibitory strength.

The negatively accelerated learning curve that has been noted in many conditioning experiments serves as a starting place for a description of Rescorla and Wagner's (1972) anlaysis of the conditioning process. First, these investigators have assumed that there is an asymptote or final performance level that the US will support. A US consisting of a 4 ma shock will support a higher asymptote than if the US is 1 ma; thus, conditioning with the 4 ma US will result in superior performance over a series of CS-US trials. It should be noted that the investigators have adopted Kamin's (1968) argument that in order to support conditioning, the US must somehow be "surprising" for the experimental subject.

Second, the rate of growth of the acquisition process is related to two learning rate parameters, one of which is determined by the salience of the CS. Here, it is assumed that different stimuli may acquire associative strength at different rates despite equal reinforcement. A second growth parameter is determined by the characteristics of the US, with the rate of learning dependent on the particular US employed. These growth values may range between 0 and 1.00. In keeping with current descriptions of the model, K has been usually employed to identify these growth parameters and has been generally limited to the salience of the CS. Finally, the amount of the increment of associative strength that is obtained on any CS-US trial is determined by multiplying the value of the growth factor, K, by the value of the difference between the performance asymptote and the level of performance that was exhibited on the previous trial.

The mathematical formula that expresses the change in associative strength on any given trial is as follows:

$$\triangle V_n = K(\lambda - V_{\text{sum}})$$

Here we may note that $\triangle$ is the increment of associative strength that will accrue on any trial represented by n; K represents the constant growth value that reflects the salience of the CS; λ identifies the value of the asymptote or the amount of learning that the US can support; V_{sum} represents the total amount of associative strength that has been previously acquired.

Let us provide a hypothetical experiment in order to work out the incremental values of excitatory strength that would be obtained for four CS-US trials in conditioning the human eyeblink. At the beginning of the study, $V = 0$; we shall assume that the value of K is .50 and $\lambda = 100$.

	Amount of Increment on Each Trial	Total Associative Strength
Trial 1: $V = 0.5 (100 - 0)$	50.00	50.00
Trial 2: $V = 0.5 (100 - 0)$	25.00	75.00
Trial 3: $V = 3.5 (100 - 75)$	12.50	87.50
Trial 4: $V = 0.5 (100 - 87.5)$	6.25	93.25

Let us examine how inhibitory strength accrues as a function of four extinction trials. We shall assume that CS-US trials have continued so that at the end of these trials, $V_n = 100$. The formula employed in determining the growth of excitatory strength would be used also to determine inhibitory strength; K value would remain at 0.5, with λ being 0 since the US is no longer present.

	Amount of Increment on Each Trial	Total Associative Strength
Trial 1: $V = 0.5 (0 - 100)$	50.00	50.00
Trial 2: $V = 0.5 (0 - 50)$	25.00	75.00
Trial 3: $V = 0.5 (0 - 75)$	12.50	87.50
Trial 4: $V = 0.5 (0 - 87.5)$	6.25	93.25

The Rescorla and Wagner model has been used to explain a number of conditioning phenomena with varying degrees of success, although the original intent of these investigators was to provide an explanation for overshadowing and blocking phenomena which are found when compound stimuli are used as the CS. It is readily apparent that the model can predict an increase in conditioning with an increase in the "surprisingness" (or intensity) of the US; such an increase will result in a higher conditioning asymptote and a greater increment taking place with each CS-US trial. Similarly, an increase in the salience of the CS will result in a larger K value, which also will result in more rapid conditioning. The popularity of the model, however, can be attributed to its success in predicting the effects of overshadowing and blocking. Interested readers can refer to Rescorla and Wagner (1972) for a description and analysis of these deductions from their model.

Many investigators have been aware that it is not likely that a conditioning model that can be summarized in a single equation can account for the large numbers of phenomena that have been identified during the past seven or eight decades of conditioning research. In fact, many classical conditioning findings have been obtained that cannot be reconciled with Rescorla and Wagner's theoretical position, although in fairness, it was not the intent of the investigators to provide such a formulation.

Prokasy's Model

Prokasy (1984, 1987) has proposed a model of classical conditioning that is so fundamentally different from Rescorla and Wagner (1972) that any comparison between the two is very difficult to make. Prokasy's major interest has been in identifying those processes that govern the conditioning of skeletal conditioned responses. He has posited that acquisition of the CR consists of four stages through which subjects must pass in moving from a base or operant level of responding to asymptotic performance.

Stage I has been identified as contingency detection; here, the subject learns about the CS-US contingency in addition to learning something about the characteristics of the experimental environment. Such learning takes place during early conditioning trials and precedes any indication of skeletal responding. A basic question is: How is the learning of the CS-US relationship revealed? Prokasy has indicated that one indicator is the appearance of the electrodermal response, which has been shown to indicate the CS-US association in only a few trials. Such rapid learning can be contrasted with the acquisition of the conditioned eyeblink response in humans, which typically does not appear for many more trials.

Additional evidence that the CS-US relationship is stored rapidly and before the emergence of skeletal CRs has been provided by Thompson, Berger, Cegavske, Patterson, Rosemer, Teyler, and Young (1976). These investigators reported increments in dorsal hippocampus multiple unit responding of the rabbit within eight conditioning trials, even though the skeletal CR (nictitating membrane) did not emerge until after considerably more CS-US trials.

Prokasy has identified the second stage also as an associative event but one that emphasizes response selection. During this period, the subject codes information about the US characteristics—its location, temporal relationship to the CS, intensity, temporal properties, and so on. It is with this information that the subject actively searches for a response. There are, however, restraints in terms of how the organism can respond. With the usual restrictions that classical conditioning operations provide, there is little left for the experimental subject to do but identify responses that are oriented to the US and that may be similar to the UR. But as Prokasy (1984) has written, "That a UR-like-CR occurs does not imply that it has been acquired because the US elicits that particular UR. It is selected as the organism's way of adjusting to the stimulus properties of the US" (p. 5). Prokasy has hypothesized that the response selection process takes place between the trial on which the subject stores the CS-US relational information (Stage I) and trial K, which represents the trial on which there is the first appearance of the CR (Stage III).

The third stage is response acquisition, a stage characterized by changes in response frequency. The transformation from base level responding to a stable response level is governed by the conditions or parameters provided by the experimenter. Prokasy's model assumed that these values are determined by, if not before, trial K. The parameter values are set by the experimental context and include the contingencies of the reinforcement schedule, the intensity of the US, and so on. It is interesting to note that Prokasy believes US intensity determines the limit or asymptote of performance rather than determining the limit of the associative strength of the CS-US relationship, as many other theorists (e.g., Hull, 1943; and Rescorla and Wagner, 1972) have proposed.

The fourth stage has been identified as response shaping. Here, Prokasy has argued that molecular conditioned response characteristics change systematically over many trials in adjusting to the particular temporal and qualitative attributes of both the CS and the US, although the US plays the more important role in determining such changes. Such response changes are analogous to those in the honing of a highly skilled motor response. Many investigators have reported on the nature of such changes. For example, Gormezano (1972) has reported that the peak amplitude of the conditioned nictitating membrane response in the rabbit gradually moves forward over CS-US trials to about the time that US onset takes place.

In his analysis of the four stages of conditioning, Prokasy has indicated that the first two stages comprise Phase 1—these represent the learning phase; whereas Phase 2, consisting of the second two stages, reveals performance. An important assumption he has made is that Phase 1 is essentially independent of Phase 2, and he has provided both behavioral as well as neurological evidence to support his position. For example, he has cited the work of Berry and Thompson (1978) who examined the effects of small medial septal lesions on the acquisition of the conditioned nictitating membrane response in rabbits. Their findings revealed that the presence of the lesion increased the number of trials required before responding occurred (Phase 1), but once responses emerged, the performance curve did not differ from that obtained with rabbits who had not had the lesion (Phase 2).

Prokasy's assumption of the independence of the operation of these phases has suggested that the performance increments, as measured in classical conditioning studies, reveal little about the relative strength of the associative network that is represented by the CS-US contingency; this linkage had been established much earlier in the experiment.

More broadly conceptualized, Prokasy has provided a two-factor theory of skeletal classical conditioning in which there is one factor or process that results in the organism acquiring knowledge about the environment and more specifically about the CS-US relationship. A second factor results in the acquisition and subsequent stabilization of the conditioned response. Moreover, these two processes are relatively independent. An interesting aspect of Prokasy's model is that he believes that the autonomic nervous system's visceral and vascular changes immediately reflect information that has been acquired about the relationship between the CS and US. Target skeletal responses are later acquired but their acquisition is neither in conjunction with nor as a consequence of the earlier modification.

Prokasy has provided a thoughtful and interesting descriptive analysis of skeletal conditioning in the human subject. His model provides some speculative answers to many of the questions that have arisen in the anlaysis of classical conditioning. Some of these include the distinction that has been made between learning and performance, the nature of the conditioned response, the identification of variables that influence performance rather than learning, and the role of prolonged training in changing the characteristics of the conditioned response. It will be interesting to see the impact of his two-stage model on future classical conditioning investigations.

The Value and Application of Classical Conditioning Experiments ▶

What value and/or objectives are achieved by psychologists who classically condition a college student's eyeblink, a dog's salivary response, or a rabbit's nictitating membrane? There are varying answers to this question, depending on the objectives of the investigator.

Some experimenters have been interested in analyzing the nature of associative learning and, as a result, have chosen as simple a form of associative learning as can be found. It has been their belief that it is necessary first to understand the simplest type before moving on to more complex forms. Dickinson and Mackintosh (1978) have written, "Conditioning is . . . as simple a form of associative learning as we are likely to find" (p. 587). Much of the value in using the conditioning task is that the experimenter can exercise excellent control over the stimuli that are used (e.g., their physical characteristics), the onset and offset of their presentations, as well as in the preciseness with which the response can be measured.

The varying physiological changes that eventually will be identified as representing the neurological basis of learning will most likely be discovered through the study of the classical conditioned response. Thompson and his associates see the examination of the classically conditioned nictitating membrane response of the rabbit as an extremely useful procedure for analyzing the relationship between certain neurological changes taking place in the brain and the development of the conditioned response. A series of studies by these investigators has made substantial progress in this important undertaking (see Thompson, 1986).

Another objective has been to use the classical conditioning paradigm as a model in order to afford a better understanding of how certain behavior problems that are of importance to society are acquired and extinguished. It will be recalled from Chapter Two that Watson and Rayner (1920) conditioned a little boy, Albert, to be afraid of a white rat—a finding that suggests how some human emotional responses may be learned. Quite possibly, severe emotional responses—those described as phobias—may arise from an environmental situation that mirrors the classical conditioning paradigm. Moreover, how can such emotional responses be eliminated or extinguished? Laboratory studies reveal that the elimination of many conditioned responses can be achieved by using an extinction procedure. However, the experimental findings of Masserman (1943) and Wolpe (1952) have indicated that the emotional responses of fear and anxiety were not eliminated by this procedure. This suggested that an appropriate way to treat anxiety might be counterconditioning—a technique that is now found in a variety of psychotherapeutic procedures.

The counterconditioning procedure consists of conditioning a new response that is incompatible with the emotional response. For example, assume a rat fears a specific location in an experimental apparatus because that location has been associated with shock. The experimenter may make the animal hungry and place food at a location in the apparatus where the animal's fear response is sufficiently weak to permit the animal to eat. Each day the food can be placed progressively nearer to the place eliciting fear, so that eventually the animal will eat from the specific location that originally elicited fear. Since a positive affective state is generated from eating and is incompatible with fear, the counterconditioning procedure effectively eliminates the animal's fear of the apparatus.

In summary, emotional responses such as anxiety and fear appear to be basic responses that are learned rapidly; since the autonomic nervous system plays an important role in the eliciting of these responses, we have only minimal control over them. An examination of the conditioning process can undoubtedly make an important contribution in better understanding how subjects acquire anxious or fearful responses to innocuous environmental stimuli.

Classical conditioning models have also been used in an effort to better understand drug addiction. Psychologists are indebted to Pavlov (1927) for his early work in demonstrating that it is possible to condition addictive behavior resulting from morphine injection. Krylov, as reported by Pavlov (1927), found that when dogs received morphine injections regularly, the preliminaries associated with injections were sufficient to produce all of the observable symptoms (nausea, salivation, vomiting, etc.) that arose from the injection of the drug itself. Krylov's findings have been replicated by early and current investigators (see Collins and Tatum, 1925; Crisler, 1930; and Wikler, 1970).

It is not likely that classical conditioning plays an important role in accounting for drug seeking or the beginning of addictive behavior. As Jaffe (1970) and others have acknowledged, instrumental conditioning serves as a better paradigm since the euphoric reaction produced by the drug serves as a reward for the beginning addict. Later, reinforcement is provided by the reduction of the tension, anxiety, and pain occasioned by the lack of the drug in the body. Much more feasible is the proposed role of classical conditioning in withdrawal responses accompanying therapy and contributing to the craving responsible for the addict's return to the habit.

It has been assumed that the subject's early withdrawal symptoms, which can be identified as URs, are produced by physiological factors (US) stemming from the absence of the drug in the nervous system. A variety of environmental stimuli are invariably associated with the US, so the withdrawal symptoms may be elicited by such stimuli long after the physiological factors cease to exist. Jaffe (1970) has written that narcotic addicts often report that they feel sensations very similar to withdrawal symptoms when they return to those environments where drugs were available. He suggests that it is not unlikely that the addicted alcoholic has similar experiences. Such conditioned abstinence phenomena may play a significant role in the frequent relapses that characterize the clinical picture of compulsive abuse. Support for Jaffe's position has been provided by Wikler (1965) who has experimentally demonstrated the elicitation of withdrawal symptoms by conditioned stimuli.

Another aspect of addiction is drug tolerance. It is generally known that the repeated administration of some drugs will result in a need for increasing amounts; thus, at the same dosage, the drug becomes less effective over continuing administrations. Increases in the original dosage are necessary in order to produce the same effect. Many investigators have held that the increased need arises from physiological factors occurring from repeated administrations (e.g., increased rapidity with which the drug is metabolized, decreased sensitivity of the drug receptors, etc.). But during the past several decades, as Kesner and Baker's (1981) review has indicated, many investigators have found that environmental variables that influence learning and memory exert similar effects on drug tolerance. For example, Mitchell and his associates (e.g., Adams, Yeh, Woods, and Mitchell, 1969; and Ferguson, Adams, and Mitchell, 1969) have demonstrated that maximum levels of morphine tolerance are obtained only when the administration of the drug and testing for tolerance are conducted in the same environment. The question to be answered is to identify the theoretical paradigm that best accounts for these environmental effects.

As a result of a series of studies examining tolerance levels of morphine, Siegel (1975b, 1976) has proposed a classical conditioning model in which the environment within which the drug is administered is conceptualized as a CS, and the morphine as the US. The UR is the pain reduction produced by the morphine. The CR that arises from CS-US pairings is a pharmacological response that is compensatory to (or opposite) the pain reduction response produced by the morphine.

Siegel's experimental procedure has been as follows: Rats are injected with low to intermediate doses of morphine over a series of trials; injections take place in a special environment. Shortly after each injection, the animals are given a pain test in order to measure the analgesic effects of the drug. In some experiments (Siegel, 1975b), pain sensitivity was measured by using a hot plate test—here the animal is placed on the surface of a carefully controlled hot plate for one minute, with measurement being made of the number of seconds that elapsed until the animal first licked its paw. In other studies (Siegel, 1976), pain tolerance was measured by an analgesiometer. This instrument is designed to increase automatically, at a constant rate, the pressure applied to a rat's paw; the animal is free to withdraw its paw from the source of pressure at any time. The amount of pressure provided just prior to paw withdrawal represents the response measure.

Experimental findings have typically demonstrated that animals that are given a series of injections with morphine will develop an increased need for the drug, as revealed by their responding more rapidly to pain as the injections continue. After demonstrating such tolerance, however, an injection provided in a different environment will result in a decreased need for the drug, thus indicating an increase in their tolerance level. Such a finding is explained by positing that since the environment has been changed, there is no CS to elicit the compensatory pharmacological response that decreases or attenuates the effectiveness of the morphine.

In support of his classical conditioning, drug tolerance model, Siegel (1978) has demonstrated that two operations that have been shown to influence classical conditioning, namely, experimental extinction and preexposure to the CS, also influence tolerance.

Drug tolerance or a lack of it has often been used in explaining deaths attributed to overdose.[9] In some instances, it can actually be shown that an overdose was administered, but in other instances, it has been found that many experienced drug users die after a dose that should not be fatal in view of their tolerance. In some instances, individuals have died following a heroin dose that was well tolerated the previous day.

Using Siegel's classical conditioning model, the failure of tolerance should occur if the drug was administered in an environment that had not in the past been associated with the drug. Thus, the model would posit that one contributing factor in death from a so-called overdose might be the absence of the conditioned compensatory pharmacological response that attenuates the drug's effectiveness. A study by Siegel, Hinson, Krank, and McCully (1982) has supported such a position. These investigators found that groups of rats with the same pharmacological history of heroin administration will differ in mortality, depending on whether a potentially lethal dose is given in the context of cues previously associated with sublethal doses or if such an environmental context is absent.

Some of the experimental work that has been directed toward the control and treatment of allergies has employed the classical conditioning paradigm. The presence of an allergen has been generally regarded as an important factor in governing the onset of bronchial asthma, but psychological factors have been acknowledged to contribute to these attacks. In fact, physicians have ranked asthma first among those diseases in which they believed psychogenic factors were important. In one case study, Luparello, Lyons, Blecker, and McFadden (1968) misled 40 asthmatic patients into believing that they were inhaling an allergen that frequently precipitated an attack, when in fact they were breathing nebulized saline. In 19 of the patients, airway resistance increased, and 12 of them developed a bona fide attack. Ottenberg, Stein, Lewis, and Hamilton (1958) and Justensen, Braun, Garrison, and Pendleton (1970) made an experimental attack on the problem by demonstrating that bronchial asthma attacks in guinea pigs can be conditioned, thus suggesting classical conditioning may be one of the psychogenic mechanisms contributing to the illness.

An even more direct application of the classical conditioning paradigm is found in the treatment of enuresis first proposed in the United States by Mowrer and Mowrer (1938). The Mowrers believed that a classical conditioning procedure could be used to prevent children from bedwetting. An apparatus was devised to detect the presence of urine through a sensing mechanism contained in a pad on which the child slept. When the child urinated, a bell or buzzer went off to awaken the child, who would then stop voiding and go to the toilet to complete the act. Viewing the process as a classical conditioning procedure, Mowrer and Mowrer paired the conditioned stimulus of the child's bladder distension with the unconditioned stimulus of the alarm, which produced an unconditioned response of awakening. After an appropriate number of

---

[9] The mean number of deaths attributable to drug overdose is surprisingly high. In urban areas, drug overdose is among the leading causes of death in individuals ages 15 to 35.

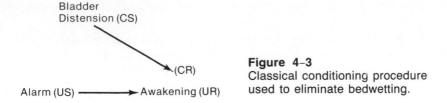

Figure 4-3
Classical conditioning procedure
used to eliminate bedwetting.

pairings, the bladder distension (CS) should result in a conditioned response of awakening, which in turn would be followed by subsequent urination in the toilet rather than the bed. Figure 4-3 illustrates the procedure.

A review by Doleys (1977) has indicated that, in a dozen studies using such a conditioning operation between 1965 and 1975, bedwetting was arrested in 75% of the experimental subjects.

Summary ▶

This chapter examined a number of basic issues that have been raised in the study of classical conditioning, as well as discussed the use of this paradigm in order to better understand a number of behavioral problems present in our society.

One issue that was raised has to do with whether the US must have motivational significance in order to be used in the conditioning experiment. Early attempts to condition pupillary responding using light as the US, and to demonstrate spinal conditioning in dogs, were unsuccessful, thus suggesting that the US had to have appetitive or aversive characteristics in order to function as a US. More recent work has demonstrated that it is possible to obtain spinal conditioning using cats, thus indicating that the US need not have motivational significance to serve in a conditioning experiment.

The events that are associated in a classical conditioning paradigm, although once believed to be between a stimulus and a response, are now believed to be between the CS and US. However, many current investigators view this association, not as between two sensations elicited by appropriate stimuli, but between central representations of the CS and US.

Although Pavlov and early investigators believed that the choice of the response in the conditioning experiment was a matter of experimenter indifference, this position has been replaced by current knowledge that one stimulus may have an unique relationship with another stimulus as well as with the response; in summary, a selective character of the associative relationship is well established in classical conditioning.

Whether or not US-CS pairings results in conditioning has been a controversial question. At present, there is no answer that is completely acceptable to all investigators, with both inhibition and excitation being posited to arise from CS-US trials.

The last issue that was discussed has to do with whether the CS-US association arises from a pairing (or contiguity) of the CS and US, or from the establishment of a contingency. Although most current investigators accept the contingency position, there is some evidence to make a case for contiguity as being the necessary condition.

Two major theoretical analyses of classical conditioning were discussed. Rescorla and Wagner (1972) attempted to describe classical conditioning in terms of a mathematical formula that includes assumptions being made concerning the amount of conditioning that a particular US can support, the saliency of the CS, and the so-called surprisingness of the US. Declining increments of associative strength are posited to arise as a result of CS-US trials, with the familiar negatively accelerated learning curve being the product of this set of assumptions. The major concern of Rescorla and Wagner, however, has been to use their model in order to better understand overshadowing and blocking. Prokasy's model is more descriptive. His major interest has been in identifying those processes that govern the conditioning of skeletal responses. Acquisition consists of four stages through which subjects must pass in moving from an operant level of responding to asymptotic conditioned responding. These four stages have been identified as (1) the detection of a contingency between the CS and US, (2) the selection of a response within the constraints placed by the experimental situation, (3) the acquisition of the conditioned response, and (4) the shaping of the conditioned response that reflects response changes analogous to the honing of a highly skilled motor response.

A variety of applications of the classical conditioning paradigm have been examined. These include use of this paradigm for a better understanding of phobias, drug addiction and drug tolerance, as well as in the treatment of allergies and enuresis.

chapter five

▶

Instrumental and Operant Conditioning: General Considerations

By the early 1930s, two general types of learning tasks were frequently used by American psychologists. As we described in Chapter One, one type was the conditioned response task as illustrated by the work of Pavlov; the second was represented by the learning as found in simple and complex mazes, puzzle boxes, and so on, in which reward for making the response was a prominent feature of the task. With these two general kinds of learning tasks being so often employed, it is not surprising that Skinner (1938) and then Hilgard and Marquis (1940) proposed that two types of learning processes were involved in their mastery.

It will be recalled from Chapter One that the taxonomy proposed by Skinner (1938) identified the operations employed by Pavlov as resulting in respondent behavior, whereas a second type, illustrated by Thorndike's experiments with cats learning to escape from a puzzle box in order to secure fish, or Skinner's own work with rats learning to press a bar for a food pellet, was characterized as operant. Respondent behavior, Skinner noted, was elicited by known stimuli as the use of the US in classical conditioning would attest. In contrast, operant responding was emitted, with the experiments being unable to identify any specific stimulus responsible for eliciting the response that led to reward.[1]

Several years later, Hilgard and Marquis (1940) indicated that Pavlov's methods and procedures should be characterized as classical conditioning. They also pointed out that

---

[1] This did not mean that an operant could not become associated with some prior stimulus; in such cases, operants were designated as *discriminated operants*. In such instances, the stimulus became only an occasion for the operant.

Pavlovian methods did not exhaust the procedures used to establish other types of learned responses. These other procedures focused on the fact that the subject's response was instrumental in securing a reward or a consequence that was pleasant, or escaping from (or avoiding) a consequence that was unpleasant. In contrast to the CS-US relationship established with classical conditioning operations, it was the response-reinforcement association that was fundamental in instrumental conditioning. Instrumental conditioning thus became the second major learning type in Hilgard and Marquis's classification system.

We should emphasize that a fundamental difference between the classical and instrumental conditioning procedure was that with classical conditioning, the presentation of the US was independent of the experimental subject's response—the US continued to be presented regardless of whether or not the subject responded. In contrast, instrumental (or operant) conditioning involved providing a consequence only if a predetermined response was made by the experimental subject. Thus, the instrumental procedure demanded that the consequence be provided only after the appropriate response had been made.

Although the classical-instrumental conditioning (or respondent-operant) distinction has been widely accepted by most contemporary investigators, a problem has remained in providing a taxonomy that would effectively organize the myriad of instrumental conditioning tasks employed in psychology laboratories. The difficulty in establishing a viable classification system has been that the varying tasks often employ different arrangements of stimuli and frequently demand different types of instrumental responses to be made by the experimental subject, which in turn result in varying kinds of stimulus consequences.

Classification systems have been provided by Hilgard and Marquis (1940), Grant (1964), Cohen (1969), and Woods (1974) but none of these has generated widespread acceptance. Nonetheless, some taxonomy is necessary if a systematic examination of the nature of instrumental conditioning is to be made. The most frequently employed taxonomy of instrumental conditioning (and the one that we will use in this text) can be described as functional with five major types of tasks being identified: (1) positive reinforcement (or reward), (2) negative reinforcement (or escape), (3) punishment, (4) avoidance, and (5) omission training. We will briefly examine the characteristics of these varying instrumental conditioning tasks.

Types of Instrumental Tasks ▶

Positive Reinforcement, or Reward Tasks

Positive reinforcement (or reward tasks) involve the experimenter providing a contingency between making an instrumental response and presenting a reward or a pleasant consequence. Early investigators used tasks that were fairly complex (e.g., the puzzle box employed by Thorndike [1898] or a model of the Hampton Court maze used by Small [1900]). Contemporary experimenters, however, utilize tasks demanding only simple responses. An often used apparatus is the runway in which hungry or thirsty white rats learn to leave a starting box, run down a straight alley, and enter a goal box in order to secure food or water.

A second type is the Skinner Box described in Chapter One, which requires that the rat make a simple lever-pressing response in order to secure a pellet of food. The Skinner Box has been modified to accommodate pigeons in which their pecking at an illuminated plastic disk on the wall of the experimental chamber will provide access to a hopper of grain for a fixed amount of time.

Negative Reinforcement, or Escape Tasks

Escape tasks have been often identified as involving negative reinforcement. With such tasks, the subject must learn to escape or terminate an aversive stimulus—the reinforcement is relief from the noxious event. Positive and negative reinforcement tasks are similar in that both types of reinforcement result in increased responding by the experimental subject; the difference, of course, is that positive reinforcers require the introduction of a reward whereas negative reinforcers increase responding by reason of their removal.

Punishment

Current investigators define punishment as the presentation of an aversive stimulus, contingent upon the execution of a specific response. If a rat, after reaching a stable level of bar pressing that results in securing food in a Skinner Box, is then shocked after making the bar-pressing response, the punishment task is illustrated. Our definition of punishment indicates that (1) the presentation of an aversive stimulus is contingent on the making of the bar-pressing response, (2) with such presentation reducing the probability that the punished response again will be made. We may note that the objective of punishment is not the acquisition of an instrumental response that characterizes positive and negative reinforcement tasks, but rather involves the weakening or the elimination of a response already in the repertoire of the experimental subject.

One type of punishment that can be subsumed under this general heading has been identified as *negative punishment,* which consists of the removal of a previously acquired reward or privilege. A mother may punish her daughter by sending her to her room for not doing her chores around the house. This procedure of isolating the daughter from her normal environment has been categorized as a *time-out procedure.* Negative punishment that involves the loss of a privilege has been also identified as *response cost.* This procedure has a basic similarity to the omission training paradigm discussed in a later section.

Avoidance

The fourth instrumental conditioning task is avoidance. Here, the presentation of a stimulus or warning signal is followed a short time later by the presentation of an aversive stimulus (e.g., shock). The subject must learn to respond appropriately when the stimulus is presented in order to avoid receiving the noxious stimulus. To illustrate, a rat is placed in one compartment of a shuttle box and a tone is presented several seconds later followed by shock. On early trials the task is one of negative reinforcement as the animal runs to the second (and safe) compartment when the shock is presented; after several trials the animal responds when the tone is presented and prior to shock onset.

One unusual type of avoidance task has been designated as *nondiscriminated* or *Sidman* (1953a, 1953b) *avoidance.* There is no signal or discriminative stimulus to predict the onset of the aversive stimulation. Rather, shock is provided on a regular interval, but an instrumental response by the subject, such as bar pressing, will delay or postpone the shock for an arbitrary length of time set by the experimenter. The interval between shock presentations has been identified as the *shock-shock interval,* whereas the amount of time that the instrumental response delays presentation of shock is known as the *response-shock interval.* It is possible for the subject to learn to respond and greatly reduce the frequency of shock although complete avoidance is rarely achieved.

Omission Training

The last instrumental conditioning task we would like to describe has been termed omission training (or negative punishment). More properly, omission training reflects a procedure rather than an instrumental conditioning task since this procedure has been employed with both classical and instrumental conditioning tasks.

In an early classical conditioning study by Sheffield (1965) (who introduced the term), the salivary response was conditioned in dogs by pairing a tone (CS) with food (US). After a stable level of conditioning has taken place, omission training was carried out in which the making of the CR prevented the subject from receiving the US. On those trials in which the CR was not made, the US was presented. It might be noted that Sheffield reported that one dog that was provided this omission contingency continued to salivate on approximately 50% of the trials provided, missing food on 800 trials. Subsequent classical conditioning studies employing appetitive as well as aversive unconditioned stimuli and using omission training have been conducted (e.g., Patten and Rudy, 1967; Gormezano and Hiller, 1972; and Coleman, 1975).

The omission procedure has been also used with instrumental conditioning tasks. To illustrate, a rat is trained to press a bar for food. After a stable level of responding has been reached, the animal is then rewarded (with food) for not pressing the bar until a certain period of time (e.g., 30 seconds) has elapsed. Omission training does not involve the presentation of a discriminative stimulus since the subject must wait for a given period of time without responding in order to receive reward. Although it might be conjectured that the rat is learning a type of temporal discrimination, inasmuch as bar pressing results in postponing reward, the omission procedure results in a decline in the rate of the previously established instrumental response.

Omission training has been rarely used in parametric studies of instrumental conditioning; rather, and as we shall note later in this chapter, it has been employed in the examination of certain theoretical issues that have arisen in the study of classical and instrumental conditioning.

Instrumental Conditioning Parameters— Nonsignaled and Signaled

The instrumental conditioning taxonomy that we have presented contains several parameters that can be related to the identification of the task. One has to do with the nature of the consequences or the type of reinforcer (e.g., appetitive or aversive) that is used. The second has to do with whether the response is instrumental in either securing, removing, or preventing the consequence. The last parameter has to do with whether conditioning takes the form of increases or decreases in the frequency of responding. But this dimensional analysis omits a basic feature that is a part of all instrumental conditioning tasks—a feature that has to do with whether or not the task employs a specific stimulus or cue for responding.

Many instrumental conditioning tasks can be categorized as simple or nonsignaled. With such tasks, the stimulus situation provides no specific cues (at least as manipulated by the experimenter) to indicate when a response will result in the appropriate consequence. The task provides the organism with contextual stimuli but a specific stimulus to cue the instrumental response cannot be identified. The use of the Skinner Box in which bar pressing will provide the rat with a pellet of food is an example of a nonsignaled task. With this task we may note that there is no external stimulus that cues the animal when to respond.

Other tasks can be described as signaled instrumental conditioning tasks, since the experimenter provides the subject with a signal or discriminative stimulus. If the organism responds appropriately, the consequence will be provided. Avoidance tasks are generally of this variety. Here, the organism must receive some cue in order to respond in time to avoid the aversive stimulus. But it is also possible to use a discriminative stimulus when employing appetitive stimuli. By placing a light above the bar in the Skinner Box, the experimenter can arrange conditions so that reward is provided for responding only during the presentation of light.

Response Measurement

The measurement of responding in instrumental conditioning tasks is similar to that employed in classical conditioning in that response measures during acquisition include: (1) latency, (2) magnitude, and (3) frequency or probability of responding.

These measures can also be obtained during extinction trials but as we have noted in our discussion of classical conditioned response measures in Chapter Two, our bias has been to stress response measures obtained during acquisition.

Operant Conditioning ▶

We have previously indicated that Skinner's (1938) concept of operant conditioning was similar to the instrumental conditioning category as described in Hilgard and Marquis (1940). In this section we will discuss operant conditioning procedures as well as several differences that set operant conditioning apart from instrumental conditioning.

The kinds of apparatus used in operant conditioning experiments have been so designed that (1) the subject's response takes only a short time to make and (2) reinforcement is received in proximity to where the response is made; after completing the response and receiving reinforcement, the subject is ready to respond again. The apparatus permits free responding, since the manipulandum is always available. An example of such free responding would be a pigeon pecking at a plastic disk thousands of times in a single experimental session.

Operant conditioning tasks differ from instrumental conditioning tasks along several procedural dimensions. One is that discrete learning trials, used with instrumental conditioning tasks, are not usually programmed with operant conditioning experiments. With operant tasks, subjects are provided with experimental sessions; the animals are placed in the experimental apparatus for a fixed length of time (e.g., 30 minutes) or until they obtain a specific number of reinforcements.

The lack of discrete trials and the rapidity with which operant responses can be made raise two other considerations. One is that the subject cannot be provided with reinforcement after each response, as would frequently be the case with instrumental conditioning tasks. This results in operant investigators using partial reinforcement schedules, or programs detailing how reinforcement shall be provided. Second, the rapidity with which responses may be made has resulted in investigators using the rate of response as their basic response measure.

In addition to these comparisons between operant and instrumental learning tasks, other differences may be noted. One is that operant investigators often place emphasis on the analysis of individual responding so that only a few experimental subjects need to be used. The basic procedure that permits this type of analysis has been described as the *operant level of responding* or the *free operant baseline.*

To illustrate, when a rat is placed in a Skinner Box equipped with a lever that can be depressed but that does not dispense food, operant experimenters are interested in measuring the number of bar depressions made by the animal when placed in that environment for a fixed period of time. The number of presses made by the animal during that period would be identified as the animal's operant level of responding, with rate of responding providing a free operant baseline. It is against each animal's baseline of responding that the effectiveness of any experimental procedure designed to increase level pressing would be measured.[2]

---

[2] It is obvious that if investigators are interested in examining effectiveness of an experimental procedure designed to *decrease* lever pressing, the use of such baseline behavior would be inappropriate. The solution to this problem would be to provide reinforcement for bar pressing until some sizeable and stable level of responding was present so that any reduction in lever pressing arising from the experimental manipulation could be readily measured.

Another difference is that operant experimenters have often been concerned with maintenance behavior; such interest is directed not toward an examination of variables that influence acquisition but rather toward how specific variables influence the maintenance of behavior. An illustration of such an interest in maintenance behavior would be as follows: After a rat acquires a bar-pressing response and reaches a stable level of responding, the operant investigator might be interested in examining how the administration of an experimental drug would influence the animal's rate of responding.

Schedules of Reinforcement

As mentioned earlier, operant conditioning tasks frequently result in the experimental subject making a large number of responses within a very short period of time. Since it is not feasible to provide reinforcement after each response, it has been necessary to place the animal on a partial reinforcement schedule—to specify which response will be reinforced through the use of a reinforcement schedule. Reinforcement may be provided after the subject has made a specified (or variable) number of responses or after a specific (or variable) amount of time has elapsed since the last response was made. Four basic reinforcement schedules have been utilized: (1) fixed interval, (2) variable interval, (3) fixed ratio, and (4) variable ratio.

Fixed Interval (FI)   With a fixed interval schedule, reinforcement is provided for the first response that the organism makes after some fixed period of time has elapsed. With a FI 20 schedule, reinforcement is provided for the first response that occurs 20 seconds or more after the previous reinforcement.

Variable Interval (VI)   With the variable interval schedule, reinforcement is provided for the first response that is made after a variable (rather than a fixed) period of time has elapsed. A 20-second variable interval (VI) schedule consists of reinforcement administered for the first response that follows selected time intervals averaging 20 seconds in duration.

Fixed Ratio (FR)   For the fixed ratio schedule, reinforcement is provided after every nth response. For example, an FR 10 schedule is defined as every tenth response being followed by reinforcement.

Variable Ratio (VR)   With the variable ratio schedule, the number of responses needed in order to secure reinforcement varies, but the varying numbers of responses are averaged to provide a descriptive statement of the type of schedule utilized. A VR 10 schedule would be produced by the following: 4 responses followed by reinforcement, 14 responses followed by reinforcement, 10 responses followed by reinforcement, 6 responses followed by reinforcement, and 16 responses followed by reinforcement.

These varying reinforcement schedules can frequently be observed to influence human behavior. An example of the VR schedule is found in the operation of slot machines programmed to pay off on some average number of operations. Since the machine has been placed on this type of schedule, it is not possible to predict which particular play will pay off. One player may win twice in succession, whereas the next player may pull the lever twenty or thirty times without a payoff. Applied psychologists have often attempted to apply these reinforcement schedules to business, factory, and school settings with an appropriate scheduling of piecework systems.

Other Operant Reinforcement Schedules

In addition to the four basic reinforcement schedules described, a number of other and more complex schedules have been used. Three of these are: (1) multiple, (2) chained, and (3) concurrent.

Multiple schedules consist of two or more schedules presented successively and correlated with external cues. A pigeon might be given a 30-second presentation of a red plastic disk, followed by a 30-second presentation of a yellow disk, and then a green disk for 30 seconds. Responding to the presentation of the red disk would be associated with a specific VI schedule, the yellow disk would be associated with a specific FI schedule, and the green disk would be associated with a VR schedule.

Chain schedules also consist of two or more cues presented successively to the subject; however, responding by the organism to the first stimulus results only in the presentation of the second stimulus. Responding to the second stimulus will result in reinforcement.

Concurrent schedules involve two or more responses, each reinforced by a separate schedule. For example, a pigeon may be reinforced for responding to a plastic disk placed on the right side of the box on a FI schedule, whereas its response to the plastic disk placed on the left side of the box will result in a VI schedule.

Two other reinforcement schedules that have been used by operant investigators are differential reinforcement for the low rates (DRL) and differential reinforcement for high rates (DRH). With the DRL schedule, the more frequently used of the two, the organism's response is reinforced only if it is made *after* a specified time period has elapsed; responses made within the time interval are not reinforced. A practical illustration would be flooding your carburetor in attempting to start your car. You must wait a sufficient period of time before it can be successfully started. As would be expected, the DRL schedule results in a very low response rate and one that is related to the length of the interval set by the experimenter.

With the DRH schedule, reinforcement depends on the subject responding a specific number of times within a designated time period (e.g., 20 pecks at a disk within five seconds). This schedule has been used only infrequently, since it is very difficult to control the subject's responding. Assume, for example, that the experimenter sets a DRH criterion of having a pigeon peck at a disk 10 times in four seconds. If responding takes place at this rate, reinforcement is received. If responding on an occasion should go below this number during the four-second time period, reinforcement is not provided. This lack of reinforcement reduces the rate of responding still more, resulting in reinforcement being withheld, which in turn results in still fewer responses being made, and so on. Eventually, the response may cease completely, since reinforcement has not been received.

Rate of Responding

The response measure used in all of the schedules is the rate of responding—the number of responses made by the organism within an experimental session. The plotting of these responses results in a cumulative curve: The number of responses made by the subject is plotted on the ordinate against time on the abscissa. Figure 5-1 shows how a cumulative record is obtained. Each time the organism responds, the pen moves vertically on the paper feeding through the apparatus.

Note that if the organism does not respond, a horizontal line occurs in the direction of the paper feed. The more frequently the organism responds, the more closely the record approaches verticality. Although the rate of responding is directly proportional to the slope of the curve, at slopes above 80° small differences in the angle represent very large differences in rate.

An Analysis of Instrumental and Classical Conditioning

Our previous and current examinations of classical and instrumental conditioning tasks now permit us to examine some of the issues that have arisen in the study of these two paradigms.

Some investigators have conjectured that classical conditioning is actually an instance of instrumental conditioning, in which the conditioned response serves as an instrumental response. For example, consider the dog conditioned to salivate to a tone (CS) prior to the delivery of the food (US). The conditioned response of salivation may

Figure 5-1
A picture of a commercial recorder and a sketch of its operation. Photo courtesy of Gerbrands Corporation, Arlington, Massachusetts.

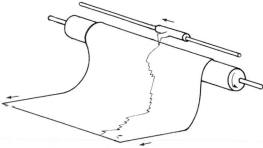

Each response made by the organism moves the pen one space in this direction.

serve as an instrumental response that aids in the animal's mastication of the dry food, or it may simply improve the food's flavor. Or, if the investigator would employ acid as the US in order to elicit salivation, the salivary response is instrumental in diluting the acid, thus making it less aversive.

It has been possible to analyze virtually all classical conditioning studies from the point of view of hypothesizing apparent reinforcement effects that follow the making of the conditioned response, thus placing such instances of classical conditioning within an instrumental conditioning framework.

Opponents of this position have raised several arguments against its acceptance. Perhaps the most telling have been the findings obtained from the use of an omission training schedule, described earlier in the chapter. It is noteworthy that if the CR is made, there is the omission of the US. This arrangement abolishes any contingency that could take place between the CR and the US. We have previously cited Sheffield's (1965) findings that omission training employed with the conditioned salivary response in dogs resulted in one animal continuing to salivate on approximately 50% of the trials provided, missing food on 800 trials. If salivation was serving as an instrumental response, the response should have eventually extinguished since reinforcement was not received when the response was made.

The use of the omission training procedure has been also used employing an aversive US, with results supporting the findings of Sheffield (1965). Coleman (1975) examined an omission schedule of reinforcement in conditioning the nictitating membrane of the rabbit. We will describe the findings for the two major experimental groups that were used.

With one group, presentation of shock (the US) was omitted when the CR was made; the second group always received shock following the CS, regardless of whether or not the CR was made. Acquisition training consisted of providing 480 trials (80 per session), with findings revealed in Figure 5-2. As may be noted, reliably poorer conditioning was exhibited by the group in which responding was instrumental in providing the presentation of the shock. Thus, the omission procedure was not as effective in enhancing the rate of conditioning as was the traditional CS-US method.

In summary, the evidence seems clear that the classical and instrumental conditioning paradigms represent different types of learning tasks and that the distinction that has been made between them is a valid one.

Can Autonomic Nervous System Responses Be Instrumentally Conditioned?

Our analysis of instrumental and classical conditioning raises an interesting question that has been a part of the classical-instrumental conditioning literature for some time. This has to do with whether the instrumental conditioning procedure can be used to modify autonomic nervous system responses. Early learning theorists hypothesized that only classical conditioning operations could be employed to modify autonomic nervous system responses. The early failure of Skinner and Delabarre (Skinner, 1938) to instrumentally condition vasoconstriction, supporting this position, deterred investigators from undertaking this type of study.

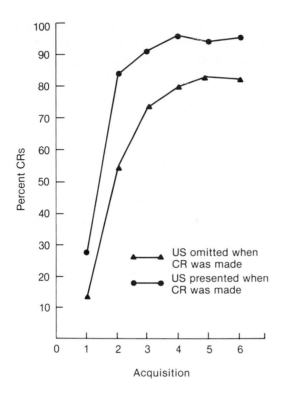

Figure 5-2
The percentage of CRs in 80-trial blocks for Acquisition Days 1–6. Adapted from S. R. Coleman, "Consequences of response-contingent change in unconditioned stimulus intensity upon the rabbit (Oryctolagus cuniculus) nictitating membrane response," *Journal of Comparative and Physiological Psychology*, 1975, *88,* 591–595. Copyright © 1975 by the American Psychological Association. Reprinted by permission.

But in the early 1960s, the problem of instrumental conditioning of autonomic nervous system responses was reopened by Kimmel and his associates. In a series of studies, many of which were summarized by Kimmel (1974), it was demonstrated that the EDR could be instrumentally conditioned using positive reinforcement. An early study by Kimmel and Kimmel (1963) illustrates the procedure. Experimental subjects, whose EDRs were monitored, were first provided with a 10-minute test period, the last five minutes of which were used to establish a base level of EDR responding. Following this period, all EDRs emitted during a 16-minute test period were reinforced by the presentation of a light. A control or noncontingent group received the same number of light presentations, but light was never associated with an elevation of the EDR. Clear evidence was obtained for the instrumental conditioning of the EDR. The experimental group revealed increases of up to 120% of their initial resting level, whereas the control group declined in rate of emission to below 80%.

The finding that various human autonomic responses can be modified by using an instrumental conditioning operation employing positive reinforcement has been confirmed in a host of studies—Engel and Hanson (1966) and Brener and Hothersall (1967) using heart rate; Snyder and Noble (1968) employing vasoconstriction; and Frezza and Holland (1971) investigating the salivary response.

Harris and Brady's (1974) survey of studies in which the autonomic responses of animals were instrumentally conditioned has provided confirmation of the results obtained with humans. Illustrative of the work with animals is an experiment conducted by Miller and Carmona (1967). Dogs who had been deprived of water for 16 hours were rewarded with water for salivating. The investigators first obtained a base rate of salivation, measured in number of drops per minute. During the experimental period, spontaneous bursts of salivation were reinforced with 20 ml of water. More specifically, water was provided for every burst of salivation of one drop or more per five-second period, with the performance criterion progressively increasing to seven drops per five-second period by the end of 40 days of training. In a second experiment, omission training was provided with the experimental animals learning *not* to salivate. Water was provided when the animals did not salivate for two seconds; the time interval progressively increased over training to 60 seconds. Figure 5–3 provides the results of Miller and Carmona's (1967) findings, which convincingly demonstrate that salivation, an autonomic response, can be instrumentally conditioned.

A methodological problem that confronts the investigator conducting this type of instrumental conditioning experiment is the possibility of the subject exercising some control over an autonomic response through skeletal muscles (voluntary responding) or cognitive activity. Attempts to examine the role of such activity have taken the form of monitoring the subject's respiration rate and obtaining electromyographic (EMG) records during the experimental period. It is then possible to determine if changes in these responses have been correlated with the receiving of reinforcement. The presence of such changes would suggest that the conditioning of the autonomic responses has been mediated by skeletal responding. In addition, postexperimental interviews have been conducted with the human subject in an effort to determine if they engaged in any cognitive activity that might be related to the receiving of reward.

Miller and his associates have suggested that one way to handle the problem of controlling muscular responses that might accompany autonomic responses would be to paralyze muscles by using the drug curare. Electrical stimulation of the brain, which Olds and Milner (1954) discovered to have reinforcing effects, could also be used as reward. In a study conducted by Trowill (1967), curarized rats were first observed in order to measure their normal or base heart rate. Following this, one group of

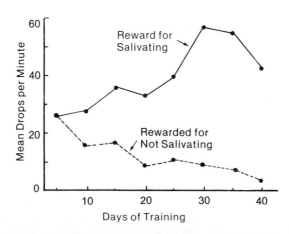

Figure 5–3
Mean curves of instrumental learning by three thirsty dogs rewarded with water for increases or decreases in spontaneous salivation. Adapted from N. E. Miller and A. Carmona, "Modification of a visceral response, salivation in thirsty dogs, by instrumental training with water reward," *Journal of Comparative and Physiological Psychology,* 1967, *63,* 1–6. Copyright © 1967 by the American Psychological Association. Reprinted by permission.

experimental animals received brain stimulation only if heart rate increased over the base rate, whereas a second group of animals received brain stimulation only if heart rate decreased below the base rate. Although rate changes were small, Trowill was able to demonstrate that heart rate could be either increased or decreased by using brain stimulation as the reinforcing agent. Control animals receiving brain stimulation uncorrelated with increase or decrease of heart rate (yoked controls) failed to show the changes observed in their experimental counterparts.

Subsequent studies by Miller and DiCara (1967), Miller and Banuazizi (1968), DiCara and Miller (1968), and Miller and DiCara (1968) provided confirmation of Trowill's (1967) earlier study. But in the early 1970s, Miller and Dworkin (1974) conducted an extensive series of experiments and were unable to replicate the positive findings that had been reported earlier. Dworkin and Miller (1986) have recently provided a detailed analysis of six of these experiments in which more than 2,500 animals served as subjects. The investigators concluded:

> The original visceral learning experiments are not replicable and that the existence of visceral learning remains unproven; however, neither the original experiments nor the replication attempt included the necessary controls to support a general negative conclusion about visceral learning (p. 299).

These authors point out:

> The incorrect conclusion that visceral learning has been demonstrated as reported by many current publications should not be supplanted by the equally incorrect assertion that it is not possible . . . and that failure to replicate the original studies in acutely curarized rats should not be taken as a signal to abandon the problem but rather as an opportunity to do more rigorously controlled and definitive experiments (p. 312).

The Role of Motivation ►

A teacher observes early in the school year that one child seems eager to learn the material presented, yet another child couldn't care less about daily lessons. Since both children have about the same intelligence, the difference in learning is attributed to differences in their motivation. Reading the sports page in the daily newspaper reveals that a professional tennis player who has generally lost to a superior player has now won, or that a weak college football team has defeated a much stronger opponent. Such sports upsets have often been attributed by coaches to the individual or team's increased motivation or desire. We may note, then, that the concept of motivation is frequently used in our everyday experiences to describe invigorated performances on the part of individuals in some specific situation.

The concept of motivation has been acknowledged by most psychologists to play an important role in learning, and in particular, instrumental conditioning. In this section we will provide a brief overview of the concept; in subsequent chapters we shall examine how instrumental and operant conditioning are influenced by motivational variables.[3]

Appetitive and Aversive Stimuli as Motivational Variables

An important aspect of the varying instrumental and operant conditioning tasks that we have described has been the role played by aversive and appetitive stimuli. Aversive stimuli such as shock will generally elicit responding by the experimental subject. When an instrumental response terminates the noxious stimulus, the subject experiences relief, which serves to act as a reward or reinforcer.

Appetitive stimuli such as food and water are also considered as rewards, although it has been recognized that there must be a need for the appetitive stimulus if it is to serve this function. (Obviously, food for a satiated rat cannot be used to reward the animal's responding.) Typically, experimenters place their experimental subjects on some deprivation schedule in order to insure that the appetitive stimulus will have reward value.

From this brief description of deprivation states, appetitive and aversive stimuli, we can identify two functions that are generally considered to be an inherent part of motivational stimuli. One of these can be described as an *eliciting* function—certain stimuli energize or elicit responding by the experimental subject. The second function assigned to a motive is a *reinforcing* function; this function serves to increase or decrease the probability of an instrumental response. But let us examine these functions in somewhat greater detail.

The Eliciting Function   Early investigators believed that the organism's need states were responsible for eliciting or producing general activity in the organism. Experimenters used the construct of *drive* to describe this function. A drive was thus regarded as a primitive motivational construct. In Hull's (1943) analysis of classical and instrumental conditioning, he considered drive states (e.g., D) as important contributors to such learning.

A drive was conceptualized as an intervening variable in which the operation of depriving the organism of some basic physiological requirement, such as food or water, represented the antecedent condition. The construct was anchored to the consequent condition or the organism's activity as measured by the amount of movement exhibited by the animal in the exercise wheel or stabilimetric cage.

The early studies of Richter (1922, 1927) indicated that increasing the rat's need for food would result in increased amounts of activity wheel behavior. These experimental

---

[3] The concept of motivation is quite complex and we can provide only a brief overview of the construct, focusing particularly on its relevance to instrumental conditioning tasks. See Cofer and Appley (1964), Korman (1974), or Mook (1986) for an extended examination of the topic.

findings lent support to the position that drive states had the function of initiating and/ or eliciting activity.

But over the years, investigators noted some basic problems involved with the use of the construct of drive. First, some psychologists employed the term indiscriminately. Curiosity, exploration, and boredom were all posited as drive states, without experimenters identifying the appropriate antecedent condition necessary for their arousal. (The use of the concept of drive in this way bears a marked similarity to the earlier employment of the concept of instinct, which was eventually abandoned because it contributed little to understanding behavior.) More important, experimental evidence accumulated to dispute the position that an inherent characteristic of an organism's physiological need state (e.g., deprivation) was to produce activity. Many studies have revealed that such needs were not always accompanied by increased activity (see Strong, 1957; Bolles and deLorge, 1962; and Treichler and Hall, 1962).

These difficulties casted doubt on the usefulness of the concept of drive. By the early 1970s, Wayner and Carey (1973) had occasion to write, "The term drive has been bandied about to the point where it is not only useless but is actually meaningless and confusing in the literature. We believe that the term serves no scientific purpose and should be abandoned" (p. 54).

The difficulties with the concept of drive, which had as one of its distinguishing features the position that deprivation states should energize the organism, do not negate the eliciting function that characterizes one aspect of motivation. Aversive or noxious stimuli result in pain or unpleasant emotional states (e.g., fear) and have an obvious eliciting function in that they prompt the organism to escape or avoid these sources of stimulation.

A second operation of the eliciting function is found in current investigators' recognition that the cognitive states of anticipation or expecting reward may also elicit responding. For example, if a deprived rat was placed in an experimental situation that resulted in its obtaining food, the hungry animal's anticipation or expectancy of receiving food would elicit responding when the animal was again placed in that experimental situation.[4] In summary, experimenters appear to be placing primary emphasis on the characteristics of rewards and the resultant expectancies of the experimental subject in accounting for the eliciting function.

The Reinforcing Function   A second function of a motive is a reinforcing function that operates to increase or decrease the probability of a response. Appetitive stimuli, such as food or water, have been readily recognized to play this role; with the aversive stimuli, as mentioned earlier, it is the relief that is experienced from the termination of such stimuli that provides reinforcement for the subject.

---

[4] It will be recalled that in Chapter One, Tinklepaugh's (1928) substitution of a lettuce leaf for a piece of banana as a reward in a delayed discrimination task resulted in eliciting emotional responses on the part of his experimental subject.

The Nature of Reinforcement ▶

Reinforcement has played such an important role in instrumental conditioning that it is not surprising that theorists have been interested in attempting to determine its nature—the identification of those characteristics which define a reinforcer.

If we examine what events can act in this capacity, we could make a very long list, beginning with those that satisfy the physiological needs of the organism (e.g., need for food and water, relief from pain, etc.). But such a list would also include foodstuffs that are not related to the organism's physiological well-being (e.g., saccharin). Moreover, the list could be expanded to include a variety of simple sensory stimuli such as light and sound onset (or offset), and to even more complex perceptual stimulation (e.g., viewing moving electrical trains). In each instance, it has been demonstrated that the presentation of such stimuli can increase the probability of an instrumental response being made.

After examining such a list, the question arises: What general property do these events have in common? A more basic query would be: What is the nature of the reinforcing process? Psychologists have attempted to answer this question for some time but without a great deal of success. We will now look at some of their answers, keeping in mind that the topic is too extensive for anything other than a brief summary of the approaches taken.

Thorndike's Law of Effect

Our everyday experiences suggest that the pleasure and pain we receive are important determinants of our behavior. Humans seeking to obtain pleasure and avoid pain is known as *hedonism*, which has been an important topic in philosophy since the Greeks. In psychology, it was Spencer (1872) writing in his *Principles* who suggested that there was a correlation between the pleasant and the beneficial, as well as a correlation between the unpleasant and the injurious. Some time later, the derivatives of pleasure and pain, satisfaction and discomfort, were provided special status by Thorndike (1911) who proposed that these constructs played important roles in determining how learning took place. The function of satisfaction and discomfort was found in Thorndike's formulation of the law of effect; an early version of this law stated:

> *Of several responses made to the same situation, those which are accompanied or closely followed by satisfaction to the animal will, other things being equal, be more firmly connected with the situation, so that when it occurs, they will be more likely to recur; those which are accompanied or closely followed by discomfort to the animal will, other things being equal, have their connection with the situation weakened so that, when it occurs, they will be less likely to occur (p. 244).*

A basic problem has been that the definition of the law of effect is circular since the only way that we can tell whether or not satisfaction is achieved is to note if the organism repeats the response that produced the satisfaction; a similar problem exists with defining discomfort. We see, then, the circularity: Satisfaction is defined in terms of increased probability of responding but the reason for such responding is accounted for by satisfaction. What is needed, of course, is an independent measure of satisfaction and discomfort—a means whereby we can determine what events are satisfying (or discomforting) prior to their manipulation in a learning study.[5]

Reinforcement as a Stimulus

One way to solve the circularity problem has been to consider reinforcers as specific categories of stimuli that follow and increase the probability of instrumental responding. An example is found in Hull's (1943) *Principles of Behavior,* in which he proposed that a reinforcer (primary) should be defined as a stimulus that reduced some basic or physiological need of the organism. But the problem with this hypothesis was that some experimenters were able to demonstrate that many stimuli, although not satisfying a basic need, could be reinforcing. For example, Sheffield and Roby (1950) found that a saccharin solution could serve as a reward for rats learning a simple T-maze. Others (e.g., Robinson, 1959; and Barnes and Kish, 1961) have shown that the presentation of a light or tone that followed the pressing of a bar in a Skinner Box would increase the probability of that response being made again.

As a further note in the search for a stimulus explanation of reinforcement, we should call attention to the pioneer study of Olds and Milner (1954), who found that brain stimulation could serve as reinforcement for a bar-pressing response. In their early study, rats had electrodes implanted in the septal region of their rhinencephalon. When placed in Skinner Boxes in which brain stimulation followed bar pressing, it was discovered that the animals would continue to make the bar-pressing response for long periods of time—in some instances until they were physically exhausted. Presumably, the physiological correlate of reinforcement had been discovered.

Olds and Milner's discovery led to a host of experimental studies, both physiological as well as behavioral in nature. Some of the most interesting of these has been the examination of similarities and differences between traditional reinforcers (e.g., food) and brain stimulation. One remarkable difference between them was found to be the persistent and very high rates of responding observed when brain stimulation was employed as the reinforcing agent; another was the temporary influence that brain stimulation had in influencing learning from one day to the next. For example, Olds (1956) found that although the use of brain stimulation resulted in the improvement of rats learning a complex maze, there was a spontaneous decrement in performance from the last trial of one day's session to the first trial on the next day.

Although opening new areas of research, the finding that brain stimulation can serve as a reinforcing agent has not, at least as yet, provided psychologists with an

---

[5] It should be recognized that Thorndike's law was one of effect, not affect. He did not relate satisfaction and discomfort to the subject's subjective emotional states of pleasure and pain. Rather, a satisfying state of affairs was defined as one which the organism does nothing to avoid, often doing such things as to attain or preserve it. By a discomforting state of affairs, he meant one that the animal avoids and/or abandons.

explanation for reinforcement. Does the receiving of food by a hungry pigeon, the reinforcing effect of a sound for the rat, or the satisfying state of affairs that accompanies the solving of a crossword puzzle, all produce essentially the same kind of neural activity that is found when an organism's brain is electrically stimulated?

Some investigators have posited that it is not the nature of the stimulus per se which serves as reinforcement but rather the capacity of the stimulus to produce in the organism a positive (or negative) affective state—a position akin to the hedonistic position discussed earlier. The difficulty is that since the emotional or affective state is known only through the subject's introspection and verbal report, there is the problem of being able to determine the presence of the affective state apart of independent from the verbal report itself. Moreover, it becomes necessary to be able to manipulate the affective state if it is to be used as an experimental variable. Experimenters are making progress in being able to measure physiological concomitants of emotion, but more research is needed if the presence and intensity of the affective state is to play any role in a definition of reinforcement.

Secondary Reinforcement

No account of reinforcement conceptualized as stimuli would be complete without providing a brief discussion of the concept of secondary reinforcement, or what operant investigators have termed *conditioned reinforcers* (Keller and Schoenfeld, 1950). Secondary reinforcement played an important role in Hull's (1943) *Principles.* Hull was aware that learning could take place without primary reinforcement being provided, but accounted for such learning by positing that neutral stimuli could acquire reinforcing characteristics by their consistent and repeated association with primary reinforcement.

Hull (1943) cited an early study by Cowles (1937) to support his position. In this experiment, chimpanzees were first trained to insert poker chips into a slot machine that delivered a raisin for each poker chip that was inserted, thus establishing an association between the chip and the food. Following such training, Cowles found that the chips could serve as a reward for new learning.

During the 1940s and 1950s, several hundred studies were conducted examining the operation of secondary reinforcement. Some of these studies indicated that traditional reward variables, such as the frequency and magnitude of reinforcement, the length of the interval separating the presentation of the secondary reinforcer from the securing of reinforcement, as so on, all contributed to conditioned reinforcer strength. Other studies viewed a secondary reinforcing stimulus as a cue or as a discriminative stimulus for the subject in the learning task—a cue which indicated that reinforcement would be forthcoming. Regardless of how secondary reinforcement was conceptualized, many of these experiments indicated that secondary reinforcing stimuli in the form of presentation of tones, visual stimuli, and so on, were quite fragile and temporary in their capacity to either strengthen or sustain learned responding over a substantial number of trials.

One interesting empirical development in the study of conditioned reinforcement has been the use of tokens as secondary reinforcers. Inasmuch as rats and pigeons have been mostly used as experimental subjects, conditioned reinforcers have usually taken the form of tones or visual stimuli. But a series of studies by Kelleher (1956, 1957, 1958) providing tokens (poker chips) to chimpanzees has demonstrated that the use of such conditioned reinforcers was quite effective in maintaining learned responding for long periods of time, providing, of course, that the animals could exchange their tokens for food from time to time. Tokens that human subjects can later exchange for candy, television watching, and so on have also been successfully used by psychologists working in mental hospitals. These tokens are provided to inmates for performing varying and useful tasks around the institution. See Chapter Eleven for a description of token economies.

Reinforcement as a Response or Related to Differential Response Probability

In view of the lack of success of a stimulus explanation of reinforcement, it is not surprising that the search to explain reinforcement shifted to examining the organism's response. In Sheffield and Roby's (1950) study, which demonstrated that a saccharin solution could serve as a reward, the authors pointed out that the "performance of a consummatory response appears to be more important to instrumental learning . . . than the drive [or need] satisfaction which the consummatory response normally achieves" (pp. 480–481). The authors hypothesized that it was the consummatory response and not the reward that produced the reinforcing effect.

Such a hypothesis had difficulty, however, when Hull, Livingston, Rouse, and Barker (1951) demonstrated that milk that had been directly injected into a dog's stomach would serve as a reward for the animal learning a T-maze. The consummatory response was eliminated by their procedure and yet the foodstuff continued to have a reinforcing function.

Fundamental to any consummatory response hypothesis has been the position that these responses are different from those responses that have been identified as instrumental. But one difficulty with this position is that consummatory responses can also serve as instrumental responses: A child may eat his spinach in order to obtain dessert. It was Premack (1959), however, who pointed out that the consummatory and instrumental response categories in traditional experiments differ only in terms of the probability of their occurrence. From such a position, he hypothesized that reinforcement involves a special relationship between these two responses—one response is being reinforced whereas the second response serves as the reinforcer. Premack's hypothesis is found in his statement that for any pair of responses the more probable one will reinforce the less probable, or "Reinforcement results when an R [response] of a lower independent rate coincides within temporal limits, with the stimuli governing the occurrence of R or a higher independent rate" (p. 219).

An explanation by Premack of the typical Skinner Box finding in which a rat's lever press is reinforced by a pellet of food would be that it is the differential probability of responding that is responsible for the reinforcing effect. That is, for the food-deprived rat, the consummatory response of eating has a higher independent rate of occurring than does bar pressing, thus enabling the eating response to reinforce bar pressing.

One interesting corollary of Premack's hypothesis is that reinforcement is relative. The most probable response of a set of responses will reinforce all members of that set; the least probable response will reinforce no member of that set. However, the relativity feature can be noted with responses of intermediate probability reinforcing those responses less probable than themselves but not those that are more probable.

In an experiment demonstrating the role of response probability as well as the interchangeability of instrumental and consummatory responses, Premack's (1962) noted that both drinking and wheel-running responses are found in the response repertoire of the rat. If the rats were made thirsty, the presentation of water would reinforce wheel running since the drinking response had a higher probability of occurrence than of wheel running. However, if the animals were not deprived of water, it was found that the higher probability response would reinforce drinking responses. (See Box 5–1.)

Not all of the experimental evidence has supported Premack's hypothesis, however. Eisenberger, Karpman, and Trattner (1967), using humans as subjects, have reported that under certain circumstances low probability responses would reinforce high probability, rather than the other way around as Premack would predict.

Premack's approach to reinforcement theory based on the examination of response probability has provided the foundation for a behavioral regulation or equilibrium

box 5–1

An interesting study using children as experimental subjects and providing support for the differential response probability hypothesis was conducted in Premack's own laboratory. Here, a pinball machine was rewired for continuous operation and placed adjacent to a candy dispenser. The subjects, 33 first-grade children, were each tested twice. The first testing session served to determine the subject's relative rate of responding to the candy and to the pinball machine when both were unrestrictedly available. The children were then told that there were two games and that they could play either or both of them as much as they cared to. Children who made more pinball responses than they ate pieces of candy were labeled "manipulators," whereas children who ate more candy than made pinball responses were labeled "eaters."

In a second session, the manipulator group and the eater group were subdivided. One half of each group was tested under an eat-manipulate contingency, and the other half of each group was tested under a manipulate-eat contingency. It was arranged that the experimental group of manipulators had to eat before they could manipulate, whereas the eaters had to manipulate before they could eat.

Results supported Premack's theory of reinforcement. It was noted that for the manipulators there was a significant increase (over the controls) in the number of pieces of candy eaten, providing such eating was followed by the opportunity to play the pinball machine. Similarly, with the eater group there was a significant increase in the number of times the pinball machine was played if such activity was followed by the opportunity to eat a piece of candy (Premack, 1959).

theory as proposed by Timberlake and Allison (Timberlake, 1980, 1984; Timberlake and Allison, 1974). These authors hypothesized that there exists a stable set of responses that an organism will attempt to maintain even under circumstances that may challenge such stability. For example, if a laboratory rat is placed in an activity wheel with food and water available, the investigator will find that after a number of days, each of the eating, drinking, and running responses over a 24-hour period will stabilize, with the distribution of these combined activities resulting in an equilibrium for the organism within the type of environment that is provided. Other environments would, of course, result in different types and distributions of activities.

A challenge to such response stability would be produced by removing food from the animal's environment since it would mean that the level of eating activity previously enjoyed in the free environment would be reduced. If the experimenter then made the presentation of food (and the consummatory response of eating) contingent on wheel running, the result would be that the animal would increase its wheel running in order to increase the amount of its eating behavior commensurate with that experienced in the free environment. Timberlake and Allison (1974) would thus posit that the increase in the instrumental response of wheel running arose from the conflict existing between the amount of the consummatory response (e.g., eating) as it was exhibited in the free environment, and the restrictions of such activity occasioned by the deprivation schedule.

More generally, these authors have proposed that the imposition of a schedule by the investigator that demands that the instrumental response be made before the contingent response can be exhibited imposes certain constraints on the animal that typically conflict with its pattern of free behavior. Thus, "instrumental performance is a result of conflict between the freely occurring behavior of the animal and the restrictions of a schedule" (p. 150). Like Premack, such a theory has as a major tenet the position that reinforcement is relative to the organism's pattern of free responding and the restrictions of responding provided by the experimental environment.

Timberlake and Allison, like Premack, do not make any basic distinction between instrumental and consummatory (or contingent) responses. In the example previously cited, if the level of running activity was restricted beyond that observed in the free environment, providing a contingency between eating and running would result in the animal increasing its eating in order to permit greater amounts of running. In such instances, the eating response would be the instrumental response, with wheel running serving as reinforcement. A study by Timberlake and Wozny (1979) has demonstrated such to be the case. After first measuring the rat's behavior in an environment permitting access to both food and the activity wheel (which permitted running), these authors then demonstrated that by restricting running, the animals would eat in order to run. Similarly, they found that by restricting eating, the animals' running behavior was increased. Instrumental and consummatory responses were thus differentiated only by the role that each response played in the contingent relationship that had been established by the investigator.

One outcome is that in some instances the nature of the instrumental response/consummatory response contingency will prevent the experimental subject from achieving equilibrium. Timberlake and Allison have proposed that when the previous state of equilibrium cannot be approximated, there is a redistribution of instrumental and consummatory responses in which a compromise is effected. The compromise can be viewed as resulting in a new state of equilibrium, given the nature of the response/ reinforcer contingency that has been imposed by the experimental situation.

The innovative approach in describing the nature of reinforcement as proposed by Premack, and Timberlake and Allison, can be viewed as a major departure from earlier conceptualizations of reinforcement, particularly those positions that have viewed reinforcers as stimuli. At this time, it is too early to make an assessment of the contribution of this new theoretical position. There is no doubt that its emphasis on the fact that reinforcement is relative and that we cannot make any basic distinctions between instrumental and consummatory responses are important contributions that must be taken into consideration by any viable reinforcement position. On the other hand, the equilibrium position has not generated very many experimental studies. One reason for this has undoubtedly been the difficulty in securing a stable measure of response probability or the distribution of responses for the experimental subjects, be they rat or humans, operating in a free environment. In fact, some investigators have reported that it has been necessary to observe rats for more than a month in a free environment before stable baseline responding was noted. In any event, it can be said that the equilibrium position has not as yet entered the mainstream of reinforcement theory.

In reviewing the difficulties that investigators have had in answering the question How can we define reinforcement? it may be concluded that the failure to answer this question has not resulted in experimenters abandoning their examination of instrumental conditioning. Most investigators have taken a pragmatic approach to the problem, adopting as their guide the empirical law of effect, which states that some consequences have the capacity to increase (or decrease) the probability of responding whereas other consequences do not. The experimenters' course of action has been to use stimulus events which in earlier studies have been demonstrated to have a reinforcing function. This position represents an implicit acceptance of a suggestion provided by Meehl (1950), who wrote that the empirical law of effect is acceptable if reinforcers are treated as transituational in their effects. That is, a stimulus that is identified in one situation as having reinforcing effects can be used to predict an increase in the probability of an instrumental response in other situations.[6]

Summary ►

It will be recalled that both Skinner (1938) and Hilgard and Marquis (1940) proposed that conditioning tasks could be divided into (1) classical conditioning (or respondent behavior) and (2) instrumental conditioning (or operant behavior). This chapter dis-

---

[6] This does not completely solve the problem since, as Timberlake and Allison (1974) have indicated, the experiments of Premack demonstrated that reinforcement is relative and not absolute as the transituational position would appear to hold.

cussed general considerations involved in the study of instrumental and operant conditioning.

Many different instrumental conditioning tasks have been used, with a variety of classifications being provided. The most frequently employed include: (1) positive reinforcement (or reward tasks), (2) negative reinforcement (or escape tasks), (3) tasks involving punishment, (4) avoidance tasks, and (5) omission training. The response measures that are used include (a) latency, (b) magnitude, and (c) frequency or probability of responding.

Operant tasks differ from instrumental conditioning tasks along several dimensions. The apparatus used for operant conditioning is so designed that the subject's response takes only a short time to make, and reinforcement is received in proximity to where the response is made. Discrete learning trials are not used in operant studies; rather, experimental sessions that permit the subject to respond freely throughout the period are provided. The rapidity with which the response can be made precludes providing reinforcement after every response. This has resulted in operant investigators employing reinforcement schedules, the basic schedules being: (1) fixed ratio, (2) fixed interval, (3) variable ratio, and (4) variable interval. The response measure employed by operant investigators is rate of responding, with a cumulative recorder being used to measure the subject's frequent and rapid responding.

In the analysis of instrumental and classical conditioning, some investigators have theorized that classical conditioning is actually an instance of instrumental conditioning. Opponents of this position have called attention to the findings obtained from omission training schedules in which such training abolishes any contingency between the CR and US. If such was the case, an instrumental response should extinguish. But extinction does not take place, with the response continuing to be made, thus identifying it as classical.

A question has been raised about whether or not autonomic nervous system responses can be instrumentally conditioned. Although experimental studies have demonstrated that such conditioning can be effected, it is possible that the associative relationship established is dependent on muscular responses mediating the learning of these visceral responses. Experimental attempts to control muscular responses by paralyzing them with curare have not been definitive.

Motivation is a basic construct that has been generally agreed to play an important role in instrumental conditioning. A motive has been hypothesized to possess two functions: an eliciting and a reinforcing function. Instrumental conditioning experimenters have been particularly interested in this latter function and have attempted to determine the nature of reinforcing events. A variety of answers have been proposed. In his law of effect, Thorndike posited that responses that were followed by satisfaction to the organisms would be strengthened, whereas those that were followed by dissatisfaction would be weakened. Recent investigators have considered reinforcement as a stimulus with special properties. Hull (1943) assumed that stimuli that reduced a physiological need should be defined as reinforcers. But a variety of experiments have demonstrated that certain stimuli, although not possessing the capacity to reduce a physiological need, could serve as reinforcers.

Other investigators have considered reinforcement as a response, or related to differential response probability. Sheffield and Roby (1950) hypothesized that consummatory responses could serve as reinforcers, but some experimenters demonstrated that consummatory responses need not be made for certain stimuli to serve as reinforcement.

Premack (1959) proposed that reinforcement involved a special relationship between pairs of responses, namely, the more probable response will reinforce the less probable. An interesting corollary of Premack's position was that reinforcement was relative: some responses are able to reinforce less probable responses but are unable to reinforce those responses that are more probable.

Most current investigators have adopted the empirical law of effect in guiding their use of reinforcers in instrumental conditioning studies. This law states that some consequences have the capacity to increase the probability of responding whereas other consequences do not. The experimenter's course of action has been to use stimulus events which in earlier studies have been demonstrated to have reinforcing effects.

chapter six

►

Instrumental Conditioning: Acquisition and Extinction of Positive and Negative Reinforcement Tasks

It will be recalled from Chapter Five that two groups of instrumental conditioning tasks were identified as those involving (1) positive and (2) negative reinforcement. Positive reinforcement tasks were defined by the establishment of an association or a contingency between the making of a response and the securing of reward. Negative reinforced tasks include those in which a response terminated or removed an aversive stimulus, thus providing reinforcement in the form of relief from pain, fear, and the like. In both instances, the reinforcement received resulted in increasing the probability of the instrumental response.

Inasmuch as reinforcement plays such a prominent role in the learning of these instrumental conditioning tasks, investigators have been interested, almost exclusively so, in determining how the manipulation of reward variables influence responding during both acquisition and extinction.

Acquisition ►

The Role of Reward Variables

How does reinforcement contribute to performance in positive and negative reinforcement tasks? Investigators have concentrated their efforts on examining three basic variables: (1) the frequency and/or percentage of reinforced trials, (2) the characteristics of the reinforcing agent, and (3) the time or delay between the making of the instrumental response and the receiving of reinforcement.

Frequency and Percentage of Reinforcement   A commonplace finding in positive and negative reinforcement studies has been that performance during acquisition is related to the frequency with which continuously reinforced trials are provided. That is, 20 continuously reinforced trials will result in better performance than if just 10 are provided; 40 will produce superior performance to 20, and so on.

When partial reinforcement schedules are employed and compared with each other as well as with continuous reinforcement, the findings have not been sufficiently consistent to draw any firm conclusions. It might be assumed that a reinforcement schedule that provides reward on less than 20% of the training trials would result in much poorer performance than a group receiving continuous (100%) reinforcement. But this assumption may be incorrect. While examining rats traversing a runway, Weinstock (1958) provided reinforcement on 17, 33, 50, 67, 83, or 100% of the trials. He found that the group receiving 83 and 100% reinforcement ran most slowly over the

Figure 6-1
Mean reciprocal latency as a function of percent reinforcement for the acquisition series. Adapted from S. Weinstock, "Acquisition and extinction of a partially reinforced running response at a 24-hour intertrial interval," *Journal of Experimental Psychology,* 1958, *56,* 151–158. Copyright © 1958 by the American Psychological Association. Reprinted by permission.

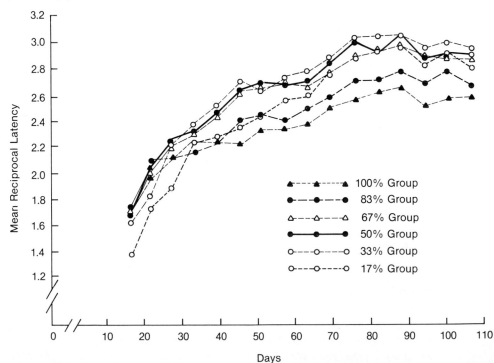

last two dozen trials. The group receiving just 17% reinforced trials ran most slowly during the early acquisition trials but appeared to catch up after about seventy trials. (See Figure 6–1.)

Although some investigators have obtained results that have, at least in part, supported Weinstock's (1958) findings (e.g., Goodrich, 1959; Haggard, 1959; and Wagner, 1959), others have found that continuous reinforcement (when contrasted with partial) produces superior runway performance (e.g., Wagner, 1961; Brown and Wagner, 1964; and Wong, 1978). The lack of consistent findings among some experimenters suggests that more research is needed in order to reconcile the divergent findings.

Operant Reinforcement Schedules   The basic procedure for examining the contribution of partial reinforcement with the operant task has been to use some type of reinforcement schedule. There is such extensive literature in this area that we can indicate only some of the important relationships existing between the type of schedule provided and the characteristics of the organism's performance. It is important to keep in mind that in these studies the experimental subjects have already acquired the response; the experimenter's objective has been to determine how different schedules of reinforcement influence maintenance behavior.

Fixed Interval and Variable Interval Schedules   It will be recalled from Chapter Five that with the fixed interval (FI) schedule, the subject received reinforcement for the first response made after a fixed or specific period of time. With the variable interval (VI) schedule, the time interval that determines when reinforcement will occur varies, with the value of the VI schedule being the average time between reinforcements.

A comparison of responding under FI and VI schedules reveals marked differences. Nevin (1973) has provided an interesting comparison of a rat's rate of lever pressing for water under a FI-1 minute and VI-1 minute schedule in Figure 6–2. Under the FI-1 schedule, an animal makes relatively few responses at the beginning of the one-minute interval but increases the rate of responding dramatically just prior to the time reinforcement is provided. This is fundamental property of FI schedules; responding takes place at very low rates at the beginning of the interval but increases rapidly as the end of the interval approaches. The effect is clearly observed in a study by Dews (1962), who provided pigeons with a standard FI-500 second schedule. Dews noted the average number of responses made by his four subjects over each 20-second period making up the 500-second schedule. The differential rate of responding produces a scalloping effect, which can be noted in Figure 6–3.

A variable interval schedule eliminates the scalloping effect, as is revealed by Nevin's use of a VI-1 minute schedule, also shown in Figure 6–2. The differences in rates of responding at the beginning and end of the interval that characterized the FI schedule is replaced by a relatively steady rate of responding with a VI schedule.

One similarity that exists between FI and VI responding is that the rate of responding is inversely related to the length of the interval. In a study by Wilson (1954), six groups of rats were trained at one of the following FI values: 0.17, 0.33, 1.0, 2.0, 4.0, or 6.0 minutes—until 240 reinforcements had been received. Wilson found that the number of responses made per minute declined as a function of the length of the fixed interval.

Figure 6-2
Cumulative records of lever pressing by rats under a FI-1 and VI-1 schedule of reinforcement. Presentation of reinforcement indicated by the diagonal marks. Adapted from *The Study of Behavior* by John A. Nevin. Copyright © 1973 by Scott, Foresman and Company. Reprinted by permission.

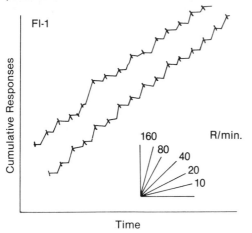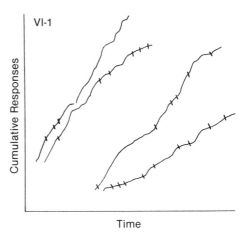

Clark (1958) obtained similar findings when using a variable interval schedule. Schedules of VI-1, VI-2, and VI-3 minutes were examined with different groups of rats placed under varying deprivations levels. At each level of deprivation, the VI-1 schedule provided the largest number of responses per minute, whereas the VI-3 schedule produced the smallest. (See Figure 6–4.)

Fixed Ratio and Variable Ratio Schedules   A fixed ratio (FR) schedule is one in which the subject must make a fixed number of responses before receiving reinforcement, with the last response of the appropriate number resulting in reinforcement. The variable ratio (VR) schedule is one in which the number of responses determining when reinforcement will occur varies over the experimental session, with the value of the

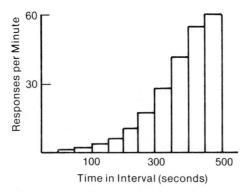

Figure 6-3
Rate of pecking in successive 50 second periods during a standard FI-500 second schedule of reinforcement. Adapted from P. B. Dews, "The effect of multiple S periods on responding on a fixed-interval schedule," *Journal of the Experimental Analysis of Behavior*, 1962, *5*, 369–374. Copyright © 1962 by the Society for the Experimental Analysis of Behavior, Inc. Reprinted by permission.

Figure 6-4
Rate of bar pressing under three different schedules of reinforcement as a function of
deprivation time. Adapted from F. C. Clark, "The effect of deprivation and frequency
of reinforcement on variable-interval responding," *Journal of the Experimental Analysis
of Behavior,* 1958, *1,* 221–228. Copyright © 1958 by the Society for the Experimental
Analysis of Behavior. Reprinted by permission.

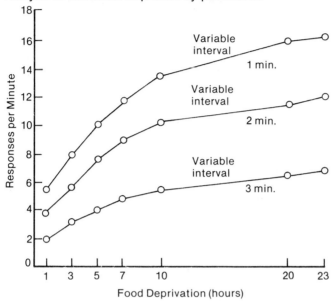

schedule being the average number of responses required for reinforcement. A comparison of an FR-45 with a VR-45 schedule can be found in a study by Nevin (1973) who
used a rat's rate of lever pressing as the response measure. (See Figure 6–5.)

Under the FR schedule, pauses in responding may follow reinforcement, with the
pause or rest on some occasions being fairly long. Once the animal begins to respond,
the number of responses required to obtain reinforcement, provided it is not an
excessive number, may be completed with a sustained burst of responding. In contrast,
the cumulative record for the VR-45 schedule reveals that pauses in responding are not
related to the receiving of reinforcement. Long pauses may appear either in the midst of
a sustained burst of responding or immediately after receiving reinforcement.

Ratio vs. Interval Schedules   When a ratio schedule is employed, whether it be
fixed or variable, the rate of responding directly determines the reinforcement rate. If
an animal responds at a rate of 20 responses per minute and a FR-60 schedule is used, the
animal will receive one reinforcement every three minutes, or 20 reinforcements per
hour. But an increase by the animal to 30 responses per minute on a FR-60 schedule will
result in one reinforcement every two minutes, or 30 reinforcements per hour. The
increase in response rate will result in a greater number of reinforcements, which in
turn will result in a greater number of responses, and so on.

In contrast, the use of an interval schedule limits the amount of reinforcement

Figure 6–5
Cumulative records of lever pressing by rats under a FR-45 and a VR-45 response schedule of reinforcement. Presentation of reinforcement is indicated by the diagonal marks. Adapted from *The Study of Behavior* by John A. Nevin. Copyright © 1973 by Scott, Foresman and Company. Reprinted by permission.

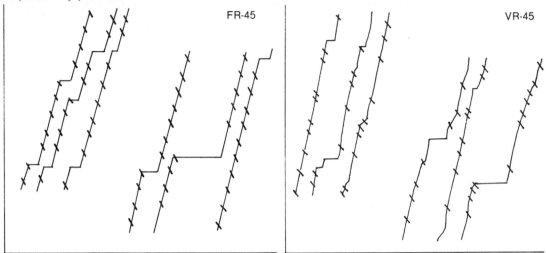

received by the organism during any one interval. Reinforcement can never be more frequent than the reinforcement value assigned to the interval and is independent of the organism's rate of responding. A VI-1 minute schedule will result in no more than 60 reinforcements in an hour, regardless of whether the animal responds 20 times per minute or 60 times. It is not surprising, then, that ratio schedules will result in higher rates of responding than interval schedules since the organism can increase the amount of reinforcement received by increasing its rate of responding.

Characteristics of the Reinforcing Agent   Early experimenters were interested in determining how the amount of reward influenced learning. Grindley (1920), using chickens, and Crespi (1942), using rats, found that performance, as measured by speed of traversing an alley, increased as a function of the amount of food placed in the goal box.

Beginning in the late 1940s, a host of investigators using the runway have confirmed the findings of Grindley and Crespi, demonstrating that the rate of responding is an increasing function of the amount of reward (e.g., Zeaman, 1949; D'Amato, 1955; Armus, 1959; Reynolds and Pavlik, 1960; Hill and Wallace, 1967; Wike and Chen, 1971; and Goomas, 1982). Goomas's study was unusual in that he was able to demonstrate that reward differences could influence performance when only a single acquisition trial was provided.

Some investigators have preferred to vary reward by using different concentrations of sucrose solution. This procedure keeps constant the number of consummatory responses that vary when different amounts of reward are employed but the use of a sugar solution changes the characteristics of the reward from quantitative to qualitative. The experimental findings obtained with varying sucrose concentrations have been similar to those reported when reward amount has varied—namely, higher concentrations of sucrose led to higher performance levels (see Guttman, 1953; Butter and Thomas, 1958; Goodrich, 1960; and Kraeling, 1961). In a study by Kraeling (1961), three groups of rats were given one trial per day for 99 days on a runway, with one of three concentrations of sucrose, 2.5, 5.0, or 10.0%, serving as a reward. The running speed of the animals over blocks of nine trials, presented in Figure 6-6, indicates performance level to be a function of the concentration of sucrose used as a reward.

Differing reductions in shock intensity have been used to examine the contribution of this variable on tasks involving negative reinforcement. A study by Trapold and Fowler (1960) illustrates the procedure and experimental findings. Five groups of rats were given 20 training trials to learn to escape a shock of either 120, 160, 240, 320, or 400 volts by traversing the charged runway to reach an uncharged goal box. The results,

Figure 6-6
Strength of instrumental response, broken down by concentration of sucrose solution. Adapted from D. Kraeling, "Analysis of amount of reward as a variable in learning," *Journal of Comparative and Physiological Psychology,* 1961, *54,* 560–565. Copyright © 1961 by American Psychological Association. Reprinted by permission.

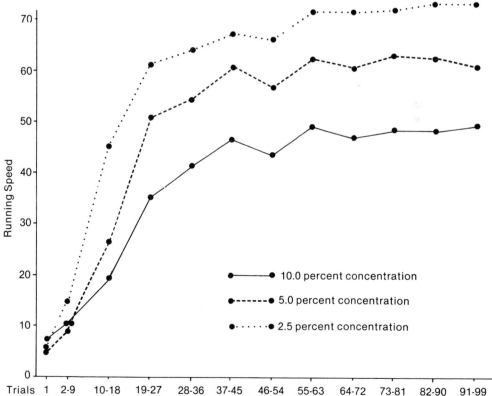

Figure 6-7
Mean performance over the last eight trials as a function of shock intensity. Adapted from M. A. Trapold and H. Fowler, "Instrumental escape performance as a function of the intensity of noxious stimulation," *Journal of Experimental Psychology*, 1960, *60*, 323–326. Copyright © 1960 by the American Psychological Association. Reprinted by permission.

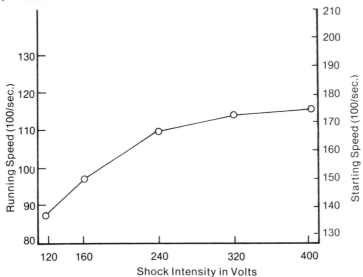

indicated in Figure 6–7, show that running speed was related to the amount of shock reduction provided.[1]

Contrast Effects   One interesting aspect of reward studies has been the investigation of how shifts in the amount of reward influence performance. Crespi (1942) examined this variable, giving rats 19 acquisition trials and providing either 16, 64, or 256 pellets as the reward for traversing a runway. This was followed by a shift to a 16-pellet reward for all animals. In a second study, subjects were given 19 trials with a one- or four-pellet reward, followed by a shift to 16 pellets. In both studies, there were abrupt or sudden shifts in runway performance. For animals given the 16-pellet reward after experiencing a larger reward, running speed slowed down dramatically; however, when an animal was shifted to 16 pellets from just one or four pellets in previous trials, running speed suddenly became more rapid.

Crespi (1942) found that the running speed of animals shifted from 256 or 64 pellets to 16 was slower than that of the constant 16-pellet group at its asymptote or limit of practice. On the other hand, for those animals shifted from one to four pellets to 16, performance rose above the level characteristic of the constant 16-pellet group, which presumably had reached its asymptote of running speed. Increased performance, as a

---

[1] The reader should be aware that many of these negative reinforcement studies are confounded; increasing the intensity of shock will make the animal more active, suggesting that the eliciting function of shock presentation also contributes to performance.

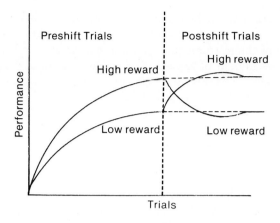

Figure 6-8
Hypothetical performance curves arising from a shift in the amount of reward and demonstrating positive and negative contrast effects.

result of going from a small to a large reward, was identified as a *positive contrast* effect, whereas poorer performance associated with shifting from a larger to a smaller amount of reward was termed *negative contrast*.[2] Many (but not all) subsequent findings have indicated the contrast effect to be transient; the elevated and depressed performance levels were eventually replaced by levels similar to those reached by control animals that had been provided only a single amount of reward. Figure 6–8 presents hypothetical performance curves illustrating this effect.

Subsequent experimenters have been able not only to replicate Crespi's findings using food pellets as reward and runway speed as the instrumental response (e.g., Zeaman, 1949; Mellgren, 1972; and Shanab and Spencer, 1978), but have been also able to demonstrate positive and negative contrast effects employing a consummatory response (licking), using a sucrose solution as the reward (e.g., Flaherty and Largen, 1975). And a host of investigators have been interested in examining positive and negative contrast effects as a function of a variety of motivational variables.[3]

What are the implications of contrast effect findings for a better understanding of this type of instrumental conditioning task? Two are noteworthy. First, the abrupt increment or decrement in responding that takes place as a result of a single reinforced

---

[2] Some investigators (e.g., Ashida and Birch, 1964; and Goodrich and Zaretsky, 1962) have had difficulty in obtaining positive contrast effects. One problem was that the experimental conditions used to examine this condition generally resulted in the constant high-reward group responding at the highest level of performance possible with this amount of reward. When the shift animals were switched from low to high reward, there was no opportunity for them to perform at a level higher than that achieved by the constant high-reward subjects. If the experimental conditions were changed so as to lower the performance level of the constant high reward group (e.g., providing them with reward delay), positive contrast findings were readily obtained.

[3] The examination of the varying experimental conditions (e.g., reward disparity, deprivation state, etc.) that influence positive and negative contrast represents a voluminous literature, which unfortunately we cannot undertake to examine in this text. The interested reader can refer to Dunham's (1968) and Black's (1968) early reviews, as well as a more recent one by Flaherty (1982).

trial strongly suggests that reward magnitude influences performance rather than the learning process. Obviously, the poorer performance following a reduction in reward does not reflect an unlearning of the instrumental response, but rather a lowering of performance in keeping with the amount of reward. And the increase in performance following reward increment appears to be too abrupt for the change to be attributed to the learning process that many studies have indicated to take place gradually. (We have noted a similar finding reported by Blodgett [1929] in our learning-performance discussion in Chapter One.)

A second implication is that the presence of contrast effects supports the position of Premack (1959) and others who have emphasized the theoretical position that reinforcement is relative. In fact, the findings provide support for the general position that experience with any stimulus influences responding to similar stimuli. It will be recalled in our examination of the role of CS intensity on classical conditioning, that an experimental design in which subjects experienced both weak and strong CSs was more sensitive in demonstrating the contribution of this variable on conditioning than if the experimental subjects experienced only a single intensity. A somewhat similar phenomenon appears to be taking place with contrast effects. Thus, most of our everyday evaluations of events appear to be influenced by the range of conditions that the individual has experienced. If we have been accustomed to eating expensive cuts of meat for dinner, the appearance of hamburger brings forth a cry of anguish and perhaps even its rejection. In contrast, to a family that is not able to afford meat for their evening meal, hamburger looks great.

How can contrast effects be explained? Flaherty's (1982) review indicates that several explanations have been proposed. The most viable of these has to do with the positing of motivational-emotional processes that are generated by the shifts in reward. Crespi (1942) identified these processes in terms of *elation* and *depression,* suggesting that it was these emotional states that contributed to the changes in performance.

As the experimental findings of Amsel (1962, 1967) have suggested, after a series of rewarded trials, the elimination of or reduced amount of reward appears to produce a frustrative or emotional state in the organism. This state elicits responses that may conflict with the instrumental response demanded by the experimenter. This results in a performance level lower than that which would be attributed to the influence of only the smaller reward. Moreover, and as Flaherty (1982) has written, the frustration explanation of negative contrast effects is appealing since many of the variables influencing frustration have been worked out in other contexts.

The accounting for positive contrast effects in terms of an elation or a positive affective state represents a more difficult hypothesis to test and the experimental work attempting to examine this intervening variable has been almost nonexistent. It is interesting, however, that subjective reports of an elation effect have been proposed by human subjects who, when experiencing a reward greater than anticipated, have responded with increased vigor and enthusiasm.

Delay of Reinforcement   In positive and negative reinforcement tasks, delay of reinforcement refers to the amount of time that elapses between making the response and securing the reinforcement or relief from the aversive stimulus. Numerous investigators, beginning with Watson (1919), have been interested in determining how this variable influences learning.

Perin (1943) found that when a delay of 30 seconds or more was introduced between the rat's pressing a bar and its receiving food, the animal was unable to learn this response. Renner's (1964) review of studies examining the role of reinforcement delay on instrumental learning indicated the central importance of this variable. Recent investigators have continued to demonstrate the contribution of reward delay to performance. For example, Capaldi (1978) trained rats to traverse a runway, providing delays of 0, 10, 15, or 20 seconds between the time the animals entered the goal box and the time they received reinforcement. Results revealed that the animal responded more rapidly as the delay interval approached 0.[4]

As with reward magnitude, the experimental evidence strongly suggests that reinforcement delay, when examined with simple positive reinforcement tasks, influences performance rather than the learning process. A study by Shanab and Biller (1972) may be cited to support this position. In employing the runway, these investigators found that when they shifted their animals from a 0-second to 15-second delay of reinforcement, performance as measured by running speed declined to a value that was approximately one quarter of that which was found under the 0-second delay. It does not seem reasonable to assume that the performance decrement arising from such a delay arose from an unlearning process; rather, the reinforcement delay appeared to be responsible for a decrement in the organism's performance.

Studies utilizing negative reinforcement tasks have also indicated the role of the delay interval. Fowler and Trapold (1962) have found that the speed of rats running a charged runway was significantly slower when shock reduction provided in the goal box was delayed. The delay interval used by these investigators was either 0, 1, 2, 4, 8, or 16 seconds. Figure 6–9 presents these findings.

Tarpy and Koster (1970) noted an even more deleterious influence of delay when a lever-pressing response was employed. These experimenters provided rats with 60 shock-escape trials in which the termination of shock was delayed for either 0, 1.5, 3, or 6 seconds following the pressing of a lever. Although learning was obtained for the 0- and 1.5-second delay groups, learning did not take place when longer delay periods were used. This finding suggests that the more difficult a response is to acquire, the more detrimental to learning will be delay of reinforcement.

It may seem unusual to the reader that experimental subjects have difficulty in learning a task when the delay of reinforcement is measured in *seconds*. One reason for these findings is that current investigators of reward delay have been careful to control for the influence of secondary reinforcing stimuli (secondary rewards). If such stimuli are not controlled in the learning task, they can provide a bridge between the instrumental response and the securing of the delayed primary reward. Watson's (1917) early finding that rats could learn an instrumental response, although reward was delayed for as long as 20 minutes, has been attributed to the action of secondary rewards present in the task.

---

[4] The influence of reinforcement delay has been much more extensively investigated with the discrimination type task. We shall review this work in Chapter Nine.

Figure 6-9
Running speed (100/time in sec.) as a function of the delay (in sec.) of shock termination. Adapted from H. Fowler and M. A. Trapold, "Escape performance as a function
of delay of reinforcement," *Journal of Experimental Psychology*, 1962, *63*, 464–467.
Copyright © 1962 by the American Psychological Association. Reprinted by permission.

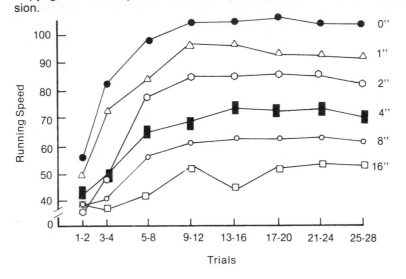

Experimental Extinction ▶

In Chapter Two, we found that the continued presentation of the CS, with the US
omitted, resulted in a gradual decline and eventual disappearance on the conditioned
response. Both the operation of omitting the US as well as the decline in responding
that accompanied the omission of the US were identified as experimental extinction. It
is not surprising that experimental extinction has also been examined with instrumental
conditioning tasks. With positive reinforcement tasks, deprivation and reward have
been used to motivate the subject during acquisition; extinction trial operations have
consisted of continuing to deprive the animal but removing the reward from the goal
box. When negative reinforcement is utilized, the removal of the aversive stimulus (e.g.,
shock) has been considered to be the appropriate extinction operation (comparable to
the removal of reward). But there is a problem with this procedure since the removal of
shock also results in the loss of the eliciting function—thus, there is no aversive stimulus
to "elicit" responding—which results in extinction taking place almost immediately.
The result has been that many experimenters have followed the procedure suggested by
Church (1971). For the extinction operation, Church presented the aversive stimulus in
the goal box, in addition to presenting it in those parts of the apparatus where it had
been provided during acquisition. As with the removal of reward, the presentation of
the aversive stimulus in the goal box also removes reinforcement, since shock termination does not take place. An example of this procedure is found in a study by Bower
(1960), who trained rats to escape from a 250-volt shock by running to a safe goal box.

Extinction trials following such training were conducted by presenting the same intensity of shock in the goal box, in addition to continuing to present it in the start box and runway.

When extinction behavior exhibited in positive and negative reinforcement tasks is examined, there is one marked difference between them. With positive reinforcement tasks, and following a series of rewarded trials, it has often been noted that the introduction of extinction trials produces a strong emotional state, which has been identified as *frustration*. A rat that has been traversing an alley and finding food on each trial appears to become emotionally upset when reward is not found in the goal box. Such emotional responding is inferred from the animal's goal box behavior, which includes frantic running from corner to corner, urination, and hostile behavior (e.g., biting the hand of experimenters when they reach into the goal box in order to place the animal in its restraining cage).

Azrin, Hutchinson, and Hake (1966) noted that after pigeons were trained to peck a response key in order to receive food, with each response resulting in reinforcement, the removal of food on extinction trials resulted in their subjects attacking another bird that had been restrained in one corner of the apparatus. Similar behavior was noted even if the restrained bird was stuffed. The authors suggested that the transition from food reinforcement to extinction was an aversive event that produced emotional responding (and aggressive behavior) in the pigeon. But it must be noted that the behavior we have just described is not found when the extinction trial procedure of providing shock in the goal box is employed with negative reinforcement tasks.[5]

Variables Influencing Experimental Extinction

The influence of stimulus and reward variables in the analysis of experimental extinction has interested investigators; reward conditions have been much more extensively examined. Accordingly, we will discuss their contribution to extinction prior to examining the role of stimulus conditions.

Reward Variables   Our examination of how reward variables influence extinction has revealed that negative reinforcement tasks have been used infrequently. In contrast, the contribution of how the conditions of positive reinforcement provided during

---

[5] A formidable question that has arisen over the past several decades has been What does extinction measure? In his *Principles of Behavior,* Hull (1943) assumed that resistance to extinction was one measure, along with several others obtained during acquisition trials, that could be used from which to infer the strength of a learned response. But it has become evident, beginning with Humphreys' (1939) demonstration of the partial reinforcement effect, that Hull's assumption was in error. But an assertion that extinction should not be used from which to infer learning does not answer the question which was originally posed—What does extinction measure? Amsel (1967) has made the very interesting proposal that extinction measures the persistence of a response—a response dimension that differs from response strength. It would appear, however, that most current investigators consider extinction to be only a particular kind of behavior in which they have an interest.

acquisition influence experimental extinction has generated most interest among investigators. This is not surprising since the removal of reward is the operation that has traditionally defined extinction.

The reward variables that have been manipulated during training trials include amount, delay, and frequency. Partial reinforcement, an aspect of frequency, has been examined so extensively that it will be discussed in a separate section.

Amount of Reward   Studies examining the effect of increasing the amount of reward on lever pressing or runway performance have yielded similar findings: Increasing the amount of reinforcement during acquisition trials (by varying the size or number of food pellets) decreases resistance to extinction (see Hulse, 1958; Wagner, 1961; Ison and Cook, 1964; Marx, 1967; Roberts, 1969; and Campbell, Batsche, and Batsche, 1972). An extensive study by Roberts (1969) illustrates this finding. Rats were provided with 48 trials in learning to traverse a runway and received 1, 2, 5, 10, or 25 pellets of food. This was followed by 31 extinction trials. All animals received one trial a day. The animals' starting times—time to get out of the start box—clearly reveal the nature of the relationship between the amount of reward obtained during acquisition and performance during extinction. Those animals who had received the largest number of food pellets during acquisition trials extinguished most rapidly, whereas those receiving the smallest number of pellets extinguished least rapidly. (See Figure 6-10.)

Delay of Reward   Investigators have found that delaying reward for a constant length of time after the subject makes an instrumental response during acquisition trials increases resistance to extinction; the control group, of course, receives reward immediately (see Fehrer, 1956; Tombaugh, 1966, 1970; and Wike and McWilliams, 1967). Using rats in a lever-pressing task, Tombaugh (1970) examined delay conditions of 15, 30, and 45 seconds, and found that the group with the 45-second delay took longest to extinguish, followed by the groups with the 30- and 15-second delays.

The increased resistance to extinction caused by delay of reinforcement is also found when the delay period is provided on some trials but not on others. In a study by

Figure 6-10
Extinction curves as measured by starting times for each amount of reward used during acquisition. Adapted from W. A. Roberts, "Resistance to extinction following partial and consistent reinforcement with varying magnitudes of reward," *Journal of Comparative and Physiological Psychology,* 1969, 67, 395–400. Copyright © 1969 by the American Psychological Association. Reprinted by permission.

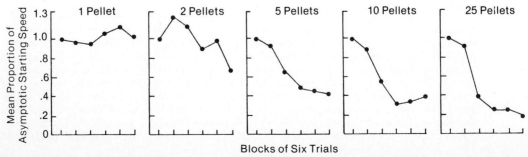

Knouse and Campbell (1971), varying groups of rats traversing a runway were provided different delays of reinforcement on half of their 50 acquisition trials; no delay of reinforcement was given on the other half. Delay periods of either 0, 8, 16, 24, 32, 40, 48, or 56 seconds were examined. Reward consisted of 15 seconds of eating wet mash. Forty extinction trials were provided after acquisition training, with increasing resistance to extinction being related to the length of the delay provided during acquisition. Figure 6–11 reveals these findings.

   Frequency of Continuously Rewarded Trials   When extinction has been examined as a function of the frequency of continuously rewarded trials, the experimental findings have been contradictory. The result is related to the kind of task that is used. When the Skinner Box has been used, most investigators have found that the extinction of a bar-pressing response is related positively to the number of reinforced responses provided during acquisition (e.g., Williams, 1938; Perin, 1942; Harris and Nygaard, 1961; Dyal and Holland, 1963; and Uhl and Young, 1967). Thus, in the Uhl and Young (1967) experiment, 180, 360, and 720 bar-pressing responses, each reinforced with a sucrose solution, were followed by extinction trials. As Figure 6–12 indicates, resistance to extinction was positively related to the number of reinforced responses.

   However, when the learning task consisted of the rat running down an alley, a different finding was obtained. Experimenters found that increasing the number of reinforced trials results in more rapid extinction, referred to as the *overlearning extinction effect* (OEE). This finding was originally reported by North and Stimmel (1960), who found that rats receiving 45 acquisition trials extinguished less rapidly than subjects receiving 90 or 135 trials. Many subsequent runway studies have confirmed this result (e.g., Ison, 1962; Siegel and Wagner, 1963; and Clifford, 1964, 1968).

   At this time, it is difficult to reconcile the disparate findings of the bar pressing and runway studies, although it can be suggested that two variables need further examination. First, investigators using a Skinner Box and the bar-pressing response typically provide only a small amount of reward; in contrast, large amounts are often used on runway studies. It may be that a large amount of reward produces frustration during extinction, which contributes in some way to the overlearning effect found in runway studies. Ison and Cook (1964) report some support for this position. In their study,

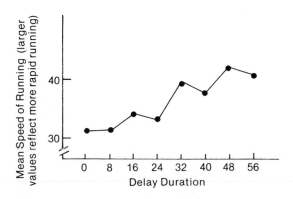

Figure 6-11
Mean running speeds for each delay duration during extinction. Adapted from S. B. Knouse and P. E. Campbell, "Partially delayed reward in the rat: A parametric study of delay duration," *Journal of Comparative and Physiological Psychology,* 1971, *75,* 116–119. Copyright © 1971 by the American Psychological Association. Reprinted by permission.

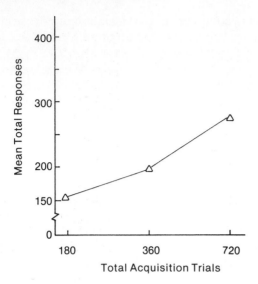

Figure 6-12
Mean total extinction responses as a function of total number of acquisition trials. Adapted from C. N. Uhl and A. G. Young, "Resistance to extinction as a function of incentive, percentage of reinforcement, and number of nonreinforced trials," *Journal of Experimental Psychology,* 1967, *73,* 556–564. Copyright © 1967 by the American Psychological Association. Reprinted by permission.

groups of rats were provided with either 30 or 75 training trials on the runway, with half of each group receiving one pellet of food (small reward) and the other half receiving 10 pellets (large reward). Fifteen trials a day were provided for either two or five days, following which the animals received 30 extinction trials. Results indicated that the animals that received 75 trials with 10 pellets of food extinguished most rapidly; animals receiving 75 trials with just one pellet of food, however, revealed the greatest resistance to extinction.

A second variable may be the difference in timing between programming extinction trials over a single session and distributing them over several sessions. Using a lever-pressing task, Senkowski (1978) was unable to obtain the overlearning extinction effect in one experiment (Experiment 1), thus confirming the findings of many other investigators; however, he was able to demonstrate this effect in a second experiment (Experiment 2). Both experiments were conducted under identical conditions except that extinction trials in the first study (which did not demonstrate OEE) were distributed over seven sessions, whereas extinction trials in Experiment 2 were provided in a single session. Such findings suggested to Senkowski that "session-related variables . . . may be important determinants of extinction performance" (p. 140).

Partial Reinforcement

Varying Partial Reinforcement Schedules   In our discussion of the contribution of partial reinforcement to the extinction of a classically conditioned response, we noted that Humphreys' (1939) study revealed that a 50% partial reinforcement schedule resulted in greater resistance to extinction than a continuous reinforcement schedule. It will be recalled that the superior resistance to extinction resulting from a partial reinforcement schedule has been identified as the partial reinforcement effect (PRE).

The PRE has been also obtained by many experimenters using positive reinforcement tasks. Weinstock's (1958) study, partially described in Chapter Five, employed a runway with rats receiving varying percentages of reinforced trials ranging from 17 to 100%. Results revealed an inverse relationship between resistance to extinction and percentage of reinforced acquisition trials. Thus, maximum resistance to extinction was obtained with the 17% reinforcement group, whereas minimum resistance was noted with the 100% group.[6]

Many other investigators, however, have found poorest resistance to extinction taking place when subjects were provided with (1) continuous reinforcement or (2) a very small percentage of reinforced trials, thus suggesting that a U-shaped function best described the relationship between percentage of reinforced trials and resistance to extinction. This conclusion was echoed by Lewis (1960) following his extensive review of the findings of partial reinforcement studies.

It will be recalled that Grant and Schipper's (1952) explanation for the U-shaped function revealed in partially reinforced classical conditioning studies was based on the operation of two conditions: (1) the amount of reinforcement and (2) the ease of discriminating acquisition from extinction trials. Thus, a group receiving only a small number of partially reinforced acquisition trials should reveal little resistance to extinction because the few reinforcements received resulted in only a small amount of learning. Response strength for the continuously reinforced group would be high; however, this group should be better able to make the acquisition-extinction trial discrimination and as a result, should also exhibit poor resistance to extinction. Thus, the poor resistance to extinction performance by both the continuously reinforced group and the low percentage partially reinforced group contributed to the U-shaped function.

Bacon's (1962) instrumental conditioning study clearly supports the Grant and Schipper (1952) position. In Bacon's experiment, 16 groups of rats were given training trials in traversing an alley with either 30, 50, 70, or 100% of these trials being reinforced. Following such training, 30 extinction trials were provided. Figure 6–13 plots the speed of running during extinction trials as a function of the two manipulated variables, namely, the number of acquisition trials and the percentage of reinforced trials. In accounting for this result, Bacon reasoned that after just 10 acquisition trials, only the reinforcement process was operating so that resistance to extinction was related to the percentage or number of reinforcements received. After 30 trials, both the reinforcement and the discrimination process were operating so the U-shaped function

---

[6] Typically, PRE studies have used a between-groups design in which one group receives partial reinforcement whereas a second group receives continuous. It is possible, however, to use a within-subjects design in which subjects are presented with a discrimination task in which one stimulus is associated with continuous reinforcement whereas a second stimulus is associated with partial reinforcement. In such experiments, Pavlik and Carlton (1965), Pavlik, Carlton, Lehr, and Hendrickson (1967), and Adams, Nemeth, and Pavlik (1982) all have reported that the employment of the partial reinforcement schedule has resulted in poorer extinction, thus producing a "reversed partial reinforcement effect." As Adams and colleagues have stated, "The within-subject reversed PRE has been shown to be a large robust phenomenon in discrete-trial and free-operant lever pressing situations" (p. 261).

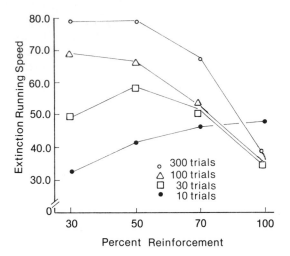

Figure 6–13
The effect of different numbers of acquisition trials on mean extinction running speed as a function of percentage of reinforcement. Adapted from W. E. Bacon, "Partial-reinforcement extinction following different amounts of training," *Journal of Comparative and Physiological Psychology,* 1962, *55,* 998–1003. Copyright © 1962 by the American Psychological Association. Reprinted by permission.

was obtained. Finally, with 100 and 300 acquisition trials, the response was well learned by all groups regardless of the percentage of reinforced trials, so only the discrimination process appeared to operate. (See Box 6–1.)

Stimulus Variables

In an examination of the role of stimulus variables on extinction, the evidence suggests that if the stimuli making up and surrounding the experimental task are changed from those found during acquisition, extinction will be facilitated. What appears to take place is that as the experimental subject becomes better able to discriminate acquisition from extinction trials, the probability of responding during extinction becomes less likely. We can observe such a result in some of the studies described in the previous section. For example, if reward is considered to be an important stimulus in the makeup of the instrumental reward task, and extinction is regarded as a condition of reward with an infinite delay, the degree of similarity of reward conditions between acquisition and extinction should help determine the rapidity with which extinction takes place. It will be recalled that investigators (e.g., Hulse, 1958) have found that extinction is facilitated if acquisition trials provide the experimental subject with a large reward in contrast to a small one. Similarly, if the subject receives reward immediately after arriving in the goal box during acquisition, thus resulting in no delay of reinforcement, extinction takes place more rapidly than if a delay of reward had been introduced during acquisition. Thus, the discrimination between acquisition and extinction trials becomes progressively more difficult as the amount of reward becomes smaller and the delay of receiving it becomes longer.

The finding of such a relationship between changing the characteristics of the reward provided during acquisition and extinction suggests that if contextual stimuli are changed, extinction responding should be similarly influenced. A study by Welker and McAuley (1978) has provided support for such a position. In this study, rats were

box 6-1

The playing of a slot machine, which provides intermittent reinforcement, has been a frequently cited example of how *partial reinforcement* influences responding.

Lewis and Duncan (1956) have used the slot machine to experimentally study the effects of partial reinforcement. Seven groups of college students served as subjects. They were provided with an unlimited number of disks with which to play the machine, and told that it would be possible to win tokens that could be cashed in for five cents apiece after they decided to stop playing. Each group was given eight acquisition trials and provided a different percentage of reinforcement on these trials—namely, 100, 75, 50, 37.5, 25, 12.5, and 0 percent. Except for the 0 percent group, all subjects received a token on the eighth trial, in addition to any tokens they received on other trials, the number depending on the percentage of reinforcement they were programmed to receive. Extinction trials immediately followed the acquisition trials, with the subjects being encouraged to play as long as they wanted.

Results indicated that the percentage of reinforcement provided the varying groups had a significant effect on the total number of plays, as shown in the figure below. It will be recalled that Bacon (1962), using rats, observed that when a well-learned response was extinguished, the percentage of reinforced trials provided during acquisition was inversely related to the animal's resistance to extinction. Lever pulling was a well-learned response among the college students, so Lewis and Duncan's finding that their subjects' resistance to extinction was inversely related to the number of reinforced responses provided during the eight acquisition trials is in keeping with Bacon's point of view.

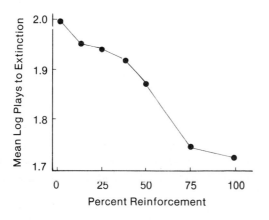

Box Figure 6-1
Mean log trials to extinction as a function of the percentage of trials reinforced during acquisition. Adapted from D. J. Lewis and C. P. Duncan, "Effect of different percentages of money reward on extinction of a lever pulling response," *Journal of Experimental Psychology*, 1956, *52*, 23–27. Copyright © 1956 by the American Psychological Association. Reprinted by permission.

trained to bar press in a Skinner Box under a VI schedule until stable responding was achieved. The influence of changing two types of stimulus conditions during extinction were examined. These stimulus conditions were identified by the authors as: (1) transportational, which was related to the kind of transportation equipment and procedure involved in transporting the animals from their home cages to the Skinner Box; and (2) contextual, which involved the stimulus conditions found in the Skinner Box itself. (It is suggested that transportational stimuli are also contextual since they are present within the context of the experimental situation.)

Although we shall not describe in detail the nature of the two types of stimulus change provided during extinction, we would indicate that they were quite marked. During acquisition, the rats were transported to the apparatus area in their home cages, whereas a transportational change during acquisition involved removing them from their home cages and transporting them in a black plywood box with cedar shavings on the floor. During acquisition of the bar-pressing response, the Skinner Box context consisted of illuminating a circular disk above the bar and providing a background of white noise. Contextual changes provided during extinction consisted of not illuminating the circular disk, covering the Skinner Box walls and ceiling with black plastic inserts, reducing the level of illumination of the box, and presenting a tone.

The changes in transportation and contextual stimuli provided during extinction resulted in four experimental groups: (1) same context, same transportation stimuli; (2) same context, changed transportation stimuli; (3) changed context, same transportation stimuli; and (4) changed context, changed transportation stimuli. The findings obtained from these four groups are presented in Figure 6–14. It will be noted that if the contextual and transportation stimuli are not changed from acquisition to extinction, extinction took place least rapidly, whereas groups that had the contextual stimuli changed, regardless of whether or not transportational stimuli were changed, extinguished most rapidly. It is of interest that the two types of stimuli had differential effects on extinction; as might be expected, changing the contextual stimuli had the greater influence in producing response decrement.

Theories of Extinction

Pavlov's classical conditioning experiments resulted in his hypothesizing that the presentation of the CS alone resulted in the growth of inhibition, which eventually masked the excitatory strength that had developed during CS-US presentations. Few investigators, however, have agreed with Pavlov and a much different explanation was proposed by Guthrie (1935) and Wendt (1936). These investigators hypothesized that the removal of reinforcement resulted in the organism learning to make other responses that were incompatible with the making of the instrumental response. These interfering responses, learned during extinction trials, eventually precluded the appearance of the instrumental response.

It was evident to many investigators, however, that Guthrie and Wendt's interference explanation of extinction was no more acceptable than one based on inhibition since a basic difficulty was in finding the source of motivation that elicited the interfering response, whereas another was in identifying the nature of reinforcement that presumably strengthened such responding.

It is of historical interest to note that several years later Hull (1943) provided an explanation of extinction that incorporated both inhibitory and interfering response constructs, but Hull's proposed explanation also ran into difficulties. It has now become evident to many investigators that no single theoretical structure can account for the diverse extinction findings obtained from the many different classical and instrumental conditioning experiments, particularly when avoidance conditioning experiments are included. The result has been that explanations for extinction provided by theorists after Hull have been limited to relatively specific types of conditioning tasks.

Figure 6-14
Mean percentage of terminal acquisition rate during successive six-minute blocks of extinction trials. Adapted from R. L. Welker and K. McAuley, "Reductions in resistance to extinction and spontaneous recovery as a function of changes in transportation and contextual stimuli," *Animal Learning & Behavior,* 1978, *6,* 451–457. Copyright © 1978 by The Psychonomic Society. Reprinted by permission.

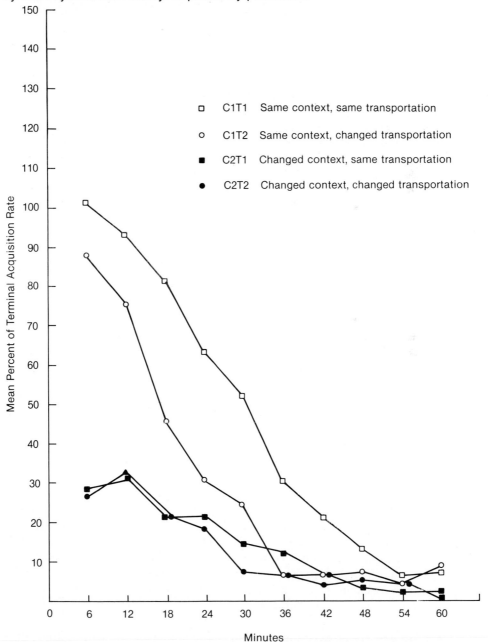

A Descriptive Account of Experimental Extinction in Tasks Involving Positive Reinforcement   In keeping with the general concern of investigators to consider extinction within a relatively restricted scope of operations, Wong (1978) has provided a descriptive account of the rat's extinction behavior in the runway following reward training.

In order to provide his animals with the opportunity to engage in a variety of responses during extinction trials, Wong drastically modified the traditional runway. Animals were placed in an entry box from which they could jump a hurdle leading into a starting box. The starting box contained a drinking tube, a model animal, and a sand-digging apparatus. A runway adjoined the starting box. Small strips of board divided the runway into 9 (Experiments 1 and 2) or 12 (Experiment 3) equal segments. All segments were numerically coded so that the animal's route in traversing the runway could be recorded. A small opening in the runway led to an exploration box. The goal box contained a sand-digging apparatus, a model animal, a can lid that the animal could bite, a door that led to a small escape box, and the food cup.

This apparatus permitted Wong to record the animal's differing behaviors in considerable detail. Wong was able to obtain measures of sniffing, grooming, immobility, and most of the experimental activities that brought the animal into direct contact with the various parts of the apparatus. These included drinking, biting, sand digging, and exploration, in addition to running the habitual and alternative routes through the runway and to the goal box.

By analyzing these varying kinds of behavior throughout extinction trials, Wong concluded that extinction involves an orderly succession of three qualitatively different stages of behavior. In the first of these, identified as a habit stage, the predominant behavior of the animal is the repetition of the response acquired during the learning trials. However, these responses are performed more vigorously than before. The second stage is characterized by investigatory behavior. Here there is considerable variation in the route taken to the goal box, coupled with exploratory behavior. Finally, the last stage consists of the animal abandoning second-stage behavior and engaging in subgoal behavior characterized by drinking, sand digging, and the like. In an apt summary of these stages, Wong (1978) noted that in case of repeated failure to secure reward it is only natural for the subject to first repeat the same response that has been successful (Stage 1) and then try to alternate responses (Stage 2) before switching to alternative goals (Stage 3). Responses that compete with the previously acquired running response are seldom found in Stage 1 but do play a major role in extinction behavior during Stage 2 and 3.

An important contribution of Wong's descriptive analysis is that it recognized that specific variables provided during acquisition (e.g., amount of reward) will influence each of the three stages of extinction behavior differently. Wong's work has also indicated that extinction is even more complex than previously believed, and that the different theoretical positions might all have validity, depending on the stage of extinction examined. As he has indicated, the task that faces current extinction theorists is to determine how a specific theoretical position is related to these different stages of extinction.

In a series of experiments using college students in which extinction behavior under partial and continuous reinforcement was examined, Nation and Cooney (1982) have obtained findings supporting Wong's stage analysis of extinction. These experimenters reported that Wong's arguments "for a multiprocess account of extinction are sound and deserve more attention at both theoretical and empirical levels" (p. 112).

Extinction Theories of Partial Reinforcement

We have noted that investigators have been unable to provide a general theory of extinction that can account for the variety of experimental findings obtained. One alternative has been for experimenters to develop mini-theories that attempt to account for why extinction takes place with a specific type of learning task or with the operation of a particular experimental condition.

The finding that partial reinforcement, in contrast to continuous, leads to greater resistance to extinction has been identified as the partial reinforcement effect (PRE). A number of explanations have been proposed to account for this finding, and we shall examine those we believe to be most viable.

The Discrimination Hypothesis An early theoretical explanation for the partial reinforcement effect (PRE), identified as the discrimination hypothesis, was provided by Mowrer and Jones (1945). These investigators conducted a study in which four groups of rats were trained in a Skinner Box on a FR 1, 2, 3, or 4 schedule. A fifth group was placed on a VR 2.5 schedule. After extensive acquisition training, several extinction sessions were provided. It was found that the total number of bar presses made during extinction was a function of the reinforcement schedule; animals provided the FR 4 schedule extinguished least rapidly, followed by the FR 3, VR 2.5, and FR 2. The continuously reinforced group (FR 1) extinguished most rapidly.

Mowrer and Jones posited that when the change in stimulus conditions (from acquisition trials to extinction trials) was difficult to discriminate, greater resistance to extinction occurred than when such a discrimination was easy. They reasoned that providing a partial reinforcement schedule during acquisition trials made it more difficult for the organism to discriminate between acquisition and extinction trials than when acquisition trials were continuously reinforced. Hence, there was greater resistance to extinction in partially reinforced subjects.

This hypothesis has been used to explain the findings of Tyler, Wortz, and Bitterman (1953), who observed that a group of rats provided with alternating reinforced and nonreinforced acquisition trials extinguished more rapidly than a group provided with randomly reinforced trials. However, one problem with this theory is that its proponents have not specified the conditions that determine whether discrimination between acquisition and extinction will be easy or difficult.

Some experimenters have argued that if partially reinforced trials are provided and then followed by a series of continuously reinforced trials, the discrimination hypothesis should predict no PRE. This follows, since the subject should be able to discriminate easily between the last of the continuously rewarded acquisition trials and the first of the extinction trials. But the findings of Theios (1962), Perry and Moore (1965), and

Gibbs, Latham, and Gormezano (1978), who used this kind of experimental design, have indicated that the PRE continues to be found.

In Theios's (1962) study, three groups of rats were each provided with a block of 70 trials with 40% random reinforcement, followed by either 0, 25, or 70 continuously reinforced trials. Two control groups received 70 or 140 continuously reinforced trials. Forty extinction trials were provided after the acquisition training. Theios found that the PRE continues to be manifested even though as many as 70 continuously reinforced trials immediately preceded extinction trials.

This challenge to the discrimination hypothesis rests on the position that only those acquisition trials immediately preceding the extinction trials are critical in any discrimination made between acquisition and extinction. And yet, there is no reason to assume that such must be the case. It could be argued that the conditions found in all of the trials in an acquisition series contribute to the discrimination response being made by the organism, although acquisition trial conditions closest to extinction trials should be most important. Dyal and Systma (1976) have demonstrated such to be the case, finding that when continuously reinforced trials are followed by a series of partially reinforced trials, extinction takes place *less* rapidly than if the acquisition series of partial and continuously reinforced trials is reversed.

Sequential Aftereffects   Capaldi (1966, 1967, 1971) has hypothesized that stimuli arising from nonrewarded trials form a long-lasting memory trace, which becomes a part of the stimulus pattern on rewarded trials. If on a rewarded Trial 2, for example, the animal remembers receiving nonreward on the previous trial, the memory of nonreward becomes a part of the total stimulus pattern that is conditioned to and acquires control over the organism's instrumental response. The organism's resistance to extinction is determined by a comparison of the memory trace formed during the acquisition trials with the memory trace generated during extinction.

Operationally, Capaldi's theory rests on the sequence of patterning of reinforced and nonreinforced trials that forms the partial reinforcement regimen. His theory has led him to identify several partial reinforcement conditions that play a role in determining the organism's resistance to extinction. One of these is the number of nonreward-reward (N-R) transitions experienced.

In a study by Capaldi and Hart (1962) examining the number of N-R transitions, two experiments were conducted. Rats were trained to traverse a runway under either continuous, random, or single alternations of reward. In the first experiment, nine training trials per day were provided for three days. A basic difference between the two partial reinforcement groups was in the number of nonreward-reward (N-R) transitions each day. The single alternation group received four N-R transitions each, whereas the random group received just one, although the percentage of reinforcement was the same for both groups. In the second experiment, similar conditions were examined, but two days of training (nine trials per day) were provided. Results from both studies indicated that the single alternation group had the greatest resistance to extinction, thus supporting the position that the number of N-R transitions contributed to the partial reinforcement effect.

Subsequent studies by Spivey (1967), who examined one versus three N-R transitions (provided over 10 acquisition trials), and Seybert, Mellgren, and Jobe (1973), who examined two versus six N-R transitions (provided over 16 acquisition trials), supported the findings obtained by Capaldi and Hart (1962).

A second condition of importance to Capaldi's theory is the number of nonreinforced trials preceding a reinforced trial, or what has been identified as *N* length (such as *N-R, N-N-R, N-N-N-R,* etc.). To examine this variable, Capaldi and Kassover (1970) trained rats to run an alley, giving either one, two, or three consecutive nonrewarded trials which were both preceded and followed by rewarded trials. The 10 days of training was followed by seven days of extinction (six trials per day). Results revealed that resistance to extinction was positively related to the number of consecutive nonrewarded trials provided. Capaldi and Kassover hypothesized that the memory trace from three consecutive nonrewarded trials would become part of the memory trace arising from the rewarded fourth trial, with superior resistance to extinction for this group being attributed to the greater similarity of that memory trace with the memory trace arising from extinction trials.

Frustration Theory   Another explanation for the partial reinforcement effect has been proposed by Amsel (1958, 1962, 1972), using frustration as his basic explanatory construct. Amsel assumed that some nominal number of reinforced trials provided animals in an instrumental conditioning task was responsible for these animals obtaining an expectancy of reward. After such an expectancy had been established, not finding reward on a given trial elicited a primary emotional response, frustration. Providing several nonreinforced trials over a training series established a conditioned form of the original frustration response (rf) and its sensory consequences (sf). This rf-sf construct was first elicited by goal box stimuli, then through stimulus generalization, and eventually by the starting box. Thus, Amsel posited that animals that were partially reinforced learned to make the instrumental response in the presence of a conditioned emotional response, frustration, whereas animals given continuous reinforcement did not acquire such learning. When continuously reinforced animals were given extinction trials, the frustration generated by nonreward elicited overt responses that interfered with the instrumental response, thus facilitating extinction. In contrast, partially reinforced animals, having learned to make the instrumental response in the presence of frustration, extinguished more rapidly.

Amsel's positing of frustration arising from nonreward after the animals has experienced reward, has had the experimental support from a host of subsequent investigators. Providing extended acquisition training, using large rewards, or providing minimum delay of rewards, all have been demonstrated to result in decreasing resistance to extinction (e.g., Bower, 1962; Daly, 1968, 1969; and Yelen, 1969). The explanation for such decremental responding has been that these experimental conditions have increased the animal's expectancy of reward, which in turn resulted in frustration being enhanced on nonrewarded trials.

Tests of Amsel's Position   Amsel's theoretical position has generated considerable experimental interest; however, his frustration explanation for the PRE has been questioned (1) when only a few acquisition trials are provided and (2) when all of the nonreinforced trials are provided prior to the animal receiving rewarded trials.

A number of investigators were able to demonstrate the PRE by using only two to five training trials—fewer than Amsel had originally anticipated that would be necessary for the animal not only to acquire an expectancy for reward but also to learn to make the instrumental response in the presence of frustration (e.g., Godbout, Ziff, and Capaldi, 1968; and McCain, 1966, 1968). On the basis of the experimental findings of Amsel, Hug, and Surridge (1968), Amsel revised his position and posited that the learning of reward expectancy and responding in the presence of frustration could take place in fewer trials than he had originally assumed.

The second question concerning the frustration explanation was raised by Capaldi and Waters (1970), who demonstrated that the PRE could be obtained when animals were given a series of nonrewarded trials followed by continuously rewarded trials. The extinction performance of rats given either 5 or 10 continuously reinforced trials traversing a runway was compared with the performance of a partially reinforced group that received 5 nonrewarded trials followed by 5 rewarded trials. Capaldi and Waters found that the partially reinforced animals were more resistant to extinction. Since all of the nonrewarded trials preceded the rewarded trials, it was difficult to see how frustration could develop and thus account for the PRE.

Perhaps a more viable explanation for some of these unusual PRE findings was provided in a series of studies by Brooks (1969, 1971, 1980). Brooks hypothesized (and experimentally demonstrated) that the expectancy for reward at the end of training trials was less for animals given partial reinforcement than for those given continuous reinforcement. With the continuously reinforced animals possessing a greater expectancy of reward, greater amounts of primary frustration was generated when extinction trials were introduced, thus resulting in more rapid extinction.

Moreover, if animals received a series of nonreinforced trials prior to rewarded ones (the procedure employed by Capaldi and Waters, 1970), Brooks noted that the early nonreinforced trials appeared to retard the growth of reward expectancy. Thus, when extinction trials were provided, smaller amounts of frustration were noted for these animals.

There appears to be little difference between Amsel's frustration theory and Capaldi's sequential position with regard to the adequacy with which they can explain the PRE findings; critical experiments to differentiate between these two theoretical positions have yet to be performed. But the use of types of apparatus more complex than the runway should be considered in an attempt to examine Amsel and Capaldi's position within the descriptive framework and stage analysis of extinction as provided by Wong (1978).

Summary ▶

In the examination of the acquisition of positive and negative reinforcement tasks, three reward variables have been extensively examined: (1) the frequency or patterning of reinforced trials, (2) the characteristics of the reinforcing agent, and (3) the time or delay interval placed between the making of the instrumental response and the receiving of reinforcement.

The patterning of reinforcement has been investigated primarily with operant conditioning tasks. Fixed and variable interval, and fixed and variable ratio reinforcement schedules have been most often examined. Many comparisons among these schedules have been made; perhaps the most basic finding is that ratio schedules result in more rapid rates of responding than interval schedules.

The characteristics of the reinforcing agent are frequently manipulated by increasing the amount of reward, which results in learning taking place more rapidly. An interesting aspect of these reward studies is the finding of contrast effects. The presentation of a large reward followed by a small reward will result in the animal responding at a performance level lower than the performance level of an animal who was given the large reward at the start of the learning trials. In contrast, the presentation of a small reward followed by a large reward will result in the animal responding at a performance level higher than the performance level of an animal who was given the large reward at the start of the learning trials. These effects have been identified as negative and positive contrast effects.

Experimenters examining delay of reinforcement have been interested in the effects of varying the time interval between making the response and securing the reward. Results generally reveal that as this interval grows longer, learning becomes more difficult.

An examination of the extinction of positive and negative reinforced tasks reveals that both reward and stimulus variables have been manipulated in order to determine their contribution to extinction. The reward conditions manipulated during training trials include amount, delay, frequency, and intermittency. When amount is manipulated, most studies indicate that an increase in the amount of reinforcement provided during acquisition decreases resistance to extinction. When delay of reinforcement is manipulated, experimental findings have indicated that a delay between the making of the response and the securing of the reward increases resistance to extinction.

Studies of the frequency of continuously rewarded trials have provided unusual findings. Some investigators have found that resistance to extinction was positively related to the number of reinforced responses; others have found that increasing the number of reinforced trials resulted in more rapid extinction, a result referred to as the overlearning extinction effect (OEE). When partial reinforcement schedules are used, the most typical finding has been that an intermittent schedule of reinforcement produces increased resistance to extinction, an effect identified as the partial reinforcement effect (PRE).

The contribution of stimulus variables to extinction has typically indicated that resistance to extinction is a function of the amount of stimulus change provided between the acquisition and the extinction trials.

The extinction theories of Pavlov (who emphasized the contribution of inhibition), Guthrie and Wendt (who assumed that extinction took place because of the interference from other responses), and Hull (whose theory of extinction incorporated both inhibition and interference constructs) have not stood the test of time so that no current theory can adequately explain the experimental findings. One limited account of extinction has been provided by Wong. He has found that extinction behavior of rats traversing an alley can be described as being composed of three stages: (1) repeating the same response as previously made, (2) trying alternative responses, and (3) switching to alternative goals that demand new responses. The failure to find a viable general theory of extinction has resulted in many investigators developing mini-theories that explain extinction in restricted situations. One such attempt has been made to account for the partial reinforcement effect. Explanations have centered around three points of view: (1) the discrimination hypothesis, (2) the sequential aftereffects theory, and (3) the frustration theory; these last two positions account for many of the experimental findings.

chapter seven

► —————————————————————————————————————

Punishment and Avoidance
Conditioning Tasks

When the instrumental conditioning task is identified as punishment, the typical operation has involved the (1) application of an aversive or noxious stimulus, (2) contingent on the subject making a previously acquired response, with (3) such stimulation resulting in reducing the probability of the occurrence of that response. We should also note that current investigators have indicated that punishment need not involve the application of an aversive stimulus but rather may consist of the removal of a previously acquired reward or privilege—a procedure defined as *negative punishment*. Thus, a father may punish his son for failure to return home at an agreed upon hour by restricting the son's use of the family car. Or, in an effort to help curb the use of drugs, some law enforcement officials have suggested that teenagers who are found guilty of using drugs have their driver's license revoked.[1] Most laboratory research examining punishment, however, has involved the presentation of an aversive stimulus since it represents a much easier procedure to manipulate.

An early study by Kamin (1959) illustrates the nature of a punishment task. Rats were first trained to avoid shock by running from one compartment to another in a shuttle box. A buzzer served as the warning signal and the shock was administered 10 seconds following the onset. After the animal had learned to avoid shock by responding when the buzzer sounded, punishment was introduced. When the buzzer sounded and the animal ran to a second compartment, it was immediately shocked. As a result, the

———————————————————

[1] Negative punishment tasks have typically involved using either response cost or time-out procedures. The loss of a privilege or a previously acquired object (e.g., money, etc.) has been identified as response cost. Time-out procedures involve the subject being isolated from his or her normal environment for a period of time. Thus, a teacher who sends a pupil to an isolated room in order to punish misbehavior is using a time-out procedure.

animals had to learn to avoid shock by remaining in the first compartment when the buzzer was presented.[2]

The effect of punishment is opposite of the effect of reinforcement. The application of reinforcement will result in increasing the number of responses or the probability of responding over operant or baseline responding. Conversely, the application of punishment will decrease the number of responses or their probability over that observed prior to punishment being administered. Note that baseline responding prior to the introduction of positive reinforcement is quite low (e.g., the experimental subject makes very few responses). In contrast, baseline behavior prior to the introduction of punishment will typically be relatively strong, which is a necessary prerequisite if the investigator is to demonstrate that the introduction of the aversive stimulus will reduce the probability of such responding.

Historical Antecedents ►

Thorndike (1911), an early investigator who examined punishment, stated that responses closely followed by discomfort to the organism will have their connection with the stimulus weakened. When the stimulus is again presented, there will be a decrease in the probability of such responding. Twenty years later, Thorndike (1932) revised his position, proposing that punishment did not weaken an S-R connection but rather, the effect of punishment resulted only in subjects varying their responses, which in turn increased the probability of the occurrence of the correct response. The action of punishment as Thorndike hypothesized was thus indirect rather than direct as posited in his earlier formulation.

The kind of study that led Thorndike to this conclusion was as follows: College students were presented with 200 rare English words. For each word they had to choose the correct meaning from five alternatives provided. The sample below offers an example of the material:

    dowlas: bowie/fabric/grief/Indian soldier/howls
    edacious: daring/tractable/sober/devouring/polite
    edolon: laziness/benefice/gift/duck/phantom
    ern: long ago/foretaste/zeal/merit/eagle

If the chosen word was correct, the experimenter rewarded the subject by saying "right"; if the chosen word was wrong, the experimenter punished the subject by saying "wrong." Twelve or more repetitions of the 200-word list were provided. Thorndike's

---

[2] Punishment tasks have sometimes been identified as *passive avoidance* since the experimental subject must remain passive in order to avoid receiving the noxious stimulus. Most current investigators, however, use the term *punishment* to describe this paradigm.

(1932) analysis of the alternatives selected suggested that although "right" strengthened the making of the response on subsequent repetitions, "wrong" had little weakening influence, thus supporting his position that punishment did not have any uniform weakening effects.

After Thorndike's (1932) reformulation of the effect of punishment, there was little consideration of this phenomenon by most psychologists for more than the next decade. One exception, however, was found in the work of Estes (1944), who trained rats to depress a lever in the Skinner Box; responses were reinforced every four minutes. After stable responding had been achieved, several extinction sessions were provided. All responses were punished with mild shock during the first extinction session; during subsequent extinction periods, shock was omitted. Results indicated the effect of shock during the first extinction session produced a temporary depression in rate of responding. When shock was discontinued, there was a compensatory increase in the rate of responding so that the total number of responses to reach the criterion was equal to the number that was present if no punishment had been administered. In a second experiment, Estes examined the influence of a more severe shock on lever pressing. Here, the effect of punishment resulted in a rapid decrease in the rate of responding until by the end of the first 10 minutes of extinction, all of the animals had stopped responding. Punishment was not provided on any of the following extinction sessions. For the next three extinction days, there was some responding on the part of the previously punished animals but the rate was markedly depressed. But on the next four extinction days, responding by the experimental subject did not differ from that of the controls.

As a result of his work, Estes came to the conclusion that the punished response was not eliminated from the organism's repertoire of responses; rather, it continued to exist with considerable latent strength. When punishment ceased, the suppression of the punished response was weakened, with the original response eventually recovering in strength. Estes hypothesized that when the punished response was being suppressed it was not only protected from extinction but also could become a source of conflict. He also posited that the most effective way to break a habit or to prevent a response from occurring was to permit it to extinguish rather than resorting to punishment.

The studies of Thorndike (1932) and Estes (1944) led many parents and educators to question whether punishment was an effective way of controlling behavior. However, other experimental evidence suggested that if the aversive stimulus was sufficiently intense, punishment could control responding. Masserman (1943) trained cats to feed in an experimental apparatus and then subjected them to a blast of air or shock at the moment of feeding. He noted that despite severe hunger, when the animals returned to the apparatus, they were unlikely to eat for a long period of time. Similarly, Lichtenstein (1950) observed that dogs that were shocked on the forepaw while eating in the experimental apparatus refused to eat when again placed in the apparatus. Such refusal lasted for weeks and sometimes months without further presentation of shock. Subsequent studies by Storms, Boroczi, and Broen (1962), Appel (1963), and Walters and Rogers (1963) have confirmed these findings. When the aversive stimulus is sufficiently intense, the punished response may be inhibited for a long period of time.

In spite of early theorists' neglect of the concept of punishment, current investigators are finding this topic to be an important one. In the following section, we will examine some of the punishment variables that have been found to contribute to the suppression of responding.

An Examination of Punishment Variables ▶

The Response-Punishment Contingency

In his classic text, *Behaviorism,* Watson (1924) wrote, "The idea that a child's future bad behavior will be prevented by giving him a licking in the evening for something he did in the morning is ridiculous." But Watson did suggest that punishment would be effective "provided the child is caught in the act and the parent can administer the rap at once in a thoroughly objective way" (p. 183). It is evident that Watson was calling attention to the need for the punishment to be contingent on the making of the response. Many contemporary experimenters have provided experimental support for this position.

One of the early studies was conducted by Azrin (1956), who trained pigeons to peck a key for food on a three-minute VI schedule. After a stable level of responding had been established, the response key was alternately illuminated with an orange light followed by blue, the duration of each stimulus being two minutes. The food reinforcement schedule was continued regardless of key color. When the orange light was presented, subjects were provided with either a noncontingent shock or a procedure that made punishment contingent on the response. Thus, under the noncontingent shock condition, an inescapable shock was administered at either a fixed or a variable time after the orange light came on. In effect, the orange light served as a warning signal for impending shock but was independent of the subject's behavior. Under the contingent condition, the shock was not administered unless the pigeon made a pecking response; if no response took place during the two-minute period that the orange light was on, shock was not provided. Results indicated that there was much greater suppression of responding when shock was made contingent on the key peck than when shock presentation was independent of the bird's responding.

Delay of Punishment   Further support for the importance of the presentation of the aversive stimulus to be contingent on making a response is found in the studies conducted on delay of punishment. As the delay period between the making of the response and the administration of punishment increases, the response-punishment relationship grows more remote, which in turn results in the experimental subject increasing its frequency of making the punished response.

Kamin's (1959) study was one of the first to examine the role of delay on response suppression. In this study, consisting of two separate experiments, rats were first trained to avoid shock by running from one compartment of a shuttle box to another. The CS was a buzzer (Experiment 1) or a buzzer plus the lifting of a gate separating the two compartments (Experiment 2). The aversive stimulus was a shock administered through the grid floor with a CS-US interval of 10 seconds. After the animals had reached a criterion of 11 consecutive avoidance responses, punishment trials were provided in which varying groups of animals received shock at either 0, 10, 20, 30, or 40 seconds after making the avoidance response. Punishment might occur immediately or as much as 40 seconds following the running response. A control group, which did not receive punishment for responding, was also used. The results of the control and experimental groups in both experiments are shown in Figure 7–1 and reveal similar delay of punishment gradients.

Kamin's (1959) study differs from many punishment experiments in that the motivation for the original responding was shock. Frequently, other studies employ positively reinforced behavior; one such study was conducted by Baron (1965). Rats were first trained to traverse a runway in order to secure water. They were shocked at varying intervals (0, 5, 10, 20, or 30 seconds) following their entrance into the goal box. For the 0 delay group, the animals were shocked immediately following the running response; on the other hand, since water continued to be present in the goal box, animals in the varying delay groups were often shocked while they were drinking. The experimental findings revealed that running speed was related to the length of the delay interval, although, as Baron has pointed out, the disruption of the consummatory

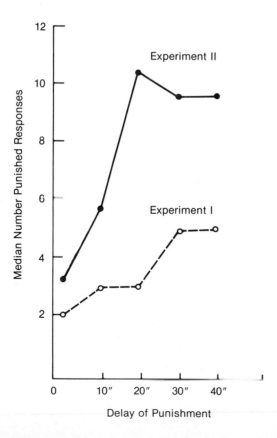

Figure 7-1
Median number of extinction responses as a function of delay of punishment. Adapted from L. J. Kamin, "The delay-of-punishment gradient," *Journal of Comparative and Physiological Psychology,* 1959, *52,* 434–437. Copyright© 1959 by the American Psychological Association. Reprinted by permission.

behavior by the presentation of shock could not be completely discounted as a factor contributing to the observed differences in performance.

Intensity and Duration of the Aversive Stimulus

When punishment tasks are examined, a frequent finding is that the degree of response suppression is a function of the intensity of shock. A study by Camp, Raymond, and Church (1967) has illustrated the nature of these findings. Following eight sessions of training rats to press a lever for food on a one-minute VI schedule, the subjects were divided into five experimental groups and given shock with intensities of either 0.1, 0.2, 0.3, 0.5, or 2.0 ma. Duration of shock was 2.0 seconds and delivered according to a FR schedule so calculated that each animal would receive an average of one shock per minute if its response rate remained unchanged. A control group did not receive shock. As Figure 7–2 reveals, the amount of response suppression was a function of the intensity of shock used. Other investigators (e.g., Azrin, Holz, and Hake, 1963) have reported similar findings.

Figure 7–2
Mean suppression ratio as a function of intensity of punishment. Adapted from D. S. Camp, G. A. Raymond, and R. M. Church, "Temporal relationship between response and punishment," *Journal of Experimental Psychology,* 1967, *74,* 114–123. Copyright© 1967 by the American Psychological Association. Reprinted by permission.

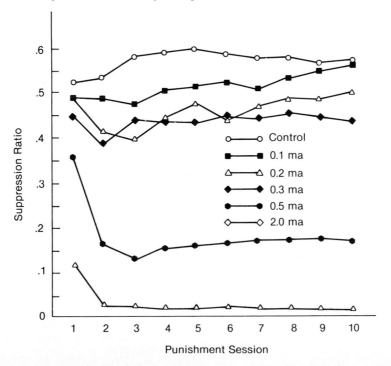

Another way of manipulating intensity would be to increase the duration of the aversive stimulus; the influence of this variable on response suppression is quite similar to an increase in intensity. Seligman and Campbell (1965), Storms, Boroczi, and Broen (1962), and Church, Raymond, and Beauchamp (1967) have all demonstrated this effect. In the latter study, following five sessions of training rats to press a lever for food on a one-minute VI schedule, 42 rats were divided into six groups and given shock for durations of either 0, 0.15, 0.30, 0.50, 1.0, or 3.0 seconds. The aversive stimulus was a 0.16 ma shock delivered according to a two-minute VI schedule. The mean suppression ratio as a function of the duration of the shock is indicated in Figure 7–3.

Method of Presentation

When a response is punished, sometimes the aversive stimulus employed is not effective in suppressing the response. When the instrumental response is again made, the experimenter may consider using a stronger or more intense stimulus in order to suppress the response. And if this level of intensity does not effect a change, a still more intense stimulus may be used. But is this gradual increase in intensity an appropriate

Figure 7–3
Mean suppression ratio as a function of sessions of punishment training for groups with 0.0, 0.15, 0.30, 0.50, 1.0, and 3.0 sec. duration of punishment. Adapted from R. M. Church, G. A. Raymond, and R. D. Beauchamp, "Response suppression as a function intensity and duration of a punishment," *Journal of Comparative and Physiological Psychology*, 1967, *63*, 30–44. Copyright© 1967 by the American Psychological Association. Reprinted with permission.

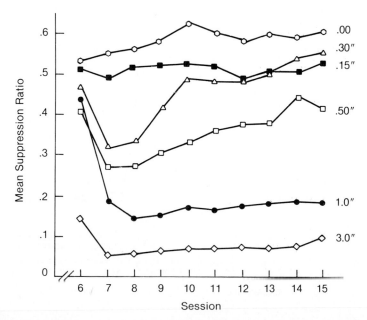

way to suppress the instrumental response? The work of Miller (1960) suggests that it is not.

In Miller's (1960) study, rats were trained to traverse a runway in order to secure a moist pellet of food. Such training continued until the animals appeared to reach their asymptote of running speed. Following such training, the animals were divided into two groups. A *gradual* group was given five trials per day. On Day 1, a 125-volt shock was presented through the grid floor of the goal box on each trials. Increasing levels of shock were provided in 15% increments throughout 14 additional training days, with shock level for the last three days being 335 volts. A *sudden* group continued the rewarded nonshock training of five trials per day for 15 days, following which both groups were given 20 test trials (five per day) with the 335-volt shock in the goal box. Results presented in Figure 7-4 reveal that the sudden group suppressed their running response significantly more than the gradual group.

Figure 7-4
Effect on speed of approach of gradual vs. sudden introduction of electric shock at the goal. Adapted from N. E. Miller, "Learning resistance to pain and fear: Effects of overlearning, exposure and rewarded exposure in context," *Journal of Experimental Psychology,* 1960, *60,* 137–145. Copyright© 1960 by the American Psychological Association. Reprinted by permission.

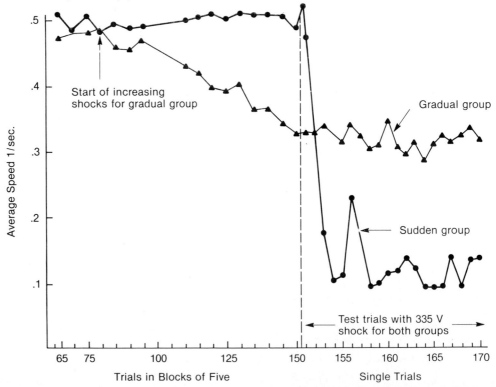

Strength of the Original Response

Our discussion of punishment has centered around an examination of the effect of varying parameters of the aversive (and punishing) stimulus on suppressing a response. But a variable often overlooked in determining whether or not punishment will result in response suppression has to do with strength of the originally trained response. It seems reasonable to assume that breaking a smoking habit would be more difficult if a strong habit was being punished rather than a weak one, with the strength of the habit being measured either by the number of cigarettes smoked each day or the number of years that the subject had smoked.

As we noted in earlier chapters, several variables (e.g., number of training trials, amount of reward, etc.) may contribute to the strength of the response. Although a systematic examination of the relationship of these variables and the amount of response suppression produced by punishment has not been made, an experiment by Azrin, Holz, and Hake (1963) is illustrative of what findings should be anticipated. In their study, pigeons were trained to peck at a key on a VI three-minute schedule of reinforcement. After every 100th response, a fairly intense 100 msec. shock was provided on the tail of the subject. The influence of such punishment was examined when the subjects had been placed on varying food deprivation schedules, namely, 60, 65, 70, 75, or 85% of their normal body weight. Results in Figure 7–5 reveal that as deprivations increased, thus resulting in a stronger pecking response, the effect of shock to suppress the key-pecking response grew progressively weaker.

Theories of Punishment

We will conclude our treatment of punishment by briefly discussing some of the theories that have been proposed to account for why the presentation of an aversive stimulus will suppress a response.

One proposal has been that reward and punishment, or appetitive and aversive stimuli, result in mutually antagonistic effects. One version of this theory was discussed by Thorndike (1913) in his early version of the law of effect in which he posited that reward would strengthen a stimulus-response connection, whereas punishment would weaken it. In this latter case, the S-R association presumably became unlearned as a result of the presentation of the aversive stimulus.

More recently, Mackintosh (1983) has suggested that instrumental conditioning involves the establishment of an association between a response and a consequence, with no difference as to "whether these consequences are appetitive or aversive." He has pointed out, however, that there is the transformation of these associations into behavior that reflects the nature of these consequences and the antagonism between them. The opposed operation of appetitive and aversive motivational effects on behavior can be noted in a study by Konorski and Szwejkowski (1956). These experiments demonstrated that the acquisition of a salivary CR to a CS paired with food was severely retarded if that stimulus had previously served as a CS signaling shock to the

Figure 7–5
Effect of food deprivation during fixed-ratio punishment of food reinforcement responses. Every 100th response is being punished (160V) at the moment indicated by the short oblique lines on the response curves. The food reinforcements (not shown) are being delivered according to a three-minute variable schedule. Adapted from N. H. Azrin, W. C. Holz, and D. F. Hake, "Fixed-ratio punishment," *Journal of the Experimental Analysis of Behavior,* 1963 *6,* 141–148. Copyright© 1963 by the Society for the Experimental Analysis of Behavior. Reprinted by permission.

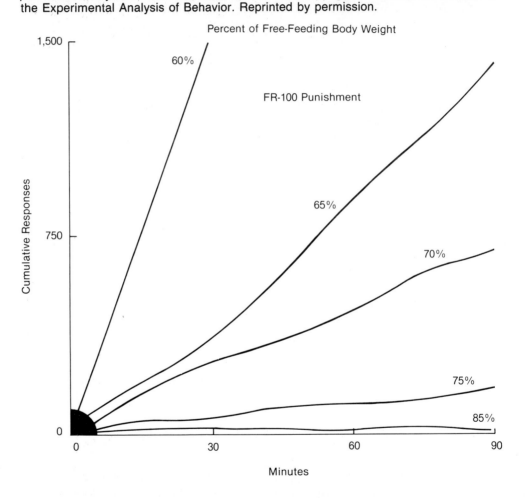

paw; conversely, the development of a leg flexion CR to a CS signaling shock to the paw was inhibited if that stimulus had previously served as a CS signaling food.

A different theory has been to assume that the suppression of responding can be attributed to the learning of new responses that compete with and eventually overshadow the punished response. In one such proposal, Estes (1944) posited that the stimuli experienced by the experimental subject just prior to making the punished response act as conditioned stimuli, which become associated with the aversive stimuli serving as the US. Since the US elicits an unconditioned response of both pain and fear, the CS, after several CS-US trials, acquires the capacity to elicit fear. It is this emotional response of fear that competes with and eventually suppresses the punished response. In a revision of his position, Estes (1969) theorized that the fear response elicited by the CS is incompatible with the appetitive motivation responsible for eliciting the punished response. With the motivation for this response thus diminished in strength by the presence of fear, the suppression of the punished response can be readily explained.

A somewhat different competing response theory is found in Mowrer's (1947) two-factor theory. Mowrer posited that the classical conditioning of fear, as indicated by Estes (1944), took place but he further indicated that the fear response also served as a stimulus to elicit a response that was instrumental in reducing such fear. As we shall note, Mowrer's hypothesis has particular relevance in accounting for avoidance conditioning. But it also has applicability to punishment tasks since it is necessary to posit only that the nonresponding by the experimental subject is a response that results in fear reduction. We will discuss Mowrer's two-factor theory in greater detail later in the chapter.

Avoidance Conditioning ▶

In the avoidance conditioning task, the experimental subject's response is instrumental in avoiding an aversive or noxious stimulus. It is important to keep in mind, however, that the procedure and the nature of the response noted in early training trials mirrors classical conditioning. As a result, investigators often use classical conditioning terminology in describing avoidance task procedures. Overall, the two paradigms are decidedly different and will often yield different findings.

A study by Church, Brush, and Solomon (1956) illustrates the discriminated avoidance conditioning paradigm. Dogs, used as experimental subjects, were placed in a shuttle box. The apparatus consisted of two compartments separated by a barrier, with a buzzer (CS) sounding for ten seconds. The termination of the buzzer was followed by a shock (US), programmed through the grid floor of one compartment. After a number of buzzer-shock presentations, the animal learned to jump over the barrier and into the safe compartment when the buzzer was sounded, thus avoiding shock.

A different type of avoidance paradigm is nondiscriminated or Sidman (1953a, 1953b) avoidance (described in Chapter Five). Here it will be recalled that there is no stimulus to predict the onset of the aversive stimulation. Rather, shock is provided on a regular interval but an instrumental response such as bar pressing will delay or postpone the shock for an arbitrary length of time set by the experimenters. The interval between shock presentations is known as the *shock-shock interval,* whereas the amount of time that the instrumental response delays presentation of the shock is known as the *response-shock interval.* It is possible for the subject to learn to respond in such a way that the frequency of shock is reduced but complete avoidance of the shock rarely occurs.

Variables Influencing Avoidance Responding

An examination of those variables that influence avoidance responding bear a marked similarity to those that we found to influence classical conditioning. Briefly, they can be related to the intensity of the aversive stimulus or US, as well as the temporal interval separating the two stimuli.

Intensity of the Aversive Stimulus (US)   The experimental findings clearly indicate that avoidance responding is a function of the intensity of the aversive stimuli that is employed. In an early study by Kimble (1955), rats were trained to turn a wheel within a five-second interval in order to avoid shock. A buzzer served as the CS; one of four intensities of shock, either 0.2, 0.5, 1.0, or 2.0 ma, was used. The response measure was latency of responding; results indicated that latency decreased as a function of shock intensity.

One-way shuttle box studies conducted by Moyer and Korn (1966), as well as others (e.g., Theios, Lynch, and Lowe, 1966; and McAllister, McAllister, and Douglas, 1971), have also demonstrated the influence of the intensity variable on avoidance responding. The one-way shuttle box procedure consists of the animals being presented with the CS in one compartment followed by shock after an arbitrary time interval (e.g., 10 seconds). The animal must run to a second compartment in order to escape or avoid the aversive stimulus. The subject thus learns to respond in one direction, leaving one compartment associated with shock and entering a second compartment associated with safety. In the Moyer and Korn (1966) study, four different shock intensities were used (e.g., 0.5, 1.5, 2.5, or 3.5 ma) with rats receiving 50 acquisitions trials in a single session. The task consisted of the animal's learning to avoid shock by running from the compartment where shock was presented to the adjoining one within five seconds. Results indicated that the mean number of trials to the first avoidance response was a functions of the intensity of shock.[3] (See Table 7–1.)

CS-US Interval   In an avoidance conditioning task, experimenters have been interested in examining performance as a function of the interval between the onset of the

---

[3] The consistent findings that reveal that avoidance conditioning in the one-way shuttle box is a function of the intensity of the aversive stimulus do not hold if the two-way shuttle box is used. This type of apparatus provides shock in both compartments. The operation is as follows: A CS is presented for several seconds followed by shock, with the animal running from compartment A to B in order to avoid or escape the aversive stimulus. After a short time in compartment B, the CS is presented again. The animals have to return to compartment A in order to escape or avoid shock. Trials continue as before. The findings using this kind of apparatus indicate that the animal has greater difficulty in learning to avoid shock than if the one-way shuttle box is utilized. Moreover, two-way shuttle box findings reveal more rapid learning accompanies weak rather than strong shock, and that learning is facilitated if both compartments are of the same color (e.g., black-black) rather than being different (e.g., black-white).

Table 7-1
Avoidance responding as a function of shock intensity

	Intensity of Shock					
Mean number of	.5	1.5	2.5	3.5	7.4	6.8
trials to first	19.7	11.5	7.2	8.2	8.0	9.2
avoidance response						

Data obtained from Moyer and Korn (1966)

CS and the presentation of the aversive stimulus. If this type of task is conceptualized as classical conditioning, the noxious stimulus is regarded as the US, so that the study becomes an examination of the CS-US interval.

In his examination of the role of this interval, Kamin (1954) employed a two-way avoidance task that required dogs to jump a barrier in order to get from one side to the other. The CS was the sounding of a buzzer for two seconds in the compartment where the animal was placed. Following an interval of either 5, 10, 20, or 40 seconds as measured from the onset of the CS, the US was presented. The two-second duration of the CS with the long CS-US intervals employed defines this procedure as *trace conditioning*. An acquisition criterion of five consecutive avoidance trials was employed. Results indicated that the briefer CS-US intervals led to the most rapid acquisition of the avoidance response.

A study by Church, Brush, and Solomon (1956) replicated Kamin's (1954) procedure except that a delay rather than a trace procedure was employed, using either a 5-, 10-, or 20-second CS-US interval. This procedure required that the CS be presented during the entire CS-US interval. Acquisition of the avoidance response was measured by the number of trials to reach a criterion of five consecutive avoidance responses. In contrast to Kamin's (1954) findings, Church and associates were unable to find that the varying CS-US intervals made any difference in rate of acquisition. The Kamin (1954) and Church, Brush, and Solomon (1956) findings together clearly indicate that when a trace conditioning procedure is used, the length of the CS-US interval contributes to the ease of conditioning; in contrast, when the conditioning procedure is one of delay, no difference in acquisition can be observed.

Mowrer's Two-Factor Theory of Avoidance Conditioning

As with other types of instrumental conditioning paradigms, experimenters have been interested in providing an explanation for the acquisition (and extinction) of avoidance responding. With this type of task, it seems logical to assume that it is the omission of the aversive event that accounts for why the avoidance response is made. But as Mowrer (1947) reasoned some years ago, not getting something can hardly in and of itself qualify as reinforcement or satisfaction. Since his early discussion of this issue, a great many experimental studies and theoretical papers have appeared in an explanation for how avoidance conditioning takes place. The extensiveness of the literature precludes a detailed examination of this topic; however, we will briefly present Mowrer's (1947) two-factor theory, which has held center stage for over the past several decades.

Mowrer posited that the aversive stimulus experienced on early trials in the avoidance conditioning task elicited not only pain but also fear. If a CS such as a buzzer was presented followed by the presentation of a US (shock), the unconditioned response to the US was pain and fear. After several CS-US trials, the CS became capable of eliciting a CR taking the form of fear. Thus, Mowrer's first factor was posited to be the acquisition of a classically conditioned response. But Mowrer reasoned that the conditioned fear response could also be conceptualized as a stimulus that had an eliciting or motivational function. Thus, fear provided motivation for the subject to make a response (e.g., avoidance), which would result in moving the subject away from the fear-producing environment. But if fear elicits responding, the so-called avoidance response is not truly avoidance but one of escape; the instrumental response is strengthened by fear reduction. The redefining of avoidance responses to escape thus solves the earlier problem we discussed of determining what reinforces avoidance responses. In summary, instrumental conditioning was identified as the second factor in Mowrer's two-factor theory.

Mowrer's (1947) explanation of avoidance conditioning incorporating both classical and instrumental conditioning paradigms has been subjected over the years to a great deal of scrutiny, resulting in a variety of questions. For example, can fear actually serve as motivation for avoidance responding? Is the termination of the CS fear reducing? And if fear can serve these functions, what is the relationship between the strength of the fear and the strength of the avoidance response? In this text, we cannot provide any extended discussion of these questions, but we will point out that several investigators (e.g., Brown, Kalish, and Farber, 1951; and Wagner, 1963) have demonstrated that stimuli associated with shock can elicit responding and that the termination of the CS can serve as reinforcement for an avoidance response. Kamin (1957) found that the avoidance response in a two-way shuttle box was much more rapidly learned if the buzzer was terminated by the running response than when the buzzer had a fixed duration of either 2.5, 5, or 10 seconds following the making of the response.

What is the relationship between the strength of fear and the strength of the avoidance response? Mowrer's two-factor theory suggested that as training trials are continued, the magnitude of the fear should increase, which in turn would result in the avoidance response growing stronger. But the experimental evidence has indicated that such is not the case. The early studies of Solomon, Kamin, and Wynne (1953) and Solomon and Wynne (1954) suggested that with continued training, a point was reached in which their animals appeared to become less afraid, although the avoidance response grew stronger. Kamin, Brimer, and Black (1963) have also noted this relationship between the magnitude of fear and the strength of the avoidance response. In their study, rats were trained to bar press in a Skinner Box on a 2.5-minute VI food reinforcement schedule until stable responding had been achieved. After such training, the animals received tone-shock pairings in a shuttle box; four groups of animals were trained to a criterion of either 1, 3, 9, or 27 consecutive avoidance responses. The animals were then returned to the Skinner Box where 24 20-second presentations of the tone were provided. The tone was presented an average of once every four minutes. The findings, confirming the suggestion of the Solomon and colleagues studies, revealed that fear of the CS, as measured by the suppression ratio, increased as the acquisition criterion increased to 9 consecutive avoidance responses. But when the very stringent criterion of 27 consecutive avoidance responses were examined, the fear response to the CS decreased markedly. Starr and Mineka (1977) have been able to replicate Kamin, Brimer, and Black's results.

In utilizing physiological indices for fear, investigators have also found that extended avoidance training is related to the presence of only small amounts of fear. Coover, Ursin, and Levine (1973) have noted that plasma-corticosterone levels in rats were quite high following early avoidance training trials, but after prolonged training sessions with avoidance performance reaching asymptote, plasma-corticosterone levels revealed only small increases over base levels.

In summary, if fear diminishes over the course of many successful avoidance trials, it should follow that avoidance performance should become weaker. And yet it does not. What is responsible for such response maintenance in light of the experimental evidence that suggests that the amount of fear present in the experimental subject after extended avoidance responding is minimal? It must be acknowledged that at present we do not have a completely acceptable theory of avoidance learning, although as Mineka (1979) has written, no one "has yet demonstrated responding can take place in the complete absence of fear of the CS" (p. 988).

Species-Specific Defense Reactions

Mowrer's analysis of avoidance conditioning was based on the assumption that such responding was conditioned or learned. And yet, many investigators have found that it has been quite difficult for their experimental animals to learn selected avoidance responses. Meyer, Cho, and Wesemann (1960), D'Amato and Schiff (1964), and others have reported that bar pressing in order to avoid shock is a very difficult response for the rat to learn, although bar pressing for food is easily acquired. Hoffman and Fleshler (1959), in their examination of pigeons learning to avoid shock by lifting their head, reported that more than 3,000 tone-shock pairings were necessary in order to achieve a 50% level of avoidance responding.

In view of such findings, it could be posited, at least in some instances, that avoidance responses may be unlearned. Bolles (1970) has supported such a position. He has argued that animals come into the world with defense reactions already a prominent part of their response repertoire. The gazelle does not flee from an approaching lion because it has been previously bitten by the lion — it runs away from any large object that approaches it because such responding is innate, one of its species-specific defense reactions (SSDR).

Bolles (1970) has indicated that the organism's SSDR generally takes one of three forms: (1) running or flying away, (2) freezing, or (3) adopting some type of pseudoaggressive response. It would follow from Bolles's hypothesis that some avoidance responses should be more easily learned than others. Thus, if the avoidance response demanded by the experimenter is an SSDR, it should be readily acquired, whereas if it is not, considerable difficulty should be experienced in its acquisition. In keeping with this position, Bolles (1969) found that rats easily learn to avoid shock by running in an activity wheel; in contrast, if the animal must learn to stand on its hind legs to avoid shock, the acquisition of such a response takes place quite slowly, if at all.[4]

The Extinction of Avoidance Responding

There has been no operation generally agreed upon for use in extinguishing an avoidance response. Traditionally, extinction has called for the omission of the US, but as noted earlier, the omission of the aversive stimulus in avoidance conditioning is inappropriate. As a result, alternative methods of extinguishing the avoidance response have been to present the US randomly during the extinction trials or to present the US whenever the subject makes the avoidance response.

When these latter two procedures are contrasted with the traditional method of omitting the US, substantial differences in extinction performance can be noted. In a study by Bolles, Moot, and Grossen (1971), rats were provided with 100 training trials in which they learned to avoid shock by running to an adjacent compartment in a shuttle box. A buzzer served as the CS; the interstimulus interval was 10 seconds. The making of an avoidance response resulted in three conditions: (1) avoidance of the shock, (2) termination of the CS (buzzer), and (3) a 10-second period of lights-out in the "safe" compartment; thus, the animals were given feedback concerning the correctness of their response. During 100 extinction trials, one or more of the three basic conditions were changed. These changes were as follows: (1) the CS continued to be presented after the avoidance response had been made, (2) the light in the safe compartment was not extinguished, and (3) shock was presented after ten-second presentations regardless of the subject's response.

In a second experiment, the shock presentation during extinction trials was further examined by (1) shocking all responses, (2) providing traditional extinction operations in which shock was not presented, or (3) shocking the avoidance response only if it occurred.

Results from both experiments revealed that changing those stimulus conditions that involved continued presentation of the buzzer and light had little influence on extinction. In Experiment 1, continuing to present the buzzer or the light in the safe compartment after the avoidance response had been made had little influence on the rate of extinction—responding continued at a relatively high level throughout the extinction trials.

Manipulating the shock contingency, however, provided different results. Findings revealed that the number of avoidance responses made during extinction for the "punish all responses" group was 25, whereas the group that was punished only when an

---

[4] The interested reader should be aware that other explanations for avoidance conditioning have been proposed. See Denny (1971) for a description of his relaxation theory.

avoidance response was made revealed just 4 responses. This result demonstrated the effectiveness of this latter method of extinguishing avoidance responding.

In summary, these findings suggest that extinction takes place quite slowly if shock is completely removed from the situation. An obvious explanation is that the experimental subjects have no direct opportunity to learn that the aversive stimulus is no longer being presented. If shock is provided for making the avoidance response, the previously acquired contingency between making a response and safety is replaced by a contingency between making a response and punishment.

For groups that are presented with an aversive stimulus with the stimulus not necessarily being contingent with any response, one factor is undoubtedly operative, which results in more rapid extinction by the traditional control group, but less than the punishment group. This factor has to do with the fact that on some trials the presentation of shock takes place shortly after an avoidance response has been made, thus resulting in a punishment trial and facilitating extinction of the response. But it is also possible that the receipt of the shock has been associated with responses made prior to the avoidance response, in which case the task becomes one of escape. The escape response is strengthened by shock reduction, which prolongs avoidance responding.

Solomon, Kamin, and Wynne's Theory of Extinction

Solomon, Kamin, and Wynne (1953), using intense shock in conducting active avoidance learning experiments with dogs, noted that when the traditional method of extinguishing the avoidance response was used (omitting the US), their experimental animals would make hundreds of responses without any decrement in responding. How could such prolonged responding be explained? They provided an explanation based on two principles: the conservation of anxiety and partial irreversibility.

Solomon and associates reasoned that in order to extinguish the instrumental avoidance response it would first be necessary to extinguish the fear response that elicited the avoidance response. But they pointed out that during extinction trials the subject removed itself from the presence of the CS so rapidly that the CS appeared to be almost ineffective in arousing fear. Since the instrumental response was not followed by fear reduction, the instrumental response started to weaken, as revealed by the animal taking a longer time to respond when the CS was presented. But the delay in responding once again allowed the CS sufficient time to elicit the fear response, so that its instrumental avoidance response was once again followed by fear reduction and decreased latency in responding. The authors posited that this state of affairs could result in the experimental subject making avoidance responses for thousands of trials.

Solomon, Kamin, and Wynne (1953) were unable to see how such prolonged extinction noted in avoidance conditioning tasks could be successfully integrated with the findings obtained from appetitive tasks, in which extinction takes place more rapidly. As a result, they posited two principles to account for their unusual findings. The first principle, the conservation of anxiety, arises when the instrumental response to the CS is made too rapidly to permit the CS to elicit fear (or anxiety). In brief, the conditioned fear response is conserved by the rapidity with which the instrumental response is made. The second principle was identified as the principle of partial irreversibility. Here, they posited that the fear or anxiety conditioned under such circumstances is so strong that it can never be extinguished. Such being the case, the instrumental response elicited by the emotional state will continue to be made.

What is the present status of Solomon, Kamin, and Wynne's (1953) position? As we noted earlier, one problem is in demonstrating the pivotal role that fear is presumed to play in eliciting the avoidance response. Black (1959), using dogs as his experimental subjects, conditioned the heart rate response, a presumed indicator of fear, in addition to having his animals learn to make a panel-pushing response in order to avoid intense shock. Black was able to condition both responses, but during extinction trials he found that the heart rate response extinguished before the avoidance response. The correlation between speed of extinction of the avoidance responding and heart rate conditioning was not significant.

Since we have observed in an earlier section that investigators have been unable to find any consistent relationship between the strength of fear and response acquisition, it is not surprising that a similar relationship exists between the strength of fear and extinction. It would appear that until an adequate hypothesis is provided for the acquisition of an avoidance response, any explanation for responding during extinction is premature.

Response Prevention or the Phenomenon of Flooding

Investigators have frequently pointed to an apparent similarity between (1) the persistence of responding in laboratory avoidance learning tasks using animals and (2) some specific human behaviors motivated by anxiety, phobias, and the like. However, many of the laboratory procedures employed to extinguish learned avoidance responses would be difficult to use in modifying human behavior. One method that has shown some promise for dealing with the problem of speeding up the extinction of avoidance responding has been called *response prevention or flooding.*

As originally employed by Solomon, Kamin, and Wynne (1953) and Page and Hall (1953), the flooding procedure consists of preventing the organism from making the avoidance response when the CS is presented, thus indicating to the experimental subject that the aversive stimulus is no longer associated with the CS. In both of these shuttle box avoidance experiments, a barrier was placed between the compartments to prevent the subject from making the instrumental response during extinction trials. Both experiments revealed that extinction of the avoidance response took place much more quickly with this method than with the traditional method of permitting the response to be made but omitting the US.

Both Marks (1972, 1975) and Kazdin (1978) have reported that variations of the flooding procedure have clinical applications. Many investigators have reported that this procedure has been successful in reducing fear and anxiety elicited by snakes, spiders, test-taking situations, and so on. A detailed examination of this topic can be found in Baum (1970) and Mineka (1979).

Learned Helplessness: The Role of Unavoidable Aversive Stimuli

In an earlier section of this chapter, we noted that it was possible for subjects to learn to avoid aversive stimuli. But what if such an avoidance conditioning task was preceded by a procedure whereby the experimental subjects were presented with an aversive stimulus from which they could neither escape nor avoid? Overmier and Seligman (1967) suggested that this type of preliminary treatment in which a series of intense shocks were given to their experimental subjects (dogs) seriously interfered with the animals learning to escape from or avoid shock.

A study by Seligman and Maier (1967) further illustrates the procedure as well as confirms the nature of the experimental findings. The training phase of their experiment consisted of strapping dogs in hammocks that were so constructed that the animal's legs hung below its body through holes cut in the canvas. The animal's head was held in position by two side panels. Three groups of subjects were run. An escape group was given 64 trials in which a five-second shock was applied to the animal's hind leg on each trial. To escape from the shock the animal had to push one of the side panels. A second group received inescapable shock—when shock was presented, the panel-pushing response (or any other response) would not terminate the shock. In order to equate shock duration for the escape and inescapable shock groups, each animal in the inescapable group was paired with an animal in the escape group. The amount of shock received by each animal in the escape group determined the amount of shock that was presented to the paired animals in the inescapable group. Thus, the only way in which the inescapable shock group differed from the escape group was in the lack of control it had over the termination of the shock. Finally, a control group was placed in the hammock but received no shock.

The second phase of the experiment consisted of avoidance/escape training in the shuttle box. A darkening of the experimental chamber served as the CS; 10 seconds later shock was presented. Jumping over a shoulder-high barrier into the adjacent chamber during or after the 10-second CS-US interval enabled the animals to avoid or escape shock. If the animal did not respond in 60 seconds following the onset of shock, the trial was terminated. Ten test trials were provided. The median latency of responding for the three groups can be noted in Figure 7–6. The animals who had received inescapable shock during training were unable to learn the jumping response that would permit them to avoid or escape from the shock.

Maier and Seligman (1976), in describing this earlier study (Seligman and Maier, 1967), have provided an interesting account of the behavior of their animals who had been placed in the avoidance conditioning task:

> [A dog that had been given inescapable shock] runs around frantically for about 30 seconds, but then stops moving, lies down, and quietly whines. After about 1 minute of this, the shock is terminated automatically. The dog fails to cross the barrier and escape from shock. On the next trial, the dog again fails to escape. At first he struggles a bit and then, after a few seconds, seems to give up and passively accept the shock. On all succeeding trials, the dog continues to fail to escape (p. 4).

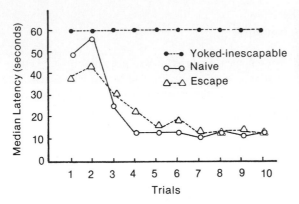

Figure 7–6
Median response latency in a shuttle box for dogs given escapable, yoked inescapable, or no shock in a harness. (Data obtained from Seligman and Maier, 1967.) Figure adapted from S. F. Maier and M. E. P. Seligman, "Learned helplessness: Theory and evidence," *Journal of Experimental Psychology: General,* 1976, *105,* 3–46. Copyright© 1976 by the American Psychological Association. Reprinted by permission.

Such responding is in marked contrast with the control animals not given inescapable shock. These animals, after considerable trial and error behavior, eventually scramble over the barrier and escape shock. On subsequent trials, the escape response occurs much more rapidly. Eventually, the animals learned to avoid shock on almost all of the trials provided near the end of the experimental session.

Seligman and his associates inferred the concept of learned helplessness from the kinds of behavior exhibited by those animals in the inescapable shock group. They assumed that such a state arose when the experimental subject perceived that a particular outcome would take place independent of any response that might be made. Their suggestion was that learned helplessness involved a motivational and cognitive deficit as well as a modification of the organism's emotionality, with depression replacing the fear originally elicited by the shock.[5]

Seligman and Maier's (1976) explanation for their earlier experimental findings has resulted in a number of clinical investigators examining the relationships between learned helplessness and the human clinical disorder of depression. Thus, when humans are used as experimental subjects, learned helplessness has been viewed as being related to an individual's expectancy that he or she cannot control future events, which in turn is responsible for producing depression. Within this context, a variety of experimental

---

[5] It should be pointed out that there is one methodological problem, only recently identified, that is present in some of these studies. It has been generally assumed that since the escape shock group animals were yoked to the inescapable shock group animals, with each group receiving the identical number of shocks, the effects of such stimulation is the same. However, Mineka, Cook, and Miller (1984) have asserted that the response made by the escape group and that terminates the shock provides them with feedback. Such feedback results in less fear for this group than that experienced by the inescapable group, which does not receive any stimulus that has been associated with shock termination. Mineka and associates (1984) have been able to demonstrate such differences in fear as well as show an equivalency of this emotional state when the inescapable group is presented with a stimulus associated with shock termination. As a result, these investigators have questioned the validity of the conclusions of some of the studies conducted in this area that have compared the effects of controllable versus uncontrollable shock, since different amounts of fear are undoubtedly present in the test task.

conditions have been investigated—the generalization of expectancies from one situation to another, how individuals perceive their inability to control future events, the perception of the kinds of helplessness, and so on.

Many investigators, however, have been reluctant to explain the performance of animals provided inescapable shock by positing the construct of learned helplessness. Rather, they have pointed out that the difficulty of the experimental animals in learning the new task might be attributed to their general inactivity, citing the work of many experimenters who have demonstrated that reduced activity does follow inescapable shock (e.g., Anisman, DeCatanzaro, and Remington, 1978; Drugan and Maier, 1982; and Jackson, Maier, and Rapaport, 1978). The Drugan and Maier (1982) study is particularly noteworthy in that inescapable shock was provided via fixed tail electrodes rather than through a grid floor, which results in the animal receiving varying intensities of shock as it moves about the experimental apparatus.

A second factor contributing to poorer performance of animals provided inescapable shock has been hypothesized to be reduced motivation arising from reduced sensitivity to pain (analgesia). A variety of investigators have shown that inescapable shock produces analgesia (e.g., Drugan and Maier, 1982; and Jackson, Maier, and Coon, 1979).

We may note then that the experimental evidence suggests that inescapable shock leads not only to decreased activity but also to reduced sensitivity to pain. Either or both of these factors contribute to poorer learning of the test task.

Recent evidence suggests, however, that another contributor to the animal's learning deficit arising from inescapable shock is due to an associative factor. More specifically, the animals learn that there is no relationship or contingency between any response that they might make and any consequence or outcome. One kind of indirect evidence supporting this hypothesis has been provided by experimenters who have found that subjects may be immunized against the effects of inescapable shock. This immunization procedure consists of providing the animals with a task that permits them to learn to escape from shock prior to experiencing inescapable shock. In a study by Seligman, Rosillini, and Kozak (1975), rats were immunized by giving them training in jumping onto a platform in order to escape shock. The second phase of the study consisted of providing these animals with inescapable shock. Phase three presented a new learning task; here, the animals received shock and had to learn to press a lever in order to terminate it. The immunized animals learned this task significantly more rapidly than animals that had been given only inescapable shock prior to learning the lever-pressing task.

The results from a series of experiments conducted by Rosellini, DeCola, and Shapiro (1982) have provided more direct support for an associative explanation of learned helplessness. Their general procedure consisted of providing rats with preliminary training in which they learned to poke their nose into two laterally positioned holes in order to receive a pellet of food. During such training, the experimenters were able to identify each animal's position preference (e.g., right or left). A stabilimeter, which formed the floor of the hole-poke apparatus, permitted the animal's activity to be measured during these sessions.

The second phase of their experiments consisted of using a shuttle box to provide escape training for one group of animals and to provide inescapable shock for another group. The experimental design employed was a "poking" procedure whereby the amount of shock received by subjects that learned to escape determined the amount of shock received by animals in the inescapable shock group. A control group, which was placed in the shuttle box but given no shock, was also employed.

Following this second phase, all three groups of animals were returned to the hold-poke apparatus where they had to learn to respond to their nonpreferred side in order to receive food.

Ten sessions of 50 trials per session were provided. In one experiment (Experiment 3), the task was extended to include three position reversals, with each reversal commencing only after the animal had reached a criterion of 90% correct on the previous discrimination. Figure 7–7 reveals the mean percentage of correct responses/ session for the (1) inescapable, (2) escapable, and (3) control groups for Experiment 2. Although reduced activity was noted for the inescapable group, it did not play a role in the learning of the discrimination since performance was calculated on the basis of only those trials on which a response occurred. It is difficult to see how an analgesic effect could play any role in the findings since the test task employed food as a reward. We may note, then, that the findings of Rosellini and associates (1982) are in keeping with an associative explanation for the performance deficit exhibited by the inescapable shock group. More specifically, it is posited that these animals learn that there is no contingency between any response that they make and the consequences or outcome that is received.[6]

An examination of the associative explanation for learned helplessness has been a continuing one; a large number of investigations have been undertaken. One interesting study was conducted by Rosillini, DeCola, Plonsky, Warren, and Stilman (1984). These experimenters pointed out that an implicit prediction of the associative explanation is that the acquisition of an expectancy of response-reinforcer independence by the inescapable shock animals should increase the sensitivity of these animals to future instances of such independence. A series of experiments were carried out using a similar apparatus and procedure as we have described earlier (e.g., Rosellini, DeCola, and Shapiro, 1982). A major difference, however, was that after being exposed to the test-task in which there was response-contingent food, test sessions were provided in which there was response-food independence. Results indicated that animals that received inescapable shock stopped responding during these sessions more rapidly than controls, thus supporting the general prediction that uncontrollable aversive events can increase an animal's awareness of noncontingent response-reinforcer relationships.

It will be recalled that in Chapter Three we indicated that US preexposure in a classical conditioning experiment would result in delaying the establishment of a CR. The use of inescapable shock, which results in a subject having difficulty in learning an

---

[6] Jackson, Alexander, and Maier (1980) were able to obtain findings similar to those obtained by Rosellini, DeCola, and Shapiro (1982) and Anisman, Hamilton, and Zacharko (1984) using inescapable shock with mice. However, they were unable to demonstrate that the acquisition of the discrimination response was retarded for those animals that had been exposed to inescapable shock.

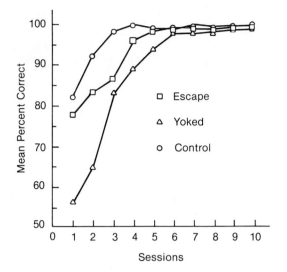

Figure 7-7
Mean percentage of correct trials per session as a function of shock treatment (escapable, yoked inescapable, or no-shock control) for the 10 sessions of the discrimination test. Adapted form R. A. Rosellini, J. P. DeCola, and N. R. Shapiro, "Cross-motivational effects of inescapable shock are associative in nature," *Journal of Experimental Psychology: Animal Behavior Processes*, 1982, *8*, 376–388. Copyright© 1982 by the American Psychological Association. Reprinted with permission.

instrumental conditioning task, would appear to be a similar phenomenon. Mackintosh's (1983) careful analysis of learned helplessness studies has convinced him, however, that in spite of the similarity between the two situations, learned helplessness appears to be a more general phenomenon. (See Box 7-1.) Thus, he writes:

> Exposure to a zero correlation between responding and reinforcement may indeed interfere with the detection of a subsequent correlation between the two, but it is reasonable to assume that the prolonged, severe stress to which subjects are exposed in experiments on learned helplessness has other consequences which are probably responsible for other characteristics of helplessness (pp. 96–97).

Summary ►

Two instrumental conditioning tasks that have interested investigators are punishment and avoidance. Examining the effect of punishment on behavior has had a long history. The writings of Thorndike, Skinner, and Estes suggest that punishment is not an effective way of controlling behavior. Many later investigators, however, have demonstrated that punished responses can be suppressed for long periods of time, provided the punishment is sufficiently severe.

Current experimenters have been interested in examining those punishment variables, namely, delay, intensity, and duration of the aversive stimulus as well as the method of presentation, which have been found to suppress responding. Aversive stimulation had been found to be effective in suppressing a response if the delay between making the response and securing the punishment is minimal, and if such stimulation is quite intense and of long duration. It has also been found that it is better

box 7–1

One interesting consequence of an inability to control aversive stimuli has been reported by Visintainer, Volpicelli, and Seligman (1982). They found that rats experiencing inescapable shock after being implanted with tumor cells were less likely to reject them than control animals. The details of this study were as follows: Sections of a cancerous tumor were injected subcutaneously into the left lower anterior flank of rats. Some 24 hours later, the animals were randomly divided into three groups: (1) those that were provided escapable shock (N#30); (2) those given inescapable shock (N#30); and (3) those not shocked at all (N#33).

Sixty shock trials were presented at random intervals. Animals in the escapable group could terminate the shock at any time by pressing a bar in the experimental chamber. If bar pressing did not occur, the shock ended after 60 seconds. Animals in the inescapable group were yoked to the animals in the escapable group, thus receiving the same amount of shock as their partners but, of course, were helpless to control it.

Tumor rejection was defined as the absence of a tumor 30 days after implantation. The 30-day period was chosen as a result of extensive pilot work showing that all rats that had this tumor 30 days after cell injection died within another 60 days and that no rat that was tumor free after 30 days developed the tumor or died within the next 60 days. Results revealed that rats receiving inescapable shock were only half as likely to reject the tumor and twice as likely to die as rats receiving escapable shock or no shock. The figure below presents this data. Thus, only 27% of the rats given inescapable shock rejected the tumor compared to 63% of the rats given escapable shock and 54% of the rats given no shock. Inescapable shock thus increased the probability that an animal would die by decreasing the rate of tumor rejection. The authors point out that immunological activity is probably an important line of defense against the development of cancer. The present study contributes to the evidence that the immune system appears to be suppressed after uncontrollable aversive events.

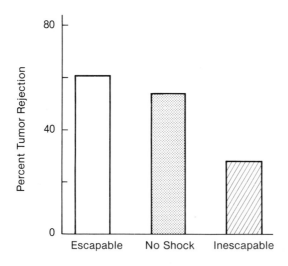

Box Figure 7–1
Tumor rejection in rats subjected to escapable shock, no shock, or inescapable shock. Adapted from M. A. Visintainer, J. B Volpicelli, and M. E. P. Seligman, "Tumor rejection in rats after inescapable or escapable shock," *Science,* 1982, *216,* 437–439. Copyright© 1982 by the American Association for the Advancement of Science. Reprinted with permission.

to provide the experimental subject with an intense aversive stimulus early in training rather than gradually increasing the intensity over presentations.

The second kind of instrumental conditioning task—avoidance conditioning—also involves aversive stimulation; however, if the subject responds to a cue provided prior to the presentation of the aversive stimulus, the response is not punished. Variables that have been shown to influence avoidance conditioning have been the intensity of the aversive stimulus that is used, as well as the interval of time separating the presentation of the cue (CS) and the aversive stimulus (US).

Mowrer's two-factor theory of avoidance conditioning has been a popular one in explaining why such conditioning takes place. Briefly, Mowrer has proposed that the presentation of the cue (CS) and aversive stimulus (US) is a classical conditioning procedure that results in the cue eliciting fear as a conditioned response. Fear also serves as a stimulus to elicit avoidance responding; such responding is reinforced by fear reduction. But many questions have been raised concerning the adequacy of Mowrer's explanation. A basic problem has been the inability of investigators to find a positive relationship between the strength of the avoidance response and the magnitude of the fear response. Solomon, Kamin, and Wynne observed that with continued avoidance training, a point was reached in which their animals appeared to become less afraid, although the avoidance response grew stronger.

Bolles's explanation for avoidance conditioning is that in many instances such avoidance responding is unlearned—animals come into the world with defense reactions already a prominent part of their response repertoire. The innate defense reactions, identified by Bolles as species, specific, defense reactions (SDDR), consist of (1) running or flying away, (2) freezing, or (3) adopting some type of pseudoaggressive response.

Providing an appropriate operation for extinguishing an avoidance response has been a problem for many experimenters. An animal that has learned to make an avoidance response does not have the opportunity to learn that the aversive stimulus is no longer presented. Several different operations for extinguishing the avoidance response have been proposed, with perhaps the most frequently used being to present the aversive stimulus after the avoidance response has been made. Solomon, Kamin, and Wynne have proposed that there are two principles that account for the difficulty of obtaining extinction with avoidance conditioning tasks. One is the conservation of anxiety that arises when the instrumental response to the CS is made too rapidly to permit the CS to elicit fear. The second principle, partial irreversibility, posits that frequently fear is so strong that it can never be extinguished.

chapter eight

▶

Stimulus Generalization
and Discrimination

Stimulus Generalization ▶

In Chapter Two stimulus generalization was acknowledged to be a process that would account for the experimental findings that a classical conditioned response could be elicited by a stimulus other than the conditioned stimulus. Such a finding provided a more extended role for the operation of classical conditioning in our everyday environment, since responding could be elicited by stimuli other than those that were involved in the original training procedure. In the United States, however, only a limited number of generalization studies have been conducted using the classical conditioning paradigm, and there has been far greater interest in examining the generalization process operating with instrumental or operant conditioning. These procedures employ a specifically defined discriminative stimulus that cues the operant or instrumental response; following training, other stimuli usually having some relationship to the discriminative stimulus, are employed to test for stimulus generalization.[1]

Early instrumental conditioning investigators assumed that it was necessary to follow Hovland's procedure of using a jnd scale—an assumption that resulted in a dearth of early animal studies since establishing a jnd scale with animals is difficult and laborious. But Grice and Saltz (1950) rejected the necessity of using a jnd scale with

---

[1] Many operant conditioning investigators do not use the term *stimulus generalization*. Rather, they employ the term *stimulus control* since the experimental operations utilized in generalization studies enable the experimenter to assess the degree to which the subject's behavior is elicited by the presentation of generalized stimuli. The operant investigator is interested in the control that both the training stimulus and the generalized stimuli have over the experimental subject's responding.

animals and proceeded to examine generalization using test stimuli that were physically similar to the training stimulus. Their apparatus was a runway ending at a white disk placed on the door leading to food. The disk served as the discriminative stimulus. One group of rats was trained to run to a 20 sq. cm. disk, whereas a second group was trained to run to a 79 sq. cm. disk. The test for stimulus generalization used disks of different size. For these test trials, the group that had trained on the 79 sq. cm. disk was divided into five subgroups; each group was given test trials using a disk of either 79, 63, 50, 32, or 20 sq. cm. The group trained on the 20 sq. cm. disk was divided into four subgroups; each of these subgroups was tested with a disk of either 20, 32, 50, or 79 sq. cm. The stimulus generalization curves obtained from these groups are shown in Figure 8–1.[2]

The Grice and Saltz (1950) study was important for several reasons. Many psychologists had assumed that the true shape of the generalization curve was concave, as Hovland (1937a) had previously found. Grice and Salt's findings indicated that the form of the generalization curve was not constant but was a function of the experimental conditions employed. Their study also demonstrated the feasibility of examining generalization using animals and scaling the test stimuli along a physical dimension.

But Grice and Saltz's study did raise one methodological problem. Since 25 nonrewarded trials were used in their test for generalization, it was likely that the extinction process was contributing to the test performance of the experimental animals, but there was no way of assessing its contribution, either in terms of overall responding or to specific stimuli. How best to overcome this difficulty? One answer was provided by operant investigators. By placing animals on some type of interval or ratio reinforcement schedule during acquisition, one could obtain a large number of generalization test responses that were relatively uninfluenced by the extinction process.

One of the early studies of this type was conducted by Guttman and Kalish (1956), who trained pigeons to peck at an illuminated key in order to receive food. Different groups were trained under a variable interval schedule. The training stimulus was presented for 60 seconds, followed by 10 seconds when the experimental lights were turned off (blackout), followed by 60 seconds of stimulus presentation, and so on. Four groups of birds were trained to respond to one of the colors, measured in nanometers (nm): 530 nm, 550 nm, 580 nm, or 600 nm. After stable responding or maintenance behavior had been established, generalization testing using extinction trials was carried out. Eleven different hues, ranging from 470 nm to 640 nm, were randomly presented in a test series; each hue appeared for 30 seconds. Twelve of these sessions were provided. The findings obtained with each training stimulus are presented in Figure 8–2. When all of these values are combined, the resultant gradient is as shown in Figure

---

[2] One methodological question must be answered in stimulus generalization studies—whether to use an absolute or relative response measure of generalization. Most experimenters, as Grice and Saltz (1950) have done, use an absolute measure. Here, the generalization curve is plotted as a function of the absolute number of responses made to the varying test stimuli that are used. If there is a great deal of response variability among subjects, a relative measure is frequently used. Here, the response data are transformed to reveal the number of responses made to the generalized stimuli as a percentage of the number of responses made to the training stimulus.

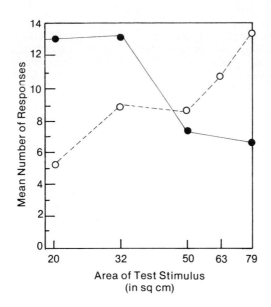

Figure 8-1
Generalization functions showing mean number of extinction responses for each test group. The solid line indicates the group trained on the 20 sq. cm. disk; the dotted line indicates the group trained on the 79 sq. cm. disk. Adapted from G. R. Grice and E. Saltz, "The generalization of an instrumental response to stimuli varying in the size dimension," *Journal of Experimental Psychology,* 1950, *40,* 702–708. Copyright© 1950 by the American Psychological Association. Reprinted by permission.

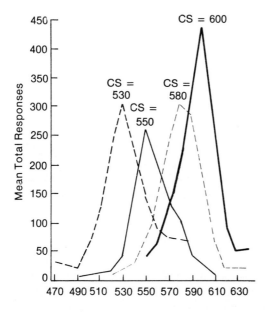

Figure 8-2
Mean total responses on the generalization test as a function of the wavelength of the stimuli for four groups for whom the original CS was either 530, 550, 580, or 600 nm. Adapted from N. Guttman and H. I. Kalish, "Discriminability and stimulus generalization," *Journal of Experimental Psychology,* 1956, *51,* 79–88. Copyright© 1956 by the American Psychological Association. Reprinted by permission.

8-3. This gradient, although concave, differs markedly from Hovland's (1937a) classic curve and thus confirms the results of Grice and Saltz (1950), whose findings indicated that stimulus generalization was a function of the experimental conditions that were employed.

Figure 8-3

The mean generalization gradient for all CS groups combined. Adapted form N. Guttman and H. I. Kalish, "Discriminability and stimulus generalization," *Journal of Experimental Psychology,* 1956, *51,* 79–88. Copyright© 1956 by the American Psychological Association. Reprinted by permission.

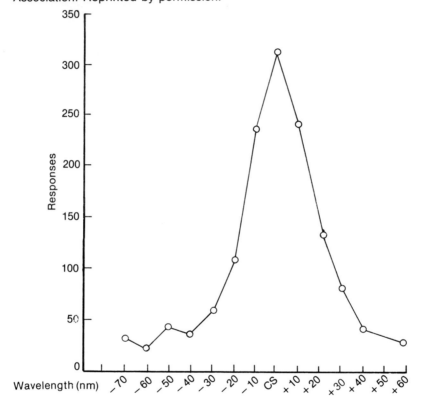

Guttman and Kalish's (1956) study was of major methodological significance. Their findings demonstrated the feasibility of using an operant procedure to investigate stimulus generalization gradients that appeared to be uninfluenced by the extinction process.

In the studies we have just cited, only visual stimuli have been used in the examination of stimulus generalization. There is no reason to assume, however, that the generalization process does not operate when stimuli received by other sense modalities are utilized. One example is found in a study by Riccio, Urda, and Thomas (1966) examining the generalization of proprioceptive stimulation. Pigeons were first trained to peck an illuminated disk using a VI schedule. The floor of the experimental apparatus was level, thus providing the pigeons with a particular pattern of proprioceptive stimulation. After responding had stabilized, the subjects were provided a stimulus generalization test in which the floor was tilted at varying amounts away from the original position experienced during training. Test trials in which the floor orientation was changed revealed that the proprioceptive stimulation during training had acquired some control over the pecking response. Thus, when the floor was oriented away from that provided during original training, there was a decrement in responding. The amount of decremental responding was a function of the difference between the floor tilt experienced during training and that provided during the test periods.

Generalization of Inhibition

Following the work of Grice and Saltz (1950), who used animals in their examination of the generalization of excitatory tendencies, studies by Kling (1952), Honig (1961), and Dubin and Levis (1973) (also using animals) examined the generalization of inhibition. Working with rats, Kling (1952) utilized the same type of apparatus and methodology employed by Grice and Saltz (1950). In contrast, Honig's (1961) experiment mirrored the method pioneered by Guttman and Kalish (1956). In this study, pigeons were placed on a VI schedule and trained to peck at a key in which 13 different colored stimuli, ranging from 510 nm to 630 nm, were presented and equally reinforced. Two experimental groups then had their responses to the 570 nm stimulus extinguished; one group was given just one extinction session and the other group was given two such sessions. A control group was not given any extinction trials. Generalization testing was then instituted; each of the 13 colored stimuli was presented without reinforcement. Results for the control group and the two experimental groups are shown in Figure 8–4. It may be noted that for the two experimental groups an orderly inhibition gradient was obtained; the smallest number of responses was made to the 570 nm stimulus that received extinction training. Dubin and Levis's (1973) study, using tones rather than color as the experimental stimuli, has confirmed the findings of Honig (1961). Church and Gibbon's (1982) study (Experiment 7), examining the generalization of temporal stimuli, manipulated by presenting house lights for varying lengths of time and using lever pressing as a response measure for their experimental animals (rats), has provided recent confirmation of the generalization of inhibition.

Stimulus Variables Influencing the Generalization Process ▶

After the stimulus generalization process had been demonstrated, it is not surprising that investigators became interested in examining a number of the conditions that contribute to this process. One thread that ties many of these studies together is how these varying conditions influence the discriminability of the stimuli that are used in the training and testing procedure. Intuitively, it would seem that any condition that made it easier for the experimental subject to discriminate between the original training stimulus and the test stimuli should produce a steeper generalization gradient; conversely, if the experimental variable resulted in discrimination becoming more difficult, the generalization gradient would become flatter.

Figure 8–4
Response rates for the two experimental and one control group at the end of training and for generalization of extinction. Adapted from Figures 1, 2, and 3, by W. K. Honig, "Generalization of extinction on the spectral continuum," *The Psychological Record,* 1961, *11,* 269–278.

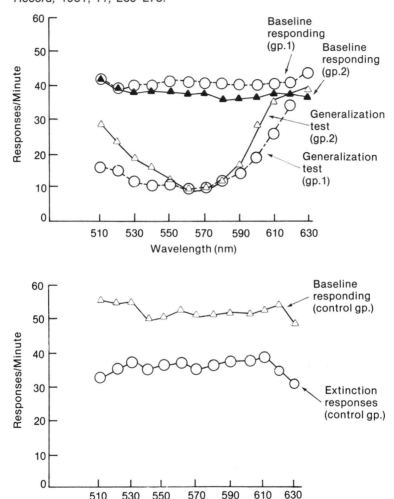

Time of Testing

If the test for generalization is provided sometime after the original training has been completed, is there greater generalization than if such testing is provided immediately following the acquisition trials? The studies of Perkins and Weyant (1958), Thomas and Lopez (1962), and McAllister and McAllister (1963) have all demonstrated a flatter generalization gradient when the testing period is delayed. The interpretation of the finding is that delay enhances the possibility of the subject confusing the original stimulus with the test stimulus.

In Perkins and Weyant's (1958) study, four groups of rats were trained to traverse a black (or white) alley in order to obtain food in a goal box. Animals then received generalization test trials immediately following the training or seven days later. Half of each group was provided trials on the same black (or white) runway as was used during training; the other half was given trials on a different runway. Running speed was used as the response measure. The findings, shown in Figure 8–5, indicate that the group not tested until seven days after the original training produced a much flatter generalization curve than the groups tested immediately after training.

One variation of the time of testing variable is found in a study conducted by Blough (1975) examining the pecking response of pigeons placed under a FI schedule. It will be recalled that in Chapter Five we indicated that stabilized responding under an FI schedule reveals that the experimental subject makes relatively few responses early in the interval, followed by increased rates of responding as the time for reinforcement approaches. In Blough's experiment, a FI schedule was used where stimulus generalization was examined over each five-second increment of a 20-second period during which time the stimuli to which the pigeon responded was tabulated. (After 20 seconds, any response during the next 10 seconds turned off the stimulus and produced a gray square, which was followed about 10 percent of the time by reinforcement.) The S+ was a 597 nm hue, with 24 generalized stimuli being utilized, ranging from 570 to 617 nm. Blough's findings are presented in Figure 8–6. Here it can be noted that during the first quarter of the 20-second period the pigeons are responding at a very low rate, and a relative steep generalization gradient is obtained. As rate of responding increases, the gradient becomes flatter so that by the last five seconds of the interval almost a flat gradient can be observed. It is obvious that the pigeons are able to make the discrimination between training and test colors since a relatively steep gradient is noted during the first five seconds of the reinforcement interval. As the interval approaches the time for reward, however, it appears that the birds' increased expectancy for reward with its accompanying increase in response rate overshadows the selectivity of responding that

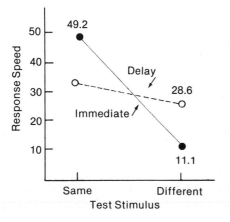

Figure 8–5
Median response speed (100/response time in seconds) for the two test conditions. Adapted from C. C. Perkins Jr. and R. G. Weyant, "The interval between training and test trials as a determiner of the slope of generalization gradients," *Journal of Comparative and Physiological Psychology,* 1958, *51,* 596–600. Copyright© 1958 by the American Psychological Association. Reprinted by permission.

Figure 8-6
Mean data from a single bird across four sessions (60 stimulus series) under a condition of food reinforcement at S+. (The 20-second trial interval is broken down into four 5-second periods.) Adapted from D. S. Blough, "Steady state data and a quantitative model of operant generalization and discrimination," *Journal of Experimental Psychology,* 1975, *104,* 3–21. Copyright© 1975 by the American Psychological Association. Reprinted by permission.

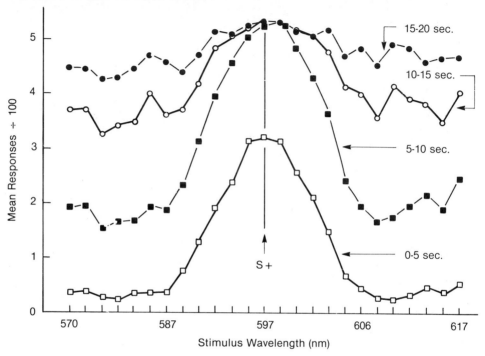

was noted during the first five-second interval. The result is that the training stimulus exerts very little control over the birds' responding.

Amount of Training

Several experimental studies have demonstrated that the possibility of confusing the training stimulus and test stimulus may be reduced by giving the subject more training with the original stimulus. In Hearst and Koresko's (1968) study, pigeons were placed on a VI schedule and trained to peck at a vertical line (0°) that was projected on a response key. Training sessions, lasting 50 minutes each, were provided each day for either 2, 4, 7, or 14 days. Following such training, generalization tests were given. Each of the eight orientations of the stimulus line—four on each side of verticality (e.g., 22.5°, 45°, 67.5°, or 90°)—was presented in random order a single time, thus forming a test series; ten such series were provided. Two experiments were conducted, one utilizing White Carneaux birds, the other using White King. Figure 8–7 presents the findings. It may be noted that as the number of days of training increased, the

Figure 8-7
Gradients of generalization for groups receiving 2, 4, 7, or 14 days of VI training. The training stimulus for all Ss was a vertical line (0°) on the response key. White Carneaux (WC) birds are shown on the left, White King (WK) on the right. Adapted from E. Hearst and M. B. Koresko, "Stimulus generalization and amount of prior training on variable interval reinforcement," *Journal of Comparative and Physiological Psychology,* 1968, *66,* 133–138. Copyright© 1968 by the American Psychological Association. Reprinted by permission.

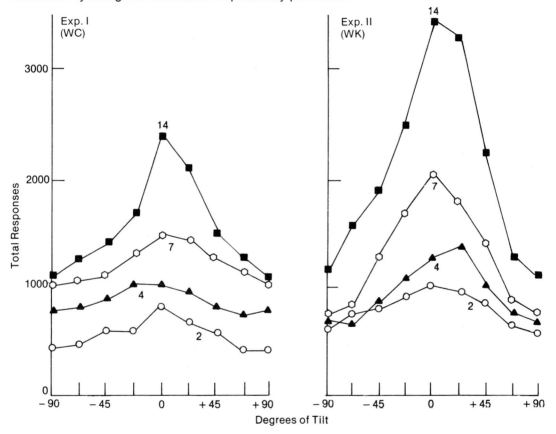

generalization gradient became steeper, thus supporting the position that more training results in increased discriminability between the training stimulus and each of the test stimuli.

The Discriminability of Stimuli

The results of many of the studies we have just described may be explained by hypothesizing that the experimental conditions manipulated served to increase or decrease the subject's ability to discriminate the stimulus used in the original training from the test stimuli. In fact, many consider generalization and discrimination to be different ways of explaining the same behavior. Brown (1965) has written that "generalization and discrimination turn out to be nothing more than two different ways of reporting the same experimental results" (p. 11).

If such is the case, then greater amounts of generalization should be obtained when it is difficult to discriminate the training and test stimuli from one another than when such stimuli are easy to discriminate. The findings obtained in an experiment conducted by Kalish (1958) confirm this. Kalish's procedure consisted of presenting a specific visual stimulus as a training stimulus or standard and instructing his college student subjects to try to remember it. Hues of 500, 560, and 580 nm were used as standards while the test stimuli presented were four hues above and four hues below the standard with each test hue separated by 10 nm. Subjects responded by lifting their hand from a telegraph key if the test stimulus was the same as the standard. Findings indicated that the shape of the stimulus generalization gradient obtained with each standard hue conformed to the discriminability curve obtained for human subjects.[3] Kalish concluded from these findings that there is "striking evidence for the supposition that the processes of generalization and discrimination, as generally defined, bear an inverse relationship dependent upon the characteristics of the underlying stimulus continuum" (p. 642). Thomas and Mitchell (1962), in a later study, obtained results confirming Kalish's findings.

Previous Discrimination Training

Discrimination has been assumed to play an important role in the stimulus generalization process, and yet, for more than two decades after Hovland's (1937a, 1937b, 1937c, 1937d) early studies, discrimination tasks were never used in generalization experiments. But just how does the learning of a discrimination during training trials influence the generalization process?

Hanson (1959) used an operant task to answer this question. Four groups of pigeons were provided discrimination training in which the S+ was a 550 nm hue and the S− was either 555, 560, 570, or 590 nm. A control group was trained to respond only to the presentation of a 550 nm hue. Following VI training, the subjects were given tests for generalization with 13 hues ranging from 480 to 620 nm. The generalization gradients for the groups are shown in Figure 8–8.

Several findings should be noted. First, the control group that did not have the benefit of discrimination training produced a much flatter gradient than those groups that were provided discrimination training. Second, discrimination training resulted in a much steeper generalization gradient being obtained on the S− side; as the S− grew more distant from the S+, the gradient became less steep. The presentation of a 560 nm test stimulus, for example, resulted in the group with an S− of 590 nm producing the largest number of responses, followed by those groups trained with S−s of 570, 560,

---

[3] It has been well established that human subjects cannot discriminate among the varying hues in the visual spectrum with equal accuracy. For example, it is more difficult to discriminate among some of the yellow-orange hues (e.g., 590–600 nm) than it is to discriminate among some of the green hues (530–540 nm).

Figure 8–8
Mean generalization gradients for the control and four discrimination groups, identified
by the values of the negative stimulus. Arrows indicate the positions of the negative
stimuli. Adapted from H. M. Hanson, "Effects of discrimination on stimulus generalization," *Journal of Experimental Psychology*, 1959, *58*, 321–334. Copyright© 1959 by the
American Psychological Association. Reprinted by permission.

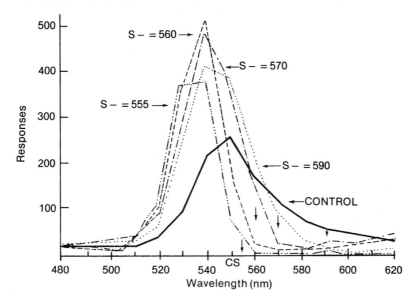

and 550 nm. Finally, it should be noted that the presentation of the discriminative
stimulus (S+) did not elicit maximum responding during the test for generalization.
Instead, there was a shift of maximum responding from the S+ in a direction away
from the S−. Thus, more responses were made to the 540 nm test stimulus than to the
550 nm hue which served as the S+. Such displaced responding to the S+ during
generalization tests has been identified as *peak shift*. This phenomenon has been of
theoretical interest, since it suggests that responding to the S− during training trials has
produced an inhibitory state that has generalized to adjacent stimuli, resulting in a
shifting of maximum responding away from the S+. Purtle (1973) has provided an
extensive review of the peak shift phenomenon.[4]

It has been obvious from Hanson's (1959) findings that discrimination training
resulted in a steeping or sharpening of the generalization gradient, with the steepening
confined primarily to the side of the S−. Subsequent studies by Hanson (1961) and
Thomas and Williams (1963) demonstrated that such steepening can be obtained on

---

[4] A theory of discrimination learning proposed by Spence (1936, 1937a, 1937b) and Hull
(1939, 1943), which we shall briefly describe later in this chapter, has been used by some
investigators to explain peak shift findings. Inasmuch as the Spence-Hull theory has proven to be
deficient on many counts in its explanation for discrimination learning, the value of any
presentation of this explanation for peak shift is questionable.

both sides of the S+ if two S−s are used. In Hanson's study, one group of pigeons was given discrimination training in which responses to a 555 nm hue were rewarded but responses to the two S− stimuli (540 and 560) were not reinforced. A control group was trained to respond only to the 550 nm hue. Following training, there were 12 generalization test sessions consisting of random presentations of stimuli ranging from 490 to 610 nm. The findings, shown in Figure 8-9, reveal a relatively symmetrical gradient for both groups of subjects, although responding by the experimental group was restricted to those stimuli bounded by the two nonreinforced stimuli.

A more recent examination of the role of discrimination training on generalization is found in a temporal generalization study conducted by Church and Gibbon (1982). Their general procedure was to turn off the house light (responsible for illuminating the

Figure 8-9
Mean generalization for a control group not given discrimination training and an experimental group trained on a discrimination with the 550 nm stimulus reinforced and the 540 and 560 nm stimuli not reinforced. Adapted from H. M. Hanson, "Stimulus generalization following three-stimulus discrimination training," *Journal of Comparative and Physiological Psychology,* 1961, *54,* 181–185. Copyright© 1961 by the American Psychological Association. Reprinted by permission.

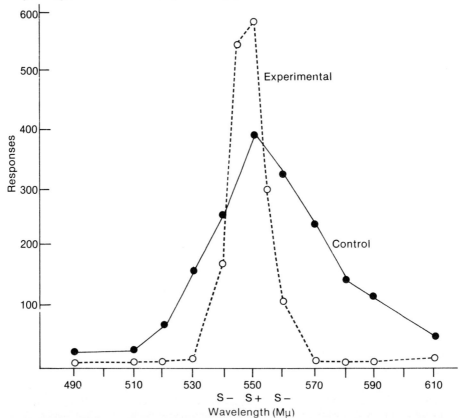

experimental chamber) for either 0.8, 4.0, or 7.2 seconds. Half of those presentations (or trials) were 4.0 seconds in length, whereas the other half of the trials were randomly selected to have dark periods of either 0.8 or 7.2 seconds. At the end of the darkened period, the house light was turned on and a response lever was inserted into the chamber. If the dark (or discriminative stimulus) period was 4.0 seconds in duration, depression of the lever resulted in reinforcement; if the signal was either 0.8 or 7.2 seconds in length, lever pressing was not followed by reward. (If a lever press was not made, the lever was withdrawn at the end of five seconds.) A second group of animals was given similar treatment except that the nonreinforced signal durations were one and 16 seconds of darkness. Following training, tests for generalizations were provided by darkening the experimental chamber for one of the nine durations, spaced at 0.8 second intervals (e.g., 0.8, 1.6, 2.4, 3.2, 4.0, 4.8, 5.6, 6.4, and 7.2 seconds). During these trials, lever pressing to the 4.0-second signal continued to result in reinforcement. Results are presented in Figure 8–10 and reveal a generalization gradient not unlike those obtained by earlier experimenters.[5,6]

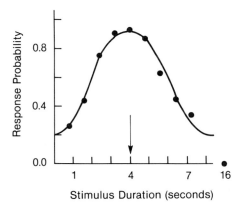

Figure 8–10
Stimulus generalization gradient obtained with rats trained to respond after a four-second stimulus presentation and then tested with stimuli of differing durations. Adapted from R. M. Church and J. Gibbon, "Temporal generalization," *Journal of Experimental Psychology: Animal Behavior Processes,* 1982, *8*, 165–186. Copyright© 1982 by the American Psychological Association. Reprinted by permission.

---

[5] Church and Gibbon (1982) conducted seven experiments in all; their general findings replicated as well as extended the results of earlier stimulus generalization studies. By adding to the number and range of darkened nonreinforced periods of time to include 11.3, 19.0 and 32.0 seconds, relatively low but similar levels of lever pressing were noted for these extended durations. The location of peak responding at the four-second period was not influenced by these additional durations. If separate groups of subjects were run with the duration of the reinforced temporal period (either two, four, or eight seconds), results indicated that response probability was highest at each reinforced duration. If a partial reinforcement regimen was introduced, there was an overall decrease in response probability of responding at both rewarded and nonrewarded temporal durations. The form of the generalization function was similar in the two conditions.

[6] Virtually all of the instrumental or operant conditioning studies examining stimulus generalization have used rats or pigeons as experimental subjects. A few investigators have employed human subjects but for the most part this work has not been integrated with the findings obtained with animals. See Brown, Bilodeau, and Baron (1951), Thomas and Jones (1962), and Thomas and DeCapito (1966) for an illustration of studies using humans.

Interpretations of Stimulus Generalization

How can the phenomenon of stimulus generalization be explained? Our examination of stimulus generalization of classical conditioned responses in Chapter Two did not include any theoretical accounts of the phenomenon. Most current theoretical positions have proposed explanations applicable to both classical and instrumental reward conditioning tasks. As a result, we delayed discussion of theory until we could examine the experimental contributions provided by instrumental reward studies.

Early Theoretical Accounts   Pavlov assumed that stimulus generalization was due to a fading wave of excitation irradiating from the point on the cortex that was stimulated by the presentation of the CS. Test stimuli whose cortical representations were contiguous to the CS could elicit the conditioned response. But Pavlov also assumed that the wave of excitation produced by the CS grew progressively weaker as a function of its distance from the cortical representations of the CS; thus, the excitation arising from the test stimuli and coming in contact with these weak excitatory represenions of the CS would elicit only a weak response.

Physiologists have found no evidence of neural excitation spreading in this fashion, so Pavlov's neurological explanation of stimulus generalization is no longer accepted. Thompson (1965) has written that Pavlov's "concepts of spreading cortical waves of excitation and inhibition become difficult to interpret with the advent of the neuron doctrine in neurophysiology" (p. 154).

Spence (1936, 1937a, and 1937b) and Hull (1943), working in the tradition of Pavlov, did not make any neurological assumptions about the stimulus generalization process. They did assume, however, that as a result of conditioning trials, the conditioned response became associated with a zone of stimuli adjacent to the CS. The development of this zone of stimuli—or afferent continuum, as Hull phrased it—arose as an innate characteristic of the organism, so the process responsible for the organism responding to a stimulus located within this zone was identified as primary stimulus generalization.

Several assumptions were important to the Spence-Hull explanation of stimulus generalization. First, it was assumed that subjects responding to test stimulus did so not because they were unable to discriminate such stimuli from the CS, but because of the excitatory tendencies that had been established between the test stimuli and the response during training. Second, inhibition was also assumed to generalize, with the shape of the generalization gradient being similar to that produced by excitation. Finally, the process of secondary stimulus generalization was posited. This accounted for responding when the connections among stimuli located along the afferent continuum had been learned rather than produced by the innate characteristics of the organism.

The Spence-Hull position was challenged by Lashley and Wade (1946), who wrote that "stimulus generalization is generalization only in the sense of failure to note distinguishing characteristics of the stimulus or to associate them with the conditioned reaction" (p. 81). From this point of view, stimulus generalization was nothing more than a failure on the part of the subject to differentiate the conditioned stimulus from the generalized stimulus presented during the test period. These authors further argued that the generalization gradients obtained were only products of the testing procedure. That is, the test trials directed the subject's attention to the relevant stimulus attributes that differentiated the conditioned stimulus from the test stimulus. When the difference between the training stimulus and test stimulus was noted by the subject, there was a decline in responding (or weaker response) that characterized the generalization gradient.

Neither theoretical position has had the support of current investigators. One of the problems with the Spence-Hull position was the fact that many investigators rejected their premise that learning consisted of the establishment of specific stimulus-response relationships. Moreover, the Spence-Hull assumption that there was a continuum of stimuli surrounding the training stimulus which automatically became associated with the response as a function of reinforced trials appeared most questionable.

Lashley and Wade's position has not fared any better. These authors emphasized the necessity for the subject to be aware of the stimulus dimension that differentiated the CS from the generalization test stimulus in order for a decremental generalization gradient to be demonstrated. This position suggested an interesting experimental test — raising experimental subjects under conditions in which the subjects would never have the opportunity to be aware of the relevant stimulus attribute (or dimension) which would be subsequently changed in a test for stimulus generalization. The Lashley and Wade position would predict that, since these organisms had never experienced changes in this attribute, a flat generalization gradient would be obtained from the findings.

A study by Peterson (1962) illustrates the frequently used experimental procedure that examines Lashley and Wade's point of view, as well as providing support for this position. Ducklings were raised from birth in cages illuminated only by a monochromatic light of 589 nm and were subsequently trained to peck at a 589 nm illuminated key. Following training, they were tested for stimulus generalization using keys illuminated with eight different wavelengths ranging from 480 to 650 nm. The obtained generalization gradient was flat; the birds responded with equal frequency to all of the stimuli used. The results for the control birds, which had been raised normally, showed the decremental stimulus generalization gradient obtained by investigators.

Unfortunately, Peterson's (1962) results have not stood the test of time; many later experimenters have been unable to replicate his findings. Mountjoy and Malott (1968) and Riley and Leuin (1971), using chicks, Rudolph, Honig, and Gerry (1969), using quail and chicks, and Tracy (1970), using ducklings, have all found decremental stimulus generalization gradients after raising their birds in an environment in which exposure to visual stimuli was carefully controlled.

The Riley and Leuin (1971) study illustrates the nature of these results. After hatching, White Leghorn chickens were maintained in a light-tight brooder illuminated by a monochromatic light of 589 nm. Beginning at 10 days of age, the birds were trained over a four-day period to peck at a translucent key illuminated with a 589 nm light. A VI-1 minute schedule was used. After training, three days of testing were provided. Each day 21 extinction trials were presented in which the key was illuminated by test stimuli of 589 nm, 569 nm, and 550 nm. One group of subjects that was

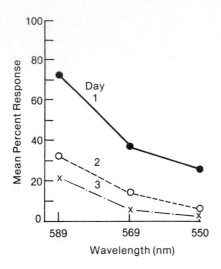

Figure 8-11
Mean relative generalization gradient for chicks tested with all three wavelength values. Adapted from D. A. Riley and T. C. Leuin, "Stimulus-generalization gradients in chickens reared in monochromatic light and tested with a single wavelength value," *Journal of Comparative and Physiological Psychology,* 1971, *75,* 399–402. Copyright© 1971 by the American Psychological Association. Reprinted by permission.

tested with all three wavelengths produced generalization curves, as indicated in Figure 8–11. The curves are not flat, as had been predicted by Lashley and Wade's hypothesis.

Current Considerations   The theoretical positions of Spence and Hull, and Lashley and Wade have undergone considerable modification over the years. These revised positions have not provided a complete explanation of the stimulus generalization process, but they have contributed to a better understanding of the phenomenon. At present, there is no single explanation of stimulus generalization that will adequately account for the myriad of findings. Since stimulus generalization has been demonstrated with almost every type of organism, using both very simple and complex stimuli and a variety of learning tasks, it is undoubtedly unrealistic for an investigator to provide an explanation that will account for all of the findings. But let us consider the thrust of some of the explanations that have been proposed.

If the training and test stimuli used in the stimulus generalization experiment can be placed along some basic sensory continuum, such as hue or brightness for visual stimuli, the presentation of a specific stimulus value during training trials will elicit a cortical response to the training stimulus and to other stimulus values that lie on the same sensory continuum. After the organism has learned to respond to the training stimulus, responding will also be elicited by these other stimulus values, thus providing a generalization gradient. One explanation was proposed by Thompson (1965) who suggested that "that the amount of behavioral stimulus generalization given by the organism to a test stimulus is a monotonic increasing function of the degree of overlap of excitation in the cerebral cortex resulting from a training and test stimulus" (p. 159). Some physiological evidence has supported Thompson's explanation. For example, if a green hue strikes the retina of the eye, retinal elements that are maximally sensitive to that cue will fire, but other hues similar to green may also fire retinal elements; the probability that a hue will fire an element is a function of its distance from the original hue. Presumably, training trials have produced differential associative strength between the response and a range of stimuli, so the presentation of a test stimulus may elicit a response, but one reduced in strength.

If the learning task utilizes a more complex discriminative stimulus, consisting of several relatively discrete stimulus elements (e.g., a white circle on a red background), some investigators have theorized that these varying stimulus elements will provide differential control over the response. Subjects tested for generalization will respond to the test stimulus to the extent that the stimulus elements contained in the first stimulus overlap elements that comprise the training stimulus. The smaller the overlap of the stimulus elements, the weaker the generalized response. For example, when a pigeon is reinforced for pecking at a red disk on which a white circle has been placed, it has been assumed that the organism's response is associated with both stimulus elements—the redness and the circularity. The presentation of a generalized stimulus, such as just one of these elements, will elicit a response that will be weaker than the one made to the presentation of both stimulus elements. The explanation for this is that smaller amounts of associative strength exist between the single element and the response. These explanations have their antecedents in the Spence-Hull position, since it has been assumed that during training trials associative strength is established between all of the varying attributes of the stimulus and the response. The strength of the response elicited by the test stimulus during the generalization test is related to the strength of the original S-R relationship.

A more cognitive oriented explanation has been proposed by Riley and Lamb (1979). They suggested that during training the experimental subject classifies or identifies the stimulus along some dimension, and then responds in keeping with the payoff that has accompanied such responding. One examination of this position was provided in an early study by Cumming and Eckerman (1965), who had pigeons learn a discrimination task. Responding to the keys on the extreme right side of a brightly illuminated (1.1 log foot-lamberts) 10-inch stimulus strip of 20 response keys would result in food; responding to the keys on the extreme left side of the strip when it was dimly illuminated (0.1 log-lamberts) would also result in food. Following such training, generalization testing was provided in which four brightness values (0.1, 0.6, 0.8, and 1.1 foot-lamberts) were presented. An examination of where the pigeons pecked along the strip of response keys when the generalized test stimuli (0.6 and 0.8 log-lamberts) were presented disclosed that the birds distributed their pecks to these two brightnesses at the two ends of the strip. Such responding suggested that they classified each generalized stimulus in terms of bright and dim and responded appropriately.

An explanation for the many examples of stimulus generalization found in human behavior may be related to Riley and Lamb's (1979) classification hypothesis and what Bruner, Goodnow, and Austin (1960) termed *categorized behavior.* Bruner, Goodnow, and Austin write that "to categorize is to render discriminably different things equivalent, to group the objects and events and people around us into classes, and to respond to them in terms of their class membership rather than their uniqueness" (p. 1). Thus, if the training stimulus and test stimulus were classified by the subject as equivalent because of identical class membership, the result would be that the subject responded to the test stimulus. But such responding could not be attributed to any stimulus generalization process, since the training and test stimuli were regarded by the subject as identical.

Summary ▶

Stimulus generalization, as originally discovered by Pavlov in his classical conditioning studies, refers to the capacity of a stimulus other than the CS to elicit the conditioned response. Most current investigators, however, have used either instrumental or conditioning procedures to examine this process.

A stimulus generalization experiment conducted by Grice and Saltz (1950) in the 1950s was important because it demonstrated that this process could operate with animals learning an instrumental task. In this study, the relationship between the discriminative stimulus and the test stimuli was based on the physical similarity of the stimuli rather than psychological similarity (as with the jnds).

Guttman and Kalish (1953) examined stimulus generalization using an operant procedure. Pigeons placed on an interval or ratio reinforcement schedule were trained to peck at an illuminated disk. The color of the disk served as the discriminative and test stimuli. Their procedure has been extensively used in generalization studies.

Pavlov was an early investigator to demonstrate the generalization of inhibitory tendencies. The method used was to condition a response to several CSs. One CS was then extinguished; the other CSs served as test stimuli. Results showed that the capacity of these other CSs to elicit the CR was diminished as a result of the one CS undergoing extinction.

Stimulus generalization has generated a great deal of interest among current investigators. Many studies have been designed to examine how selected conditions influence the generalization process. Time of testing, amount of training, and the discriminability of the stimuli are three variables that have been found to influence generalization. Discrimination training provided prior to the generalization test has also been of experimental interest; findings indicate that such training produces a much steeper gradient than that of control groups not provided discrimination training.

Several theoretical explanations for stimulus generalization have been provided. Pavlov believed that generalization was due to a fading wave of excitation that irradiated from the point on the cortex stimulated by the presentation of the CS; however, physiologists have found no evidence for neural excitation spreading in this fashion. Hull (1943) assumed that as a result of conditioning trials, the conditioned response became associated with a zone of stimuli, making up an afferent stimulus continuum. Presentation of a test stimulus that was located along this continuum elicited generalized responding. Lashley and Wade (1946) posited that stimulus generalization resulted from a failure on the part of the subject to differentiate the conditioned stimulus from the test stimulus presented during the test period.

Current research findings suggest that stimulus generalization is a complex phenomenon for which there may be several explanations. When basic sensory stimuli are used, there may be a physiological base for responses that are made to test stimuli. In other instances, the response may arise from learning, the subject having learned to categorize different stimuli as equivalent.

chapter nine

▶

Discrimination Learning: General Considerations

We have chosen to consider discrimination learning apart from the classical and instrumental conditioning sections although, quite obviously, the basic classical and instrumental conditioning operations are utilized when discrimination learning is examined. Our reason for treating discrimination learning separately rests on both empirical and theoretical considerations. Empirically, we shall note that a number of variables that contribute to discrimination learning cannot be manipulated in either the simple classical conditioning task or in the nonsignaled (or signaled) stimulus instrumental conditioning experiment. Theoretically, explanations proposed for discrimination learning do not have relevance for classical or instrumental conditioning tasks.

Discrimination Operations, Tasks, and Discriminanda ▶

It will be recalled from Chapters Two and Five that investigators can employ either classical or instrumental conditioning operations in their employment of a discrimination task. With classical conditioning, two CSs are employed. On some trials, presentation of a positive stimulus (CS+) is followed by the presentation of the US; on other trials, presentation of a negative stimulus (CS−) is never followed by the US. Such differential conditioning demands that a successive procedure be used: The CS+ and CS− must be presented singly and in random sequence over the conditioning trials.

When an instrumental conditioning operation is used, as in the case of a two-choice discrimination task, reinforcement follows the subject's responses to one stimulus (S+), but responses to the other stimulus (S−) are not reinforced. The S+ and S− may be presented successively (as in classical conditioning) but most investigators present the

S+ and S− together (or simultaneously) so that the subject must choose between them. Simple T-mazes, discrimination boxes, and the Wisconsin General Test Apparatus (WGTA) are the kinds of apparatus most frequently used. Figure 9–1 illustrates one type of discrimination apparatus frequently used with rats. The animal is placed in the start box; the lifting of a gate permits the animal to move to the adjoining chamber. A choice between the two discriminanda is made by the animal who pushes the hinged discriminanda card aside, permitting access to the goal box and reinforcement if the choice is correct. Many modifications of this basic design have been made depending on the specific requirements of the experiment.

The WGTA is illustrated in Figure 9–2. With the WGTA, two (or more) stimulus objects are placed on the stimulus tray, with each object covering a small food well. When the tray is placed in front of the subject, the subject responds by moving one of the objects to the side. If correct, the subject secures a reward found in the food well.

More complex discrimination tasks have also been used; two types are (1) oddity and (2) matching to sample. With the oddity task, three stimulus objects are presented together—two of these are identical, whereas the third stimulus is different. If the subject chooses the odd stimulus object, a reward is provided.

The matching to sample task has been frequently used by current experimenters and consists of presenting a single stimulus, designated as the sample, followed by two stimuli, one of which is identical to the sample whereas the other is not. The subject must learn to respond to the stimulus in the discrimination task which is the same as the sample. One variation of the task, identified as simultaneous matching to sample, consists of keeping the sample stimulus visible, along with the discriminative stimuli. Thus, if pigeons are used as subjects, a three-key apparatus would be used, with a specific colored (or patterned) middle key (e.g., blue) serving as the sample. After the key has been exposed for several seconds, the two side keys are illuminated, with one key illuminated by the sample color (e.g., blue) and the other key with a different color (e.g., yellow). The pigeon must peck the particular side key that matches the color of the middle key in order to receive reinforcement. If the experimenter chooses to employ the delayed matching to sample task, the sample stimulus is removed prior to the discriminative stimuli being presented. The delayed matching to sample task is not an easy one for the animals to master, although two variables can influence the ease

Figure 9-1
Top view of a discrimination apparatus. The discriminanda or cue cards are placed on hinged doors that lead to the goal box. In order to control for position preferences often exhibited by rats, the position of the cue cards are randomly changed from right to left.

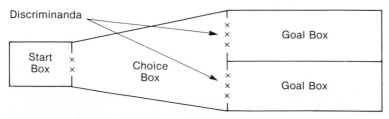

Figure 9–2
Wisconsin General Test Apparatus. Adapted from H. F. Harlow, "The formation of learning sets," *Psychological Review,* 1949, *56,* 51–65. Copyright © 1949 by the American Psychological Association. Reprinted by permission.

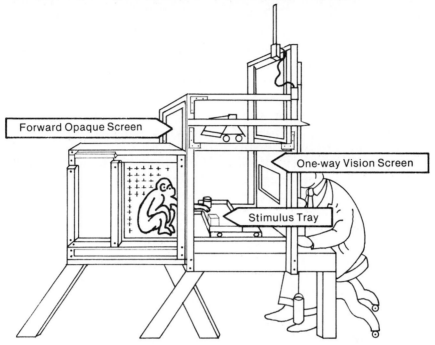

with which the task is learned: the length of the delay placed between the offset of the sample stimulus and the onset of the discriminative stimuli as well as the nature of the stimuli employed. D'Amato, Salmon, and Colombo (1985) have reported that in order for their monkeys to achieve a criterion of 90% correct on 96 trials in which a triangle and red disk served as the stimuli (and with a nine-second delay), training trials ranged from 373 to 1185.

The Nature of the Discriminanda ►

Simple discriminanda are used in most discrimination tasks, the specific type being adapted to the experimental subject and the kind of discrimination apparatus employed. Wooden objects of different shapes, sizes, and colors are often used with monkeys in the WGTA. Illuminated keys or disks in a variety of colors and lines generally serve as the discriminanda for pigeons, whereas the discrimination task apparatus for rats may utilize discriminanda consisting of flat pieces of light metal or cardboard that differ in brightness (e.g., black vs. white) or pattern (e.g., black and white vertical stripes vs. black and white horizontal stripes).

Natural Concepts

The discriminanda used in laboratory studies are characterized by a simplicity that sets them apart from the kinds of stimuli confronting most organisms in natural discrimination situations. Laboratory stimuli will vary along only a few basic dimensions, such as color, shape, or size. In contrast, open-ended variability characterizes the discriminanda found in natural settings. For example, we can discriminate dogs from all other animals, although dogs come in all shapes, sizes, and colors, and other animals may appear to have all of the attributes that characterize the dog.

Herrnstein and his associates have called such open-ended stimuli *natural concepts*. They have examined discrimination learning in pigeons and humans using such stimuli (see Herrnstein and Loveland, 1964; Herrnstein, Loveland, and Cable, 1976; Herrnstein, 1979; Herrnstein and deVilliers, 1980). Herrnstein, Loveland, and Cable (1976) used 920 different pictures of trees, 880 different pictures of water, and 800 different pictures of a single person. Thus, each group of pictures dealt with a natural concept (e.g., trees, water, or a human being) that would serve as a S+ in an operant discrimination study. The pictures representing a single natural concept were quite diverse—the concept was photographed in whole or in part, from near or far, obstructed or unobstructed, and so on. For example, the pictures of trees were of many different types of trees, and the pictures of water included everything from an aerial view of the Atlantic Ocean to a close-up of a very small puddle.

The photographs serving as negative stimuli (S−) were comparable to the positive stimuli (S+) except for the presence of the natural concept item. In Experiment 1, 920 negative pictures were combined with 920 pictures of trees to form a pool of 1,840 photos. From this pool, sets of 40 S+ and 40 S− pictures were randomly drawn for use during each experimental session. Pools of pictures were also made up for the examination of water in Experiment 2 (1,960 pictures) and a human being in Experiment 3 (1,600 pictures).

The experimental procedure consisted of presenting a single picture, either an S+ or S−. If the pigeon pecked at the key light placed below the picture when the S+ was presented, reinforcement was provided; pecking at the key light when the S− was presented did not result in reward. In each experiment pigeons were run for more than 100 sessions. Results clearly revealed the ability of pigeons to discriminate pictures of a tree, water, or a person from those not containing these natural concepts.

Findings such as these raise many questions for which psychologists, at least at the present time, have no completely adequate answers. A traditional explanation for the ability of the pigeon to make these discriminations would be a theory in which trees, water, and the like were each identified as representing a class of stimuli (or a natural concept) because each photograph contained some element common to the concept. For example, all trees should have in common a particular color, shape, structure, and so on, or possibly some combination of them. And yet, according to the experimenters, specific attributes were not common to all of the examples of a natural concept. In examining the pictures of trees, for example, the pigeons did not require that the tree be green, leafy, vertical, woody, branching, and so on. Moreover, for a picture to be recognizable as a nontree, the picture did not have to eliminate greenness, woodiness, verticality, and the like. Thus, a picture of a large stalk of celery, in spite of its many treelike characteristics, was rarely identified as a tree.

A second explanation could be that Herrnstein, Loveland, and Cable's (1976) pigeons did not learn the concept of a tree during the experiment—that trees were viewed in all sizes, shapes, and configurations by the pigeon in its natural environment; as a result of this experience the birds had already learned about the characteristics or features of trees. But a subsequent study by Herrnstein and deVilliers (1980), in which underwater photographs of fish were used as stimuli, resulted in pigeons acquiring the capacity to also successfully discriminate between slides containing fish and nonfish. The pigeons' success in so doing was approximately the same as that noted in the Herrnstein, Loveland, and Cable (1976) study. Inasmuch as fish, certainly viewed in an underwater setting, are not a part of the pigeon's natural environment, an explanation of discriminability based on experience is not tenable.

In this text we cannot provide an extended discussion of the proposed solutions, although one approach is noteworthy: In the identification of a natural concept, the organism will identify a number of features that are common to the concept; varying combinations of these features will be used to identify a specific instance as belonging to the general category. Such a position demands that no single feature, either alone or in combination with other features, be considered as critical in the determination that a particular instance be identified as an example of the natural concept (see Lea and Harrison, 1978; and Lea, 1984).

Blough (1982) has acknowledged that the perception of natural concepts is difficult to analyze but he has taken one preliminary step in such an examination by studying the capacity of pigeons to learn to discriminate each letter of the alphabet from all the other letters. Alphabetical letters cannot be regarded as natural concepts but they do represent a series of stimuli that can be differentiated one from the other, are all of a single class, but with a variety of features making up the class. Blough observed that the errors made by his subjects during the discrimination task could be analyzed in terms of the type of error made. When this was done, it was noted that four confusion discriminations could be identified: (1) confusion among letters that were closed (e.g., *O* vs. *D*); (2) confusion among letters that were open at the right side (e.g., *F* and *E*) (3) confusion among letters that were open at the top (e.g., *U* and *V*); and finally, (4) confusion among letters that involved straight lines (e.g., *T* and *L*). Blough noted that the pigeons' perception of the letters as indicated by such errors was similar to those made by human subjects. He has pointed out that the perceptual processes of the pigeon and the human appear to have much in common, and has suggested that his findings call attention to universal or fundamental aspects of recognition processes, which in turn may permit the manipulation of training or physiological variables that would be difficult with human subjects.

Variables Influencing Discrimination Learning ▶

In keeping with our organization presented in Chapter One, we shall examine the role of stimulus or task variables, motivational variables, and cognitive processes in the learning of discrimination tasks.

Stimulus or Task Variables

The Role of Stimulus Salience   As the difference between the stimuli used in a simultaneous discrimination task increases, the task becomes easier to learn. It takes the rat only a few trials to learn a black-white discrimination task; the animal has much more difficulty learning a light grey-medium grey discrimination. The characteristics of the discriminanda have been called *stimulus salience.*

To manipulate salience, the physical characteristics of the stimuli may be changed. For example, Broadhurst (1957) provided three levels of difficulty in a discrimination task by differentially illuminating the two alleys of a Y-maze. The difference in illumination between these alleys was represented by the ratios of 1:300, 1:60, and 1:15. Broadhurst found that the discrimination task with the largest difference in illumination (1:300) yielded the most rapid learning, whereas the one with the smallest difference (1:15) resulted in the slowest learning.

Another procedure for manipulating physical differences between stimuli has been to vary the number of different elements comprising the discriminanda. Hara and Warren (1961) examined how increasing the number of cues in the discriminanda influenced a simultaneous discrimination learning task in cats. The stimulus objects they used varied with regard to visual form, size, and/or brightness. The authors found that if two stimuli making up the discrimination task differed on all three dimensions (e.g., if one stimulus was a large, bright square and the other stimulus was a small, dark circle), the cat's performance level reached 99% correct during the training/trials provided. On the other hand, if the stimuli differed on just two dimensions (e.g., large, dark triangle vs. large, bright circle) or on just one dimension (e.g., large, dark triangle vs. large, dark circle), performance declined to 90 and 82%, respectively.

Hara and Warren's (1961) findings are noteworthy, since they demonstrate that the ease of learning a discrimination problem can be related to the number of different stimulus elements that make up the discriminanda. But it should be acknowledged that some of the elements that make up the discriminanda may play a more dominant role in determining the difference between discriminanda than other elements.

One example is found in a study by Spetch and Wilkie (1981) employing a successive (rather than simultaneous) discrimination procedure. The task was for pigeons to learn to discriminate between temporal intervals of 5 seconds (S−) versus one of 10 seconds (S+). During either the 5- or 10-second interval, the subjects were presented with food or had the house lights turned off. In effect, the learning of two discrimination tasks was compared; one consisted of the subject learning to differentiate 5 seconds versus 10 seconds of food presentation, whereas the second task consisted of the subject learning to make this differentiation when the house lights were on for these differing durations. Inasmuch as a within subjects design was used, four different stimulus presentations were randomly provided: (1) food presentation for 5 seconds (S−); (2) food presentation for 10 seconds (S+); (3) house light presentations for 5 seconds (S−); and (4) house light presentations for 10 seconds (S+). Following the presentations of one stimulus arrangement, the single pecking key (it will be recalled that a successive discrimination task was used) was illuminated with green light for 10 seconds. A peck that occurred during the last two seconds produced reinforcement if the preceding stimulus had been 10 seconds in duration, whereas responding following 5-second durations of food or house light was never reinforced. Results revealed that the temporal discrimination was more rapidly learned when food was used as a part of the discrimination stimulus than when the house light served this function. As Spetch and Wilkie (1981) have written, since stimuli differ in effectiveness, it seems reasonable that stimuli important for survival (e.g., food) should be effective as discriminative stimuli.

The Role of the S−   It has been assumed that in the learning of a discrimination task, it is important for the subject to learn *not* to respond to the S−, in addition to learning *to* respond to the S+. Many investigators have demonstrated that the organism's response to the negative stimulus plays an important role in the learning of the correct response. One such example can be noted in a study by Harlow and Hicks (1957). Their procedure consisted of having monkeys learn a series of discrimination problems using the Wisconsin General Test Apparatus. On the first training trial, only a simple stimulus object was presented. With Group 1, the stimulus object was always rewarded on Trial 1; with Group 2, the stimulus object was never rewarded on this trial. On Trials 2 through 6 (only six trials were provided on each problem), the object presented on the first trial was paired with a new stimulus object to form the discrimination problem. If the original stimulus object had been the S+ on Trial 1, it continued to be positive on the following five trials; if it was negative on Trial 1, it continued to serve as the S−. See Figure 9–3 for an outline of this procedure. Figure 9–4 presents the percentage of correct responses on Trial 2 over the 90 problems provided the animals. Note that the presentation of the S− on the first trial, in contrast to the presentation of the S+, resulted in superior learning.

One problem that arises with this type of study is that the new stimulus object that is paired with the previously experienced object (as an S+ or S−) to form the discrimination task may have properties that influence the subject's responding. Thus, the novelty of a new stimulus may elicit approach or avoidance responding, which, of course, could confound the contribution of any associative process that had developed during earlier exposure to either the S+ or S−. Mason, Stevens, Wixon, and Owens (1980) and Stevens, Mason, and Wixon (1981), cognizant of this problem and utilizing rats as subjects, employed a transfer test in their experiments that eliminated novelty as a confounding condition. We shall not describe the specific methodology used by these investigators; however, in their assessment of the stimulus control exerted by the S+ and S− during discrimination training, results demonstrated the importance of the subject responding to the S−. Mason, Stevens, Wixon, and Owens (1980) concluded

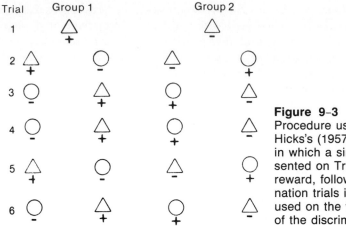

Figure 9-3
Procedure used in Harlow and Hicks's (1957) discrimination study in which a single object was presented on Trial 1, with or without reward, followed by five discrimination trials in which the object used on the first trial was a part of the discrimination task.

that "learning what to avoid, or 'where not to go,' contributes at least as much to performance as does learning what to approach, or 'where to go' [and] nonreinforced responses evidently are at least as important as reinforced responses in producing efficient discrimination performance" (p. 59).

An examination of the role of the S− in discrimination learning has led some investigators to ask if there is any specific ratio of positive (S+) to negative stimulus (S−) presentations that will lead to optimal learning. The experimental findings have suggested that no such ratio can be identified (e.g., Fitzwater, 1952; Birch, 1955; and Lachman, 1961). The answer appears to be specific to the kind of experimental subject used, the type of task employed, as well as procedural and methodological considerations.

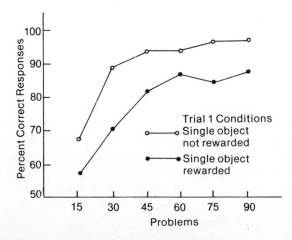

Figure 9-4
Discrimination learning set curves based on Trial 2 responses following rewarded and unrewarded Trial 1 responses. Adapted from H. F. Harlow and L. H. Hicks, "Discrimination learning theory: Uniprocess vs. duo-process," *Psychological Review*, 1957, *64*, 104–109. Copyright © 1957 by the American Psychological Association. Reprinted by permission.

The Role of Distinctive Features–The Feature Positive Effect (FPE)   The experimental findings demonstrating the importance of the S− in discrimination learning is in contrast to the operation of a distinctive stimulus feature condition, the findings from which have been identified as the *feature positive effect* (FPE). In an early study, Jenkins and Sainsbury (1970) were interested in determining if using a distinctive feature as a part of a discriminative stimulus would influence learning as a function of whether that feature was found on the positive (S+) or the negative (S−) discriminada. Their experiment consisted of providing pigeons with a successive discrimination task in which a dot on a homogeneous background served as the distinctive feature and was used as the S+ (feature positive) for one group, whereas a second group found the dot on the homogeneous background to be part of the S− (feature negative). The homogeneous background served as the other stimulus in making up the discrimination task. Results revealed that when the S+ contained the distinctive feature, the learning of the discrimination took place more rapidly than when the S+ contained the distinctive feature, thus demonstrating what the authors have termed as the feature positive effect (FPE).

Subsequent studies by Sainsbury (1971, 1973) confirmed these findings by using a simultaneous discrimination task and employing children four and five years of age. When older children (nine years old) served as subjects, the FPE was not obtained, thus raising the question as to whether this effect was a phenomenon found only with animals and young children.

Newman, Wolff, and Hearst (1980) suggested that Sainsbury's failure to obtain the FPE in older children was undoubtedly due to a ceiling effect–the task Sainsbury used was so easy that differences between groups could not be obtained. In a series of experiments, Newman and colleagues (1980) were able to obtain the effect with adults (college students); moreover, they noted the broad generality of the FPE, obtaining feature positive superiority in tasks involving both simultaneous and successive discriminations, immediate or delayed feedback, different kinds of features, and so on. The FPE has been obtained with adults by many subsequent investigators (e.g., Richardson and Massel, 1982; Brown, Nallan, Gerdes, Dykeman, Sanders, and Lamb, 1983; and Nallan, Sanders, Dykeman, Hughes, Rauth, McCann, and Morrison-Nallan, 1986). Although all of the factors that contribute to FPE findings have not been identified, Brown and associates (1983) have isolated one variable that does appear to account for some of the FPE results–the tendency for the subjects to attend to only the S+. Thus, when subjects are instructed to attend to the S−, as well as the S+, the FPE is not obtained.

Errorless Discrimination Learning   The organism's response to the S− has been found to be of considerable value in learning a discrimination problem. However, some investigators have shown that it is possible for a subject to learn a discrimination task without ever responding to the S−. This effect has been demonstrated in several operant studies conducted by Terrace (1963a, 1963b), teaching pigeons to discriminate between different colored plastic keys. Terrace's procedure consisted of presenting his subjects with a single stimulus, S+, for a fixed amount of time, followed by the presentation of the S−. Two basic conditions were manipulated in his first study. The first of these was the way in which the S− was presented. A *constant* procedure consisted of presenting the S− (green key) for the same length of time that the S+ (red key) was presented, with the brightness of the two keys being the same. In contrast, a *progressive* procedure consisted of gradually changing the S− from a nonilluminated key of five seconds' duration to a bright green key of three minutes' duration. These changes in duration and intensity were made in progressive stages.

The second condition was whether the S− should be introduced early or late in the training trials. For the early condition, the S− was introduced during the first conditioning session, and for the late condition, several weeks of training on the S+ alone preceded the introduction of the S−. The two basic training sessions provided four experimental groups: (1) constant-early, (2) constant-late, (3) progressive-early, and (4) progressive-late. Twenty-eight discrimination training sessions were provided. As Figure 9–5 indicates, the subjects in the progressive-early group acquired the discrimination with virtually no responding to the S−, their range of errors being 5 to 9.

In contrast, the range of errors for the progressive-late group was 35 to 760; for the constant-early group, the range of errors was 191 to 210; for the constant-late group, it was 1922 to 4135. The second experiment, in which Terrace made a few modifications in the procedure, produced similar findings. A third study revealed that a more difficult discrimination task could also be learned without errors using the early-progressive introduction of the S−.

In summary, there appear to be two necessary conditions for the acquisition of a discrimination without the subject responding to the S−: (1) the introduction of the S− immediately after conditioning of the response to the stimulus correlated with reinforcement and (2) provision of an initially large difference between the S+ and S−, which is progressively reduced to a smaller and constant difference.

The second condition used by Terrace (1963a), in which the difference between the S+ and S− was gradually reduced by increasing the brightness of the S− key, has been termed *fading;* it represents an important procedure in obtaining errorless discrimination performance. Moore and Goldiamond (1964) have confirmed the importance of fading by examining discrimination learning with children. In their study, six nursery school children were given a matching to sample task in which a triangle was projected on a milk glass window for four seconds using full (110 volt) intensity. The children were asked to "look at the picture in the top window." This picture was then turned off, and three triangles were presented in three windows located below the first window. The children were asked to point to the triangle that was the same as the first one they had viewed.

Two experimental conditions were examined. In one, the illumination of all of the test triangles was the same as that of the originally presented triangle. The second condition, which examined the contribution of fading, consisted of presenting the correct test triangle at the same intensity as the originally presented triangle; the other two were presented at a lower intensity. Throughout the trials, the illumination was increased, beginning with 0 volts and increasing through 16 steps until all the test triangles had the same intensity as the sample. Results from all six subjects indicated that the fading procedure aided discrimination performance. Other investigators work-

Figure 9-5
The number of responses to S− made by each bird during all 29 S+ and S− sessions. Adapted from H. S. Terrace, "Discrimination learning with and without 'errors,'" *Journal of the Experimental Analysis of Behavior,* 1963, *6,* 1–27. Copyright © 1963 by the Society for the Experimental Analysis of Behavior, Inc. Reprinted by permission.

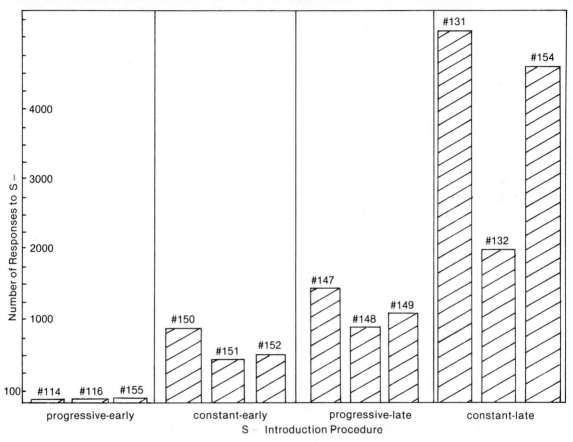

ing in school situations have demonstrated the role of fading in errorless discrimination learning. (See Box 9–1.)

What is the value of demonstrating that a discrimination task can be learned without the subject making errors? First, errorless discrimination findings contrast markedly with the findings of other investigators that we reviewed earlier who indicated that the organism's response to the S− is necessary for the discrimination task to be learned with the optimum efficiency. It is obvious that the differences between the two procedures should be further investigated to determine under what circumstances each method will result in superior performance. Second, there has been some evidence to indicate that the responses that are not followed by reward may result in the subject becoming frustrated and experiencing decreased motivation to continue to learn. The

box 9-1

An interesting application of errorless discrimination training and the use of the fading procedure—to teach children to discriminate letters of the alphabet—was reported by Egeland (1975).

In his study, the subjects were children, aged four to five years, enrolled in a pre-kindergarten program and unfamiliar with letters. A matching to sample format was employed in which the child was required to discriminate between two similar letters by selecting the letter that matched the sample previously presented. The pairs of letters used were *R-P, Y-V, G-C, Q-O, M-N,* and *K-X.*

The procedure used with the errorless training group on early trials was to highlight in red the cue that differentiated one letter from the other. Thus, the stem of the *R* in the *R-P* discrimination was colored red; the rest of the letter was black. During the course of training trials, the red highlighting was gradually faded until the stem of the *R* was black. A second group of subjects learned to discriminate between the letters using a traditional discrimination procedure; here, subjects were informed after making a choice whether their response was correct or incorrect. Egeland provided 10 training trials, followed immediately by 5 posttest trials, with 5 additional test trials given one week later. Egeland found that the errorless training group made significantly fewer errors than the traditional discrimination learning group on both the immediate and the delayed posttest trials. He reported that many of the children in the traditional discrimination group had considerable difficulty in understanding why an incorrect choice was wrong. Egeland has indicated the educational value of errorless discrimination training as a technique for dealing with many of the problems young children have in learning to discriminate letters or words.

use of the errorless discrimination procedure may be of value in minimizing such effects. Finally, the finding that it is possible to learn a discrimination problem without making errors has some implication for those theoretical analyses of discrimination learning positing that discrimination performance is related to the development of inhibition produced by the subject responding to the S−.[1]

Motivational Variables

Motivational variables (primarily those involving reward) have been extensively investigated with instrumental learning tasks, so it is not surprising that experimenters have also been interested in the contribution of these variables to discrimination learning. The reinforcement parameters that have been investigated have included (1) frequency,

---

[1] Terrace (1972) has argued that errorless discrimination learning is a process fundamentally different from learning with errors. Rilling (1977) has taken issue with this position. Rilling's research has indicated that the behavior of subjects who make no errors (or very few errors) in learning a discrimination task is not fundamentally different from the behavior of subjects who make many errors except, of course, for differences in error production. The research of Rilling and his associates suggests that it is the procedure used in errorless discrimination training rather than the making (or not making) of errors that is responsible for apparent behavior differences found between the two conditions (see Rilling and Caplan, 1973; Rilling, Caplan, Howard, and Brown, 1975; and Rilling, Richards, and Kramer, 1973).

(2) amount or intensity, and (3) temporal delay between the response and the presentation of the reward or aversive stimulus.

Frequency   An examination of the learning curves obtained for discrimination tasks almost always reveals increased discriminability as a function of increasing the frequency of reinforcement to the S+. There is little doubt that such learning is a function of the number of rewards to the S+, although, as was noted earlier, the number of nonrewarded trials may also make a contribution.

Amount of Reward   Much of the experimental evidence reveals discrimination learning to be an increasing function of the amount of reward provided. Cowles and Nissen (1937), using small and large pieces of banana and orange as rewards for chimpanzees learning a discrimination task, found that learning took place more rapidly when large rewards were used. Subsequent experiments have confirmed the findings of Cowles and Nissen (1937) (e.g., Greene, 1953; Schrier and Harlow, 1956; Leary, 1958; and Davenport, 1970).

Can these findings be generalized to human subjects? We would assume so, since our everyday experiences frequently suggest that individuals learn more rapidly if large rewards are provided rather than small. But surprisingly, the little experimental evidence we have does not support our assumption. Miller and Estes (1961) used as a reward (1) knowledge of results, (2) 1 cent, or (3) 50 cents; whereas Estes, Miller, and Curtin (1962) used as a reward (1) knowledge of results, (2) 1 cent, or (3) 25 cents. These investigators found that these differing rewards did not influence discrimination task learning for either nine-year-olds or college students. But one must be cautious when considering findings obtained from reward studies using students as subjects. For many students, pleasing the instructor or doing well in a school-related task is an intangible but potent reward. As a result, the influence of the small and tangible rewards provided by the experimenter may be obscured by the contribution of an intangible one. (See Box 9–2.)

Motivational Intensity and Task Difficulty: The Yerkes-Dodson Law   The most frequently used procedure to manipulate the motivational variable of reward with animals has been to vary the amount of food. It is also possible to vary motivation by providing subjects with different intensities of shock, followed by shock termination.

When shock intensity has been varied with discrimination tasks, some experimenters have found an interaction between differences in intensity and task difficulty. More specifically, they have found that although very intense shock results in the most rapid learning of an easy discrimination task, a less intense shock provides optimal learning when the discrimination is more difficult. This relationship between level of motivation and task difficulty was first noted by Yerkes and Dodson (1908).

These investigators had mice learn three visual discrimination tasks of increasing difficulty. In addition, three different levels of shock intensity were used to motivate the animals. The authors found that with the easiest task (i.e., when there was a large difference between the brightness of the two grey papers that were used as the discriminanda) increasing the intensity of shock resulted in increasing performance. But

box 9-2

Some investigators believe that external rewards (money, toys, candy, etc.) used in human learning situations may have deleterious consequences for later learning. Deci (1975) has assumed that persons' intrinsic need for feelings of competence and self-determination makes them aware of potential satisfactions, which in turn provide the energy for them to set goals and strive to achieve them. The achievement provides an intrinsic reward, an outcome that Deci has contrasted with outcomes involving extrinsic or external rewards.

The interesting aspect of Deci's position is that if a person who is intrinsically motivated to do something begins to receive an extrinsic reward for such behavior, a loss of intrinsic motivation ensues. Thus, when a child enters school and begins to receive As and gold stars for doing well in tests, what happens to the intrinsic motivation for learning?

One type of experimental study that has been used to examine the role of intrinsic and extrinsic rewards on learning has been as follows: Experimental subjects are first asked to work on a presumably interesting task (e.g., solve puzzles, etc.) for a period of time during which they are paid for the successful completing of each item that comprises the task. Control subjects are paid a fixed amount for their participation in the session. Following the work period, a free time period is then made available to subjects in which they are free to do as they please, including working on task items. No pay is given for an activity during this free time. Intrinsic motivation is measured by the amount of free time spent working on the task items, with the predicted outcome being that the experimental subjects who were paid to work on an intrinsically interesting task would spend less time working on this task when they were not paid for doing so than control subjects. Boal and Cummings's (1981) examination of Deci's hypothesis has indicated that it has had only modest success. Their review indicated that of 24 studies designed to test Deci's position, 10 of these failed to do so.

when the discrimination became more difficult, optimal learning took place with lower shock intensities. Yerkes and Dodson concluded, "An easily acquired habit . . . may be readily formed under strong stimulation, whereas a difficult habit may be acquired readily only under relatively weak stimulation" (p. 482).

Subsequent studies using rats by Hammes (1956), Broadhurst (1957), and Dennenberg and Karas (1960) have confirmed Yerkes and Dodson's findings.

The deleterious effect of an aversive stimulus on the *maintenance* of a reasonably complex task by human subjects has been reported in a study by Patrick (1934). In this study, college students were placed in a room that had four doors, only one of which was unlocked. It was only through this unlocked door that the subject could leave the room. Which door was unlocked varied, but the subject could learn that the door that was open on any given trial would be locked on the next. Thus, it was possible to increase the probability of finding the unlocked door on the first guess from 25 to 33%. Subjects were given 10 trials a day for 10 days in order to obtain a control measure of performance. Following these trials, the subjects were again placed in this problem situation, but this time a specific type of aversive stimulation was provided during each trial—namely, a cold shower of water or a blast of a klaxon horn. Patrick found that when the subjects were performing under the aversive stimulus conditions, in contrast to their control performance, the probability of their responding correctly decreased significantly. It was also observed that a great deal of emotional responding appeared to be in evidence; the subjects would repeatedly pull on the locked doors, dash frantically from one door to another, and so on.

One explanation for the Yerkes-Dodson law would be that the organism's emotionality increases with the onset of the aversive stimulation. These strong emotional responses, elicited by intense stimulation, are more likely to interfere with the learning of difficult tasks or their maintenance than with the learning or maintenance of easy ones.

If such an explanation is correct, it would be expected that the Yerkes-Dodson law would not be operable when motivation was manipulated by varying the amount of reward or level of deprivation. Increases in these motivational conditions would not be accompanied by the strong emotional responses that could interfere with the learning of a complex task. And neither Fantino, Kasdon, and Stringer (1970) nor Hochhauser and Fowler (1975) were able to obtain experimental findings supporting the Yerkes-Dodson law when manipulating such conditions. Fantino and colleagues (1970) varied the level of food deprivation of pigeons while requiring these subjects to learn detour problems of varied complexity. Hochhauser and Fowler (1975) placed rats on moderate or high levels of food deprivation, provided rewards of one, two, or four pellets of food, and had their animals learn discrimination tasks that varied in difficulty. Both studies revealed that as task complexity increased, increasing the level of motivation resulted in increasing the level of performance.

In summary, and in agreement with Fowler's (1982) assessment, the Yerkes-Dodson law is not a general law encompassing all types of motivation; "rather its operation is limited to aversive motivational states" (p. 172).

Delay of Reward and Acquisition Training   The effects of delaying reward, found with positive and negative reinforcement tasks, are also observed with discrimination tasks. In an early and classic study by Grice (1948), groups of rats were given training on a black-white discrimination problem, with a delay of either 0, 0.5, 1.2, 2.0, 5.0, or 10 seconds introduced between the animal's correct response and its reward of food. The criterion of learning was 18 correct responses out of 20 trials. Performance for the varying groups, as indicated in Figure 9–6, reveals that the 0 delay group learned most rapidly, followed by the 0.5, 1.2, and 2.0 delay groups. When a delay of 5 seconds was introduced, the animals in this group experienced considerable difficulty in learning. The animals provided with a delay of 10 seconds were unable to learn the discrimination, even though in some cases they were given as many as 1,400 trials.

Subsequent studies by Keesey (1964), Topping and Parker (1970), and Culbertson (1970) provided confirmations of Grice's (1948) findings. In these studies, brain stimulation was used as the reward. This type of reinforcement permits the experimenter to exercise more precise control over the length of the delay interval than when traditional rewards such as food or water were employed. In Culbertson's (1970) study, rats learned a discrimination problem in which their receiving brain stimulation for making a correct response was delayed for either 0, 0.5, 1.0, 2.0, 3.0, or 5.0 seconds. Results from 500 acquisition trials revealed that the 0- and 0.5-second delay groups were clearly superior to all of the other experimental groups.

The delay of reward variable was responsible for stimulating a great deal of research

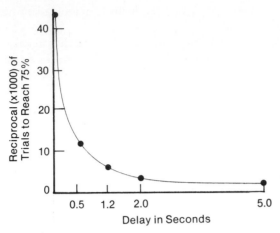

Figure 9-6
Rate of learning as a function of delay of reward. The experimental values are represented by black dots, and the smooth curve is fitted to these data. Adapted from G. R. Grice, "The relation of secondary reinforcement to delayed reward in visual discrimination learning," *Journal of Experimental Psychology,* 1948, *38,* 1–16. Copyright © 1948 by the American Psychological Association. Reprinted by permission.

using children. In a study by Terrell and Ware (1961), kindergarten children and first graders were asked to solve concurrently two easy discrimination problems. With one problem, there was an immediate reward (light flash) after the correct response; with the second problem, the reward was delayed for seven seconds. Training trials were provided until the subject reached a criterion of six consecutive correct responses. In a second experiment, more difficult discrimination tasks were provided, although the same immediate and delayed reward conditions were examined. Results from both experiments indicated that the subjects learned significantly more rapidly when rewarded immediately than when given the delayed reward. In Experiment 1, the mean number of trials to criterion was 6.6 and 16.6 for the immediate and delayed conditions respectively, whereas in Experiment 2, the means were 16.6 and 22.7.

The effect of the delay of reward variable on performance appears to decline for older children, particularly when easy tasks are used. Perhaps this is because the children are better able to use the delay period to rehearse the correct response. Hockman and Lipsitt (1961) used fourth-grade children as subjects in learning an easy (two-stimulus) and a difficult (three-stimulus) discrimination problem. Correct responding was rewarded by the presentation of a red light; an incorrect response was accompanied by a buzzer. The time interval between the subject's response and the presentation of the red light or buzzer varied—either 0, 10, or 30 seconds. The criterion was 12 correct responses or a maximum of 36 trials. Results indicated that the learning of the easy discrimination task was not influenced by the delay interval; however, the delay did influence the learning of the difficult task.

Delay of Reward and Maintenance Responding   We have noted that experimental interest in delay of reward has centered around how this variable has influenced acquisition. Cox and D'Amato (1977) have demonstrated that reinforcement delay can also disrupt the maintenance of discrimination responding. In their study, monkeys were first given extensive training on a simple two-choice discrimination problem. The procedure consisted of having the animals learn to push a microswitch 15 times, with the last response causing a projector to produce two discriminative stimuli on a screen. Pressing a key below the S + resulted in the immediate presentation of a pellet of food, whereas pressing the S − key produced dimming of the illumination in the experimental chamber for one minute.

After extensive training resulted in the animals responding to the S + at a high level of accuracy, a delay of reinforcement procedure was instituted. After the animal had made a discriminative response, delay periods of 2, 4, 8, 16, and 32 seconds were provided, in increasing order. Utilizing these varying intervals of delay of reinforcement, 24 trial sessions were provided. A high level of maintenance responding was noted when 2-, 4-, and 8-second delay intervals were used, but as the interval was increased from 8 to 16 seconds, a decrement in correct responding gradually appeared. With a 32-second delay interval, correct responding declined to below 70%.

Delay of Reward Explanations   In the analysis of the role of reward on learning, Spence (1956), Mowrer (1960), and Revusky (1971), all in one form or another, have proposed a behavioristic explanation. More specifically, these investigators have proposed that the delay of reinforcement provides the experimental subject with the opportunity to make other responses. It is these other responses that interfere with the subject's identification of the specific response that has been associated with reward, and thus contributes to poorer learning.

A somewhat different analysis of why delay of reward contributes to poorer learning has been provided by D'Amato and his associates who have chosen to examine the role of this variable in the learning of preferences. In an early study conducted by D'Amato and Buckiewicz (1980), monkeys were permitted to explore a small T-maze for 5 minutes; their preference for either the striped or black arm of the maze was measured. On the next day, each experimental animal was placed in the nonpreferred arm for one minute, following which it was removed from the apparatus and provided a 30-minute delay. It was then returned to the start box of the maze where it received a supply of raisins. The animal was then returned to the maze a minute later where it was given a preference test identical to that originally provided. Control Group 1 animals were treated like the experimental animals except they did not receive the raisins; Control Group 2 animals were also given treatment similar to that provided to the experimental group except that these control animals did not receive the 1-minute placement in the nonpreferred arm.

Results indicated that the experimental animals preferred the arm associated with reward; in contrast, control animals did not reveal such a preference. The authors have indicated that as a result of a single placement experience followed 30 minutes later by food reward, the experimental animals more than doubled the amount of time spent in the originally preferred arm. On the other hand, there was virtually no change of preference in either of the control groups.

A second experiment conducted by D'Amato and Safarjan (1981) using water-deprived rats and a sucrose solution as reward has confirmed the earlier findings of D'Amato and Buckiewicz (1980). Experimental animals that had been given access to a sucrose solution after having been earlier exposed to a distinctive arm of the T-maze spent significantly more of their time on that arm than did control subjects.

D'Amato has likened his delay of reward findings to those obtained with the taste aversion paradigm discussed in our classical conditioning chapters, as well as raising the important question of whether the poor instrumental learning that has invariably taken place with a substantial delay of reward is due to the failure of the supporting affective response to become conditioned on early trials.

A Little Theory

At this point, with our examination of the influence of stimulus and motivational variables completed, let us see how investigators accounted for discrimination learning. Lashley (1929) posited that the rat, in learning a brightness discrimination task, attempted various solutions before it hit upon the correct one. A few years later, Krechevsky (1932a, 1932b, 1938), in keeping with Lashley's point of view, observed that his experimental rats, prior to learning a discrimination task, appeared to engage in a number of systematic modes of responses. That is, the animal might first respond to position, and if such responding did not lead to consistent reinforcement, would respond to another stimulus dimension in an effort to solve the problem. The critical elements of Lashley and Krechevsky's discrimination theory was that the learning of the discrimination task was related to the adoption of hypotheses by the experimental subject. Such being the case, it meant that the actual learning of the discrimination took place very rapidly—as soon as there was substantial correspondence between consistency of reinforcement and the particular hypothesis that had been adopted by the experimental subject. Thus, learning did not take place in a step-by-step fashion or incrementally, but rather occurred very rapidly, with performance on earlier trials guided by incorrect hypotheses, not contributing to the solution of the problem. Moreover, as Lashley and Wade (1946) reiterated some years later, it meant that in discrimination learning tasks, the experimental subject responded only to what was perceived to be the dominant cue while all other cues became irrelevant. As these experimenters wrote, "If a monkey is trained to choose a large red circle and avoid a small green one, he will usually choose any red object and avoid any green but will make chance scores when colored large and small circles are presented" (p. 82). Under such circumstances, color was the dominant cue while size was irrelevant.

Opposed to this hypothesis testing, nonincremental theory of discrimination learning was a different point of view proposed by Spence (1936, 1937a, 1937b) and Hull (1943) and based on Pavlov's postulation of excitation and inhibition. In addition to accepting Pavlov's assumption that excitatory and inhibitory strength develop to the CS+ and CS−, Spence and Hull proposed that:

1. Both excitatory and inhibitory tendencies generalize to other stimuli on the same stimulus continuum as the CS+ and CS−.
2. These excitatory and inhibitory tendencies interact algebraically.
3. The subject's response is determined by the product of this algebraic interaction.

Moreover, Spence and Hull made the assumption that excitatory and inhibitory strength developed between the organism's responses and each stimulus element of the discriminanda. Thus, if a pigeon had to discriminate between a white triangle placed on a red background (S+) and a white square placed on a green background (S−), reinforcing the S+ would result in excitatory strength being established between the instrumental response and (a) the white triangle as well as the (b) red background; nonreinforcement of the S− would result in inhibitory strength developing between nonresponding and (a) the white square as well as the (b) green background.

Spence and Hull's account of discrimination learning taking place as a function of reinforced and nonreinforced trials that resulted in increments of associative and inhibitory strength was experimentally supported by the findings obtained in a variety of studies conducted in the late 1940s and 1950s.[2] But a careful analysis of their theory revealed many problems, only a few of which we shall identify. For example, the characteristics of the excitatory and inhibitory generalization gradient could take any shape that the theorist desired. And it was the algebraic summation of these generalized excitatory and inhibitory strengths that determined the subject's performance. Moreover, to assume that all generalization curves were basically similar was obviously an error.[3]

Although the Spence-Hull theory has been used in accounting for certain current experimental findings (e.g., peak shift), it is no longer a viable explanation, and new conceptualizations of discrimination learning have been proposed (e.g., Lovejoy, 1968; and Sutherland and Mackintosh, 1971). These explanations have posited the operation of two constructs or processes; a brief description follows.

One process is related to the assumption that different tendencies are learned in the presence of the S+ and S−. The process of reinforcement is responsible for increasing the probability of responding to the S+, whereas nonreinforcement will result in increasing the probability of not responding to the S−. The second construct is selective attention, which is responsible for determining to what stimulus elements the subject will attend during the course of training trials. It is assumed that as a function of the reinforced and nonreinforced trials taking place during training, there will be changes in the capacity of each stimulus element to elicit the attention of the subject, which in turn will result in the subject eventually learning the discrimination. Our description of these processes has been quite abbreviated; a more complete presentation can be found in Lovejoy (1968) or Sutherland and Mackintosh (1971). Although these models are more adequate than that provided by the Spence-Hull formulation, a theoretical model that can account for most of the experimental findings that have been obtained remains to be developed.

---

[2] The increment position of Spence and Hull, and the nonincremental points of view provided by Krechevsky and Lashley has been identified as the *continuity-noncontinuity controversy.*

[3] The reader can examine Mackintosh (1983) for an excellent critique of the Spence-Hull theory of discrimination learning.

Summary ▶

Discrimination tasks are considered a part from the nonsignaled and signaled tasks discussed in earlier chapters because some variables that contribute to discrimination learning do not operate with these other types of tasks. Several theoretical explanations have been proposed for discrimination learning.

Stimulus salience, or the characteristics of discriminanda, represents the most important stimulus variable that has been investigated with discrimination learning tasks. Not surprisingly, virtually all researchers have found that as the discriminanda become more salient, discrimination learning takes place more rapidly.

A second stimulus variable investigated has been the contribution of responding to the S−. It has been assumed that in the learning of a discrimination task, it is important for the subject to learn *not* to respond to the S−, in addition, of course, to learning *to* respond to the S+. Several studies have demonstrated such to be the case. Experience with the S− results in learning taking place more rapidly than if the experimental subject did not have experience with the S−.

It is possible for a subject to learn a discrimination task without responding to the S−. Terrace (1963a) has demonstrated that if the S+ is presented only on early trials and then the S− is made gradually more perceptible, it is possible for the organism to learn the discrimination without ever responding to the S−. This process has been identified as errorless discrimination learning.

Three motivational variables have been investigated: (1) frequency, (2) amount or intensity, and (3) temporal delay between the response and the presentation of the aversive stimulus. Virtually all investigators have found that discrimination learning is a function of the frequency with which reward is provided, the S+. Most of the experimental evidence indicates that such learning is also related to the amount of reward employed. As the amount of food or time during which the animal is permitted to eat is increased, discrimination learning takes place more rapidly.

In studies of the motivational variable of shock (and the termination of shock), an interaction between shock intensity and task difficulty has been discovered. That is, increasing the intensity of shock when an easy discrimination task is used results in learning taking place more rapidly; however, an intermediate level of shock provides optimal learning if the discrimination task is more difficult to learn. This relationship between level of motivation and task difficulty has been described as the Yerkes-Dodson law.

Delay of reinforcement has also interested experimenters. They have found that as the time interval between the making of the response and the securing of reward is increased, discrimination learning becomes poorer.

An area of experimenter interest has been the determination of the nature of discrimination learning. Hull and Spence were advocates of the position that excitatory and inhibitory strength accrued to the S+ and S−, with the discriminatory response learned being related to the algebraic summation of these two values.

Other issues that arose in the analysis of discrimination learning included: (1) did the subject associate with the response all the stimuli it perceived at the time the correct response was made? and (2) did discrimination learning take place gradually, with an accumulation of excitatory strength occurring over trials, or did such learning take place very rapidly, with the animal testing varying hypothesis until one of them resulted in the solution of the problem? These issues have coalesced into the continuity-noncontinuity controversy. Early tests of the two rival positions favored the continuity position, but more recent studies have supported a modified noncontinuity position.

chapter ten

▶

Discrimination Learning:
Cognitive Variables and
the Concept of Choice

In Chapter Nine we examined the contribution of stimulus and motivational variables to discrimination learning. In this chapter, and in keeping with the conceptual framework outlined in Chapter One, we will examine the role of cognitive processes. In the latter portion of this chapter, we shall consider another discrimination topic—the concept of choice.

Cognitive Processes ▶

The Learning of Relationships

The impetus for some of the early investigators positing the contribution of cognitive-like processes was the inference from animal discrimination task findings that such a process best explained their data. One such example is found in the early experimental studies of Köhler, a German investigator, conducted in 1918. This work was eventually translated and published in English in 1939. Köhler (1939) pointed out that animals that were provided a discrimination task could learn that a relationship existed between or among the stimuli—a relationship that would aid in the learning of that task.

In one study, Köhler trained chickens to peck for grain placed on the darker side of two grey papers. Following such training, the birds were then tested on a new pair of stimuli: (1) the original grey paper to which they had been previously trained to respond and (2) still darker paper. (Providing different test stimuli or the transposing of stimuli after training identifies this problem as a transposition task.) Köhler found that the birds pecked at the darker paper. From such a finding, he argued that his subjects had learned during the original training to respond, not to a specific brightness of the paper, but to the relationship between the stimuli—the difference in brightness.

Later studies by Baker and Lawrence (1951) and Lawrence and DeRivera (1954) have confirmed Köhler's findings. Animals can learn relationships between stimuli, which in turn could be used to provide solutions to discrimination tasks.

Further evidence for the acquisition of a relational construct was noted in a different type of transposition task identified as an *intermediate size problem*. In a study conducted by Gonzales, Gentry, and Bitterman (1954), chimpanzees were presented with three different sized boxes and were reinforced for selecting the intermediate or mid-sized one. The spatial arrangement of the boxes was systematically varied on each trial. After reaching a criterion of 16 correct responses, the animals were then tested on each of two new sets of stimuli. One set consisted of three different sized boxes. The intermediate size was smaller than the originally reinforced box; the second set consisted of three different sized boxes with the intermediate size box being larger than the original. Results supported Köhler's earlier findings in that Gonzales, Gentry, and Bitterman's (1954) chimpanzees revealed a significant tendency to select the intermediate sized box during both test series.[1]

It seems evident from the findings that we have reported that relational learning involves the operation of a cognitive process—a process that is perhaps similar to a hypothesis or strategy adopted by the experimental subject during the course of the training trials. The positing of such a process (as well as the experimental findings supporting it) provided one difficulty for the Spence-Hull theory of discrimination learning.

Learning to Learn

A second difficulty noted with the Spence-Hull model was indicated by the work of Harlow (1949). Harlow observed monkeys learning a series of object discrimination problems with increasing efficiency. He posited that his subjects had acquired a learning set—a cognitive construct arising from experience—and firmly disavowed any explanation based on the establishment of associations between stimuli and responses.

Harlow's procedure consisted of having monkeys learn a series of object discrimination tasks using the Wisconsin General Test Apparatus. In this study, 344 discrimination problems were provided to each of eight monkeys, with a different pair of stimuli being used with each problem After extended training was provided for the first 32 problems, only six trials per problem were provided for the next 200 problems. For the last 112 problems, an average of just nine trials per problem were provided. Figure 10–1 presents the learning curves revealing the percentage of correct responses on the first six

---

[1] We do not want to give the impression that all subjects placed in a transposition experiment will reveal relational responding. Most investigators have noted that some subjects will respond to the absolute characteristics of the stimulus rather than responding relationally.

Figure 10-1

Discrimination learning curves obtained from successive blocks of problems. Adapted from H. F. Harlow, "The formation of learning sets," *Psychological Review,* 1949, *56,* 51–65. Copyright © 1949 by the American Psychological Association. Reprinted by permission.

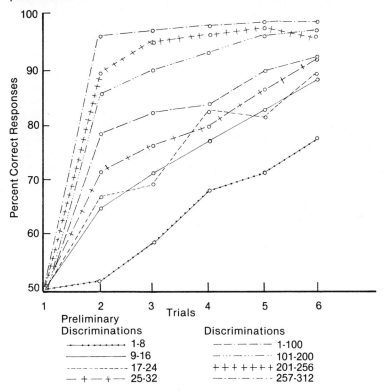

trials of the discrimination task; whereas Figure 10–2 plots the percentage of correct responses on Trials 2 to 6 as a function of the number of problems previously presented. It may be observed that both figures indicate an increase in learning efficiency as more and more problems are provided for the monkey to solve.

As mentioned earlier, Harlow (1949) described his findings in terms of his subjects acquiring a learning set or learning to learn, an undefined cognitive process arising from the monkeys' experience with learning specific discrimination problems that enabled them to solve later problems with astonishing efficiency.

Subsequent studies have demonstrated that organisms other than primates (e.g., rats, cats, and pigeons) can learn a series of discrimination problems with increasing rapidity. But there appears to be a substantial performance difference between primates and these other organisms. Sutherland and Mackintosh (1971) have suggested that primates appear to learn rules or adopt strategies that represent a specific cognitive process not found in these other subjects. These authors have proposed that there is the adoption of a "win-stay, lose-shift" strategy. Thus, after being given trials on an object

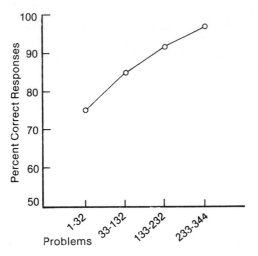

Figure 10-2
Discrimination learning set curve based on responses for Trials 2–6. Adapted from H. F. Harlow, "The formation of learning sets," *Psychological Review,* 1949, *56,* 51–65. Copyright © 1949 by the American Psychological Association. Reprinted by permission.

discrimination task, if the stimulus object that has been chosen results in reward, the subject should stay with that choice. If, however, the object chosen does not result in reward, the strategy calls for a shift to the other object on the next trial. Support for this position is found in a study by Schusterman (1962). Chimpanzees were first trained on an object-alternation discrimination task. With this task, the same stimulus object is rewarded on alternate trials, thus demanding a win-shift, lose-stay strategy. When these animals were switched to an object discrimination task demanding a win-stay, lose-shift strategy for the optimal performance, poorer performance was observed.

The Role of Attention

It is obvious that when an experimental subject is placed in the discrimination task situation, it must attend to the discriminanda in order to observe the difference between them. But what is the nature of such attending? Early psychologists such as James (1890) considered attention to be a cognitive state—a process of the mind or consciousness. Thus, attention "is the taking possession by the mind, in clear and vivid form, or one out of what seem several simultaneously possible objects or trains of thought. Focalization, concentration of consciousness are of its essence" (p. 403). But with the advent of behaviorism, attention was one of the cognitive concepts which Watson rejected.

By the early 1930s, the need to posit some type of attentional process, particularly if animal discrimination learning was to be understood, was evident. It was not surprising, however, that behavioristic investigators of this era defined attention in terms of specific overt responses made by the organism. Frequently, these responses were identified as *preparatory* responses. Thus, attending was conceptualized as a muscular response which resulted in orienting the subject's sensory apparatus in such fashion that certain aspects of the discriminanda would be perceived (and responded to). It seems reasonable to assume that one aspect of the concept of attention may be conceptualized in terms of receptor orientation, but there is a problem in assuming that this function represents the complete picture. The findings from an experiment by Reynolds (1961) provides evidence for this position.

In Reynolds's study, two pigeons were given discrimination training in which the positive stimulus key was a white triangle on a red background (S +) whereas a negative stimulus key was a white circle on a green background (S −). Six three-hour sessions of training with the two stimulus keys presented concurrently resulted in the pigeons achieving stable responding to the S +, and not responding to the S −. Two subsequent test sessions, separated by a training session, were provided in which the triangle, circle, red background, and green background lights were presented separately for one-minute sessions with more than 200 minutes of testing time being provided for all stimuli. No responses were reinforced during these test trials.

During training, both subjects came to respond predominantly to the white triangle on the red background. The discriminative control acquired by these stimuli is shown in Figure 10–3. The results of the test session in which each stimulus was presented separately are also indicated in Figure 10–3. It may be noted that for one of the pigeons there was little responding to the red background, whereas for the other pigeon, there was little responding to the triangle. Inasmuch as both color (red) and form (triangle) were projected on the response key, it is not likely that a particular receptor orientation could be used to account for why the birds responded to only a single stimulus element. It must be assumed that the birds saw both attributes of the stimulus—color and form—but for some reason, attended exclusively to only one of these. Tennant and Bitterman (1975) have obtained similar findings with fish. More specifically, carp were given training with discriminanda differing in both color and in the orientation of a line superimposed on the color. The fish responded almost totally to color when these stimulus elements were presented singly. The authors demonstrated, however, that if the discriminanda consisted of only different line orientations, learning of the discrimination took place readily.

The early findings of Reynolds (1961) indicated that attentional processes had to be considered as playing an important role during discrimination learning. It will be recalled that Lovejoy (1969) and Sutherland and Mackintosh (1971) have included the process of attention in their model describing how such learning takes place.

The role of attention in discrimination learning has been identified by current experimenters as a cognitive construct, and more specifically, as selective attention. As we have just noted, if the discriminanda contains multiple stimulus elements, one element may play a more dominant role on the discrimination process than another. Other examples of selective attention mechanisms are found in the experimental studies of overshadowing and blocking, which we have discussed in our examination of classical conditioning. Overshadowing refers to a situation in which, if a response is conditioned to a strong (A) and weak (B) stimulus presented simultaneously, AB, testing with each stimulus, A and B individually, would result in stimulus A eliciting the response at almost full strength, whereas the stimulus B, being overshadowed by stimulus A, will not elicit the response. In such instances, it is assumed that the subject during the simultaneous presentation of A and B has attended only to stimulus A, thus precluding B from serving as a CS. With blocking, there is the training with a single

Figure 10-3

The rate of responding of each pigeon in the presence of each of the key illumina-
tions in the training and testing phases of the experiment. Adapted from G. S.
Reynolds, "Attention in the pigeon," *Journal of the Experimental Analysis of Behavior,*
1961, *4,* 203–208. Copyright © 1961 by the Society for the Experimental Analysis of
Behavior. Reprinted by permission.

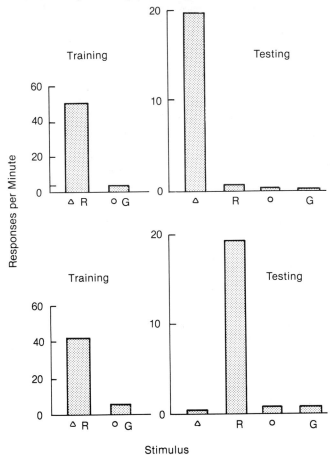

stimulus, A, followed by continued training with a stimulus compound, AB. When the
subject is tested by presenting stimulus B alone, there is virtually no responding. Here
again, it is assumed that having been conditioned to stimulus A during the first training
period, the experimental subject continues to attend only to that stimulus during the
presentation of A and B, thus precluding stimulus B from serving as a CS.

The Construct of Memory

The investigator's objective, as revealed in the studies we have just presented, has
attempted to better understand discrimination learning by positing the contribution of
cognitive processes. The willingness of these experimenters to infer the presence of such

processes has undoubtedly contributed to the readiness of current experiments also to employ cognitive constructs, and in particular, the construct of memory. One way individuals have used this construct has been in providing a conceptual understanding of findings obtained in earlier discussed topics. One of these is the delay of reinforcement.

Delay of Reinforcement Revisited

In Chapter Nine we noted the findings of Grice (1948), Keesey (1964), and others who demonstrated that providing rats with an extremely short reinforcement delay (e.g., 0.5 second) would result in a learning decrement, and that a 10-second delay would make a simple black-white discrimination task unsolvable. But a recent series of experiments conducted by Lieberman, McIntosh, and Thomas (1979) have demonstrated discrimination learning using delays as long as 60 seconds with an explanation for these findings being related to the operation of the cognitive construct of memory. Let us examine the nature of the apparatus employed, the procedure, and the experimental findings. The black-white discrimination apparatus used in an earlier study by Lieberman and colleagues is illustrated in Figure 10–4. The procedure consisted of animals in the experimental group being picked up by the experimenter immediately after making a choice and placed in a delay box for 60 seconds. After the control subjects made the correct response they were permitted to run into the delay box undisturbed. Animals in both groups were contained in the delay box for 60 seconds after which they were placed in the goal box to obtain food. If the correct response was made, the same handling or nonhandling procedure was used except that a correction procedure was utilized in which the animal was immediately given another trial. Such trials continued until a correct response was made. Results revealed that the handled animals reached a 90% level of correct responding after 50 trials; nonhandled animals responded at chance throughout these trials.[2]

The identification of handling as the apparent critical variable in this experiment suggested that the presentation of any novel stimulus might serve to reduce the effect of reinforcement delay; a later study (Experiment 4) provided confirmation of this position. If a brief, loud sound or a bright light, a marking stimulus, was presented immediately after the animals had made an instrumental response, the learning of the discrimination was facilitated although reward was delayed for 60 seconds.

---

[2] The impetus for the Lieberman, McIntosh, and Thomas (1979) study was an earlier series of experiments conducted by Lett (1973, 1974, 1975), who found that rats could learn a right-left discrimination task with delay intervals of either 1, 20, or 60 minutes if the animals spent the delay interval in their home cage. Animals that spent the same length of delay in the apparatus did not learn. Lett attributed the ability of her rats to learn with such long delay intervals to the fact that the responses made by the animals in their home cage did not interfere with the instrumental response that was made in the apparatus. (It will be recalled from Chapter Nine that Spence [1956] and others have proposed a similar explanation for the earlier delay of reinforcement findings obtained by Grice [1948], and so on.) Since it was necessary for Lett to handle her experimental animals in placing them back into the home cage for the delay interval and then back again to the apparatus, Lieberman and colleagues (1979) were interested in examining the contribution of such handling to the experimental findings.

Figure 10-4
Discrimination apparatus used in examining delay of reward. Adapted from D. A. Lieberman, D. C. McIntosh, and G. V. Thomas, "Learning when reward is delayed: A marking hypothesis," *Journal of Experimental Psychology: Animal Behavior Processes,* 1979, *5,* 224–242. Copyright © 1979 by the American Psychological Association. Reprinted by permission.

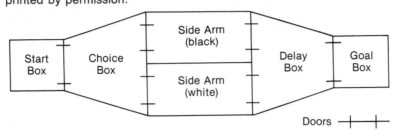

In a series of experiments, Thomas, Lieberman, McIntosh, and Ronaldson (1983) continued to examine the role of stimulus markers in facilitating discrimination learning with delayed reward. Since two markers had been used in their earlier studies—a stimulus presented (1) immediately following the making of the choice and (2) prior to receiving reward—the investigators were interested in determining if the presentation of only a single stimulus marker immediately after making the choice response would be equally effective in facilitating the discrimination. Using the same apparatus and virtually the same procedure as in their earlier studies, one experimental group received a 2-second burst of noise immediately after the choice response and immediately upon entering the goal box, whereas a second group received only the 2-second burst of noise after the choice response. Control animals did not receive the noise at either time. Results indicated that at the end of 50 trials, the one- and two-stimulus marker groups were responding equally well, and at a level of more than 80% correct, whereas the control animals were responding at chance. Thus, findings indicated that it was not necessary to present the marking stimulus on two occasions in order for marking stimuli to mitigate the effects of reward delay.

In another experiment, the authors noted that it was possible to present a marking stimulus just *prior* to the animal making its choice in order for the stimulus to be effective in enhancing discrimination learning; in fact, the performance of these animals was no different than the performance of a second group of animals that had received the burst of noise just after making their choice. Finally, Lieberman, Davidson, and Thomas (1985) were able to demonstrate that a different type of marking stimulus could be used in facilitating the discrimination learning in pigeons when reward was delayed. Since similar results were obtained with a different species, apparatus, marking stimulus, and response, the authors have suggested that the marking phenomenon is a robust one.

In accounting for their findings, Lieberman and his associates have proposed that when an unexpected stimulus is presented, it will trigger a search through memory to identify preceding events that might have caused or predicted it. The extra attention or rehearsal devoted to whatever event is so identified marks that event in memory so that subjects will be more likely to recall it subsequently. Applying this analysis to their experimental findings, the presentation of the burst of noise would have been particularly likely to direct attention to the choice response that immediately preceded it, thereby marking it in memory. When food is presented at the end of the delay interval, the rats again search their memories for a possible cause, and those animals whose choice response had been marked would now remember it and associate it with food.

Other Examinations of Memory

We have noted how some investigators have employed the construct of memory in an effort to account for reinforcement delay in discrimination learning. Other experimenters, however, have not been interested in gaining insight about how a particular type of discrimination task is learned; rather, their primary interest has focused on examining the nature and operation of the memory process itself—the discrimination task serves only as a means by which the process can be examined.

It has been suggested from human experimental studies that memory is not unitary but rather there are several memorial processes. One of these is long-term memory in which it is hypothesized that the traces that are formed are lost very slowly; in fact, in some instances, they have been retained for the lifetime of the individual. In contrast, short-term or working memory refers to a memory store in which the trace appears to be lost rather quickly. We shall discuss this distinction in greater detail in Chapter Fourteen.

Working Memory

Almost all experimenters working with animals have been interested in the operation of working memory, with the delayed matching to sample task (DMTS) being frequently used from which working memory has been inferred. It will be recalled that with this task, a sample stimulus is first presented for a fixed period of time (e.g., 4 seconds), following which a delay period or retention interval is provided (e.g., 10 seconds), during which time the stimulus is no longer present. When the delay period is terminated, two test stimuli are presented—one is the sample stimulus previously presented and the other is a new stimulus. Responding to the sample stimulus results in reward.

We cannot describe in this text all of the variables that have been shown to influence performance on the DMTS task (and the inferred memory process) but two have been extensively investigated. One has been the length of the delay period between the offset of the sample stimulus presentation and the presentation of the discrimination task. Some experimenters have referred to this delay as the *retention interval.*

In an early study, D'Amato and O'Neill (1971) had monkeys begin each DMTS trial by pressing a microswitch that resulted in the sample stimulus (e.g., triangle) being projected on the screen. The image remained there until the subject pressed a key which removed it. After an appropriate retention interval, the discrimination task was presented with the sample being projected on one side of the screen and a new stimulus (e.g., square) being projected on the other side. The two stimuli remained on the screen until the subject made a choice by pressing a lever beneath one stimulus. A correct response was followed by the delivery of a food pellet, whereas an incorrect response was followed by a dimming of the house light for one minute. At the end of this period, the house light was returned to full illumination and the subject was free to begin the next trial.

The experimenters were interested in examining performance as a function of the length of the retention interval, which was 15, 30, 60, or 120 seconds. An added concern was whether performance would be influenced by the subjects spending the delay interval in either darkness or normal illumination. D'Amato and O'Neill's results, as Figure 10–5 reveals, indicated that percent responding was substantially above chance when the 15-second delay interval was used, but it may be noted that performance

Figure 10–5
Delayed matching to sample performance as a function of the duration and lighting conditions of the delay (retention) interval. House light on (●—●) house light off (0—0). Adapted from M. R. D'Amato and W. O. O'Neill, "Effect of delay-interval illumination on matching behavior in the capachin monkey," *Journal of the Experimental Analysis of Behavior*, 1971, *15*, 327–333. Copyright © 1971 by the Society for the Experimental Analysis of Behavior. Reprinted by permission.

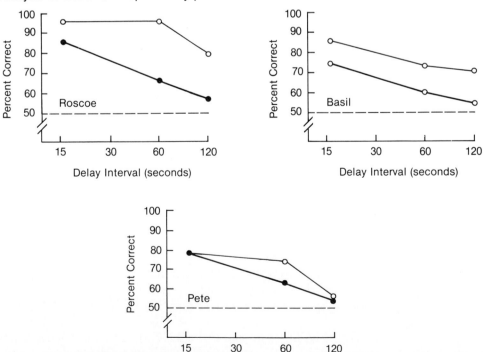

gradually declined as the retention interval grew longer until subjects were responding at only slightly better than chance when the 120-second delay interval was employed. In addition, it will be noted that spending the delay interval in darkness aided correct responding.

A second DMTS variable of interest to experimenters has been the duration of the presentation of the sample stimulus. A study by Grant (1976), using pigeons as experimental subjects, has examined this condition as well as manipulated the duration of the retention interval. Four levels of sample stimulus presentation time (e.g., 1, 4, 8, or 14 seconds) were examined and combined with four durations of the retention interval (e.g., 0, 20, 40, or 60 seconds). The sample and test stimuli were pairs of colors (e.g., red and green, and yellow and blue). A within-subjects experimental design was used with each subject serving under all conditions. As Figure 10–6 shows, matching accuracy was a negatively accelerated increasing function of sample presentation time. Thus, the longer the time that the sample stimulus was presented, the better the performance. In addition, D'Amato and O'Neill's (1971) retention interval findings were confirmed since it was noted that performance was a decreasing function of the length of the delay interval.

Many experimenters have replicated the stimulus presentation time and length of the retention interval findings, with Guttenberger and Wasserman (1985) obtaining these results using the DMTS go/no go task.

Some experimenters have assumed that working memory can best be described by hypothesizing that the memorial representation of the sample stimulus is a memory

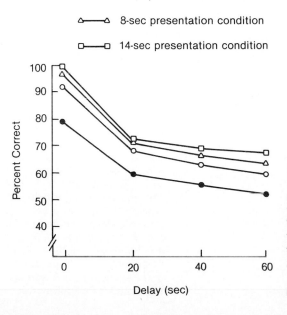

o——o 1-sec presentation condition

o——o 4-sec presentation condition

△——△ 8-sec presentation condition

□——□ 14-sec presentation condition

Figure 10-6
Retention curves for the 1-, 4-, 8-, and 14-second presentation conditions. Adapted from D. S. Grant, "Effect of sample presentation time on long-delay matching in the pigeon," *Learning and Motivation*, 1976, 7, 580–590. Copyright © 1976 by Academic Press. Reprinted by permission.

trace, the strength of which decays over time. When the discrimination task is presented, the subject compares each test stimulus with the trace and responds to the stimulus that matches the trace. By increasing the duration of sample stimulus presentation, the strength of the trace is increased, thus leading to improved performance. Conversely, as the duration of the retention interval is decreased, the strength of the trace becomes weaker, making the matching operation more difficult and resulting in poorer performance.

As we shall also note in Chapter Fourteen, the postulation of a memory trace weakening as a function of the length of the delay interval has been referred to as a *decay theory*; thus, some investigators have assumed that the decaying or weakening of the trace (and revealed in poorer retention) can be attributed solely to the passage of time. An alternative point of view has been that retention decrement (or forgetting) can be explained in terms of interference—material that the subject has learned or stimulation that has been experienced either prior to participation in the task or during the retention interval interferes with correct responding when the discrimination task is presented.

D'Amato and O'Neill's findings that superior DMTS task performance was obtained when their monkeys experienced the retention interval in darkness (in contrast to the same length of time in normal illumination) is difficult to reconcile with the assumption that working memory decays as a function of time. D'Amato and O'Neill's results have been confirmed by Roberts and Grant (1978) who, using pigeons as their experimental subjects, provided retention interval delays of either 0, 0.5, 1, 2, 4, 6, or 12 seconds. On some trials the retention interval was spent in darkness, whereas on other trials the house lights were on. Figure 10-7 indicates the significant differences in correct responding over the varying delay intervals as a function of whether the interval was spent in darkness or in light.

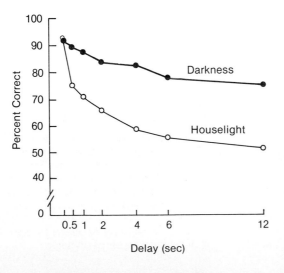

Figure 10-7
Retention curves for delays filled with darkness and delays filled with houselight. Adapted from W. A. Roberts and D. S. Grant, "An analysis of light-induced retroactive inhibition in pigeon short-term memory," *Journal of Experimental Psychology: Animal Behavior Processes*, 1978, 4, 219–236. Copyright © 1978 by the American Psychological Association. Reprinted by permission.

Worsham (1975) has noted also that animals perform better when there is a large set of stimulus items from which the experimenter selects sample and nonmatching stimulus items than when the selection is from a small set of items. This suggests that the animal's previous experience with stimulus items that serve as both matching and nonmatching stimuli plays an important role in influencing performance. Zentall and Hogan (1977) have confirmed this position, finding that the more experience a subject has had with the nonmatching stimulus as a sample, the poorer performance is. And a DMTS task study conducted by Medin, Reynolds, and Parkinson (1980) has revealed that stimuli that were presented to their subjects during the retention interval either facilitated or interfered with the discrimination task performance as a consequence of the characteristics of the interpolated stimuli. An explanation of the weakening of working memory based on interference rather than decay appears to be more in accord with the experimental evidence.

One other variable that has been shown to contribute to DMTS task performance has been the characteristics of the stimuli. Typically, pigeons, and to a lesser extent monkeys, are provided relatively simple types of stimuli to match to sample (e.g., colored disks, vertical and horizontal lines, basic shapes such as triangles or squares, etc.). A study by Wilkie and Summers (1982), using pigeons, employed sample and test stimuli consisting of a series of three lights located within a 3×3 array. Thus, the spatial position of the lights represented the sample that had to be matched when the discrimination task was presented. Results indicated that memory for the position of the illuminated lights was significantly superior when they were placed either horizontally or vertically, in contrast to a diagonal placement. A second finding was that linear patterns produced fewer errors than nonlinear discontinuous patterns even though the discontinuous patterns were presented for five times as long as the line pattern.[3]

The Nature of the Mental Representation

What is the nature of the mental representation in working memory? A variety of possibilities can be suggested with the kind of tasks, as well as the stimuli used with the task, being important determinants.

In the DMTS task where the subject must match the sample stimulus with one of the test stimuli, it seems reasonable to assume that the mental representation is identical to the sample stimulus. Thus, when a subject is provided with a homogeneous red sample stimulus and has the representation of *red* in its working memory, and when the test stimuli are presented, the subject matches the representation of red with the appropriate stimulus. There is the suggestion from D'Amato, Salmon, and Colombo (1985), however, that the representation present on early training trials may change—

---

[3] The authors believed that their finding that pigeons remember three-light locations with some difficulty reflects the effects of procedural variables rather than a working memory limitation. In support of their position, they have called attention to field foraging studies in which nectar-feeding birds avoid returning to depleted flowers even when the flowers number in the hundreds and the foraging bout extends over a period of hours.

perhaps something is added—as the experimental subject acquires greater experience with the task.

The added component, the authors have posited, is the learning of a concept, in this instance the sameness of stimuli, that enables these subjects to learn DMTS task more easily with experience. The evidence to support their position is as follows: D'Amato and colleagues (1985) have found that monkeys require a large number of trials in order to learn the first DMTS task that is presented, reporting, for example, that the number of trials necessary for their subjects to reach a criterion of 90% correct on 96 trials has ranged from 373 to as many as 4,673. Following the learning of the first DMTS task, they presented their subjects with a second DMTS problem and found that it took their monkeys considerably fewer trials to learn this new task. In order to account for the superior learning of the second task, D'Amato and colleagues assumed that their animals had acquired a strategy based on the concept of sameness. Thus, any perceived stimulus (in the discrimination task) that was the same as the stimulus representation which they held in memory should be responded to.

In this DMTS task previously described, there was an identity between the mental representation of the sample stimulus and one test stimulus. We should be aware, however, that such an identity need not always occur. One example is found with conditional discrimination. Here, the cue or stimulus only designates the correct response. For example, the task may consist of presenting two black cards at the choice point as a cue for a rat to turn right in a T-maze in order to secure reinforcement, whereas two white cards cue the animal to turn left. Note that the animal does not obtain reward for approaching a particular stimulus, as would be the case in a traditional black-white discrimination task. Rather the two black and two white stimulus cards serve as cues for choice responses that are related to other stimuli (e.g., kinesthetic cues) that have been associated with correct responding. Since rats are capable of learning such conditional discriminations, it has been assumed that the mental representations of the sample stimulus must be transformed into some other representation which leads to correct responding.

An example of pigeons learning a conditional discrimination in the DMTS study has been noted by Urcuioli and Zentall (1986). In one experiment, four groups of pigeons learned to respond to sample and test stimuli with delay intervals of 0, 1, 2, 4, or 8 seconds provided between the presentation of the sample stimulus and the test stimulus. The pigeons were provided with 25 sessions consisting of 100 trials per session. The sample and test stimuli were as follows:

Group 1: Sample stimulus: red or green hue
          Test stimuli: vertical and horizonal lines

Group 2: Sample stimulus: vertical or horizonal lines
          Test stimulus: red and green hues

For these groups it was necessary for the pigeons to transform (or code) the sample stimulus into a mental representation different from that provided by the sample stimulus in order to facilitate acquisition of the task.

Two traditional DMTS groups were employed in order to examine how discrimination learning would take place when there was direct representation of the stimuli.

Group 3:   Sample stimulus: red or green hue

Test stimulus: red and green hue

Group 4:   Sample stimulus: vertical or horizonal lines

Test stimulus: vertical or horizonal lines

Figure 10-8 provides the performance gradients for the four groups averaged over all sessions and as a function of the length of the delay interval. It is interesting to note that the use of the very discriminable sample stimuli for pigeons, hues, with the test stimuli consisting of vertical and horizontal lines, resulted in better performance than if both the sample and test stimulus were vertical lines.

Some investigators have given the name *prospective coding* to the inferred transformation process in which the subject can use a representation that mirrors the sample

Figure 10-8
Retention gradients for the four groups averaged over all sessions of delayed matching-to-sample with long delays (in seconds). (L = line; H = hue.) Adapted from P. J. Urcuioli and T. R. Zentall, "Retrospective coding in pigeons' delayed matching-to-sample," *Journal of Experimental Psychology: Animal Behavior Processes*, 1986, *12*, 69–77. Copyright © 1986 by the American Psychological Association. Reprinted with permission.

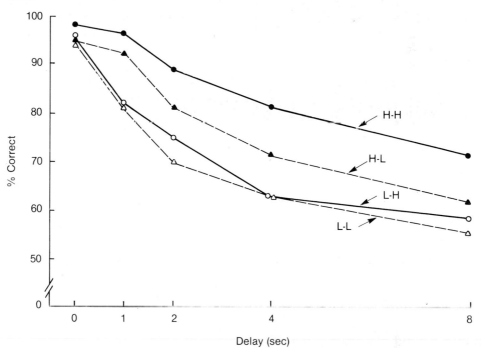

stimulus to solve the discrimination task. In contrast, retrospective coding has been used to identify the process whereby the subject must transform the representation that mirrors the sample stimulus to another representation that does not provide such identity, but at the same time enables the subject to acquire the discrimination. Urcuioli and Zentall (1986) have indicated that the results of their study suggest that coding processes inferred from their findings appear to be flexible—that the discriminability of the stimuli can make an important contribution as to whether prospective or retrospective coding will result in superior discrimination performance.

A second type of task that has been used to examine the nature of working memory is the *radial maze*. This type of apparatus consists of a number of arms (e.g., 8, 12, or 16) radiating out from a central platform. At the end of each arm is a small hole that serves as a food cup. Olton and Samuelson (1976) have conducted a series of experiments using a maze containing 8 arms, seen in Figure 10-9. The general procedure consisted of placing rats on a food-deprivation schedule and first adapting them to the apparatus. Test sessions consisted of placing each animal on the platform where it was permitted to choose freely among all of the arms on the maze. At the beginning of each session, a pellet of food was placed on each arm; once an arm had been chosen and the pellet was consumed, it was not replaced during the session.

The most efficient strategy would be for the animals to select only those arms that contained food. One result obtained from the authors' investigation (experiment 4) indicated that this is what the animals learned to do. The choosing of an arm that contained food was considered as a correct response. Figure 10-10 illustrates the number of correct responses made during the first 8 choices over the 20 test days that were provided. Thus, the mean number of correct responses for the first five days was 6.9, with performance improving to a mean of 7.5 during days 6-10, then increasing to an asymptote at 7.6 on days 11-30. Although the animals' early performance began at significantly better than chance, a significant amount of learning did take place over the first ten test days.

Inasmuch as Olton and Samuelson's (1976) animals performed quite well at the beginning of the experiment, it was necessary first for the authors to consider explanations for their performance that did not include the construct of memory. One

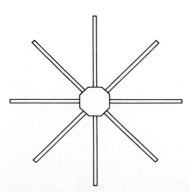

Figure 10-9
Radial maze of the type used by Olton and Samuelson (1976). Animals are placed on the center platform and may enter any arm. Food is placed at the end of each arm.

Figure 10-10
Mean number of correct responses made during the animals' first eight choices as a function of test days. Plotted from data provided by Olton and Samuelson (1976).

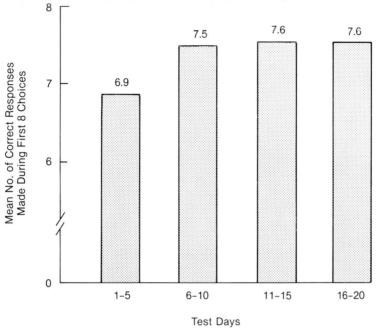

possibility would be that the animals left an odor when they ran over a maze arm to secure food; a second possibility was that they could pick up the scent of food located on specific arms. In one experiment the authors sprinkled aftershave lotion on all of the arms just prior to testing each rat and found that although the smell appeared to disturb the general activity of the animals on early trials, it had no effect on the correctness of their responding. It might be added that Zoladek and Roberts (1978), using the radial arm maze, surgically disrupted the animals' sense of smell and found that the accuracy of responding was not influenced. Olton and Samuelson also observed that the animals did not use any fixed sequences of responding (e.g., responding to the arm on their immediate left [or right] after returning from a rewarded pathway), which could explain their unusual performance. With these explanations for their animal's performance thus ruled out, Olton and Samuelson (1976) inferred the operation of "spatial memory" in their animals in order to account for their experimental findings.

There is a problem, of course, in such an inference since the concept of spatial memory only describes that their animals were successful in choosing arms that contained food (or avoiding those that did not). In addition, this type of inference raises the specter of investigators inferring a specific kind of memory for each type of learning problem that can be mastered. To illustrate, Menzel (1978) found that a young chimpanzee, who had been carried around in an open field viewing where an experimenter hid food, was able, after an interval of time, to go directly to the varying hidden locations, in fact, following a path more direct than that used by the experimenter. Menzel posited that the animal had acquired a cognitive map that enabled it to retrieve food successfully in a minimum amount of time. The inference of a cognitive map presumably represents a different kind of mental representation than that inferred from the DMTS studies.

Summing Up

We have provided only an introduction to the identification of cognitive processes presumed to operate in animals learning discrimination tasks; many other examples could have been cited. Church and his associates (e.g., Church, Getty, and Lerner, 1976; Church, 1978; Church and Gibbon, 1982; and Roberts, 1983) have inferred the presence of an internal clock in rats learning to make temporal discriminations; Hulse (1978) has identified cognitive mechanisms operating in serial pattern learning of rats; and Gardner and Gardner (1974) have employed cognitive constructs in understanding language learning in chimpanzees. Our primary purpose, however, has been to illustrate the work of investigators who believe that the positing of cognitive constructs, and in particular the concept of attention and memory, can lead to a better understanding of the nature of discrimination learning.

It must be acknowledged, however, that the postulation of such constructs has its difficulties, and there is not universal acceptance among the scientific community that this approach is always profitable. Frequently, the definition of the posited construct is circular (e.g., spatial memory accounts for the findings that rats are able to learn to take different paths in the radial maze), but such findings are used to support the existence of spatial memory. In the last analysis, the investigators are speculating (often based on their own experiences or intuition) about the existence and operation of these processes.[4]

Perhaps the answer to whether or not the positing of cognitive processes is helpful is a pragmatic one. If such hypothesizing leads to better learning and memory models, provides new insights, and suggests important experiments, it can be considered as a worthwhile enterprise. On the other hand, if the psychology of learning is inundated by the positing of a multitude of cognitive processes presumed to be operating in conditioning tasks, with little or no attempt to define them independently of the experimental findings they are presumed to explain, and to the extent that the end result is nothing more than a mere listing of these processes, it is likely that we shall return to the problem that has plagued investigators who had used the concept of instinct to "solve" the problem of motivation.

---

[4] Universal agreement has not been achieved with regard to the hypothesizing of cognitive processes in animals. One only has to examine Roitblat's (1982) "The Meaning of Representation in Animal Memory" and the many commentaries this article has elicited to be aware of the diversity of opinions regarding the usefulness of cognitive constructs.

Choice Behavior ►

In the late 1960s a new area emerged from the examination of discrimination learning—the study of choice behavior. It has been a subject matter of growing interest and although extensive coverage of the area will be left to more advanced texts, we will provide the reader with a brief introduction to the topic.

It is obvious that the study of discrimination learning and the study of choice are interrelated. One difference however, is that with discrimination learning, the experimenter places emphasis on the acquisition process—how discrimination learning proceeds over trials. Thus, in the typical two-stimulus discrimination task, the experimental operation is so arranged that responding to one stimulus leads to reinforcement, whereas responding to the other stimulus does not. In many instances, the experimental subjects have had little, if any, experience with the discriminanda so that it is necessary for them to learn to differentiate between them prior to their learning that responding to one stimulus is associated with reinforcement, whereas responding to the other is not.

Although the study of choice involves employing a discrimination task, responding to the discriminanda has been previously established; if not, preliminary training provides such learning. In addition, reinforcement is associated with both discriminanda, with the variable of interest being related to reinforcement differences that are experimentally arranged and associated with each stimulus. For example, an investigator may be interested in examining how choice responding is related to providing a rat in a Skinner Box with a one-pellet reward for responding to the lever on the right side of the box, in contrast to giving the animal three pellets for responding to the lever on the left side. Or another experimenter may be interested in determining how choice responding is influenced by providing pigeons immediate access to a hopper of grain for pecking at one visual stimulus, whereas pecking at the other will result in access to food only after a four-second delay. In each instance, the subjects receive reinforcement for either choice; however, experimental interest is directed toward how the distribution of the subjects' responses can be related to the differences in reinforcement that are provided. Considering the extent that choice is involved in virtually all of both human and infrahuman behavior, it is not surprising that studies of choice can be found in as diverse subject matter areas as ethology and economics.

The examination of choice behavior has been undertaken primarily by operant investigators using concurrent and concurrent chain schedules of reinforcement as their basic methodology. The experimental work has been quite extensive so our presentation shall be limited to a few of the basic findings.

Use of Concurrent Schedules

It will be recalled that a concurrent schedule consists of two response keys made available to the subject, frequently pigeons, with each key being associated with a specific reinforcement schedule with the subject free to switch from one key to the other. By manipulating the reward schedule associated with each key, it is possible to examine how differences between schedules influence the frequency or distribution of responses. (See Figure 10–11.)

The measurement of choice is reflected in the distribution of the pecking response made to each discriminanda. A common procedure has been to calculate the relative frequency or rate of responding to each key. This measure is obtained by dividing the rate of responding on one key by the total rate of responding obtained by measuring the number of responses on both keys. Thus, if the pigeon responds equally often on both keys, the ratio will be 0.5; however, if the response frequency on the first key is less than the frequency of responding on the second key, the ratio will be less than 0.5.

The Matching Law

It has been noted that a pigeon's rate of responding appears to be related to the VI reinforcement schedule associated with each stimulus. If the same schedule is provided for each key, the subject will respond to each key equally often. But what if a disparity between reinforcement schedules exists? In answering this question, Herrnstein (1961) has found that a proportional relationship between the responses and reinforcement holds over a wide range of variable interval values. For example, he found that if the proportion of reinforcements available to the pigeon on Key 1 was 0.25, the proportion of responses the pigeon would make to this key would also be 0.25. However, if the proportion of reinforcements available on this key was increased to 0.75, the proportion of responding by the pigeon to this key would also increase to 0.75. This led to his postulation of a matching law which states that the relative frequency of a response will match the relative frequency of the reinforcement obtained by the response. This relationship has been expressed as follows:

$$\frac{\text{Response to Stimulus 1}}{\text{Responding to Stimulus 1} + \text{Responding to Stimulus 2}} = \frac{\text{Reinforcement Obtained from Stimulus 1}}{\text{Reinforcement Obtained from Stimulus 1} + \text{Reinforcement Obtained from Stimulus 2}}$$

An interesting demonstration of the matching law, as it operates with humans, has been provided by Schroeder and Holland (1969), who used eye movements as a

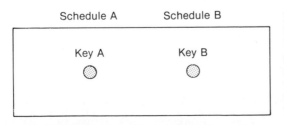

Schedule A   Schedule B

Key A   Key B

Figure 10–11
Diagram of a concurrent schedule. Pecking on Key A is reinforced according to a FI 30-second schedule of reinforcement, whereas pecking on Key B is reinforced according to a VR 25 reinforcement schedule.

response measure. The task of the subject was to match for deflections of a pointer, which could appear on any of four dials. Two dials were placed on the right side of the apparatus and two dials were placed on the left side. The task of the subjects was to detect as many deflections as possible. When the deflection was noted, the subject used a button to reset the pointer, an act that could be considered reinforcement. Looking at the two dials on one side of the apparatus was considered to be equivalent to responding to a single key, whereas looking horizontally or diagonally was analoguous to switching from one key to another, as would be done with a concurrent schedule. Varying numbers of reflections were provided on the right and left dials. The experimenters found that their subjects matched their rate of eye movements to the rate of reinforcement.

Bradshaw, Szabadi, Bevan, and Ruddle (1976) were also able to obtain support for the matching law by using a procedure that involved just one response key. In this study, human subjects were told that they could earn money by pressing a button when one of five amber disks arranged in horizontal fashion was illuminated. Illumination of a green light beneath the amber one indicated to the subjects that they had earned a monetary reward. The amber disks were illuminated for 10 minutes followed by a 5-minute rest period. Fifteen experimental sessions were provided, with each of the five disks being illuminated during each session. Each amber disk was associated with a different VI schedule; thus $A - 1 = 720$ seconds; $A - 2 = 157$ seconds; $A - 3 = 51$ seconds; $A - 4 = 25$ seconds; and $A - 5 = 17$ seconds. Results revealed that the subject's button-pressing performance conformed to the matching law.

We have discussed just two studies that have resulted in the response frequency of human subjects conforming to the matching law but others could also have been cited. In fact, Pierce and Epling's (1983) review indicated that 13 out of 16 experimental investigations using human subjects supported the position that performance on a concurrent interval schedule could be described by the matching law where relative responding matched the relative rate of reinforcement.

Undermatching and Overmatching

DeVillier's (1977) review of many of the matching experiments has indicated that Herrnstein's matching law can account for most, although not all, of the experimental findings. Two types of deviations have been noted: overmatching and undermatching. An example of undermatching, which is the more frequent of the two, would be when the proportion of reinforcers for responding to the left key was 0.9, when the actual proportion of the left key responses would be 0.75, or if the proportion of reinforcers to the left key was 0.3, and the proportion of left key responses would be .45. In summary, undermatching describes a situation in which a subject's preferences are closer to 0.5 than they would be according to the matching law.

Overmatching is the opposite of undermatching. Here, the subject's response proportions are more extreme than the reinforcement proportions that have been provided. For example, a reinforcement proportion of 0.7 produces a response proportion of 0.8, whereas a reinforcer proportion of a 0.4 produces a response proportion of 0.2.

Although overmatching and undermatching have been reported, some of these findings can undoubtedly be accounted for by making an analysis of the conditions under which these experimental findings have been obtained. Perhaps the most basic of these is related to being sure that the two response alternatives are truly independent. In some studies the experimental procedure has been so arranged that the pigeon received reinforcement for its first response after switching from one key to another. Such a procedure will often result in reinforcing the switching response, which of course, is not the objective of the experimenter. In order to solve this problem, some constraints on providing reinforcement after switching are typically provided. One such restraint is that reinforcement will not be provided following a switch until after several responses have been made or a certain time period has elapsed. This procedure has been identified as the *change over delay* (COD). Herrnstein (1961), Shull and Pliskoff (1967), and others have demonstrated that some minimum COD duration is necessary if matching is to be obtained.

The Examination of Other Reinforcement Variables

We have noted that choice, or response frequency, as measured with a concurrent schedule, is related to the frequency of reinforcement. Can variations of reward amount and reward delay also reflect differential response frequency? Experimenters have demonstrated such to be the case—the manipulation of both of these variables can influence choice responding.

In a study by Catania (1963a), amount of reinforcement provided on a VI schedule was manipulated by permitting pigeons access to a feeder for either 3.0, 4.5, or 6.0 seconds with the following combinations utilized:

Left key 4.5 seconds; right key 4.5 seconds

Left key 6.0 seconds; right key 3.0 seconds

Left key 3.0 seconds; right key 6.0 seconds

Left key 4.5 seconds; right key 4.5 seconds

With the concurrent procedure, response rate was linearly related to the duration of reinforcement. The sensitivity of the choice procedure was indicated by the finding that if only a single key was used and the responding was related to reinforcement amounts of either 3.0, 4.5, or 6.0 seconds, no difference in responding was noted.

A study by Chung (1965) (with her findings extended by Chung and Herrnstein, 1967) has demonstrated that reinforcement delay on the concurrent task also influences choice responding. In Chung's (1965) study, pigeons learned to peck at one of two response keys for reinforcement on a VI-1-minute schedule, with reinforcement delay intervals on one key (the experimental key) being either 0, 1, 4, 6, 8, 12, 20, 24, or 28 seconds, presented in irregular order. The other key (a standard key) resulted in the subjects receiving reinforcement immediately but, of course, in keeping with the VI-1-minute schedule that was in operation. In Chung and Herrnstein's (1967) experiment, a similar procedure was utilized except that for some subjects, the standard key was reinforced after an 8-second delay, whereas for other subjects, the standard key was reinforced after a 16-second delay. Reinforcement for responses on the experimental key were provided at the following delay intervals: 1, 2, 4, 6, 8, 12, 16, 20, 24, and 30 seconds. As in the Chung (1965) study, between the response-to-be reinforced and the delivery of reinforcement, the experimental chamber was darkened and responses produced no auditory feedback.

Both Chung (1965) and Chung and Herrnstein's (1967) findings are presented in Figure 10–12, which reveals the relative frequency of responding on the experimental key. It may be noted that when the delay of reinforcement is the same on both keys, responding with a 0- and 8-second delay approximates 0.5—an expected finding. Results obtained when responding to the standard key resulted in a 16-second delay period, suggesting that there was some degree of artifactual key-preference for this group. Nonetheless, the findings clearly support the position that choice responding can be related to the duration of the reinforcement delay.

Concurrent Chain Schedules

In the choice experiments we have described, it may be noted that the pigeon is free to switch from one response key to another at any time. We frequently find choice situations of this type. At the salad bar in a restaurant, for example, we are free to switch from one kind of foodstuff to another at any time. Or during an evening of studying, we are free to switch from one subject to another whenever we wish.

Other choice situations can be more complex, however. In some cases, choosing

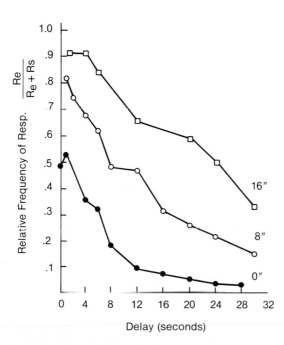

Figure 10-12
Relative frequency of responding on the experimental key as a function of the reinforcement delay for that key, averaged across subjects. The parameters refer to the duration of the standard delay. The bottom curve was taken from Chung (1956). Adapted from S. H. Chung and R. J. Herrnstein, "Choice and delay of reinforcement," *Journal of the Experimental Analysis of Behavior*, 1967, *10*, 67-74. Copyright © 1967 by the Society for the Experimental Analysis of Behavior. Reprinted by permission.

one alternative means that we are no longer free to switch since the alternative is no longer available. Choosing between vacationing at the seashore or backpacking in the mountains means that a choice of the seashore foregoes the opportunity of backpacking.

This kind of choice situation has been examined most frequently by operant investigators using pigeons as experimental subjects and employing concurrent chain schedules of reinforcement. In the typical concurrent chain, the initial link consists of providing equal independent fixed or interval schedules programmed on each of two keys, with the subject making a choice by appropriately responding to one of them. The reinforcement for this response is entrance into a particular terminal link that has been associated with that key. This terminal link generally consists of presenting only a single key that must be responded to; thus, the opportunity for choice by the subject is absent. We may say that the initial choice keys will determine the nature of the reinforcing event provided during the terminal link of the chain. For example, if an experimenter is interested in determining whether a pigeon will choose between the presentation of a small reward or a large reward, the procedure would be as illustrated in Figure 10–13.

An example of the use of a concurrent chain schedule is found in a study by Ito and Asaki (1982) examining how a rat's preference for a large reward is influenced by the

Figure 10–13
Diagram of a concurrent chain schedule.

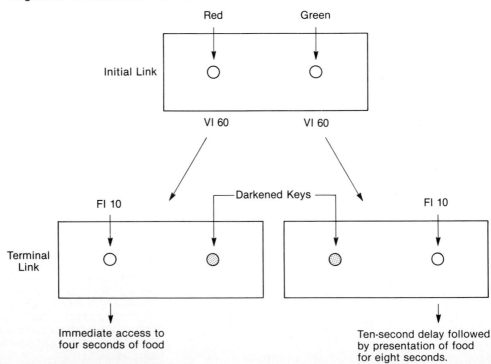

length of the delay of reinforcement provided in a terminal FI schedule. Their procedure consisted of providing rats with two levers; the initial link had a VI-60-second schedule. Appropriate responding on the left lever resulted in the introduction of an FI schedule (terminal link) of a given length followed by a large reward of three food pellets. If the right lever was chosen in the initial link, appropriate responding also resulted in an FI schedule of the same duration as that provided on the right lever. However, the reinforcement that followed consisted of only a single food pellet. The variable of interest for the experimenters was the length of the FI interval (terminal link) with the intervals chosen being 5, 10, 20, or 40 seconds. The experimental findings are presented in Figure 10–14. It may be noted that with the smallest FI interval (5 seconds), there was only a slight preference for responding to the left lever, which provided three pellets. But as the length of the FI interval increased to 40 seconds, there was an increasing preference for that lever. Thus, we may note that the subjects' performance reflects an interaction between the length of the terminal link and the amount of reinforcement provided, with the reinforcement variable reflecting substantial performance differences only when the terminal link of the concurrent chain had an extended duration.

One interesting extension of the concurrent chain schedule is found in a study by Rachlin and Green (1972), who provided a model of what they identified as self-control and commitment. One manifestation of what we normally mean by self-control is the capacity of an individual, when given the opportunity to obtain immediate gratification, to refrain from such responding in order to secure a delayed reward of greater consequence. Thus, dieters exercise self-control when they choose a delayed reward of personal and social consequence—losing weight—over the immediate pleasure derived from eating a dish of ice cream.

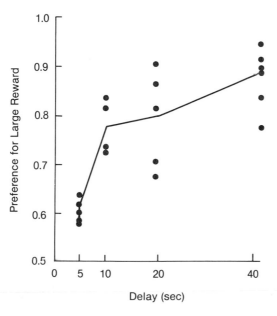

Figure 10–14
Percent choice of the large reward as a function the length of the delay period provided during the terminal link of the chain. Filled circles refer to responses by individual animals. Adapted from M. Ito and K. Asaki, "Choice behavior of rats in a concurrent-chains schedule: Amount and delay of reinforcement," *Journal of the Experimental Analysis of Behavior*, 1982, *37*, 383–392. Copyright © 1982, by the Society for the Experimental Analysis of Behavior. Reprinted by permission.

These investigators provided what they believed to be a laboratory model or analogue of this situation by using pigeons that were provided with a choice of experiencing an immediate small reward or a delayed reward. During the initial link, their experimental procedure consisted of presenting left and right white keys with passage to the terminal link governed by a FR 25, which could be distributed in any manner on the two keys. If the 25th peck was on the right key, both keys and the house lights were blacked out for a variable length of time. Following the blackout, the keys were reilluminated, one key with a red light, and the other with green. A single peck on the red key produced two seconds of access to food, followed by six seconds of blackout. A single peck on the green key produced four seconds of blackout, followed by four seconds of access to food.

During the initial link, if the 25th peck was on the left key, there was a blackout for

Figure 10-15
Concurrent chain schedule used by Rachlin and Green. The 25th peck on the right key in the initial link leads to the upper branch, which presents a choice between delayed, greater reinforcement (green key) vs. immediate, lesser reinforcement (red key). The 25th peck on the left key in the initial link leads to the lower branch, which presents the green key only (greater, delayed reinforcement), the other key being darkened. *T* represents the length of the delay between the end of the initial link and the presentation of the red and green key (choice) or green key only (no choice). Adapted from H. Rachlin and L. Green, "Commitment, choice and self control," *Journal of the Experimental Analysis of Behavior*, 1972, *17*, 15–22. Copyright © 1972, by the Society for the Experimental Analysis of Behavior. Reprinted by permission.

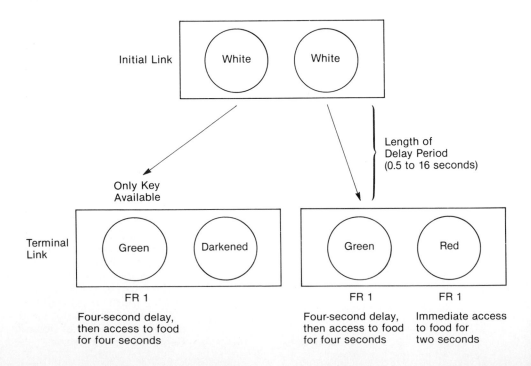

Initial Link   White   White

Length of Delay Period (0.5 to 16 seconds)

Only Key Available

Terminal Link   Green   Darkened   Green   Red

FR 1   FR 1   FR 1

Four-second delay, then access to food for four seconds

Four-second delay, then access to food for four seconds

Immediate access to food for two seconds

a variable length of time, followed by reillumination of only the green key. The other remained dark. A single peck of the green key produced a 4-second blackout, followed by 4 seconds of access to food. Following preliminary training in which a 10-second blackout period was used, 10 sessions of 50 trials each were provided utilizing each of the following time periods in turn: 0.5, 1, 2, 4, 8, 16, 8, 4, 2, 1, and 0.5 seconds. (See Figure 10–15.)

The number of times (or proportion of pecks) that the pigeons responded to the left key in the initial link (or what the investigators considered to be a commitment) represented the basic response measure. Figure 10–16 presents the findings. It may be noted that as the duration of the blackout period increased, the proportion of pecks on the left key gradually increased until, at 16 seconds, almost all of the pigeon's responding was to the left key. The analysis of these findings suggests that if the length of the blackout period is minimal, the pigeons will choose the right key, which gives them a choice of a small immediate reward or a large delayed reward and they invariably choose the small immediate reward. Lengthening the blackout period to 16 seconds, however, results in the pigeons choosing the left key during the initial link. It will be recalled that this does not result in the terminal link providing the subjects with any choice—they must wait four seconds prior to receiving a large reward. By choosing the left key, they have, in effect, made a commitment to wait for the larger reward.

In summary, if reward is provided soon after the subjects make a choice, they will respond to the stimulus that provides them a small but immediate reward. However, if a delay is added to the delivery of the reward, subjects are likely to forgo the immediate

Figure 10–16
Proportion of choices on the left key as a function of the duration of the delay period imposed between responding during the initial link and terminal link responding. Adapted from H. Rachlin and L. Green, "Commitment, choice and self control," *Journal of the Experimental Analysis of Behavior*, 1972, *17*, 15–22. Copyright © 1972, by the Society for the Experimental Analysis of Behavior. Reprinted by permission.

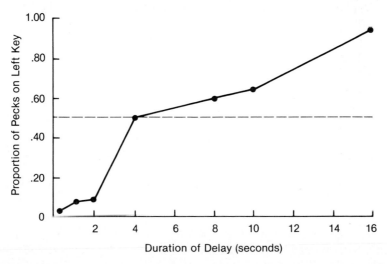

small reward and respond to the stimulus that provides the delayed large one. Thus, there is a reversal of preference from an immediate small reward to a delayed large reward as the duration of the delay of reward increases. This finding has been replicated by Ainslie and Herrnstein (1981).

Summary ►

In this chapter we continued to discuss discrimination learning, examining the contribution of cognitive processes as well as investigating the related topic of choice.

Early investigators found that it was possible for animals to learn about relationships existing among stimuli. The transposition experiment represents one paradigm from which relationship learning was inferred. A second cognitive process, learning to learn, was posited by Harlow, who found that monkeys could solve object discrimination problems with increasing efficiency as a function of their previous experience with this type of task.

Two cognitive processes that have interested current investigators are: attention and memory. In the experimental studies of Reynolds, he observed that pigeons, when presented with a complex stimulus that was reinforced (e.g., white triangle on red background), did not attend to each stimulus element equally. Rather, his pigeons appeared to pay attention to only a single element (e.g., white triangle). Such selective attention was assumed to be a cognitive process operative in discrimination learning.

The construct of memory has been another cognitive process that was posited, with several discrimination paradigms being used to investigate this construct. One of these is the delayed matching to sample (DMTS); the other is the radial maze. One DMTS has been identified as the retention interval or the length of the delay period placed between the offset of the sample stimulus presentation and the presentation of the discrimination task. The second is the length of time that the sample stimulus is presented. The findings from several studies have indicated that as the length of the retention interval increases, performance deteriorates; in contrast, as the length of time that the sample stimulus is presented increases, performance also increases.

The radial maze is an apparatus with a number of arms radiating out from a central platform. Each arm is baited with food. The choice of arms by rats over the course of a series of responses has been observed. The most efficient strategy would be for the animal to select only those arms that contain food, and investigators have found that this is what animals have learned to do. Investigators have posited the presence of spatial memory in order to account for the animal's ability to refrain from choosing those arms that have already been selected (and do not contain food) and to choose only those arms that have food.

The study of choice behavior has been of interest to investigators for several decades. It differs from an examination of discrimination learning in that all choices of the subject will lead to reinforcement; however, experimental interest is related to reinforcement differences that are associated with each stimulus. A concurrent schedule is often used to examine choice. With such a schedule, two response keys are made available to the subject, typically pigeons, with the birds free to switch from one key to the other. One of the basic findings has been the matching law. Here, it has been found that the pigeon's rate of responding is related to the kind of reinforcement schedule associated with each stimulus. If the same schedule is provided for each key, the subject will respond to each key equally often. Disparities between reinforcement schedules are reflected in the different number of responses made to each key.

Concurrent chain schedules have also been used to examine choice situations. With this paradigm, after the choice has been made, the subject is no longer free to switch to another response key. Using this type of procedure, Rachlin and Green have provided a model of what they have identified as self-control and commitment.

chapter eleven

▶

Generalization and
Application of
Basic Learning Principles

The kinds of learning tasks and procedures that we have described in previous chapters have been especially adapted for laboratory investigations, designed to illuminate the relationships that can be established among stimuli, responses, and reinforcement. But the findings from laboratory tasks, generally employing animals as experimental subjects, raise several interrelated questions. One has to do with whether learning and memory processes play as important a role in determining behavior, particularly in animal responding, as learning theorists have believed. Another question is whether laboratory findings can be generalized to the nonlaboratory environment. The third question, and perhaps the most basic, is whether the experimental results obtained with animals can be generalized to humans.

The Role of Learning and Memory
Processes in Behavior ▶

Many investigators have made the assumption that learning and memory are basic processes that play a very important and pervasive role, not only in determining human behavior but animal behavior as well. But all behavioral scientists have not been in accord with this position. Ethologists, particularly those working in Europe, have approached the study of animal behavior from a markedly different position. We will examine their contribution in some detail.

The Ethological Approach

Ethology, the comparative study of behavior, was brought to the attention of psychologists with the publication of Tinbergen's (1951) book *The Study of Instinct.* This volume, along with the writings of another European, Lorenz (1935, 1950, 1958), provided a different way of studying behavior; it also indicated some of the shortcomings of the point of view that has been adopted by psychologists in the United States. Ethologists stressed the *adaptive* significance of an animal's behavior, an emphasis similar to the prominence physiologists have placed on the adaptive significance of structure. Moreover, ethologists assumed that a genetic factor, passed from generation to generation, was responsible for the transmission of behavior patterns needed for the organism's survival. Evolution selects those anatomical features that lead to survival, and behavior patterns are selected in much the same way.

The ethologist's general approach has been first to observe the animal in a naturalistic setting, and in so doing, become familiar with the animal's activities, undisturbed by outside distractions. Goodall's (1963, 1986) widely publicized description of the behavior of wild chimpanzees is one example. Following such observation, an ethogram is constructed, which consists of a cataloging of the various activities engaged in by the subject. Since it is not practical to obtain a complete cataloging of all of these, investigators usually select more restricted behavior patterns (e.g., feeding, courtship) to study, along with a description of the stimuli that appear to elicit them.

Many of the animal's activities have been identified as fixed-action patterns— sequences of behavior assumed to be innate or instinctive. A counterpart of the fixed-action pattern was hypothesized to be the *innate releasing mechanism* (IRM), which was posited to consist of two parts: (1) a standard external stimulus or releaser, and (2) an internal state that was basically responsible for the appearance of the instinctive response. Such fixed-action patterns could take place without any apparent awareness by the animal of the particular function that the act was presumed to play. Examples of such behavior are: a dog hiding a bone in the living room of a home, with the animal attempting to cover it as if it were burying it in the ground, or a cat urinating in a litter box without litter, responding by scratching the bottom of the box as if litter were present.

As we have just noted, ethologists assumed that releasers, or sign (or key) stimuli play an important role in an animal's activities, since it is the sign stimulus that is responsible for instigating or eliciting the fixed-action pattern. Eibl-Eibesfeldt (1970) has written:

> In analogy to a key that opens a lock, the key stimuli act upon a mechanism . . . that normally prevents the release of central impulses when it is not appropriate and will open the way to the musculature when the appropriate key stimuli are received. Each functional cycle has its own key stimuli, and the animal reacts to correspondingly different key stimuli (pp. 67–68).

Ethological research has indicated that a variety of sign stimuli release many different fixed-action patterns in a host of species. For instance, the movement of small insects appears to be a sign stimulus for the toad's prey-catching response—the toad will fixate on the spot where the insect was last seen moving but will rarely snap if the insect remains motionless. In sharks, the odor of blood releases the search-for-prey pattern;

for the mosquito and bedbug, the key stimulus is the heat radiated from warm-blooded animals. A complete listing of all such stimuli would indeed be a long one. (See Box 11–1.)

box 11–1

Ethologists have been especially interested in identifying the stimuli that elicit instinctive responses found in animals. Their position has been that many of these responses appear to be elicited or released by specific attributes of a complex stimulus—stimuli that they have identified as *sign stimuli.*

Tinbergen's (1951) examination of the fighting behavior in the male stickleback fish is a classic example of this type of work. The fighting of male sticklebacks in the spring is directed especially against other male sticklebacks. Tinbergen was interested in determining what stimulus characteristics of the male were responsible for eliciting the fighting behavior. His procedure was to construct a number of models, some of which are illustrated in the figure below. The model identified as N was an accurate imitation of the fish except that it lacked the red throat and belly found in the male. The other models, labeled R, are very crude imitations lacking many of the characteristics of the species, but all possessing a red belly. When these models were placed in the water, Tinbergen found that the sticklebacks reacted vigorously only to the red models, although the fish were perfectly able to see the other details of these crude imitations. Redness in the male was thus identified as a sign stimulus that elicited fighting behavior.

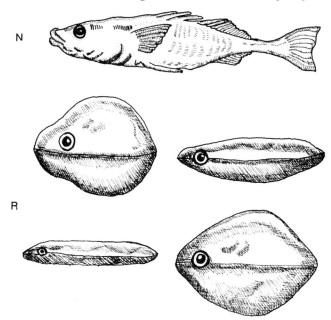

Box Figure 11–1
Models used in eliciting fighting behavior in the male stickleback. The top model, N, is an accurate reproduction of the male fish except that it lacks a red throat and belly. The four lower models, R, are crude imitations but all have the appropriate color. Adapted from N. Tinbergen, *The Study of Instinct,* published by Oxford University Press, 1951.

Another important contribution of the ethological movement was the description of behavior described as *imprinting*. The origin of imprinting theory was found in the early observations of Spalding (1873) who found that as soon as a chick could walk, it would follow any moving object, whether it was the hen that hatched it, a duck, or even a human. Lorenz (1935), who shared the Nobel Prize in 1973 for his contributions to ethology, drew attention to the behavior of young ducklings or goslings who exhibited this type of behavior by following him rather than their mother.

Lorenz noted that the bird's behavior arising from the imprinting process consisted of (1) first perceiving the object and following it, (2) a tendency to approach the object in preference to other objects, and (3) the uttering of distress cries as the object escaped perceptual contact, coupled with sounds of contentment when contact was reestablished.

A number of attributes were identified by Lorenz which he believed differentiated imprinting from the learning process. First, imprinting appeared to operate at only a certain stage or particular time in the bird's development, a time that has been called the *sensitive* or *critical period*. Second, the external stimulus that elicited the behavior had to possess certain well-defined characteristics. Finally, he posited that the imprinting process was irreversible; imprinting responses could not be reversed by subsequent learning.

The early ethologists provided a cogent critique of the learning theorists' (and also comparative psychologists') assumptions about the role of learning in animal behavior as well as their methodology and species examined. Learning was not a general process, they averred, but rather, it was a specific mechanism that interacted with the animal's innate response capacities in order to enable each species to survive in its particular environment. Moreover, the ethologists pointed out that an animal's behavior should be examined in a natural setting; laboratory experiments provided only contrived problems in an artificial environment that was too restrictive and confining. These conditions resulted in the animal being unable to reveal any of its natural ways of responding or employing those processes that were basic to its behavior. Inferences from laboratory experiments were thus apt to be erroneous. Finally, they objected to the very limited number of species that were employed in experiments; most learning theorists utilized rats, pigeons, or monkeys—hardly a representative sample of the animal kingdom.

In an earlier chapter we noted the psychologists' surprise at the findings that the delay of reinforcement gradient for rats learning to avoid a toxic substance could be measured in hours, rather than in seconds, as a number of earlier laboratory discrimination learning studies had found. But such a finding would cause no consternation among ethologists because they would never assume that a learning principle generated from an artificial laboratory task would have relevance for a more naturally occurring one.[1]

---

[1] Learning theorists responded to the ethologists' criticisms by calling attention to a number of difficulties found in the ethological theory of instinctive behavior. An important one was the difficulty of determining what constituted innate behavior as well as noting that the use of the terms *innate* or *instinctive* added little to understanding the origins of any behavior pattern. In

Current Considerations

Contemporary ethologists have discarded some of the hypothesized processes provided by earlier investigators, as well as recognizing the difficulty of providing precise definitions for others. Their most basic concept—instinct, which Lorenz indicated to be a form of innate behavior that is characteristic of the species and is internally motivated—has been abandoned. Hinde's (1982) text, *Ethology,* does not include instinct in its index or glossary. The *innate relearning mechanism* (IRM), which suggests a physiological basis for instinctive behavior, has also been discarded. And there has been the recognition that some of their concepts such as *sign stimulus* and *fixed-action patterns,* although basic to many ethological endeavors, are "slippery at the edges."

Nonetheless, as Gould (1986) has recently written, there are a number of basic constructs found in the early work of Tinbergen and Lorenz that continue to provide a conceptual framework for many contemporary ethologists and comparative psychologists.[2]

The first is the idea of an animal's recognition of important stimuli in the environment. We have already noted how ethologists have catalogued an almost endless list of releasers or sign stimuli. Our growing understanding of the mechanics of sensory processing suggests that most sign stimuli are relatively simple sorts of cues for which ensembles of visual-acoustic-olfactory feature-detectors in the central nervous system are known to code.

A second concept is the fixed-action pattern. A good deal of animal behavior appears to be highly stereotyped; once triggered, it proceeds to completion even if the situation no longer demands it. These units have often been termed *motor programs,* which emphasize their neural basis, but at the same time removing the implication that the units need to be innate or immune to sensory feedback. Fixed-action patterns are of importance to ethologists because they are readily identifiable units that break up the stream of behavior. They have been especially valuable in comparative studies since they can be treated like morphological characters and the small differences between related species can be used to establish hypotheses about their evolution.

A third concept has to do with endogenously generated motivation. As Gould (1986) has indicated, if we assume that much of the lower animal's behavior is triggered and directed by sign stimuli and accomplished by a motor program, it becomes evident

---

addition, laboratory examinations of imprinting by a variety of investigators (e.g., Fabricius and Boyd, 1954; Sluckin and Salzen, 1961; Moltz and Stettner, 1961; and Bateson, 1966) did not always reveal findings that were in keeping with Lorenz's description of the imprinting process. After conducting an extensive series of experimental studies examining the imprinting of ducklings, Hoffman (1978) concluded, "Our findings ... reveal that most, if not all of the seemingly distinctive features of imprinting are in fact the product of a limited number of well-known, if not yet thoroughly understood, behavioral processes" (p. 33). Of these processes, Hoffman pointed out, "It seems clear that the classical conditioning process ... is the heart of imprinting" (p. 19).

[2] Gould (1986) has made the interesting observation that although ethologists are seen as being preoccupied with innate behavior, the Nobel Prize winning trio of early ethologists—von Frisch, Tinbergen, and Lorenz—all began with and frequently returned to studies of learning.

that some of these behavior patterns take place only during certain periods of an animal's life. For example, the behavior that characterizes the Greylag goose's retrieving an egg that has rolled out of the nest occurs only seasonally, appearing about a week before incubation begins and lasting until about a week after hatching. The motivation of such behavior must arise from within the organism, rather than from without.

The fourth concept derived from early ethological theory is imprinting. The temporal sensitivity of the process, its innate triggering by specific sign stimuli, the difficulty in reversing imprinting behavior, as well as the lack of an obvious external reward suggests that imprinting is a pervasive process in animal behavior.

It should be noted that in the past decade, the philosophical and experimental differences existing between the ethologist, and the comparative psychologist and learning theorist, particularly those in the United States, have been markedly reduced. In fact, Snowdon (1983) has pointed to a synthesis of ethology and comparative psychology, whereas Hinde (1982) has suggested that prospects for increased cooperation between ethologists and learning theorists appears bright. The need for such cooperation, Hinde has indicated, is emphasized by a traditional difference in orientation between these two groups of scientists. Ethologists still like to classify types of behavior into groups on the basis of causal or functional grounds (e.g., sexual, aggressive, feeding, etc.). In contrast, psychologists have been concerned with the characteristics of such processes as perception, motivation, and learning, which permeate the ethologists' categories. Hinde points out that the ethologists' bias may lead to shortcomings in their approach to development where such categories can be misleading, and in studies of higher organisms, where cognitive functions may link causal or functional categories of behavior. The psychologists' bias has appeared to retard their recognition of the importance of situation-specific constraints on learning. The integration between these approaches is clearly essential.[3]

Foraging

The ethologists' reservations of learning theorists' attempts to derive general learning principles from animal behavior observed in restricted laboratory settings has at least partially been responsible for psychologists examining some of the functional behavior of animals taking place in specialized laboratory environments that have been so

---

[3] We should not become overly optimistic about any complete rapprochement between ethologists and learning theorists since basic differences continue to exist. For example, the restrictiveness of the laboratory task as well as the limitation of response measurement has resulted in Barnett (1981) writing, "The most obvious limitation of CRs is that the experimental condition in which they are observed allow hardly any behavior. The other popular method, that of the problem [Skinner] box allows the animal to move but ignores all its movements except those that activate a device and provide reinforcement. Usually, the movement recorded is pressing a bar. Behavior is then presented as a set of response rates that vary with the outcome of bar pressing; that is, all the behavior that is acknowledged depends on the 'schedule of reinforcement' provided by the environment. And the environment is, of course, the experimenter and his special equipment. There is little connection between a 'cumulative record' of instrumental movements, on the one hand, and an account of an animal moving around in natural environment, on the other" (p. 626).

arranged as to provide a number of natural environmental components. One of these functional behaviors examined has been *foraging,* which involves the response patterns found in an animal operating in its natural environment, searching for, finding, and consuming food. We cannot provide a detailed description of the variety of experimental findings that have been obtained by investigators working in the area, but we would like to describe some of the significant features of this general area, and in particular, the work of Collier and his associates (e.g., Collier and Rovee-Collier, 1981; and Collier, 1983).

Historically, the study of feeding behavior has largely been confined to an examination of differences among species as to their physiological mechanisms, comparative anatomy, and so on—an area that Collier (1983) has described as *feeding tactics.* Recently, there has been considerable interest in the examination of another area— feeding strategies inferred from the organism's behavior. Interest in this topic was first provided by the papers of MacArthur and Pianka (1966) and Emlen (1966), in which they asked the question of how many food items, ranked in terms of their quantity and nutritional quality, should be included in the diet of an efficiently foraging predator. Foraging costs were divided into those associated with (1) search and (2) pursuit, capture, and consumption. It was hypothesized by these investigators that the optimal diet was one that would include all of the highest ranked down to that particular foodstuff for which reduction in search costs resulting from its inclusion would be less than the increase in the other costs that would be realized as a result of including it.

From this general approach, a number of optimal foraging models have been proposed, with their basic assumption being that the efficiency of foraging, or the net energy yield of feeding relative to the time and/or energy required to feed, is maximized by natural selection.[4]

Collier's (1983) approach has been to identify the behavior patterns or components which make up foraging, with those consisting of (1) the search for food; (2) the identification of food, which involves discriminating food from nonfood, as well as choice between available foods; (3) procurement or the actual securing of food; (4) handling, which includes any preparation necessary for consumption; and (5) food consumption. The experimental apparatus he has employed is illustrated in Figure 11-1. One notable feature of this apparatus environment is that the animal lives in a closed economy. Its total daily food requirement is obtained as a result of its interaction with the experimental conditions that are provided.[5]

---

[4] The maximization hypothesis arises from the assumption that animals engage in a number of activities in addition to feeding, all of which are essential to their reproductive capacity, and these varying activities compete for time and energy allocation. Thus, the more time and energy invested in any one activity results in less time or energy being available for another. It is assumed that there is an optimal solution to this problem of appropriate allocation of activities.

[5] In contrast, an open economy is one in which the subject does not control its total daily intake; such intake is determined and controlled by the experimenter through restricted feeding, deprivation schedules, and so on. The significance of the distinction, as Hursh (1980) has pointed out, is that some familiar parameters of operant reinforcement schedules (e.g., FR, VI) appear to have quite different behavioral effects in a closed economy in contrast to the almost exclusively used open economy.

Figure 11–1

The experimental cage in which animals live around-the-clock. The animal searches for a food item by completing the operant requirement on the search bar, which is active when the cue light mounted above it is illuminated. That a food item has been encountered as a result of search is signaled by the illumination of a pattern of cue lights at the opposite end of the cage, the particular pattern of lights indicating the cost to the animal of procuring the item that has been encountered. The animal identifies the nature of the prey encountered in terms of its cost and either procures it by completing the prescribed number of presses on the procurement bar or renews searching on the search bar, which may result in the encounter of a less costly food item. When the item has been procured, the door to the feeder tunnel opens and the animal is free to eat a meal of any size (i.e. for as long as it wishes), with the feeder door closing only after the animal has remained out of the feeder tunnel for ten or more consecutive minutes. Water is continuously available, and weights can be placed on either bar in order to manipulate the energetic cost of foraging independent of the time required to complete the bar-press requirement. Adapted from G. H. Collier, "Life in a closed economy," in M. D. Zeiler and P. Harzem (Eds.), *Advances in analysis of behavior,* Vol. 5. Chichester, England: Wiley, 1983. Reprinted by permission.

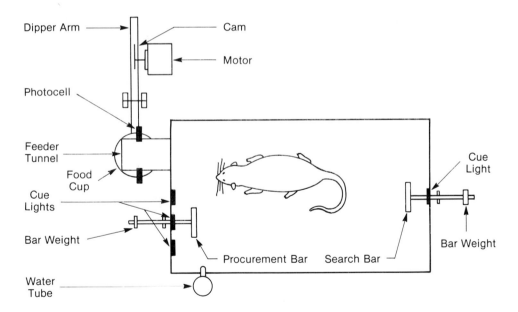

Relating the characteristics of the apparatus to the behavior patterns that comprise foraging, the animal must first press the search bar (only when it is illuminated) the number of times demanded by the experimenter.[6] It is thus possible for the experimen-

---

[6] Collier (1983) has addressed the issue of whether an arbitrary response such as bar pressing is representative of foraging behavior. He has noted that if other responses (e.g., wheel turning) are substituted for bar pressing, findings similar to those obtained with bar pressing are obtained.

ter to require the animal to make few or many bar presses, which it is assumed corresponds to a small or large amount of energy expended by the animal in a natural environment in its search for food. Following the completion of the required number of presses on the search bar, the search bar light is extinguished, and there is the illumination of one of two cue lights which are located over the procurement bar found at the opposite end of the apparatus. The particular cue light illuminated will indicate to the animal the "cost" (as represented by a number of required bar presses) of securing food. If the animal chooses to procure food, it will make the required number of bar presses, following which the feeder door opens and the animal is free to eat a meal of any size. (The feeder door closes only after the animal has remained out of the feeder tunnel for ten or more consecutive minutes.)

It should be kept in mind that under some circumstances when one particular light over the procurement bar is illuminated, the animal may choose not to press the bar the required number of times in order to secure food. (The cost may be too great.) If such is the case, the procurement light will go off and the cue light over the search bar will go on. The animal is then free to press the search bar the requisite number of times again, which may result in the illumination of the other procurement bar light. Since, typically, each light over the procurement bar will demand a different number of bar presses to provide access to food, it is possible that the second light will indicate to the animal that a fewer number of bar presses need to be made in order to secure food.

It is not within the scope of this text to describe in detail all of the studies conducted by Collier and his associates, but one study by Kaufman (1979) (described by Collier, 1983) can be cited. In this experiment, search and procurement cost were varied. More specifically, a rat was faced with meals that cost either 5 or 100 presses on the procurement lever, with these two different meal costs being signaled by the two lights placed above the procurement bar. The animal thus had a choice of accepting the meal by pressing the procurement level the required number of times, or of rejecting the meal and beginning the search over again. Search cost was manipulated by varying the number of presses on the search bar.

The results, indicated in Figure 11-2, reveal that the animal always accepted the low-cost meals (5 presses on the procurement bar) when the opportunity was provided, regardless of whether the search cost was 5 or 100 presses. The high-cost meal (100 presses on the procurement lever) was rejected the great majority of time when the search cost was low, but as search behavior increased in cost, the animals were more likely to accept any meal, regardless of procurement cost. These findings suggest that when the energy expenditure required to search for a meal was high, the animal will be likely to accept any meal that is obtainable, regardless of the cost of procurement. On the other hand, if the expenditure of energy required is minimal, then the animal can afford to be selective in the meals that it takes, rejecting those that are energy expensive.

It is too early to assess the impact of such studies on current conceptualizations and investigations of learning theory, although these studies represent an interesting and provocative approach in the analysis of behavior.

Figure 11-2
Percent of high- and low-cost meal opportunities procured by two rats (S2, S3) as a function of different search costs over pairs of procurement costs when the higher procurement cost was either 50 bar presses (top panel) or 100 bar presses (bottom panel). Adapted from G. H. Collier, "Life in a closed economy," in M. D. Zeiler and P. Harzem (Eds.), *Advances in analysis of behavior*, Vol. 3. Chichester, England: Wiley, 1983. Reprinted by permission.

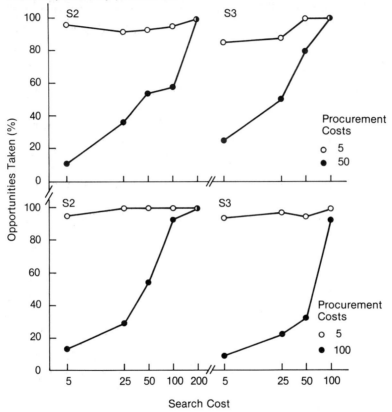

The Generality of Learning and Memory Principles ▶

One of the questions we asked at the beginning of the chapter had to do with whether laboratory findings can be generalized to the nonlaboratory environment. Some of the empirical evidence that has accumulated suggests that the learning principles that appear to operate in the laboratory do not always seem to "work" when the experimental subject is placed in a different environment.

One example is anecdotal evidence cited by Breland and Breland (1961). These psychologists have made it a business of teaching a wide variety of tricks to animals who then are exhibited at zoos, department stores, fairs, trade conventions, and even on television shows. The training procedures used by the Brelands have been quite successful, but there have been some unusual failures.

One failure occurred when they attempted to teach a pig how to pick up a large wooden coin and deposit it in a piggy bank. Coins were placed a few feet from the bank and the pig was required to carry each coin to the bank and deposit it, receiving a reward for every four or five coins deposited. However, it was discovered that although the pig would learn the task quite rapidly, over a period of weeks the animal would deposit the coins in the bank at a progressively slower pace. The animal might run eagerly to get the coin, but on its way to deposit it, it would repeatedly drop it, root it, drop it again, pick it up, toss it in the air, drop it, root it, and so on.

This type of behavior, the authors have written, is not that which would normally be expected on the basis of the operation of learning principles generated in the laboratory. Breland and Breland observed that after their animals learned a specific behavior pattern, they gradually *drifted* into patterns that were entirely different from those learned. They called this phenomenon *instinctive drift*. The general principle states that whenever an animal has strong instinctive behavior that bears some similarity to the learned response, the animal's learned responding will drift toward the instinctive behavior. Such drifting will take place even though it could delay or preclude the receiving of reinforcement. Thus, the pig's rooting behavior with the wooden coin was similar to what the pig would have done with a piece of food. Powell and Curley (1976) have noted a similar drifting effect when working with Mongolian gerbils and cotton rats, thus indicating that the phenomenon has some generality.

A second failure of laboratory learning principles in nonlaboratory situations occurred when the Brelands attempted to train a chicken to play a modified baseball game. The game was arranged so that a ball would roll toward home plate and the chicken would pull a chain to swing a bat (a small metal bar). If the ball was hit, a bell would ring and the chicken would run to first base, receiving food at that location. Preliminary work in teaching the bird to pull the chain and run to the sound of the bell went well, but when a ball was introduced, there was chaos. If the ball was hit, the chicken would not run to the base to get food but would chase the ball around the field.

These misbehaviors, as cited by Breland and Breland (1961), must be acknowledged. What has been conveniently forgotten is that more than 6,000 animals, representing a variety of species, have successfully transferred many types of skills learned in a laboratory setting to successful performance as exhibited in television shows, fairs, and many other types of public presentations, as the Brelands' work attests.

Principles of Animal Learning Applied to Man

Undoubtedly of greater importance is the issue of whether we can generalize those principles that have been discovered in learning studies using animals as experimental subjects to human behavior.[7] Historically, the proposed applicability of behavioral

---

[7] This problem has not been of great concern to biologists and physiologists since the findings of many studies investigating biological functions in animals have been shown to be applicable to human beings. The respiratory properties of hemoglobin are similar in mice, whales, and humans; a basic knowledge of human nerve physiology was obtained from the frog and squid. Mice, rats, monkeys, and even armadillos have been used in laboratory studies in an effort to find cures for polio, cancer, diabetes, and leprosy, as well as a host of other diseases, with such research being readily accepted by the public. It is when animals are used to learn something about human behavior that skepticism seems most likely to arise.

principles generated from experiments conducted with animals to human behavior was discussed by Pavlov (1927), who wrote that since "higher nervous activity exhibited by the cortex rests, undoubtedly, on the same foundation in man as in the higher animals, some very general and tentative inferences can even now be drawn from the latter to the former" (p. 395).

It was Thorndike (1911), however, who exercised the most influence on psychologists in the United States and for laying the foundation that there was little difference in the learning process between man and animals. Thorndike assumed that all animals were "systems of connections subject to change by the law of exercise and effect, and they differ only in the particular connections formed as well as in the efficiency of the connections" (p. 280). Writing of his own research, Thorndike reported that "experiments have been made on fishes, reptiles, birds, and various mammals, notably dogs, cats, mice and monkeys, to see how they learned to do certain simple things in order to get food. All these animals manifest fundamentally the same sort of intellectual life. Their learning is after all the same general type" (pp. 282–283). Since Darwin's evolutionary principles had been accepted by virtually all scientists, and since there was an obvious relationship between the organism's structure and its function, it is not surprising that Thorndike's working assumption eventually became a basic operating principle for many investigators, coming full flower in Hull's (1943) *Principles of Behavior* and in the operant conditioning movement initiated by Skinner (1938).

As we noted in Chapter One, Hull (1943) proposed a series of learning principles that, although generated primarily from experiments with animals, were purported to be basic behavioral laws having generality for all organisms. And more than a decade later, Skinner (1959) wrote:

> *Pigeon, rat, monkey, which is which? It doesn't matter. Of course, these three species have behavioral repertoires which are as different as their anatomies. But once you have allowed for differences in the ways they make contact with the environment, and in the ways they act upon the environment, what remains of their behavior shows astonishingly similar properties (pp. 374–375).*

Many current investigators are in accord with this general position; we shall cite only a sampling of the arguments they have made. For example, Dinsmoor (1970) has written:

> *The question remains, of course, whether experimental findings obtained with rats, pigeons, and monkeys can be applied to human beings. The similarities in anatomical structure and biological functioning would suggest that the fundamental principles should be much the same. The pigeon, to be sure, is not a mammal, and his physiology is somewhat different from that of man, but the correspondence between the behavioral processes observed with birds and with mammalian species adds to our confidence in the degree of biological continuity that prevails. The rat and the monkey might also be considered to be smaller humans with fur and tails (p. 3).*

Estes (1975) has taken a similar position: "Again and again aspects of learning formally assumed to be reserved for the higher position on the scale of intellect turn out to be demonstrable at progressively lower levels" (p. 5).

Not all investigators have found the generality argument convincing. As we indicated earlier, European ethologists have considered learning to be a very specific process that interacts with the animal's capacities and its environment. An increasingly large number of American investigators have become skeptical that the learning principles discovered with animals have generality to human responding. Warren (1972) echoing the ethological position, has written:

> *Behavioral observations indicate that the learning abilities of animals are as specialized and as closely related to ecological factors as their sensory capacities are. Every species appears to have its own set of special learning abilities, each one evolved to facilitate adaptation to specific ecological and social requirements (p. 582).*

And Finkelman (1978) has stated that studying rat behavior in mazes provides much information about rat behavior in mazes and not much else.

Experimental answers to the generality question have provided mixed findings. Some operant researchers have noted that the providing of basic operant schedules employing positive reinforcement have resulted in substantial performance differences between animals and humans. Lowe's (1979) review of many of these studies has resulted in his concluding that when either a fixed ratio (FR) or fixed interval (FI) schedule is employed, marked differences in responding between animals and humans can be observed. It will be recalled that the response pattern of animals under a FR schedule reveals a pause after each reinforcement, and under a FI schedule, there are relatively few responses at the beginning of the interval but many near the end, resulting in the familiar scalloping effect. But neither of these response patterns are typically observed when human subjects are placed on the same schedules.

To these findings can be added the results of studies by Weiner (1969) and Matthews, Shimoff, Catania, and Sagvolden (1977), who found a difference in rate and pattern of responding between humans and animals when variable ratio (VR) and variable interval (VI) reinforcement schedules have been employed.

But other operant investigators have noted a similarity of findings from animals to man. Higgins and Morris (1984) surveyed the results obtained from operant avoidance tasks in their search for the generality of findings between human and animal responding. Five experimental areas were reviewed: response acquisition, response maintenance, extinction, the use of external or signaling stimuli, and pharmacological studies. The overall conclusion of the authors was that the generality of responding between humans and animals is robust with respect to four of the five areas examined; only the extinction area has revealed incongruent findings. Moreover, they have pointed out that none of the studies that reveal differences in responding between humans and animals requires explanations that must fall outside of existing behavioral principles, or override the basic tenets of the experimental analysis of behavior.

Can the Generality Question Be Resolved?

Many contemporary investigators, such as Harlow, Gluck, and Suomi (1972) or Logan and Ferraro (1978), see an empirical answer to the problem of assessing the generality of learning principles. That is, any generalization that is extended to include a new species or a different environment remains a hypothesis to be tested, and is subject equally to disconfirmation or confirmation. Confirmation presumably indicates the existence of generality, whereas disconfirmation, although suggesting that a generalization of findings cannot be made, may reflect nothing more than the limitations of the method used.

Consider those studies attempting to determine whether human language data can generalize to the chimpanzee. The experimental evidence indicates that chimpanzees cannot acquire vocal language. The reason is that their mouth and throat were not designed to permit human-like vocalizations. Can it be concluded, then, that the chimpanzee cannot acquire language? Such a conclusion would be premature, since many investigators are convinced that these animals can communicate with words and word combinations transmitted by means of the American sign language, use of computers, or symbols placed on a magnetic blackboard.

Must empirical tests always be conducted in order to determine whether or not a learning principle will generalize to another species? Probably, although two other criteria might be used to provide a tentative answer to the question. One criterion suggested by Harlow and associates (1972) is anatomical similarity between species, although all analogous brain structures should not be given equal consideration. Probably the most sophisticated criterion for assessing the capacity of an organism to learn complex tasks is the cytoarchitectonic structure of the neocortex—not the mass of the brain but the delicate organization of cells in or near the cortical outer fringe. There is, however, one anomaly: Birds have little or no cortex and yet are successful at solving problems at a level of complexity equal to or beyond that achieved by rats, cats, and dogs.

A second criteria may be related to what Warren and Kolb (1978) have called *class-common behaviors.* Many species share common behaviors as well as common structures. An examination and comparison of an animal's natural behavior should help identify class-common behaviors, which in turn would provide a basis for generalizing experimental findings from one species to another.

One important consideration concerning the generality of experimental findings has been frequently neglected. This has to do with the role that animal research and experimental findings can play in the formulation of hypotheses or "best guesses" about problems arising in human behavior. Snowdon (1983), citing the work of Kaufman and Rosenblum (1969), has provided an interesting illustration of this point of view—one that has to do with different responses to infant separation made by two different but closely related species of old world monkeys. Pigtail macaque infants reveal high levels of behavior pathology when separated from their mothers, whereas infant bonnet macaques show very little evidence of disturbance. One cause of these behavioral differences appears to arise in the nature of the maternal behavior experienced by the infants. Bonnet macaque mothers allow their infants to be very independent and to interact with other members of the group, whereas pigtail macaque mothers are very restrictive of their infants, tolerating very little interaction with the infant by other group members. Snowdon suggests that these animal findings could be translated to a testable hypothesis that could be useful to working human mothers. Allowing infants to experience a variety of caretakers from a very early age should make them more accepting of separation when the mother returns to work. In contrast, infants whose mothers spend the early postnatal months as the almost exclusive caretakers are likely to experience distress when the mothers return to work.

The Application of Learning Principles

Another approach in helping to answer the question of generality can be found in those studies by experimenters who have attempted to determine if laboratory principles, particularly those generated from animal experiments, can be applied to everyday situations.

Reinforcement Procedures

Undoubtedly, the oldest application of learning principles is in situations in which the experimenter views the organism's behavior as an instrumental response (or as an operant) that can be modified by providing an appropriate response-reinforcement contingency. Literally thousands of studies have been conducted using various types of reinforcers to change a variety of behavior patterns in a host of different environments. (See Box 11–2.)

To illustrate the general procedure, Schulman, Suran, Stevens, and Kupst (1979) have demonstrated the effectiveness of reinforcement in reducing the excessive (and disruptive) activity level of emotionally disturbed children in a day hospital program. Their subjects were 11 children, ages 9 to 13. During the entire period of the experiment, all of the children wore a biomotometer—an electronic device that measured their general motor activity. When a child's movements exceeded a certain level of activity over a designated period of time, feedback was provided in the form of an auditory signal (beep) transmitted through an earphone worn by the child.

Following the establishment of a baseline activity level over five sessions, the children were informed that they could earn a reward if they would slow down whenever they heard a beep. They were not told, however, what level of activity would result in reinforcement, only that the fewer signals they heard the better the chance they would have to earn a reward. If during the hour-long classroom session the children's activity level was below 80% of their baseline activity level, the children were rewarded by being given a choice of candy or a toy. Following the five periods in which

box 11–2

An interesting and early use of the operant procedure is illustrated in a story about Benjamin Franklin, as related by Knapp and Shodahl (1974). While Franklin was on a fort-building expedition, the chaplain complained to him of low attendance at prayer meetings. Franklin knew that when the men enlisted they had been promised, in addition to pay and provisions, a gill of rum a day, half of which was regularly served to them in the morning and half in the evening. Since the men were most punctual in receiving it, Franklin suggested to the chaplain, "It is, perhaps, below the dignity of your profession to act as steward of the rum, but if you were to deal it out and only just after prayers, you would have them all about you" (p. 656). The chaplain liked the idea, and, with the help of a few men to measure out the liquor, the procedure was implemented. Never were prayer meetings more generally and more punctually attended.

the experimenters provided reward for appropriate behavior, there were five additional sessions in which reward was not contingent upon activity. During these sessions, the children wore the apparatus without the earphone, and they were told that they would earn a reward just for wearing it. Rewards were provided after each session. Figure 11–3 summarizes the mean activity of the subjects for the baseline, contingent reward, and noncontingent reward sessions. Providing a reward significantly reduced activity, but when the response-reward contingency was removed, increased activity similar to baseline responding was obtained.

Table 11–1 provides a summary of only a few of the large number of studies that have been conducted using rewards to modify behavior. One could point out that the only restriction that can be placed on the diversity of responses that are changed, and the kinds of rewards that are provided, is the imagination of the investigator. (See Box 11–3.)

The Use of Tokens and Token Economies

In many instances it is not feasible to provide immediate reinforcement in the form of toys, candy, money, and the like following the making of the instrumental response; as a result, investigators have provided reward in the form of tokens later redeemable for a

Figure 11–3
Summary of mean activity for all children across baseline, contingent reinforcement, and noncontingent reinforcement trials. Adapted from J. L. Schulman, B. G. Suran, T. M. Stevens, and M. J. Kupst, "Instructions, feedback, and reinforcement in reducing activity levels in the classroom," *Journal of Applied Behavior Analysis,* 1979, *12,* 441–447. Copyright © 1979 by the Society for the Experimental Analysis of Behavior, Inc.

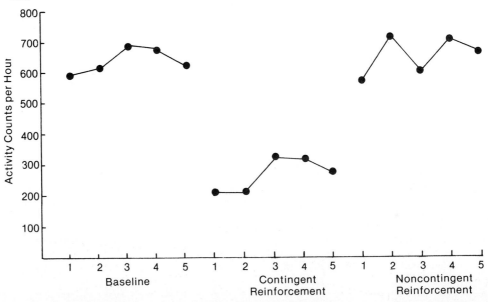

Table 11-1
A summary of selected studies in which investigators have used rewards to
modify behavior

Type of Subject	Experimental Environment	Type of Behavior Change Sought	Kind of Reward	Results	Investigators
Factory employees	Manufacturing company	Reduction in tardiness	Bonus vouchers	Significant decrease in tardiness	Hermann, deMontes, Dominguez, Montes, and Hopkins (1973)
Anorexic patients	Hospital	Gain in weight	Six-hour pass	Mean gain of four pounds/week	Brady and Rieger (1975)
Hospital employees	Hospital	Reduction in absenteeism	Chance in lottery	Significant decrease in absenteeism	Stephens and Burroughs (1978)
Students in elementary & junior high school	School	Reduction in vandalism	Praise for good work	Mean reduction of 78% in vandalism for experimental schools over control schools	Mayer, Butterworth, Nafpaktitis, and Sulzer-Azaroff (1983)
Factory employees	Munitions plant	Wearing of seat belts	Chance to win prizes	Significant increase in seat belt wearing	Geller (1983)
Normal adults	Family home	Reduction of rapid eating	Praise	Reduction of rapid eating to normal	Britt and Singh (1985)
7-11-year-old children	Family home	Improve dental flossing	Praise	Improvement in reduction of plaque	Dahlquist and Gil (1986)
Hospital employees	Hospital	Reduction of smoking	Monetary rewards	Substantial decline in smoking	Stitzer, Rand, Bigelow, and Mead (1986)

reward. Laboratory research in the 1950s and 1960s, following the earlier token reward studies of Wolfe (1936) and Cowles (1937) using chimpanzees, indicated the feasibility of using tokens (which could be subsequently exchanged for candy or trinkets) to reinforce responding. And Ferster and DeMyer (1961, 1962) found tokens to be effective reinforcers for key pressing in autistic children. It is not surprising, therefore, the current experimenters have continued to use tokens to reinforce the acquisition and maintenance of a wide variety of behaviors outside the laboratory—behavior that has ranged from improving meal-time behavior (e.g., Sisson and Dixon, 1986) to reducing children's excessive television watching (Wolfe, Mendes, and Factor, 1984). We will cite a few examples of these studies.

DesLauriers (1977) established a token reinforcement procedure in order to get more individuals to ride a university bus system that served 30,000 students and 6,000

box 11-3

The number of real-life situations in which reinforcement has been used to change behavior are many. One important example is noted in the work of Guthrie, Guthrie, Fernandez, and Estrera (1982), who used reinforcement to improve the nutritional status of young children living in primitive, rural communities in the Philippines. Millions of poor people live in poverty, disease, and malnutrition, in spite of the fact that surplus food is frequently available. Although it would appear that simply giving people food would alleviate the problem, such is not the case. Most experts agree that the ultimate solution to the problem is quite complex, having political, economic, sociological as well as psychological ramifications.

The solution proposed by these investigators to improve the nutritional status of poor Philippine children was to reinforce mothers for child-care behavior that would improve the health of their offspring. In their experiment, the mothers and children in three rural villages were selected for study. In all three villages, a medically supervised health clinic was established. Children were brought regularly to the clinic and examined for their health status; in addition, the others were given advice on how to best care for their children. All clinic workers emphasized concrete physical indexes (plotting of growth curves, weight gains, etc.). Mothers in one of the villages, serving as a control group, received treatment that was limited to the care and advice provided by clinic workers. Mothers in the other two villages served as experimental subjects. Here, reinforcement was provided contingent on the clinic workers finding increased growth and better health of their children as reflected in regular visits to the clinic. For mothers in one village, reinforcement was a ticket that purchased chances in a drawing held at the end of the study; the prize was food. For mothers in the other villages, photographs of their children were used as reinforcement. Results revealed that after one year of testing, substantially better growth and less malnutrition was observed in the children in the two villages where reinforcement was provided the mothers, compared to the control village subjects who experienced medical care alone. No differences, however, were noted between children living in the two experimental villages.

If these results are generalized, it may be concluded that providing poor, rural people only with information about health care is not sufficient to obtain optimal health care for their children. Some other incentive must be offered to the mothers in order to promote such care.

faculty and administrative personnel. Two treatment conditions, one providing continuous reinforcement and the other providing partial, were utilized in an effort to increase the riding of the campus bus. Continuous reinforcement provided a token on every boarding of the bus; partial reinforcement provided a token that averaged out to one token for every three boardings. The tokens could be traded at local businesses for a variety of goods and services (e.g., candy bars, record albums, etc.). Results revealed that there was a 27 to 30% increase in ridership when tokens were provided, in contrast to the control condition of ridership without reinforcement.

Little would be gained by describing the varying token economies that have been established since Ayllon and Azrin's (1965) early studies. Token economies have been employed across a wide range of populations, including psychiatric patients, mentally retarded children and adults, drug addicts, alcoholics, prisoners, juvenile delinquents, and public school students. Kazdin's (1977) volume may be consulted for an in-depth treatment of the topic. (See Box 11-4.)

box 11–4

One interesting aspect of the use of a token economy in institutions has to do with legal restrictions placed on the nature of reinforcement. In *Wyatt* v. *Stickney*, the court ruled that the rights of patients included access to a variety of items and activities that had traditionally been used as reinforcing stimuli for appropriate behavior. The court held that a patient was entitled to a comfortable bed, a closet or locker for personal belongings, a chair and table in the room, a nutritionally balanced meal, as well as the right to have visitors, wear one's own clothes, and attend religious services. In addition, patients were entitled to exercise several times weekly, interact with the opposite sex, and look at television in the day room.

The rulings of the court concerning the basic amenities to which the institutionalized population is entitled have obvious implications for token economy programs. In such programs, many of these amenities have been used as privileges that can be purchased with tokens that were earned by appropriate behavior. The court ruling makes these amenities rights rather than privileges, and presents some problems for the establishment and maintenance of a token economy. It is likely that the future of token economies in institutionalized settings will depend on providing new reinforcing events over and above those basic rights to which patients are entitled, as ruled by the courts.

Other Learning Paradigm Applications

Providing reinforcement to modify behavior has been the most extensively used procedure, but other instrumental conditional paradigms have been also employed to change responding.

Experimental Extinction and Desensitization   It will be recalled that one laboratory procedure designed to eliminate an established instrumental response was to remove the reinforcement, a process that was identified as *experimental extinction*. Since humans sometimes acquire undesirable habits that are difficult to break, the use of extinction has been employed to help individuals modify their behavior.

Another example has been reported by Wolfe, Mendes, and Factor (1984), who reported that it was possible to reduce children's excessive television viewing by making television watching contingent on the use of tokens. Children were given 20 unearned tokens each week that they could exchange for up to 10 hours of viewing time. A gold token was earned for viewing in accordance with the rules for four consecutive weeks; this token was exchangeable for a reward (e.g., trip to zoo, an amusement park, etc.). The experiment was terminated after three months with a significant reduction in children's excessive television viewing being noted.

The use of tokens has been most notable, however, in the establishment of token economies, with the early work of Ayllon and Azrin (1964, 1965) providing widespread attention. These investigators had their experimental subjects (patients in a mental hospital) perform a variety of activities that were necessary and/or useful in the institution, such as serving meals, washing dishes, cleaning floors, and so on. Reinforcement for such activity was provided in the form of tokens that could be subsequently exchanged for rewards. Results included consumable goods such as candy or milk at a cost of from 1 to 5 tokens, a choice of television programs for 3 tokens, a private audience with the ward psychologist at 20 tokens, or even a trip to town for 100 tokens. Eight experiments conducted in two studies (Ayllon and Azrin, 1964, 1965) all demonstrated that the use of tokens was effective in maintaining desired performance. The effect of tokens was clearly demonstrated, since the patients' performance in formally rewarded tasks deteriorated markedly when they were discontinued.

One example of using extinction to modify a child's tantrum behavior is found in a study by Williams (1959). He reported that the parents of a 21-month-old child would become quite distressed when the child threw tantrums if they left the room before he was asleep. The parents were requested to attempt to extinguish the response by putting the child to bed and leaving the room, not to return when the child cried. On the first occasion, the tantrum lasted for 45 minutes before the child went to sleep. The next night no tantrum ensued, and for the next six nights there was a gradual cessation of crying until it completely stopped. However, the next evening the child became agitated when put to bed by his aunt, who then stayed in the room until he went to sleep. The following evening the tantrum returned, but this behavior was again extinguished by the parents refusing to enter the room. Figure 11–4 reveals the amount of crying for the two series of extinction trials.

The extinction procedure, as utilized by Williams (1959), has not been particularly effective in eliminating fear or anxiety, since an avoidance response does not provide the subject with the opportunity to learn that the aversive stimulus is no longer presented. As a result, Wolpe (1958) used counterconditioning or desensitization to help eliminate these undesirable responses.

It is interesting that Wolpe's discovery of the desensitization procedure resulted from his work with cats. Severe trauma was first produced in these animals by

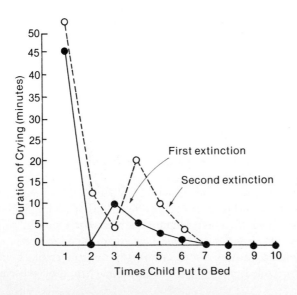

Figure 11-4
Duration of crying as a function of the number of times the child was put to bed. Adapted from C. D. Williams, "The elimination of tantrum behavior by extinction procedures," *Journal of Abnormal and Social Psychology*, 1959, *59*, 269. Copyright © 1959 by the American Psychological Association. Reprinted by permission.

depriving them of food and then shocking them when they began to eat. This resulted in emotional responses being made in the presence of the environmental stimuli that had been associated with shock. Wolpe then began to feed cats in an environmental situation distinctly dissimilar from the original environment where they received shock. By gradually moving toward situations that approximated the environment where the animals had been fed originally, Wolpe found that he was able to overcome the animal's neurotic responses and restore them to apparent normality. Conceptually, he had retrained or counterconditioned the emotional response, replacing it with the positive affective state that generally accompanies eating.

It was obvious that feeding responses could not be used when using this procedure with humans. Wolpe's search for a response that would be antagonistic to anxiety and fear led him to the work of Jacobson (1938), who recommended the use of relaxation as a treatment for helping his anxious and fearful patients. Briefly, Wolpe's desensitization procedure consists of having the subject learn to relax deeply and then imagine, rather than actually experience, a series of anxiety-evoking stimuli. Prior to having the subject actually begin therapy, the therapist develops a collection of a number of anxiety-evoking events, hierarchically arranged from those eliciting very weak emotional responses to those eliciting strong responses. The therapeutic procedure then consists of the therapist asking the subject to imagine the weakest event in the hierarchy repeatedly until no more anxiety is elicited by that event. The next item in the hierarchy is then presented, and so on, until after a number of sessions, even the strongest anxiety-provoking stimulus fails to elicit any anxiety. To illustrate this emotional-provoking sequence of the stimuli, Wolpe used the following situations, hierarchically arranged from weak to strong, to treat a housewife suffering from claustrophobia: (1) reading about miners trapped underground, (2) being told of somebody in jail, (3) going on a journey by train, (4) traveling in an elevator alone, (5) being locked in a small room, and (6) being stuck in an elevator.

Wolpe (1961) has analyzed the effectiveness of this procedure, reporting success with 35 of 39 patients. A follow-up covering from six months to four years indicated that 20 of these did not experience any relapse or emergence of new symptoms. Subsequent evaluative reviews by Rachman (1967), Bandura (1969), and Paul (1969) have indicated that desensitization appears to be an effective treatment for adults with a variety of anxiety-based problems. Hatzenbuehler and Schroeder (1978) examined this procedure with children and came to the same conclusion. Snakes, rats, spiders, mice, loud noises, darkness, reading, and test taking are some of the fear-provoking stimulus situations that have yielded to the desensitization procedure.

Aversion Therapy   The use of aversive stimuli in controlling undesirable behavior has taken a variety of forms in attempts to eliminate such habits as cigarette smoking, compulsive eating, and alcoholism. The aversion therapy procedure is similar to the operations used in the laboratory when examining punishment. The aversive stimulus, usually shock, is presented after an undesirable response is made, with such punishment being provided for a series of trials. Rachman and Teasdale's (1969) volume, devoted solely to the examination of the varieties of aversion therapy, illustrates the popularity of this procedure.

An unusual example of aversion therapy is found in a study by Lang and Melamed (1969). A nine-month-old infant was plagued with chronic vomiting which had persisted for more than four months. The infant was actually starving to death in spite of a variety of methods being used to attempt to alleviate the condition. The experimenter's first task was to distinguish initial chewing, sucking, and swallowing responses from the first weak sign of reverse peristalsis, which preceded the vomiting reflex. Once this sign or cue was identified, the treatment was deceptively simple. It consisted of a brief but intense electric shock applied to the child's leg at the first sign of regurgitation, and repeated at one-second intervals until the vomiting had stopped. According to the authors, success was achieved with the first treatment, although five additional treatments were subsequently administered. Over the next two weeks body weight increased by 20%, and follow-up examinations after one and two years revealed that the child's weight was normal.

Alcoholism has been treated frequently with aversion therapy. Here, the aversive stimulus generally consists of the injection of a drug such as emetine or apormorphine. With this procedure, the subject ingests the drug (or is injected with it) and then drinks alcohol. The drug alone, or in combination with alcohol, produces severe physical discomfort accompanied by retching and vomiting. After several pairings of the drug and alcohol, the subject develops a negative affective state at the sight and smell of alcohol, resulting in avoidance of its use.

Covert Sensitization and Covert Conditioning   When using aversion therapy procedures, some therapists have had difficulty in handling and controlling the presentation of the physical stimuli (US) used to elicit the avoidance response. Drugs must be administered by a physician, whereas using an electric shock involves a relatively elaborate apparatus. Moreover, it is difficult to provide a drug dosage or intensity of shock that is effective as an aversive stimulus and yet does not harm the patient.

An alternative to the employment of such physical stimulation has been the use of covert stimuli. Cautela (1966) has identified this procedure as *covert sensitization.* Briefly, this technique consists of having a subject *imagine* that the appetitive stimulus eliciting the undesirable response has become aversive, and that it is now accompanied by a feeling of revulsion. When the appetitive stimulus is avoided, the subject is instructed to feel calm and relaxed. These trials of imagining the appetitive stimulus becoming aversive are alternated with feelings of calm and relaxation that accompany the making of the avoidance response.

Cautela's (1966) early report illustrated how this procedure was used in treating obesity. A 200-pound school teacher was interested in losing weight. First, she was taught to relax in a training session. Then:

> [She was asked to visualize that] while she was preparing the supper she started to reach for a piece of bread to make a peanut butter sandwich. Just as she reached the bread she would begin to feel sick to her stomach. She could feel the vomit come into her mouth and then she would vomit all over the supper she was preparing. She would then have to clean it all up. When she could visualize the complete scene and feel a little sick to her stomach she was to signal with her finger. This was repeated three or more times using cake, cookies, and pie as the tempting foods. On the next trial she was asked to visualize that when she was tempted to eat a piece of cake she felt a little

sick but this time she would say to herself, "Oh, I don't want the food." She would then feel immediately calm and relaxed. Ten additional trials (scenes) were presented. On every trial she would resist the temptation and feel calm and relaxed. She was asked to repeat this procedure at home, every day until the next therapy session (p. 39).

Cautela reported that the subject's imagined aversion to eating when preparing food was subsequently coupled with an imagined aversion to eating snacks. At the end of therapy, the subject had reduced her weight to 134 pounds.

Cautela's (1966) description of the covert sensitization procedure coupled with its successful application in treating obesity (a successful case of treating alcoholism was also reported) was followed by a host of experimenters using this technique to treat a variety of behavioral disorders.[8]

Cautela (1977, 1986) has identified covert sensitization as representing just one procedure that can be subsumed under the general paradigm of covert conditioning, a paradigm that includes overt reinforcement, covert extinction, covert negative reinforcement, and covert modeling. He has reported success in modifying problem behavior using each of these procedures (e.g., Cautela, 1970a, 1970b, 1971, 1976). Recently, he has suggested that each of these procedures may be combined with other behavior techniques to modify pain (e.g., Cautela, 1986).

A basic problem has been that many of the published findings employing covert conditioning procedures are difficult to evaluate since appropriate controls are lacking. Little and Curran's (1978) careful examination of covert sensitization studies has indicated that, in spite of occasional successes, it remained to be demonstrated that this procedure provided a consistently successful method of treating the behavior problems of obesity, alcoholism, and smoking.

Summary ►

Experimental studies of learning laboratory tasks frequently raise three questions: (1) Do learning processes play as important a role in determining behavior as learning theorists believe? (2) Can laboratory findings be generalized to the nonlaboratory environment? (3) Can results using animals as subject be generalized to human beings?

Ethologists have stressed the adaptive significance of an animal's behavior and have assumed that learning is not a general process, as many learning theorists have assumed.

---

[8] One exception is a study by Janda and Rimm (1972) who used the covert sensitization to treat obesity. In addition to the experimental group, two control groups were employed. One control group was informed that they had been placed on a waiting list for therapy and so would not receive treatment for a period of time. The other control group, identified as "realistic attention," attended the same number of therapy sessions (six) as the experimental group but only received relaxation therapy coupled with a general discussion of personal problems. Results indicated that by the end of the six therapy sessions, the experimental group lost 9.5 pounds in contrast to a 4.5-pound loss by the nontreated control group and a 0.7 pound gain for the "realistic attention" group.

Rather, learning represents a special mechanism that interacts with the animal's innate response capacities in order to enable each species to survive in its particular environment. They have objected to the examination of behavior in a laboratory setting, pointing out that laboratory experiments provide only contrived problems placed in an artificial environment, with little useful information being derived from the findings. The ethological position has called attention to a number of areas that investigators in the United States had previously ignored, such as the role of key stimuli, imprinting, and so on.

The second question was whether laboratory findings could be generalized to the nonlaboratory environment. Although Breland and Breland pointed to the number of failures of their animals to transfer learned behavior acquired in the laboratory to nonlaboratory settings, the bulk of their work has demonstrated that such failures are rare.

The third and perhaps most important question was whether principles discovered in the laboratory using animals can be generalized to humans. Reviews of the literature suggest mixed findings; some investigators report success and others indicate failure. Many current investigators see an empirical answer to the problem of assessing the generality of learning principles. That is, any generalization that is extended to include a new species or a different environment remains a hypothesis to be tested.

The oldest application of learning principles has been in situations in which the experimenter views the organism's behavior as an instrumental response that can be modified by providing an appropriate response-reinforcement contingency. Literally thousands of studies have been conducted using various types of reinforcers, and many of the experimental results suggest that reinforcement can change a variety of behavior patterns. The use of secondary rewards, or tokens, in modifying the behavior of patients in mental institutions has been examined with the establishment of token economies where patients earn tokens that can be later exchanged for privileges (e.g., television watching, receiving of snacks, etc.). Token economies have proven to be quite successful, although recent court decisions that do not permit institutions to withhold some of these amenities raise some questions about the continuance of such economies. The use of experimental extinction and aversion therapies have also been successfully used to modify human behavior.

chapter twelve

▶

Verbal Learning:
A Functional Approach

The landmark experiments of Ebbinghaus (1913) demonstrated that it was possible to use the scientific method to examine a higher mental process, thus changing the study of memory from an art to a science. Although he entitled his monograph *Memory*, he used the term *learning* for the process in which a list of nonsense syllables, or consonant-vowel-consonant units, was acquired through repetitive reading and recitation. When he placed varying time intervals (e.g., 5 minutes, 24 hours, 31 days, etc.) between such learning and the relearning of these lists, the relearning scores were identified as measuring retention.

Many of the experimental studies of verbal learning that followed Ebbinghaus's (1885/1913) monograph (and which have continued to be conducted) can be characterized as representing a functional approach to the study of learning. Early psychologists who were members of this movement (e.g., John Dewey, who has been generally recognized as its founder) were interested in the function of the mind as it was related to the organism's adaptation to its environment. Later investigators, using a stimulus response analysis of behavior, centered their attention on human verbal learning, with their primary interest being in determining how such learning was a function of stimulus and motivational variables that could be manipulated in the laboratory.

The difference between the approach adopted by functional psychologists in contrast to other learning theorists can be illustrated by comparing Hull's *Principles of Behavior* (1943) with John McGeoch's (1946) *The Psychology of Human Learning*, both volumes being published at about the same time. Hull was concerned with providing a theory of learning in which learning principles were deduced from a variety of experimental studies. The principles that were posited presumably had generality for all organisms.

McGeoch's text, on the other hand, was concerned with examining functional relationships between learning and stimulus (or motivational) variables. List learning by human subjects represented the basic experimental task. It was only after a stable, functional relationship between a specific independent variable and learning had been established that a theoretical position that accounted for the findings would be proposed. In contrast to Hull's deductive approach to the study of learning, the functionalists' position was inductive.

Beginning in the 1950s, investigators began to adopt a new approach to the study of learning and retention—a "new look," which has been identified as the study of memory and which we will present in considerable detail in Chapter Fourteen. Their approach was to examine learning and retention from an information processing point of view, positing the basic construct investigated was memory that incorporated the processes of encoding, storage, and retrieval. Over the next several decades, this point of view has grown rapidly, and can now be described as probably the most popular approach to the study of this subject matter.

In view of the popularity of the information processing point of view, it is reasonable to ask why we should acquaint the reader with the functional approach. There are two reasons. First, investigators working over a period of five decades have obtained a great deal of basic information about learning and retention which must be explained and integrated with the findings obtained by current experimenters if the study of learning and retention, or memory, is to be complete.

Second, and as Postman (1975) has written, the point of departure for answering current theoretical questions is often found in the experimental findings of functional studies. For example, in the examination of the nature of memory, the resolution of this question has hinged in large measure on the reexamination of the effects of old and familiar variables examined by functional investigators. Thus, theorists knew what the expected effects in conventional rote-learning situations were. By showing that these findings did not materialize in certain newly established experimental procedures, a case was made for a different (and distinct) memory system.

Basic Considerations: Materials, Tasks, and Response Measures ▶

Regardless of the approach to the study of learning and retention, or memory, that is adopted, similar kinds of materials, tasks, and response measures have been used by investigators adopting either the functional or the information processing point of view.

Materials

Ebbinghaus, aware that learning material differed in its meaningfulness, invented the nonsense syllables in an attempt to eliminate this problem. Virtually all learning texts describe the material utilized by Ebbinghaus as nonsense syllables consisting of two consonants separated by a vowel (or a CVC). But as Gundlach (1986) has written, authors have been in error in describing Ebbinghaus's material as nonsense syllables. The translator of Ebbinghaus's *Memory* identified the experimental material as a "series of nonsense syllables" when the translation should have been a "meaningless series of syllables." Thus, it was the *series* of items that was hypothesized by Ebbinghaus to be meaningless, and any individual syllable that was a part of the series could or could not be meaningful. In the 2,299 different syllables that Ebbinghaus used, three-, four-, five-, and even six-lettered words were included among them. It should be acknowledged, however, that the current use of consonant, vowel, consonant (CVC) units, in which three-lettered words are omitted, provides investigators with a more homogeneous list of material than if Ebbinghaus's population of syllables continued to serve as the basic source of such material.

Over the years, investigators have utilized single letters, bigrams (two-lettered items), consonant syllables (e.g., RTX), digits, isolated words, and prose as material to be learned. A wide variety of other visual materials (e.g., varying types of pictures, faces, figures, digits, etc.) has also served as experimental material.

Types of Tasks

List-learning tasks have been enlarged from the serial-learning task utilized by Ebbinghaus; they now include free recall, paired associate, and verbal discrimination tasks.

In serial learning tasks, the subject must learn the items in the order in which they were presented. When the anticipation procedure is used, each item on the list is assumed to serve as a stimulus or cue which the subject uses to anticipate the next item and respond with it. When the next item is presented, it indicates to the subject the correctness of the response as well as serves as a stimulus for the following item. The first item on the list is cued by an asterisk or some other arbitrary visual stimulus. Items, generally presented with a memory drum, slide projector, or video monitor, are exposed for a fixed period of time, usually one to five seconds. In a different serial learning procedure, the list is presented either in an item-by-item fashion or by showing the complete list of items at once, following which the subject is instructed to write down or verbally report the items in the same order in which they were presented. This is known as the study-test procedure. We should note that serial learning tasks involve two components. First, it is necessary for the subjects to recall the items that have been presented; second, the items are to be remembered in the order in which they were presented.

The free recall task, although infrequently used by traditional investigators, has been extensively employed by information processing experimenters. It consists of the investigator presenting, usually in an item-by-item fashion, the material to be learned or placed in memory, followed by the subject being asked to recall as many of the items as possible and without regard to the order of presentation. If more than a single trial is provided, the order of presentation of the items is randomized from one trial to the next; in some instances, order over trials may remain the same.

A different procedure in conducting the free recall study has been described by Battig (1965) as a "drop out" procedure, and by Buschke (1973) as "selective reminding."

With both procedures, items that are correct on a given trial are removed from presentation on the next trial. The basic argument made for selective reminding is that dropping out correct items—items already in the subject's memory—speeds up study trials because fewer items need to be presented. In addition, the subject does not overlearn those items that are recalled on early trials since they are removed from the list of presented items. In comparing the selective reminding procedure against the standard procedure in which all items were presented on all trials, MacLeod (1985) reported that the two methods were identical on virtually all learning and retention measures (e.g., trials to reach an acquisition criterion, number of items correct on each recall trial during acquisition, number of items correct on a three-week delayed recall test, etc.).

The selective reminding procedure has much to recommend it; perhaps the most basic problem is that when material is presented to groups of subjects, differences on each trial among each subject's pattern of recall precludes its use.

A cued recall task is similar to free recall except that the experimenter provides the subject with some specific cue about the nature of the material to be recalled. For example, in a study by Tulving and Watkins (1973) subjects were presented with lists of five-lettered words, following which the cued recall test consisted of presenting the first two, three, or four letters of each word, with the task of the subject to recall the missing letters.

The paired associate (PA) task is made up of lists of pairs of items, usually CVCs or words, such as *XED-TIV, MUL-HEV, JOX-FUP*. The subject is asked to recall the second item after the first item on the pair is presented. The list frequently consists of 10 to 15 pairs of items; the position of each pair in the list is changed from one trial to the next. This procedure requires the subject to learn to associate the first item of the pair with the second; it prevents the subject from learning the responses in serial order, as might be done if each pair remained in the same position from one trial to the next. Anticipation and study-test procedures have been used with paired associate tasks, as well as with the serial-learning tasks.

The PA task was first used by Calkins (1894, 1896) shortly after Ebbinghaus's experiments employing serial learning, but it was not used extensively until the early 1950s. The task can be conceptualized as a series of stimulus and response relationships, since the first item of the pair can be considered as a stimulus used to cue the subject's response (represented by the second item).

The last type of list task is verbal discrimination. The list consists of a number of pairs of verbal items (frequently 40 or more). The subject has to learn which item of each pair was designated by the experimenter as correct. The task is similar to the discrimination learning task discussed in Chapter Five, except that the stimuli are words or verbal symbols.

Illustrations of the varying tasks using CVCs, CCCs, or words as the materials to be learned are provided in Table 12–1. In all of the learning tasks, the experimenter can provide the subject with a predetermined number of presentations of the material (or trials), or continue trials until the subject reaches some arbitrary criterion, such as one errorless trial.

Table 12-1
Types of tasks, materials, and requirements used in list-learning experiments

Type of Task	Material	List		Requirement
Serial Learning	CVCs	ZUH CEJ GEC KOJ QEM VEH		Subject must learn the items in the order in which they were presented.
Free Recall	Words	viand torque pinnace excise despot		Subject is not required to learn the items in any particular order.
Paired Associate	CCCs	ZGF-DNT FJH-PNK BFM-HZL TZL-LRD		Subject must learn to associate the second item of the pair with the presentation of the first item.
Verbal Discrimination	Words	pencil sheath *careen* inure	*patrol* levee beguile *recoil*	Subject must learn to choose the item which the experimenter has arbitrarily designated as correct.

Response Measures

The basic response measures in verbal learning and memory experiments are (1) relearning, (2) recall, and (3) recognition. The relearning measure is generally converted into a savings score by computing the difference between the number of trials required to relearn it to the same criterion. It is obvious that the use of this measure demands that the investigator employ a criterion, and that at least several trials are necessary in order to achieve it. The savings score formula is:

$$Savings = \frac{\text{No. of trials for original learning} - \text{No. of trials required to relearn the material}}{\text{No. of trials required for original learning}}$$

Although originally employed by Ebbinghaus (1913), the savings method has been infrequently used. One reason is that it takes much more time to obtain this measure than any of the others. Some interest in the savings methods, however, has been expressed by Nelson and his associates (see Nelson, 1971, 1978; Nelson and Rothbart, 1972; and Nelson, Fehling, and Moore-Glascock, 1979).

The recall method requires the subject to reproduce or generate the materials or target items that have been presented. The number or percentage of correct responses is typically used as the performance measure. For example, the presentation of a list of 50 words might be followed with instructions to the subject to recall as many as possible. The number of words correctly recalled would be used as the recall measure.

Recognition means knowing that a particular event has been experienced on an earlier occasion. In everyday situations, individuals experiencing a given stimulus situation will state that they do (or do not) recognize the situation. It is possible in such instances for so-called dishonest individuals to indicate that they have recognized the situation when actually they have not. In verbal learning tasks, experimenters have assumed it necessary to keep their subjects honest—to have them refrain from claiming to recognize any item when they have not. This has been accomplished by combining the target item with a number of distractors to form a recognition test. Here, the subject is instructed to recognize or choose the previously experienced item from the alternatives provided. Wallace (1980) has defined such measures as *recognition-discrimination measures,* to distinguish them from measures of recognition memory in which distractors are not used.[1]

The sensitivity of recognition memory for verbal material, as measured by a recognition-discrimination test, has been demonstrated by Shepard (1967). In one part of his study, 540 common nouns and adjectives were presented (such as *child, office*) and 612 sentences (such as *A dead dog is no use for hunting ducks*). Following the presentation of such material, a recognition test consisting of 68 pairs of an original item and a distractor was administered. The mean percentage of correct answers was 88.4 for the words and 89.0 for sentences.

Recognition memory performance for visual material, as reported by Standing (1973) and Standing, Conezio and Haber (1970), is also quite high. In the Standing, Conezio, and Haber (1970) study, students viewed 2,500 slides containing vacation scenes. Each slide was presented for 10 seconds, with four daily two-hour sessions being required to complete the task. Subsequently, the subjects were shown pairs of slides consisting of a slide that had been previously shown and a new one (distractor), with the task of the student to identify the previously presented slide. Results indicated that approximately 90% of the subjects' choices were correct.

Many studies, beginning with Luh's (1922) very early investigation which was replicated by Postman and Rau (1957), have indicated that recognition memory, as measured by the discrimination task, is superior to recall memory. But investigators today are aware that any comparison between these response measures is tenuous at best, since all performance measures are dependent on the experimental procedures employed. In the case of recognition-discrimination memory, it is obvious that this measure is related to the characteristics of the distractors used in the discrimination test.

---

[1] It is possible that experimenters have erred in assuming that subjects will invariably claim to recognize many more items than they actually do. Wallace (1978) has found that his subjects recognized target words without distractors, and provided a level of performance only slightly higher than that obtained when distractors were used. Ley and Long (1987) have reported that their use of a distractor-free recognition test resulted in recognition performance almost identical with that of the conventional recognition test which employed distractors.

This problem can be illustrated by conducting the following hypothetical experiment. Two groups of subjects are presented with identical lists of CVCs, following which each group is given a different recognition test. Group 1 is given a test in which the distractors are other CVCs, whereas Group 2 is given a test in which common words are the distractors. All would agree that recognition performance for Group 2 should be superior to that for Group 1. In fact, it is likely that recognition performance for Group 2 should approximate 100%.

The role of distractors on recognition-discrimination memory has been experimentally demonstrated by many investigators. McNulty (1965) has shown that recognition memory declines when the distractors are orthographically (physically) similar to the target word (for instance, *plunger–plunder*). Underwood (1965) and Anisfeld and Knapp (1968) have shown that recognition test performance is adversely influenced when the distractors are related associatively to the target items (for example, *rough–smooth*) or are synonyms (such as *girl–female*). Since the characteristics of the distractors used in the recognition-discrimination test play such an important role in determining the performance level, any comparison of performance on this task with recall performance should be recognized as being specific to that particular experiment, and of limited generality (see Hall, 1983).

Learning and Retention as Viewed by Functional Investigators ▶

Having reviewed the materials, tasks, and response measures employed by most experimenters working in the area of learning and memory, we will devote the remainder of the chapter to an examination of some of the contributions made by functional investigators who have been guided primarily by a stimulus-response analysis of their experimental findings. These experimenters have distinguished learning from retention by inferring the operation of the learning process from changes taking place in the subject's performance over varying number of trials or presentations of the material. In contrast, the operation of the retention process was inferred from the persistence of such behavior over a period of time, with hours, days, or weeks being placed between the original learning and the test for retention.

Stimulus Attributes of Verbal Material ▶

It is not surprising that one of the primary concerns of investigators has been to identify the varying attributes or dimensions of verbal materials. An early study by Glaze (1928) demonstrates the nature of such inquiry. Glaze (1928) was interested in examining the association value or meaningfulness of many of the nonsense syllables that Ebbinghaus (1913) used in his early work. And when such association values were obtained from some 2,000 CVCs, Glaze found large differences among them. Investigators used Glaze's CVC association values in their experiments for more than the next three decades. Archer (1960) and Noble (1961) have provided more current association measures of CVCs. See Box 12–1 for a description of Glaze's (1928) study.

Meaningfulness and Other Attributes

Guided by Glaze's (1928) work with nonsense syllables, Noble (1952b) used words in obtaining an association measure which he defined as *meaningfulness*. Noble secured this measure by having his subjects write down as many free associations as they could generate in 60 seconds to each of 96 words. Noble found that the number of associations elicited by these words varied, thus suggesting that a word, like a nonsense syllable, could be calibrated on the dimension of association value or as he defined this measure, meaningfulness. Table 12–2 provides meaningfulness values for some of the words that Noble used. It was later determined that a similar measure of meaningfulness could be obtained by having subjects indicate on a five-point rating scale, the frequency of associations (as provided by the verbal descriptors of *none, below average, average, above average,* and *very many*) that a specific word elicited.

box 12–1

Early investigators of verbal learning assumed that at least some of the nonsense syllables they used in their experiments were meaningful in that they elicited associations of one type or another. Cason (1926) and Glaze (1928) experimentally demonstrated the validity of this assumption. Glaze's study was more extensive, and his calibration of the meaningfulness of more than 2,000 syllables served as a standard of reference for the next 25 years. His population of 2,019 syllables included all of the nonsense syllables that could be constructed from the English alphabet, with the letter *Y* serving as both a consonant and a vowel. Words were eliminated from the population.

Fifteen college students served as subjects. A tachistoscope was used to present 252 syllables to each subject in one sitting; a number of sittings were required for presentation of all the syllables. Subjects were instructed that when the syllable appeared they should indicate with one or two words what the syllable meant. If the syllable meant something that could not be expressed, they were to respond with the word *yes*. If the syllable meant nothing, the subject was instructed not to say anything.

An association value for each nonsense syllable was obtained and expressed as a percentage of the number of subjects who had indicated that the syllable elicited an association. Below is a sampling of the association values obtained by Glaze for a number of the nonsense syllables.

100%	73%	53%	33%	20%	0%
BAL	BOV	CAZ	DAH	BEJ	GUQ
DEP	HEV	KOB	JOD	FUP	QIJ
ROV	MUL	SUB	VUP	SAJ	XUK
WIL	VAM	WEM	ZON	WEQ	ZIW

gojey	.99	kennel	5.52
attar	1.71	insect	7.39
femur	2.09	money	8.89
rostrum	2.73	kitchen	9.61
argon	3.34		

Table 12-2
Meaningfulness values for a sampling of verbal items obtained from Noble (1952b)

Experimenters working in the 1950s and 1960s identified a host of other word attributes. The more frequently used of these are included here.

Pronounceability   Underwood and Schulz (1960) measured pronounceability of words by instructing their subjects to rate words on the relative ease or difficulty of pronouncing each item.

Concreteness   In a study by Gorman (1961), almost 1,800 nouns served as the population of words to be rated, with judges classifying them on the basis of (1) concreteness—those words that had reference to objects, material, or sources of sensation that were relatively direct; and (2) abstract—those words that had reference to objects, material, or sources of sensation that were relatively indirect. Later investigators (e.g., Paivio, Yuille, and Madigan, 1968) had subjects use seven-point rating scales to make this same kind of judgment.

Vividness and Imagery   Tulving, McNulty, and Ozier (1965) and Paivio (1965) had subjects rate nouns as to the ease with which these words produced a picture or a visual image. Subsequently, Paivio, Yuille, and Madigan (1968) had subjects provide imagery ratings for 925 nouns. Table 12-3 illustrates ratings that were obtained for a sample of these words.

Pleasantness   Silverstein and Dienstbier (1968) had subjects rate 101 nouns on a seven-point rating scale in which the categories ranged from very unpleasant through neutral to very pleasant. Toglia and Battig (1978) have also identified this word attribute in their research.

Objective Word Frequency   The objective word frequency measure was obtained from one of several word frequency counts that are available. These include Thorndike and Lorge (1944), Kucera and Francis (1967), and the American Heritage (1971)

interim	1.97	fatigue	5.05
context	2.13	paper	6.30
virtue	3.33	orchestra	6.77
profession	3.83	grass	6.96
salary	4.70		

Table 12-3
Imagery values for a sampling of words obtained from Paivio, Yuille, and Madigan (1968)

frequency counts. These counts indicate the frequency with which a word appears in print.[2]

The Interrelatedness of Word Attributes and Their Relation to Learning

Since words can be classified by a variety of attributes, one may ask "Are these attributes measuring unique characteristics, or do they all appear to be measuring a similar component?" There is the suggestion from the experimental studies of Noble (1953), Paivio (1965), Hall (1967), and Paivio, Yuille, and Madigan (1968) that meaningfulness, objective frequency, and pronounceability are all reflections of one attribute that can be defined as *meaningfulness,* and that a second attribute can be identified as *imagery.* Frincke's (1968) factor analytic study is in keeping with this point of view; his findings indicated that the varying word attributes which he examined could be grouped into two conceptual categories: (1) meaningfulness—familiarity and (2) imagery—concreteness.

A next step by investigators was to determine if the word attribute that had been identified influenced the acquisition of word lists; it is not surprising that positive findings have been obtained. A sampling of these results follow.

Noble demonstrated that when three serial lists were constructed with each list differing in meaningfulness and with subjects required to learn each list to a criterion of one perfect trial, results indicated that the list containing words high in meaningfulness was most easily acquired, whereas the list containing words low in meaningfulness was the most difficult to learn. Figure 12-1 illustrates these findings. Other investigators (e.g., Kimble and Dufort, 1955; and Noble and McNeely, 1957), using lists of paired associates that varied in meaningfulness, have also found meaningfulness to influence acquisition.

Vividness or imagery has also been demonstrated to be a significant variable influencing list learning. Tulving, McNulty, and Ozier (1965) constructed three lists (16 words per list) that differed in vividness; meaningfulness of the words were held constant. Each subject learned all three lists using free recall; eight trials per list were provided. Significant differences in recall scores were obtained with the material rated highest in imagery being the easiest to learn. (See Figure 12-2.) Paivio (1965) and Yarmey and Paivio (1965) have confirmed the importance of imagery in the learning of paired associates.

A New Look at Word Attributes and Learning

The experimental findings of investigators, first identifying word attributes and then determining how they were related to learning, were broadened and also challenged by

---

[2] To illustrate, Kucera and Francis (1967) examined 500 samples of words, with approximately 2,000 words/sample, covering a wide variety of subject matters. Their count is based on the tabulated frequencies of all of the words included in their samples.

Figure 12–1
Mean number of trials required to anticipate correctly 12 successive items. The (m) parameters denote average meaningfulness on the lists. Adapted from C. E. Noble, "The role of stimulus learning (m) in serial verbal learning," *Journal of Experimental Psychology,* 1952, *43,* 437–446. Copyright © 1952 by the American Psychological Association. Reprinted by permission.

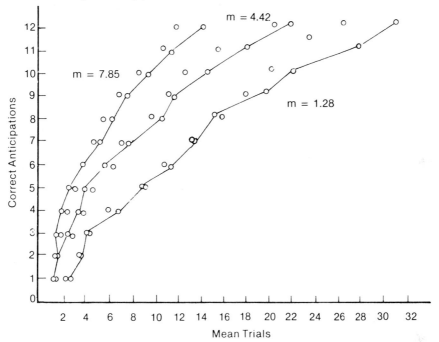

the work of Rubin (1980, 1983, 1985) and Rubin and Friendly (1986). This last study best describes the nature of this work.

A population of 925 words was obtained from the listing of words provided by Paivio, Yuille, and Madigan (1968). Scale values for these words included the attributes of imagery, concreteness, meaningfulness, pronounceability, and objective word frequency. Based on an earlier study conducted by Rubin (1980), three additional word attributes were added to the list. These included:

1. Availability or associative frequency. (Instead of measuring how many associates were given to a word that would measure meaningfulness, availability measured the number of times a word was given as a first associate to a sample of stimulus words.)
2. Emotionality. (Here, a word was given a rating of 1 through 7 based on how intense the emotional meaning of the word was.)
3. Goodness in which a word was rated as to how intensely good or bad a word's meaning was. (The scale ranged from (1) bad to (4) average to (7) good.)

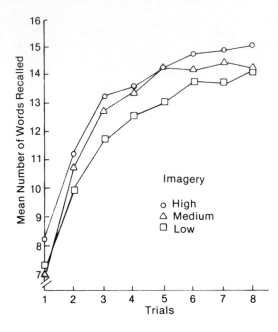

Figure 12-2
Mean number of words recalled as a function of trials for three lists differing in imagery of words listed. Adapted from E. Tulving, J. A. McNulty, and M. Ozier, "Vividness of words and learning to learn in free-recall learning," *Canadian Journal of Psychology,* 1965, *19,* 242–252. Copyright © 1965, by the Canadian Psychological Association. Reprinted by permission.

Thirteen multitrial free recall list-learning experiments were conducted. Each of the lists contained words sampled from the 925 original word list. Recall scores were obtained for each experiment, and these scores related to the presence of those attributes of the words that made up each list. Statistical analysis of the data revealed that there were three major factors of the recalled words: imagery, availability, and emotionality. The identification of availability was a distinct surprise, although Rubin's (1980) early study had indicated that this attribute was a significant contributor to recall. Rubin (1983), in support of the availability attribute, found that 64 high-availability words were easier to recall than 64 low-availability words when both sets of words equated for meaningfulness, imagery, and differences in objective word frequency were minimized.

Rubin's identification of the attribute of word availability suggests that investigators employ other word populations in order to determine the generality of these findings.

Stimulus Position

The serial-learning task demands that the subject recall the items in the same order in which they were presented. It has been found that errors (or correct responses) are not equally distributed over all of the positions in the list. Rather, a bow-shaped curve is obtained; items located at a position just beyond the middle of the list are subject to the most errors, and items at the end of the list are subject to more errors than those items at the beginning of the list. Subsequent studies have indicated that the serial position effect (SPE) is found over a wide range of conditions. The characteristics of the material, the type of presentation procedure, and the kind of subject have been some of the conditions examined, with the SPE continuing to be demonstrated. For example, in learning a list of common names in serial order, McCrary and Hunter's (1953) subjects revealed the familiar SPE. Using lists of 12 common words, Underwood, Boruch, and Malmi (1978) were also able to demonstrate the SPE when the familiar anticipation method was replaced with a study-test procedure. In their study, lists of 12 common words were presented, 2 seconds allowed per word, followed by a test trial in which subjects were given 60 seconds to write down as many words as possible in their correct order. Figure 12–3 presents the findings obtained on the first trial for 200 subjects. Finally, a study by Cornell and Bergstrom (1983) has demonstrated the SPE with seven-month-old infants using a recognition test—an interesting finding since these subjects are not capable of speech and thus are unable to use speech-related strategies to assist them in learning.

The SPE has also been obtained with free recall tasks. More errors were found for items in the middle of the list than for those words at the beginning or at the end. But unlike the findings obtained with serial learning tasks, free recall findings reveal fewer errors for items located at the end of the list than for items located at the beginning.

Murdock's (1962) findings are typical of the results obtained with free recall tasks. In this most comprehensive study, the serial position effect was examined as a function

Figure 12–3
Correct responses on Trial 1 as related to position of items in the serial lists. The data were combined for two lists of twelve common words learned by 200 subjects using a study-test procedure. Adapted from B. J. Underwood, *Attributes of memory* (Glenview, Ill.: Scott, Foresman and Co.), © 1983. Reprinted by permission.

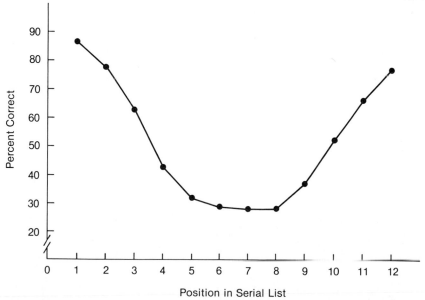

of the length of the list as well as the presentation time. Lists of 10, 15, and 20 words were presented at a rate of two seconds per item; other lists of 20, 30, and 40 items were presented at a rate of one second per item. A 1.5-minute recall period followed the presentation of a list, during which time the six groups of subjects were requested to write down as many of the words as they could remember, without regard to the order of presentation. The serial position curves, shown in Figure 12–4, all have the same general form. The items located at the end of the list were recalled best (the recency effect); items located at the beginning of the list were learned next best (the primacy effect); and items located in the middle of the list were the most difficult to learn.

The serial position effect can be readily obtained outside the laboratory, being noted in the learning of a poem, a speech, or even a motor skills task. Jensen (1962) has shown that misspellings are much more frequently found in the middle of a word than at the beginning or the end. Gymnasts and other competitors whose serially presented activities are recalled and graded by judges would be wise to place their most difficult and spectacular feats at the beginning or at the end of their routine, thus increasing the probability that the judges will remember them.

Figure 12–4
Serial position curves for six free-recall groups. Adapted from B. B. Murdock, "The serial position effect of free recall," *Journal of Experimental Psychology,* 1962, *64,* 482–486. Copyright © 1962 by the American Psychological Association. Reprinted by permission.

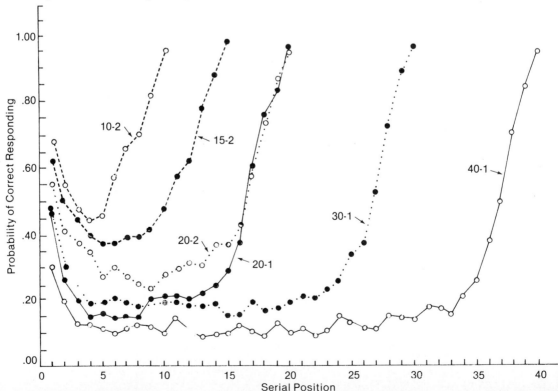

The search for at least a partial explanation of the SPE has resulted in experimenters examining several assumptions that have been made about the nature of serial learning. Perhaps the most basic of these has been that in the learning of a serial list, the subject acquires a series of associations between adjacent items (e.g., 1 to 2, 2 to 3, 3 to 4, etc.). If such associations are formed in serial list learning, it would suggest that a paired associate task should then be learned quite rapidly, providing the items in the PA task consisted of the same items used with the serial list. Thus, if a serial list consisting of items A, B, C, D, E, and F was first learned, a subsequently presented PA task consisting of the pairs of items, A-B, B-C, D-E, and E-F should be more rapidly acquired than an appropriate control group. But Young (1959), carrying out such a study, was unable to find any facilitation of PA learning produced by the previous learning of the same items learned in serial order.[3]

A second assumption that has been made is that the distinctiveness or isolation of the first and last items on the list, brought about by the temporal interval traditionally placed between trials, contributes to the SPE. And such a variable has been shown by Glanzer and Peters (1962) to have a significant effect on the nature of the experimental findings. In this study, subjects learned a serial list of 10 items using either a 0-, 2-, 4-, 8-, or 16-second intertrial interval. These experimenters found that as time between trials decreased, the distribution of effort approached linearity, with the traditional bow-shaped curve virtually disappearing when the 0-second intertrial interval was used.

However, if the serial list contains some distinctive cue when the 0-second intertrial interval is examined, the bow-shaped curve reappears. Coppage and Harcum's (1967) study illustrates this finding. Subjects serially learned a list of 10 CVCs with no intertrial interval provided. However, one syllable was typed in red and all others were in black. The red syllable was located in either the first, third, fifth, seventh, or ninth position. The learning criterion was 20 successive correct responses. An analysis of the errors made by each of the five experimental groups revealed typical bow-shaped curves, with the red syllable appearing to serve as the first item on the list and yielding the fewest number of errors.

Explanations for the SPE have been provided by experimenters who have eschewed the traditional stimulus-response position and we shall return to this issue in a subsequent chapter. We would suggest, however, that Underwood's (1983) position that "the mechanisms underlying serial learning remain one of the enigmas waiting around for a fresh approach" (p. 196) characterizes the status of this problem.

The Isolation Effect

The last stimulus condition to be discussed is called the isolation effect. Von Restorff (1933) demonstrated that a two-digit number was more easily learned if it was placed among a list of CVCs than if it was placed among a list of other two-digit numbers. Von

---

[3] Some investigators have pointed out that Young's (1959) study suffered from the fact that when an item serves as both a stimulus and a response (a double function), the PA task becomes very difficult to learn. In a subsequent study by Young (1962), in which serial list items previously learned had only a single function, the same conclusion was reached.

Restorff attributed her findings to the isolation of the digit among the CVCs, which provided a homogeneous background. This isolation effect has been called the *von Restorff phenomenon.*

The isolation of an item can be carried out using a variety of procedures. One method is to make the physical presentation of the isolated item different from that of the other list items. For example, Jones and Jones (1942) examined the isolation effect by having one item in their experimental list printed in red and the remaining items printed in black. A second procedure has been to provide semantic isolation. Kimble and Dufort (1955) produced an isolation effect by using an item low in meaningfulness (Noble's *m*) and the remaining items high in meaningfulness values.

Research has revealed that the learning of the isolated item is a function of the amount or degree of its isolation. Gumenik and Levitt (1968) provided subjects with a serial-learning task consisting of nine CVCs projected on a screen. For one condition, the size of each control item was small (2.3 × 4.5 inches), whereas the size of the isolated item was much larger—either (a) 3.3 × 6.4, (b) 4.7 × 9.1, or (c) 6.7 × 13.0 inches. For a second condition, the size of each control item was represented by the largest projection (6.7 × 13.0 inches), with the isolated item being smaller—namely (a) 4.7 × 9.1, (b) 3.3 × 6.4, or (c) 2.3 × 4.5 inches. The results, as indicated by the mean number of errors in noting the isolated item over 30 learning trials, are presented in Table 12–4. As the difference between the isolated item and the control item increased, the number of errors made on the isolated item decreased.

A question arose almost immediately after the isolation effect had been discovered: How does the learning of the isolated item influence the learning of the remaining items on the list? In the early serial-learning study by Jones and Jones (1942), two lists of 10 CVCs were used. All of the items on the control list were printed in black, whereas on the experimental list the seventh CVC was printed in red but all the other CVCs were in black. Subjects were required to learn the material to a criterion of one errorless trial. A week later they were asked to relearn the material to the same criterion. Findings indicated that although the red CVC was more rapidly learned and better retained than its control, thus confirming the isolation effect, no difference was obtained between the experimental and control list when overall learning or retention was examined. Subsequent studies conducted by Newman and Saltz (1958), Jensen (1962), Roberts (1962), and Lippman and Lippman (1978) have confirmed this finding.

Table 12–4
Number of errors as a function of the size of the isolated item

Size of Unisolated CVCs in Inches	Number of Errors by Size of Isolated CVCs in Inches			
	2.3 × 4.5	3.3 × 6.4	4.7 × 9.1	6.7 × 13.0
Small (2.3 × 4.5)	15.5	13.2	11.0	7.8
Large (6.7 × 13.0)	11.9	15.5	14.4	21.2

Adapted from W. E. Gumenik and J. Levitt, "The von Restorff effect as a function of difference in the isolated item," *American Journal of Psychology*, 1968, *81*, 247–252. Copyright © 1968 by the University of Illinois Press.

Isolation effects have also been demonstrated with paired associate learning tasks. One problem has been to determine if such learning is aided more by the isolation of the stimulus or of the response. Research conducted by Kimble and Dufort (1955) and Newman (1962) revealed equivocal findings; Erickson (1963) found that, although isolating either the stimulus or the response item alone facilitated the learning of the pair, the isolation of the stimulus produced the greater facilitation.

Wallace's (1965) review and evaluation of the varying explanations for the isolation effect have revealed inadequacies in all of them. As Lippman and Lippman (1978) acknowledged, "An adequate theory of the isolation effect has yet to be offered" (p. 49).

Cognitive Variables ►

Early investigators, working within the confines of a behavioristic model, were reluctant to extend their search for learning variables to include processes operating inside the organism's head. The emphasis on stimulus or task variables, a topic we have just discussed, was in keeping with this point of view. But it became apparent that many unusual findings obtained in learning studies could not be accounted for by reference to the contribution of only stimulus variables. Some type of cognitive activity had to be operating in order to account for the results. Moreover, the intuitive experience of investigators themselves suggested that cognitive-like processes were often brought into play in order to facilitate learning. The result was that some experimenters began to explain their findings by positing the operation of cognitive activities on the part of their experimental subjects. Some experimenters considered the subject's cognitive activities as covert responses (often with stimulus characteristics), thus preserving the stimulus-response framework, but others have considered these cognitive activities only as processes that could be described with such terms as *intention, stimulus selection, mediation,* and *organization.*

Intent to Learn

A cognitive activity with which most of us have some familiarity is intention—a topic that has been closely associated with the concept of motivation. It has been recognized that this construct plays an important role in determining how an individual performs. But how can intention be manipulated? Operationally, experimenters have accomplished this by providing different types of instructions to their subjects. Intentional learning subjects may be provided with instructions indicating that they should learn the presented material since there will be a subsequent test to determine how well they have learned. The performance of those individuals who have been given such instructions is compared with a group not given such instructions; in fact, these latter subjects are generally misled about the purpose of the experiment and as a result, are not aware that there is anything to be learned.

Two different types of incidental learning procedures can be delineated. One has been to expose the material to the subject with no instructions to learn. For example, Biel and Force (1943) used CVCs with six different types of print (Bodoni, Caslon, etc.). With a tachistoscope, subjects were presented with 12 different CVCs and were asked to indicate the print they found most legible. At the end of the session, the subjects were asked to recall as many of the CVCs as possible.

A second "incidental" procedure has been to have the subject learn a task, but during the learning period the subject is shown material not covered by the learning instructions. When the task has been learned, the subject is asked to recall the material not covered by the instructions. In a study by Bahrick (1954), 14 geometric forms, filled with seven colors, served as the experimental material. The subjects were instructed to learn the forms using a serial anticipation procedure, but the role of color was not mentioned. After the subjects had reached a criterion of one perfect trial, they were asked to indicate which color was associated with which form.

Investigators have found that subjects can learn without intent to do so—that is, under incidental learning conditions. However, intentional learning frequently results in superior performance. One study illustrating this result was conducted by Postman, Adams, and Phillips (1955), who had two groups of subjects rate 30 adjectives with respect to their frequency of use in the subject's daily speech. An intentional learning group was asked to remember as many of the items as possible, whereas the incidental group was not given these instructions. After the adjectives had been rated, the subjects were given five minutes to recall as many as possible. Results indicated that the intentional group recalled 12.62 items and the incidental group recalled 9.41, thus demonstrating superior recall for the intentional group but also revealing that the incidental group had learned more than 30% of the items presented.

An examination of the literature reveals that although intentional learning groups generally reveal superior performance, this finding is not always obtained and in some instances, no difference can be observed between the groups (see Hyde and Jenkins, 1973).

In his analysis of the findings obtained with incidental and intentional learning procedures, Postman (1964) has concluded that we should not look at "intention" (or a lack of it) as the significant construct in this type of learning experiment. Rather, differences in recall between intentional and incidental learners can be explained by the different kinds of cognitive activity or strategies adopted by each group while learning the material. For example, given a list of words to rate for frequency of usage, along with instructions to remember the words, the "intent to learn" subject may attempt to devise some story that incorporates each of the words on the list into a coherent whole. The subject not given instructions to remember would be unlikely to construct such a narrative. The difference in recall between the two subjects would reflect a difference in their cognitive activity rather than a difference between incidental and intentional learning. It is possible, of course, that the incidental learner may engage in an activity that also contributes to subsequent recall. When such is the case, the incidental learner's recall performance on the learning task would be similar to that obtained by the intentional learning group. As a result of Postman's analysis, investigators have shifted their interest from an examination of the intentionality of the subject to examining the kind of cognitive activity or processing that is demanded by the task to be learned.

Stimulus Selection

In our examination of discrimination learning it was noted that many investigators hypothesized that animals learning a discrimination task engaged in selective perception. The animal does not respond to all of the stimulus elements that make up the discriminanda; some elements are ignored and others are used to cue the response.

A similar effect is observed in verbal learning tasks, but this process has been called *stimulus selection.* An excellent demonstration of the stimulus selection process can be found in one part of the paired associate study by Underwood, Ham, and Ekstrand (1962). Each paired associate item consisted of a trigram placed on a colored background, paired with a single digit that served as the response. The stimulus components can be seen in Table 12-5. Learning trials were provided until each subject reached a criterion of one perfect trial. Ten transfer trials were then provided in order to determine that stimulus element the subjects had used in their learning trials to cue their responses. For one transfer group, only the background colors were presented as stimuli; whereas for a second group, the trigrams were presented without their distinctive background colors. A control group was used in which the transfer task involved presenting each trigram with its appropriate colored background. Figure 12-5, which indicates acquisition curves for the three experimental groups, clearly reveals the operation of the stimulus selection process. When the colors were presented alone, virtually complete transfer resulted, but when the trigrams were presented, there was a marked decline in performance. Quite obviously, most subjects had selected the background colors as stimuli to cue their responses.

Many current information processing investigators have considered stimulus selection as an encoding operation. We shall discuss this topic in Chapter Fourteen.

Mediation

Another cognitive process has been identified as mediation, a concept used by early associationists. They assumed that an association between two contiguous events took place only because of the role of a mediator. Thus, an association between events A and C could be established by associating A with B and B with C, with event B serving to mediate the A–C association. For example, a subject learning to associate the stimulus

Trigrams	Colors
GWS	Red
DWK	Brown
NXQ	Yellow
DHX	Blue
BWD	Orange
GVS	Black
BXD	Green

Table 12-5
Stimulus components used in the paired-associate task

Figure 12-5
Acquisition curves on the ten transfer trials. Adapted from B. J. Underwood, M. Ham, and B. R. Ekstrand, "Cue selection in paired-associate learning," *Journal of Experimental Psychology,* 1962, *64,* 405–409. Copyright © 1962 by the American Psychological Association. Reprinted by permission.

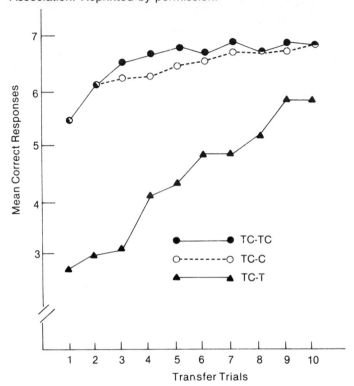

word *dog* with the response *nine* might use the word *cat* as a mediator. When *dog* was presented, the subject would think *cat,* which in turn would elicit *nine.* Since there were previous associations between *dog* and *cat* and *nine,* the learning of the *dog–nine* association should take place quite rapidly.

Underwood and Schulz (1960) have examined mediation in paired associates learning. These experimenters asked their subjects how they went about associating specific stimulus and response pairs. They found that almost 75% of such associations were reported to have been acquired by means of a mediated association. Moreover, these investigators found that learning took place more rapidly for those pairs of items for which their subjects had reported the use of mediators, in contrast to those pairs of items for which mediators were not required.

A study by Wood and Bolt (1968) has demonstrated the facilitative effect of mediators. In their experiment, subjects learned a paired associate task in which the stimuli were single letters and the responses were high-frequency words. An experimental group of subjects were told that they would be given a mediator in order to help them associate each letter with its appropriate response. The mediator was written out and placed in parenthesis between the stimulus and the response on each of the study trials. Each mediating response started with the same letter as the stimulus and was a strong associate of the response. For example, the stimulus-response pairs *T-chair*, *K-queen*, and *M-lamb* had the mediating responses *table*, *king*, and *mutton*, with the presentation of the paired associates appearing as: *T(table)–chair; K(king)–queen; M(mutton)–lamb*. A control group was not provided with mediators. Subjects received four alternating study and test trials. The test trials consisted of presenting only the stimulus letter, with the subject required to call out the appropriate response. Table 12–6, which presents recall scores for the experimental and control groups for the four test trials, clearly indicates the facilitative effect of the use of mediators.

Most frequently, subjects make up their own mediators. When this is done, they are called *natural language mediators* (NLM). The facilitative effect of natural language mediators has been demonstrated in a study conducted by Adams, McIntyre, and Thorsheim (1969). In this study, subjects learned a list of 10 paired associates. After each pair had been presented, the subjects were asked to report the mediator they had used to associate the items. If they did not use any, they were to report *Rote*. Eight trials were provided. The percentage of correct responses for mediated and rote responses is shown in Figure 12–6. Obviously, the use of natural language mediators facilitated the learning process.

Organized Mediation: Mnemonics   A formal, well-organized system of mediators is an example of a mnemonic, which is a technique or strategy used by individuals as a memory aid. Their operation can be seen in the stage performance of professional mnemonists who demonstrate extraordinary acts of memory. These performers can go through a deck of cards, pausing only long enough to see each one briefly, and then name the cards in the precise order in which they were presented. Or they can meet 100 people, associate each face with a different name, and shortly thereafter proceed to identify each person in the group correctly. The secret of their success is in the use of an elaborate mnemonic system.

Yates (1966) traced the history of the use of these techniques and found that they were invented by the ancient Greeks. In an age before printing, mnemonics were

	Trials			
	1	2	3	4
Control	3.25	6.25	8.42	10.17
Experimental (mediating)	5.92	9.50	12.08	13.17

Adapted from data provided by G. Wood and M. Bolt, "Mediation and mediation time in paired associate learning," *Journal of Experimental Psychology*, 1968, 78, 15–20. Copyright © 1968 by the American Psychological Association. Reprinted by permission.

Table 12-6
Mean number of correct responses

Figure 12-6

A comparison of mediated and rote verbal learning. Adapted from J. A. Adams, J. S. McIntyre, and H. I. Thorsheim, "Natural language mediation and interitem interference in paired-associate learning," *Psychonomic Science*, 1969, *16*, 63–64. Copyright © 1969 by the Psychonomic Society. Reprinted by permission.

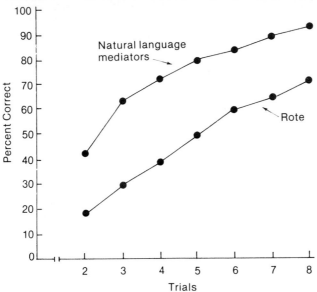

invaluable aids for orators who had to talk for hours without recourse to notes. Even today, many people use these techniques. We remember the number of days in each month by recalling the familiar "Thirty days hath September . . . ," or we remember the notes on the line of the treble clef by reciting "Every good boy does fine" (EGBDF). More elaborate systems have been provided in specialized texts such as Lorayne and Lucas's (1974) *The Memory Book,* which appeared on the best-seller list for a number of months.

The foundation for any mnemonic system is the learning of a sequential series of words that may be visualized and firmly fixed in the individual's memory. Once these images have been established, new items to be remembered are associated with each of the original images. When it becomes necessary to recall these new items, the previously visualized items are recalled as cues for those items that were more recently acquired.

One technique, mentioned earlier in this book, is the method of loci. Here the sequential series of items are familiar geographical locations that permit the individual to figuratively "walk" from one place to another in a fixed order. In learning a list of words, for example, a learner would associate each word with a different location. The individual then "walks" through the varying places in order to recall the word associated with each location.

A second technique has been described as the peg-word system. It is illustrated by the following rhyme: "One is a bun, two is a shoe, three is a tree, four is a door, five is a hive, six are sticks, seven is heaven, eight is a gate, nine is a line, and ten is a hen." More elaborate peg-word systems have been devised in which the peg-words have been associated with the first 100 digits. The general procedure is similar to that employed with the method of loci. Each word on a list of words to be remembered is associated with a peg-word. When the word is recalled, the well-learned peg-words serve as cues for the list words.

The study of mnemonics was disdained by early psychologists. In fact, as recently as 1960, Miller, Galanter, and Pribram (1960) wrote that experimental psychologists believed that mnemonic devices were immoral tricks suitable only for stage magicians. Hoffman and Senter's (1978) review of mnemonic techniques has indicated that experimental interest in mnemonics began in the mid to late 1960s with the studies of Bugelski, Kidd, and Segman (1968), Bugelski (1968), and Ross and Lawrence (1968) all demonstrating the superiority of recall when mnemonic techniques were used.

In an extensive study by Bugelski (1968), experimental subjects learned the rhyme, "One is a bun . . ." and were then given six different paired associate lists to learn. Each list had the same stimulus numbers, 1 through 10, and the responses were 10 concrete nouns. Different nouns were used with each list. Subjects were instructed to learn each list by forming a visual image linking each noun to the peg-word associated with each number. Control subjects were not taught the rhyme, nor were they told anything about using images to help them learn the list of words. All subjects studied the first list and were then given an immediate recall test. The second list was then studied and followed by an immediate recall test, and so on until all six lists had been learned and recalled. A final recall test was provided in which the subjects were asked to provide the words from all lists associated with "number 1," all "number 2 words," and so on. The results of Bugelski's (1968) study are shown in Figure 12–7. Recall performance for the experimental group on the six lists was statistically superior to that for the control; on the final recall test, the number of words correctly recalled by the experimental group was almost twice that of the control.

Ross and Lawrence (1968) have reported similar findings using the method of loci. In one experiment (Study 2), subjects learned 52 sequential locations following a walk through the grounds of a university campus. Subjects were then required to learn a list

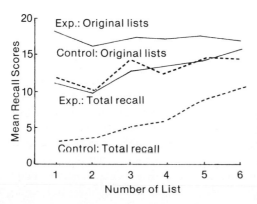

Figure 12–7
Learning scores for original learning of each of the six lists and total recall scores for experimental and control groups. Adapted from B. R. Bugelski, "Images as mediators in one-trial paired-associate learning. II. Self-timing in successive lists," *Journal of Experimental Psychology,* 1968, *77,* 328–334. Copyright © 1968 by the American Psychological Association. Reprinted by permission.

of 40 words on each of four consecutive days, with the words on each list being presented only once. With each trial, each word was to be associated with a specific location. At the beginning of the second, third, and fourth sessions, subjects were asked to recall the words from the previous day's list before learning a new list. Results indicated that the mean number of words recalled for the four sessions ranged from 35.8 to 38.4. The 24-hour delay in recall produced some decrement, with the mean number of words recalled for each of the four sessions ranging from 30.2 to 38.4 words. Although the experiment lacked a control group, these recall scores are considerably higher than those obtained by subjects participating in similar experiments who did not use mnemonic techniques.

Visual Imagery in the Mnemonic System   The importance of using visual imagery in the mnemonic system has been readily acknowledged. Professional mnemonists have added the so-called principle that when the subject forms a visual image of the peg-word with the item to be learned, the resultant image should have the two items interacting and should be quite bizarre.

Wollen, Weber, and Lowry (1972) have experimentally examined the role of interaction and bizarreness. They found that interaction did indeed contribute to recall, but bizarreness did not. In their study, 18 high-imagery nouns were used to form nine paired associates. For each pair, line drawings were made depicting the objects in four different ways: (1) noninteracting-bizarre, (2) interacting-bizarre, (3) interacting-non-bizarre, and (4) noninteracting-nonbizarre. Below each drawing, the words corresponding to the objects were printed. An example of the piano–cigar pair is presented in Figure 12–8. These four different types of drawings were made into slides and presented to four experimental groups of subjects. A control group saw only the word pairs without the pictures. All subjects were given one study trial, two seconds long, followed by a test trial in which the stimulus word was presented along with instructions that the subject should recall the appropriate response. Results are presented in Table 12–7. Those subjects who had seen pictures with interaction recalled a significantly greater number of responses than those who saw pairs of pictures with no interaction. The bizarreness of the picture, however, did not enhance recall. An interesting finding was that the control group, which had been presented with only pairs of words without pictures, recalled a larger number of correct responses than either of the groups with noninteracting conditions. It is possible, as the authors suggest, that the presentation of noninteracting pictures inhibited subjects from using mediators, which in turn contributed to the poorer recall scores.

Senter and Hoffman (1976) were able to replicate Wollen, Weber, and Lowry's (1972) findings that interactiveness was an important variable in recall. But Webber and Marshall (1978) have shown that bizarreness can make a contribution when relatively long retention intervals are used. In their study, bizarreness did not result in superior retention when immediate recall was demanded; however, when a retention interval of seven days was utilized, the bizarreness of the picture did contribute to superior recall.

An interesting replication of the role of interaction on memory has been provided by Lutz and Lutz (1977) using brand names and their products. After using the yellow pages of a telephone directory to obtain the names of 48 companies and their products,

Figure 12-8
Adapted from K. A. Wollen, A. Weber, and D. H. Lowry, "Bizarreness versus interaction of mental images as determinants of learning," *Cognitive Psychology,* 1972, *3,* 518–523. Reprinted by permission of the Academic Press.

Noninteracting, nonbizarre

PIANO   CIGAR

Noninteracting, bizarre

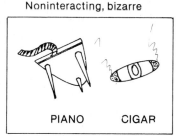

PIANO   CIGAR

Interacting, nonbizarre

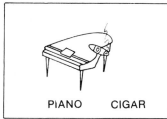

PIANO   CIGAR

Interacting, bizarre

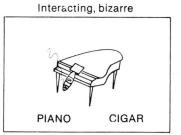

PIANO   CIGAR

the experimenters made up interactive and noninteractive pictures of each word pair to serve as the experimental material. Subjects looking at the interactive pictures were able to recall significantly more brand names than a group viewing the noninteractive pictures.

A Case History of a Professional Mnemonist—Mr. S.   Performers who exhibit unusual memories on stage usually employ extensive mnemonic systems that were developed through many hours of study. But from time to time, individuals have been found who have an apparently innate ability to remember extraordinary amounts of

		Bizarreness	
		Present	Absent
Interaction	Present	6.67	6.60
	Absent	3.05	3.50
	Control	5.50	

Adapted from K. A. Wollen, A. Weber, and D. H. Lowry, "Bizarreness versus interaction of mental images as determinants of learning," *Cognitive Psychology,* 1972, *3,* 518–523. Reprinted by permission of the Academic Press.

Table 12-7
Mean number of correct responses for each condition

material. One such man, S, is described in *The Mind of a Mnemonist,* written by the Russian psychologist A. R. Luria (1968), who observed and tested S for almost 30 years. S was able to remember long lists of words, nonsense material, tables of numbers, mathematical formulas, and so on, after only a single reading and for very long periods of time. (See Box 12–2.)

An unusual aspect of S's mental operations was that the remembering of material was generally accompanied by a marked degree of synesthesia, a condition in which a sensation obtained from one modality will elicit a sensation in another modality. Some synesthetic experience is found with most individuals. The hearing of a high tone, for example, may be accompanied by "seeing" bright red and yellow colors. But for S, the synesthetic response was much more elaborate. If he was asked to listen to a 30 Hz tone, he reported that at first he saw a strip 12–15 cm wide in the color of old tarnished silver. Gradually, this strip narrowed and was converted into an object that glistened like steel. The presentation of a 50 Hz tone, on the other hand, resulted in S "seeing" a brown strip against a dark background that had red tongue-like edges. Accompanying this tone was a sense of a taste like that of sweet and sour borscht, a sensation he described as gripping his entire tongue.

These added sensory components seemed to play an important role in S's recall, since he reported that he recognized words not only by the images they evoked but by the whole complex of sensations that were present. S reports:

box 12–2

An interesting example of how S was able to remember material is described by Luria (1968) in the following example. A "mathematical" formula that had no meaning was presented for study:

$$N \cdot \sqrt{d^2 \times \frac{85}{vx}} \cdot \sqrt{\frac{276^2 \cdot 86x}{n^2 v \cdot \pi 264}} \; n^2 b \; = \; sv \; \frac{1624}{32^2} \cdot r^2 s$$

Luria reports that S examined the formula closely, lifting the paper up several times to get a closer look at it. Then he put it down, shut his eyes, and after seven minutes came through with an exact reproduction of the formula.

The following is an account of S's procedure in recalling the first part of the formula:

Neiman (N) came out and jabbed at the ground with his cane (.). He looked up at a tall tree which resembled the square root sign ($\sqrt{}$), and thought to himself: "No wonder the tree has withered and begun to expose its roots. After all, it was here when I built these two houses" (d^2). Once again he poked with his cane (.). Then he said: "The houses are old, I'll have to get rid of them ($\times$); the sale will bring far more money." He had originally invested 85,000 in them (85). Then I see the roof of the house detached (_____), while down below on the street I see a man playing the Termenvox (vx). He's standing near a mailbox, and on the corner there's a large stone (.) which has been put there to keep carts from crashing up against the houses. (pp. 49–50)

Fifteen years later, S was still able to trace his pattern of recall in precise detail, even though he had been given no previous indication that he would be tested on this material.

Usually I experience a word's taste and weight, and don't have to make an effort to remember it— the word seems to recall itself. But it is difficult to describe. What I sense is something oily slipping through my hand . . . or I'm aware of a slight tickling in my left hand caused by a mass of tiny, light-weight points. When that happens I simply remember, without having to make the attempt (p. 28).

In spite of his unusual ability to remember verbal materials, S had a poor memory for faces because he said that they were so changeable. Unlike most individuals, who tend to single out certain features by which to remember faces, S saw faces as changing patterns of light and shade, which varied as the individual's face changed with his or her mood. S also had difficulty grasping entire passages of prose, since each word would call up a different image, and working out some order for these images was frequently a difficult and exhausting job. Moreover, if the material was read to him at a fairly rapid pace, the images would collide, with the result that the face would register confusion and finally utter bewilderment.[4]

Organization

The last variable to be discussed in this section is organization, a cognitive construct that is inferred from a subject's performance in a learning task and that reveals an integration or arrangement of the stimulus material which provides greater coherence, unity, and/or understanding.

Chunking   In a paper describing one such organizational process, chunking, Miller (1956) posited that an individual's immediate memory span was quite limited and could hold only about seven items. But the memory span could be increased or expanded, Miller pointed out, not by increasing the number of items that could be retained but by increasing the size of the unit. By organizing the material and combining smaller units into larger ones or *chunks*, as Miller has termed them, an individual could retain larger and larger amounts of material.

An example that Miller used to illustrate the chunking operation involved an individual just beginning to learn telegraphic code. At first, the telegrapher hears each dit and dah as a separate chunk. Soon, he is able to organize these sounds into letters so that he deals with letters as chunks; after some practice, the letters are organized into words that represent larger chunks. Finally, the telegrapher begins to hear whole phrases. Larger and larger chunks thus emerge as the telegrapher learns the code. Some investigators consider this process of chunking, in which items are combined or organized to form still larger units, to be a basic cognitive process operating in many learning tasks.

In verbal learning tasks, Bower (1969) considered a chunk of verbal material to be a

---

[4] Hunt and Love (1972) report the case history of VP who appeared to have a memory capacity rivaling that of Luria's subject, S. One interesting difference between VP and S was that with VP, visual imagery did not appear to play an important role in his ability to remember vast amounts of material.

highly integrated or coherent group of words, indexed by a strong tendency of the subject to recall the words together as a unit. Miller's chunking hypothesis would predict that the number of chunks and not the number of words would be critical in a free-recall task. In a study by Bower (1969) examining this hypothesis, subjects were provided one trial in which they were presented and asked to recall (1) 12 unrelated nouns, presented singly, such as *flag, sun, couch,* etc.; (2) 12 triplets—combinations of 3 unrelated nouns, such as *baby, cabin, fur;* and (3) 12 familiar cliches of 3 words, such as *ball point pen, mail order catalogue, Rose bowl parade.* Results were in keeping with the chunking hypothesis; there was no difference in the number recalled between the single presented nouns and the 3-word cliches, which were always remembered as a unit. The number of triplets recalled, however, was significantly lower. Bower (1969) has concluded, "In almost every aspect, pre-established word groups (cliches) behave like single words in recall. . . . Recall limits are expressible in chunks, not words" (pp. 612–613).

Clustering   A second organizational process, somewhat related to chunking and observed in free-recall tasks, is clustering. In a study by Bousfield (1953) in which clustering was first noted, subjects were first presented with a randomized list of 60 words consisting of 15 items obtained from each of four different categories: animals, vegetables, names, and professions. Immediately following the presentation of items, subjects were given 10 minutes to write down all of the words they could recall. Bousfield found that the subject revealed a greater than chance tendency to place items in clusters or groups that contained members of the same category. Thus, a subject's written recall might be *dog, cat, cow, bean, pea, John, Bob, doctor, dentist,* and so on. Since the varying words forming a cluster can be described in terms of their membership in a general class or category, the name category clustering has been given to this type of organizational category.

The phenomenon of clustering has been studied extensively, with many more conditions being investigated than can be presented in this introduction. Two examples, however, will illustrate the general nature of these studies. Mathews (1954) and Tulving and Pearlstone (1966) examined clustering as a function of the number of categories that comprised the word list. These experimenters found that as the number of categories increased, at least up to six, recall also increased. The kind of categories used was a second topic of interest. Bousfield and Wicklund (1969) and Fagan (1969) have found that when subjects are presented with sets of words that rhyme, such as *dead, led, wed, head,* they will tend to group them in their recall protocols, thus revealing acoustical clustering. Similarly, Freund and Underwood (1969) have reported that subjects will cluster their recall if alphabetical categories—sets of words all beginning with the same letter—are employed. But not all experimenter-identified categories have resulted in clustering, as Cofer and Bruce (1965) found when using clusters of words based on grammatical form class, such as nouns, verbs, and adjectives. In this study, subjects did not cluster these sets of words any more than would have been expected by chance.

Subjective Organization   In clustering experiments, the organization of the subject's recall protocols is related to the categories of items provided by the experimenter. The material in most learning tasks, however, is not so organized. In fact, the experimenter attempts to use words that are quite unrelated. Nonetheless, as noted in the examination of natural language mediators (NLM), subjects will frequently attempt to generate some natural or subjective kind of organization for the material they are asked to learn.

Tulving (1962) has found evidence of this type of organization in his examination of free recall learning. His experimental procedure consisted of selecting 16 unrelated words and arranging them in 16 different trial orders so that each word appeared just once in each position. Sixteen trials were provided, with the words presented at intervals of 1 second. Following each trial, the subjects were given 90 seconds to write down in any order as many words from the list as they could remember.

In Tulving's analysis, a subject's subjective organization (SO) score was a measure of the actual organization obtained compared to the maximum that could be achieved. Maximum organization was indicated by a score of 1.00, a value obtained by the subject who recalled all of the words on all trials in the same order. In contrast, a score of 0 would be obtained if the subject recalled each word in a different position on each trial. As can be noted from Figure 12–9, subject organization, as indicated by the subject recalling words in the same order, increased over successive blocks of trials. Tulving's (1962) study demonstrates that subjects do organize their recall sequentially, even in the absence of any kind of organization that is provided by the list itself.

Summary ▶

Many of the experiments in the area of verbal learning and memory have been conducted by investigators, identified as functionalists, who have been interested in examining the functional relationship existing between the stimulus and/or cognitive variables and ease of learning. The experimental materials have been lists of nonsense syllables (CVCs) or words with serial, paired associate, and free recall tasks being employed. Response measures have been either recall or recognition.

The stimulus attributes of words that have been identified have been (1) meaningfulness, (2) objective word frequency, (3) pronounceability, (4) vividness or imagery, and (5) concreteness. A factor analytic study indicates that all of these attributes could be encompassed by two factors—meaningfulness and imagery. Investigators have demonstrated that each of the listed attributes can be related to ease of learning. Recently, Rubin and Friendly have suggested that availability (the number of times a word was given as a first associate to a sample of stimulus words) and emotionality (how intense the emotional meaning of a word was) are important attributes that can be related to ease of learning.

Other stimulus characteristics that have been related to ease of learning are stimulus position and isolation. When the position of a word in a list is examined, it has been found that items at the beginning of the list and at the end of the list are learned most rapidly. The isolation effect refers to the finding that a word that is unique or

Figure 12-9

Mean performance (upper curve) and mean subjective organization (SO) (lower curve) as a function of trials. (Values of performance are to be read from the left ordinate, SO from the right ordinate.) Adapted from E. Tulving, "Subjective organization in free recall of 'unrelated' words," *Psychological Review,* 1962, *69,* 344–345. Copyright © 1962 by the American Psychological Association. Reprinted by permission.

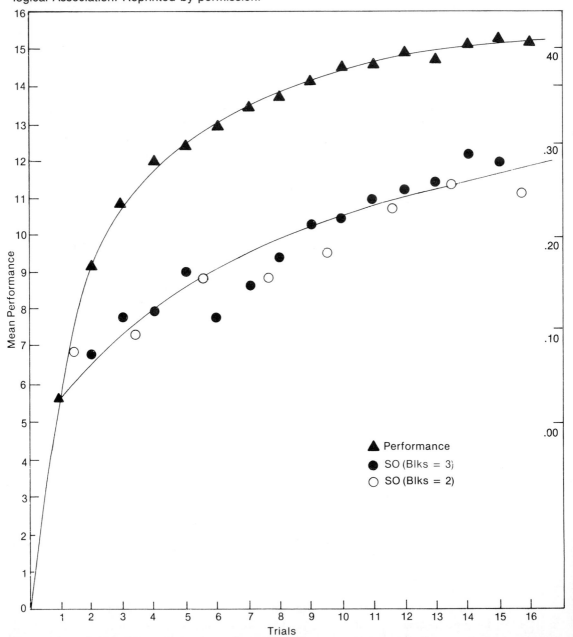

distinctive in an otherwise homogeneous list of words is learned more rapidly than a word that does not have this uniqueness.

The contribution of cognitive variables represents a recent interest of investigators, with such constructs as stimulus selection, mediation, chunking, and clustering being examined. Stimulus selection is a process whereby experimental subjects select and respond to only some of the stimulus elements that make up the discriminanda. Mediation refers to the subject's use of ideas, thoughts, or covert responses as an aid in learning to associate one item with another. In the learning of paired associates, for example, most subjects use mediators in order to more readily associate one item with another.

Another cognitive variable has been identified as an organizational process; it refers to the general tendency on the part of the subject to integrate or arrange the material to be learned in order to facilitate such learning. One specific organizational process is chunking—the subject organizes items into larger and larger units. Another organizational process is clustering—the tendency on the part of the subject to group similar items together in recall, although the items were not originally presented in groups. In the absence of some type of experimenter-provided organization of the material, it has been found that experimental subjects will provide their own (subjective) organization.

chapter thirteen

▶

Retention and Forgetting: The Functional Approach Continued

Functional investigators have been interested not only in the learning of verbal material but, following the lead of Ebbinghaus (1885/1913), also in their retention and forgetting. As is readily apparent, measures of retention and forgetting reflect different sides of the same coin. Assume, for example, that a subject, after having learned a list of 20 words to a criterion of one perfect recall, is able to recall just eight of the items 24 hours later. A retention score would reflect a value of 8, a forgetting score 12, with one of these values used in the plotting of a retention or a forgetting curve.

Operationally, retention and forgetting have been examined by interpolating a period of time and/or certain events (e.g., another learning task) between the reaching of a learning criterion (or a fixed number of learning trials) and the subsequent test for retention. Experimenters, beginning with Ebbinghaus, have generally examined retention as a function of varying time periods that have been placed between the last acquisition trial and the retention test. Experimental interest in forgetting has centered around an examination of the specific conditions that have been interpolated between the last acquisition trial and the subsequent measure of retention.

Retention ▶

The Length of the Retention Interval

A first step taken by investigators in their study of retention has been to describe how the amount of material that is retained changes as varying time or retention intervals are placed between the original learning and the test for retention. For most material that is learned, the amount retained is a function of the length of the retention interval.

The earliest experimental demonstration of this relationship was provided by Ebbinghaus (1885/1913). In his study, lists of nonsense syllables (13 per list) were learned until a criterion of two errorless recitations was reached. Following an interval of either 20 minutes, 1 hour, 9 hours, 1 day, 2 days, or 31 days, each list was relearned to the original learning criterion. Different lists were learned and retained for each of the retention intervals examined.

Figure 13-1 shows a retention curve in which Ebbinghaus's saving scores have been plotted as a function of the varying retention intervals. It may be noted that after a rather precipitous drop in performance for retention intervals up to nine hours, the subsequent decline in performance was quite small over the remaining intervals.

Williams's (1926) early retention study is noteworthy since more than 4,200 subjects, broken down into four distinct age groups (e.g., 9+ years, 12+ years, 16+ years, and adult) served as subjects. Fifty unrelated, monosyllabic words were used as the experimental material; the procedure consisted of presenting all of the words at the same time. Five minutes were provided for study, followed by a recall test. Varying groups then attempted to recall the words a second time after a retention interval of either one, two, three, five, or seven days. The value of immediate recall scores was used as a base from which to determine the percentage of recall for these varying retention intervals. Figure 13-2 provides Williams's findings for each of the age groups—an interesting note is that the retention curves for all groups are quite similar.

Figure 13-1
Retention as a function of the amount of time elapsing between learning and the test for retention. Based on data from Ebbinghaus (1913).

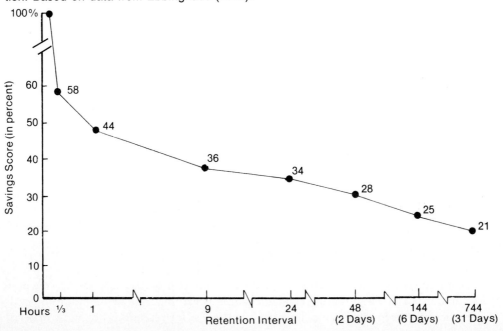

Figure 13-2
Retention curves for monosyllabic words. The varying curves, A, B, C, and D represent four different age groups (ages 9+, 12+, 16+, and adult). Adapted from O.
Williams, " A study of the phenomenon of reminiscence," *Journal of Experimental Psychology,* 1926, *9,* 368-387. Copyright © 1926 by the American Psychological Association. Reprinted by permission.

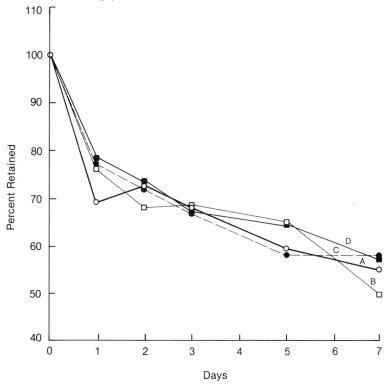

Early investigators assumed that Ebbinghaus's results indicated the general nature
of retention (or forgetting). However, psychologists today know that the slope of any
retention curve, like the slope of any learning curve, is related to the experimental
materials and conditions that are employed. This is illustrated by the findings of
Postman and Rau (1957), who had their subjects learn lists (12 items each) of CVCs and
words to a criterion of one perfect recitation, with retention of this material measured
either 20 minutes, 24 hours, or 48 hours later. Figure 13-3 presents retention curves
using recognition, free recall, and relearning measures as a function of the kind of
experimental material utilized.

It is readily apparent that different curve slopes were obtained by these experimenters as a function of the kind of experimental material used and how retention was
measured. But contrary to the conclusions arrived at by some experimenters, no general
statement can be made about the sensitivity of the varying retention measures that
Postman and Rau (1957) employed. Such comparisons among retention measures are

Figure 13-3
Retention curves for nonsense syllables and words as a function of the method of measurement. Adapted from L. Postman and L. Rau, "Retention as a function of the method of measurement," *University of California Publications in Psychology*, 1957, *8*, 217–270. Reprinted by permission.

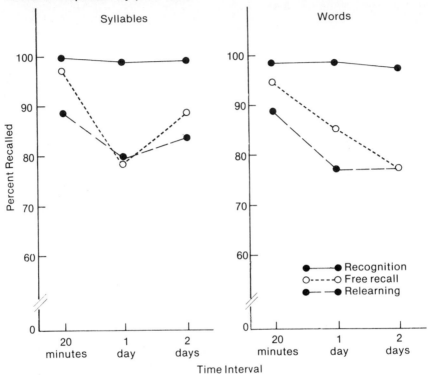

tenuous since any response measure is a function of the experimental conditions employed. There is little doubt that the retention curves for recognition obtained by Postman and Rau (1957) could have been changed by using different types of distracters.

The retention intervals examined by most investigators have been quite short, typically measured in hours. Although a general interest has been expressed in determining the course of retention over longer intervals of time, such as years, few investigators have conducted such experiments because of the problem of subject availability. Rarely are subjects who originally learned the experimental material available to be tested for retention years later. A study by Burtt (1941) represents an exception. (See Box 13-1.)

Current Long-Term Retention Studies– The Cross-Sectional Approach

Long-term retention studies are difficult to conduct because of the difficulty of keeping subjects available for very long periods of time. A study by Squire and Slater (1975), as

box 13–1

If you read material to your infant son or daughter, would you expect to find any retention of that material 5, 10, or 15 years later? We would not expect to discover any remembering, but such a result is possible, according the findings obtained in a study by Burtt (1932, 1937, 1941). The materials he used consisted of varying selections from Sophocles' Oedipus Tyrannus in the original Greek, with each selection consisting of approximately 20 lines or about 240 syllables. When his son Benjamin was 15 months of age, Burtt read to him three of these selections once daily for a period of three months—a total of 90 repetitions of each passage. These selections were then replaced with three other passages that were read to him each day for the next three months. This procedure of reading three selections/day for a three-month period, followed by a different set of selections, etc., was continued until the child was three years old, and 21 different selections had been presented. At this point the readings were discontinued.

When Benjamin was 8¹/₂ years old, seven selections, one from each three-month period, were selected and, along with three new selections, were used to measure retention using a relearning method. Another one-third of the original passages plus three control passages were used to measure retention when the subject was 14 years old, and finally the remaining one-third of the selections plus three control passages were used to measure retention when Benjamin was 18¹/₂ years old. Each retention period consisted of first reading all 10 passages—seven old and three new—for 18 trials. (The reading of all 10 passages constituted one trial.) Beginning with the nineteenth trial, every third trial employed a prompting method in which the experimenter read each section slowly, with the subject attempting to anticipate the next syllable in the passage. The number of trials required by the subject to recite the entire section verbatim and without prompting served as the measure of retention.

Burtt's findings were as follows: at age 8¹/₂ years, Benjamin required a mean of 317 trials to recite the previously presented selections of material, whereas for control materials he required a mean of 435 trials. At 14 years of age, the mean was 149 trials for the previously presented material and 162 trials for the new material. At age 18¹/₂ years, the mean number of trials for relearning and learning the experimental and control passages was 189 and 191 respectively. It may then be noted that a savings score of 27% was obtained when the retention interval was over five years in length. Savings declined to just 8% when the retention interval approximated 10 years. Finally, a retention interval of about fifteen years resulted in no savings, and Burtt (1941) concluded that the last retention interval was "sufficient to eradicate completely any trace of the original stimulation in infancy" (p. 437).

well as a series of experiments by Bahrick and his associates (e.g., Bahrick, Bahrick, and Wittlinger, 1975; Bahrick, 1983; and Bahrick, 1984b), are noteworthy because these experimenters solved the problem of subject availability by using a cross-sectional approach. This procedure employs retention tests given at approximately the same time to all subjects serving in the study. Variations in the time that the material was originally learned, however, provide the varying retention intervals, which in turn typically result in differing levels of performance.

Several long-term cross-sectional retention studies conducted by Bahrick and his associates represent landmarks in the study of long-term retention. The subject matters include (1) memory for the names and faces of high school classmates; (2) memory for a cognitive map of a small college town involving street names, locations of buildings, and so on; and (3) memory for the subject matter, Spanish, obtained in either a high school or college classroom. Bahrick's work is also noteworthy since it includes an examination of the retention of information acquired both casually as well as formally. All of these studies have included impressively large numbers of subjects, ranging from almost 400 used in examining memory for names and faces, to more than 850 employed in the cognitive map study.

The general procedure employed by Bahrick in all three studies is similar, and can be illustrated in his examination of the retention of Spanish (e.g., Bahrick, 1984). Subjects numbered 773, with 146 of these being students who at the time of testing were enrolled in a high school or college-level Spanish course. The bulk of the subjects, consisting of 587, however, had previously taken one or more Spanish courses during either high school or college, with such instruction varying from 1 to 50 years (retention interval) prior to being tested. In addition, 40 individuals who had no instruction in Spanish were included in order to establish a performance baseline.

We shall not describe in detail the varying subtests that were used but they included a knowledge of English-Spanish, and Spanish-English vocabulary, reading comprehension, grammar, idioms, and word order, with both recognition and recall measures being used. In addition to these varying subtests, subjects were asked to complete a questionnaire asking the extent of their formal language training, grades received, as well as inquiring about the use of Spanish taking place during the retention interval. Of the many conditions that were examined only the level of Spanish training, mean grades received, and the level of training in other Romance languages were found to contribute significantly to the test scores that were obtained.

From these significant contributors to performance, Bahrick grouped his subjects into three levels of Spanish expertise, which we shall identify as elementary, intermediate, and advanced. Test scores involving Spanish-English recall and recognition, reading comprehension, and word order for these three groups of subjects are presented in Figures 13–4 and 13–5.

The general form of these retention curves found for Spanish has been also found with memory for names and faces (e.g., Bahrick, Bahrick, and Wittlinger, 1975), and for the location of streets and buildings in a college town (e.g., Bahrick, 1983). In addition to providing a descriptive account of the course of retention over a 50-year retention interval, as well as demonstrating that such retention is a function of the strength of the original learning, Bahrick (1984a) has noted a most unusual finding. This has to do with the fact that after an exponential decline in performance for the first 3 to 6 years of the retention interval, retention then remains virtually unchanged for periods of up to 30 years before revealing a final decline. Thus, a large portion of the originally acquired information remains accessible for up to 50 years, even though it has been neither used nor rehearsed. Bahrick (1984a) has described such information as being in "permastore," which in turn results in the two parts of the retention curve being discontinuous.

From a methodological point of view, the cross-sectional approach does not provide the control of extraneous variables that can be provided by laboratory investigations of memory. But the cross-sectional method does permit investigations of retention that cannot be adequately or conveniently conducted within the confines of a laboratory. This approach is not a substitute for laboratory investigations of retention, but is an addition that investigators will surely find valuable in the future.

Figure 13-4
The effects of level of training on the recall and recognition of Spanish-English vocabulary. Adapted from H. P. Bahrick, "Semantic memory content in permastore: Fifty years of memory for Spanish learned in school," *Journal of Experimental Psychology: General*, 1984, *113*, 1–29. Copyright © 1984, by the American Psychological Association. Reprinted by permission.

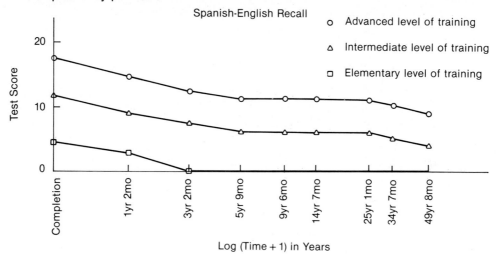

Spanish-English Recall

o   Advanced level of training

△   Intermediate level of training

□   Elementary level of training

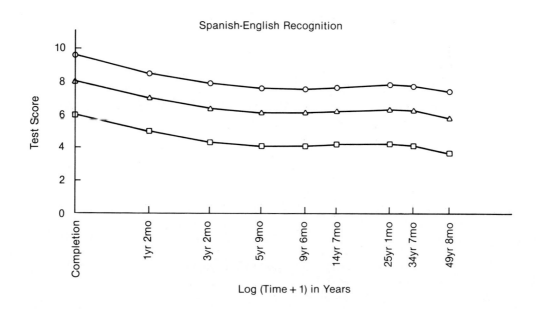

Spanish-English Recognition

Figure 13–5
The effects of level of training on the retention of reading comprehension and word order. Adapted from H. P. Bahrick, "Semantic memory content in permastore: Fifty years of memory for Spanish learned in School," *Journal of Experimental Psychology: General,* 1984, *113,* 1–29. Copyright © 1984, by the American Psychological Association. Reprinted by permission.

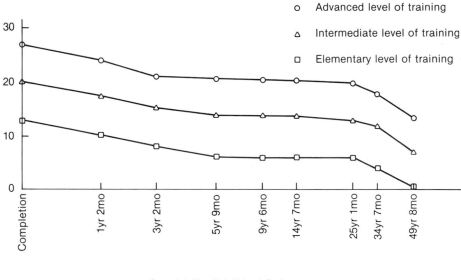

Spanish-English Reading Comprehension

o   Advanced level of training

△   Intermediate level of training

□   Elementary level of training

Spanish-English Word Order

Log (Time + 1) in Years

Hypermnesia

Our examination of retention curves has revealed that as the retention interval increases, there is a decline in performance. But an interesting contradiction in this relationship is found with the phenomenon of hypermnesia. A series of studies conducted by Erdelyi and his associates (e.g., Erdelyi and Becker, 1974; Erdelyi, Finkelstein, Herrell, Miller, and Thomas, 1976; Erdelyi, Bushke, and Finkelstcin, 1977; and Erdelyi and Kleinbard, 1978) has revealed a performance increment rather than a decrement over the retention interval.

To illustrate the nature of the procedure and the experimental findings, we will describe the Erdelyi and Kleinbard (1978) experiment. These investigators presented 60 slides containing either (1) simply sketched pictures of objects, such as a fish or phone; or (2) the names of these same objects, to two groups of subjects at the rate of one slide/ five seconds. After the slides had been presented, subjects were given seven minutes to recall as many of the items as they could. Following this recall period, subjects were requested to relax and think about the items for seven minutes, following which another recall period was provided. This was then followed by a second seven-minute relaxation/seven-minute recall period. Subjects were then given 37 recall sheets, each containing space for 60 items, with instructions to attempt to recall the experimental items three or more times each day so as to provide 37 additional recall protocols. These recall periods were conducted outside the laboratory, but subjects were asked to scrupulously limit them to seven minutes. (It should be pointed out that the individuals who comprised the experimental subjects were acquaintances of the experimenter and judged to be highly reliable and honest). About a week later, when the subjects returned to the laboratory to hand in the completed recall forms, three more recall sessions were provided, interspersed with "relax and think" intervals. All subjects were required to write the names of 60 nonrepeating items on all recall sheets, guessing if necessary in order to complete the protocol.

Figure 13–6 presents the retention curves of the picture and word groups across some 164 hours. It may be observed that the recall of pictures systematically increased over time, increasing from 26.7 items of the first recall trial to 38.3 items some 164 hours later—an increase of 44%. There was no recall growth beyond the first take-home recall trial for words, although there was some indication of recall increasing within the first 10-hour period.

The findings from Erdelyi and his associates' research, although originally indicating that recall did not improve over time for concrete words, did reveal that if subjects were asked to image the concrete words that were presented, hypermnesia effects could be obtained.

In view of these most unusual findings, which are at variance with most of the traditional retention studies, beginning with Ebbinghaus (1913), it is not surprising that the phenomenon of hypermnesia has generated a host of studies by other investigators. Roediger and Payne (1985) have attempted to answer several basic questions that were raised in Erdelyi's research. These were: (1) Can hypermnesia be found with concrete words when subjects were not given instructions to form images? (2) Can semantic rather than imaginal instructions result in hypermnesia? and (3) Can hypermnesia be obtained with low-imagery words? In their study, a mixed list of 70 words consisting of 35 low-imagery and 35 high-imagery words were used as the experimental material. One group of subjects were given imaginal instructions ("form a clear and vivid" image of the referent of the word), whereas a second group of subjects were given semantic instructions. Here, they were instructed to repeat the word to themselves, but also to

Figure 13-6

Average "forgetting" curves for picture and word lists. Adapted from M. H Erdelyi and J. Kleinbard, "Has Ebbinghaus decayed with time? The growth of recall (Hypermnesia) over days," *Journal of Experimental Psychology: Human Learning and Memory,* 1978, 275–289. Copyright © 1978 by the American Psychological Association. Reprinted by permission.

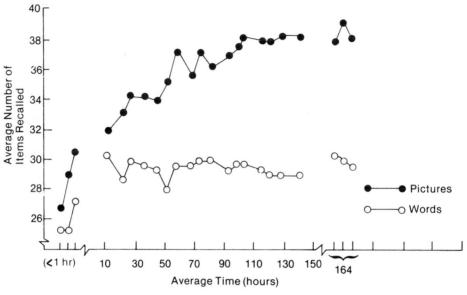

think of the meaning of the word. Presentation of the word list was first provided (e.g., five seconds per word) followed by three eight-minute sessions for recall, with approximately two minutes being provided between sessions. Results revealed that hypermnesia effects were obtained since there was consistent improvement over the three test periods. Ederlyi's position of the central role of imaging the material was not confirmed, however, since both sets of instructions (e.g., semantic vs. imaginal) resulted in producing improved performance over the testing session. In addition, hypermnesia was obtained with both high and low-imagery words, although the improvement for high-imagery words was superior to the improvement exhibited for words with low imagery.

In his review of many studies examining hypermnesia, Payne (1987) has concluded that hypermnesia is a reliable memory phenomenon, since he has noted that more than 100 experiments (many investigators have reported the findings of more than a single experiment in the same published study) have yielded positive results. In keeping with Roediger and Payne's (1985) findings, Payne concluded that hypermnesia can be obtained with verbal materials and without imaginal processing; however, he has also pointed out that hypermnesia is more readily obtained with pictorial stimuli and that such stimuli produce larger effects than when words are used as the experimental material. Finally, he has indicated that hypermnesia appears to depend critically on the subject repeatedly attempting to retrieve the previously studied information. These retrieval attempts may be induced either by administering several recall tests, or by permitting the subject to retrieve the list of items during the retention interval. If such retrieval opportunities are prevented, or are unlikely to occur spontaneously, however, the effect cannot be obtained.

Since the operations used to produce hypermnesia require that the subject actively attempt to retrieve the material throughout the retention interval, it becomes apparent that these operations differ from traditional retention operations in which retrieval of the to-be-remembered material is not encouraged, and in some instances actively prevented. From this perspective, hypermnesia operations can be viewed as "rehearsal trials" which have a basic similarity to traditional learning trials.

Strength of the Original Learning

One variable that has interested investigators of retention has been the strength of the original learning. One would expect to find that the amount of retention is related to how well the material was originally learned, and the experimental evidence supports this expectation. An early study demonstrating this effect was conducted by Underwood (1954), who had subjects learn a serial list of 14 CVCs to a criterion of either 7 or 13 correct responses on a single trial. In a second study, subjects learned a paired associate list of adjectives (10 pairs) to a criterion of either 5 or 10 correct responses on a single trial. Retention scores obtained 24 hours later revealed that those groups that learned the list to a more rigorous criteria recalled the greater number of items.

What has not been recognized as frequently, however, is that continued practice beyond the criterion of one perfect trial will have an effect on subsequent retention. Such continued practice past the point of complete mastery has been defined as *overlearning*. The classic overlearning study was performed by Krueger (1929) more than fifty years ago. Lists of nouns (12 nouns/list) were learned by subjects to either (1) a criterion of one perfect trial; (2) a criterion of one perfect trial plus 50% additional (overlearning) trials; or (3) a criterion of one perfect trial plus 100% additional (overlearning) trials. The lists were then relearned 1, 2, 4, 7, 14, or 28 days later, with the first trial providing a recall score. Table 13–1 indicates these recall scores obtained as a function of the degree of learning and the retention interval. It may be observed that overlearning trials significantly aided retention, although the increase in recall scores was less when overlearning trials were increased from 50 to 100% than when they were increased from 0 to 50%.

Few investigators have attempted to replicate Krueger's results or extend his findings to other types of material or different tasks. A study by Postman (1962b) is an exception. In his study, high- and low-frequency nouns were used to construct two serial lists (12 items/list) which subjects learned by the anticipation method. Following Krueger's procedure, groups of subjects learned these lists to a criterion of one perfect trial (0% overlearning) or 50 or 100% overlearning. Seven days after the original learning had taken place, groups relearned the original list to a criterion of one perfect trial.

Postman, like Krueger, found that overlearning significantly influenced retention

Retention Interval (days)	Mean Words Recalled Degree of Learning		
	0%	50%	100%
1	3.10	4.60	5.83
2	1.80	3.60	4.65
4	.50	2.05	3.30
7	.20	1.30	1.65
14	.15	.65	.90
28	.00	.25	.40

Adapted from W. C. F. Krueger, "The effect of overlearning on retention," *Journal of Experimental Psychology,* 1929, *12,* 71–78. Copyright © 1929 by the American Psychological Association. Reprinted by permission.

Table 13-1
Recall scores as a function of degree of learning and retention interval

of both types of materials as measured by the mean number of trials required to relearn the material. For the high-frequency words, the mean number of trials to relearn the list was, respectively, 6.12, 4.69, and 3.69 after 0, 50, and 100% overlearning trials. The corresponding mean number of trials required to relearn the low-frequency words was 7.31, 5.44, and 3.75. Postman's findings, which confirm Krueger's results, point to the value of practicing beyond the point of complete mastery in order to increase retention.

The overlearning effect would appear to have considerable practical value since continued practice on material already learned to a point of mastery can take place with a minimum of effort, and yet will prevent significant losses in retention. One such application is found in a study by Schendel and Hagman (1982). These investigators, working with the U.S. Army Research Institute, were interested in examining the cost effectiveness of providing soldiers with overtraining on the procedure for assembling machine guns. The Army's regular program was to train recruits to a specified criterion, following which retraining was instituted when the soldier's retention of the procedure dropped below the minimum level. Such retraining was costly since it meant that the soldier's current activity had to be interrupted, as well as involving the additional expense of providing transportation back to the training facility. Schendel and Hagman hypothesized that if soldiers were provided 100% overlearning during the initial training, the cost of retraining could be considerably reduced. Results of their study in which overtrained subjects were compared with controls who received no overtraining resulted in these investigators concluding that the cost and effectiveness weighed heavily in favor of the overlearning group.

Forgetting ▶

Many early investigators believed that forgetting arose from two interrelated conditions—disuse and time. Forgetting took place because the previously learned material was not used. The neural trace that had been laid down during the learning of the material decayed or deteriorated with time and disuse, so eventually the previously learned material was lost or forgotten.

   Although some experimenters have continued to assume that deterioration of the neural correlate of learning is responsible for some of our forgetting, much of the experimental analysis of forgetting has centered around an examination of three conditions that are presumed to account for a loss in retention. Thus, forgetting arises from (1) interference from material that has been previously learned, (2) stimulus conditions present during the learning trials being changed during the test for retention, and (3) a change in the subject's central state from learning trials to the test for retention trials.

The Role of Interference

In contrast to explanations based on time or disuse, many investigators argued that forgetting took place because specific activities that were learned by the subject during the retention interval interfered with the material to be recalled.

   One examination of this hypothesis was undertaken by Jenkins and Dallenbach (1924), who assumed that if the disuse theory was correct, it should make no difference what kind of activity the subject engaged in during the retention interval. On the other hand, an interference position would predict that an activity such as sleep should provide less interference (and greater recall) for earlier learned material than a waking activity. In Jenkins and Dallenbach's experiment, subjects first learned a list of 10 CVCs to a criterion of one perfect trial. After one, two, four, or eight hours of either (1) normal waking activity or (2) sleeping, the subjects were asked to recall the material. Results, as Figure 13-7 indicates, show that the CVCs were better retained after

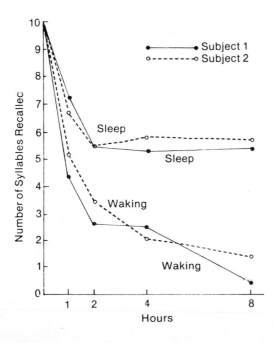

Figure 13-7
Mean number of syllables recalled after intervals of sleeping and waking. Adapted from J. G. Jenkins and K. M. Dallenbach, "Obliviscence during sleep and waking," *American Journal of Psychology,* 1924, 35, 605–612. Copyright © 1924, by the University of Illinois Press. Reprinted by permission.

intervals of sleeping than after corresponding periods of wakefulness. Since the same amount of time had elapsed between the original learning and the test for recall for both groups, the disuse theory was unable to account for the differential forgetting that took place. Jenkins and Dallenbach concluded that forgetting is "a matter of the interference, inhibition, or obliteration of the old by the new" (p. 612), with sleep insulating the newly learned material from the interfering activities. Later experimenters confirmed these findings (see Van Ormer, 1932; Newman 1939; and Lovatt and Warr, 1968).

Several years after Jenkins and Dallenbach's (1924) experimental findings were published, McGeoch (1932) attacked disuse theory by arguing that it was the characteristics of the events taking place during the retention interval that determined the amount of forgetting that would occur. The passage of time, he wrote, was not an explanation for forgetting but rather a condition within which causative events took place. More specifically, he wrote, "In time iron, when unused, may rust, but oxidation, not time, is responsible. In time organisms grow old, but time enters only as a logical framework in which complex biochemical processes go their ways" (p. 359). McGeoch's paper not only appeared to silence those theorists who assumed that forgetting could be attributed to disuse or decay of the neural trace but provided the foundation for what current investigators have designated as an interference theory of forgetting.

An interfering event is the learning of other material that competes with the material to be recalled. If the interfering material is learned prior to the learning and recall of the experimental material, the operation is identified as proactive inhibition (PI). If the interfering material is learned between the last learning trial of the experimental material and its subsequent recall, the operation is designated as retroactive inhibition (RI). The two experimental designs describing these paradigms are found in Table 13–2.

Two aspects of these experimental designs should be noted. The first is that the "rest" condition does not mean that control subjects really rest. In most instances, they are given some task to perform in order to prevent the rehearsal of the previously learned material. For instance, the rapid naming of colors, repeating of digits, and so on has often been used as a "rest" task. In other instances, control subjects have been asked to learn a second task, but one that has been judged to be irrelevant to the originally learned task.

Second, in keeping with the Ebbinghaus tradition, list-learning tasks have been used, with many investigators employing lists of paired associates. When these tasks are used, a specific notation denotes the stimuli and responses that comprise the pairs. The

Table 13–2
Experimental designs for proactive and retroactive inhibition

	Proactive Inhibition			Retroactive Inhibition		
Experimental Group	Learn Task 1	Learn Task 2	Recall Task 2	Learn Task 1	Learn Task 2	Recall Task 1
Control Group	Rest	Learn Task 2	Recall Task 2	Learn Task 1	Rest	Recall Task 1

notation A-B is used to indicate the stimulus and response items employed in the original learning task, whereas the notation used to denote the interfering task will vary, depending on the kind of stimuli and responses provided by the experimenter. If the stimuli in the interfering list are identical to those in the original but the responses are different, an A-B, A-C notation is used. If the responses in the interfering list are identical to those in the original list but the stimuli are different, an A-B, C-B notation would be used. In some instances, the stimuli and responses in the original list may be re-paired to provide different paired associates in the interfering task. In such instances, the notation used is A-Br. Finally, an A-B, C-D notation indicates that the stimuli and responses on the interfering list are completely different from those used in the original learning. Table 13–3 illustrates four of the basic experimental procedures.

It should be noted that intervening activities in proactive or retroactive paradigms do not necessarily result in inhibition and forgetting. In some instances, the learning of such intervening material facilitates retention. It has been generally found that the A-B, A-C and A-B, A-Br paradigms result in inhibition, and they have been used almost exclusively in proactive and retroactive inhibition studies. The A-B, C-B paradigm, on the other hand, facilitates retention. Theoretically, the A-B, C-D paradigm, which has been used by many experimenters as a control condition, should result in neither inhibition nor facilitation, although Newton and Wickens (1956) observed that, at least in their study, the A-B, C-D paradigm produced inhibition.

An Analysis of Retroactive Inhibition

Following the lead of McGeoch (1932), most early psychologists believed that forgetting could be attributed to retroactive inhibition. Proactive inhibition was given little consideration. Moreover, it was assumed that the basic source of interference with the RI paradigm arose from the two sets of responses competing during the recall of the original list. For example, if an originally learned paired associate item was active-pencil, and the interpolated pair was active-sugar, it was assumed that the responses of *pencil* and *sugar* would compete with each other when the stimulus active was presented during the recall test. If the originally learned response, pencil, was forgotten in such

Original Task		Interfering Task	
Stimulus	*Response*	*Stimulus*	*Response*
A Active	B Pencil	A Active	C Sugar
A Active	B Pencil	C Bright	B Pencil
A Active Engine	B Pencil Lower	A Active Engine	Br Lower Pencil
A Active	B Pencil	C Bright	D Sugar

Table 13-3
Notation and examples used to indicate varying stimulus-response relationships in proactive and retroactive inhibition experiments

circumstances, it was attributed solely to the action of the competing response, sugar. Thus, the A-B, A-C paradigm became an important one for investigating the contribution of RI to forgetting. (See Box 13–2.)

Melton and Irwin (1940) made an interesting discovery regarding the contribution of response competition to retroactive inhibition. In their RI study, 18 CVCs were presented in serial order to the subjects for 5 trials, following which a second list was presented for either 5, 10, 20, or 40 trials. These second list learning trials were followed by relearning trials on the first list to a criterion of two perfect recitations. In an examination of their subject's performance during these relearning trials, the experimenters made special note of the number of overt responses that belonged to the second list. Melton and Irwin believed that the overt responses or intrusions would provide an index of the amount of response competition between the original and interpolated responses. Admittedly, the number of overt intrusions would not reflect the total amount of forgetting, since it was assumed that forgetting could also be attributed to covert response competition. Nonetheless, it was believed that there should be a positive relationship between the total amount of retroactive inhibition observed and the number of overt intrusions. As retroactive inhibition increased, so should the number of overt intrusions.

When Melton and Irwin compared the total amount of RI with the number of intrusions, they were surprised to find that no consistent relationship could be noted between these measures. Figure 13–8 presents their results. The total amount of RI increased to an asymptote at approximately the level of 20 trials of second-list learning, whereas the amount of RI attributed to overt competition declined after 10 trials of interpolated learning and was virtually nonexistent at 40. Melton and Irwin reasoned that some process other than response competition must contribute to forgetting. They identified this process as *Factor X;* it was later called an *unlearning process.* When first-list responses intruded during the learning of second-list responses, these first-list responses were not reinforced and were thus unlearned or extinguished.

box 13–2

An interesting demonstration of response competition and an interference effect is found in what is known as the Stroop effect (1935). With this procedure, an experimental group of subjects is presented with a list of names of colors. However, each name (or word) is printed in a color that is inappropriate for the color name. For example, the word *blue* would be printed in red, the word *green* would be printed in orange, and so on. The task of the subject is to name the color of the word and not use the word itself. Individuals who participate in such a task actually become aware of the interference that arises from wanting to respond to the word rather than the color. The interference of the presence of such interference can be made by comparing the experimental groups' latency of responding with a control group in which subjects name a list of color patches as rapidly as possible. In keeping with the varying paired associate paradigms previously described, the Stroop effect describes an A-B, A-C situation, with the visual presentation of the word being the stimulus (A) in each association. The previously learned verbal response of pronouncing the word made to the visual presentation of the word would be B, whereas responding with the name of the color would be C.

Figure 13-8
Relationship between the amount of retroactive inhibition and the degree of learning
of the interpolated material. Adapted from A. W. Melton and J. M. Irwin, "The influence of degree of interpolated learning on retroactive inhibition and the overt transfer
of specific responses," *American Journal of Psychology*, 1940, *53*, 173–203. Copyright
© 1940 by the University of Illinois Press. Reprinted with permission.

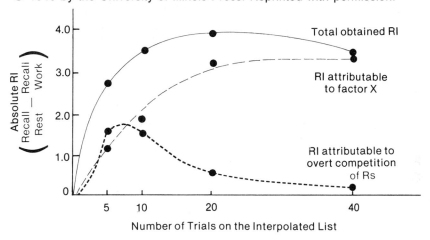

The result was that these first-list responses were not available when first-list
relearning or recall trials were provided. A two-factor theory of RI thus emerged;
competition taking place between responses during relearning or recall was one factor,
whereas the unlearning of first-list responses during second-list learning was the second.
Note that the unlearning process should not operate with proactive inhibition, since
this paradigm does not provide the opportunity for second-list responses to be unlearned. Moreover, since two factors contribute to RI and only a single factor to PI, this
supported the position emphasizing the greater contribution of retroactive inhibition
to the process of forgetting.

Experiments by Underwood (1948a, 1948b) contributed to a further understanding
of the operation of the unlearning factor. In one study, Underwood (1948a) had
subjects learn two lists of paired adjectives (A-B, A-C), each to a criterion of one perfect
trial. Recall of either the first or second list took place under the following conditions:
(1) List 1 recalled after 5 hours (RI); (2) List 2 recalled after 5 hours (PI); (3) List 1
recalled after 48 hours (RI); and (4) List 2 recalled after 48 hours (PI)

Underwood found that after 5 hours the recall of first-list responses (RI paradigm)
was significantly less than the recall of second-list responses (PI) paradigm, a finding in
keeping with the two-factor theory that posited RI to be more important to forgetting
than PI. A surprising finding, however, was that after 48 hours there was no difference
in the recall of the two lists. As can be noted from Figure 13–9, an increase in the recall
score for the RI condition from 5 to 48 hours was accompanied by a decline in the recall
score for the PI condition. Underwood suggested that if the concept of unlearning was
enlarged to include spontaneous recovery of associations that had been unlearned
during the presentation of the second list, the increased recall for the RI condition

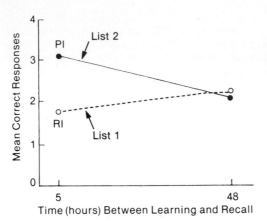

Figure 13-9
Mean number of correct anticipations on the first relearning trial after 5 and 48 hours. RI refers to the recall of the first list, PI to recall of the second. Adapted from B. J. Underwood "Retroactive and proactive inhibition after five and forty-eight hours," Journal of Experimental Psychology, 1948, *38*, 29-38. Copyright © 1948 by the American Psychological Association. Reprinted by permission.

could be adequately explained. Later, experimental evidence suggested that such spontaneous recovery, as inferred from increases in recall of first-list responses over time, could be obtained with intervals as short as a half-hour (see Abra, 1969; and Kamman and Melton, 1967).

A Further Examination of Two-Factor Theory

For at least two decades following Melton and Irwin's (1940) work, a host of experiments were conducted, all concerned with exploring the nature of the unlearning and response competition processes.

In the typical retroactive inhibition experiment, many subjects who were asked to respond with first-list responses during the final recall period did not do so. Did their failure arise because they assumed first-list responses were inappropriate in that setting, or because such responses were actually unavailable? Presumably, following Melton and Irwin's (1940) analysis, first-list responses were unavailable because they had been unlearned during the subject's learning of the second-list. But how was it possible to determine that such unlearning actually took place?

An approach to this problem was provided by Barnes and Underwood (1959) who devised a procedure designated as the *modified modified free recall* (MMFR). Here, after having learned the different list responses to a common stimulus, experimental subjects were asked to recall both responses if possible.

In an experiment conducted by Barnes and Underwood (1959) using the MMFR procedure, subjects learned two paired associate lists in which CVCs served as stimuli and two syllable adjectives as responses. An A-B, A-C design was used. Following the learning of the A-B list, the A-C list was presented for either 1, 5, 10, or 20 trials. Following the appropriate number of A-C trials, each subject was provided with a piece of paper on which each stimulus CVC was printed and was asked to write down the two responses that had been associated with it. Results are presented in Figure 13–10. As the number of trials of the A-C list increased, the number of correct responses from this second list also increased, but the number of correct responses appropriate for the

Figure 13-10
Mean number of responses correctly recalled in the A-B, A-C paradigm. Adapted from J. M. Barnes and B. J. Underwood, " 'Fate' of first-list associations in transfer theory," *Journal of Experimental Psychology,* 1959, *58* 97–105. Copyright © 1959 by the American Psychological Association. Reprinted by permission.

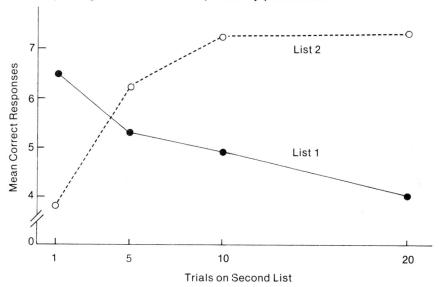

A-B list showed a gradual decline. Since the subjects were instructed to recall the adjectives from both lists if at all possible and not pressed to respond rapidly during this recall period, any competition between responses should have been eliminated. The decline of the first-list responses was attributed to the unlearning of these responses during second-list learning. Thus, Barnes and Underwood's (1959) experiment provided important support for the existence of an unlearning process operating in retroactive inhibition studies.

A second area of concern was with the construct of response competition which most investigators assumed was present when different responses used on the first and second list were attached to the same stimulus. Newton and Wickens (1956), however, noted that their use of an A-B, C-D paradigm produced a substantial amount of forgetting even though different stimuli were employed with each list. As a result, they suggested that during the recall of the original list responses there was a tendency on the part of subjects to restrict their responses to those that had been learned on the interpolated list, a phenomenon that they identified as *generalized response competition.*

Subsequently, Postman, Stark, and Fraser (1968) identified this tendency as *response-set interference.* They believed that this developed not during the recall of the original responses, as Newton and Wickens had suggested, but during the learning of the second-list responses.

In a further elaboration of this construct, Postman and Underwood (1973) have written that subjects established a set for giving responses from a particular list during a particular learning session—this makes it difficult for the subject to switch almost instantaneously to provide responses from another list. Thus, there is a tendency for the subject in the RI experiment to respond with second-list responses during the recall period designed to elicit first-list responses.

One might assume that if the original-list responses were made available to the subject during or prior to the recall period, the interference arising from an inappropriate set to recall second-list responses might be minimized.

Several different procedures were used to do this (e.g., Postman, 1976; Cofer, Failie, and Horton, 1971; and Postman and Gray, 1978), but the results were disappointing. The reduction in forgetting produced by the procedures used to make first-list responses available was small, suggesting that conditions in addition to response set interference was contributing to the forgetting process.

The Role of Proactive Inhibition in Forgetting

Of the varying processes hypothesized to operate with retroactive inhibition, only response competition and response set interference have been assumed to operate with proactive inhibition. The process of unlearning, which has played a prominent role in RI, cannot take place since there is no opportunity for second-list responses to be unlearned. It is not surprising, then, that most psychologists, at least until the late 1950s, assumed that PI was less important than RI.

In a most important paper, Underwood (1957) suggested that this position was incorrect and that PI made a much greater contribution to forgetting than had been previously assumed. Underwood noted that if a subject learned a list of CVCs and then was asked to recall them after an interval of 24 hours, a substantial amount of forgetting was observed. Traditionally, such forgetting had been attributed to RI, with the interfering activities being assumed to take place between the original learning and the subsequent test for recall. But Underwood reasoned that this was an incredible stretching of interference theory to believe that such forgetting was produced by the learning of material that subjects had learned outside the laboratory.

Underwood believed that it made more sense to assume that the interference arose from proactive inhibition—responses that the subject had learned prior to learning the experimental material. But a basic problem was to identify the nature of these responses. Underwood and Postman (1960) reasoned that such responses had to be acquired outside the laboratory and that they consisted of (1) letter-sequence habits and (2) word-sequence habits. *Letter-sequence habits* were defined as habits that developed through the normal course of learning a language. For example, if a two-lettered combination, QJ, was used as a response term in a paired associate task, the subject's previously learned letter-sequence habit, QU should make the learning of QJ difficult. Moreover, after QJ had been acquired, the older QU habit would recover in strength with the passage of time and interfere with any subsequent recall of QJ.

Word-sequence habits were defined as the learning of sequences of words that frequently occur in the language. If the sequence "black-rubber" was to be learned and subsequently recalled, the previously learned word-sequence habit "black-white" would have to first be unlearned; moreover, the subsequent recovery of the "black-white" sequence would interfere with the recall of the "black-rubber" sequence.

A number of investigators have attempted to obtain experimental support for the contribution of extra-experimental interference in the recall of list-learning material. We shall not provide the details of these studies other than to point out that they have been uniformly unsuccessful (see Underwood and Postman, 1960; Postman 1962, Ekstrand and Underwood, 1965; and Underwood and Ekstrand, 1966, 1968).

The Present Status of Interference Theory

For more than the past decade, interference theory has been under attack; in fact, some investigators have expressed doubt that this theory will survive. Although this is undoubtedly an exaggeration, some very legitimate problems exist with this explanation of forgetting.

First, questions have been raised about the operation of some of the basic interference constructs that have been posited. For example, the operation of unlearning has been examined using the MMFR procedure—presumably, the opportunity for subjects to provide both responses in the RI experiment has been assumed to eliminate response competition so that any failure of recall must be due to unlearning. But Koppenaal's (1963) demonstration that PI effects may be detected using the MMFR procedure raises a basic problem. Since PI is assumed to reflect the operation of only response competition—there is no opportunity for second-list responses to become unlearned—it is difficult to explain how unlearning, as measured by the MMFR, could be a contributor to the PI findings. Postman and Underwood (1973) have acknowledged the difficulty, writing, "Attempts to specify the exact mechanisms of associative unlearning have met with only indifferent success" (p. 23).

A second problem has to do with the demonstration of PI and RI effects with single-list learning tasks. When subjects learn only a single-list of words or CVCs in the laboratory (interfering lists are not provided), forgetting appears to take place at a relatively uniform rate, regardless of the characteristics of the material learned. For example, after a subject learns a list of high- or low-frequency words or high- or low-association CVCs to the same criterion, a recall test provided 24 hours later will reveal that these lists have been forgotten at about the same rate. If interfering materials, presumably arising from an extra-experimental source such as natural language habits, are held accountable for the forgetting that has been observed over the 24-hour period, it is necessary to assume that the interference provided by natural language habits is the same regardless of the kind of material learned.

Underwood (1983) has indicated that it is necessary to demonstrate that the forgetting of the singly learned list is due to RI and PI. But as he indicated, it is necessary to be more specific than that.

> We must say that the forgetting is produced either by interference from an interpolated task learned outside the laboratory or from a prior task learned outside the laboratory, or from both. ... [And] at the present time the theorizing is "stuck" at this point. We have not been able to

identify the interfering associations acquired outside the laboratory which produce the loss in the single-earned list. It is an act of faith in nature's consistency that we generalize the facts of interference as observed in RI and PI saying that all forgetting must be due to interference (p. 238).

A more general problem has to do with the failure of many investigators to demonstrate either proactive or retroactive inhibition using prose as the experimental material (e.g., McGeoch and McKinney, 1934; Deese and Hardman, 1954; Hall, 1955; and Ausubel, Robbins, and Blake, 1957). Some investigators have been able to demonstrate such an effect (e.g., Anderson and Carter, 1972; and Bower, 1978. But an analysis of these studies reveals that the basic paradigm used to demonstrate inhibition effects was in keeping with paired associate studies which have indicated the necessity of attaching different responses to identical or similar stimuli. Although Anderson and Myrow (1971) were successful in demonstrating the operation of RI with prose, they have wondered how frequently forgetting analogous to RI occurs in educational settings since students are seldom taught different answers to the same question. Thus, these authors have indicated that if RI is found in the recall of prose only when the materials to be learned are quite similar, the efficacy of the interference model as an inclusive explanation of forgetting must be questioned.

A final inadequacy has been noted in the puzzling experimental findings of Ekstrand and his associates, who have resumed the work of Jenkins and Dallenbach (1924) in examining the role of sleep on retention. Since there is now much more information about the characteristics of sleep, Ekstrand was interested in how such information might add to a better understanding of the effects of sleep on recall.

Five different stages of sleep have been identified through the use of electroencephalographic features. Stages 1 through 4, collectively known as *non-REM,* are each indicated by specific EEG features and the absence of rapid eye movements (REM) on the part of the sleeping subject. The fifth state, the REM stage, is similar to Stage 1 except that there are periodic bursts of rapid eye movements. Typically, REM sleep occupies about 20% of a normal night's sleep. Most of REM sleep takes place in the second half of the typical eight-hour sleep period.

Yaroush, Sullivan, and Ekstrand (1971) examined how recall was affected by the first four hours of sleep (small amounts of REM) verses the second four hours (large amounts of REM). The first group of subjects learned a list of 15 paired associates to a criterion of 10 out of 15 correct responses just before retiring. Four hours later, they were awakened and provided several recall tests. The second group of subjects went to bed shortly after appearing at the laboratory, but four hours later they were awakened, learned the experimental material to the same criterion, returned to bed, and then four hours later were awakened and tested for recall. (See Table 13–4 for this design.) Results, which were confirmed in a subsequent study by Barrett and Ekstrand (1972), indicated that performance was superior for the group that recalled the material after the first four hours of sleep. Thus, the first group revealed an absolute recall decrement of 1.50 items in contrast to a decrement of 3.50 items for the second group.

Ekstrand has acknowledged that it is difficult to reconcile these findings with an interference theory of forgetting, since it is necessary to assume that the second four hours of sleep creates greater interference than the first four hours. Such greater interference effects would appear to be attributed to different neural activities that are

Table 13-4
Experimental design examining first four hours of sleep versus second four hours on recall

		8 hours of sleep			
Experimental Group A	Learn PA list	Sleep 4 hours	Recall PA list	Sleep 4 hours	
Experimental Group B		Sleep 4 hours	Learn PA list	Sleep 4 hours	Recall PA list

found in the varying stages of sleep. This explanation stresses the fact that physiological conditions must at least in part account for the forgetting process.

The Role of Contextual Stimulus Change ►

A second variable that has been found to influence forgetting was identified by McGeoch (1942) who wrote that a "fundamental condition in the psychological account of forgetting is an alteration of the stimulating conditions from the time of learning to that of the measurement of retention" (p. 501). As Riccio, Richardson, and Ebner (1984) have indicated, "More contemporary forms of this principle generally refer to 'contextual cues'" (p. 152).

Many laboratory investigations employing human subjects have demonstrated that retention is maximized when the environment or context during retention is the same as it was during learning. Conversely, any change in the retention environment will result in forgetting (e.g., Bilodeau and Schlosberg, 1951; and Greenspoon and Ranyard, 1957).[1]

A study by Smith, Glenberg, and Bjork (1978) illustrates this kind of experiment (Experiment 2). Subjects learned two lists of paired associates. List 1 was learned on Day 1 in one environment (location A), and List 2 was learned the next day in a different environment (location B). Location A was a small windowless room, containing a large blackboard and glass cabinets and located in an old building off the main campus. Here, the list of paired associates was presented using a slide projector. Location B was a small room containing windows and a mirror located in a large modern central campus building; the experimental material was presented with a tape recorder. On Day 3, subjects were asked to recall words from both lists; however, some subjects recalled

---

[1] Results obtained from the experiments employing animals have been in accord with human subject findings. Spear and his associates (e.g., Klein and Spear, 1970; Spear, Klein, and Riley, 1971; and Spear, 1978) have convincingly demonstrated the contribution of contextual cue changes on forgetting. These studies have led Spear (1978) to write, "The effectiveness of memory retrieval depends on the similarity between events noticed at the time of retrieval and those presented as attributes of the critical memory. The greater the similarity, the better the retention" (p. 56).

these items in Location A, the others in Location B. Results indicated that more words were recalled from List 1 than from List 2 when recall took place in Location A (where List 1 words had been originally learned), whereas more words were recalled from List 2 than from List 1 when recall took place in Location B (where List 2 words had been originally learned). Godden and Baddeley (1975) have reported similar findings in their examination of changes in natural environments. (See Box 13–3.)

Investigators have provided several explanations for the effects of a changed context on retention. A performance explanation assumed that when subjects attempt to recall material in an unfamiliar context, they attend to their changed surroundings with anxiety or suspicion, which in turn depresses performance. A second explanation, based on associative relationships, assumes that an association is established between the material that is learned and the context in which such learning takes place. When the learning and recall contexts are the same, the subject is able to use those associations that had been established between the learned items and the location to aid in the recall of those items. The changed context does not make such associations available, thus depressing performance.

The results obtained from most studies cannot be used to distinguish between these explanations, but a series of experiments by Smith (1979) does support the associative position. Smith found that when subjects were placed in a changed environment for the recall test but were asked to remember the characteristics of the room in which the original learning had taken place, or were shown slides of the original learning room, thus reinstating contextual associations, their performance was similar to that of subjects who learned and recalled the items in the same environment.

In spite of the positive findings by earlier investigators, a series of experiments conducted by Fernandez and Glenberg (1985) have raised some basic questions about the reliability of these laboratory findings. The first seven experiments conducted by Fernandez and Glenberg examined the role of incidental learning. Their Experiment 3 illustrates the nature of this type of task, their procedure, and the kinds of environments employed for the learning and recall sessions. An easy task, consisting of easily related pairs of common nouns, and a difficult task, consisting of difficult-to-relate pairs, were employed. Subjects were presented with single cards, each containing a word pair, and instructed to use the words in each pair to create a sentence that conformed to certain criteria (e.g., order of the words in the sentence had to correspond to the words presented on the card, the words could not be used together, etc). Two different rooms provided the different contextual settings. One room was large, with the walls painted black and gray, and contained electronic equipment in addition to tables, chairs, and the like. The other room was a much smaller basement room, and furnished with carpeting, pictures, plants, and so on. Context was additionally changed by using a tape recorder to present the instructions in one room, whereas the experimenter presented the instructions in the other. Following the completion of the task, subjects returned a day later and were instructed to write down as many words as they could remember. The general procedure used in the examination of context was employed with groups of subjects either learning and recalling in the same context, or learning and recalling in different contexts.

box 13-3

Most learning and retention experiments are conducted in unimaginative environmental locations, generally a college classroom or research cubicle. But the environmental settings of an experiment conducted by Godden and Baddeley (1975) examining context effects were a far cry from the college campus. In this study, members of a university diving club learned lists of 36 unrelated words on shore (dry environment) and also underwater (wet environment), and were then asked to recall these words either in the same environment in which the words were learned or in the other environment. In summary, the 16 students who participated performed under each of four experimental conditions: (1) learn dry, recall dry; (2) learn dry, recall wet; (3) learn wet, recall wet; and (4) learn wet, recall dry; with 24 hours separating each experimental session. The words in each list were auditorily presented twice, with 10 seconds between presentations. After the last word in the second presentation had been given, subjects were asked to copy digits for 30 seconds. Four minutes later, remaining in either the same environment or having moved to the other, they were given two minutes to write down as many words as they could recall.

When subjects were in the dry environment, they sat by the edge of the water, with their masks tipped back, breathing tubes removed, listening to the words over their underwater-communication earphone. When in the wet environment, subjects dove to approximately 20 feet, taking with them a formica board on which the words could be written and two pencils. Heavy weighting enabled them to sit on the bottom of the open water site to participate in the experiment.

Results clearly revealed that superior recall took place when subjects learned and recalled the words in the same environment. See Box Table 13-1.

But could the decrease in performance be attributed to the disruption produced by a diver moving from a wet environment to dry, or vice versa? Such a possibility exists, and it was investigated in another experiment conducted by Godden and Baddeley. In their second study, in which the word lists and conditions were similar to the first, subjects were required to learn and recall in the dry environment. In one condition they rested between the learning and recall conditions, while in the second they first learned the words but were then asked to enter the water and dive to a depth of 20 feet before recalling them. Results indicated that this disruption had no effect on their subsequent recall.

Learning Environment	Recall Environment		
	Dry	Wet	Total
Dry	13.5	8.6	22.1
Wet	8.4	11.4	19.8
Total	21.9	20.0	

Adapted from D. R. Godden and A. D. Baddeley, "Context-dependent memory in two natural environments: On land and underwater," *British Journal of Psychology*, 1975, 66, 325–331.

Box Table 13-1
Recall of words by divers as a function of learning and recall environment

Results indicated that the only significant difference obtained was related to the difficulty of the task. Whether learning and retention took place in the same room or in different rooms played no role in determining the number of words recalled.

The investigator's eighth experiment was a replication of Smith's (1979) study and one in which the incidental learning type of task was replaced by one in which subjects were told that their task was one of learning and recalling verbal materials. But here again, and using many more subjects than employed in Smith's study, positive findings were not obtained. In summary, findings from all of their experiments provided no support for a conclusion, which indicated that superior recall was associated with learning and recall in the same context.

In a most provocative discussion of context effects on retention, the authors have not rejected the role of context in facilitating retention, since anecdotal reports are far too frequent to relegate them to fiction. Rather, an examination of these natural occurring incidents suggested that (1) such improvements in memory are typically associated with long retention intervals; (2) such improvement was associated with a unique context in terms of the physical qualities of the context at the time during which the event was experienced; and (3) the improvement was associated with multiple retrieval attempts over an extended period of time.

In their examination of laboratory studies, they have indicated that the match between typical study and test rooms does not capture the critical feature of natural changes in context that are responsible for producing the same-context advantage. Moreover, these tasks do not preserve the strong link between naturally occurring events and their environment, which presumably underlies the anecdotal reports of context effects. Finally, they indicate that from the experimenter's point of view, changing the room from learning to recall may be perceived as a massive change in stimulation, but this may not be so for the subject. It has been proposed that future studies should deal with memory for events that are perceived to be related to the environment, and that manipulations of the environmental context should involve components of the context that are likely to be perceived by the subject as relevant to the memory task.

The Contribution of State-Dependent Variables

The last variable to be discussed that influences forgetting is state-dependent effects, which bear a striking similarity to context effects. Specifically, a state-dependent effect refers to the phenomenon whereby material that has been learned under the influence of one physiological or emotional state is forgotten if the subject attempts recall under a different state. Anecdotes abound testifying to the validity of this phenomenon. Goodwin, Powell, Bremer, Hoine, and Stern (1969) have reported clinical evidence that alcoholics, when sober, were not able to find money or alcohol that they had hidden when they were drunk, but they did remember the hiding places when they were again intoxicated.

In an experiment designed to examine state-dependent effects produced by the ingestion of alcohol, Weingartner, Adefris, Eich, and Murphy (1976) had 11 female subjects participate in each of four experimental conditions: (1) learn and recall while sober; (2) learn and recall when they were intoxicated; (3) learn while sober, recall when intoxicated; and (4) learn while intoxicated, recall when sober. The experimental lists were composed of high- and low-imagery words. Following a presentation and immediate recall of the items, the subjects were asked to recall the words four hours later. Intoxication, as indicated by blood alcohol levels of 0.060–0.95, was produced by having the subjects drink vodka and fruit juice prior to the learning and/or recall of the word lists. State-dependent effects were obtained; the subjects recalled a significantly greater number of words when the learning and recall took place under the same condition—either sober or intoxicated—than when learning took place under one condition and recall the other. As might be anticipated, greater amounts of recall were found for high-imagery words than for low-imagery words. (See Figure 13–11.)

A state dependent variable that has aroused considerable interest has been the role of the emotionality or mood of the subject. Basically, the experimental paradigm is similar to that we have just described; moreover, the amount of retention (or forgetting) is related to the similarity of the mood present during recall and that which was present when the learning task was undertaken.

Bower, Monteiro, and Gilligan (1978) have demonstrated state-dependent effects by manipulating the mood or emotionality of their subjects by using hypnosis to induce the moods of happiness and sadness in subjects while they were learning and recalling word lists. Although unsuccessful in their first two experiments, the investigators were able to obtain findings that revealed the state-dependent effect in Experiment 3 using an experimental design where their subjects learned one list of words while happy, and a second list while they were sad. After reading and summarizing a chapter from a book, which represented the distractor task, the subjects reentered the hypnotic state, reacquired either the happy or sad emotional state, and then were asked to recall the items from both lists. Results revealed that maximum recall was obtained when the learning and recall of the material took place under the same emotional state.

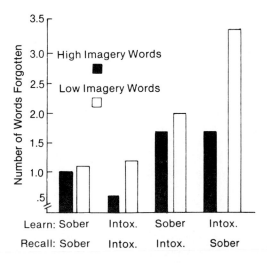

Figure 13-11
Number of words forgotten in relation to whether the subject's recall state was the same as or different from the learning state. Adapted from H. Weingartner, W. Adefris, J. E. Eich, and D. L. Murphy, "Encoding-imagery specificity in alcohol state-dependent learning," *Journal of Experimental Psychology: Human Learning and Memory,* 1976 *2,* 83–87. Copyright © 1976 by the American Psychological Association. Reprinted by permission.

Summary ►

Retention and forgetting have been basic areas of interest for functional investigators who have continued to use list-learning tasks consisting of words or CVCs as their experimental material. Although retention and forgetting represents different sides of the same coin—what is not retained is forgotten—each topic has retained a separate experimental identity.

Early experimenters of retention were interested in describing how performance declined as a function of the length of the retention interval. Ebbinghaus's retention curve, obtained in his classic study, was considered by some to reflect the course of retention for all material. Experimenters are now aware that the slope of the retention curve is related to the specific experimental conditions employed.

A major problem in examining very long retention intervals is obtaining subjects. Seldom is it possible to have subjects learn material at one time and then have those same subjects available for a retention test many years later. One solution to this problem has been to use a cross-sectional approach. This procedure uses only a single retention test given at approximately the same time to all subjects. Variations in the time that the material was originally learned provides the experimenter with different retention intervals. Bahrick and his associates have been quite successful in using this procedure to examine the capacity of individuals to remember different types of material (e.g., names and faces, locations of streets and buildings, foreign languages).

One interesting retention phenomenon is hypermnesia—defined as an *increase* in retention over time. Early work by Erdelyi and his associates found that individuals were able to recall greater amounts of material after a retention interval than they could immediately after learning. A host of hypermnesia studies have been conducted, with the general conclusion being that it is a reliable memory phenomenon and more readily obtained with pictorial stimuli than with verbal materials. Payne's (1987) review of this work has suggested that increased recall appears to depend critically on the subject repeatedly attempting to retrieve the previously studied information.

Why do we forget? This question has puzzled individuals for a very long time and psychologists have attempted to answer it. An early position posited that forgetting took place because of disuse and a decaying of the neural trace. But later studies by Jenkins and Dallenbach (1924) and Van Ormer (1932) demonstrated that there was less forgetting when the retention interval was filled with sleep than when it was filled with activity. This finding suggested that forgetting arose from activity that interfered with the material to be recalled and provide the foundation for an interference theory of forgetting. If the interfering activity had been learned prior to the original learning and subsequent recall of the experimental material, it was identified as proactive inhibition (PI). If the interfering activity had been learned during the retention interval, it was identified as retroactive inhibition (RI).

A great many experiments have examined the types and characteristics of these interfering activities. One of these has been identified as response competition, and is assumed to occur when the subject attempts to recall one set of responses but finds interference from another set that has been previously learned.

A second kind of interference, called unlearning or extinction, is assumed to take place in RI studies when the subject responds with first-list responses during the learning of responses from the second list. Inasmuch as these first-list responses are incorrect and are not reinforced, they are unlearned or extinguished and not available for subsequent recall.

Response competition and unlearning have thus been posited to be the two factors that create interference and produce forgetting.

Although an interference position is the most developed theoretical explanation of forgetting, this theory does have a number of problems. One problem has been that forgetting appears to take place at a relatively uniform rate, regardless of the characteristics of the material learned. Thus, low-frequency words are forgotten at about the same rate as high-frequency words, although one would assume that the kind of material learned between the original learning and the test for retention should result in differences in the amount retained for the two types of material.

A second problem has been that many investigators have failed to demonstrate either PI or RI using prose as the experimental material. And when experimenters have been able to demonstrate such an effect, the experimental material is so artificial that they have questioned the generality of interference theory as an inclusive explanation of forgetting.

A third difficulty has been in accounting for why different sleep periods provide differential forgetting. Thus, the first four hours of sleep will result in less forgetting than the second four.

Two other variables have been demonstrated to influence forgetting. One is contextual stimulus change, with a variety of studies demonstrating that any change form the learning to the retention environment will result in forgetting. The other variable has been identified as state dependent effects. This refers to the phenomenon whereby material that has been learned under the influence of one physiological or emotional state is forgotten if the subject attempts to recall that material under a different state.

chapter fourteen

▶

The Nature and
Functioning of Memory

Our organization of the experimental studies examining human learning and retention in the two previous chapters has been described as functional; thus, a major objective of investigators beginning with Ebbinghaus (1885/1913) was to delineate the functional relationships that existed among various experimental variables and learning and retention.

But during the past several decades, it was possible to note several concerns that investigators had with the functional approach. One such concern was with the functionalists' almost exclusive use of serial and paired associates as the experimental tasks assumed to be most appropriate for the investigation of verbal learning and retention. A related concern was with the use of CVCs and words as the experimental material. In addition, there appeared to be a reluctance on the part of many of these investigators to consider seriously the contribution to performance of cognitive variables.

One response to these concerns was the employment by some experimenters of a wider range of experimental materials, including phrases, prose, connected discourse, faces, geometric patterns, and so on. In addition, list-learning tasks using free recall became a standard and frequently employed verbal learning paradigm.

An example of this kind of task can be found in a study by Bousfield (1953), who presented subjects with a randomized list of 60 words made up of four 15-item categories: animals, names, vegetables, and professions. Immediately following the presentation of the last item, subjects were given 10 minutes to write down all of the words they could recall. The findings indicated that subjects, when given a list of randomly arranged words, will in their recall reveal a greater-than-chance tendency to group the items in clusters containing members of the same general category. More important, however, was the fact that it introduced to contemporary experimenters a much different type of learning-retention task.

A somewhat similar paradigm was employed by Peterson and Peterson (1959). In this experiment, a single CCC was visually presented for half a second, followed by a three-digit number. Subjects were instructed to count backwards by threes or fours from this number until a cue for recall of the trigram was provided. This response of counting backwards seriously interfered with any rehearsal of the trigram that the subjects might undertake. Each subject was tested a number of times at recall intervals of 0, 3, 6, 9, 12, 15, and 18 seconds. Correct recall, defined as a subject responding with a latency of less than 2.83 seconds, was found to be a function of the length of the recall interval. (The authors indicated that they used the value of 2.83 seconds since the mean latency of all correct responses was 2.83.) Figure 14–1 illustrates Peterson and Peterson's (1959) findings.

These single presentations—single retention trial procedures used in free recall studies—invariably raised the question for investigators: Was learning or retention being measured? Since the methodological distinction between these constructs used by functional investigators could not be made, the use of the construct *memory* could readily accommodate both processes.[1]

A second factor in promoting an alternative memory position was the belief of experimenters that learning and retention should be analyzed in terms of how the subject processes the material. This position placed emphasis on cognitive variables (or processes) and could be contrasted with an earlier emphasis on the stimulus properties of the material to be learned. It will be recalled that some investigators did occasionally exhibit an interest in cognitive variables but "new look" psychologists considered this

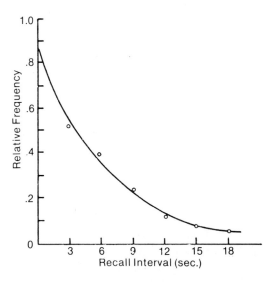

Figure 14-1
Correct recalls with latencies below 2.83 seconds as a function of recall interval. Adapted from L. R. Peterson and M. J. Peterson, "Short-term retention of individual items," *Journal of Experimental Psychology,* 1959, *58,* 193–198. Copyright © 1959 by the American Psychological Association. Reprinted by permission.

---

[1] It will be recalled that functional investigators distinguished learning from retention by inferring the operation of the learning process from changes taking place in the subject's performance over varying numbers of trials or presentations of the material. In contrast, the operation of the retention process was inferred from the persistence of such behavior over a period of time, with hours or days being placed between the original learning and the test for retention.

approach only as an appendage to the position that emphasized a stimulus-response analysis of the learning process. The study of cognitive processes, these psychologists argued, should occupy center stage.

The most important change, however, was the adoption of a different conceptual approach to the study of memory. Here, the operation of human memory could be likened to the functioning of a computer that receives information from tapes or disks and stores it for subsequent use. The information can be retrieved later either in the form of its input or in some other form as determined by the operator. The introduction of the computer concepts of encoding, storage, and retrieval as reflecting memorial constructs, was a radical departure from earlier investigators' conceptualization of memory.

The Information Processing Position ►

At the present time, the most frequently employed framework for the study of memory is the information processing position that involves the constructs of encoding, storage, and retrieval. Thus, when verbal material is perceived by the experimental subject, it is first encoded, then stored, and subsequently retrieved. The following sections will review some of the experiments that have been conducted that have examined these constructs.

A caution: This text's separate consideration of encoding, storage, and retrieval may provide the impression that the operation of an independent variable in an experiment can be readily identified as contributing to or reflecting the operation of one of these processes. This must be done with the utmost caution, because investigators are working with only two observables: (1) the stimulus condition or characteristics of the material that is to be placed in memory and (2) some performance or response measure from which the presence of a memory has been inferred. But the processes of encoding, storage, and retrieval have been assumed to operate serially and between the two observables. Thus, it is generally not possible to examine the operation of just one of these processes separate and apart from the other two.

We prefer to think of the processes of encoding, storage, and retrieval as metaphors; they are representations of what the theorists believe is taking place when material is placed in memory and later remembered. The identification of any given independent variable as contributing to just one of these processes most generally cannot be done experimentally but depends on the experimenter's theoretical position or judgment as to the locus of the effects.

The Nature of Encoding

Most generally, *encoding* has been defined as a process responsible for transforming an external stimulus into a cognitive or memorial representation of that stimulus. Such representation may be almost identical to the external stimulus, but it need not be; in fact, it is likely that only rarely does the representation mirror the external stimulus. Experimenter interest has been in the categorizing or identifying the different methods and procedures involved in this transformation process.

An examination of the literature has revealed that encoding is also used to refer to the employment of specific procedures employed by subjects (or experimenters) to provide memory enhancement. To illustrate, rehearsal, a frequently used procedure individuals use to help them remember an event, has been often identified as an encoding process. There can be, of course, a relationship between these two approaches to the study of encoding, in that the kind of transformation that takes place may contribute to the characteristics of enhancement.

The Transformation of External Stimuli into Cognitive Representations   We cannot, in this text, present a detailed description of all of the hypothesized encoding processes (or experimental procedures used to make such inferences) that have been used to examine the subject's transformation of external stimuli into cognitive representations. Bower (1972) has provided a succinct summary of some of these, identifying four as (1) stimulus selection, (2) rewriting, (3) elaboration, and (4) componential description.

Stimulus Selection   A specific stimulus component is encoded and selected out of a complex pattern of external stimuli. The Underwood, Ham, and Ekstrand (1962) experiment, which we described in an earlier chapter, demonstrates the operation of this process. In this study, it will be recalled that seven different trigrams were each placed on a different colored background, with such complex stimuli being used in a paired associate task. It was observed that subjects in learning this task ignored the trigram, selecting the background color as the stimulus to which to attach the response.

Rewriting   This type of encoding involves the rewriting or reformulation of an external stimulus into a type or form that has greater relevance for the subject. In some instances, it may be the translation of visual information into auditory, as illustrated in a study by Conrad (1964) who, in a memory span experiment, visually presented a series of letters, and then noted the errors made in remembering them were often similar in sound to the correct letter (e.g., *B* for *T, M* for *N*). The subject seemed to have auditorially encoded the visually presented letters.

Elaboration   This involves an external stimulus being transformed into a qualitatively different kind of item to be remembered. The use of natural language mediators, which we discussed in an earlier chapter, is one example of this type of encoding process. A second example would be the subject using a mental image for a word having the same referent (e.g., in learning a pair of words, *piano-cigar,* images or pictures of a large cigar are placed on the keys of a piano.

Component Description   In some instances, an external stimulus is represented in terms of a list of components, attributes, or features. The presentation of a work to be placed in memory may be encoded by the subject in terms of the word's frequency of occurrence, as well as its physical characteristics (e.g., whether upper- or lower-case letters were used). This type of encoding has been of interest to both Underwood (1969, 1983) and Wickens (1972) in their attempt to provide a taxonomy of encoded attributes. We will now examine the work of these investigators in some detail.

Underwood's Attributes of Memory   In his examination of the concept of encoding, Underwood (1969, 1983) posited that any memory consists of a collection of attributes derived from the external stimulus. He had suggested that some attributes appear to be an inevitable part of the stimulus input over which we have little control (automatic encoding), whereas others are volitional in that they become part of the mental representation resulting from the effort expended by the experimental subject. We shall not discuss all of the attributes posited by Underwood but shall describe several in some detail.

One attribute identified by Underwood is *acoustical*. The visual presentation of words will often involve an acoustical attribute that becomes a part of the mental representation of the material. For example, Underwood (1983) has reported that the high similarity among the acoustical properties of the visually presented words, *ham, hum, ram, rum*, and so on, results in an acoustical encoding that contributes to the recall of this material.

A second posited attribute is *orthographic*. The structural features of a visually presented word, like its acoustical properties, become a part of the word's mental representation. If the word is capitalized, the feature of capitalization may also become a part of the word's cognitive representation.

A third attribute Underwood has identified as *spatial*. Verbal material, in its visual presentation, may occupy different spatial positions so that the location of such information may be encoded, in some cases without the intent of the learner to do so. Rothkoph (1971) and Zechmeister and McKillip (1972) have shown that after reading several pages of prose, the subject acquired some knowledge of the page location of particular statements.

These examples provide the reader with what Underwood considers to be the attributes of memory. Other attributes that Underwood has posited have to do with frequency of occurrence, temporality, modality, and context, as well as the affective and semantic characteristics of the verbal material. In summary, Underwood has conceptualized the memorial representation of an external stimulus as being comprised of a number of attributes. Moreover, each memory is unique, consisting of a different collection of attributes. The task of the memory researcher, Underwood has suggested, is to determine the role that various attributes play in the functioning of memory (e.g., is there a relationship between the permanence of memories and the number of attributes which constitute memory?).

Wicken's Release from Proactive Inhibition (PI)   A different approach to the examination of the encoding process, but one that also emphasizes those attributes that are placed in memory, is found in a series of studies conducted by Wickens and his associates. An early study by Wickens, Born, and Allen (1963) illustrates the methodology, experimental findings, and general rationale of this approach. Peterson and Peterson's (1959) short-term memory procedures were used with experimental and control subjects being presented with a consonant syllable (CCC) for half a second. Following a brief retention interval, all subjects were asked to recall the syllable. Three presentations, or trials, each involving a different CCC, were provided. On the fourth trial, control subjects continued to be presented with still another CCC; experimental subjects, however, were presented with a three-digit number. A number of similar four-trial presentations were provided both experimental and control subjects, with each presentation consisting of the same type of experimental materials. Results indicated a gradual performance decrement for both groups over the first three trials. On the fourth trial, it was noted that performance continued to decline for the control group but there was a performance increment for the experimental group. Figure 14–2 presents the kind of experimental findings obtained with this type of study.

Wickens (1972) has accounted for the findings obtained in this type of study as follows: For the control group, there is an accumulation of PI on each of the four trials. For the experimental group, the first three trials reveal the accumulation of PI; on the fourth trial, however, a performance increment is obtained and is attributed to a release from the effects of PI. Wickens has assumed that the presentation of similar experimental material on the first three trials results in the subject encoding a specific characteristic of the material that can be identified by the investigator. Obtaining a performance increment when a noun is printed in the upper case on Trial 4, following the presentation of lower-case nouns on the first three trials, would suggest that the encoding attribute was the physical characteristics of the material. In describing the encoding process, Wickens has written that in the split second during which the word is processed by the subject, it is encoded on many dimensions, assuming that the encoding process is both simultaneous and automatic.

Wickens (1972) has summarized an extensive series of experiments conducted in his laboratory by identifying at least three major classes of encoding attributes: (1) semantic features, as indicated by the use of words followed by a shift to a three-digit number; (2) physical features, as revealed by the use of words printed in the upper case, followed by a shift to a word printed in the lower case; and (3) syntactic features, as demonstrated by the use of verbs followed by a shift to a noun.

As release from PI experiments have continued to increase, the number of encod-

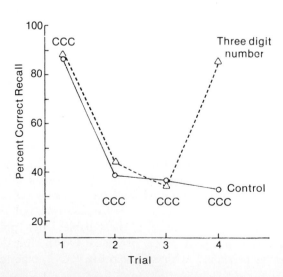

Figure 14–2
Illustration of release from PI. Both experimental and control groups are presented with CCCs on the first three trials; on the fourth trial, the experimental group is presented with a three-digit number while control subjects are presented with another CCC.

ing dimensions that appear to be activated during the presentation of a word keeps growing; one must question whether the procedure does reflect different types of encoding on the part of the subject. And some experimenters (e.g., Postman, 1975) have questioned whether the dimensions for which the release from PI has been observed are simultaneously encoded during the presentation of a word.

Encoding Processes and the Enhancement of Memory   In our earlier discussion of encoding processes, we pointed out that the concept of encoding has been also used to refer to the employment of specific procedures that individuals (or experimenters) may use to enhance memory. Those we shall examine in this section include (1) rehearsal, (2) generation, and (3) varying types of orienting instructions.

Rehearsal   Rehearsal, or more specifically, *maintenance rehearsal,* is the overt or covert repetition of material that the subject desires to remember.[2] The findings from Peterson and Peterson's (1959) short-term memory study suggests that preventing the rehearsal of the trigram by having the subject count backward interferes with the retention of the experimental material. Moreover, in their short-term memory study, Dillon and Reid (1969) have shown that such interference is a function of the type of interfering task used. A complex interfering task results in poorer retention than if the interfering task is a simple one.

Many investigators have found that the active rehearsing of the material to be learned enhanced retention when long-term memory operations are employed. Rundus and Atkinson (1970) asked their subjects to rehearse aloud so that the experimenters could analyze the nature of the rehearsed responses after the experiment had been completed. The investigators presented lists of 20 unrelated nouns, with each noun being exposed for five seconds. During this time, subjects were asked to study the list by rehearsing—repeating aloud items from the list. A tape recorder was used to obtain rehearsal protocols for the subjects. After each presentation of the list (there were usually three), the subjects were asked to recall as many of the nouns as possible.

The characteristics and role of the rehearsed responses were examined by looking at a rehearsal set. A rehearsal set was defined as all of the overt nouns that the subject made during the five-second interval during which each word was presented. Thus, the second rehearsal set comprised those responses that were rehearsed when the second noun on the list was shown; the third rehearsal set included those responses that were rehearsed when the third noun on the list was being presented, and so on. Rundus (1971) found that with the exception of the first rehearsal set, the rehearsed items in

[2] It has been frequently assumed that in the examination of memory, either overt or covert rehearsal can be used without differentially influencing the experimental findings. The evidence for this assumption, as Johnson's (1980) review has indicated, is controversial. He has found two studies that have revealed retention superiority for overt rehearsal (e.g., Izawa, 1976; and Whitten and Bjork, 1977), whereas three experimenters have reported superior postrehearsal remembering arising from covert rehearsal (e.g., Jeffery, 1976; Murray, 1967; and Reynolds, 1967). Two other studies revealed nonsignificant differences between the two methods (e.g., Horton, 1976; and Murdock and Metcalf, 1978).

each set remained relatively constant, ranging from 4.0 to 4.9. The number of *different* items that were rehearsed in a set increased until the fourth item was presented, at which point it stabilized except for the last few items. When the probability of recalling an item is plotted as a function of the mean number of rehearsals of that item, the relationship between these variables is quite high for the first 15 items on the list. It may also be noted that the last items of the list are recalled quite well in spite of relatively few rehearsals. In such instance, it has been posited that subjects keep these items in their consciousness as these items are the first to be recalled. (See Figure 14-3.) The evidence strongly suggests that overt rehearsal aids recall—a conclusion that has been supported by other investigators (e.g., Nelson 1977; and Glenburg, Smith, and Green, 1977).

Some investigators (e.g., Darley and Glass, 1975; and Maki and Schuler, 1980) have been interested in examining rehearsal with the "memory" aspect of the experiment masked. When this is done, the experimental findings continue to support the efficacy of rehearsal. To illustrate this type of experimental procedure, Maki and Schuler (1980) had subjects participate in a reaction time experiment. Here, a word was presented on a

Figure 14-3
The mean probability of recall, P(R), and the mean number of rehearsals of an item as a function of its serial input position. Adapted from D. Rundus, "Analysis of rehearsal processes in free recall," *Journal of Experimental Psychology,* 1971, *89,* 63–67. Copyright © 1971 by the American Psychological Association. Reprinted by permission.

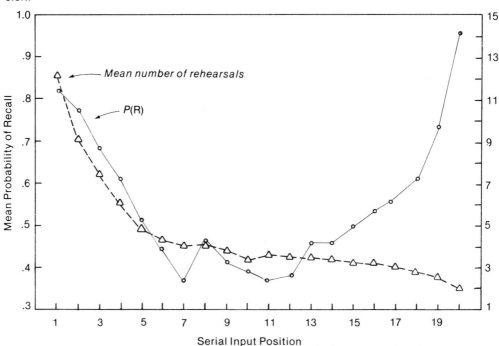

screen for two seconds, after which a set of eight words was shown on a screen and subjects were asked to determine if the set contained the target word. The time to decide whether or not the target word was among those shown was recorded. Subjects were required to search through one, two, or four sets of words in order to find the target word. Once the target word was found among the set, a new target word was shown, followed by presentations of more word sets, and so on. At the conclusion of the presentation of all of the target words and their appropriate word sets, subjects were asked to recall as many of these target words as possible. In keeping with the earlier findings obtained by Darley and Glass (1975), results indicated that the probability of recalling the target words was a function of the number of sets or words that were searched. The larger the number of sets searched for a particular word, the greater the probability was that the subject would recall that word. The authors reasoned that the probability of recall increased as a function of the length of time that the subjects kept in mind (rehearsed) the target word. Two additional experiments by the same authors have confirmed these findings.

The Nature of Maintenance Rehearsal   What is the basic nature of maintenance rehearsal? Naveh-Benjamin and Jonides (1984a, 1984b) have suggested that such rehearsal is composed of two stages. Stage 1 consists of the retrieval of an appropriate motor program for a rehearsal sequence and the initiation of the program; this stage demands some cognitive functioning and effort on the part of the subject. With the continued repetition of the material, Stage 2 evolves, which appears to take place automatically, demands little cognitive functioning, and consists only of the continuous execution of the program. Naveh-Benjamin and Jonides (1984a, 1984b) have hypothesized that long-term memory may be established only during Stage 1 of maintenance rehearsal, and that with the absence of cognitive functioning during Stage 2, it is unlikely that rehearsal during this stage has any effect on long-term memory.

The experimental procedure the authors have used to examine their model has been to use a slide projector to present either two, three, or four two-digit numbers for two seconds of silent study, followed by a pair of words. The viewing of these words was followed by presentation of a blank slide which remained on for varying lengths of time and which permitted subjects either 1, 5, or 10 overt rehearsals of the word pair. The subjects were then given 10 seconds to write down the two-digit numbers. Following a number of trials, subjects were given an unexpected self-paced recognition test for the words that had been presented. An examination of the mean percent correct recognition responses revealed findings that were in keeping with the investigator's hypothesis. When the primary task load was either two or three two-digit numbers, correct recognition responses increased as a function of the number of rehearsals, thus indicating that maintenance rehearsal did play a role in aiding memory for the words. However, when the primary task for the subject was to recall the four two-digit numbers, increasing the number of rehearsals did not result in increased correct responding. As the capacity for cognitive functioning taking place during word rehearsal diminished as a result of the increased load of remembering the four two-digit numbers, only the first few rehearsals appear to be of consequence in the establishment of a permanent memory for the words.

Generation   A second encoding process that has been related to memory enhancement (and inferred from performance) is generation. Studies by Anderson, Goldberg,
and Hidde (1971), and Slamecka and Graf (1978) have indicated that memory for
information generated by the subject was superior to memory for the same information
that was only visually presented to the subject. If one group of subjects was asked to
generate a word that rhymed with *cart* (e.g., *dart*), whereas another group was asked
only to verify that the words *cart* and *dart* rhymed, the experimental evidence has
indicated that *cart* was better remembered by the group which generated the word.

Slamecka and Graf's (1978) study, which consisted of five different experiments, has
indicated the specific characteristics of the procedure and the nature of the experimental
findings. In their Experiment 1, 100 words were each placed on a separate index card. In
the *generate* condition, on each card was placed a stimulus word and the initial letter of
the response (e.g., *rapid-f_ _ _*). For the visual presentation or *read* condition, both
words were presented (e.g., *rapid-fast*). Five different categories or rules for generating
responses to each of the stimulus words was examined: association (lamp-light); category (ruby-diamond); opposite (long-short); synonym (sea-ocean); and rhyme (save-
cave). The procedure consisted of presenting five sets of 20 cards per set,
with each set representing one of the above categories. When each card was presented,
the stimulus and the read or generate response had to be uttered aloud just once.
Following presentation of the last card, a recognition test was provided in which
subjects were asked to select the presented or generated word that had been placed
among two distracters. Differences in recognition probability are provided in Figure
14–4 and reveal significant recognition performance for the generated condition. Four
additional experiments provided confirmation for the generality of the findings.

Substantial interest in the generation phenomenon has been noted over the last
decade with the effect being demonstrated by investigators employing a variety of
procedures and materials. In one interesting study, Glisky and Rabinowitz (1985) were
able to demonstrate the generation effect with subjects who were required to generate
words from single words that contained one or more letters missing (e.g., fen _e [fence]
or al_oho_ [alcohol]).

McElroy and Slamecka (1982) noted that the generation effect was not obtained

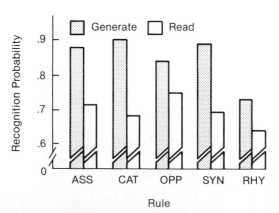

Figure 14–4
Mean recognition probabilities for
each condition for each rule of
Experiment 1. (ASS = associate;
CAT = category; OPP = opposite; SYN = synonym; RHY =
rhyme.) Adapted from N. J.
Slamecka and P. Graf, "The generation effect: Delineation of a
phenomenon," *Journal of Experimental Psychology; Human Learning and Memory*, 1978, 4,
592–604. Copyright © 1978 by
the American Psychological Association. Reprinted by permission.

when meaningless or low-frequency words were used as the to-be-remembered items. A more recent examination of the effect by Nairne, Pusen, and Widner (1985) has confirmed these findings. These experiments, in which either nonwords or low-frequency words were used, had experimenters using different procedures to have subjects generate the experimental material. For example, in Experiment 1, a rhyming procedure was employed with the nonwords. One group of subjects was asked only to read the experimental material (e.g., *frab-prab*), whereas a second group was asked to generate the response word by rhyming it with the stimulus word (e.g., *frab-p_ _ _*). Results from this study as well as two other experiments failed to obtain the generation effect. Nairne and colleagues (1985) have hypothesized that the generation effect is more "effortful" and activates an item's location in the subject's lexical network to a greater extent than does reading. This activation then spreads to related entries, enhancing the activated item's retrieval network, with the end result being that a greater number of retrieval routes are established from the generated items. In contrast, if an item is not represented in the individual's lexicon, no generation effect can be demonstrated. The extent to which an item is represented in the individual's lexical network will play an important role in determining whether or not the generation effect can be found.

Support for the role of effort in accounting for the generation effect can be found in the earlier studies of Kolers (1973), who found that if the words in a sentence are presented upside down or backwards, the sentences are better remembered than if the words are presented normally. Lockhart, Craik, and Jacoby (1976) have also indicated that if material is uncommon, unfamiliar, or difficult to process, conditions all of which would lead to more effort during the time of encoding, memory is enhanced.

Another operation that is related to the generation effect is semantic processing. Using homographs (two or more words that are spelled alike but differ in meaning) as words to be generated, McElroy (1987) found that it was possible to obtain the generation effect "only when retrieval cues biased the same meaning as was encoded at study" (p. 152). Her findings from two experiments suggested that the response of generating a word involves the processing of the word's semantic memory attributes. She has found, however, that if such processing is not subsequently related to the retrieval cue, the generation effect will not be obtained. For example, for rhyme generation such as *luck-d_ _ _*, a simple substitution of *d* for *l* in luck will produce the required response. Once the work *duck* is generated, it is more likely to be semantically processed (e.g., defined as a swimming bird) than if it is only read. If the retrieval cue that is provided at recall is related to another meaning of the word (e.g., "to quickly lower the head"), McElroy's findings indicate that the generation effect will not be found.

It is possible that the concepts of effort and semantic processing are interrelated so that obtaining the generation effect is dependent on either or both of these variables being present in the experimental situation. An important consideration, however, is providing an appropriate definition of both of these constructs.

The Role of Orienting Instructions   Several investigators have demonstrated that the type of orienting instructions that are provided to the experimental subject can also play a role in the enhancement of memory. An example can be found in the work of

Jenkins and his associates (e.g., Hyde and Jenkins, 1969, 1973; Walsh and Jenkins, 1973; and Till and Jenkins, 1973). In the Hyde and Jenkins (1973) study, five groups of subjects were asked to recall a list of 24 words which were orally presented at three-second intervals. Prior to the presentation of the words, each group received a different set of task instructions, with subjects being asked to process or encode the words in one of the following ways:

1. Rate each word as to how pleasant or unpleasant it was.
2. Rate each word as to how frequently it was used.
3. Determine if either an *E* or a *G* or both of these letters appeared in the word.
4. Identify the part of speech of each word.
5. Determine whether the word fit (or did not fit) into the frame ("It is _____" or "It is the _____").

Each of the five groups was subdivided into (a) an intentional learning group in which subjects were informed that they would be asked to recall the words at the end of the session and (b) an incidental learning group—subjects did not receive these instructions. A sixth group, serving as a control, was instructed just to listen and attempt to recall the words. The results of this study are shown in Table 14–1. The incidental versus intentional learning conditions resulted in little difference in performance regardless of the type of orienting instructions. Of primary concern was the performance difference found between the first two sets of instructions (rating a word for pleasantness or unpleasantness and for frequency of use) and the last three. The first two types of instructions produced a semantic type of processing or encoding, which in turn resulted in better performance than the nonsemantic type of encoding produced by the last three types of instructions.[3]

Performance as Related to Kind of Encoding and Type of Task   There is implied in the experimental findings of Jenkins and his associates that one type of encoding (e.g., semantic), in contrast to another type (e.g., nonsemantic), will invariably result in superior retention of the to-be-learned material regardless of the nature of the material, kind of task, and so on. A similar position was taken by Craik and Lockhart (1972), who proposed that rehearsal, which represented one level of processing, would always result in poorer retention than if some higher processing level was employed. But as the studies of McDaniel and Kearney (1984) and Hall (1985) attest, such is not always the case. These investigators have proposed that there is an interaction between the type of processing and the kind of material to be placed in memory.

In Hall's (1985) free recall study, three 20-item lists having either high-frequency,

---

[3] Interest has also been directed to an examination of encoding differences within the semantic domain. Some investigators have proposed that varying types of semantic processing can be identified and that these can be related to differences in retention. It has been proposed that if a greater number of features of the material to-be-remembered are encoded, thus producing an elaboration effect, better recall of the material takes place. See Hasher, Griffin, and Johnson (1977), Johnson-Laird and Bethell-Fox (1978), and Hashtroudi (1983) for representative studies.

Condition	Learning	
	Intentional	Incidental
Rating words for pleasantness	12.7	11.2
Rating words for frequency of usage	10.4	10.2
Identifying words as a part of speech	8.1	8.1
Checking of letters E and G	8.2	6.6
Does word fit into sentence frame?	6.2	6.6
Control	10.9	

Adapted from data provided by Hyde and Jenkins (1973).

Table 14-1
Mean number of words recalled as a function of the type of processing

low-frequency, or rare words served as material to be recalled. One type emphasized rehearsal of the words, whereas with the second type, subjects were encouraged to try to associate one word with another, using phrases, sentences, and stories in order to do so. The presentation of the material was designed to facilitate rehearsal or the semantic type of processing provided by the instructions. Rehearsal groups were always presented with a single word appearing three times in column form on each slide. Semantic processing groups had a modified serial presentation with most generally three different words appearing on a slide—a type of display that should encourage an association among items. Following presentation of the last slide and a one-minute digit-matching task designed to minimize rehearsal, all subjects were provided three minutes to recall as many words as possible. Table 14-2 presents the number of words recalled as a function of word frequency and type of instructions. Of primary importance was the significant interaction that was found between the type of encoding and word frequency. It may be observed that using a repetitive or rehearsal-like encoding process is more beneficial for recalling rare words than is semantic processing; however, if high-frequency words are used, semantic processing provided superior recall scores.

Type of Processing	Word Frequency		
	Rare	Low	High
Rehearsal	4.13	6.31	8.88
Semantic	2.50	5.44	10.00

Adapted from J. F. Hall, "Free recall as a function of type of encoding and word frequency," *Bulletin of the Psychonomic Society*, 1985, *23*, 368–370. Copyright © 1985 by the Psychonomic Society. Reprinted by permission.

Table 14-2
Number of words recalled as a function of word frequency and type of processing

Summary   We can view the studies cited in this section as providing a beginning in the study of encoding but it is obvious that much additional work is needed if this construct is to provide basic help in our understanding of memory. The identification of encoding attributes has been closely tied to the operations that experimenters have used. The problem is that literally hundreds of such operations can be undertaken with presumably a like number of encoding attributes being inferred from the operations. As Tulving (1983) has acknowledged, "The ingenuity of experimenters has known few bounds in creating variations in learners' mental activities that define encoding operations" (p. 154).

It is also apparent that any given type of encoding cannot always be directly related to amount of retention; rather, such retention is a function of both type of encoding and kind of experimental material employed.

Storage

Storage refers to the holding or storing of information that has been received or encoded by the individual. The tapes in a musical library are stored representations of concerts that took place years ago, but are nonetheless available when one wishes to listen to them. Storage has been generally thought of as a passive process; it has been often conceptualized as consisting of traces or engrams, neurological correlates of the stimulus event as encoded by the subject and that can be subsequently retrieved.

Questions concerning the nature of the storage process and the characteristics of the neural trace have been asked for probably as long as people have been interested in the area of memory. Thus, many of the issues raised by current information processing theorists have had a long experimental history, with an important one being whether the memory trace is permanent. That is, once laid down, does the trace remain forever as a part of the organism's neural structure?

This question may appear foolish, since it is obvious that there are many occasions on which one is unable to remember material that had once been learned. But failure to remember an event at a particular time does not mean that the memory of that event has been lost, since the event may come to mind perhaps an hour or a day later. Clearly, the earlier failure to remember cannot be used as evidence that the event had been irretrievably lost or that the memory trace was transient. Such failure to remember might be related to difficulty with the retrieval process rather than storage. This illustration reveals the basic problem that confronts investigators in attempting to determine whether memory is permanent. Failure to remember may not reflect the fact that the appropriate memory trace has been erased or has decayed; it may simply reflect an inability of the individual to retrieve the information at a particular time. Until appropriate physiological evidence is obtained, it is impossible to provide an experimental answer to the question. No one can demonstrate that memories are not permanent since all failures to remember can be attributed to retrieval failure. Nonetheless, there is some interesting clinical evidence that bears on the problem.

The Case of S   Chapter Thirteen mentioned the clinical observations of Luria (1968), who for more than 30 years systematically observed S, a man whose ability to remember vast amounts of material was truly remarkable. Luria was convinced that the capacity of S's memory was virtually unlimited—he did not have to memorize the data presented but merely had to register an impression, which he could "read" at any subsequent point of time. Luria reports instances in which S was able to reproduce material 10 or even 16 years after its original presentation and without apparent or obvious rehearsal of this material during the interim.

Luria has indicated that there were instances of S forgetting material. But such forgetting consisted of omissions of elements within the material to be remembered, and there was a simple explanation for these omissions. In "reading" off the impressions during the recall period, S might omit a particular element because it was not discernible. Luria believed that these omissions were not defects of memory but, rather, defects of perception. In these instances, failure to recall could not be explained in terms of traditional explanations—the decay of memory traces, or interference, provided by other material that had been learned—but by certain factors that influenced S's perception, such as clarity of the perception, contrast, the amount of lighting available, and so on. As Luria (1968) has written, "His errors could not be explained, then, in terms of the psychology of memory but had to do with the psychological factors that govern perception" (p. 35).

Penfield's Conceptualization of Memory   Early physiological evidence on the permanence of memory has come from the work of Penfield (1955), a Canadian neurosurgeon. As a result of his surgical observations with patients who had epilepsy, Penfield suggested that information that has been placed in memory (storage) is localized there permanently. In the course of operations, patients were given only a local anesthetic, and when the brain was exposed, Penfield explored the cortex by applying a weak electrical current from place to place in an effort to reproduce the beginning of the patient's attack and thus verify the appropriate place to make a surgical excision. Penfield noted that when such gentle electrical stimulation was applied to the temporal lobes, it resulted in some of his patients remembering experiences from the past—a phenomenon that he defined as *psychical responses*. In some cases there was a detailed reenactment of a single experience which presumably had been long available to the normal recall of the patient. Such experiences included many different elements of thought, including auditory, visual, and somatic sensations as well as emotional responding. Penfield likened these psychical responses to a stream of consciousness and attempted to indicate their nature by means of the following analogy:

> Among the millions and millions of nerve cells that clothe certain parts of the temporal lobe on each side, there runs a thread. It is the thread of time, the thread that had run through each succeeding wakeful hour of the individual's past life. Think of this thread if you like, as a pathway through an unending sequence of nerve cells, nerve fibers, and synapses. It is a pathway which can be followed again because of the continuing facilitation that has been created in the cell contacts.
>
> When, by chance, the neurosurgeon's electrode activates some portion of that thread, there is a response as though that thread were a wire recorder, or a strip of cinematographic film, on which are registered all those things of which the individual was once aware, the things he selected for his attention in that interval of time. Absent from it are the sensory impulses he ignored, the talk he did not heed.
>
> Time's strip of film runs forward, never backward, even when resurrected from the past. It

seems to proceed again at time's own unchanged pace. It would seem, once one section of the strip has come alive, that a functional all-or-nothing principle steps in so as to protect the other portions of the film from activation by the electric current. As long as the electrode is held in place, the experience of a former day goes forward. There is no holding it still, no turning back. When the electrode is withdrawn it stops as suddenly as it began.[4]

It is tempting to assume that Penfield's neurological findings represent the place and mechanism of storage, thus supporting the position that the memory trace is permanent. But challenges to his physiological conceptualization of memory have come from several sources. Barbizet (1970) has reported that only a small percentage of patients (less than 8%) provide such recollections when their temporal lobes are stimulated. In addition, Mahl, Rothenberg, Delgado, and Hamlin (1964) found that the psychical responses of one of their patients, electrically stimulated in the temporal lobe, were related to specific events that had taken place just prior to the time she received the stimulation, and were not literal recollections of earlier events. Finally, Neisser (1967) has suggested that a careful examination of recollections obtained with temporal lobe stimulation frequently reveals that they are comparable to dreams, which are generally accepted to be synthetic constructions and not literal recall of earlier events.

Hypnosis and the Phenomenon of Age Regression   A last bit of evidence having to do with the permanence of memory comes from the phenomenon of hypnotic age regression. Many of us are familiar with stage and parlor demonstrations of hypnosis. A hypnotist suggests to a hypnotized subject that he or she is much younger, perhaps a child of six or seven years of age. Upon receiving the suggestion, the subject provides information or behaves in a way that seems characteristic of children that age. This hypnotic phenomenon had been described as *age regression.* The fact that an individual who is unable to respond appropriately when in a normal state is apparently able to do so when hypnotized suggests that the forgotten event did not decay with time but instead is permanent.

In an early clinical study of age regression, Erickson (1937) reported the experiences of a police informer who had survived a homicidal assault that occurred two years previously. The subject had complete amnesia for virtually all of the details of the experience; through the use of hypnosis, the individual was able to recount the incident with remarkable vividness and richness of detail. Moreover, the accuracy of the subject's recollections of the event was verified by the police for whom the subject had served as an informer and by attendants at the hospital where the individual had been taken after the assault.

Hypnosis is currently being used by police officers as a procedure designed to help individuals remember information that presumably they cannot recall in their waking state. One example is found in the case of a school bus driver and 26 children who disappeared from the small town of Chowchilla, California. Subsequent information indicated that the driver of the bus and the children had been kidnapped by three

---

[4] Reprinted by permission of the publisher from "The Permanent Record of the Stream of Consciousness" by W. Penfield, Proceedings of the Fourteenth International Congress of Psychology, Montreal, June 1954, pp. 67–68. Copyright© 1955 by Elsevier North Holland, Inc.

masked men. They had been driven to a gravel quarry located more than 100 miles away and forced to stay in an abandoned trailer that had been buried six feet under the ground. Eventually, the driver and children were rescued unharmed but questioning of the victims by the police gave them little information about the kidnappers. A professional hypnotist was asked to help in the case. Under hypnosis, the bus driver was able to recall all but one digit of the license plate on the white van that the kidnappers had used in committing the abduction. This information was primarily responsible for locating the suspects and their eventual conviction.

A more recent example of the use of hypnosis in obtaining critical information about a crime has been reported by Kroger and Douce (1979), which involved two girls aged 7 and 15 being abducted by a man describing himself as a member of the Symbionese Liberation Army. The girls, picked up in San Francisco, were driven to Mexico where the 15-year-old was raped in a motel near the border. The girls were released shortly thereafter, with the warning that if they informed the police, it would mean death to their parents. In interviews with the police in which the girls were not hypnotized, it was found that they remembered little about the abduction, even having difficulty in remembering the chronology of events, although the older girl did succeed in identifying the motel room where the suspect had registered under an assumed name. The investigation stalled until the older girl was hypnotized. Under hypnosis, she was able to recall many details about the car. Of greatest value was the girl's recall of a meeting of the abductor with the operator of a San Diego gasoline station on a hilltop where the suspect had had his car repaired. The girl remembered a conversation between the gas station operator and the suspect that had to do with the nature of the repairs, as well as the fact that the transaction was paid for by the use of a red, white, and blue credit card. FBI agents located the gasoline station and the attendant, and through the credit card transaction, were able to identify and arrest the suspect. Of particular importance was the fact that an examination of the car confirmed every single detail supplied by the older girl when she was under hypnosis.

These anecdotes are only two of many that illustrate the usefulness of hypnosis to the police. Schafer and Rubio (1978) have discussed 14 cases of interrogation of witnesses and victims of crimes under hypnosis in and around Orange County, California, during the years 1972–1973. They have reported that in 10 cases, information obtained when the individual was hypnotized substantially helped investigators to solve the crime; moreover, such information was not obtainable when the victims and witnesses were in their normal waking state. Yarmey (1979) has indicated that hypnotists associated with the Israeli National Police Force have reportedly solved 25 cases and assisted in 60 others between the years 1972–1976.

Although the anecdotal reports we have just described may be persuasive in indicating the value of hypnosis in certain prescribed situations, unfortunately such reports are of little value in answering the question as to whether or not memories are permanent. It is important to keep in mind that there may be other explanations for the superior recollection of events under hypnosis (e.g., the more relaxed atmosphere in which the recall of the event took place). In any event, a control group is necessary in order to rule out these other explanations. Control groups are routinely used in laboratory explanations of hypnosis, but as Smith's (1983) survey of the experimental evidence examining the enhancement of memory by hypnosis has revealed, there is no clear documentation that hypnosis improves memory.

Retrieval

After information is encoded and placed in storage, it becomes necessary for the subject to retrieve it. Some theorists have considered retrieval to be synonymous with overt responding but most frequently, like encoding and storage, *retrieval* has been considered to be a conceptual process operating within the general information processing model of memory.[5]

Tulving (1983) assumed that the retrieval process consists of two basic elements. One is that the system must be in what he has referred to as a "retrieval mode." He has suggested that the role that the retrieval mode plays in memory is demonstrated by casual observation of our everyday experiences. There are few things that take place that make us think of previous happenings—individuals spend very little time reminiscing. In addition, many specific stimulus events that could serve as potential reminders or cues do not do so. Our everyday functioning seems so structured that it would be possible to have constantly recurring memories, and yet we do not. The retrieval mode, or set to remember, appears to be of basic importance, but as Tulving has indicated, it has escaped the notice of most experimenters and its functioning is largely unknown.

The second element is the contribution that cues play in the retrieval process. Experimenters, both traditional as well as those identified with the information processing position, have been interested in examining the contribution and role of retrieval cues on memory. Many of the functional investigator's findings have been considered in Chapter Thirteen, where we discussed retention (which obviously reflects the operation of a retrieval process) as a function of such variables as stimulus change, context, and state dependent effects. In this chapter we shall consider primarily the contributions from information processing experimenters, although not exclusively so. The literature has been so voluminous in this area that our presentation shall reflect only a sampling of the studies conducted on this topic.

The Role of Retrieval Cues   Many experimenters have demonstrated that retrieval, as inferred from recall, can be related to the presence and/or absence of retrieval cues.

---

[5] In some instances it is possible to relate the contribution of an experimental variable to the functioning of the retrieval process. Consider two groups of subjects, an experimental and a control, who have been given a list of words to remember under some type of standard presentation. It would be assumed in this situation that the encoding and storage process would be the same for both groups. Just prior to the recall test, the experimental group receives specific information (e.g., retrieval cues) about the characteristics of the words that had been presented. This information indicates that the words to be recalled can be grouped into four categories: precious gems, kinds of metal, pieces of furniture, and types of vegetables. The control group does not receive this information. If the recall score obtained by the experimental group is superior to the control, investigators assume that the information provided after the words had been presented and prior to recall, had a facilitative effect only on the retrieval process and that encoding and storage processes were not involved.

In a paired associate study by Bahrick (1969), 20 pairs of unrelated common nouns served as the material to be learned. After the subjects had reached a criterion of six correct anticipations, a retention interval of either zero or two hours, two days, or two weeks was provided, followed by a retention test in which the subjects were given a list of stimulus terms and asked to write the responses they could recall opposite the appropriate stimuli. Subjects were then told that they would be given a second trial in which retrieval cues would be presented to help them recall each response word that they had missed on the previous trial. The experimental variable that interested Bahrick was the associative relationship existing between the retrieval cues presented and the response words that had been forgotten. Five progressively higher associative relationship levels were examined. At the lowest level, the retrieval cue elicited the response word approximately 4% of the time, as with the retrieval cue *print* and response word *book*. At the highest level, the retrieval cue elicited the response word approximately 74% of the time (e.g., the retrieval cue *hot* and the response word *cold*).

Results indicated that regardless of the length of the retention interval (zero or two hours, two days, or two weeks), the recall of forgotten responses was aided by the presentation of retrieval cues. Moreover, as the associative level of the retrieval cue–response word increased, recall of the forgotten words also increased. Table 14–3 presents the results of the five levels of associative relationships as related to the duration of the retention interval.[6]

Table 14–3
Percent correct responding as a function of the associative level between the retrieval cue and the to-be-remembered word

Associative Level of Retrieval Cue	*Retention Interval*				
	0	*2 hours*	*2 days*	*2 weeks*	*Mean*
1	18	16	13	14	15
2	48	43	42	27	40
3	49	55	58	50	53
4	79	72	62	63	69
5	86	80	70	80	79
Mean	56	53	49	47	

Adapted from H. P. Bahrick, "Measurement of memory prompted by recall," *Journal of Experimental Psychology,* 1969, *79,* 213–219. Copyright © 1969 by the American Psychological Association. Reprinted by permission.

---

[6] Our discussion has centered around the facilitative effect that cues may have on retrieval; we should point out that in some instances, cues may have a detrimental effect as well. Studies by Slameka (1968), Rundus (1973), and others have demonstrated that if, in a free recall study, the subject is provided with some words actually taken from the original list during the recall period, and is asked to recall the remainder, the probability of recalling these remaining words is poorer than a control group that had not been given those words. In effect, the presentation of some of the list words as cues has reduced, rather than increased, the probability of recalling the remaining words on the list.

The Principle of Encoding Specificity   Functional investigators had generally assumed that the effectiveness of a cue (or stimulus) in being able to elicit a response was a function of the strength of the association between the cue and its to-be-elicited response. The findings of Bahrick (1969), which we just reported, demonstrating that the recall of forgotten words was a function of the strength of the association between the cue word and the response, was in keeping with this assumption.

But Tulving adopted a different position in his analysis of the role of retrieval cues on to-be-remembered material. He hypothesized that a cue that was present when the information was encoded must also be present during retrieval if it was to be effective in eliciting a response. This relationship between encoding cues and the presence of those cues at retrieval, has been identified as the principle of *encoding specificity*. Early studies by Tulving and Pearlstone (1966) and Tulving and Osler (1968) illustrate its operation.

In the Tulving and Pearlstone (1966) study, lists of either 12, 24, or 48 words were constructed. Each list also included additional words that indicated the presence of either one, two, or four classes of categories of list words. In the oral presentation of these words, the category word would be presented, followed by the words to be recalled (*CRIMES: theft, treason; WEAPONS: bomb, cannon,* etc.). After such a presentation, the subjects were asked to recall as many of the words as possible, either with the category words being present, which could serve as retrieval cues, or without them.

As may be noted from Figure 14–5, the findings indicate that cued recall was higher than uncued recall in all comparisons, with such cueing assuming greater influence as the length of the list increased. But it should be noted that some recall was obtained for the noncued group.

In a subsequent study, Tulving and Osler (1968) examined the characteristics of the cues in relation to the words to be recalled. Rather than using category names, as in the Tulving and Pearlstone (1966) study, Tulving and Osler (1968) utilized the weak associates of the experimental words. For example, the cue for the to-be-remembered word *city* would be *dirty* or *village*. Instructions, similar to those provided by Tulving and Pearlstone (1966), informed the subjects that the associated cues might aid them in their subsequent recall. Their results supported the earlier findings. The use of word associates as cues increased recall if the cue was present during both the original presentation of the material and the subsequent recall test; however, the cue had no effect when presented only during recall. Moreover, no effect was obtained if different cues were present during presentation and recall. For example, recall for the word *city* was not influenced if *dirty* was used when *city* was originally presented, and *village* was used during the test for recall. In summary, the authors stated the principle of encoding specificity to be as follows: "Specific retrieval cues facilitate recall if and only if the information about them and their relation to the to-be-remembered word is stored at the same time as the information about the membership of the to-be-remembered word in a given list" (Tulving and Osler, 1968, p. 593). Over the years, additional support for the operation of encoding specificity has accumulated as Tulving's (1983) summary of the results of a dozen list learning experiments attests.

In spite of the impressive list of supporting experiments, some investigators have obtained findings that have not been in keeping with the encoding specificity principle. It will be recalled that the retrieval cues used by Bahrick (1969) were not present during

Figure 14–5
Mean number of words recalled as a function of list length and number of items per category. Adapted from E. Tulving and Z. Pearlstone, "Availability versus accessibility of information in memory for words," *Journal of Verbal Learning and Verbal Behavior,* 1966, *5,* 381–391. Reprinted by permission of the Academic Press.

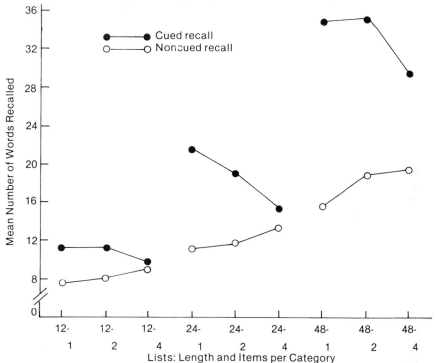

the original presentation of the target words, and yet his results indicated that recall was aided by their presence. Subsequent studies by Reder, Anderson, and Bjork (1974) and Kochevar and Fox (1980) have also provided findings that do not support Tulving's encoding specificity hypothesis. Kochevar and Fox's (1980) experiment is interesting since these investigators used the same paired associates (P-A) previously employed by Bahrick (1969). In this study, immediately following a single presentation of the material, four different retention tests were given in sequence: (1) the standard P-A test in which the stimulus word served as a cue for the to-be-remembered response; (2) free recall of the response words; (3) a test in which extra list cues were provided in order to cue the responses; and (4) a matching test whereby subjects were presented with randomized lists of the stimulus and response words and instructed to pair each response with its appropriate stimulus word.

Results indicated that with each successive retention test, subjects continued to recall new responses—responses which had not been recalled on prior tests. The authors suggested that with continued probing, it may be possible to effect nearly complete recall of input information, regardless of how poorly subjects performed on the initial retention test. Of particular interest was the general finding that the continued probe technique can be effective when retrieval cues are used that differ from those present during acquisition—a result that is not in keeping with the encoding specificity principle.

In view of the conflicting findings that have been obtained, some reconciliation of the experimental findings may be provided by suggesting that retrieval is a function of two conditions. The first condition is that cue retrieval is related to the effectiveness of the cue that is present. This acknowledges the contribution of Bahrick (1969) and others who have found that retention was related to the strength of the association that existed between the cue and the target item. The second condition is a modification of Tulving's principle of encoding specificity in that cues that are present at both encoding and retrieval will be more effective than cues that are present only at retrieval.

Recall versus Recognition   One topic that has frequently arisen in the examination of the retrieval process has been to determine the nature of the relationship between the two basic measures of retrieval: recognition and recall.

Many experimenters have assumed that recall and recognition each tap the same storage construct, but with different thresholds. Recognition has been found in most studies to have the lower threshold of the two measures employed. (Comparisons between response measures are tenuous since both recall and recognition scores are dependent upon the experimental methodology employed.)

Many information processing investigators, however, have not accepted the differential threshold position. Rather, they have assumed that the retrieval process involved in recall is qualitatively different from that operating in recognition. When material is to be recalled, retrieval consists of a generation and a discrimination-decision process; in contrast, if the information needs to be recognized, only the discrimination-decision process is involved. In order to illustrate this position, assume that one is interested in remembering the numerical value of pi. In attempting to recall this value, one may generate a variety of numerical values (i.e., 3.20, 3.12, 3.19, etc.). As each value is generated, a discrimination-decision process takes place whereby a given value may be (1) rejected, and in such a case, a new value is generated; or (2) accepted, with the subject overtly responding with that value. In contrast, if retention is measured by recognition, it is necessary only to recognize the correct value of pi; the generation process is not necessary, and only a discrimination decision needs to be made.

Investigators supporting the generation discrimination-decision process have argued that if the traditional position is correct and if recall and recognition differ only in the sensitivity with which they measure memory, experiments using both of these measures should reveal retention scores that are only quantitatively different one from the other. But this has not been the case. High-frequency words have been shown to be more easily recalled than low-frequency words (e.g., Hall, 1954; and Bousfield and Cohen, 1955), but experimenters have frequently found that low-frequency words are more easily recognized (e.g., Gorman, 1961; Shepard, 1967; and Wallace, Sawyer, and Robertson, 1978).[7] In addition, Kintsch (1968) has found that lists made up of highly

---

[7] The evidence is not completely unequivocal on this issue since Hall (1979) has demonstrated that low-frequency words are less easily recognized than high-frequency words when

associated or conceptually similar words are recalled better than lists containing unrelated words, but that no such difference between lists is found when retention is measured with a recognition test.

Rabinowitz, Mandler, and Patterson (1977) and Rabinowitz, Mandler, and Barsalou (1979) have suggested, however, that the generation and discrimination-decision hypothesis for explaining recall, at least in its pure form, is untenable. They noted that introspectively, free recall does not generally consist of the generation of candidate items coupled with a discrimination-decision phase. Our illustration of a subject attempting to remember the value of pi is not a typical case; an individual does not normally retrieve the value of pi (or any other kind of information) by generating varying alternative values. The experimental findings of Rabinowitz and his associates have suggested that the generation process can be conceptualized only as an auxiliary strategy. It may be used at times, but its usefulness is limited, since it is most effective when employed shortly after target items have been presented. Rabinowitz, Mandler, and Barsalou (1979) have concluded, "Since in the real world auxiliary retrieval strategies are typically used after some time interval and only after direct access has failed, generation-recognition seems to be a poor candidate for trying to recall the name of a town one had visited some time ago or the name of a guest at a party" (p. 70).

During the 1970s, Tulving and his associates proposed that neither the differential threshold nor the two-process position was correct, suggesting that the retrieval process operating in both recognition and recall was the same. When differences in retention were found between the two measures, they were assumed to be related to the number and/or characteristics of the retrieval cues that overlapped with the memory trace or engram. This position has been now revised, and a new theoretical position has been put forth in Tulving's General Abstract Processing System. But these is too little experimental evidence available to determine whether Tulving's new position describing the relationship between recognition and recall will be any more successful than his earlier one.

Classification Schemes of Memory ▶

The information processing position has been accompanied by a concern on the par some psychologists who have been interested in providing a classification sche describing our memorial system. One of the earliest (and most notable) has been distinction between short-term and long-term memory, but more recent classificat systems have been also proposed. The topic is an extensive one and we shall provide reader with only a brief introduction to a few of the topics that have assumed spe importance.

---

appropriate distractors are used. Recognition test scores depend on the nature of the distractors utilized. Since it is necessary to use different types of distractors in the high- and low-frequency word recognition tests, it is possible that the findings of Gorman (1961) and other experimenters were related to the differences between the types of distractors used, rather than any qualitative differences existing between the two performance measures.

Short-Term and Long-Term Memory Systems

In the late 1940s, Hebb (1949) assumed that a basic memory process could be inferred from the findings of memory span studies.[8] He proposed that after stimuli were perceived, for a very short time thereafter such stimuli continued to reverberate in the organism's nervous system. This short reverberation period was distinct from a second memory process that operated in those retention studies, where substantial intervals of time were placed between the learning of material and its subsequent recall. Hebb's two-memory classification was similar to the position of William James (1890), who had suggested that human memory consisted of two separate components—a primary memory, which was believed to contain material that had not left the individual's consciousness, and a second memory system, which was assumed to contain material that was not in consciousness but was available if needed.

Almost ten years later, Broadbent (1958), in his text, *Perception and Communication,* formally proposed a long-term memory (LTM) and short-term memory (STM) system, hypothesizing that material entering the short-term memory store formed a trace that decayed rapidly but could be maintained by rehearsal. Since all of the items could not be rehearsed simultaneously, there was a limit to the number of items that could be maintained in short-term memory by rehearsal.

For the next decade, a good deal of evidence accumulated that appeared to support Broadbent's position of a dual memory system. It was generally assumed that the learning and retention studies of earlier investigators reflected the operation of long-term memory so that much attention was concerned with representation and functioning of short-term memory.

Miller (1956) had proposed that an individual's memory span, as noted in traditional memory span studies that were assumed to examine short-term memory, would hold only about seven items, or chunks as he termed them. This proposal was supportive of Broadbent's position that the capacity of short-term memory was quite limited. (See Box 14–1.)

Other experimental evidence was provided by Peterson and Peterson (1959) and Glanzer and Cunitz (1966). Peterson and Peterson's findings, which we described earlier in the chapter, supported the operation of a short-term memory system since these experimenters found that recall of the CCCs declined as the length of the retention interval increased. Moreover, these investigators ruled out proactive inhibition as a contributor to their findings since a subject's recall of the trigrams at the end of the experimental session was no different than that observed at the beginning.

Glanzer and Cunitz (1966) proposed that the U-shaped serial position curve found in many list-learning studies reflected the output from two separate storage systems. The recall of items from the beginning of the list represented output from long-term

---

[8] A memory span task consists of presenting a number of items, typically digits, to the subject who is asked to repeat them immediately following the presentation of the last item. Beginning with the correct recall of three (or four) digits, the experimenter increases the number presented by one digit until the subject is unable to correctly repeat all of the items. The subject's memory span is represented by the number of digits that can be correctly recalled.

box 14-1

Miller's (1956) proposal that an individual's memory span would hold only about seven unrelated items stands in apparent contrast to the documented feats of memory experts who have demonstrated a remarkable ability to remember strings of items numbering 50 or more. In an effort to determine if such a memory skill could be acquired with practice, Ericsson, Chase, and Faloon (1980) provided S. F., an undergraduate who was a good long-distance runner and of average intelligence, with memory span practice for about one hour a day, three to five days a week, for more than 1 1/2 years The procedure was to read S. F. random digits at the rate of one digit per second, following which the sequence was recalled. If the sequence was reported correctly, the next sequence was increased by one digit; if incorrect, it was decreased by one digit. Immediately after half of the trials, S. F. provided verbal reports of his thoughts during the trial.

During the course of 20 months of practice, involving more than 230 hours of laboratory testing, S. F.'s digit span steadily improved from 7 to almost 80 digits. Box Figure 14-1 presents these findings.

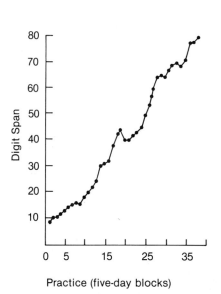

Practice (five-day blocks)

Box Figure 14-1
Average digit span for S. F. as a function of practice. Digit span is defined as the length of the sequence that is correct 50% of the time; under the procedure followed, it is equivalent to average sequence length. Each day represents about 1 hour's practice and ranges from 55 trials per day in the beginning to 3 trials per day for the longest sequences. The 38 blocks of practice shown here represent about 190 hours of practice; interspersed among these practice sessions are approximately 40 hours of experimental sessions (not shown). Adapted from K. A. Ericsson, W. G. Chase, and S. Faloon, "Acquisition of a memory skill," *Science,* 1980, *208,* 1181–1182. Copyright © 1980 by American Association for the Advancement of Science. Reprinted by permission.

In analyzing S. F.'s skill, it was noted that the most essential ingredient was his development of mnemonic associations, described in great detail in his verbal reports. What S. F. did first was to categorize three- and four-digit groups as running times for various races. Thus, 3,492 was recoded as "3 minutes and 49 point 2 seconds, near world-record mile time." This procedure, however, was not sufficient to account for long-digit span performance since the grouping of digits into three- and four-digit categories demanded that he remember the order in which the digits were presented. The order of the categories had to be organized. Early organization consisted of S. F. subdividing the material into varying groups of running times. Thus, the presentation of 18 or so digits resulted in his organizing groups of digits into two four-digit groups, followed by two three-digit groups, with the last four, five, or six digits presented being rehearsed while recall of the others was taking place. When the length of the digit span presented

(continued)

totaled 80 items, S. F.'s organization retrieval structure could be described as a hierarchy with three levels, and illustrated as follows, with spaces corresponding to levels in the hierarchy:

444-444   333-333   444-333   444 + last 5 digits rehearsed

In their analysis of S. F.'s skill, Ericsson and associates (1980) concluded that S. F. had not increased his memory span (or short-term memory) capacity but, rather, the increase in the length of his memory span could be attributed to the use of mnemonic associations that he had developed. It was noted that the size of the mnemonic groups S. F. formed were almost always three and four digits; a rehearsal group never exceeded six digits, and a supergroup generally consisted of three groups and never more than four. In addition, it was noted that in one experiment, S. F., after three months of digit span practice, was switched to letters of the alphabet and exhibited no transfer; his memory span had dropped back to about six consonants.

memory, whereas the recall of items from the end of the list represented output from short-term memory. Support for their position was provided by experimentally demonstrating that it was possible to decrease recall of the last few items by increasing the length of the delay interval provided between the presentation of the last item on the list and the test for recall. But the retention of items found at the beginning of the list was not influenced by changing the length of the delay interval.

Clinical evidence used to support the two-memory system was provided by Milner (1968), who indicated that bilateral surgical lesions in the hippocampal region produced a severe and persistent memory disorder in human patients. The operation resulted in no loss of preoperative acquired skills—long-term memories acquired prior to the surgery were left intact. In addition, there was the immediate registration of new information, as assessed, for example, by digit span tests. But it appeared that these patients could not transfer newly acquired information to long-term memory, thus also suggesting the involvement of two memory systems.

Difficulties with the STM-LTM Distinction

All psychologists were not convinced that short-term and long-term memory represented two functionally and conceptually different systems. Melton (1963), in a classic paper, rejected the STM-LTM distinction and argued for the desirability of considering short-term and long-term memory as representing a continuum, thus providing a unitary system. Postman (1975), Lewis (1979), and Crowder (1982), after a careful examination of the evidence that had accumulated, have also argued that dividing memory into short-term and long-term stores was in error. But what was the nature of the evidence that casted doubt on this conception of memory?

Hebb (1949) and Broadbent (1958) had theorized that forgetting in STM arose from the short-term trace decaying over time. And Peterson and Peterson (1959) had provided experimental support for this position by not being able to obtain proactive inhibition effects in their STM study. But Keppel and Underwood (1962) and many subsequent experimenters were able to demonstrate that proactive inhibition did contribute to the forgetting of material in short-term memory experiments.

Glanzer and Cunitz's (1966) explanation of the role of short-term memory in accounting for the excellent recall of items at the end of the list noted in serial learning studies (a finding identified as a *recency effect*) was also found to be specious. In a study by Baddeley and Hitch (1977), subjects were presented with a series of 12 four-lettered anagrams and were permitted a 30-second solution time for each item. After 12 anagrams had been presented, subjects were asked to count backwards for either 10 or 30 seconds, followed by instructions to recall all of the anagrams presented. Since the test was quite unexpected, the subjects did not have any reason to maintain the items in short-term memory; moreover, the backward counting task should have reduced if not eliminated any short-term memory effect. Nonetheless, large recency effects were found in their study. Other investigators (e.g., Bjork and Whitten, 1974; and Glenberg and Kraus, 1981) have noted that the absolute length of the delay interval provided just prior to recall is not of critical importance. Large recency effects can be observed as long as the delay interval provided just prior to recall is small relative to the length of the delay which separates each item on the list. Greene's (1986) comprehensive review of recency effects in free recall has resulted in his stating, "The safest conclusion that can be reached . . . is that primary or short term memory theories are no longer an adequate explanation for the recency effect in recall" (p. 226).

Finally, subsequent examination of amnesia patients or individuals who had brain surgery revealed problems in the earlier accounts of how these deficiencies were presumed to influence memory. Corkin (1968) demonstrated that patients who presumably had lost the capacity to transfer material in short-term to long-term memory can do so. (See Box 14–2.) Moreover, other investigators have reported that amnesic patients show considerable retention of classical conditioned responses (e.g., Weiskrantz and Warrington, 1979).

Short-Term Memory Revisited

The experimental evidence we have reviewed led many investigators to reject the theoretical distinction that had been made between short-term and long-term memory. However, the evidence did not result in the term *short-term memory* being abandoned. Many experimenters have used the concept to denote a specific experimental operation or research paradigm, roughly defined as the brief presentation of within-memory span material, followed by a retention interval measured in seconds or at the most minutes, with recall or recognition of the material then requested. Investigators operating within this framework have directed their interest toward an examination of how a variety of experimental variables influence performance.[9]

---

[9] A revised approach to the concept of short-term memory has been proposed by Baddeley (1976, 1983) who has suggested that there is a short-term storage system—material that we can keep in consciousness—that functions as working memory. He has used the term *working* since he believes that emphasis should be placed on the fact that this is a temporary storage system that we can use as a "work place," while attempting to arrive at the solution of mental problems. Baddeley's concept of working memory is only gradually achieving popularity but it cannot be said to have entered the mainstream of memory research in the United States.

box 14-2

Brain operations can provide interesting and suggestive evidence, although not necessarily conclusive, concerning how memory functions. The effects of one brain operation have been reported by Milner and her colleagues in a series of studies; see Milner (1963, 1965, 1968); Milner and Teuber (1968); Milner, Corkin, and Teuber (1968). All the studies examined the residual learning capacities of H. M. following the bilateral removal of his medial temporal lobes. Prior to his operation, H. M. had severe epilepsy, suffering major convulsions about once a week, combined with many minor attacks each day. In order to alleviate this condition, an operation was performed to bilaterally remove the medial temporal lobes. Once this was done, major convulsions were almost entirely eliminated, while minor seizures were reduced to one or two a day. But the improved physical condition was accompanied by an unusual memory deficit. H. M. could not remember information obtained after the operation. He was unable, for example, to recognize people who became close neighbors or family friends, or to remember the address of the house to which his family had moved after the operation. He revealed little awareness of major national or international events. Laboratory testing involving memory functions, as reported by Milner, Corkin, and Teuber (1968), confirmed this type of memory loss.

But H. M.'s memory deficit was not accompanied by general intellectual loss. Prior to his operation he had an IQ of 104; two years after his operation, his IQ was 112; seven years later, it was 118. Moreover, the operation did not appear to change H. M.'s capacity to recall remote events antedating his operation. He was able to remember incidents from his early school years and positions that he had held during his late teens and early twenties. His interaction with individuals in social settings revealed that he had not lost any of the social graces he had acquired in his youth.

Tulving's Semantic-Episodic Distinction of Memory

It is not surprising that many theorists have attempted to replace the short-term–long-term conception of human memory with memory systems of their own. One such conceptualization that has aroused a great deal of interest has been provided by Tulving (1972, 1983, 1984, 1985). In an early paper (1972) he identified two types of memory that had primary relevance for verbal material. One type, semantic memory, was defined as a system "which receives and stores information about temporally dated episodes or events, and temporal-spatial relations among these events" (p. 385). A second type was episodic memory— "the memory necessary for the use of language" (p. 386).[10]

Semantic memory thus represented general knowledge about the world; an example would be knowing that the chemical symbol for water was H_2O. Episodic memory,

---

[10] Tulving (1983) has incorporated the semantic-episodic distinction into a more general classification scheme of memory described in his monograph *Elements of Episodic Memory*. In this volume, he has hypothesized two basic types of memory: (1) procedural and (2) propositional, with semantic and episodic memory subsumed under propositional memory. A theoretical framework for the operation of episodic memory, identified as a General Abstract Processing System, has been proposed. A description of this system is beyond the scope of this introductory presentation.

in which Tulving had a particular interest, was represented by autobiographical episodes, an example of which would be the remembering of a personally experienced event such as meeting an attractive member of the opposite sex while on a holiday or recalling attending a World Series baseball game. Traditional list-learning studies in which familiar words were used as material to be remembered were considered to represent investigations of episodic memory since Tulving argued that the words to be placed in memory were already there—they had to be remembered only in the context of the specific experiments in which they were participating.

Critics have generally agreed that Tulving's distinction between semantic and episodic memory has had considerable heuristic value. But Tulving's claim that semantic and episodic memory were functionally different, with the two systems operating independently, has been frequently disputed. Many investigators have questioned whether it is possible to make a distinction between the two systems (see McClosky and Santee, 1981; Hintzman, 1984; Hirst, 1982; Klatsky, 1984; Morton and Bekerian, 1984; and Wolters, 1984). Baddeley (1976) has reported a study of Byrne who asked housewives to produce menus for a meal under certain constraints, and then recorded a description of their activity. Byrne noted that the recall of general principles (semantic memory) and the remembering of specific meals that had been prepared on earlier occasions (episodic memory) were inextricably interwoven. Byrne's conclusion was that Tulving's distinction was not very useful, at least for this type of task. Anderson and Ross's (1980) survey of experimental studies that examined the semantic-episodic difference has resulted in their concluding that the experimental evidence is not in keeping with the making of a functional distinction between the two memory systems, writing, "There are numerous demonstrations of similar effects in episodic and semantic memory" (p. 477).

Summary ►

Growing impatience and disaffection with the functionalist's approach to the study of learning and retention resulted, beginning with the 1950s, with many investigators adopting an information processing model of memory. This model was likened to the operation of a computer in which encoding, storage, and retrieval presented the basic memorial constructs. During the past several decades, a host of experimental investigations have been undertaken examining how memory is influenced by the operation of these constructs.

Encoding refers to those processes responsible for transforming external stimuli into internal information. Several encoding taxonomies have been proposed. Bower (1972) identified four encoding processes as (1) stimulus selection, (2) rewriting, (3) elaboration, and (4) componential description. Underwood (1983) put forth a different point of view in which he has hypothesized that any memory consists of a collection of attributes derived from the external stimulus, with each of these attributes being related to the encoding process. Wickens used a particular type of experimental design—release from proactive inhibition—to identify the operation of three major classes of encoding attributes, namely, (1) semantic features, (2) physical features, and (3) syntatic features of the external stimulus.

The work of Bower, Underwood, and Wickens has been concerned with identifying the nature of the encoding process. Other investigators, however, have been interested in relating different encoding operations to differential recall or recognition. Thus, when the encoding operation of (1) rehearsal, (2) generation, and (3) orienting instructions are employed, it has been found that each of these can influence memory.

The second construct, storage, refers to the holding or storing of information that has been received or encoded by the subject. Little experimental information is available about the operation of the storage process. Some theorists have assumed that material placed in storage remains there permanently and that difficulties in remembering arise not from a decay or deterioration of the memory trace, but from an inadequate functioning of the retrieval process. Neurological evidence obtained by Penfield (1955), who found that his surgical patients would remember forgotten events when their cortex was stimulated with a weak electrical current, suggested that the human storage system could be likened to a tape recorder, with memories being permanent. However, other investigators have pointed to inadequacies in Penfield's hypothesis.

Hypnotic age regression has also been used to provide support for a permanent memory system. It has been shown that hypnotized subjects are able to remember forgotten information from an earlier time. In the last analysis, however, every human organism forgets—the question of whether or not memory is permanent is unanswerable since any failure to remember, which presumably would negate the notion of permanence, can always be attributed to retrieval failure rather than to the impermanence of the memory trace.

Retrieval, the third memory construct posited by information processing investigators, refers to the subject recovering previously presented material from storage. It is now acknowledged that the retrieval process can be enhanced by a number of different types of probes. One theory of retrieval proposed by Tulving and his associates, identified as the principle of encoding specificity, refers to the fact that retention is maximized when the cues that were present when the material was encoded are also present during the test for retention. The inadequacy of the encoding specificity principle has been demonstrated, however, by studies in which retention was enhanced through the presentation of specific cues that were not present during encoding.

Another retrieval issue has to do with the employment of recall and recognition measures. Considerable debate exists as to whether these measures are qualitatively or only quantitatively different. The qualitative position holds that recall depends on two processes—generation and discrimination-decision—whereas recognition depends on only the discrimination-decision process. Since recall involves two processes, in contrast to just one demanded by recognition, the dual position posits that recognition should always be superior to recall. In contrast, the quantitative position states that recognition and recall are merely different ways to measure the same storage content, with recognition being the more sensitive of the two measures. The experimental evidence is conflicting so that a resolution of this controversy cannot be provided.

The information processing position was accompanied by an interest of some psychologists in providing a classification or taxonomy describing the various types of memory. One of the earliest of current positions was the distinction made between short-term and long-term memory. It was assumed that the short-term store could hold only a limited number of items in which the memory for those items decayed rapidly with time. Although early experimental evidence tended to support the short-term–long-term memory distinction, problems with this conceptualization of memory are now apparent. Current use of the concept of short-term memory denotes only a specific experimental operation, more specifically, the brief presentation of within-memory span material, followed by a retention interval measured in seconds, with recall or recognition of material then requested.

Another memory system has been proposed by Tulving (1983), who hypothesized that memory be divided into two basic categories: procedural and propositional. Procedural memory enables the subject to retain learned connections between stimuli and responses and represents a type of memory related to the remembering of what has been traditionally identified as skills behavior in which muscular movement plays an important role.

The second memory type, propositional memory, is concerned with memory for units of language, and can be divided into two subcategories: semantic and episodic. Semantic memory refers to a system of receiving and retaining information about the meaning of words, concepts, and classification of concepts. Episodic memory is represented by autobiographical episodes. Traditional list-learning studies, in which familiar words are used as material to be remembered, are considered to be investigations of episodic memory since it has been argued that the words to be placed in memory are already there—they have only to be remembered in the context of the specific experiment in which the subjects were participating.

chapter fifteen

▶

Memory for Prose

In Chapter Fourteen we noted that many investigators who had adopted the information processing approach to the study of memory continued to employ list-learning tasks. Other experimenters believed that the study of memory should encompass a wider range of materials—a position in keeping with a growing belief among many psychologists that experimental findings should have ecological significance.

During the past decade or two, considerable attention has been focused on an examination of memory for people's faces, places, and events, as well as on special types of material (e.g., prose, court testimony, autobiographies). As Johnson and Hasher (1987) have observed, "Each year, research in learning and memory comes closer to reflecting the wide range of functions that memory serves" (p. 632). It is not possible to provide a comprehensive account of each of the many topics that investigators of memory have researched. As a result, we have selected just one of these topics for presentation in this chapter: memory for prose.

The Study of Prose ▶

Up until the 1960s, with the exception of the experiments conducted by Bartlett (1932) which we shall describe in a later section, prose and meaningful material was rarely used in verbal learning experiments. Traditional experimenters were reluctant to use this type of material for several reasons. One was the difficulty of calibrating prose. It was obvious that prose materials differed in their complexity, intelligibility, and so on, but the difficulty in defining and calibrating these characteristics contributed to the reluctance of experimenters to use them.

A second problem was how to measure memory for a sentence or longer passages of prose. Verbatim recall, used in list-learning experiments, did not seem to be a viable response measure for prose; recognition measures provided difficulty for the experimenter in constructing appropriate distractors. Measuring retention by having the subject give the essence or gist of a passage is perhaps the most practical, but it does permit a variety of interpretive judgments, which may result in scoring difficulties. (See Box 15–1.)

box 15–1

When the study of prose was undertaken by functional investigators, the usual approach was to examine the contribution of a list-learning variable and use verbatim recall of the material as a measure of retention. A study by Deese and Kaufman (1957) examining the effect of serial position illustrates this approach. In this study, three passages selected from the *World Almanac* were used. Each passage consisted of 10 sentences, with 10 words per sentence. By a minor rewording of the sentences, it was possible to present them in a number of different serial orders. The material was presented with a tape recorder, following which the subjects were asked to recall as many of the sentences as possible. Retention was measured by counting the number of words in each sentence recalled at each position. Box Figure 15–1 presents the findings. Note the familiar bow-shaped curve, revealing retention to be a function of the position of the sentences making up the list.

Box Figure 15–1
Mean frequency of recall per passage per *S* for statements in textual passages as a function of position of statements in original passages. Adapted from J. Deese and R. A. Kaufman, "Serial effects in recall of unorganized and sequentially organized verbal material," *Journal of Experimental Psychology,* 1957, *54,* 180–187. Copyright© 1957 by the American Psychological Association. Reprinted by permission.

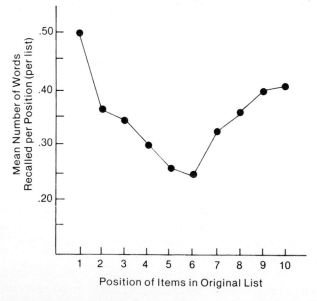

Bartlett's Contributions

Psychologists are indebted to Bartlett (1932) for his early contributions to the study of prose, many of which are found in his volume *Remembering*. One part of his research was to present a story to his subjects following which they were asked to recall the material. Let us examine one example of the kind of story Bartlett used and the characteristics of his subjects' protocols.

The War of the Ghosts

One night two young men from Egulac went down to the river to hunt seals, and while they were there it became foggy and calm. Then they heard war-cries, and they thought: "Maybe this is a war-party." They escaped to the shore, and hid behind a log. Now canoes came up, and they heard the noise of paddles, and saw one canoe coming up to them. There were five men in the canoe, and they said:

"What do you think? We wish to take you along. We are going up the river to make war on the people."

One of the young men said: "I have no arrows."

"Arrows are in the canoe," they said.

"I will not go along. I might be killed. My relatives do not know where I have gone. But you," he said, turning to the other, "may go with them."

So one of the young men went, but the other returned home.

And the warriors went on up the river to a town on the other side of Kalama. The people came down to the water, and they began to fight, and many were killed. But presently the young man heard one of the warriors say: "Quick, let us go home; that Indian has been hit." Now he thought: "Oh, they are ghosts." He did not feel sick, but they said he had been shot.

So the canoes went back to Egulac, and the young man went ashore to his house, and made a fire. And he told everybody and said: "Behold I accompanied the ghosts, and we went to fight. Many of our fellows were killed, and many of those who attacked us were killed. They said I was hit, and I did not feel sick."

He told it all, and then he became quiet. When the sun rose he fell down. Something black came out of his mouth. His face became contorted. The people jumped up and cried.

He was dead.[1]

In some instances, Bartlett examined his subject's recall of the story on several different occasions. A methodological problem with this procedure is that when the narrative is recalled more than once, it is virtually impossible to know whether subjects are basing their recall on the memory acquired during the original presentation or on the memory of a subsequent recall. In other instances, Bartlett had different groups of subjects recall the material at retention intervals that varied from a few hours to many months. Methodologically, such a procedure is much sounder than the method of repeated reproductions. Two of these recall protocols are illustrated.

A subject's recall 20 hours later:

Two men from Edulac went fishing. While thus occupied by the river they heard a noise in the distance.

---

[1] F. C. Bartlett, *Remembering* (London: Cambridge University Press, 1972), p. 65. Reprinted with permission of Cambridge University Press.

"It sounds like a cry," said one, and presently there appeared some men in canoes, who invited them to join a party on their adventure. One of the men refused to go, on the ground of family ties, but the other offered to go.
"But there are no arrows," he said.
"The arrows are in the boat," was the reply.
He thereupon took his place, while his friend returned home. The party paddled up the river to Kaloma, and began to land on the banks of the river. Presently some one was injured, and the cry was raised that the enemy were ghosts.
The party returned down the stream, and the young man arrived home feeling none the worse for his experience. The next morning at dawn he endeavoured to recount his adventure. While he was talking something black issued from his mouth. Suddenly he uttered a cry and fell down. His friends gathered around him. But he was dead.[2]

A subject's recall six months later:

Four men came down to the water. They were told to get into the boat and to take arms with them. They inquired, "What arms?" and were answered "Arms for battle." When they came to the battlefield they heard a great noise and shouting, and a voice said, "The black man is dead." And he was brought to the place where they were, and laid on the ground. And he foamed at the mouth.[3]

In an analysis of his experimental findings, Bartlett noted that his subjects omitted much of what had been originally presented; moreover, the recall protocol was an abstraction of the narrative. In addition, there frequently appeared to be a radical transformation of the original material, with subjects recasting parts of the narrative in a form that was compatible with their own cultural background and social conventions. To illustrate, Zangwill (1972) has indicated that the phrase "went down to the river to hunt seals" was changed by one of Bartlett's subjects to indicate that the two young men involved went fishing. Bartlett considered these transformations to reflect the process of *rationalization*, although current experimenters use the term *construction* or *reconstruction*.

Finally, in attempting to account for how such material was remembered, Bartlett (1932) introduced the concept of a schema. He assumed that our knowledge of the world was made up of a set of models or schemata derived from our past experience. New material that was perceived, as in reading a narrative, was integrated into the model so that recall was related to the schema that was generated. If the new material was in conflict with the schema, the process of construction resulted, which changed the memorial representation in such a way as to provide a consistent schema.

The Heritage of Bartlett

For more than two decades following the publication of *Remembering*, Bartlett's (1932) contributions were largely ignored by American psychologists whose research was guided largely by the work of Ebbinghaus (1885/1913). McGeoch's (1946) authoritative

---

[2] Ibid., p. 66.
[3] Ibid., pp. 71–72.

text on human learning, as well as a subsequent revision (e.g., McGeoch and Irion, 1952), devoted only a few brief paragraphs to Bartlett's work. But investigators in the 1950s, skeptical of the generality of list-learning studies using isolated words and nonsense syllables, widened their experimental material to include the study of prose; in so doing they rediscovered Bartlett. Bartlett's analysis of prose pointing to the role of schemata and to the concepts of abstraction and construction provided experimenters with the impetus for the further study of these constructs.

The Abstraction Process

Bartlett's (1932) work, which indicated that omission characterized the recall of prose, led Gomulicki (1956) to examine the nature of the abstractive process in considerable detail. In his study, the experimental material consisted of 37 prose passages that varied in length from 13 to 95 words. The recall of each passage was requested immediately after the experimenter had finished reading it. Subjects were instructed to repeat orally as much of the presented material as they could recall. Results indicated that the percentage of words omitted increased as the presented passages grew longer, with the nature of these omissions increasing from single-adjective phrases to longer phrases that might encompass a whole sentence being eliminated. Gomulicki further pointed out that what was omitted was not determined by random selection by the subject; rather, the material placed in memory appeared to be ordered in terms of relative importance, with enough of the less important material eliminated to bring the content of the passage within the scope of the subject's recall.

Gomulicki's hypothesis that the unit of forgetting, whenever reasonably long passages were presented, was the intact phrase rather than individual words, has been described by some as *holistic forgetting,* and can be contrasted with the position of associative theorists (e.g., Anderson and Bower, 1973) who have assumed that the words that appear in a sentence are associated via independent links that are formed piecemeal and part by part. These various linkages have differing probabilities of being stored in memory, and as a result, associative theorists would predict that fragmentary remembering would be frequent, particularly when overall levels of recall were not very high.

Johnson (1986) has conducted a series of studies in an attempt to obtain evidence on the occurrence of holistic or fragmentary forgetting taking place in the learning of prose. Five experiments examined a variety of conditions in the learning of such material: short vs. long passages; short vs. long retention intervals; and three different measures of retention—recognition, completion recall, and free recall. We will not describe the varying experimental procedures employed nor describe peripheral findings, but will concentrate on the central focus of the investigation, namely, "whether words within a phrase are remembered independently or as a holistic unit."

Johnson's findings indicated that little or no holistic forgetting was found when either recognition or completed recall measures were employed; however, strong support for a holistic interpretation of forgetting was obtained when free recall was used. Inasmuch as free recall was the retention measure used by Gomulicki (who provided a holistic interpretation of forgetting) and calling attention to other studies that have supported a holistic forgetting interpretation (e.g., Johnson and Scheidt, 1977; Owens, Bower, and Black, 1979; and Mandler and Goodman, 1982), Johnson concluded that the occurrence of holistic forgetting appears to be a phenomenon of considerable generality.

The Process of Construction

It will be recalled that the second memory process Bartlett (1932) had called attention to was construction. Observing that many modifications took place in a subject's memory for his narratives, Bartlett suggested that memory was constructive, writing:

> Remembering is not the re-excitation of innumerable fixed, lifeless and fragmentary traces. It is an imaginative reconstruction, or construction, built out of the relation of our attitude towards a whole active mass of organized past reactions or experiences. . . . It is thus hardly ever really exact, even in the most rudimentary cases or rote recapitulation (pp. 213–214).

Bartlett's position can be contrasted with an earlier and more prevalent memory position, often referred to as a *trace theory*, which held that a learning experience resulted in a neurological trace being laid down that remained essentially unchanged. This did not mean that forgetting did not take place but if memory losses were observed, it was assumed that they were primarily quantitative in nature. What was remembered was a replica of that which had been originally presented. Many investigators using list-learning material and demanding verbatim recall adopted such a position.[4]

Bahrick (1984b) has recently identified this position as a *replication hypothesis* since it has been posited that the content of recall closely matches the target material. An example of this position can be found from Wickelgren (1979), who wrote that there was no evidence for qualitative changes in memory: ". . . time does not 'rewrite the lines' in our memories, it only makes what is written on some lines fade or get smudged faster than what is written on other lines" (p. 392).

One outcome of the trace versus construction view of memory was an interest on the part of investigators to determine the nature of the representation that was placed in memory.

In an early study, Sachs (1967) attempted to determine whether the grammatical structure or syntax, an obviously integral part of prose, would become a part of the memorial representation. In her study, students listened to 28 passages of prose, one of which was as follows:

> There is an interesting story about the telescope. In Holland, a man named Lippershey was an eye-glass maker. One day his children were playing with some lenses. They discovered that things seemed very close if two lenses were held about a foot apart. Lippershey began experimenting and his "spyglass" attracted much attention. He sent a letter about it to Galileo, the great Italian

---

[4] This position does not make any assumptions about the nature of forgetting, since quantitative losses could be attributed to a decay process or to interference arising from previously learned material.

scientist. *Galileo at once realized the importance of the discovery and set about to build an instrument of his own. He used an old organ pipe with one lens curved out and the other in. On the first clear night he pointed the glass toward the sky. He was amazed to find the empty dark spaces filled with brightly gleaming stars! Night after night Galileo climbed to a high tower, sweeping the sky with his telescope. One night he saw Jupiter, and to his great surprise discovered near it three bright stars, two to the east and one to the west. A few nights later there were four little stars (pp. 438–439).*

Following the presentation of the passage, a test sentence, which was related to the non-italicized sentence, was presented. Subjects were asked to indicate whether a test sentence was identical to the one originally heard, or whether it had been changed. The test sentences were of four types. Two types were syntactically different from the original, although the meaning was not changed. One such change was to make the test sentence passive (e.g., "A letter about it was sent to Galileo, the great Italian scientist."). The other syntactic change was identified as formal since only words were rearranged (e.g., "He sent Galileo, the great Italian scientist, a letter about it."). The third form of the sentence consisted of changing the meaning of the sentence (e.g., "Galileo, the great Italian scientist, sent him a letter about it."). Finally, the last type was identical to the sentence found in the original passage.

A second objective of Sachs was in determining how the amount of material presented after the critical sentence had been presented influenced retention. Either 0, 80, or 160 syllables were presented after the critical sentence had been heard and before the test sentence was presented.

Results are indicated in Figure 15–1. Note that when the test sentences were presented immediately following the presentation of the original sentence, the three types of test sentences which differed from the original were correctly recognized as being different from the original. When 80 or 160 syllables were interpolated between

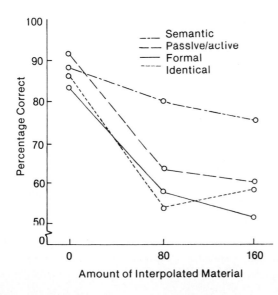

Figure 15-1

Percentage of judgments *identical* and *changed* that were correct for each test type. Adapted from J. S. Sachs, "Recognition memory for syntactic and semantic aspects of connected discourse," *Perception and Psychophysics,* 1967, 2, 437–442. Reprinted by permission of the Psychonomic Society.

listening to the original sentence and the presentation of the sentence that differed in meaning, subjects correctly recognized that it was different, thus indicating that the meaning of the original sentence had been placed in memory, thus permitting the subject to know that the test sentence was "different." But when syntactic arrangement differed, recognition performance dropped to almost chance. These findings suggest that with this sample of prose, the meaning of the material was placed in memory, although its syntactic structure was not.

That meaning is represented in memory has been also demonstrated in an interesting study by Bransford and Franks (1971). In their study, sentences were constructed that contained four related ideas. One such sentence was "The rock which rolled down the mountain crushed the tiny hut at the edge of the woods." The four ideas were "The rock rolled down the mountain"; "The rock crushed the hut"; "The hut was tiny"; and "The hut was at the edge of the woods." In one experiment, four different four-idea sentences were used from which Bransford and Franks (1971) made up 24 sentences containing either one, two, or three ideas. Each sentence was orally presented. After each presentation, subjects were asked to answer a question about the sentence—a procedure that was used to make sure that the subjects had listened to the sentence and would hold it in memory for a period of time. At the end of this phase of the study, the experimenters then read 28 related sentences to their subjects. Four of these contained four-idea units—a type of sentence that had not been presented. Four other sentences were identical to those used in the first phase of the study, and 20 others were used that had not been seen previously. Subjects were asked to indicate Yes or No as to whether or not the sentence had been seen before; in addition, they were asked to indicate how confident they were in their choice, with confidence ratings ranging from 1 to 5.

One of the most interesting results from the study was that subjects indicated that they had seen the four-idea sentences previously, expressing a greater amount of confidence in their decision than they had when presented with sentences containing one, two, or three ideas. Thus, Bransford and Frank's (1971) subjects did not recall the specific sentences that had been presented but had placed in their memory the ideas that were expressed in them. After describing this study, Cofer (1973) wrote that these results "lend powerful support to a view of memory much like that proposed by Bartlett. That is to say that people integrate information into a more of less coherent organization of schema which then governs their judgment as to whether or not statements have been encountered before" (p. 542).

As Bartlett's view of memory gained favor, investigators became interested in demonstrating that the operation of the constructive process resulted not only in capturing the meaning of prose, but in showing that the memory of an event could include information that had not been presented in the original learning situation. The experimental findings obtained by a number of investigators (e.g., Pompi and Lachman, 1967; Sulin and Dooling, 1974; Kintsch, 1977, and Loftus and her associates) have supported this position.

In the Sulin and Dooling (1974) study, two very similar experiments were conducted. The findings from both revealed the operation of the constructive process. The experimental material consisted of a short biographical passage, so written that the material was true of a noted person, namely, Helen Keller. An identical passage was used, although it portrayed the biography of a fictitious character, identified as Carol Harris.[5] The Helen Keller (Carol Harris) passage was as follows:

> *Helen Keller's (Carol Harris's) need for professional help. Helen Keller (Carol Harris) was a problem child from birth. She was wild, stubborn, and violent. By the time Helen (Carol) turned eight, she was still unmanageable. Her parents were very concerned about her mental health. There was no good institution for her problem in her state. Her parents finally decided to take some action. They hired a private teacher for Helen (Carol).*

The procedure consisted of having two groups of subjects read the story. One group learned that the person was Helen Keller; whereas the individual was identified as Carol Harris for the second group. After the material had been read, half of each group was dismissed and asked to return at the same time one week later. The remaining subjects were given a recognition test that contained seven sentences taken from the passage, intermingled with seven sentences that served as foils or distractors. The critical foil sentence asserted a well-known central fact about Helen Keller, namely, "She was deaf, dumb and blind." Two other distractor sentences less related to the historical character were also used. One of these was "She helped other people overcome their handicap," and the second one was "A book was written about Helen's (Carol's) life." In addition, four other distractor sentences were used that were considered to be neutral with regard to the theme of the paragraph.

In taking the recognition test, subjects were instructed to read each sentence and decide whether or not the sentence was the same or different from any of the sentences that were read in the story. In addition, they were asked to rate their degree of confidence in each judgment on a five-point scale. Results demonstrated that there was a significantly large number of false recognitions of the thematically related sentences, demonstrating that memory for prose involved a constructive process. Of special relevance was the demonstration that thematic effects increase with the passage of time. At the seven-day interval, subjects appeared to have less memory for specific information and relied to a greater extent upon their memory for the theme.

A somewhat different demonstration of the operation of a constructive process was provided by Kintsch (1977) who read to his experimental subjects the biblical story of Joseph and his brothers. Kintsch found that if a retention test immediately followed presentation of the story, his subjects' recall faithfully followed the presented material. But if the recall test was delayed for 24 hours, Kintsch found that his subjects were unable to differentiate between what he had presented and their general knowledge of Joseph. Many individuals wrote down just about all of the information they had about Joseph's life.

In the studies of Sulin and Dooling (1974) and Kintsch (1977), which we have just reviewed, the new information that was incorporated into the subject's recall protocol had been in the individual's memory prior to the presentation of the narrative. It is also possible to demonstrate the operation of a constructive process by providing the subject with new information between the original presentation of the experimental material

---

[5] In order to provide some generality to the findings, the experimenters employed a second passage using Adolph Hitler as the noted individual.

and the subsequent test of recall. A series of studies by Loftus and her associates had demonstrated such an effect.

The procedure and the kind of findings obtained are illustrated by Loftus's (1975) Experiment 2. In this experiment, students were shown a three-minute videotape that depicted the disruption of a school classroom by 8 demonstrators. At the end of the videotape presentation, the subjects received one of two questionnaires, each containing 19 filler questions and 1 key question. One form of the key question asked "Was the leader of the 4 demonstrators who entered the classroom a male?" The other form asked the question "Was the leader of the 12 demonstrators who entered the classroom a male?" One week later, all subjects answered a series of 20 questions about the disruption, with the critical question being, "How many demonstrators did you see entering the classroom?" Results from those subjects who had been previously asked the question presupposing 12 demonstrators averaged 8.85 individuals, whereas for those subjects who had been asked the question presupposing 4 demonstrators, the average was 6.40. The difference between the two values was statistically significant.

The same basic effect—that additional information influences a subsequent reporting of an event—was obtained in another study in which students viewed a brief videotape of an automobile accident and then answered a questionnaire that presupposed that there was (or was not) a barn in the picture. One week after seeing this film, the subjects were asked if they had seen the barn. Again, results indicated that by providing information about the previously perceived event, one could influence the subsequent reporting of what had taken place.

The Loftus (1975) study raises several questions, some theoretical and others procedural. In the studies reported, the subjects were presented with a visual event and were asked to verbally remember it. But does the transformation from a visual presentation to a verbal response contribute to the experimental findings? Did the subjects actually "see" the barn in the slide? Moreover, was it not possible that Loftus's experimental subjects, although actually seeing 8 demonstrators or not seeing the barn, "went along" with the experimenter, assuming that what was presented in the questionnaire was correct?

A series of experiments by Loftus, Miller, and Burns (1978) attempted to answer these questions. Their procedure consisted of presenting a series of 30 color slides that depicted successive stages of an automobile-pedestrian accident. One key slide featured a sign located at the intersection. For half of the subjects it was a stop sign and for the remaining subjects it was a yield sign. The usual questionnaire was administered, in which the key question presupposed either a stop sign or a yield sign. Following an interval of 20 minutes, the subjects were given a forced-choice recognition test in which 15 pairs of slides were presented. The subjects were asked to select the slide that had previously been presented. Choices made by the subjects of the pair of slides that depicted the stop sign on one side and a yield sign on the other provided the basic data. The data supported earlier findings; the interpolated questionnaire predisposed subjects to select the slide representing the sign that had been indicated on the questionnaire.

In other experiments, the investigators found that most subjects actually encoded or "saw" the sign in the slide. Thus, when they were asked to draw the details of the accident rather than choose the appropriate slide, a majority of them actually sketched in the presence of a yield sign (Experiment 4). This did not appear to be a result of either confusion on the part of the subjects or a desire to please the experimenter. When experimental subjects were given a debriefing questionnaire in which they were asked to indicate if there was a discrepancy between what they had seen in the slide and what the questionnaire indicated, only 12% stated that they had noted the difference (Experiment 2). Finally, in an effort to determine when misleading information should be provided in order to maximize the effect, the questionnaire was presented either immediately following the presentation of the original slides depicting the accident or immediately preceding the recognition test, with the interval between the slide presentation and the recognition test being either 20 minutes or 1, 2, or 7 days. Results indicated that the questionnaire had a larger impact on retention if it was introduced just prior to the recognition test rather than immediately following the slide presentation (Experiment 3).

A Current Controversy

During the past decade, some theorists have proposed that the constructive process consists primarily of a qualitative change in the memorial representation of the to-be-remembered material. Such a change arises from the interaction of the original with other stored representations and also from the nature of the conditions that are present during retrieval.

Neisser (1984), a staunch advocate of this position, has pointed out that autobiographical memory content can be so strongly altered by existing schemata and expectations that the content of recall may bear little resemblance to the objective content that it presumably reflects. He has suggested that remembering is like problem solving; that constructive recall is the rule, whereas literal or verbatim recall is the exception. In the previous section, we cited some of the experimental evidence that supports the constructive process view of memory.

It is unfortunate that Neisser and others have concluded that virtually all of our memories reflect primarily the operation of a constructive process. There is no doubt that this process contributes to our memorial representations, but as Bahrick (1984) has pointed out in rejecting Neisser's conclusion:

> There is no indication of reconstructive change in remembering one's name, the answer to simple arithmetic problems, the meaning of common words in our native language, and thousands of other overlearned facts, rules, or meanings that constitute much of our general knowledge. These instances of literal recall are not the exception; they are the rule for overlearning memory content (p. 56).[6]

Inasmuch as our memorial representations involve both replicative and constructive processes, it seems evident that the task of current investigators should be to

---

[6] Bahrick's position could be made stronger by noting carefully all of the activities that individuals engage in throughout the day. If we then determined whether the memories that were involved in each activity were replicative or constructive in nature, it would be obvious that most of our activities would fall into the replicative category.

identify those conditions that determine when constructive or replicative processes are operative. One such condition has to do with the characteristics of the material that is placed in memory. In examining the role of lexical and semantic contributions to memory, Begg and Paivio (1969) found that there was a much greater probability of subjects remembering lexical content, or word order, than semantic content, or meaning, when abstract sentences were used as the experimental material. In contrast, the use of concrete sentences resulted in these investigators finding that semantic content was better remembered than lexical content—a finding also reported by Sachs (1967).

A different approach to the problem was undertaken by Rubin (1977), who examined the recall of undergraduate students of five often-quoted passages from Psalm 23, Hamlet's soliloquy, the Gettysburg Address, the Preamble to the Constitution, and "The Star Spangled Banner." Rubin found that with few exceptions, subjects either recalled portions of the passage correctly and in their original wording or not at all. One explanation for such responding could be that a demand for verbatim recall generally accompanies the learning of this type of material. The demand may arise from precedent—it is customary to learn such material verbatim—or from the individual responsible for the subject learning the material.

The characteristics of demand need not be provided by precedent, however, but may result from the recall situation itself. One example is found in an experiment by Hasher and Griffin (1978), whose experimental material consisted of the two paragraphs in Table 15-1. We may note that each passage represents an ambiguous description of either of two events: Passage A describes (1) a man in the woods on a hunting trip or (2) a man escaping from prison; whereas passage B describes a long voyage, either that of (1) Columbus or (2) an early manned space flight. Subjects were first asked to read one of the two passages with the experimenter presenting one of the titles to indicate to the experimental subjects the theme (or schema) of what was being read.

Following the reading, the experimenter indicated to one of their experimental groups that the title that had been given was in error, and the "correct" (alternative) title was provided. Subjects in the second experiment group did not have the title of their passage changed; thus, the title that was provided at the beginning of the session was repeated prior to a recall test that was given either five minutes, two days, or one week after the original reading.

Hasher and Griffin (1978) hypothesized that recall under the same-theme condition would result in constructive process errors in retention because subjects would rely on the theme to aid them in remembering the passage; but when recall was attempted under changed-theme conditions, subjects should discard the theme when generating recall. This should result in these subjects making fewer constructive process errors. In addition, these changed-theme subjects should recall more of the actual material in the passage (than the same-theme subjects) since, realizing that a mistake had been made, would edit their recall carefully. Moreover, they should work harder to retrieve more details of the original passage, since the original theme could not be used to generate recall.

Results from the two experiments supported the authors' hypotheses, and were in keeping with the general position that the demands imposed upon the system, some of

Table 15-1
Ambiguous passages used by Hasher and Griffin in their study of reconstructive and reproductive recall

Titles	Initial Paragraph
"Going Hunting" "An Escaped Convict"	Passage A: The man walked carefully through the forest. Several times he looked over his shoulder and scrutinized the woods behind him. He trod carefully trying to avoid snapping the twigs and small branches that lay in his path, for he did not want to create excess noise. The gay chirping of the birds in the trees almost annoyed him, their loud calls serving to distract him. He did not want to confuse those sounds with the type he was listening for.
"Columbus Discovers a New World" "First Trip to the Moon"	Passage B: The voyage was long and the crew was full of anticipation. No one really knew what lay beyond the new land that they were heading for. There were, of course, speculations concerning the nature of the new place, but this small group of men would be the only ones who would know the real truth. These men were participating in an event that would change the shape of history.

From I. Hasher and M. Griffin, "Reconstructive and reproductive process in memory," *Journal of Experimental Psychology: Human Learning and Memory,* 1978, *4,* 318–330. Copyright © 1978 by the American Psychological Association. Reprinted by permission.

which were related to the retention situation, determined whether the representation of memory should be characterized as replicative or constructive.

Spiro (1977, 1980a, 1980b) has pointed to two other conditions that contribute to the operation of the constructive process. He has hypothesized that this process frequently operates in natural or practically relevant situations where the material to-be-remembered is not carefully separated by the experimental subject from general knowledge available about the same topic. Although only the presented material is demanded for recall, material from the general source is also found in the recall protocol. Kintsch's (1977) examination of protocols for subjects remembering the story of Joseph and his brothers is in keeping with this hypothesis.

A second condition that Spiro believes contributes to the development of a constructive process is contradictory information in the passage to be recalled. In instances where the contradictory material appears, the subject will add material to the recall protocol in order to reconcile the contradiction. Spiro (1977) termed this process *accommodative reconstruction.* A lengthy and complex study conducted by Spiro has provided experimental support for his assumptions.

The Concept of a Schema

It will be recalled that Bartlett (1932), as a result of his observations with subjects attempting to remember the narratives he provided them, introduced the concept of a schema.[7] This concept has been a popular one among many current investigators although, as Alba and Hasher (1983) have acknowledged, there has not been general agreement regarding a definition of the concept. The definition that we believe encompasses what a schema is has been provided by Rumelhart (1980). It is a theoretical construct for representing the generic concepts that are stored in memory. Schemata represent our knowledge about all concepts: those underlying objects, situations, events, sequences of events, actions, and sequences of actions. A schema contains, as part of its specification, the network of interrelations that is believed to hold normally among the constituents of the concept in question.

Rumelhart and Ortony (1977) have suggested that schemata consist of a number of properties, the most important of which are as follows:

1. Schemata include a variety of variables or features. A restaurant schema should include (a) the individuals involved (customers, waitresses, etc.); (b) objective variables (chairs, tables, etc.); and (c) specific actions (customer is seated, orders food, eats, leaves tip, and pays bill).
2. Schemata may vary in abstractness, with some being quite concrete and others being much more general. The characteristics of the constructs presented and the amount of information provided undoubtedly contribute to this property.
3. Schemata represent knowledge rather than definitions. The components, attributes, and relationships involved in a schema are not always necessary, certain, and universal; rather, they are possible or have some probability of being present. Our inclusion of tipping in the schema for a restaurant episode may be typical but it is not a necessary component of this schema.

Graesser (1981) has identified two functions of a schema. One has been described as identification. At some point in time, the comprehender secures sufficient information from the input to identify a particular schema as being relevant. As Graesser (1981) has written, "Stated metaphorically, all the schemas (sic) in long-term memory are waiting around to be identified and called to duty by the information that has been accrued" (p. 33).

A second function of a schema is application, with theorists identifying a number of processes that the schema executes during such application. One process is that it provides the background knowledge or context needed for guiding the interpretation of specific input that is relevant to the schema. A second process is to provide background

---

[7] Some investigators have proposed similar constructs described as scripts and/or frames, but differences among the three constructs—schemata, frames, and scripts—have not been made explicit. As a result, experimenters frequently provide their own idiosyncratic definitions of these constructs.

knowledge that is relevant for generating inferences. A third process is to generate expectations; a fourth is to guide the comprehender's attention; and a fifth process is relevant when the schema corresponds to goal-oriented action and skills.

Variables Influencing Schemata

The importance of a schema in understanding and remembering prose has resulted in investigators attempting to manipulate several conditions that they believe influence the schema generated by the individual. One of the most important has been identified as previous knowledge.

Previous Knowledge   Studies by Dooling and Lachman (1971) and Bransford and Johnson (1972) are illustrative of a host of studies in which investigators have demonstrated that by providing the title of a narrative (which would provide a context for the generation of a particular schema), memory for prose can be enhanced.

In the Dooling and Lachman (1971) study, subjects were provided with a metaphorical passage that was related to (1) Christopher Columbus discovering America or (2) The first space trip to the moon. The Columbus passage is reproduced below to indicate the nature of the material.

WITH HOCKED GEMS FINANCING HIM/OUR HERO BRAVELY DEFIED ALL SCORNFUL LAUGHTER/THAT TRIED TO PREVENT HIS SCHEME/YOUR EYES DE-CEIVE/AN EGG/NOT A TABLE/CORRECTLY TYPIFIES THIS UNEXPLORED PLANET/NOW THREE STURDY SISTERS SOUGHT PROOF/FORGING ALONG SOMETIMES THROUGH CALM VASTNESS/YET MORE OFTEN OVER TURBULENT PEAKS AND VALLEYS/DAYS BECAME WEEKS/AS MANY DOUBTERS SPREAD FEAR-FUL RUMORS ABOUT THE EDGE/AT LAST/FROM NOWHERE/WELCOME WINGED CREATURES APPEARED/SIGNIFYING MOMENTOUS SUCCESS (p. 217).

Dooling and Lachman found that presenting the title immediately prior to the reading of the passage produced 18% greater recall than when the title was omitted. Moreover, it was found that when subjects were asked to write out the story in their own words, more than 65% of those subjects who had been told the title were judged able to do an acceptable job, in contrast to less than 3% of those who had not been told the title.

In a subsequent study by Bransford and Johnson (1972), several experiments were conducted each of which also demonstrated the role of previous knowledge in the comprehension and recall of prose. Experiment II is illustrative of their procedure and experimental findings. Acquisition consisted of a single auditory presentation of the paragraph reproduced below.

The procedure is actually quite simple. First you arrange things into different groups. Of course, one pile may be sufficient depending on how much there is to do. If you have to go somewhere else due to the lack of facilities that is the next step, other wise you are pretty set. It is important not to overdo things. That is, it is better to do too few things at once than too many. In the short run this may not seem important but complications can easily arise. A mistake can be expensive as well. At first the whole procedure will seem complicated. Soon, however, it will become just another facet of life. It is difficult to foresee any end to the necessity for this task in the immediate future, but then one can never tell. After the procedure is completed one arranges the materials into different groups again. Then they can be put into their appropriate places. Eventually they will be used once more and the whole cycle will then have to be repeated. However, that is a part of life.

Subjects then completed a seven-point rating scale in which they indicated their comprehension of the paragraph, followed by a retention test in which they were asked to recall the passage as accurately as they could and write down as many ideas as possible. Three groups of subjects were used: (1) a *No Topic* group in which subjects heard only the passage and were given no additional information; (2) a *Topic After* group in which the topic sentence "Washing clothes" was provided after the paragraph had been presented, and (3) a *Topic Before* group in which the topic sentence was provided prior to the paragraph being presented. The mean comprehension ratings and mean number of ideas recalled are provided in Table 15–2. These findings, in addition to similar results obtained from two other studies conducted by the authors, indicate that providing information prior to the presentation of the material will result in significantly greater amounts of recall than if no information is provided or if the information is provided after the material has been presented.

Amount of Information   A second condition that has been found to contribute to the nature of the schema and subsequent recall is the amount of information that the subject has about the topic or the particular domain that is represented by the schema. A series of experiments by Chiesi, Spilich, and Voss (1979) was conducted using groups of subjects who had either high (HK) or low (LK) domain knowledge of baseball. (A 40-item completion test examining an individual's knowledge of the terminology and principles of the game was used to identify the LK and HK groups.) In one experiment (Experiment 3), the authors hypothesized that the immediate memory for sequences of baseball events, as indicated by presenting varying passages of baseball information, should be greater for the HK subjects. The findings supported their hypothesis, with the HK group revealing approximately 20% greater recall than the LK group's recall. These results, in addition to the results of several other experiments conducted by Chiesi and associates, have indicated that schema-related prior knowledge produces improved memory for new information that is in the same domain. If such information

	No Topic	Topic After	Topic Before
Comprehension	2.29	2.12	4.50
Recall	2.82	2.65	5.83

Adapted from data provided by J. D. Bransford and M. K. Johnson, "Contextual prerequisites for understanding: Some investigations of comprehension and recall," *Journal of Verbal Learning and Verbal Behavior*, 1972, 11, 717–726.

Table 15–2
Mean comprehension ratings and mean number of ideas recalled

is not present (as would be anticipated in the LK groups), there is no available schema into which new information can be integrated and is therefore quickly forgotten.

In general, the interpretation of the finding we have presented is relatively straight-forward. In the Dooling and Lachman (1971) and Bransford and Johnson (1972) studies, the introduction of the topic sentence or title of the narrative, prior to the presentation of the material to be recalled, brings to mind the general information that the subject has about the domain of the schema. Such information aids in the organization and comprehension of the experimental material for which recall is demanded at a later time. In the Chiesi, Spilich, and Voss (1979) study, the schema for a high knowledge group is more extensive, elaborate, and better organized, which in turn results in facilitating retention for material in that domain.

The Role of Information Processing ►

The approach adopted by many of the experimenters whose work we have just presented can be described as descriptive since their objective has been to describe what appears to be taking place when prose is placed in memory. Some investigators, however, have assumed that the information processing position, described in Chapter Fourteen and which represented such a viable foundation for the examination of memory for lists of words, should be equally valuable in studying memory for prose. Of the three basic information processing constructs that have been posited, the concept of encoding has generated the most experimental interest.[8]

The Encoding Process

It will be recalled that the concept of encoding has been considered to be a process responsible for transforming external stimuli into internal information. We are not able to discuss all of the variables that have been posited to contribute to encoding of prose, but we would like to identify several of these.

Significance of the Material

In our earlier discussion of Gomulicki's (1956) research, we noted that he concluded that material placed in memory appeared to be ordered in terms of its relative impor-tance. Subsequent studies by Johnson (1970), Meyer and McConkie (1973), as well as others have also demonstrated such to be the case. Johnson's procedure was to divide a prose passage into linguistic units and then obtain measures of the importance of these

---

[8] Some of the concepts used in a descriptive analysis of prose, and constructs used in the information processing point of view, are not necessarily incompatible. For example, variables that have been related to the operation of the encoding process can also be considered as contributing to the establishment of a schema.

units, following which he related such importance to their probability of being recalled. Bartlett's (1932) "The War of the Ghosts" was the prose passage used with subjects first dividing this narrative into "pause acceptable" units. A pause was defined as a temporary suspension of the voice designed to allow readers to catch their breath and to give emphasis to the story or enhance meaning. These units were then given to other subjects who were asked to eliminate the unimportant ones without destroying the essence of the story. A rating of the importance of each unit was obtained by determining the number of times each unit was regarded by subjects as essential to the story. Six levels of importance were derived from the ratings. The last phase of the study consisted of asking groups of subjects to read the complete story twice at their normal reading rate. After retention intervals of either 15 minutes, 7 days, 21 days, or 63 days, these subjects were asked to recall the story as accurately as possible. Recall as a function of the structural importance of the linguistic units is plotted in Figure 15–2. Findings demonstrate the importance of the hierarchical unit as a basic variable in the recall of prose. Two additional experiments using other material and controlling reading time replicated these findings.

The role of importance of linguistic units in prose was also examined by Meyer and McConkie (1973). Two prose passages were obtained from articles found in a popular magazine. Judges then selected the most important idea in each of the paragraphs; secondary and tertiary ideas that described or provided additional information about the main idea were also designated. Each idea unit selected was assumed to be a single meaningful piece of information. The logical interrelationship among these idea units was then demonstrated by arranging them hierarchically—main idea at the top, units of lesser importance under the main ideas, and then units of still lesser importance under these. From this hierarchical structure, a depth score was obtained for each of the idea units. Experimental subjects were presented with the first passage and then asked to recall as much of the material as possible. The second passage was then presented and recalled. Results indicated that the proportion of idea units recalled was a function of the hierarchical depth score of the idea units. More main ideas were recalled than idea units of either medium or low value.

In summary, when the significance of the linguistic units that comprise a narrative

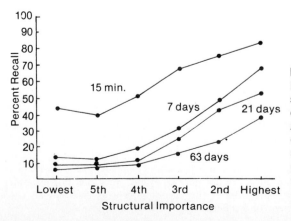

Figure 15–2
Percentage of recall of linguistic subunits of "Ghosts" as a function of levels of structural importance. Adapted from R. E. Johnson, "Recall of prose as a function of the structural importance of the linguistic units," *Journal of Verbal Learning and Behavior,* 1970, 9, 12–20. Reprinted by permission of the Academic Press.

can be judged and measured, the experimental evidence suggests that those that are rated to be highest in significance are encoded more readily, thus resulting in better recall than those units that are judged to be of lower significance.

Concreteness or Imagery

Many investigators have demonstrated memory to be a function of word concreteness, or its closely related construct, imagery, with words rated high on this dimension being more readily remembered than words rated low. It is not surprising that some experimenters have been interested in extending this finding to sentences. The experimental findings obtained by Yuille and Paivio (1969) and Marschark and Paivio (1977) have demonstrated that concrete sentences are better recalled than those that are abstract. But Marschark (1985) has suggested that there is a basic difference in the processing of unrelated sentences (which have been traditionally used), in contrast to connected discourse or prose. This difference, he has argued, is that the learning and recall of prose maximizes the relational processing among sentences—a type of processing that is minimized when unrelated sentences are used. When such relational processing takes place, Marschark has hypothesized that the role of concreteness or imagery in supporting recall is markedly reduced.

In a series of experiments designed to examine this hypothesis, paragraphs differing on two levels of concreteness (e.g., high or low) were constructed. Groups of subjects were instructed to read one type of the material for either comprehension or memory.[9] Following such reading, all subjects were asked to recall as much of the material as possible.

Scoring of the recall protocols was undertaken by dividing paragraphs into idea units; the number of units recalled was the response measure. Results revealed that significant differences were not obtained as a function of paragraph concreteness. A second study, which mirrored the first except that the material was presented in a slightly different form, confirmed these findings. The results of both studies were consistent with Marschark's (1985) suggestion that the influence of concreteness depended on the extent to which there was relational processing among the to-be-remembered items. In order to examine this explanation, Experiment 3 consisted of providing groups of subjects with the same high and low concreteness paragraphs that were used in Experiment 2. For one group, however, the ordering of the sentences within the paragraph was randomized, whereas for the other group, there were not. Here, the ordering of the sentences provided a coherent picture of the narrative.

Results for both high and low concreteness paragraphs as a function of whether the sentences were randomized or formed a coherent grouping are presented in Figure 15-3. As can be noted, the role of concreteness appears to be dependent on the lack of contextually related processing. In fact, presenting the sentences in the paragraph in

---

[9] Memory instructions to subjects emphasized that there would be a recall test, whereas comprehension instructions indicated that questions about the paragraph would be asked. Results revealed no difference in recall between the two sets of instructions.

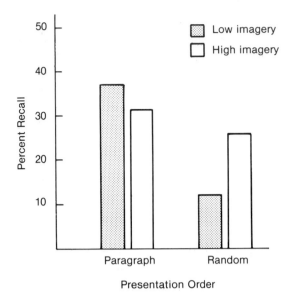

Figure 15-3
Mean recall: Experiment 3. Adapted from M. Marschark, "Imagery and organization in the recall of prose," *Journal of Verbal Learning and Verbal Behavior,* 1985, *24,* 734–745. Copyright© 1985 by Academic Press. Reprinted by permission.

random order produced a 2:1 advantage in recall for paragraphs rated high in concreteness in contrast to those which were rated low.

Wattenmaker and Shoben (1987) have identified Marschark's findings as a contextual availability model. In three separate studies, these investigators have obtained findings supporting the role of context in eliminating the role of concreteness, concluding, "The normally robust effects of concreteness observed with individual words and sentences disappeared when concrete and abstract sentences were embedded in a thematic context" (p. 148).

These results suggest that in certain instances, experimental findings may have relevance only for a particular type of material; thus the conclusion that a given variable has an effect on a particular type of material does not necessarily mean that such findings can be generalized to other classes of material. The problem of generality, which we discussed in Chapter Eleven, has relevance to this area of research as well.

The Role of Elaboration   Another encoding variable can be identified as elaboration. The concept of elaboration, as proposed by Anderson and his colleagues, can be related to the subject receiving a set of multiple propositions during the learning phase, which results in a deeper processing of the material and which in turn facilitates recall. Thus, Bradshaw and Anderson (1982) have suggested that if the subject generates a memory episode that encodes a set of multiple propositions that are partially redundant with the to-be-remembered information, the individual would have a much better chance of recalling the information at the time of test.

This hypothesis was examined in a series of experiments. Subjects were presented with a basic fact (e.g., "Newton became emotionally unstable and insecure as a child."). Two elaboration groups received additional information that was relevant to this proposition: (1) a "caused-by" condition in which the following statements were provided: "Newton's father died when he was born," and "Newton's mother remarried and left him with his grandfather"; and (2) a "resulted-in" condition which consisted of the following: "Newton became irrationally paranoid when challenged by colleagues," and "Newton had a nervous breakdown when his mother died." In addition, a third group was presented with two unrelated statements: "Newton was appointed Warden of the London mint," and "Newton went to Trinity College in Cambridge." Finally, a fourth group received only the basic proposition that we presented earlier.

Three similar experiments were conducted. Groups of subjects were presented with the kind of material illustrated, followed by immediate and/or seven-day retention test. The authors reported, "In every experiment, we found recall performance for the central fact to be best when it was supported by related facts, next best when [the statement was presented] alone, and worst when studied along with unrelated facts" (p. 172).

Lockhart, Craik, and Jacoby (1976) and Jacoby and Craik (1979) have provided a different conceptualization of elaboration, positing that task difficulty will result in the processing of many features and/or associations. Because of the multiple or elaborate processing that takes place, those parts of the text that are difficult should be better remembered than the less difficult.

In a series of studies, McDaniel and his associates have used task difficulty from which to infer the process of elaboration. Most interestingly, they have attempted to integrate the contribution of elaboration with the construct of a schema, which, as we noted earlier, also makes an important contribution to retention. In two experiments, (McDaniel, 1984—Experiments 2 and 3), the contributions to retention of both (1) elaboration (inferred from task difficulty) and (2) a schema was investigated. A narrative was used as the experimental material. Reading from the perspective of either a thief who specialized in burglarizing private homes, or a prospective home buyer, judges identified 24 idea units that were most important to the story and 24 idea units that were of least importance. The story was then typed so that half of the most important, and half of the least important idea units were composed of words with deleted letters.[10] One group of experimental subjects was instructed to adopt the perspective of a burglar, thus providing them with a schema or general idea of the theme of the story. A second group was provided with a different schema since they were instructed to adopt the perspective of a home buyer. In addition, all subjects were informed that they would encounter some words with missing letters and that, while reading the story, they should fill in the missing letters. Subjects were not forewarned about the recall task, but after completing the reading and solving arithmetic problems for five minutes they were asked to write down as much of the story as they could remember.

Experiment 3 was a replication of Experiment 2 except that a narrative about the activities of two sea gulls was used as the experimental material. Judges rated the

---

[10] The deletion operation was designed to prevent subjects from immediately recognizing these words, thus resulting in the subjects having some difficulty in comprehending the material. The deletion operation had been used previously by McDaniel (1981), who found that it did result in increasing recall.

importance of 60 idea units contained in the story; one group adopted the perspective (schema) of a florist, and the second group adopted the perspective (schema) of a shipwrecked person. On the basis of these ratings, the 20 most important and least important units relevant to each perspective was identified. Half of the important and half of the unimportant idea units were composed of words with deleted letters. Instructions to the experimental subjects were similar to those provided in Experiment 2. The findings from both experiments revealed that deleting the letters of words contained in the idea units increased the difficulty of comprehension and resulted in increased recall of that information. These findings are in keeping with results of an earlier study by the author (e.g., McDaniel, 1981) and agree with the findings obtained by Bradshaw and Anderson (1982). McDaniel (1984) has also suggested that increased recall was related to the increased accessibility of memorial representations resulting from the schema provided by having subjects adopt a particular perspective. But since groups of subjects were not used to control for the addition of the schema, this latter conclusion is gratuitous.

The contribution of task difficulty in facilitating memory has been further explored by Einstein, McDaniel, Bowers, and Stevens (1984), and has resulted in their hypothesizing that memory for prose involves two qualitatively different types of processing. One type, relational processing, involves the encoding of relationships existing among the ideas contained in the passage. The second type of processing involves the encoding of proposition-specific information. The operation of these two encoding operations was assumed to take place in the following manner: With the reading of normal prose, relational information is readily encoded so that extensive encoding of the individual items or propositions is maximized. In contrast, if the prose passage is difficult to comprehend, extensive relational processing must be undertaken in order to make sense of the material—a factor that results in minimizing the encoding of proposition-specific information.

In an experiment designed to examine this general position, two operations manipulating task difficulty were carried out. One was the letter deletion task, which the authors believed facilitated proposition-specific processing; the second difficulty task was to provide an ambiguous passage of prose that would encourage relational processing. The experimental material for this latter task consisted of the passage taken from Bransford and Johnson (1972) which describes washing clothes. Four different conditions involving the two difficulty operations were provided: (1) letters deleted, with the title of the ambiguous passage provided; (2) letters deleted, no title for the ambiguous passage; (3) no letters deleted, with the title of the ambiguous passage provided; and (4) no letters deleted, with no title for the ambiguous passage.

Following the presentation of these modifications of the text, subjects were asked to recall as much of the material as possible. There were 37 propositions contained in the passage; recall for the gist of these propositions were the response measure employed. In keeping with the author's hypotheses, results indicated an interaction between the type of processing and passage structure; thus, the effectiveness of the different difficulty tasks in facilitating recall was dependent on the structure of the passage. As Table 15–3 reveals, relational processing led to higher recall than proposi-

Passage Structure	Types of Processing	
	Proposition Specific	Relational
Explicit	14.9	12.0
Ambiguous	4.9	10.0

Adapted from data provided by G. O. Einstein, M. A. McDaniel, G. A. Bower, and D. T. Stevens, "Memory for prose: The influence of relational and proposition-specific processing," *Journal of Experimental Psychology: Learning, Memory and Cognition*, 1984, *10*, 133–143. Copyright © 1984 by the American Psychological Association. Reprinted by permission.

Table 15-3
Mean recall as a function of processing and passage structure

tion-specific processing with the ambiguous passage, whereas proposition-specific processing produced higher recall than relational processing with the explicit passage.

The authors have indicated that these findings provide support for their general position that prose memory can be best explained through the combined influence of proposition-specific and relational information processing. Each type of encoding is beneficial to recall but each influences recall through a different mechanism.

Summary ▶

Many experimenters in the verbal learning area have extended their investigations to an examination of prose or connected discourse. Current investigators have taken as their point of departure the early work of Bartlett (1932) who, in his examination of subjects learning prose, suggested that memory for this material was related to the use of a schema, as well as two basic memory processes: (1) abstraction or reproduction and (2) construction.

Abstraction refers to a process in which the number of omissions in recall increases as the amount of prose presented to the subject increases. The studies of Gomulicki (1956) and Johnson (1986) have suggested that it is intact phrases rather than isolated words that are omitted, particularly when free recall is used to measure retention.

Bartlett noted that many of his subjects introduced new material into the recall protocols in order to have the story make sense and identified such changes as arising from a process, which he identified as construction. Thus, he believed that remembering was not the reexcitation of innumerable, fixed, fragmentary traces but represented an imaginative reconstruction built from the subject's organized past experiences.

Current investigators have demonstrated the construction process operating in many different types of experiments. For example, Kintsch read to his subjects the biblical story of Joseph and his brothers. If a retention test immediately followed presentation of the story, the subject's recall faithfully followed the material. But if recall was delayed for 24 hours, subjects were unable to differentiate between what Kintsch had presented and their general knowledge of Joseph. Although some psychologists believe that most remembering can be related to the operation of a construction process, others believe that this process does not play a particularly important role in remembering.

Bartlett was also responsible for introducing the concept of a schema—a complex concept derived from past experiences that guides the organization of incoming material that is placed in memory. Many investigators have demonstrated the importance of providing the experimental subject with a schema that effectively facilitates the remembering of material.

Some experimenters have adopted an information processing approach to the study of prose; encoding represents the construct that has been most frequently examined. The role of (1) importance of the varying units that make up the passage and (2) the process of elaboration, both of which have been hypothesized as encoding processes, have been shown to influence recall.

chapter sixteen

▶

The Learning and Performance of Motor Skills

This last chapter is concerned with the learning and performance of motor skills—a topic of basic importance for all humans since it is necessary to use motor skills of one variety or another all of our lives. Walking, riding a bicycle, typing, driving an automobile, operating a lathe, and playing golf and tennis are only a few of the large number of motor skills that individuals may acquire. Motor skills tasks, at least those that are quite simple, differ markedly from the verbal learning and memory tasks examined earlier, hence our separate consideration of them in this chapter.[1]

A Bit of History ▶

In his review of motor skills learning, Adams (1987) has pointed to three historical periods that can be identified with the research efforts of investigators interested in this topic. The early period began with Bryan and Harter's (1897, 1899) study of the

---

[1] Investigators working in the area of motor skills have made a distinction between the (1) learning of motor skills and (2) control processes operating in motor skills tasks. Studies in this latter area can be related to answering such questions as, What are the conditions that are operative when individuals are controlling their limbs during the performance of a skilled response? or How do individuals control their limbs during such performance? Motor skills learning is concerned with an examination of those variables that contribute to the acquisition of the skill.

acquisition of the sending and receiving of Morse code and was conducted about the same time that Pavlov and Thorndike were investigating animal learning. During this period, interest was directed toward the examination of specific skills (e.g., Book, 1925, studied the acquisition of typing) although simple tasks such as line drawing were also used. Much experimental interest was directed toward an examination of learning curves that were derived from the acquisition of these skills.

The middle period of motor skills research was marked by two events taking place in the early 1940s. The first was World War II, during which the United States found it necessary to select thousands of inductees for pilot training. Previously, pilot selection was conducted by flight surgeons who interviewed candidates and judged their competence for flight training on the basis of an Adaptability Rating for Military Aeronautics. The need to train thousands of flight crews dictated that a more efficient selection procedure be used—a need that was answered by the construction of test batteries which included motor skills tasks.

The second event was the publication of Hull's *Principles of Behavior*. This volume, as we indicated in Chapter One, was directed primarily at the analysis of classical and instrumental conditioning, but there were parts of it, notably Hull's theoretical section on inhibition, that had relevance for motor skills research.

These events resulted in motor skills research laboratories being established all over the United States during the late 1940s and 1950s. But there was a rapid decline of these programs in the 1960s, an important reason being the lack of federal support for research. A second reason was that there was a decline of interest in providing a theoretical framework for motor skills learning since Hullian theory, which had been a primary source of experimenter interest, was no longer viable. Finally, there was a growing emphasis on information processing and the role of cognitive constructs, and investigators were slow in recognizing that motor skills tasks could also be used in the examination of these processes.

The 1970s ushered in the present or current period of motor skills research. The decline in interest noted in the 1960s was reversed by the concern of physical education specialists, as well as by a few dedicated psychologists who continued to be interested in the learning of motor skills. Adams (1987) has written:

> *Physical education specialists had been training skills since the games of ancient Greece and they have both a great deal of interest in it and practical wisdom on how it is done. ... The movement's philosophy was that experimental science is a source of new insights into the training of skills. The research that came from this movement was rationalized by the needs of physical education, but often it fit the mold of experimental psychology (p. 58).*

A Definition of Motor Skills Learning ►

When the learning of a motor skills task is examined, the experimenter is interested in determining how the organism's muscular responding or response movement changes as a function of the subject's practice or experience. The novice golfer does not know how to swing a golf club correctly; similarly, the aspiring quarterback lacks the skill to throw an adequate forward pass. It is only after long hours of practice that proficiency in these skills is acquired.

Motor skills learning can be defined as a neurological process that arises from experience or practice and is inferred from the behavior that is identified as a "skill."[2] A problem has been in differentiating what is meant by a skill from those types of responding that have been subsumed under other learning categories (e.g., instrumental conditioning, etc.).[3] Fitts and associates (1959) provided probably the best solution when they wrote that motor skills learning emphasized the acquisition of temporal-spatial organization of muscular movement in a precise and consistent manner. *Spatial organization* refers to the fact that appropriate muscles must be selected and used in a graded manner in skilled performance, whereas *temporal organization* refers to muscular contraction and/or relaxation that must occur at the precise moment. Fitts and colleagues further pointed out that motor skills learning places emphasis on three specific conditions: (1) response constancy, (2) timing and anticipation, and (3) feedback.

Fitts and colleagues used the concept of response constancy to mean that on successive occasions, individuals are able to select from a number of available response patterns, the specific response that will enable them to achieve a uniform outcome. The student is able to throw crumpled pieces of paper into a wastebasket using a variety of throwing motions and from different places in the room; thus, these differing response patterns enable him to hit the target consistently. Or one can vary the size of one's signature as the occasion demands, yet legibility is not lost and all of these signatures reveal a basic similarity.

Timing and anticipation is the second condition that helps to define a motor skill. Appropriate timing is obviously a critical aspect of the muscle pattern that characterizes skilled motor activities. In describing a good golf swing, for example, the golf instructor emphasizes the proper timing of the action of the hands, arms, shoulders, hips, and so on. But timing, at least with externally paced tasks, is impossible unless one can anticipate the pattern of the stimulus events to be presented; anticipation thus becomes an important correlate to timing.

Feedback represents the last condition that Fitts and associates posited to play an important role in motor skills learning. Most skilled performance provides the individual with some sensory feedback; that is, the individual obtains information from the

---

[2] We have assumed the neurological process related to the acquisition of motor skills to be basically the same regardless of the type of learning paradigm under consideration (e.g., classical conditioning, etc.). Recently, theorists have suggested that this assumption is undoubtedly false, and that different learning paradigms can be related to different neurological processes. See Oakley (1983), Pribram (1984), Ruggiero and Flagg (1976), and Tulving (1985) for a discussion of this topic.

[3] One solution has been proposed by Adams (1987) who, in his discussion of motor skills learning, has identified three basic characteristics of a skill: (1) the skill has a wide behavioral domain, with such behaviors almost always being complex; (2) the skill is learned; and (3) the goal attainment is importantly dependent on motor behavior.

action of his or her muscles, as well as other sense organs. Feedback provides the subject with cues or internal stimuli which, as we shall demonstrate in a subsequent section, can make an important contribution to the learning process. But we would suggest that what some investigators have identified as extrinsic feedback, or knowledge of results, is also important in motor skills tasks. This refers to the learner obtaining some information about the success (or failure) of the motor skills response in reaching a given criterion.[4]

Motor Skills Tasks ►

It becomes very difficult to provide a definition of a motor skill which in the abstract will successfully discriminate this type of activity from the kinds of responding that have been intimately associated with other learning tasks. For example, maze learning has rarely been considered to be a motor skill, and yet many definitions of motor skill would include it. Some years ago, Hilgard (1951) indicated that it was the learning experiments themselves that defined the field of learning; so it may be said that the kinds of motor skills tasks that are used by investigators in the field also define what has been traditionally considered to be the motor skills domain.

An examination of current research reveals experimenter interest in two general categories of motor skills tasks. The first category includes those tasks that, for the most part, are found in our normal everyday experiences. Obvious examples are learning to type, drive an automobile, play a musical instrument, or participate in some sports activity such as golf, tennis, and the like. The second category of learning tasks can be described as laboratory-designed tasks, and the motor skills literature reveals a large array of them. Many of these tasks have been designed to examine simple types of activity such as linear movement, tracking, rate of tapping, or muscular coordination and equilibrium. Some of the more frequently employed are discussed here.

Linear Movement

In an early study, Thorndike (1927) asked blindfolded subjects to draw a straight line of a given length. The instructions were quite simple: "Draw a three inch line." The subject proceeded to draw a line that he or she believed was this length.

Investigators have long been interested in how linear movements are made with the hand and/or arm. One type of apparatus used to examine this response consists of a knob or handle that slides along a long metal bar. The task of the subject, who is blindfolded, is to grasp the knob with the preferred hand and move it along the bar for

---

[4] Any completely satisfactory definition of skill should undoubtedly include the concept of efficiency. Sparrow (1983) has concluded that efficiency of performance should be viewed as a property which emerges from some more fundamental organizing principle of muscular responding.

a distance that the subject believes matches the distance asked for by the experimenter. By using such a simple task, the experimenter can focus interest on the operation of specific motor skills variables, such as muscular feedback and knowledge of results, which contribute to the individual learning to respond correctly.

Tracking

Another laboratory task requires the subject to track a moving target—the rotary pursuit is an excellent example of this kind of motor skills task. Here, the subject attempts to keep a hinged stylus on a small brass target that revolves on a turntable at a constant speed. (See Figure 16–1.)

Reciprocal Tapping

Here, subjects must tap two rectangular metal plates alternatively with a stylus. Movement tolerance and amplitude are controlled by adjusting the width of the plates and the distance between them. (See Figure 16–2.)

Equilibrium

Some investigators have been interested in using tasks examining muscular activity involved in maintaining equilibrium. One of these involves the stabilimeter. The subject stands on a small platform and attempts to maintain body balance for a fixed interval of time (trials). The extent of the subject's movement in maintaining balance is recorded. (See Figure 16–3.)

Figure 16–1
Rotary pursuit apparatus. The subject attempts to keep the stylus on the small metal disk that revolves with the turntable. Contact time is recorded on a clock. The stylus is hinged to prevent the subject from exerting pressure on the disk. Courtesy of Lafayette Instrument Company.

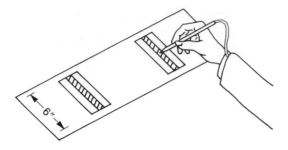

Figure 16-2
Illustration of a reciprocal tapping apparatus. The task for the subject is to hit the center plate on each side alternately without touching the adjacent plates.

A somewhat different way of examining balance is to use the Bachman (1961) ladder-climbing task. The apparatus is a free-standing ladder in which the subject must climb the ladder without skipping rungs until balance is lost and the subject and ladder topple over. The subject is instructed to return to the starting point position and continue to climb again, continuing until there is the termination of a fixed time interval which defines a trial. Figure 16–4 illustrates this apparatus.

Complex Skills

The tasks that we have described involve simple muscular skills; however, some investigators have been interested in more complex tasks, many of which have had their origins in the United States Air Force Psychology Program for pilot selection. One of

Figure 16-3
Stability platform. This instrument is used to evaluate the individual's ability to maintain bodily balance or equilibrium over a period of time. Courtesy of Lafayette Instrument Company.

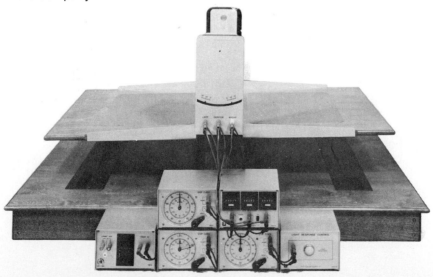

these, the Mashburn Complex Coordinator (Melton, 1947), or a modification of it (Lewis and Shephard, 1950) simulates a cockpit. It is composed of three double banks of lights: a slightly curved upper bank, a vertical bank, and a lower horizontal bank. Each bank consists of a row of red and a row of green pilot lamps, 13 per row. When lighted, the red lamps served as stimuli, whereas the green lamps can be separately illuminated by the subject through the movement of a handstick and a footbar—movements that simulate control of the aileron, elevator, and rudder of an airplane. On each trial, three red lights are lighted, one in each of the three double banks of lights, and the subject is

Figure 16–4
Bachman ladder

required to manipulate the controls so that the green lights match the red ones. When a match is made, a new combination of red lights is presented. (See Figure 16–5.)

The Course of Motor Skills Learning ▶

Many of the motor skills tasks performed in our everyday environment or studies in the laboratory are reasonably complex, requiring a long time for an individual to attain proficiency. Intuitively, it appears that in learning such a skill one moves through a number of steps or transitions. Beginning as only a crude approximation of the desired skill, the responses become more coordinated and appropriate to the task as practice continues, finally evolving into the smooth, coordinated set of muscular responses that characterize skilled performance. These steps or transitions, also called stages, were first investigated by Bryan and Harter (1897).

Stages of Acquisition

Bryan and Harter (1897) noted an interesting phenomenon in their study of students learning to use Morse code. After observing a steady improvement in their subjects' receiving the code, they found "a long period [in] which the student can feel no improvement when objective tests show little or none." This was the discovery of the plateau phenomenon—defined as a period of no change in performance that has been preceded by and is followed by learning increments.

The authors hypothesized that in the learning of a complex skill, there is a hierarchy of habits that must be mastered by the subject. During certain phases of

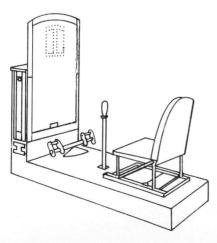

Figure 16–5
Complex coordination instrument. The stick and pedals are used by the subject to match a pattern of lights displayed on the panel. Adapted from E. A. Fleishman, "A comprehensive study of aptitude patterns in unskilled and skilled psychomotor performance," *Journal of Applied Psychology*, 1957, 41, 263–272. Copyright © 1957 by the American Psychological Association. Reprinted by permission.

learning a skill, it is necessary to replace lower-order habits with higher-order ones if performance increments are to continue. Bryan and Harter's interpretation of the plateau in the learning curve was that lower-order habits were approaching their maximum efficiency but were not yet sufficiently automatic to leave the individual free to attack the higher-order habits. Few current psychologists accept the position that the plateau phenomenon is bonafide. One reason has been that, as Adams (1987) has indicated, Bryan and Harter's findings cannot be replicated. Others believe that plateaus may be found because the method of measuring learning is not sufficiently sensitive to indicate that progress is being made. However, most investigators have accepted Bryan and Harter's position that the acquisition of a complex motor skill appears to take place in different stages.

Fitts and Posner (1967) have described three stages in the acquisition of a skill: a cognitive stage, an associative stage, and an autonomous stage. These experimenters have posited that in the early stages of learning any new motor skill, the primary task of the subject is to understand the problem and learn what needs to be done. During this stage, the subject attends to a variety of cues, many of which will be subsequently ignored. Considerable cognitive activity is manifest, since the subject must not only try to remember how similar responses were made in the past, but also use verbal responses to guide the motor activity. For example, the novice golfer, in preparing to hit the ball, may verbalize, "Bend your knees," "Head down," "Keep your left arm straight," and so on.

The second, or associative stage, consists of trying out new responses; it is during this stage that most of the erroneous responses are eliminated. Schmidt (1975a) has described this phase as the individual shifting from learning "what to do" to "how to do it." How long this intermediate phase lasts depends on the complexity of the skill and the extent to which it demands new subroutines and new integrations.

In the third phase, an automatic or autonomous one, the subject responds efficiently with errors greatly reduced and a relatively high level of proficiency. What is involved in this stage of learning? Behaviorally, the subject does not have to pay as much attention to the task as he or she had to previously in order to perform at an acceptable level of proficiency. There is some consensus that during this transition the subject's behavior comes under the control of proprioceptive stimulation, so that attention formerly directed to the task at hand can now be directed to other kinds of stimulation.

Learning to drive an automobile illustrates the operation of these stages. In the first stage, the individual learns what must be done to operate a car, whereas the second stage is one of learning how to do it. The individual often guides his or her behavior vis-à-vis self-instructions. Moreover, a variety of external stimuli control the individual's responding. The speedometer must be looked at in order to determine at what speed the clutch must be depressed and the gear shift moved, and so on. The subject's attention is directed to all of the external stimuli that are a part of the driver's environment, and there is little time to listen to the radio or engage in conversation or other activities that frequently accompany driving. Finally, the third stage is one in which the individual's driving responses are virtually automatic. The subject is able to engage in a variety of behaviors at the same time that he or she is driving.

Stages of Practice and Ability

The fact that there appear to be different stages of learning a complex motor skill suggests the possibility that the abilities the subject uses to maximize performance early in practice are not the same as those that result in optimal performance late in practice. In a series of studies, Fleishman and his associates have provided experimental evidence to support this position (e.g., Fleishman and Hempel, 1954, 1955; Fleishman, 1957, 1960; and Fleishman and Parker, 1962).

The experiment by Fleishman and Hempel (1955) illustrates the methodology and typical findings, although it should be acknowledged that these investigators did not use a task demanding a graded muscular response on the part of their experimental subjects. In the first part of their study, the experimenters used a discrimination reaction-time test in which the subject had to make different manual responses (pushing one of four toggle switches) to different visual patterns. These visual patterns were made by four lamps arranged in a square; the upper left and lower right lamps were red and the upper right and lower lamps were green. Different combinations of red and green lamps were presented, requiring different switches to be pushed; the subject's reaction time was the response measure. Twenty stimulus patterns were presented on each trial, with all subjects receiving 16 trials. The score for each trial was the total time taken to make a correct response to each of the 20 stimulus presentations. Results revealed that the mean amount of response time for the first trial was 0.45 minute, with reaction time on the fifteenth and sixteenth trials being reduced to approximately 0.25 minute/trial—a marked improvement in responding over the course of trials provided.

The second part of the study was to measure abilities that were believed to have some relevance to the subject's performance on the discrimination task that had been used. The experimenter used 9 different printed tests as well as 10 apparatus tests. Discrimination-task performance on Trials 1, 3, 5, 7, 9, 11, 13, and 15 was correlated with scores obtained on each of the 19 tests, and these findings were then subjected to a factor analysis. The results revealed nine general factors (or abilities) that contributed to discrimination-task performance.

Figure 16–6 shows the amount various factors contributed at different stages of practice. It may be noted that some of the abilities important early in practice became less so later on, and vice versa. For example, early in the training trials it was necessary for the subject to be able to identify the patterns that were arranged spatially, so a spatial-relations factor made a large and important contribution to performance on these early trials; the subject's speed of movement and reaction time, on the other hand, made a negligible contribution at this time. Later in training, however, the subject's reaction time and speed of responding made a basic contribution to performance, whereas spatial-relations ability declined in importance. What appears to have taken place was a shift over trials from a perceptual and cognitive ability to a motor ability, a finding that is in keeping with Fitts and Posner's (1967) analysis of stages of motor skills learning that we described previously.

We should indicate, however, that Fleishman's findings have not had universal acceptance since a careful analysis of his experimental results, as Adams (1987) has pointed out, reveals several problems. We shall not discuss these in detail other than to indicate that some statisticians have suggested that (1) Fleishman's use of factor analysis

Figure 16-6
Percentage of variance represented by loadings on each factor at different stages of practice on the discrimination reaction-time task. Note: Percentage of variance is represented by the size of the shaded areas for each factor. Adapted from E. A. Fleishman and W. E. Hempel, Jr., "The relation between abilities and improvement with practice in a visual discrimination reaction task," *Journal of Experimental Psychology,* 1955, *49,* 301–312. Copyright © 1955 by the American Psychological Association. Reprinted by permission.

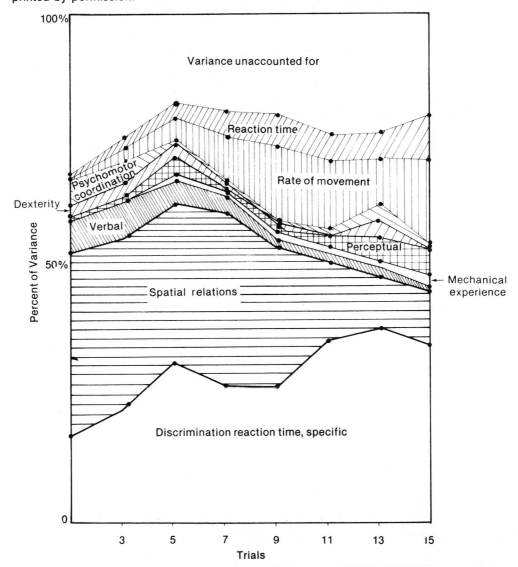

is not appropriate (e.g., Bechtoldt, 1962; Corballis, 1965; and Humphreys, 1960) and (2) there has been no independent definition of a factor or an ability. That is, the factors or abilities that Fleishman has posited are used to explain variations in the criterion learning task, but are also derived from it.

Intuitively, Fleishman's results make sense, at least to the extent that abilities that may play an important role early in training may play an unimportant role in very skilled performance. Sage (1977) has written that Fleishman's findings have some interesting implications for coaches, since some coaches assume that initial performance is related to ultimate proficiency and the rate at which it will be attained. Sage has found that some athletic coaches have selected their teams on the basis of player performance on a few practice sessions because they believe that the best performers at that point had the best potential for further improvement. The findings, he suggests, consistently reveal that the abilities that underlie this early superiority are not necessarily the abilities that underlie later proficiency levels. As a result, coaches should pause before they quickly dismiss the poorly skilled.

Variables Contributing to Motor Skills Learning ▶

The experimental variables operating with conditioned response and verbal learning tasks provide a convenient framework around which to organize those conditions that contribute to the learning and performance of motor skills. Task or stimulus and cognitive variables have been the major areas of interest for most investigators.

Task or Stimulus Variables ▶

Two task or stimulus variables that have a long experimental history are related to the conditions of practice. The first is how practice sessions should be scheduled, whereas the second is whether the task should be practiced in its totality—or whether it should be broken up into its component parts, with practice devoted to each of the parts. A third stimulus variable, which has had a much shorter experimental history, is stimulus-response compatibility.

Massed versus Distributed Practice

When a subject is given trials or practice in the learning of a motor skill, it is possible to vary the interval of time placed between trials. The terms *massed* and *distributed practice* indicate whether the intertrial interval employed is nonexistent or relatively short (e.g., 5 or 10 seconds), indicating massed practice, or long (e.g., 30 seconds or more), indicating such practice to be distributed.[5]

---

[5] In the last analysis, the concepts of massed and distributed are relative and specific to the experimental situation. Thus, if one investigator compares a 15-second intertrial interval with one of 60 seconds, the 15-second interval would be described as massed; if, however, a second experimenter examined the contribution of a 5-second intertrial interval with one of 15 seconds, the latter intertrial interval would be described as distributed.

A survey of the literature reveals that hundreds of motor skills experiments have examined performance as a function of massed and distributed practice. One of the most extensive of these was conducted by Ammons (1950) using the rotary pursuit. Some 36 trials, 30 seconds in length, were each followed by intertrial intervals of either 0, 20, or 50 seconds, 2, 5, or 12 minutes, or 24 hours. Results disclosed that the massed practice group performed most poorly. But as Figure 16–7 reveals, an examination of the varying distributed practice groups indicated no systematic relationship between the length of the intertrial interval and performance level.

There was and continues to be some unanimity among investigators that performance under some form of distributed practice is superior to that under massed practice. But the results of many of these studies, at least those conducted up until the mid-1950s, did not reveal whether performance under the massed practice condition was poorer because the learning process took place less rapidly or because there was an accumulation of fatigue (or some other type of inhibitory construct) which depressed performance. If this latter explanation is true, providing a massed practice group with an appropriate rest period should result in the dissipation of the inhibition so that their performance would "catch up" with the performance of a distributed practice group.

The results of studies by Stelmach (1969) and Whitely (1970) designed to answer this question have suggested that the *learning* that takes place under massed and distributed practice is similar, but that the massed practice condition contributes to a depression or lowering of *performance.* In Stelmach's study, two types of apparatus were employed: a stabilimeter and a Bachman ladder. Groups provided distributed practice received 16 trials consisting of 30 seconds of practice and 30 seconds of rest prior to receiving a four-minute rest period. The massed practice group received eight minutes of continuous practice prior to receiving a four-minute rest period. Following the rest period, both groups received six trials of distributed practice. Results obtained with both tasks were similar, with the findings obtained from the stabilimeter being presented in Figure 16–8. Although there was a significant difference in performance at the end of the 16 trials, the performance for both groups over the six trials following the rest period was not statistically different.

Whitley (1970) has confirmed Stelmach's (1969) findings using a fine motor learning task—a foot twist-tracking task. In contrast to Stelmach, who did not provide any rest for his massed practice group, Whitley employed 5 seconds that clearly distinguished one practice trial from the next. In this study, 25 trials of either massed or distributed practice were provided prior to providing a 5-minute rest period. The distributed practice group performed on a 25-second work/35-second rest schedule, whereas the massed practice group performed on a 25-second work/5-second rest schedule. Following the 5-minute rest period, both groups were given 10 additional distributed practice trials. Results revealed significant differences in favor of the distributed practice group at the end of the first 25 trials; performance differences between the groups were not obtained on trials following the 5-minute rest period.

Part versus Whole Methods of Practice

A subject learning a motor skill by the whole method practices the complete task from beginning to end. In contrast, the part method has the subject perform separate parts of

Figure 16-7
Performance as a function of the intertrial interval. Adapted from R. B. Ammons, "Acquisition of motor skill: III. Effects of initially distributed practice on rotary pursuit performance," *Journal of Experimental Psychology,* 1950, *40,* 777–787. Copyright © 1950 by the American Psychological Association. Reprinted by permission.

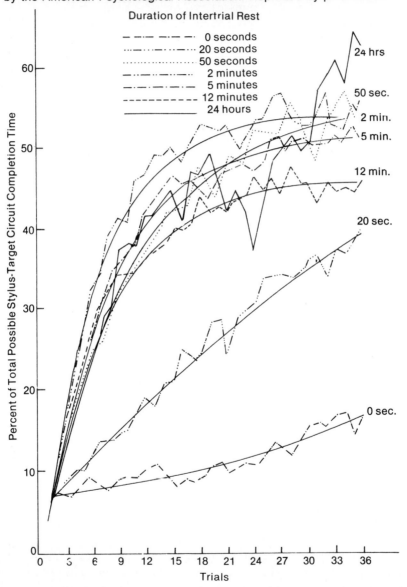

the task, with several "part" procedures being employed. A pure part method would involve the subject practicing each part of the skill prior to putting them altogether. A progressive part method would involve learning the first part of the skill, followed by the learning of the second, with the first and second parts then being practiced,

Figure 16–8
The performance curves for the distributed and massed groups on the stabilimeter.
Adapted from G. E. Stelmach, "Efficiency of motor learning as a function of intertrial
rest," *Research Quarterly,* 1969, *40,* 198–202. Copyright © 1969 by American Alliance
for Health, Physical Education and Recreation. Reprinted by permission.

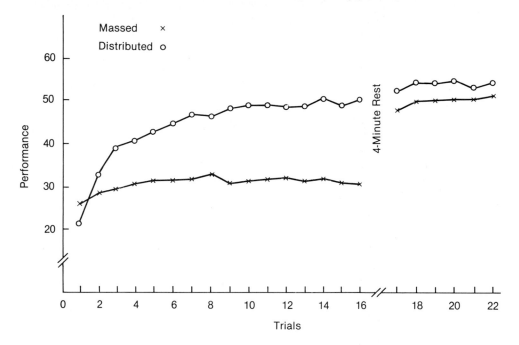

followed by practicing the third part, with parts one, two, and three being practiced,
and so on. Other variations of the part procedure have also been used. The results of
early psychological studies did not demonstrate that either the whole or part method
was superior. This inability to find a so-called best method undoubtedly contributed to
the fact that there is little interest in the topic among current psychologists.

Physical education specialists, however, have shown a continuing interest in the
problem of part versus whole methods, particularly in the practicing of sport skills.
Beginning with Cozens's (1931) early work on track and field events, a variety of skills
have been investigated in an effort to determine the superior method of practicing
them—these skills include gymnastics and tumbling (Shay, 1934; Wickstrom, 1958);
three-ball juggling (Knapp and Dixon, 1952); golf (Purdy and Stallard, 1967); and
swimming, badminton, and volleyball (Neimeyer, 1959).

The experimental findings of sports skills studies have been quite mixed, thus few
conclusions can be drawn. For example, Neimeyer (1959), in examining the effects of a
whole versus part method on the learning of swimming, volleyball, and badminton,
found that the use of the part method resulted in significantly superior learning for
volleyball, whereas the whole method was superior for swimming. No difference
between the two methods was noted in the learning of badminton.

Newell (1981) has recently advocated that if the total skill sequence can be assimilated by the subject, it should be practiced as a whole unit. In addition, many investigators have expressed the belief that training by the whole method is most efficient if the task involves some synchrony among the components—if the speed and timing of one part of the skill are critical to the operation of another. The reasoning has been that the integration of the parts is an important aspect of learning the skill and that the practice of these parts in isolation neglects the integrative component. The basketball jump shot and the golf swing are composed of almost inseparable links of muscular movement, with one link blending into and providing cues for the next link in a sequential manner. To practice such activities in a part-by-part fashion ignores the timing relationship that exists among the parts, and it is timing that is of utmost importance if optimal performance is to be achieved.

In contrast, experimenters have suggested that if the parts or the components of the skill are relatively independent of one another, it is better to practice each component separately. An obvious advantage of such part practice is that easily learned components need not be repeated, and the learner can devote most of his or her practice time to the most difficult parts of the task. Examining part versus whole methods in training individuals to operate the capstan lathe, Seymour (1954) found the part method superior because it enabled the subjects to concentrate on those parts of the task that were most difficult to perform.

Newell (1981) has also pointed out that the part method is superior if "the complexity of the action sequence is so demanding that even a basic approximation of it is beyond the scope of the learner, some breakdown of the skill into parts is probably inevitable and desirable" (p. 218).

In summary, the experimental work in the area yields only the conclusion that we cannot generalize from one skill to another as to whether one method is superior to the other. And the superiority of a particular method for a specific skill will depend upon a host of conditions, some of which are related to the length and complexity of the skill, whether the parts that make up the skill are relatively independent, and so on.

Stimulus-Response Compatibility

A more recently investigated task variable is stimulus-response compatibility. This concept is used to describe the fact that some S-R sequences can be learned more rapidly than others by nearly all of the general population. In brief, it is a kind of habitual responding or behavioral stereotype.

A commonplace example of such compatibility is found with the use of the turn signal found in automobiles. When experimental stimuli dictate that a right turn should be made, the individual responds by pushing the turn signal clockwise, whereas a proposed left turn is followed by a push of the turn signal counter-clockwise. The operation of the turn signal appears to be an obvious kind of mechanism, but it is surprising the number of times that controls devised for moving vehicles have produced stimulus-response incompatibility, with accidents a common result.

A number of experimental studies have revealed the importance of stimulus-response compatibility. One of the earliest was conducted by Fitts and Deininger (1954). The subject placed a stylus in contact with a small metal button located at the intersection of eight pathways which radiated from this point like the spokes on a wheel. The angle between each pair of adjacent paths was 45°. Figure 16–9 illustrates the apparatus. With the presentation of a specific stimulus, the subject moved the stylus in one of eight directions; reaction time was measured from the onset of the stimulus until the time when the stylus was moved into the appropriate pathway.

Although a number of stimulus sets—stimuli to which the subject had to respond in an appropriate way—were used, just two of these have interest for us. One can be described as spatial and the other as symbolic. Within each of these two stimulus sets, stimulus-response correspondence, or compatibility, can be described as (1) maximum, (2) mirrored, or (3) random. The two figure sets, along with three types of S-R compatibility, are illustrated in Figure 16–10.

Results, as indicated in Figure 16–11, reveal that stimuli that were congruent with or corresponded to the direction of the correct response yielded optimal performance, Similarly, symbolic stimuli, presented in terms of clockface numbers, also resulted in superior performance. Both of these relationships could be described as being S-R compatible. On the other hand, poorest performance arose when there was random correspondence between the stimuli and appropriate responses. Interestingly, the spatial stimulus sets resulted in significantly better performance than the symbolic ones.

An interesting aspect of compatibility involves the role of stress. It has been hypothesized that if a subject is trained to make a response that is not in keeping with the behavioral stereotype, or that it is not S-R compatible, the subject may regress to the stereotyped response when placed under stress. Fitts and colleagues (1959) report that Miquelon and Briggs have obtained some experimental support for this position. First, they trained subjects in a tracking task that required subjects to respond to targets moving either at a constant rate or with constant acceleration. Early performance on this task indicated that the subjects responded to the position of the target in space, rather than to where it would be based on its rate of movement. After training, however, the subjects learned to respond to the rate or acceleration of movement of the

Figure 16–9
Schematic of the apparatus. The example shows a stimulus from the symbolic set and a response, down and to the right, which represents maximum S-R correspondence for this stimulus. (The stimulus numeral is not drawn to scale.) Adapted from P. M. Fitts and R. L. Deininger, "S-R compatibility: Correspondence among paired elements within stimulus and response codes," *Journal of Experimental Psychology,* 1954, *48,* 483–492. Copyright © 1954 by the American Psychological Association. Reprinted by permission.

Figure 16-10
The S-R ensembles investigated. The arrows indicate the directions of response movement designated by each stimulus. Response directions were different for each subject in the case of random S-R pairing. Adapted from P. M. Fitts and R. L. Deininger, "S-R compatibility: Correspondence among paired elements within stimulus and response codes," *Journal of Experimental Psychology*, 1954, *48*, 483–492. Copyright © 1954 by the American Psychological Association. Reprinted by permission.

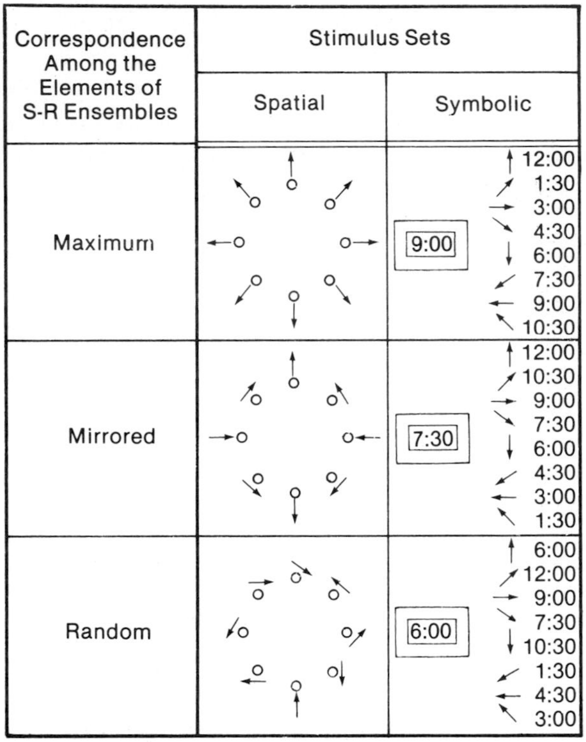

Correspondence Among the Elements of S-R Ensembles	Stimulus Sets	
	Spatial	Symbolic
Maximum	(arrows radiating in eight directions around circles)	12:00, 1:30, 3:00, 4:30, 6:00, 7:30, 9:00, 10:30 (with boxed 9:00)
Mirrored	(arrows radiating in eight directions around circles)	12:00, 10:30, 9:00, 7:30, 6:00, 4:30, 3:00, 1:30 (with boxed 7:30)
Random	(arrows radiating in eight directions around circles)	6:00, 12:00, 9:00, 7:30, 10:30, 1:30, 4:30, 3:00 (with boxed 6:00)

target. When a secondary task was introduced, making tracking more difficult and inducing stress, the experimenters noted that the subjects regressed to their early stage of training and responded to target position. This kind of finding is relevant to the accumulating evidence indicating that pilots make a number of reversal errors in interpreting their aircraft flight instruments when they are under stress (see Fitts and associates, 1959).

The Role of Sensory Stimulation—Feedback

In our examination of the contribution of stimulus conditions to motor skills learning, we have not been concerned with the role of internal stimuli, and in particular, kinesthesis. Such sensory information, associated with movement, and arising from muscles, tendons, and joints of the body, has been identified as feedback, with the role

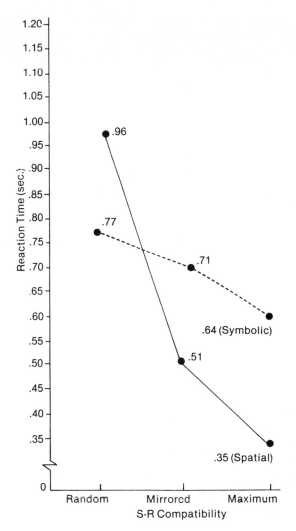

Figure 16-11
Performance as measured by reaction time as a function of varying types of S-R compatibility. Plotted from data obtained from Fitts and Deininger (1954).

some time. Kinesthesis does not, however, represent a stimulus variable that can be manipulated, but nonetheless has been accorded an important place in explanations for how skilled movement takes place. We shall delay consideration of this topic until we examine some of the varying theoretical explanations for movement.

Motivational and Cognitive Variables ►

The investigation of motor skills learning has undergone a transition from being primarily an examination of stimulus variables that can be related to performance and the contribution of reinforcement, to an orientation in which focus has been on the underlying mental or cognitive events that contribute to movement. Thus, the cognitive and information processing position, which has played such an important role in current verbal learning and memory studies, is playing a similar role in the examination of motor skills. Nowhere is the transition from an S-R reinforcement position to the cognitive explanation for behavior better illustrated than with the concept of knowledge of results (KR).

Knowledge of Results

Let us examine the concept of KR by first describing an early study by Thorndike (1927). Blindfolded subjects were asked to draw lines of either three, four, five, or six inches long. If the lines were drawn within one-eighth inch of the correct length in the case of three-inch lines, or within one-fourth inch of the correct length in the case of the other three lengths, the experimenter said, "Right." When the length of the line did not meet this criterion, the experimenter said, "Wrong." Presentation of the words *right* and *wrong* thus served as KR. Subjects were required to draw all four lines, with the number of successive repetitions of a single length varying between four and eight. In all, 600 lines were drawn, 150 of each length. Other subjects were tested without KR. Results indicated that the experimenter's statement of *right* or *wrong* significantly improved the subjects' accuracy, whereas the control groups' performance did not improve.

Thorndike viewed his results as support for his law of effect and many subsequent investigators have likened KR to the use of a reward or reinforcement in that KR has been assumed to have the function of increasing the probability of a (correct) response being made. But other investigators, particularly those supporting an information processing position have defined KR as "information that is presented to the individual from an external source after the response is completed" (Magill, 1986, p. 52). Although we may note some disagreement with regard to a completely acceptable definition of KR, there is virtual unanimity that KR is one of the most important variables contributing to the acquisition of a motor skill, with Annet and Kay (1957) referring to KR as the *sine qua non* in the acquisition of such skills.

Hundreds of experiments have followed the work of Thorndike (1927), many of which have been designed to examine how KR is influenced by a variety of conditions, with frequency, precision, and delay of KR being undoubtedly the most frequently investigated. Salmoni, Schmidt, and Walters (1984) have indicated that many investigators (like those working with massed versus distributed practice) have not used experimental designs that enable one to determine whether KR influences learning or performance. Salmoni and colleagues' analysis of appropriately designed experiments, however, as indicated by their summary of the various effects of KR on performance and learning, has revealed that in most instances, learning and performance are influenced by KR in a similar fashion. As a result, we shall call attention to the distinction between learning and performance only when disparate findings have been reported.

Frequency

It is not surprising to find that the motor skills performance can be improved by increasing the frequency with which KR is provided, with a number of investigators demonstrating this effect. To illustrate a typical finding, Bilodeau and Bilodeau (1958) asked their subjects to move a lever for a distance of approximately 33° of arc. Since a force of 20 pounds against the lever handle was necessary to move the lever, the response provided the subject with considerably more kinesthetic stimulation than one would expect to find in linear movement studies. Subjects were not informed of the specific distance they were required to move the lever, but only that their task was to find how far the lever had to be moved in order to get a "hit." On trials where KR was provided, the subject was given a verbal report on the magnitude of the error. The procedure consisted of providing 100 trials, with four groups receiving KR on every trial, or every third, fourth, or tenth trial.

The authors found that performance, as measured by reduction in error was related to the frequency with which KR was provided.

Precision

Trowbridge and Cason (1932), modeling their experimental procedure after Thorn-dike's (1927) line-drawing study, found that precise and informative KRs aided perfor-mance. More specifically, they found that subjects who were blindfolded and learning to draw a three-inch line produced less error as a result of receiving quantitative KR as opposed to either qualitative, irrelevant, or no KR. A quantitative KR was the report-ing of the amount and direction of the subject's error (e.g., plus 2, minus 3, etc.), whereas a qualitative KR was the same as reported by Thorndike (1927) (e.g., right or wrong). Trowbridge and Cason's findings have been replicated by many subsequent investigators.

Ammons (1956) has suggested that there is an optimum precision level of KR—a reasonable position since providing more precise information (e.g., going from a qualitative to quantitative KR) should be of greater aid to the subject in guiding his or her responding. But there would appear to be a point where greater amounts of precision might not be beneficial, however, and in fact, could be detrimental if the reporting was confusing or could not be related to the response. One study by Rogers (Exp. 1, 1974) has been in keeping with this position. A micrometer-positioning task was employed in which the subject had to learn to rotate a knob (attached to a hidden micrometer) a certain number of revolutions. Four groups of subjects received KR which varied in the number of digits of information that was provided. The 0-digit condition provided a qualitative KR—"too far" or "too short." The 1-, 2-, and 4-digit groups were provided KRs that were rounded to either the nearest whole unit, tenth of a unit, or thousandth of a unit. Ten acquisition trials were provided. All groups improved over the course of training; however, best performance was provided by the group receiving KR in tenths, followed by the group receiving KR in whole units.

Performance for the group receiving the most precise information was quite similar to the group receiving the qualitative KR. Figure 16–12 presents these findings.

But Newell's (1977) review has indicated that many inconsistent findings have been obtained when precision of KR has been manipulated. He has suggested that task, performance, and procedural variables undoubtedly interact with the precision variable in producing the conflicting findings. The validity of Newell's (1977) position is supported by the findings of Rogers's (1974) second experiment, which was a replication of his first except that he lengthened the time interval that followed the receiving of KR. Rogers believed that the increased time period following presentation of the KR gave his subjects more opportunity to process such information, thus suggesting an interaction between precision of the KR and the amount of time provided to process it. Results supported the experimenter's position, with the group being presented with KRs to the nearest thousandth of a unit being superior to the two other groups which were given KR to the nearest whole unit or the nearest tenth.

Delay

Delay of KR refers to manipulating the amount of time placed between the subject completing the motor skills movement and the receiving of information that is related

Figure 16–12
Mean absolute error as function of KR precision. Adapted from data obtained from C. A. Rogers, Jr., "Feedback precision and postfeedback interval duration," *Journal of Experimental Psychology,* 1974, *102,* 604–608.

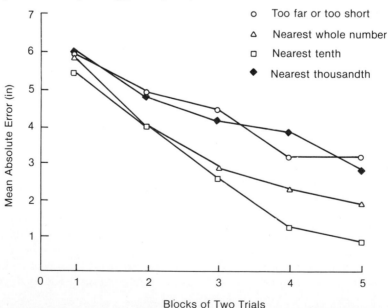

to the correctness of the response. An early study by Lorge and Thorndike (1935) illustrates the operation of this variable. Subjects were required to throw a ball at a target for 40 trials, with delays of zero, one, two, four, or six seconds interpolated between the subjects' throwing of the ball and securing the KR. Surprisingly, results indicated that the length of the delay period did not have any influence on performance, with a delay of zero seconds resulting in performance that was not any better than that found when a delay of six seconds was utilized. This was a most unusual finding since delay of reinforcement in animal learning studies generally result in poorer performance than if a no delay period is provided.

A host of subsequent studies examining the role of KR delay has provided controversial findings, with some investigators confirming Thorndike and Lorge's (1935) "no difference" result but others finding that performance was a function of the length of the KR delay. To illustrate, Greenspoon and Foreman (1956) had blindfolded subjects draw 50 three-inch lines, using a 30-second interval between trials. For Group I, the information of "long" was provided for lines longer than $3^{1}/_{4}$ inches and "right" for lines between $2^{3}/_{4}$ and $3^{3}/_{4}$ inches in length, "short" for lines shorter than $2^{3}/_{4}$ inches in length, with such information provided immediately upon completion of the response. Subjects in three other groups were also provided this information but delayed for either 10, 20, or 30 seconds following the making of the response. A control group received no information concerning the correctness of their response. As Figure 16–13 reveals, the mean number of "right" responses was a function of the length of the delay period.

Bilodeau and Bilodeau (1958) subsequently called attention to a methodological consideration that had been frequently ignored by KR delay investigators and that undoubtedly contributed to the unstable findings that characterized the area. This had to do with how the KR delay interval was filled.[6]

Although Lorge and Thorndike (1935) found that the length of the delay interval did not influence performance, they did find that if the KR referred to a previous toss, rather than the one that had been just completed, performance was quite poor. A later replication of this effect was found in an experiment (Experiment 2) by Bilodeau (1956) who had subjects pull a lever for approximately 33° of arc. The time for each trial was approximately 20 seconds, with 5 seconds between the "ready" and "pull" signals, 4 seconds for the response, and approximately 11 seconds between the end of the response and the next "ready" signal. Knowledge of results was provided 5 seconds prior to each signal. However, the experimental procedure consisted of providing either a zero-, two-, or five-trial KR delay. Thus, a two-trial KR meant that the score for the first

---

[6] Another methodological consideration to which Bilodeau and Bilodeau (1958) called attention (but which we shall not discuss in this abbreviated presentation) is the relationship existing among the three experimental time periods found in KR delay studies: (1) the time between the response and the KR, (2) the post-KR interval which involves the time between the KR and the beginning of the next trial, and (3) the interval between trials which included both the delay of the KR and the post-KR interval. See Schmidt (1982) for a discussion of this topic.

Figure 16–13
Mean number of "right" responses of the control and experimental groups for successive blocks of five trials. Adapted from J. Greenspoon and S. Foreman, "Effect of delay of knowledge of results on learning a motor task," *Journal of Experimental Psychology*, 1956, *51*, 226–228. Copyright © 1956 by the American Psychological Association. Reprinted by permission.

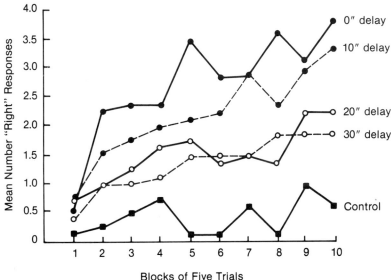

response was not given until the third response was made; for those subjects receiving a five-trial delay, KR was provided after the sixth response had been made. Thirty KR trials were provided. Figure 16–14 reveals the influence of the "trial delay" procedure. What is remarkable is that there was any change in responding over trials for the five-trial delay condition.[7]

It is apparent that with the trials-delay method of manipulating KR, there is a pairing of KR with an inappropriate response. But identifying the source of the performance decrement that takes place with the trial delay procedure is difficult. One result has been that several investigators have been interested in interpolating different types of activities between trials in an effort to determine the influence of these activities on performance.

To illustrate this approach, Shea and Upton (1976) have demonstrated that requir-

---

[7] We should alert the reader to the results of studies by Lavery (1962) and Lavery and Suddon (1962) who have found that a trials delay procedure, although producing poorer performance than KR provided immediately after each trial, resulted in superior performance during retention trials—a situation in which KR was not provided. The retention measure was used from which to infer the contribution of the previously presented KRs on learning. It should be acknowledged, however, that the trials delay procedure employed by Lavery (1962) and Lavery and Suddon (1962) was much different from those other trial delay procedures used in the earlier cited studies.

Figure 16–14
Mean absolute error in lever placement for successive pairs of KR trials. (Each data point is the mean of the mean errors of the pair of trials.) Adapted from I. M. Bilodeau, "Accuracy of a simple positioning response with variation in the number of trials by which knowledge of results is delayed," *American Journal of Psychology*, 1956, *69*, 434–437. Copyright © 1956 the University of Illinois Press.

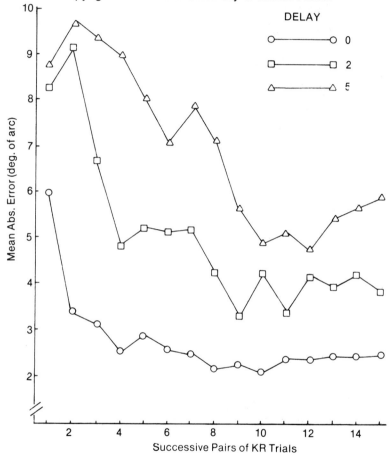

ing specific motor responses to be made during the KR delay interval can result in a performance decrement. In their study, blindfolded subjects were asked on each trial to make two separate linear responses in their moving a handle along a pair of steel rods. Response A was for a distance of 100 mm; response B was a distance of 200 mm. Approximately 30 seconds following the making of the second response, all subjects were provided a quantitative KR for both their first and second responses. It was the experimenter-determined activity taking place during each 30-second interval between trials that differentiated the two groups. The control group sat quietly; experimental subjects were asked to make two additional responses that were different from those demanded on the learning trials. All subjects were given 21 acquisition trials, and after a two-minute rest, 12 retention trials were provided without KR. As Figure 16–15 reveals, when the delay interval before receipt of KR was filled with additional movements, performance was much poorer than when such activity was not provided. It is interesting to note that when KR was discontinued (as well as the additional movements for the experimental group), performance began to deteriorate.

What seems to be taking place in this task is that subjects learn to associate the KR with a specific kinesthetic sensation which is then related to some idea of the length of the movement that was made. When there is a KR delay, it is necessary for the subject to retain in memory this associative relationship that has been (or is in the process of being) established. There is no problem in remembering the KR provided by the experimenter since it may be rehearsed. It may be more difficult to remember the

Figure 16–15
Mean absolute error scores computed over trial blocks for acquisition (KR trials) and retention trials (no KR trials). (UI = unfilled interval, FI = filled interval.) Adapted from J. B. Shea and G. Upton, "The effects on skill acquisition of an interpolated motor short-term memory task during the K-R delay interval," *Journal of Motor Behavior,* 1976, *8,* 277–281. Copyright © 1976 by Heldreth Publications. Reprinted by permission.

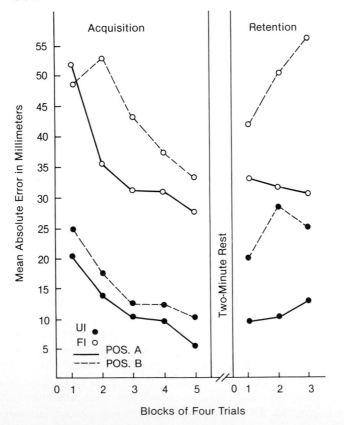

kinesthetic feeling. Moreover, it is likely that the making of other similar responses (but which generate different kinesthetic feelings) prior to receiving the KR contributes to the forgetting of the kinesthetic sensitivity that has been associated with a particular KR. We would suggest that the process operating is similar to the inhibitory process that verbal learning investigators have posited to operate in their examination of proactive and retroactive inhibition.

Kinematic Knowledge of Results or Knowledge of Performance

The early work of Thorndike (1927) using a simple linear movement followed by KR, as an example of motor skill learning, was in the tradition of those animal learning studies that involved the instrumental learning of an act that resulted in reward; thus, motor skill investigators following Thorndike directed their interest to response outcome and KR rather than the nature of the movement. Adams (1984) has pointed out that the emphasis on response acts did not reveal very much about the learning of movement sequences.

Recently, some investigators have directed their attention to skills involving movement sequences (or segments); in particular they have been interested in examining the role of KR after the completion of a segment of the skill. This area has been frequently identified as kinematic KR (KKR), which refers to information received by the subject about the correctness of the movement itself, rather than the outcome of movement that defines KR. Gentile (1972) has identified kinematic KR as knowledge of performance (KP).

An early study by Howell (1956) describes one method to examine KKR as well as the experimental findings that were obtained. The response examined was the start of the sprint race which involves series of movements taking place during the half second that elapses between the sound of the starting gun and the time that the sprinter clears the blocks.[8] Howell used an apparatus that consisted of spring-loaded starting blocks connected to a chronograph equipped with ink pens that automatically drew a graph of the force exerted as a function of time in units of 0.01 second. This response measure provided a measure of the subjects' force-time pattern of the front foot and could be compared with a theoretically ideal pattern of movement sequences that had been found to characterize the performance of experienced sprinters.

The experiment consisted of using two groups of college students with no previous track experience. An experimental group was shown their front foot, force-time pattern produced by the chronograph, along with a theoretical pattern that was considered "ideal," with instructions to subjects to try to achieve the ideal pattern during practice

---

[8] During this half-second period, the runner will have reacted to the starting gun as follows: The back leg will have thrust with pressure of perhaps 160 pounds and been swung forward, whereas the front foot commencing a fraction of a second later, will have exerted possibly 100 pounds of pressure for a longer fraction of time, and maintained until the runner has cleared the blocks.

trials. A control group was given training as provided by typical teaching and coaching techniques. Practice consisted of providing 8 to 11 running starts/day for 10 days, with the last start on each day's training being used to obtain data from which to evaluate performance differences between groups. Results revealed that the experimental group made significant increases over the practice periods in reaching the ideal force-time pattern of movement, whereas the control group did not, with performance differences between the groups being statistically significant. (See Box 16–1.)

A later study by Hatze (1976) examining a much different movement pattern has confirmed the findings of Howell (1956) in demonstrating the contribution of KKR. The task used by Hatze was quite simple—raising the right leg forward and upward with sufficient force to strike a target as rapidly as possible. Speed of movement was the response measure. A 10 kg. mass was attached to the right foot during performance trials. Traditional KR movement time information was provided for the first 120 trials of practice, with speed of responding gradually reaching a plateau of about 760 msec. Following the last trial, position-time curves of the movement of the upper and lower limb segments were superimposed on a computer-derived optimal position-time model for these respective limb parts. Performance speed immediately improved when the subject received this form of movement feedback. After 100 additional trials, the movement time approximated the time as predicted by a theoretical formulation as provided by Hatze. We may note from Figure 16–16 that the impact on performance of the movement information was most striking.

box 16–1

An interesting and early example of the use of kinematic knowledge of performance has been provided by English (1942) who has reported the procedures and results of a study undertaken shortly after World War I at an army camp in which factors involved in success at rifle shooting were examined. Recruits were instructed to squeeze the stock of their rifles as well as the trigger, with the whole hand participating in the movement as if one was squeezing a sponge. (This procedure was contrasted with a "pulling of the trigger"). As a result of the recruits' inability to comply with verbal instructions, the investigators hollowed out the stock of a rifle under the area against which the last three fingers should press in making the appropriate squeeze. In this space, a rubber bulb and tube was inserted, with a wooden plate, supported by a spring, closed over the space so that a casual inspection of the field was unaltered. The rubber tube led to a glass U-tube containing a small amount of red liquid.

The recruit was instructed to shoot in his usual fashion. A proper squeeze depressed the wooden plate and caused a change in the level of the liquid in the U-tube, which enabled the recruit to compare visually his own squeeze with that of an expert. If the recruit's squeeze was inappropriate, he continued to practice firing, at first watching the tube, but then aiming at a target without watching the tube but informed each time of his squeeze reaction. Trials continued until the recruit could fire with the proper squeeze.

English (1942) reports that positive findings were obtained using the modified rifle which provided subjects with kinematic knowledge of results (KKR). He has written, "Excellent results were obtained. Men given up as hopeless by their officers and noncommissioned officers showed rapid improvement in a large percentage of cases . . . . Nearly all, after about seven hours' drill in the laboratory, were brought up to the minimum standards for efficiency in actual range tests— much to the astonishment of the small arms instructors of their regiment" (p. 4).

Figure 16-16
Performance as a function of the subject receiving KR and KP. A small value of △ (*r*) indicates that the response is near the optimal movement. Adapted from H. Hatze, "Biomechanical aspects of a successful motion optimization," in P. V. Komi (Ed.), *Biomechanics V-B,* 1976. Copyright © 1976. Baltimore: University Park Press. Reprinted by permission.

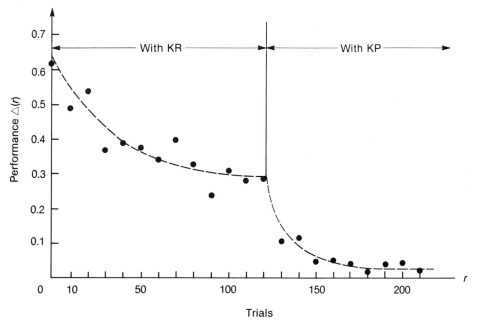

The findings from subsequent studies have not been as unequivocal in demonstrating the effectiveness of KKR as those of Howell (1956) and Hatze (1976), but nonetheless, have indicated the effectiveness of KKR. To illustrate, Newell, Quinn, Sparrow, and Walter (1983) in two experiments examined the performance of a task involving a simple arm flexion response. Here, subjects grasping the handle of a lever had to move the lever forward through a target point, with movement time being the response measure. The findings from Experiment I indicated that the presentation of discrete movement information did not provide the subjects with any information that was of greater usefulness in minimizing movement time than the presentation of KR provided after the response had been made. In a second experiment, however, when subjects were given a continuous kinematic trace of the movement, which was presented on a TV screen, the investigators' findings indicated that such information was more effective than traditional response outcome KR in improving performance.

Other procedures that have been used to provide KP have been to use videotapes of the subject in performing the required task, and another—the area of observational learning—has been to have subjects observe someone else perform, either through the use of videotapes or utilizing live models. Neither of these areas has had extensive investigation, at least as applied to motor skills tasks, and perhaps this is one reason why neither procedure has exhibited a great deal of success in facilitating levels of performance that are higher than those achieved by other procedures (e.g., use of KR).

Rothstein and Arnold's (1976) review of the literature on videotaping a subject's sequence of movement has indicated that having the subject watch his or her videotape makes a contribution to better performance; a superior procedure, however, is to draw the subject's attention to specific aspects or portions of the movement sequence. The watching or observing of one's performance can be related to the topic of observational learning, which has had a long history in experimental psychology but a neglected investigative area as well. Until Bandura's (1977) contributions, this type of learning had never entered the mainstream of learning theory. One reason was the difficulty that prominent psychologists (e.g., Thorndike, 1898, 1901; and Watson, 1908) had in demonstrating it; a second was the problem of including this type of learned behavior into the familiar stimulus-response paradigm that emphasizes the importance of reinforcement for the acquisition of S-R relationships.

Bandura's (1977) work on observational learning has influenced some motor skills investigators, and some interesting work has been done (e.g., Landers and Landers, 1973; Landers, 1975; and Martens, Burwitz, and Zuckerman, 1976), but as Newell, Morris, and Scully (1985) have suggested, the contribution of observation in influencing motor skills learning appears to be limited since it is difficult for this type of presentation to indicate to the subject the nature of the muscular tension and kinesthetic sensitivity that plays such an important role in motor skills tasks. Nonetheless, the widespread distribution of videotapes by noted sports figures demonstrating the appropriate ways to perform in such skills as golf, tennis, basketball, and the like suggest that this area is a fertile one for experimental work.

Adams has provided a model of movement sequences for the study of KKR and KR in which the movement sequence was posited to consist of a series of segments that terminated in a goal. Each segment, which may be provided with KR, makes a differential contribution to the outcome.

To illustrate, an examination of the movement sequence (or segments) that make up putting a golf ball (hopefully into the cup) might be: (1) the position of the club at the start of the swing, (2) the back swing, followed by (3) the swing forward, with the speed and direction of both the backward and forward swing being integral aspects of the movement. The KR would be determining how close the ball went into the hole, but in addition to the goal KR, it would be possible to provide KR on one or more of the segments, with such KR being related to some referent for correctness.

Adams (1987) has called attention to the importance of the sequential approach in the learning of complex skills (e.g., golf, tennis, diving, etc.) since typically only outcome KR is available, and it becomes virtually impossible for the individual to make appropriate inferences about the pertinent segments of the skill, segment weights, and segment errors in relation to goal error. He has written

> That most performers attain only a modest level of performance for popular skills over a lifetime of practice is testimony to the difficulty of this inference process. The complexities of problem solving can be greatly reduced if the performer receives segment knowledge of results along with outcome knowledge of results because he or she will then have little left to figure out alone. The

task is even easier if the trainee has an instructor who also tells him or her what to do about segment errors (p. 62).

Devising a three-segment task with speed of responding being the performance measure, Adams (1985) was interested in making a laboratory examination of his movement sequence model. The experimental variables examined were (1) the contribution of each segment to the outcome (segment weight), (2) knowledge of results provided to each segment, and (3) outcome KR. Adams found that learning took place for the entire movement sequence when only outcome KR was provided; however, the additional segment knowledge of results to outcome KR resulted in the best task performance.

Theoretical Considerations: Closed-Loop versus Open-Loop Positions

The area of control and learning of motor skills has not been without its theoretical positions. The question, How can we account for the successful completion of a sequence of movements? sets the stage for an early controversy. Psychologists were aware that kinesthetic stimulation, or what we have identified earlier as feedback, invariably accompanied movement; thus, it was not surprising that such feedback was assumed to play an important role in controlling sequential responding. William James (1890) wrote, "In action grown habitual, what instigates each new muscle contraction to take place in its appointed order is not a thought or perception, but the sensation occasioned by the muscular contraction just finished" (p. 115). Subsequently, Watson (1919) and other stimulus-response psychologists adopted a similar position in accounting for serial activity. Watson hypothesized that the specific responses that made up a serial task were chained together by kinesthetic stimulation.

But not all psychologists agreed that the response-chaining hypothesis was correct. Lashley (1917) observed a man with a spinal injury who had almost complete anesthesia in one leg. Although there were some inadequacies in his responding, he did have normal accuracy in the direction and extent of movement of the affected leg. Lashley reasoned that since the injury had eliminated kinesthetic feedback and yet there was normal movement in the leg, such movement was undoubtedly controlled by the brain and unrelated to such stimulation.

The two points of view that we have described have evolved into what psychologists have identified as *closed-loop versus open-loop positions.* The closed-loop position proposes that during the performance of skilled, sequential movements, sensory feedback is responsible for controlling as well as correcting and modifying the continuing response. One analogy for the closed-loop hypothesis is provided by the thermostatically controlled furnace. The thermostat is set for a particular temperature and the heat from the furnace is fed back into the house until the warmth of the room reaches the setting of the thermostat. At that point, the furnace cuts off and does not start again until there is another discrepancy between the thermostat setting and room temperature.

In contrast, the open-loop position hypothesizes that a motor program is structured in the brain before the movement sequence begins. This program permits the entire sequence of movements to be carried out, uninfluenced by the sensory feedback that arises from the subject's responding. Unlike the closed-loop position, the open-loop hypothesis does not specify the mechanism for correcting errors.

What kind of evidence has been brought to bear on this controversy? The closed-loop position is supported by the behavior of individuals who have tabes dorsalis, a disease that prevents them from receiving proprioceptive feedback from the limbs. As a result, walking becomes very difficult unless they are guided by visual stimulation. The individual literally has to see where to place his or her feet. The use of a procedure called delayed auditory feedback (DAF) also provides some support for the closed-loop position. Under normal circumstances, auditory feedback is received as one speaks, with such feedback making a contribution to further speech. But Lee (1950, 1951) found that delaying feedback to his experimental subjects by about a half a second caused a marked deterioration of speech fluency. More specifically, the subjects slowed down their speech, with some slurring and a kind of stuttering. This effect has been frequently replicated, as a review by Yates (1963) indicates.

But open-loop theorists have also obtained evidence to support their position. A basic argument they have made is that with some activities, particularly those involving a rapid series of movements, the speed and complexity of the skilled response is too high for the subject to receive and use proprioceptive stimulation to guide further responding. Lashley (1951) pointed out that a pianist's fingers can move at a rate of 16 movements per second in passages that call for a definite and changing order of successive finger movements. Such a succession of movements is too rapid even for visual reaction time. And Lenneberg (1967) has reported that single muscular events occur in the speech apparatus during speech production at a rate of several hundred events per second. Again, it is obvious that the activation of so many muscles within such a short time span cannot depend upon the reception of kinesthetic stimulation prior to each muscular response. Rather, there must be some complete train of events that is programmed and run off automatically.

Take the case of a subject making a very simple linear movement. Beginning with the hand at rest, movement is initiated via an abrupt acceleration followed by the hand slowing down so that it comes to rest on a target 10 cm away, all within a movement time of 100 milliseconds or less. The problem: From where do the deceleration instructions arise? It may be argued that subjects use kinesthetic feedback for information about where their hands are in space. But by the time such instructions could be issued and get to the muscles involved in stopping the hand, the hand is already at rest. Clearly, the instructions to stop the movement must be planned prior to the beginning of the movement. Such planning is assumed to arise from a motor program—defined as a set of prestructured muscle commands permitting movement to be carried out, uninfluenced by peripheral feedback.

Perhaps the strongest support for the open-loop position has been obtained from biological studies. The general approach of these investigators has been to isolate the organism's nervous system from all possible sources of sensory feedback, and then demonstrate that appropriate stimulation will elicit the normal pattern of rhythmic bursts in the motor neurons, and therefore in the muscles. Several procedures have been used to achieve this experimental objective, one of these being deafferentation. With this technique, all or some of the sensory nerves that carry information into the nervous system are severed. The effect of this operation on the capacity of the nervous system to produce the rhythmic behavior is then examined. Wilson's (1961) study illustrates the procedure and experimental findings. The desert locust was used as his experimental subject, since it can be induced to fly in the laboratory for extended periods of time and has almost constant cyclical and coordinate movements of its two pairs of wings. Wilson found that removal of portions of the insect's wings, or in fact removal of one whole wing, had no effect on the patterning of movement of the remaining wings. This finding would not be predicted if proprioceptive feedback played an important role in determining the patterning or sequencing of wing movement. Wilson concluded, "The evidence here supports strongly the notion that there is an innate central pattern for the production of flight movements in the locust" (p. 487).

Delcomyn's (1980) review of the result of experimental studies gathered over the past two decades has resulted in his concluding that the central nervous system does not require feedback from the sense organs in order to generate properly sequenced, rhythmic movement during repetitive behaviors such as locomotion. A variety of behavior patterns exhibited in many experimental subjects all have been shown to operate independently of sensory feedback; these include walking in the cat and cockroach, hopping in the rabbit and toad, swimming in the eel and shark, and flying in the dragonfly and locust.

The closed-loop theorist's rebuttal to this kind of evidence has been to acknowledge that some behavior patterns in lower animals may be controlled by the central nervous system, but certainly not all. Griffin's (1959) examination of how bats locate objects in space in order to avoid obstacles and secure insects for food reveals such activity functions by means of a closed-loop system. Griffin has indicated that certain species of bats track flying insects by means of echolocation—there is the emission of short pulses of high frequency sounds, with the echoes of such sounds serving to inform these mammals about the nature and position of objects in space, thus permitting their capture.

The Dual-Position Model

An examination of the evidence marshalled in support of either the closed-loop or the open-loop position suggests that neither of these explanations for the control of motor skills behavior can successfully account for all of the experimental findings. Both open-loop and closed-loop systems operate in guiding the behavior of infrahumans, so it would seem most unusual if both systems were not operative in human behavior.

Glencross (1977) has proposed a two-stage model of human motor skills responding which incorporates both closed- and open-loop explanations. In the first stage, the control system depends on feedback, whereas the second stage incorporates an open-loop system in the form of a motor program which, once initiated, will normally run its full course without the need for feedback. A basic problem, however, has been to examine the role of open- and closed-loop positions with humans because feedback, and in particular kinesthesis, is difficult to experimentally manipulate.[9]

A few studies, however, have suggested that the acquisition of a skill depends on both sensory stimulation as well as some type of motor program, thus supporting Glencross's (1977) two-stage model. In an experiment by Pew (1966), the apparatus consisted of a cathode ray display in which a target moved continuously from right to left of a midpoint. It was the subject's task to keep the target at midpoint by proper timing of alternating presses on a right-hand and left-hand response key. The speed of the target was one variable that the experimenter manipulated; as one might anticipate, as target speed increased, performance in keeping the target at midpoint became poorer. What Pew also found was that subjects developed two different strategies over the course of the practice trials. Early in practice, responding was slow, with the subject depending on feedback from responses made to the movement of the target. For example, the right-hand key would be depressed and the subject would wait for feedback concerning the effectiveness of the response. This would then be followed by a corrective left response, and so on. A closed-loop position would best describe such responding since such activity depended on feedback from the subject observing the position on the target. Later in practice, however, a different kind of strategy developed—the subject responded continuously with both the right and left keys. If the target drifted to the left, the subject would continue to maintain dual responding by increasing the length of time the right key was active relative to the left. Through a series of alternating responses, the subject could make the target drift back toward the center. This strategy, in contrast to the one adopted earlier in practice, would be in keeping with an open-loop program, since the subject was responding at a more rapid rate than would have been possible if such responding depended on feedback.

Current Theory

In recent years, the closed- and open-loop positions have been incorporated into more general theoretical positions designed to answer the question, How are motor skills learned? Theories proposing to answer this question have been provided by Adams (1971, 1976, 1984) and Schmidt (1975b, 1982).

---

[9] One exception to this is a procedure identified as the ischemic nerve block technique, whereby the continued application of a pressure cuff to a limb blocks sensory information. Laszlo and her colleagues have made extensive use of this procedure in examining the closed-loop and open-looped positions (e.g., Laszlo, 1966, 1967; Laszlo, Shamoon, and Sanson-Fisher, 1969; and Laszlo and Bairstow, 1971). But Glencross and Oldfield (1975) and Scott-Kelso and Stelmach (1974) have reported that this technique results in extensive motor impairment as well as sensory loss. Glencross (1977) has written, "The motor deficit observed following ischemic nerve block is not solely the result of blocked kinesthetic sensation, and thus its relevance to the issue of central versus peripheral control of movement cannot be directly assessed" (p. 21).

Adams's Closed-Loop Theory

Adams (1971, 1976, 1984) has proposed a closed-loop theory that emphasized perceptual and cognitive constructs. He has posited that a subject's movements certainly in the
form of kinesthetic stimuli provide feedback to the subject, thus providing a memorial
representation on each trial. This representation is called the *perceptual trace*. At the
start of trials, beginning with the second, the perceptual trace is aroused, and as the
subject responds, the response-produced feedback that has been elicited by the movement is compared with the perceptual trace. The appropriate matching of the feedback
and the perceptual trace is a signal that the correct movement has taken place. It should
be emphasized that the perceptual trace is not a unitary construct but rather reflects the
mode of the distribution of traces that have been formed over trials. If the response was
wrong, a knowledge of results will report it; in addition, the mismatch of the feedback
and the perceptual trace will also produce a subjective feeling of error. The subject will
then see the necessity for changing the response on the next trial.

We may note then that Adams (1987) has posited that knowledge of results and
feedback—perceptual trace comparison—are both sources of error information and
complement each other on acquisition trials in which KR is provided. In the absence of
KR, the subject still has information available, providing the perceptual trace is developed and responses produced feedback is sufficient to respond appropriately.

This aspect of Adams's theory emphasizes that motor learning is at heart a
perceptual process. The subject relies on the perceptual trace whether he or she is asked
to generate a response in recall or to recognize a response that has been made before.

But a second postulate qualifies the first by stating that another construct, the
memory trace, which is nonperceptual, is required to start the movement. There can be
no feedback before the response begins, so the perceptual trace as an instigator of action
cannot be used. The memory trace is hypothesized to be a brief motor program that
selects and initiates the response, thus preceding feedback and the use of the perceptual
trace.

Adams believes that motor learning does not always require KR. Knowledge of
results is required early in learning inasmuch as the subject has no idea of what the
correct response is to be and so it must be shaped by an external source. As learning
advances, and the perceptual trace becomes well developed, the subject on the basis of
internal error sensing can rely less on KR. Theoretically, KR, as an external source of
error information, can then be withdrawn and the subject proceed with learning using
the internal source of error alone. Learning that takes place without KR and from an
internal error source is identified as subjective reinforcement.

A crucial aspect of Adams's theory is the strong role that he provides for feedback.
Performance on acquisition trials with KR and on trials without KR should be
positively related to the amount of feedback. In addition, the greater the experience
with feedback over trials, the more stable performance should be on trials when KR is
withdrawn, since learning should occur as a function of subjective reinforcement. What
is most important is that feedback should be related to error detection and correction,
which is a requirement of a closed system.

Schmidt's Schema Theory

Schmidt (1975a, 1975b, 1982) has used the concept of a schema, borrowed from the work of Bartlett (1932) which we have described in Chapter Fifteen, to describe his theory of motor skills learning. As we have earlier noted, Bartlett, examining the recall protocols from *The War of the Ghosts,* came to the conclusion that a memory is primarily an abstraction rather than a verbatim remembrance of a previous event. Schmidt has taken a similar position for motor skills memory, positing that individuals do not retain specific information about the actions or movements that they have made but rather, develop recall and recognition schemata that represent relationships among a variety of specified conditions, which in turn aid them in making responses appropriate for the conditions that exist at the time.

At the heart of Schmidt's theory is the positing of a motor program that refers to centrally stored representations that form the basis for the performance of action or movement sequences. Schmidt (1982) has not held that there is a memory for every separate motor program—such a position not only seems implausible but would have difficulty in accounting for novel variations of performance. Rather, Schmidt has indicated that the hypothesized motor program is generalized—a basic program may be stored but certain parameters or conditions must be provided that define how the program is to be executed on any particular occasion. Inasmuch as the program's output (as reflected in action) changes according to the parameters chosen on any particular trial, the program is defined as a generalized one.[10]

Several parameters have been posited. One, the overall duration of the action or movement specifies the time required to go through the total sequence of the action. A second parameter, force, is responsible for defining the level of intensity with which the muscular action is to be carried out. Finally, a muscle selection parameter defines which muscles or limbs will be involved. When these parameters have been chosen, the movement can be carried out by the program.

Once the action has been taken, the individual stores four bits of information:

1. The initial conditions that existed before the action
2. The parameters that were assigned to the generalized program
3. The outcome of the action in the environment in terms of KR

---

[10] Schmidt has provided an example of what he means by a generalized program by using an example of a computer that is provided a statistical program capable of calculating a mean and a standard deviation. Such a program can be so constructed that it is capable of producing these statistics for various numbers of subjects, and for varying numbers of scores made by the subject. Thus, if the numbers of subjects range from 1 to 10,000, and the number of scores for each subject can range from 1 to 10,000, there is the opportunity for this program to provide means and standard deviations for combinations of subjects and scores up to 10,000,000.

Schmidt's theoretical position, which gives a central place to a generalized motor program, has been identified by some as an open-loop position since such a position hypothesized that such a program is structured in the brain before the movement sequence begins. This program permits the entire sequence of movements to be carried out, uninfluenced by the sensory feedback that arises from the subject's responding.

4. The sensory consequences of the action; that is, how the action felt, looked, and so on.

These four items are not stored permanently but only long enough so that the subject can abstract certain relationships among them. Two such relationships, or schemata, are assumed to become manifest. One of these is the recall schema, and is concerned with the production of movement. With repeated responses using different parameters and producing different outcomes, the subject begins to define and establish a relationship between the characteristics of the parameters and the nature of the action outcome. With each successive response being made, new information is generated, with the relationship being adjusted. After each adjustment, the stored data are discarded so all that remains of the movement is the revised relationship. But Schmidt has also posited that the recall schema is believed to comprise information about the initial conditions of the movement. Here, the relationship between the parameters used and the outcome produced is also related to the nature of the initial conditions, so that one can assume a relatively more complex relationship being formed among the initial conditions, the response parameter, and the outcome in the environment that has resulted from these combined factors.

The second schema that Schmidt has posited is the recognition schema. In this instance, the schema is comprised of the relationship among the initial conditions, the environmental outcome, and the sensory consequences. Since these elements are assumed to be present after each trial, a relationship among them is established. The recognition schema is assumed to be used in a way analogous to the recall schema. Before the response is made, the individual decides which movement is desired, and determines the nature of the initial conditions. As a result, the individual can estimate the sensory consequences that will be present if that movement outcome is produced. These have been identified as expected sensory consequences and serve as the basis for determining, after the action has been taken, whether or not the movement that will be produced is correct.

In summary, the relation between the recall and schema is, as Cummings and Caparola (1986) have written:

> The recall schema is responsible for those cues needed to start a movement and the recognition schema is responsible for error correction and those cues needed to keep the movement ongoing. Each memory state is hypothesized to develop through the formation of rules. Information from initial conditions, sensory consequences and actual outcomes formulate the rule for recall schema and initial conditions, sensory consequences and actual outcomes comprise the rule for recognition schema (p. 52).

Schmidt's schema theory assumes that we acquire skills by learning rules about the functioning of our bodies. With experience, we come to form relationships between how our muscles are activated, what they actually do, and how these actions feel. But a response that is made when any of the four stored elements are missing (e.g., initial conditions prior to the movement, parameters assigned to the generalized motor program, knowledge of results, and sensory consequences of the action) will result in degraded learning, with probably the most critical of these elements being knowledge of results.

General Considerations

Schmidt's schema theory posits that positive benefits are derived from the production of all movements whether they be correct or incorrect. This is because the development of the recall and recognition schemata is based on the relationship among the stored elements, and this relationship is present for incorrect movements as well as for correct ones. Producing an incorrect response provided additional information about how the body functions. Thus, an important prediction from Schmidt's theory is that variability of responding or practicing a variety of movements with the same program is beneficial since it will provide a widely based set of experiences upon which a rule or schema can be built.

When this position is translated into experimental operations, the typical procedure has been to train an experimental group on varied instances of a motor response, whereas a control group is provided training on the same motor response. Both groups are then provided a variation of the motor response that has not been previously experienced, with the prediction that the experimental group's performance should be superior to that of the control. Shapiro and Schmidt's (1982) review of such studies has indicated that the findings are mixed, and the results of several recent studies have been in keeping with this general conclusion. Cummings and Caprarola (1986), using a linear positioning task and male subjects 18 to 45 years of age, were not able to demonstrate that transfer to a novel task was enhanced by variable practice. In contrast, Turnbull and Dickinson (1986), also using a linear positioning task and examining both amount of training and degree of variability, were able to find that extremely variable practice did enhance the transfer for some groups although statistically significant differences were not in evidence.

It seems reasonable to assume that any basic conclusion regarding the role of varied versus constant practice on the learning of a novel task may be dependent upon a host of variables (e.g., kind of task, amount of practice, extent of variation of practice, etc.), so that future experimental work will be undoubtedly exploring these kinds of interaction. But one other issue also needs to be resolved—an issue having to do with the definition of a response class. As Zelaznik (1977) has suggested and as Adams (1984) has written:

> *Without a definition of response class, a failure of varied training to produce the advantage expected from schema theory may mean only that the varied training has unwittingly spanned two or more response classes, not that schema theory is wrong (p. 61).*

Summary ►

The acquisition and retention of motor skills represents another major area of interest for psychologists interested in the area of learning. To learn a motor skill, one must acquire a temporal-spatial organization of muscular movement which takes place in a precise and consistent manner. Motor skills tasks demand a graded response, with emphasis on (1) response latency, (2) timing and anticipation, and (3) feedback.

Investigators have been interested in describing how motor skills tasks are acquired. It has been suggested that the individual goes through three stages in learning these tasks. First, there is a cognitive stage in which the learner develops understanding of the task and perhaps uses verbal responses to guide the motor activity. In the second or associative stage, the subject tries our new responses and eliminates old and inefficient ones. In the third or autonomous stage, the subject responds with a high level of proficiency. Often, the subject's behavior comes under the control of proprioceptive stimulation so that it is possible for him or her to engage in other activities while performing the task. One finding derived from the stage analysis is that the contribution of a specific condition or variable to performance may depend on the subject's stage of practice.

As with other learning paradigms, experimenters have been interested in identifying the specific variables that contribute to learning and performance. Two stimulus variables that have been extensively investigated have been (1) massed versus distributed practice and (2) part versus whole methods of training. The findings from studies examining these variables have been mixed, and few generalizations can be provided. A third stimulus variable, stimulus-response compatibility, however, has been shown to contribute to performance.

Knowledge of results, although originally identified as a motivational condition, is now considered as an information processing variable, in which KR is considered as information to be processed. Frequency, precision, and delay of KR all have been demonstrated to influence the course of motor skills acquisition.

Current investigators have become interested in knowledge of performance (KP) or kinematic knowledge of results (KKR). Here, the focus of inquiry has been on the correctness of the motor movement itself. Some research in this area has suggested that this approach to motor skills performance makes an important contribution to a better understanding of these skills.

The feedback that arises from the making of a response has been assumed by some investigators to play an important role in controlling sequential responding but other experimenters have pointed to several problems with this explanation. These two positions have evolved into what has become a closed- versus open-loop controversy. The closed-loop position proposes that during the performance of skilled, sequential movements, sensory feedback is responsible for controlling as well as correcting and modifying the continuing response. In contrast, the open-loop position has hypothesized that a motor program is structured in the brain before the movement sequence begins. This program permits the entire sequence of movements to be carried out, uninfluenced by the sensory feedback that arises from the subject's responding. Experimental findings have provided support for both positions; as a result, a dual- or two-stage model has been posited in which it has been proposed that human motor skills incorporates both closed- and open-loop functions.

The closed- and open-loop positions have been recently incorporated into the more general theoretical position designed to answer the question, How are motor skills learned? Adams (1984) and Schmidt (1982) have provided theoretical structures that have attempted to answer this question.

References

Abra, J. C. List-1 unlearning and recovery as a function of the point of the point of interpolated learning. *Journal of Verbal Learning and Verbal Behavior,* 1969, *8,* 494–500.

Adamic, R., and Melzack, R. The role of motivation and orientation in sensory preconditioning. *Canadian Journal of Psychology,* 1970, *24,* 230–239.

Adams, J. A. A closed-loop theory of motor learning. *Journal of Motor Behavior,* 1971, *3,* 111–150.

Adams, J. A. *Learning and memory: An introduction.* Homewood, Ill.: Dorsey, 1976.

Adams, J. A. Learning of movement sequences. *Psychological Bulletin,* 1984, *96,* 3–28.

Adams, J. A. The use of a model of movement sequences for the study of knowledge of results and the training of experts. *Journal of Human Movement Studies,* 1985, *11,* 223–236.

Adams, J. A. Historical review and appraisal of research on the learning, retention, and transfer of human motor skills. *Psychological Bulletin,* 1987, *101,* 41–74.

Adams, J. A., McIntyre, J. S., and Thorsheim, H. I. Natural language mediation and inter-item interference in paired-associate learning. *Psychonomic Science,* 1969, *16,* 63–64.

Adams, J. F., Nemeth, R. V., and Pavlik, W. B. Between- and within-subjects PRE with sucrose incentives. *Bulletin of the Psychonomic Society,* 1982, *20,* 261–262.

Adams, W. H., Yeh, S. Y., Woods. L. A., and Mitchell, C. L. Drug-test interaction as a factor in the development of tolerance to the analgesic effect of morphine. *Journal of Pharmacology and Experimental Therapeutics,* 1969, *168,* 251–257.

Ader, R., and Cohen, N. Behaviorally conditioned immunosuppression. *Psychosomatic Medicine,* 1975, *37,* 333–340.

Ader, R., and Cohen, N. Conditioned immunopharmacologic responses. In R. Ader (Ed.), *Psychoneuroimmunology.* New York: Academic Press, 1981.

Ader, R., and Cohen, N. Behaviorally conditioned immunosuppression and murine systemic lupus erythematosus. *Science,* 1982, *215,* 1534–1536.

Ainslie, G., and Herrnstein, R. J. Preference reversal and delayed reinforcement. *Animal Learning & Behavior,* 1981, *9,* 476–482.

Alba, J. W., and Hasher, L. Is memory schematic? *Psychological Bulletin,* 1983, *93,* 203–231.

Alvarez-Buylla, R., and Carrasco-Zanini, J. A conditioned reflex which reproduces the hypoglycemic effect of insulin. *Acta Physiology of Latin America,* 1960, *10,* 153–158.

Amiro, T. W., and Bitterman, M.E. Second-order appetitive conditioning in goldfish. *Journal of Experimental Psychology: Animal Behavior Processes,* 1980, *6,* 41–48.

Ammons, R. B. Acquisition of motor skill: III. Effects of initially distributed practice on rotary pursuit performance. *Journal of Experimental Psychology,* 1950, *40,* 777–787.

Ammons, R. B. Effects of knowledge of performance: A survey and tentative theoretical formulation. *Journal of General Psychology,* 1956, *54,* 279–299.

Amsel, A. The role of frustrative nonreward in noncontinuous reward situations. *Psychological Bulletin,* 1958, *55,* 102–119.

Amsel, A. Frustrative nonreward in partial reinforcement and discrimination learning. *Psychological Review,* 1962, *69,* 306–328.

Amsel, A. Partial reinforcement effects on vigor and persistence: Advances in frustration theory derived from a variety of within-subject experiments. In K. W. Spence and J. T. Spence (Eds.), *The psychology of learning and motivation.* New York: Academic Press, 1967.

Amsel, A. Behavioral habituation, counterconditioning, and a general theory of persistence. In A. Black and W. F. Prokasy (Eds.), *Classical conditioning II.* New York: Appleton-Century-Crofts, 1972.

Amsel, A., Hug, J. J., and Surridge, C. T. Number of food pellets, goal approaches, and the partial reinforcement effect after minimal acquisition. *Journal of Experimental Psychology,* 1968, *77,* 530–534.

Anderson, J. R., and Bower, G. H. *Human associative memory.* New York: Wiley, Halstead Press, 1973.

Anderson, J. R., and Ross, B. H. Evidence against a semantic-episodic distinction. *Journal of Experimental Psychology: Human Learning and Memory,* 1980, *6,* 441–465.

Anderson, R. C., and Carter, J. F. Retroactive inhibition of meaningful learned sentences. *American Educational Research Journal,* 1972, *9,* 443–448.

Anderson, R. C., Goldberg, S. R., and Hidde, J. L. Meaningfulness processing of sentences. *Journal of Educational Psychology,* 1971, *62,* 395–399.

Anderson, R. C., and Myrow, D. L. Retroactive inhibition of meaningful discourse. *Journal of Educational Psychology,* 1971, *62,* 81–94.

Anisfeld, M., and Knapp, M. Association, synonymity, and directionality in false recognition. *Journal of Experimental Psychology,* 1968, *77,* 171–179.

Anisman, H., DeCatanzaro, D., and Remington, G. Escape performance following exposure to inescapable shock: Deficits in motor response maintenance. *Journal of Experimental Psychology: Animal Behavior Processes,* 1978, *4,* 197–218.

Anisman, H., Hamilton, M., and Zacharko, R. M. Cue and response-choice acquisition and reversal after exposure to uncontrollable shock: Induction of response perseveration. *Journal of Experimental Psychology, Animal Behavior Processes,* 1984, *10,* 229–243.

Annau, Z., and Kamin. L. J. The conditioned emotional response as a function of intensity of the US. *Journal of Comparative and Physiological Psychology,* 1961, *54,* 428–432.

Annett, J., and Kay, H. Knowledge of results and "skilled performance." *Occupational Psychology,* 1957, *31,* 69–79.

Appel, J. B. Punishment and shock intensity. *Science,* 1963, *141,* 528–529.

Archer, E. J. Re-evaluation of the meaningfulness of all possible CVC trigrams. *Psychological Monographs,* 1960, *74,* No. 10.

Archer, T., Sjoden, P., Nilsson, L., and Carter, N. Role of exteroceptive background context in taste aversion conditioning and extinction. *Animal Learning & Behavior,* 1979, *7,* 17–22.

Armus, H. L. Effect of magnitude of reinforcement on acquisition and extinction of a running response. *Journal of Experimental Psychology,* 1959, *58,* 61–63.

Ashida, S., and Birch, D. The effects of incentive shift as a function of training. *Psychonomic Science,* 1964, *1,* 201–202.

Atkinson, R. C., and Shiffrin, R. M. Human memory: A proposed system and its control processes. In K. W. Spence and J. T. Spence (Eds.), *The psychology of learning and motivation.* New York: Academic Press, 1968.

Ausubel, D., Robbins, K., and Blake, F., Jr. Retroactive inhibition and facilitation in the learning of school materials. *Journal of Educational Psychology,* 1957, *48,* 334–343.

Ayllon, T., and Azrin, N. H. Reinforcement and instructions with mental patients. *Journal of the Experimental Analysis of Behavior,* 1964, *7,* 327–331.

Ayllon, T., and Azrin, N. H. The measurement and reinforcement of behavior of psychotics. *Journal of the Experimental Analysis of Behavior,* 1965, *8,* 357–383.

Ayres, J. J. B., Haddad, C., and Albert, M. One-trial excitatory conditioning as assessed by conditioned suppression of licking in rats: Concurrent observations of lick suppression and defensive behaviors. *Animal Learning & Behavior,* 1987, *15,* 212–217.

Azrin, N. H. Some effects of two intermittent schedules of immediate and non-immediate punishment. *Journal of Psychology,* 1956, *42,* 3–21.

Azrin, N. H., Holz, W. C., and Hake, D. F. Fixed-ratio punishment. *Journal of the Experimental Analysis of Behavior*, 1963, *6*, 141–148.

Azrin, N. H., Hutchinson, R. R., and Hake, D. F. Extinction-induced aggression. *Journal of the Experimental Analysis of Behavior*, 1966, *9*, 191–214.

Bachman, J. C. Specificity vs. generality in learning and performing two large muscle motor tasks. *Research Quarterly*, 1961, *32*, 3–11.

Bacon, W. E. Partial-reinforcement extinction following different amounts of training. *Journal of Comparative and Physiological Psychology*, 1962, *55*, 998–1003.

Baddeley, A. D. *The psychology of memory.* New York: Basic Books, 1976.

Baddeley, A. D. Working memory. *Philosophical Transactions Royal Society of London*, 1983, *B 302*, 311–324.

Baddeley, A. D., and Hitch, G. J. Recency re-examined. In S. Dornic (Ed.), *Attention and Performance*, Vol. 5, 1977. Hillsdale, N.J.: Erlbaum.

Bahrick, H. P. Incidental learning under two incentive conditions. *Journal of Experimental Psychology*, 1954, *47*, 170–172.

Bahrick, H. P. Measurement of memory by prompted recall. *Journal of Experimental Psychology*, 1969, *79*, 213–219.

Bahrick, H. P. The cognitive map of a city—50 years of learning and memory. In G. Bower (Ed.), *The psychology of learning and motivation.* New York: Academic Press, 1983.

Bahrick, H. P. Semantic memory content in permastore: Fifty years of memory for Spanish learned in school. *Journal of Experimental Psychology: General*, 1984a, *113*, 1–29.

Bahrick, H. P. Long-term memories: How durable, and how enduring? *Physiological Psychology*, 1984b, *12*, 53–58.

Bahrick, H. P., Bahrick, P. O., and Wittlinger, R. P. Fifty years of memory for names and faces: A cross-sectional approach. *Journal of Experimental Psychology: General*, 1975, *104*, 54–75.

Baker, L. E. The pupillary response conditioned to subliminal auditory stimuli. *Psychological Monographs*, 1938, *50*, No. 223.

Baker, R. A., and Lawrence, D. H. The differential effects of simultaneous and successive stimuli presentation on transposition. *Journal of Comparative and Physiological Psychology*, 1951, *44*, 378–382.

Balsam, P. D. The functions of context in learning and performance. In P. D. Balsam and A.

and A. Tomie (Eds.), *Context and learning.* Hillsdale, N.J.: Erlbaum, 1985.

Bandura, A. *Principles of behavior modification.* New York: Holt, Rinehart and Winston, 1969.

Bandura, A. *Social learning theory.* Englewood Cliffs, N.J.: Prentice-Hall, 1977.

Barbizet, J. *Human memory and its pathology.* San Francisco: Freeman, 1970.

Barnes, G. W., and Kish, G. B. Reinforcing properties of the onset of auditory stimulation. *Journal of Experimental Psychology*, 1961, *62*, 162–170.

Barnes, J. M., and Underwood, B. J. "Fate" of first-list associations in transfer theory. *Journal of Experimental Psychology*, 1959, *58*, 97–105.

Barnett, S. A. *Modern ethology,* New York: Oxford University Press, 1981.

Baron, A. Delayed punishment of a runway response. *Journal of Comparative and Physiological Psychology*, 1965, *60*, 131–134.

Barrett, T. R., and Ekstrand, B. R. Effect of sleep on memory: III. Controlling for time-of-day effects. *Journal of Experimental Psychology*, 1972, *96*, 321–327.

Bartlett, F. C. *Remembering.* London: Cambridge University Press, 1932.

Bass, M. J., and Hull, C. L. The irradiation of a tactile conditioned reflex in man. *Journal of Comparative Psychology*, 1934, *17*, 47–65.

Bateson, P. P. B. The characteristics and context of imprinting. *Biological Review*, 1966, *41*, 177–220.

Battig, W. F. Procedural problems in paired-associate learning research. *Psychonomic Monograph Supplements*, 1965, *1* (No. 1).

Baum, M. Extinction of avoidance responding through response prevention (flooding) in rats. *Psychological Bulletin*, 1970, *74*, 276–284.

Bechtoldt, H. P. Factor analysis and the investigation of hypotheses. *Perceptual and Motor Skills*, 1962, *14*, 319–342.

Begg, I., and Paivio, A. Concreteness and imagery in sentence meaning. *Journal of Verbal Learning and Verbal Behavior*, 1969, *8*, 821–827.

Beggs, A. L., Steinmetz, J. E., Romano, A. G., and Patterson, M. M. Extinction and retention of a classically conditioned flexor nerve response in acute spinal cat. *Behavioral Neuroscience*, 1983, *97*, 530–540.

Benedict, J. O., and Ayres, J. J. B. Factors affecting conditioning in the truly random control procedure in the rat. *Journal of Comparative and Physiological Psychology*, 1972, *78*, 323–330.

Berger, B. D., Yarczower, M., and Bitterman, M. E. Effect of partial reinforcement on the extinction of a classically conditioned response in the goldfish. *Journal of Comparative and Physiological Psychology*, 1965, *59*, 399–405.

Bernstein, A. L. Temporal factors in the formation of conditioned eyelid reactions in human subjects. *Journal of General Psychology*, 1934, *10*, 173–197.

Bernstein, I. I. Learned taste aversions in children receiving chemotherapy. *Science*, 1978, *200*, 1302–1303.

Berry, S. D., and Thompson, R. F. Prediction of learning rate from the hippocampal electroencephalogram. *Science*, 1978, *200*, 1298–1300.

Berry, S. D., and Thompson, R. F. Medial septal lesions retard classical conditioning of the nictitating membrane response in rabbits. *Science*, 1979, *205*, 209–210.

Best, M. R., Batson, J. D., Meachum, C. L., Brown, E. R., and Ringer, M. Characteristics of taste-mediated environmental potentiation in rats. *Learning and Motivation*, 1985, *16*, 190–209.

Best, P. J., Best, M. R., and Mickley, G. A. Conditioned aversion to distinct environmental stimuli resulting from gastrointestinal distress. *Journal of Comparative and Physiological Psychology*, 1973, *85*, 250–257.

Biel, W. C., and Force, R. C. Retention of nonsense syllables in intentional and incidental learning. *Journal of Experimental Psychology*, 1943, *32*, 52–63.

Bilodeau, E. A., and Bilodeau, I. McD. Variations of temporal intervals among critical events in five studies of knowledge of results. *Journal of Experimental Psychology*, 1958, *55*, 603–612.

Bilodeau, I. McD. Accuracy of a simple positioning response with variation in the number of trials by which knowledge of results is delayed. *American Journal of Psychology*, 1956, *69*, 434–437.

Bilodeau, I. McD., and Schlosberg, H. Similarity in stimulating conditions as a variable in retroactive inhibition. *Journal of Experimental Psychology*, 1951, *41*, 199–204.

Birch, D. Discrimination learning as a function of the ratio of non-reinforced to reinforced trials. *Journal of Comparative and Physiological Psychology*, 1955, *48*, 371–374.

Bjork, R. A., and Whitten, W. B. Recency-sensitive retrieval processes in long term free recall. *Cognitive Psychology*, 1974, *6*, 173–189.

Black, A. H. Heart rate changes during avoidance in dogs. *Canadian Journal of Psychology*, 1959, *13*, 229–242.

Black, R. W. Shifts in magnitude of reward and contrast effects in instrumental and selective learning: A reinterpretation. *Psychological Review*, 1968, *75*, 114–126.

Blackman, D. E. Conditioned suppression or facilitation as a function of the behavioral baseline. *Journal of the Experimental Analysis of Behavior*, 1968, *11*, 53–61.

Blackman, D. E. Conditioned suppression and the effects of classical conditioning on operant behavior. In W. K. Honig and J. E. R. Staddon (Eds.), *Handbook of operant behavior*. Englewood Cliffs, N.J.: Prentice-Hall, 1977.

Blaney, P. H. Affect and memory: A review. *Psychological Bulletin*, 1986, *99*, 229–246.

Blodgett, H. C. The effect of the introduction of reward upon the maze performance of rats. *University of California Publications in Psychology*, 1929, *4*, 113–134.

Blough, D. S. Steady state data and a quantitative model of operant generalization and discrimination. *Journal of Experimental Psychology: Animal Behavior Processes*, 1975, *1*, 3–21.

Blough, D. S. Pigeon perception of letters of the alphabet. *Science*, 1982, *218*, 397–398.

Boal, K. B., and Cummings, L. L. Cognitive evaluation theory: An experimental test of processes and outcomes. *Organization Behavior and Human Performance*, 1981, *28*, 289–310.

Bolles, R. C. Avoidance and escape learning: Simultaneous acquisition of different responses. *Journal of Comparative and Physiological Psychology*, 1969, *68*, 355–358.

Bolles, R. C. Species-specific defense reactions and avoidance learning. *Psychological Review*, 1970, *77*, 32–48.

Bolles, R. C., and deLorge, J. Explorations in a Dashiell maze as a function of prior deprivation, current deprivation, and sex. *Canadian Journal of Psychology*, 1962, *16*, 221–227.

Bolles, R. C., Moot, S. A., and Grossen, N. E. The extinction of shuttlebox avoidance, *Learning and Motivation*, 1971, *2*, 324–333.

Book, W. F. *The psychology of skill*. University of Montana Studies in Psychology (Vol. 1), 1908. (Reprinted, New York: Gregg, 1925).

Bousfield, W. A. The occurrence of clustering in the recall of randomly arranged associates. *Journal of General Psychology*, 1953, *49*, 229–240.

Bousfield, W. A., and Cohen, B. H. The occurrence of clustering in the recall of randomly arranged words of different frequencies of usage. *Journal of General Psychology*, 1955, *52*, 83–95.

Bousfield, W. A., and Wicklund, D. A. Rhyme as a determinant of clustering. *Psychonomic Science*, 1969, *16*, 183–184.

Bower, G. H. Partial and correlated reward in escape learning. *Journal of Experimental Psychology*, 1960, *59*, 126–130.

Bower, G. H. The influence of graded reductions in reward and prior frustrating events upon the magnitude of the frustration effect. *Journal of Comparative and Physiological Psychology*, 1962, *55*, 582–587.

Bower, G. H. Chunks as interference units in free recall. *Journal of Verbal Learning and Verbal Behavior*, 1969, *8*, 610–613.

Bower, G. H. Stimulus-sampling theory of encoding variability. In A. W. Melton and E. Martin (Eds.), *Coding processes in human memory*. Washington, D.C.: Winston, 1972.

Bower, G. H. Interference paradigms for meaningful propositional memory. *American Journal of Psychology*, 1978, *91*, 575–585.

Bower, G. H., Monteiro, K. P., and Gilligan, S. G. Emotional mood as a context for learning and recall. *Journal of Verbal Learning and Verbal Behavior*, 1978, *17*, 573–585.

Bradshaw, C. M., Szabadi, E., Bevan, P., and Ruddle, H. V. Behavior of humans in variable-interval schedules of reinforcement. *Journal of the Experimental Analysis of Behavior*, 1976, *26*, 135–141.

Bradshaw, G. L., and Anderson, J. R. Elaborative encoding as an explanation of levels of processing. *Journal of Verbal Learning and Verbal Behavior*, 1982, *21*, 165–174.

Brady, J. P., and Rieger, W. Behavior treatment of anorexia nervosa. In T. Thompson and W. S. Dockens (Eds.), *Applications of behavior modification*. New York: Academic Press, 1975.

Bransford, J. D., and Franks, J. J. The abstraction of linguistic ideas. *Cognitive Psychology*, 1971, *2*, 331–350.

Bransford, J. D., and Johnson, M. K. Contextual prerequisites for understanding: Some investigations of comprehension and recall. *Journal of Verbal Learning and Verbal Behavior*, 1972, *11*, 717–726.

Braud, W. G. Effectiveness of "neutral," habituated, shock-related and food-related stimuli as CSs for avoidance learning in goldfish. *Conditional Reflex*, 1971, *6*, 153–156.

Breland, K. and Breland, M. The misbehavior of organisms. *American Psychologist*, 1961, *16*, 681–684.

Brener, J., and Hothersall, D. Paced respiration and heart rate control. *Psychophysiology*, 1967, *4*, 1–6.

Britt, E., and Singh, N. N. Reduction of rapid eating by normal adults. *Behavior Modification*, 1985, *9*, 116–125.

Broadbent, D. D. *Perception and communication*. New York: Pergamon, 1958.

Broadhurst, P. L. Emotionality and the Yerkes-Dodson law. *Journal of Experimental Psychology*, 1957, *54*, 345–352.

Brogden, W. J. Higher order conditioning. *American Journal of Psychology*, 1939a, *52*, 579–591.

Brogden, W. J. Sensory pre-conditioning. *Journal of Experimental Psychology*, 1939b, *25*, 323–332.

Brogden, W. J., Lipman, E. A., and Culler, E. The role of incentive in conditioning and extinction. *American Journal of Psychology*, 1938, *51*, 109–117.

Brooks, C. I. Frustration to nonreward following limited reward experience. *Journal of Experimental Psychology*, 1969, *81*, 403–405.

Brooks, C. I. Frustration considerations of the small-trials partial reinforcement effect: Experience with nonreward and intertrial reinforcement. *Journal of Experimental Psychology*, 1971, *89*, 362–371.

Brooks, C. I. Effect of prior nonreward on subsequent incentive growth during brief acquisition. *Animal Learning & Behavior*, 1980, *8*, 143–151.

Brown, J. Some tests of the decay theory of immediate memory. *Quarterly Journal of Experimental Psychology*, 1958, *10*, 12–21.

Brown, J. S. Generalization and discrimination. In D. Mostofsky (Ed.), *Stimulus generalization*. Palo Alto, Calif.: Stanford University Press, 1965.

Brown, J. S., Bilodeau, E. A., and Baron, M. R. Bidirectional gradients in the strength of a generalized voluntary response to stimuli on a visual-spatial dimension. *Journal of Experimental Psychology*, 1951, *41*, 52–61.

Brown, J. S., Kalish, H. I., and Farber, I. E. Conditioned fear as revealed by magnitude of startle response to an auditory stimulus. *Journal of Experimental Psychology*, 1951, *41*, 317–328.

Brown, M., Nallan, G. B., Gerdes, J., Dykeman, C., Sanders, R., and Lamb, J. Feature positive effect in adults and attention to portion of the stimulus array. *American Journal of Psychology*, 1983, *96*, 201–209.

Brown, P. L., and Jenkins, H. M. Auto-shaping of the pigeon's key peck. *Journal of the Experimental Analysis of Behavior*, 1968, *11*, 1–8.

Brown, R. T., and Wagner, A. R. Resistance to punishment and extinction following training with shock or nonreinforcement. *Journal of Experimental Psychology*, 1964, *68*, 503–507.

Bruner, J. S., Goodnow, J. J., and Austin, G. A. *A study of thinking*. New York: Wiley, 1960.

Bryan, W. L., and Harter, N. Studies in the physiology and psychology of the telegraphic language. *Psychological Review*, 1897, *4*, 27–53.

Bryan, W. L., and Harter, N. Studies on the telegraphic language: The acquisition of a hierarchy of habits. *Psychological Review*, 1899, *6*, 345–375.

Buerger, A. A., and Dawson, A. M. Spinal kittens: Long-term increases in electromyograms due to a conditioning routine. *Physiology and Behavior*, 1968, *3*, 99–103.

Buerger, A. A., and Dawson, A. M. Spinal kittens: Effect of clamping of the thoracic aorta on long-term increases in electromyograms due to a conditioning routine. *Experimental Neurology*, 1969, *23*, 457–464.

Bugelski, B. R. Images as mediators in one-trial paired-associate learning. II. Self-timing in successive lists. *Journal of Experimental Psychology*, 1968, *77*, 328–334.

Bugelski, B. R., Kidd, E., and Segmen, J. Images as a mediator in one-trial paired-associate learning. *Journal of Experimental Psychology*, 1968, *76*, 69–73.

Burkhardt, P. E. One-trial backward fear conditioning in rats as a function of US intensity. *Bulletin of the Psychonomic Society*, 1980, *15*, 9–11.

Burtt, H. E. An experimental study of early childhood memory. *Journal of Genetic Psychology*, 1932, *40*, 287–295.

Burtt, H. E. A further study of early childhood memory. *Journal of Genetic Psychology*, 1937, *50*, 187–192.

Burtt, H. E. An experimental study of early childhood memory: Final report. *Journal of Genetic Psychology*, 1941, *58*, 435–439.

Buschke, H. Selective reminding for analysis of memory and learning. *Journal of Verbal Learning and Verbal Behavior*, 1973, *12*, 543–550.

Butter, C. M., and Thomas, D. R. Secondary

reinforcement as a function of the amount of primary reinforcement. *Journal of Comparative and Physiological Psychology*, 1958, *51*, 346–348.

Calkins, M. W. Association. *Psychological Review*, 1894, *1*, 476–483.

Calkins, M. W. Association: An essay analytic and experimental. *Psychological Review Monograph Supplements*, 1896, *2*.

Camp, D. S., Raymond, G. A., and Church, R. M. Temporal relationship between response and punishment. *Journal of Experimental Psychology*, 1967, *74*, 114–123.

Campbell, D., Sanderson, R. E., and Laverty, S. G. Characteristics of a conditioned response in human subjects during extinction trials following a single traumatic conditioning trial. *Journal of Abnormal and Social Psychology*, 1964, *68*, 627–639.

Campbell, P. E., Batsche, C. J., and Batsche, G. M. Spaced-trials reward magnitude effects in the rat: Single versus multiple food pellets. *Journal of Comparative and Physiological Psychology*, 1972, *81*, 360–364.

Cannon, D. S., Berman, R. F., Baker, T. B., and Atkinson, C. A. Effect of preconditioning unconditioned stimulus experience on learned taste aversions. *Journal of Experimental Psychology: Animal Behavior Processes*, 1975, *1*, 270–284.

Capaldi, E. J. Partial reinforcement: A hypothesis of sequential effects. *Psychological Review*, 1966, *73*, 495–477.

Capaldi, E. J. A sequential hypothesis of instrumental learning. In K. W. Spence and J. T. Spence (Eds.), *The psychology of learning and motivation*. New York: Academic Press, 1967.

Capaldi, E. J. Memory and learning: A sequential viewpoint. In W. K. Honig and P. H. R. James (Eds.), *Animal memory*. New York: Academic Press, 1971.

Capaldi, E. J. Effects of schedule and delay of reinforcement on acquisition speed. *Animal Learning & Behavior*, 1978, *6*, 330–334.

Capaldi, E. J., and Hart, D. Influence of a small number of partial reinforcement training trials on resistance to extinction. *Journal of Experimental Psychology*, 1962, *64*, 166–171.

Capaldi, E. J., and Kassover, K. Sequence, number of nonrewards, anticipation, and intertrial interval in extinction. *Journal of Experimental Psychology*, 1970, *84*, 470–476.

Capaldi, E. J., and Waters, R. W. Conditioning

and nonconditioning interpretations of small-trial phenomena. *Journal of Experimental Psychology,* 1970, *84,* 518–522.

Cason, H. The conditioned pupillary reaction. *Journal of Experimental Psychology,* 1922, *5,* 108–146.

Cason, H. Specific serial learning: A study of backward association. *Journal of Experimental Psychology,* 1926, *9,* 195–227.

Catania, A. C. Concurrent performances: A baseline for the study of reinforcement magnitude. *Journal of the Experimental Analysis of Behavior,* 1963a, *6,* 299–300.

Catania, A. C. Concurrent performances. Reinforcement interaction and response independence. *Journal of the Experimental Analysis of Behavior,* 1963b, *6,* 253–263.

Cautela, J. R. The problems of backward conditioning. *Journal of Psychology,* 1965, *60,* 135–144.

Cautela, J. R. Treatment of compulsive behavior by covert sensitization. *Psychological Record,* 1966, *16,* 33–41.

Cautela, J. R. Covert negative reinforcement. *Journal of Behavior Therapy and Experimental Psychiatry,* 1970a, *1,* 273–278.

Cautela, J. R. Covert reinforcement. *Behavior Therapy,* 1970b, *1,* 33–50.

Cautela, J. R. Covert extinction. *Behavior Therapy,* 1971, *2,* 192–200.

Cautela, J. R. The present status of covert modeling. *Journal of Behavior Therapy and Experimental Psychiatry,* 1976, *1,* 323–326.

Cautela, J. R. Covert conditioning and the control of pain. *Behavior Modification,* 1986, *10,* 205–217.

Cautela, J. R. The problem of backward conditioning: Revisited. In F. J. McGuigan and T. A. Ban (Eds.), *Critical issues in psychology, psychiatry, and physiology: A memorial to W. Horsley Gantt.* New York: Gordon and Breach, 1987.

Cegavske, C. F., Thompson, R. F., Patterson, M., and Gormezano, I. Mechanisms of efferent neuronal control of the reflex nictitating membrane response in rabbit (Oryctolagus cuniculus). *Journal of Comparative and Physiological Psychology,* 1976, *90,* 411–423.

Chacto, C., and Lubow, R. E. Classical conditioning and latent inhibition in the white rat. *Psychonomic Science,* 1967, *9,* 135–136.

Champion, R. A., and Jones, J. E. Forward, backward, and pseudoconditioning of the GSR.

Journal of Experimental Psychology, 1961, *62,* 58–61.

Cheatle, M. D., and Rudy, J. W. Analysis of second-order odor aversion conditioning in neonatal rats: Implications of Kamin's blocking effect. *Journal of Experimental Psychology: Animal Behavior Processes,* 1978, *4,* 237–249.

Chiesi, H. L., Spilich, G. J. and Voss, J. F. Acquisition of domain-related information in relation to high and low domain knowledge. *Journal of Verbal Learning and Verbal Behavior,* 1979, *18,* 257–273.

Chung, S. H. Effects of delayed reinforcement in a concurrent situation. *Journal of the Experimental Analysis of Behavior,* 1965, *8,* 439–444.

Chung, S. H., and Herrnstein, R. J. Choice and delay of reinforcement. *Journal of the Experimental Analysis of Behavior,* 1967, *10,* 67–74.

Church, R. M. Aversive behavior. In J. W. Kling and L. A. Riggs (Eds.), *Woodworth and Schlosberg's experimental psychology.* New York: Holt, Rinehart and Winston, 1971.

Church, R. M. The internal clock. In S. H. Hulse, H. Fowler, and W. K. Honig (Eds.), *Cognitive processes in animal behavior.* Hillsdale, N.J.: Erlbaum, 1978.

Church, R. M., Brush, F. R., and Solomon, R. L. Traumatic avoidance learning: The effects of CS-US interval with a delayed-conditioning procedure in a free-responding situation. *Journal of Comparative and Physiological Psychology,* 1956, *49,* 301–308.

Church, R. M., Getty, D. J., and Lerner, N. D. Duration discrimination by rats. *Journal of Experimental Psychology: Animal Behavior Processes,* 1976, *2,* 303–312.

Church, R. M., and Gibbon, J. Temporal generalization. *Journal of Experimental Psychology: Animal Behavior Processes,* 1982, *8,* 165–186.

Church, R. M., Raymond, G. A., and Beauchamp, R. D. Response suppression as a function of intensity and duration of a punishment. *Journal of Comparative and Physiological Psychology,* 1967, *63,* 39–44.

Clark, F. C. The effect of deprivation and frequency of reinforcement on variable interval responding. *Journal of the Experimental Analysis of Behavior,* 1958, *1,* 221–228.

Clifford, T. Extinction following continuous reward and latent extinction. *Journal of Experimental Psychology,* 1964, *68,* 456–465.

Clifford, T. Runway length and failure of expected rewards: The OEE. *Canadian Journal of Psychology,* 1968, *22,* 417–426.

Cofer, C. N. Constructive processes in memory. *American Scientist,* 1973, *61,* 537–543.

Cofer, C. N., and Appley, M. H. *Motivation: Theory and research.* New York: Wiley, 1964.

Cofer, C. N., and Bruce, D. R. Form-class as the basis for clustering in the recall of nonassociated words. *Journal of Verbal Learning and Verbal Behavior,* 1965, *4,* 386–389.

Cofer, C. N., Failie, N. F., and Horton, D. L. Retroactive inhibition following reinstatement or maintenance of first-list responses by means of free recall. *Journal of Experimental Psychology,* 1971, *90,* 197–205.

Cohen, J. *Operant behavior and operant conditioning.* Chicago: Rand-McNally, 1969.

Cohen, D. H. Effect of conditioned stimulus intensity on visually conditioned heart rate change in the pigeon: A sensitization mechanism. *Journal of Comparative and Physiological Psychology,* 1974, *87,* 495–499.

Coleman, S. R. Consequences of response-contingent change in unconditioned stimulus intensity upon the rabbit (Orycotlagus cuniculus) nictitating membrane response. *Journal of Comparative and Physiological Psychology,* 1975, *88,* 591–595.

Collier, G. H. Life in a closed economy: The ecology of learning and motivation. In M. D. Zeiler and P. Harzem (Eds.), *Advances in the analysis of behavior.* New York: Wiley, 1983.

Collier, G. H., and Rovee-Collier, C. K. A comparative analysis of optimal foraging behavior: Laboratory simulations. In A. C. Kamil and T. Sargent (Eds.), *Foraging behavior: Ecological, ethological and psychological approaches.* New York: Garland STPM Press, 1981.

Collins, K. H., and Tatum, A. L. A conditioned reflex established by chronic morphine poisoning. *American Journal of Physiology,* 1925, *74,* 14–26.

Conrad, R. Acoustic confusions in immediate memory. *British Journal of Psychology,* 1964, *55,* 75–84.

Cook, R. G., Brown, M. F., and Riley, D. A. Flexible memory processing by rats: Use of prospective and retrospective information in the radial maze. *Journal of Experimental Psychology: Animal Behavior Processes,* 1985, *11,* 453–469.

Cooks, S. W., and Harris, R. E. The verbal conditioning of the galvanic skin reflex. *Journal of Experimental Psychology,* 1937, *21,* 202–210.

Coover, G. D., Ursin, H., and Levine, S. Plasma-corticosterone levels during active-avoidance learning in rats. *Journal of Comparative and Physiological Psychology,* 1973, *82,* 170–174.

Coppage, E. W., and Harcum, E. R. Temporal vs. structural determinants of primacy in strategies of serial learning. *Journal of Verbal Learning and Verbal Behavior,* 1967, *6,* 487–490.

Corballis, M. C. Practice and the simplex. *Psychological Review,* 1965, *72,* 399–406.

Corkin, S. Acquisition of motor skills after bilateral medial temporal-lobe excision. *Neuropsychologia,* 1968, *6,* 255–265.

Cornell, E. H., and Bergstrom, L. I. Serial-position effects in infants recognition memory. *Memory & Cognition,* 1983, *11,* 494–499.

Corson, J. A. Observational learning of a lever pressing response. *Psychonomic Science,* 1967, *7,* 197–198.

Cowles, J. T. Food tokens as incentives for learning by chimpanzees. *Comparative Psychological Monographs,* 1937, *14,* No. 5.

Cowles, J. T., and Nissen, H. W. Reward expectancy in delayed responses of chimpanzees. *Journal of Comparative Psychology,* 1937, *24,* 345–358.

Cox, J. K., and D'Amato, M. R. Disruption of overlearning discriminative behavior in monkeys (Cebus apella) by delay of reward. *Animal Learning & Behavior,* 1977, *5,* 93–98.

Cozens, F. W. Three research studies in physical education. II. A Comparative study of two methods of teaching class work in track and field events. *Research Quarterly,* 1931, *2,* 75–79.

Craik, F. I. M., and Lockhart, R. S. Levels of processing: A framework for memory research. *Journal of Verbal Learning and Verbal Behavior,* 1972, *11,* 671–684.

Craik, F. I. M., and Watkins, M. J. The role of rehearsal in short-term memory. *Journal of Verbal Learning and Verbal Behavior,* 1973, *12,* 599–607.

Crespi, L. P. Quantative variation of incentive and performance in the white rat. *American Journal of Psychology,* 1942, *55,* 467–517.

Crisler, G. Salivation is unnecessary for the establishment of the salivary conditioned reflex induced by morphine. *American Journal of Physiology,* 1930, *84,* 553–556.

Crowder, R. G. The demise of short-term memory. *Acta Psychologica,* 1982, 291–323.

Culbertson, J. L. Effects of brief reinforcement delays on acquisition and extinction of brightness discrimination in rats. *Journal of Comparative and Physiological Psychology*, 1970, *70*, 317–325.

Culler, E. A., Finch, G., Girden, E., and Brogden, W. Measurements of acuity by the conditioned response technique. *Journal of General Psychology*, 1935, *12*, 223–227.

Cumming, W. W., and Eckerman, D. A. Stimulus control of a differentiated operant. *Psychonomic Science*, 1965, *3*, 313–314.

Cummings, J. F., and Caparola, M. A. Schmidt's schema theory: Variability of practice and transfer. *Journal of Human Movement Studies*, 1986, *12*, 51–57.

Dahlquist, L. M., and Gil, K. M. Using parents to maintain improved dental flossing skills in children. *Journal of Applied Behavior Analysis*, 1986, *19*, 255–260.

Daly, H. B. Excitatory and inhibitory effects of complete and incomplete reward reduction in the double runway. *Journal of Experimental Psychology*, 1968, *76*, 430–438.

Daly, H. B. Learning as a hurdle-jump response to escape cues paired with reduced reward or frustrative nonreward. *Journal of Experimental Psychology*, 1969, *79*, 146–157.

D'Amato, M. R. Secondary reinforcement and magnitude of primary reinforcement. *Journal of Comparative and Physiological Psychology*, 1955, *48*, 378–380.

D'Amato, M. R., and Buckiewicz, J. Long-delay, one-trial conditioned preference and retention in monkeys (Cebus apella). *Animal Learning & Behavior*, 1980, *8*, 359–362.

D'Amato, M. R., and O'Neill, W. Effect of delay-interval illumination on matching behavior in the capuchin monkey. *Journal of the Experimental Analysis of Behavior*, 1971, *15*, 327–333.

D'Amato, M. R., and Safarjan, W. R. Differential effects of delay in reinforcement on acquisition of affective and instrumental responses. *Animal Learning & Behavior*, 1981, *9*, 209–215.

D'Amato, M. R., Salmon, D. P., and Colombo, M. Extent and limits of the matching concept in monkeys (Cebus apella). *Journal of Experimental Psychology: Animal Behavior Processes*, 1985, *11*, 35–51.

D'Amato, M. R., and Schiff, D. Further studies of overlearning and position reversal learning. *Psychological Reports*, 1964, *14*, 380–382.

Damianopoulos, E. N. Necessary and sufficient factors in classical conditioning. *Pavlovian Journal of Biological Science*, 1982, *17*, 215–229.

Darley, C. F., and Glass, A. L. Effects of rehearsal and serial list position on recall. *Journal of Experimental Psychology: Human Learning and Memory*, 1975, *104*, 455–458.

Davenport, J. W. Species generality of within-subject reward magnitude effects. *Canadian Journal of Psychology*, 1970, *24*, 1–7.

Davis, R. C. Patterns of muscular activity during 'mental work' and their constancy. *Journal of Experimental Psychology*, 1939, *24*, 451–465.

Dawson, M. E. Cognition and conditioning: Effects of masking the CS-UCS contingency on human GSR classical conditioning. *Journal of Experimental Psychology*, 1970, *85*, 389–396.

Dawson, M. E., and Biferno, N. A. Concurrent measurement of awareness and electrodermal classical conditioning. *Journal of Experimental Psychology*, 1973, *101*, 55–62.

Dawson, M. E., and Grings, W. W. Comparison of classical conditioning and relational learning. *Journal of Experimental Psychology*, 1968, *76*, 227–231.

Dawson, M. E., and Satterfield, J. H. Can human GSR conditioning occur without relational learning? *Proceedings of the 77th Annual Convention of the American Psychological Association*, 1969, *4*, 69–70.

Dawson, M. E., Schell, A. M., and Banis, H. Greater resistance to extinction of electrodermal responses conditioned to potentially phobic CSs: A noncognitive process? *Psychophysiology*, 1986, *23*, 552–561.

Deane, G. E. Human heart rate responses during experimentally induced anxiety. *Journal of Experimental Psychology*, 1961, *61*, 489–493.

Deci, E. L. *Intrinsic motivation*. New York: Plenum, 1975.

Deese, J., and Hardman, G. W., Jr. An analysis of errors in retroactive inhibition of rote verbal learning. *American Journal of Psychology*, 1954, *67*, 299–307.

Deese, J., and Kaufman, R. A. Serial effects in recall of unorganized and sequentially organized verbal material. *Journal of Experimental Psychology*, 1957, *54*, 180–187.

Deese, J., and Kellogg, W. N. Some new data on the nature of 'spinal conditioning.' *Journal of Comparative and Physiological Psychology*, 1949, *42*, 157–160.

Delcomyn, F. Neural basis of rhythmic behavior in animals. *Science*, 1980, *210*, 492–498.

Dennenberg, V. H., and Karas, G. C. Supplementary report: The Yerkes-Dodson law and shift in task difficulty. *Journal of Experimental Psychology,* 1960, *59,* 429–430.

Denny, M. R. Relaxation theory and experiments. In F. R. Brush (Ed.), *Aversive conditioning and learning.* New York: Academic Press, 1971.

DesLauriers, B. C. A behavioral approach to transportation: A study of commuting by university employees. Ph.D. dissertation. The Pennsylvania State University, 1977.

DeVilliers, P. A. Choice in concurrent schedules and a quantitative formulation of the law of effect. In W. K. Honig and J. E. R. Staddon (Eds.), *Handbook of operant behavior.* Englewood Cliffs, N.J.: Prentice-Hall, 1977.

Dews, P. B. The effect of multiple S △ periods on responding on a fixed-interval schedule. *Journal of the Experimental Analysis of Behavior,* 1962, *5,* 369–374.

DiCara, L. V., and Miller, N. E. Changes in heart rate instrumentally learned by curarized rats as avoidance responses. *Journal of Comparative and Physiological Psychology,* 1968, *65,* 1–7.

Dickinson, A. *Contemporary animal learning theory.* Cambridge: Cambridge University Press, 1980.

Dickinson, A., Hall, G., and Mackintosh, N. J. Surprise and the attenuation of blocking. *Journal of Experimental Psychology: Animal Behavior Processes,* 1976, *2,* 313–322.

Dickinson, A., and Mackintosh, N. J. Classical conditioning in animals. In M. R. Rosenzweig and L. W. Porter (Eds.), *Annual review of psychology.* Palo Alto, Calif.: Annual Reviews, Inc., 1978.

Dillon, R. F., and Reid, L. S. Short-term memory as a function of information processing during the retention interval. *Journal of Experimental Psychology,* 1969, *81,* 261–269.

Dinsmoor, J. A. *Operant conditioning: An experimental analysis of behavior.* Dubuque, Iowa: W. C. Brown Co., 1970.

Doleys, D. M. Behavioral treatments for nocturnal enuresis: A review of the recent literature. *Psychological Bulletin,* 1977, *84,* 30–54.

Domjan, M. Biological constraints on instrumental and classical conditioning: Implications for general process theory. In G. H. Bower (Ed.), *The psychology of learning and motivation.* New York: Academic Press, 1983.

Dooling, D. J., and Lachman, R. Effects of comprehension on retention of prose. *Journal of Experimental Psychology,* 1971, *88,* 216–222.

Drugan, R. C., and Maier, S. F. The nature of the activity deficit produced by inescapable shock. *Animal Learning & Behavior,* 1982, *10,* 401–406.

Dubin, W. J., and Levis, D. J. Generalization of extinction gradients: A systematic analysis. *Journal of Experimental Psychology,* 1973, *100,* 403–412.

Dunham, P. J. Contrasted conditions of reinforcement: A selective critique. *Psychological Bulletin,* 1968, *69,* 295–315.

Durkovic, R. G. Classical conditioning, sensitization and habituation in spinal cat. *Physiology and Behavior,* 1975, *14,* 297–304.

Dworkin, B. R., and Miller, N. E. Failure to replicate visceral learning in the acute curarized rat preparation. *Behavioral Neuroscience,* 1986, *100,* 299–314.

Dyal, J. S., and Holland, T. A. Resistance to extinction as a function of the number of reinforcements. *American Journal of Psychology,* 1963, *76,* 323–333.

Dyal, J. S., and Sytsma, D. Relative persistence as a function of order of reinforcement schedules. *Journal of Experimental Psychology: Animal Behavior Processes,* 1976, *2,* 370–375.

Dykman, R. A., and Shurrager, P. S. Successive and maintained conditioning in spinal carnivores. *Journal of Comparative and Physiological Psychology,* 1956, *49,* 27–35.

Ebbinghaus, H. *Memory: A contribution to experimental psychology* (translated by H. A. Ruger and C. E. Bussenius). New York: Teachers College, Columbia University, 1885/1913.

Egeland, B. Effects of errorless training on teaching children to discriminate letters of the alphabet. *Journal of Applied Psychology,* 1975, *60,* 533–536.

Eibl-Eibesfeldt, I. *Ethology: The biology of behavior.* New York: Holt, Rinehart and Winston, 1970.

Eikelboom, R., and Stewart, J. Conditioning of drug-induced physiological responses. *Psychological Review,* 1982, *89,* 507–528.

Einstein, G. O., McDaniel, M. A., Bowers, C. A., and Stevens, D. T. Memory for prose: The influence of relational and proposition-specific processing. *Journal of Experimental Psychology: Learning, Memory, and Cognition,* 1984, *10,* 133–143.

Eisenberger, R., Karpman, M., and Trattner, J. What is the necessary and sufficient condition for reinforcement in the contingency condition? *Journal of Experimental Psychology*, 1967, *74*, 342–350.

Ekstrand, B. R., and Underwood, B. J. Free learning and recall as a function of unit-sequence and letter-sequence interference. *Journal of Verbal Learning and Verbal Behavior*, 1965, *4*, 390–396.

Elkins, R. L. Bait-shyness acquisition and resistance to extinction as functions of US exposure to conditioning. *Physiological Psychology*, 1974, *2*, 341–343.

Emlen, J. M. The role of time and energy in food preference. *The American Naturalist*, 1966, *100*, 611–617.

Engel, B. T., and Hansen, S. P. Operant conditioning of heart rate slowing. *Psychophysiology*, 1966, *3*, 176–187.

English, H. B. How psychology can facilitate military training—A concrete example. *Journal of Applied Psychology*, 1942, *26*, 3–7.

Erdelyi, M. H., and Becker, J. Hypermnesia for pictures: Incremental memory for pictures but not words in multiple recall trials. *Cognitive Psychology*, 1974, *6*, 159–171.

Erdelyi, M. H., Bushke, H., and Finkelstein, S. Hypermnesia for Socratic stimuli: The growth of recall for an internally generated memory list abstracted from a series of riddles. *Memory & Cognition*, 1977, *5*, 283–286.

Erdelyi, M. H., Finkelstein, S., Herrell, N., Miller, B., and Thomas, J. Coding modality vs. input modality in hypermnesia: Is a rose rose? *Cognition*, 1976, *4*, 311–319.

Erdelyi, M. H., and Kleinbard, J. Has Ebbinghaus decayed with time? The growth of recall (Hypermnesia) over days. *Journal of Experimental Psychology: Human Learning and Memory*, 1978, *4*, 275–289.

Erickson, M. H. Development of apparent unconsciousness during hypnotic reliving of a traumatic experience. *Archives of Neurology and Psychiatry*, 1937, *38*, 1282–1288.

Erickson, R. L. Relational isolation as a means of producing the vonRestorff effect in paired-associate learning. *Journal of Experimental Psychology*, 1963, *66*, 111–119.

Ericsson, K. A., Chase, W. C., and Faloon, S. Acquisition of a memory skill. *Science*, 1980, *208*, 1181–1182.

Estes, B. W., Miller, L. B., and Curtin, M. E. Supplementary report: Monetary incentive and motivation in discrimination learning—Sex differences. *Journal of Experimental Psychology*, 1962, *63*, 320.

Estes, W. K. An experimental study of punishment. *Psychology Monographs*, 1944, *57*, No. 3.

Estes, W. K. Outline of a theory of punishment. In B. A. Campbell and R. M. Church (Eds.), *Punishment and aversive behavior*. New York: Appleton-Century-Crofts, 1969.

Estes, W. K. Introduction to volume 2. In W. K. Estes (Ed.), *Handbook of learning and cognitive processes, Vol. 2, Conditioning and behavior theory*. Hillsdale, N.J.: Erlbaum, 1975.

Estes, W. K., and Skinner, B. F. Some quantitative properties of anxiety. *Journal of Experimental Psychology*, 1941, *29*, 390–400.

Fabricius, E., and Boyd, H. Experiments on the following-reaction of ducklings. *Wildfowl Trust Annual Report* (1952–53), 1954, *6*, 84–89.

Fagan, J. F. Clustering of related but nonassociated items in free recall. *Psychonomic Science*, 1969, *16*, 92–93.

Fantino, E., Kasdon, D., and Stringer, N. The Yerkes-Dodson law and alimentary motivation. *Canadian Journal of Psychology*, 1970, *24*, 77–84.

Fechner, G. T. *Elemente der psychophysik*. Leipzig: Breitkopf und Hartel, 1860.

Fehrer, E. Effects of amount of reinforcement and of pre- and postreinforcement delays on learning and extinction. *Journal of Experimental Psychology*, 1956, *52*, 167–176.

Ferguson, R. K., Adams, W. J., and Mitchell, C. L. Studies of tolerance development to morphine analgesia in rats tested on the hot plate. *European Journal of Pharmacology*, 1969, *8*, 83–92.

Fernandez, A., and Glenberg, A. M. Changing environmental context does not reliably affect memory. *Memory & Cognition*, 1985, *13*, 333–345.

Ferster, C. B., and DeMyer, M. K. The development of performances in autistic children in an automatically controlled environment. *Journal of Chronic Diseases*, 1961, *13*, 312–345.

Ferster, C. B., and DeMyer, M. K. A method for the experimental analysis of the behavior of autistic children. *American Journal of Orthopsychiatry*, 1962, *32*, 89–98.

Finkelman, D. Science and psychology. *American Journal of Psychology,* 1978, *91,* 179–199.

Fitts, P. M., Bahrick, H. P., Briggs, G. E., and Noble, M. E. *Skilled performance* (Technical Report, Project No. 7707, Contract No. AF 41 (657)-70). Ohio: Wright-Patterson Air Force Base, 1959.

Fitts, P. M., and Deininger, R. L. S-R compatibility: Correspondence among paired elements within stimulus and response codes. *Journal of Experimental Psychology,* 1954, *48,* 483–492.

Fitts, P. M., and Posner, M. I. *Human performance.* Belmont, Calif.: Brooks-Cole, 1967.

Fitzgerald, L. A., and Thompson, R. F. Classical conditioning of the hindlimb flexion reflex in the acute spinal cat. *Psychonomic Science,* 1967, *8,* 213–214.

Fitzgerald, R. D. Effects of partial reinforcement with acid on the classically conditioned salivary response in dogs. *Journal of Comparative and Physiological Psychology,* 1963, *56,* 1056–1060.

Fitzwater, M. E. The relative effect of reinforcement and nonreinforcement in establishing a form discrimination. *Journal of Comparative and Physiological Psychology,* 1952, *45,* 476–481.

Fitzwater, M. E., and Reisman, M. N. Comparison of forward, simultaneous, backward, and pseudo-conditioning. *Journal of Experimental Psychology,* 1952, *44,* 211–214.

Flaherty, C. F. Incentive contrast: A review of behavioral changes following shifts in reward. *Animal Learning & Behavior,* 1982, *10,* 409–440.

Flaherty, C. F., and Caprio, M. Dissociation between instrumental and consummatory measures of incentive contrast. *American Journal of Psychology,* 1976, *89,* 485–498.

Flaherty, C. F., and Largen, J. Within-subjects positive and negative contrast effects in rats. *Journal of Comparative and Physiological Psychology,* 1975, *88,* 653–664.

Flaherty, C. F., Uzwiak, A. J., Levine, J., Smith, M., Hall, P., and Schuler, R. Apparent hyperglycemic and hypoglycemic conditioned responses with exogenous insulin as the unconditioned stimulus. *Animal Learning & Behavior,* 1980, *8,* 382–386.

Fleishman, E. A. A comprehensive study of aptitude patterns in unskilled and skilled psychomotor performance. *Journal of Applied Psychology,* 1957, *41,* 263–272.

Fleishman, E. A. Abilities at different stages of practice in rotary pursuit performance. *Journal of Experimental Psychology,* 1960, *60,* 162–171.

Fleishman, E. A., and Hempel, W. E., Jr. Changes in factor structure of a complex psychomotor test as a function of practice. *Psychometrika,* 1954, *18,* 239–252.

Fleishman, E. A., and Hempel, W. E., Jr. The relation between abilities and improvement with practice in a visual discrimination reaction task. *Journal of Experimental Psychology,* 1955, *49,* 301–312.

Fleishman, E. A., and Parker, J. F. Factors in the retention and relearning of a perceptual-motor skill. *Journal of Experimental Psychology,* 1962, *64,* 215–226.

Fowler, H. Facilitating stimulus effects of reward and punishment: Discriminability as a general principle. In D. K. Routh (Ed.), *Learning speech and the complex effects of punishment.* New York: Plenum, 1982.

Fowler, H., and Trapold, M. A. Escape performance as a function of delay of reinforcement. *Journal of Experimental Psychology,* 1962, *63,* 464–467.

Frcka, G., Beyts, J., Levey, A. B., and Martin, I. The role of awareness in human conditioning. *Pavlovian Journal of Biological Science,* 1983, *18,* 69–76.

Fredrikson, M., and Öhman, A. Cardiovascular and electrodermal responses conditioned to fear-relevant stimuli. *Psychophysiology,* 1979, *16,* 1–7.

Freund, J. S., and Underwood, B. J. Storage and retrieval cues in free recall learning. *Journal of Experimental Psychology,* 1969, *81,* 49–53.

Frezza, D. A., and Holland, J. G. Operant conditioning of the human salivary response. *Psychophysiology,* 1971, *8,* 581–587.

Frincke, G. Word characteristics, associative-relatedness, and the free recall of nouns. *Journal of Verbal Learning and Verbal Behavior,* 1968, *7,* 366–372.

Fuhrer, M. J., and Baer, P. E. Cognitive processes in differential GSR conditioning: Effects of a masking task. *American Journal of Psychology,* 1969, *82,* 168–180.

Fulton, J. F. *Howell's textbook of physiology.* Philadelphia: Saunders, 1946.

Furedy, J. J., and Poulos, C. X. Short-interval classical SCR conditioning and the stimulus-sequence-change-elicited OR: The case of the empirical red herring. *Psychophysiology,* 1977, *14,* 351–359.

Furedy, J. J., Riley, D. M., and Fredrikson, M.

Pavlovian extinction, phobias, and the limits of the cognitive paradigm. *Pavlovian Journal of Biological Science,* 1983, *18,* 126 135.

Gaioni, S. J. Blocking and nonsimultaneous compounds: Comparison of responding during compound conditioning and testing. *Pavlovian Journal of Biological Science,* 1982, *17,* 16–29.

Galef, B. G., Jr., and Osborne, B. Novel taste facilitation of the association of visual cues with toxicosis in rats. *Journal of Comparative and Physiological Psychology,* 1978, *92,* 907–916.

Gamzu, E., and Schwam, E. Autoshaping and automaintenance of a key-press response in squirrel monkeys. *Journal of the Experimental Analysis of Behavior,* 1974, *21,* 361–371.

Gamzu, E. R., and Williams, D. R. Associative factors underlying the pigeon's key pecking in auto-shaping procedures. *Journal of the Experimental Analysis of Behavior,* 1973, *19,* 225–232.

Garcia, J., and Koelling, R. A. Relation of cue to consequence in avoidance learning. *Psychonomic Science,* 1966, *4,* 123–124.

Gardner, E. *Fundamentals of neurology.* Philadelphia: Saunders, 1952.

Gardner, B. T., and Gardner, R. A. *Comparing the early utterances of child and chimpanzee.* Minnesota symposium on child psychology, Vol. 8. Minneapolis: University of Minnesota, 1974.

Geller, E. S. Rewarding safety belt usage at an industrial setting: Tests of treatment generality and response maintenance. *Journal of Applied Behavior Analysis,* 1983, *16,* 189–202.

Gentile, A. M. A working model of skill acquisition with application to teaching. *Quest,* 1972, *17,* 3–23.

Gerall, A. A., Sampson, P. P., and Boslov, G. L. Classical conditioning of human pupillary dilation. *Journal of Experimental Psychology,* 1957, *54,* 467–474.

Gibbon, J., Farrell, L., Locurto, C. M., Duncan, H. J., and Terrace, H. S. Partial reinforcement in autoshaping with pigeons. *Animal Learning & Behavior,* 1980, *8,* 45–59.

Gibbs, C. M., Latham, S. B., and Gormezano, I. Classical conditioning of the rabbit membrane response: Effects of reinforcement schedule on response maintenance and resistance to extinction. *Animal Learning & Behavior,* 1978, *6,* 209–215.

Glanzer, M., and Cunitz, A. R. Two storage mechanisms in free recall. *Journal of Verbal Learning and Verbal Behavior,* 1966, *5,* 351–360.

Glanzer, M., and Peters, S. C. Re-examination of the serial position effect. *Journal of Experimental Psychology,* 1962, *64,* 258–266.

Glaze, J. A. The association value of nonsense syllables. *Journal of Genetic Psychology,* 1928, *35,* 255–269.

Glenberg, A. M., and Kraus, T. A. Long-term recency is not found on a recognition test. *Journal of Experimental Psychology: Human Learning and Memory,* 1981, *7,* 475–479.

Glenberg, A. M., Smith, S. M., and Green, C. Type I rehearsal: Maintenance and more. *Journal of Verbal Learning and Verbal Behavior,* 1977, *16,* 339–352.

Glencross, D. J. Control of skilled movements. *Psychological Bulletin,* 1977, *84,* 14–29.

Glencross, D. J., and Oldfield, S. R. The use of ischemic nerve block procedures in the investigation of the sensory control of movements. *Biological Psychology,* 1975, *2,* 165–174.

Glisky, E. L., and Rabinowitz, J. C. Enhancing the generation effect through repetition of operations. *Journal of Experimental Psychology: Learning, Memory, and Cognition,* 1985, *11,* 193–205.

Godbout, R. C., Ziff, D. R., and Capaldi, E. J. Effect of several reward exposure procedures on the small trial PRE. *Psychonomic Science,* 1968, *13,* 153–154.

Godden, D. R., and Baddeley, A. D. Context-dependent memory in two natural environments: On land and underwater. *British Journal of Psychology,* 1975, *66,* 325–331.

Gomulicki, B. R. Recall as an abstractive process. *Acta Psychologica,* 1956, *12,* 77–94.

Gonzalez, F. A. Effects of partial reinforcement (25%) in an auto-shaping procedure. *Bulletin of the Psychonomic Society,* 1973, *2,* 299–301.

Gonzalez, R. C., Gentry, G. V., and Bitterman, M. E. Relational discrimination of intermediate size in the chimpanzee. *Journal of Comparative and Physiological Psychology,* 1954, *47,* 385–388.

Goodall, J. My life among wild chimpanzees. *National Geographic Magazine,* 1963, *125,* 272–308.

Goodall, J. *The chimpanzees of Gombe.* Cambridge, Mass.: Harvard University Press, 1986.

Goodrich, K. P. Performance in different segments of an instrumental response chain as a function of reinforcement schedule. *Journal of Experimental Psychology,* 1959, *57,* 57–63.

Goodrich, K. P. Running speed and drinking rate as functions of sucrose concentration and amount of consummatory activity. *Journal of Comparative and Physiological Psychology,* 1960, *53,* 245–250.

Goodrich, K. P., and Zaretsky, H. Running speed as a function of concentration of sucrose incentive during pre-training. *Psychological Reports,* 1962, *11,* 463–468.

Goodwin, D. W., Powell, B., Bremer, B., Hoine, H., and Stern, J. Alcohol and recall: State-dependent effects in man. *Science,* 1969, *163,* 1358–1360.

Goomas, D. T. Reward effects following single-trial acquisition training. *American Journal of Psychology,* 1982, *95,* 275–285.

Gordon, W. C., McGinnis, C. M., and Weaver, M. S. The effect of cuing after backward conditioning trials. *Learning and Motivation,* 1985, *16,* 444–463.

Gorman, A. M. Recognition memory for nouns as a function of abstractness and frequency. *Journal of Experimental Psychology,* 1961, *61,* 23–29.

Gormezano, I. Investigators of defense and reward conditioning in the rabbit. In A. H. Black and W. F. Prokasy (Eds.), *Classical conditioning II: Current research and theory.* New York: Appleton-Century Crofts, 1972.

Gormezano, I., and Hiller, G. W. Omission training of the jaw-movement response of the rabbit to a water US. *Psychonomic Science,* 1972, *29,* 276–278.

Gormezano, I., and Kehoe, E. J. Classical Conditioning: Some methodological issues. In W. K. Estes (Ed.), *Handbook of learning and cognitive processes, Vol. 2, Conditioning and Behavior Theory.* Hillsdale, N.J.: Erlbaum, 1975.

Gormezano, I., Kehoe, E. J., and Marshall, B. S. Twenty years of classical conditioning research with the rabbit. *Progress in Psychobiology and Physiological Psychology,* 1983, *10,* 197–275.

Gormezano, I., Prokasy, W. F., and Thompson, R. F. *Classical conditioning.* Hillsdale, N.J.: Erlbaum, 1987.

Gould, J. L. The biology of learning. In M. R. Rosenzweig and L. W. Porter (Eds.), *Annual review of psychology.* Palo Alto, Calif.: Annual Reviews, Inc., 1986.

Graesser, A. C. *Prose comprehension beyond the word.* New York: Springer-Verlag, 1981.

Grant, D. A. Classical and operant conditioning. In A. W. Melton (Ed.), *Categories of human learning.* New York: Academic Press, 1964.

Grant, D. A. Cognitive factors in eyelid conditioning. *Psychophysiology,* 1973, *10,* 75–81.

Grant, D. A., and Schipper, L. M. The acquisition and extinction of conditioned eyelid responses as a function of the percentage of fixed-ratio random reinforcement. *Journal of Experimental Psychology,* 1952, *43,* 313–320.

Grant, D. A., Schipper, L. M., and Ross, B. M. Effect of intertrial interval during acquisition on extinction of the conditioned eyelid response following partial reinforcement. *Journal of Experimental Psychology,* 1952, *44,* 303–310.

Grant, D. A., and Schneider, D. E. Intensity of the conditioned stimulus and strength of conditioning: I. The conditioned eyelid response to light. *Journal of Experimental Psychology,* 1948, *38,* 690–696.

Grant, D. A., and Schneider, D. E. Intensity of the conditioned stimulus and strength of conditioning. II. The conditioned galvanic skin response to an auditory stimulus. *Journal of Experimental Psychology,* 1949, *39,* 35–40.

Grant, D. S. Effect of sample presentation time on long-delayed matching in the pigeon. *Learning and Motivation,* 1976, *7,* 580–590.

Gray, T., and Appignanesi, A. A. Compound conditioning: Elimination of the blocking effect. *Learning and Motivation,* 1973, *4,* 374–380.

Greene, J. E. Magnitude of reward and acquisition of a black-white discrimination habit. *Journal of Experimental Psychology,* 1953, *46,* 113–119.

Greene, R. L. Sources of recency effects in free recall. *Psychological Bulletin,* 1986, *99,* 221–228.

Greenspoon, J., and Foreman, S. Effect of delay of knowledge of results on learning a motor task. *Journal of Experimental Psychology,* 1956, *51,* 226–228.

Greenspoon, J., and Ranyard, R. Stimulus conditions and retroactive inhibition. *Journal of Experimental Psychology,* 1957, *53,* 55–59.

Grice, G. R. The relation of secondary reinforcement to delayed reward in visual discrimination learning. *Journal of Experimental Psychology,* 1948, *38,* 1–16.

Grice, G. R., and Hunter, J. J. Stimulus intensity effects depend upon the type of experimental design. *Psychological Review,* 1964, *71,* 247–256.

Grice, G. R., and Saltz, E. The generalization of

an instrumental response to stimuli varying in the size dimension. *Journal of Experimental Psychology,* 1950, *40,* 702–708.

Griffin. D. R. *Echoes of bats and men.* Garden City, N.Y.: Anchor Books, 1959.

Grindley, G. C. Experiments on the influence of the amount of reward on learning of young chickens. *British Journal of Psychology,* 1929, *20,* 173–180.

Grings, W. W. Orientation, conditioning, and learning. *Psychophysiology,* 1977, *14,* 343–350.

Grings, W. W., and O'Donnell, D. E. Magnitude of response to compounds of discriminated stimuli. *Journal of Experimental Psychology,* 1956, *52,* 354–359.

Gumenik, W. E., and Levitt, J. The von Restorff effect as a function of difference in the isolated item. *American Journal of Psychology,* 1968, *81,* 247–252.

Gundlach, H. U. K. Ebbinghaus, nonsense syllables, and three letter words. *Contemporary Psychology,* 1986, *31,* 469–470.

Guthrie, E. R. *The psychology of learning.* New York: Harper, 1935.

Guthrie, G. M., Guthrie, H. A., Fernandez, T. L., and Estrera, N. O. Cultural influences and reinforcement strategies. *Behavior Therapy,* 1982, *13,* 624–637.

Guttenberger, V. T., and Wasserman, E. Effects of sample duration, retention interval, and passage of time in the test on pigeons' matching-to-sample performance. *Animal Learning & Behavior,* 1985, *13,* 121–128.

Guttman, N. Operant conditioning, extinction, and periodic reinforcement in relation to concentration of sucrose used as a reinforcing agent. *Journal of Experimental Psychology,* 1953, *46,* 213–224.

Guttman, N., and Kalish, H. I. Discriminabilty and stimulus generalization. *Journal of Experimental Psychology,* 1956, *51,* 79–88.

Haggard, D. F. Acquisition of a simple running response as a function of partial and continuous schedules of reinforcement. *Psychological Record,* 1959, *9,* 11–18.

Hall, J. F. Learning as a function of word frequency. *American Journal of Psychology,* 1954, *67,* 138–140.

Hall, J. F. Retroactive inhibition in meaningful material. *Journal of Educational Psychology,* 1955, *46,* 47–52.

Hall, J. F. Recognition as a function of word frequency. *American Journal of Psychology,* 1979, *92,* 497–505.

Hall, J. F. Recall vs. recognition: A methodologi-

cal note. *Journal of Experimental Psychology: Learning, Memory and Cognition,* 1983, *9,* 346–349.

Hall, J. F. Backward conditioning in Pavlovian type studies: Reevaluation and present status. *Pavlovian Journal of Biological Science,* 1984, *19,* 163–168.

Hall, J. F. Free recall as a function of type of encoding and word frequency. *Bulletin of the Psychonomic Society,* 1985, *23,* 368–370.

Hall, J. F. The conditional emotional response as a model of Pavlovian conditioning. *Pavlovian Journal of Biological Science,* 1986, *21,* 1–11.

Hall, J. F. Gantt's principle of schizokinesis: The acquisition of classical conditioned autonomic responses. In F. J. McGuigan and T. A. Ban (Eds.), *Critical issues in psychology, psychiatry, and physiology: A memorial to W. Horsley Gantt.* New York: Gordon and Breach, 1987.

Hall, J. F., and Kobrick, J. L. The relationship among three measures of response strength. *Journal of Comparative and Physiological Psychology,* 1952, *45,* 280–282.

Hammes, J. A. Visual discrimination learning as a function of shock-fear and task difficulty. *Journal of Comparative and Physiological Psychology,* 1956, *49,* 481–484.

Hankins, W. G., Garcia, J., and Rusiniak, K. W. Dissociation of odor and taste in bait shyness. *Behavioral Biology,* 1973, *8,* 407–419.

Hanson, H. M. Effects of discrimination on stimulus generalization. *Journal of Experimental Psychology,* 1959, *58,* 321–334.

Hanson, H. M. Stimulus generalization following three-stimulus discrimination training. *Journal of Comparative and Physiological Psychology,* 1961, *54,* 181–185.

Hara, K., and Warren, J. M. Stimulus additivity and dominance in discrimination performance in cats. *Journal of Comparative and Physiological Psychology,* 1961, *54,* 86–90.

Harlow, H. F. The formation of learning sets. *Psychological Review,* 1949, *56,* 51–65.

Harlow, H. F., Gluck, J. P., and Suomi, S. J. Generalization of behavioral data between nonhuman and human animals. *American Psychologist,* 1972, *27,* 709–716.

Harlow, H. F., and Hicks, L. H. Discrimination learning theory: Uniprocess vs. duo-process. *Psychological Review,* 1957, *64,* 104–109.

Harris, A. H., and Brady, J. V. Animal learning—Visceral and autonomic conditioning. In M. R. Rosenzweig and L. W. Porter (Eds.), *An-*

nual review of psychology. Palo Alto, Calif.: Annual Reviews, Inc., 1974.

Harris, J. D. Forward conditioning, backward conditioning, and pseudo-conditioning, and adaptation to the conditioned stimulus. *Journal of Experimental Psychology,* 1941, *28,* 491–502.

Harris, P., and Nygaard, J. E. Resistance to extinction and number of reinforcements. *Psychological Reports,* 1961, *8,* 233–234.

Hartman, T. F., and Grant, D. A. Differential eyelid conditioning as a function of the CS-UCS interval. *Journal of Experimental Psychology,* 1962, *64,* 131–136.

Harvey, C., and Wickens, D. D. Effects of instructions on responsiveness to the UCS in GSR conditioning. *Journal of Experimental Psychology,* 1971, *87,* 137–140.

Harvey, C. B., and Wickens, D. D. Effects of cognitive control processes on the classically conditioned galvanic skin response. *Journal of Experimental Psychology,* 1973, *101,* 278–282.

Hasher, L., and Griffin, M. Reconstructive and reproductive processes in memory. *Journal of Experimental Psychology: Human Learning and Memory,* 1978, *4,* 318–330.

Hasher, L., Griffin, M., and Johnson, M. K. More on interpretive factors in forgetting. *Memory & Cognition,* 1977, *5,* 41–45.

Hashtroudi, S. Type of semantic elaboration and recall. *Memory & Cognition,* 1983, *11,* 476–484.

Hatze, H. Biomechanical aspects of a successful motion optimization. In P. V. Komi (Ed.), *Biomechanics V-B.* Baltimore: University Park Press, 1976.

Hatzenbuehler, L. C., and Schroeder, H. E. Desensitization procedures in the treatment of childhood disorders. *Psychological Bulletin,* 1978, *85,* 831–844.

Hearst, E., and Jenkins, H. M. *Sign tracking: The stimulus reinforcer relation and directed action.* Austin, Texas: Monograph of the Psychonomic Society, 1974.

Hearst, E., and Koresko, M. B. Stimulus generalization and amount of prior training on variable interval reinforcement. *Journal of Comparative and Physiological Psychology,* 1968, *66,* 133–138.

Hebb, D. O. *The organization of behavior.* New York: Wiley, 1949.

Hermann, J. A., deMontes, A. I., Dominguez, B., Montes, F., and Hopkins, B. L. Effects of bonuses for punctuality on the tardiness of industrial workers. *Journal of Applied Behavior Analysis,* 1973, *6,* 563–570.

Herbert, M. J., and Harsh, C. M. Observational learning in cats. *Journal of Comparative and Physiological Psychology,* 1944, *37,* 81–95.

Herrnstein, R. J. Relative and absolute strength of response as a function of frequency of reinforcement. *Journal of Experimental Analysis of Behavior,* 1961, *4,* 267–272.

Herrnstein, R. J. Acquisition, generalization, and discrimination reversal of a natural concept. *Journal of Experimental Psychology,* 1979, *5,* 116–129.

Herrnstein, R. J., and deVilliers, P. A. Fish as a natural category for people and pigeons. In G. H. Bower (Ed.), *The psychology of learning and motivation.* New York: Academic Press, 1980.

Herrnstein, R. J., and Loveland, D. H. Complex visual concept in the pigeon. *Science,* 1964, *146,* 549–551.

Herrnstein, R. J., Loveland, D. H., and Cable, C. Natural concepts in pigeons. *Journal of Experimental Psychology: Animal Behavior Processes,* 1976, *2,* 285–302.

Heth, C. D., and Rescorla, R. A. Simultaneous and backward fear conditioning in the rat. *Journal of Comparative and Physiological Psychology,* 1973, *82,* 434–443.

Higgins, S. T., and Morris, E. K. Generality of free-operant avoidance conditioning to human behavior. *Psychological Bulletin,* 1984, *96,* 247–272.

Hilgard, E. R. Methods and procedures in the study of learning. In S. S. Stevens (Ed.), *Handbook of experimental psychology.* New York: Wiley, 1951.

Hilgard, E. R., and Marquis, D. G. *Conditioning and learning.* New York: Appleton-Century-Crofts, 1940.

Hilgard, E. R., Miller, J., and Ohlson, J. A. Three attempts to secure pupillary conditioning to auditory stimuli near the absolute threshold. *Journal of Experimental Psychology,* 1941, *29,* 89–103.

Hill, F. A. Effects of instructions and subjects' need for approval on the conditioned galvanic skin response. *Journal of Experimental Psychology,* 1967, *73,* 461–467.

Hill, W. F., and Wallace, W. P. Effects of magnitude and percentage of reward on subsequent patterns of runway speed. *Journal of Experimental Psychology,* 1967, *73,* 544–548.

Hinde, R. A. *Ethology, its nature and relation with other sciences.* New York: Oxford University Press, 1982.

Hintzman, D. L. Episodic versus semantic memory: A distinction whose time has come—and gone? *Behavioral and Brain Sciences,* 1984, *7,* 240–241.

Hirst, W. The amnesic syndrome: Descriptions and explanations. *Psychological Bulletin,* 1982, *91,* 435–462.

Hobson, G. N. Effects of UCS adaptation upon conditioning in low and high anxiety men and women. *Journal of Experimental Psychology,* 1968, *76,* 360–363.

Hochhauser, M., and Fowler, H. Cue effects of drive and reward as a function of discrimination difficulty: Evidence against the Yerkes-Dodson law. *Journal of Experimental Psychology: Animal Behavior Processes,* 1975, *1,* 261–169.

Hockman, C. H., and Lipsitt, L. P. Delay-of-reward gradients in discrimination learning with children for two levels of difficulty. *Journal of Comparative and Physiological Psychology,* 1961, *54,* 24–27.

Hoffeld, D. R., Thompson, R. F., and Brogden, W. J. Effect of stimuli time relations during preconditioning training upon the magnitude of sensory pre-conditioning. *Journal of Experimental Psychology,* 1958, *56,* 437–442.

Hoffman, H. S. Experimental analysis of imprinting and its behavioral effects. In G. H. Bower, (Ed.), *The psychology of learning and motivation.* New York: Academic, 1978.

Hoffman, H. S., and Fleshler, M. Aversive control with the pigeon. *Journal of the Experimental Analysis of Behavior,* 1959, *2,* 213–218.

Hoffman, R. R., and Senter, R. J. Recent history of psychology: Mnemonic techniques and the psycholinguistic revolution. *The Psychological Record,* 1978, *28,* 3–15.

Holland, P. C. Conditioned stimulus as a determinant of the form of the Pavlovian conditioned response. *Journal of Experimental Psychology: Animal Behavior Processes,* 1977, *3,* 77–104.

Holland, P. C., and Rescorla, R. A. Second-order conditioning with food unconditioned stimulus. *Journal of Comparative and Physiological Psychology,* 1975a, *88,* 459–467.

Holland, P. C., and Rescorla, R. A. The effect of two ways of devaluing the unconditioned stimulus after first- and second-order appetitive conditioning. *Journal of Experimental Psychology: Animal Behavior Processes,* 1975b, *1,* 355–363.

Honig, W. K. Generalization of extinction on the spectral continuum. *Psychological Record,* 1961, *11,* 269–278.

Horton, K. D. Phonemic similarity, overt rehearsal, and short-term store. *Journal of Experimental Psychology: Human Learning and Memory,* 1976, *2,* 244–251.

Hovland, C. I. The generalization of conditioned responses. I. The sensory generalization of conditioned responses with varying frequencies of tone. *Journal of General Psychology,* 1937a, *17,* 125–148.

Hovland, C. I. The generalization of conditioned responses. II. The sensory generalization of conditioned responses with varying intensities of tone. *Journal of Genetic Psychology,* 1937b, *51,* 279–291.

Hovland, C. I. The generalization of conditioned responses. III. Extinction, spontaneous recovery, and disinhibition of conditioned and of generalized responses. *Journal of Experimental Psychology,* 1937c, *21,* 47–62.

Hovland, C. I. The generalization of conditioned responses. IV. The effects of varying amounts of reinforcement upon the degree of generalization of conditioned responses. *Journal of Experimental Psychology,* 1937d, *21,* 261–276.

Howe, M. J. A. *Introduction to human memory: A psychological approach.* New York: Harper and Row, 1970.

Howell, M. Use of force-time graphs for performance analysis in facilitating motor learning. *Research Quarterly,* 1956, *27,* 12–22.

Hudgins, C. V. Conditioning and the voluntary control of the pupillary light reflex. *Journal of General Psychology,* 1933, *8,* 3–51.

Hull, C. L. *Principles of behavior.* New York: Appleton-Century-Crofts, 1943.

Hull, C. L. Stimulus intensity dynamism (V) and stimulus generalization. *Psychological Review,* 1949, *56,* 67–76.

Hull, C. L. *The essentials of behavior.* New Haven: Yale University Press, 1951.

Hull, C. L. *A behavior system.* New Haven: Yale University Press, 1952.

Hull, C. L., Livingston, J. R., Rouse, R. O., and Barker, A. N. True, sham, and esophageal feeding as reinforcements. *Journal of Comparative and Physiological Psychology,* 1951, *44,* 236–245.

Hulse, S. H., Jr. Amount and percentage of reinforcement and duration of goal confinement in conditioning and extinction. *Journal of Experimental Psychology*, 1958, *56*, 48–57.

Hulse, S. H. Cognitive structure and serial pattern learning by animals. In S. H. Hulse, H. Fowler, and W. K. Honig (Eds.), *Cognitive processes in animal behavior*. Hillsdale, N.J.: Erlbaum, 1978.

Humphreys, L. G. The effect of random alternation of reinforcement on the acquisition and extinction of conditioned eyelid reactions. *Journal of Experimental Psychology*, 1939, *25*, 141–158.

Humphreys, L. G. Investigations of the simplex. *Psychometrika*, 1960, *25*, 313–323.

Hunt, E., and Love, T. How good can memory be? In A. W. Melton and E. Martin (Eds.), *Coding processes in human memory*. Washington: V. H. Winston & Sons, 1972.

Hunt, E. L. Establishment of conditioned responses in chick embryos. *The Journal of Comparative and Physiological Psychology*, 1949, *42*, 107–117.

Hunt, H. F., and Brady, J. V. Some effects of electro-convulsive shock on a conditioned emotional response ("anxiety"). *Journal of Comparative and Physiological Psychology*, 1951, *44*, 88–98.

Hupka, R. B., Kwaterski, S., and Moore, J. W. Conditioned diminution of the UCR: Differences between the human eyeblink and the rabbit nictitating membrane response. *Journal of Experimental Psychology*, 1970, *83*, 45–51.

Hursh, S. R. Economic concepts for the analysis of behavior. *Journal of the Experimental Analysis of Behavior*, 1980, *34*, 219–238.

Hurwitz, H. M. B., and Davis, H. The description and analysis of conditioned suppression: A critique of the conventional suppression ratio. *Animal Learning & Behavior*, 1983, *11*, 383–390.

Hyde, T. S., and Jenkins, J. J. The differential effects of incidental tasks on the organization of recall of a list of highly associated words. *Journal of Experimental Psychology*, 1969, *82*, 472–481.

Hyde, T. S., and Jenkins, J. J. Recall for words as a function of semantic, graphic, and syntactic orienting tasks. *Journal of Learning and Verbal Behavior*, 1973, *12*, 471–480.

Ince, L. P., Brucker, B. S., and Alba, A. Reflex conditioning in a spinal man. *Journal of Comparative and Physiological Psychology*, 1978, *92*, 796–802.

Ison, J. R. Experimental extinction as a function

of number of reinforcements. *Journal of Experimental Psychology*, 1962, *64*, 314–317.

Ison, J. R., and Cook, P. E. Extinction performance as a function of incentive magnitude and number of acquisition trials. *Psychonomic Science*, 1964, *1*, 245–246.

Ito, M., and Asaki, K. Choice behavior of rats in a concurrent-chains schedule: Amount and delay of reinforcement. *Journal of the Experimental Analysis of Behavior*, 1982, *37*, 383–392.

Izawa, C. Vocalized and silent tests in paired-associate learning. *American Journal of Psychology*, 1976, *89*, 681–693.

Jackson, R. L., Alexander, J. H., and Maier, S. F. Learned helplessness, inactivity, and associative deficits: Effects of inescapable shock on response choice escape learning. *Journal of Experimental Psychology: Animal Behavior Processes*, 1980, *6*, 1–20.

Jackson, R. L., Maier, S. F., and Coon, D. J. Long-term analgesic effects of inescapable shock and learned helplessness. *Science*, 1979, *206*, 91–93.

Jackson, R. L., Maier, S. F., and Rapaport, P. M. Exposure to inescapable shock produces both activity and associative deficit in the rat. *Learning and Motivation*, 1978, *9*, 69–98.

Jacobson, E. *Progressive relaxation*. Chicago: University of Chicago Press, 1938.

Jacoby, K. E., and Dawson, M. E. Observation and shaping learning: A comparison using Long Evans rats. *Psychonomic Science*, 1969, *16*, 257–258.

Jacoby, L. L., and Craik, F. I. M. Effects of elaboration of processing at encoding and retrieval: Trace distinctiveness and recovery of initial context. In L. S. Cermak and F. I. M. Craik (Eds.), *Levels of processing in human memory*. Hillsdale, N.J.: Erlbaum, 1979.

Jaffe, J. H. Drug addiction and drug abuse. In L. Goodman and A. Gilman (Eds.), *The pharmacological basis of therapeutics*. New York: Macmillan, 1970.

Jakubowski, E., and Zielinski, K. Stimulus intensity effects on acute extinction of the CER in rats. *Acta Neurobiologae Experimentalis*, 1978, *38*, 1–10.

James, W. *Principles of psychology*. New York: Holt, 1890.

Janda, L. H., and Rimm, D. C. Covert sensitization in the treatment of obesity. *Journal of Abnormal Psychology*, 1972, *80*, 37–42.

Jeffery, R. W. The influence of symbolic and motor rehearsal in observational learning.

Journal of Research in Personality, 1976, *10,* 116–127.

Jenkins, H. M. Animal learning and behavior theory. In E. Hearst (Ed.), *The first century of experimental psychology.* Hillsdale, N.J.: Erlbaum, 1979.

Jenkins, H. M., and Moore, B. R. The form of the autoshaped response with food or water reinforcers. *Journal of the Experimental Analysis of Behavior,* 1973, *20,* 163–181.

Jenkins, H. M., and Sainsbury, R. S. Discrimination learning with the distinctive feature on positive or negative trials. In D. Mostofsky (Ed.), *Attention: Contemporary theory and analysis.* New York: Appleton-Century-Crofts, 1970.

Jenkins, H. M., and Shattuck, D. Contingency in fear conditioning: A reexamination. *Bulletin of the Psychonomic Society,* 1981, *17,* 159–162.

Jenkins, J. G., and Dallenbach, K. M. Obliviscence during sleep and waking. *American Journal of Psychology,* 1924, *35,* 605–612.

Jensen, A. R. The von Restorff effect with minimal response learning. *Journal of Experimental Psychology,* 1962, *64,* 123–125.

Johnson, M. K., and Hasher, L. Human learning and memory. In M. R. Rosenzweig and L. W. Porter (Eds.), *Annual review of psychology.* Palo Alto, Calif.: Annual Reviews, Inc. 1975.

Johnson, R. E. Recall of prose as a function of the structural importance of the linguistic units. *Journal of Verbal Learning and Verbal Behavior,* 1970, *9,* 12–20.

Johnson, R. E. Memory-based rehearsal. In G. H. Bower (Ed.), *The psychology of learning and motivation.* New York: Academic Press, 1980.

Johnson, R. E. Remembering of prose: Holistic or piecemeal losses. *Journal of Memory and Language,* 1986, *25,* 525–538.

Johnson, R. E., and Scheidt, B. J. Organizational encodings in the serial learning of prose. *Journal of Verbal Learning and Verbal Behavior,* 1977, *16,* 575–588.

Johnson-Laird, P. N., and Bethell-Fox, C. E. Memory for questions and amount of processing. *Memory & Cognition,* 1978, *6,* 495–501.

Jones, F. M., and Jones, M. H. Vividness as a factor in learning lists of nonsense syllables. *American Journal of Psychology,* 1942, *55,* 96–101.

Justensen, D. R., Braun, E. W., Garrison, R. G., and Pendleton, R. B. Pharmacological differentiation of allergic and classically conditioned asthma in the guinea pig. *Science,* 1970, *170,* 864–866.

Kalish, H. I. The relationship between discriminability and generalization. *Journal of Experimental Psychology,* 1958, *55,* 637–644.

Kamin, L. J. Traumatic avoidance learning: The effects of CS-US interval with a trace conditioning procedure. *Journal of Comparative and Physiological Psychology,* 1954, *47,* 65–72.

Kamin, L. J. The gradient of delay of secondary reward in avoidance learning. *Journal of Comparative and Physiological Psychology,* 1957, *50,* 457–460.

Kamin, L. J. The delay-of-punishment gradient. *Journal of Comparative and Physiological Psychology,* 1959, *52,* 434–437.

Kamin, L. J. Apparent adaptation effects in the acquisition of a conditioned emotional response. *Canadian Journal of Psychology,* 1961, *15,* 176–188.

Kamin, L. J. Temporal and intensity characteristics of the conditioned stimulus. In W. F. Prokasy (Ed.), *Classical conditioning.* New York: Appleton-Century-Crofts, 1965.

Kamin, L. J. Attention-like processes in classical conditioning. In M. R. Jones (Ed.), *Miami symposium on the prediction of behavior: Aversive stimulation.* Miami: University of Miami Press, 1968.

Kamin, L. J. Predictability, surprise, attention and conditioning. In B. A. Campbell and R. M. Church (Eds.), *Punishment and aversive behavior.* New York: Appleton-Century-Crofts, 1969.

Kamin, L. J., and Brimer, C. J. The effects of intensity of conditioned and unconditioned stimuli on a conditioned emotional response. *Canadian Journal of Psychology,* 1963, *17,* 194–198.

Kamin, L. J., Brimer, C. J., and Black, A. H. Conditioned suppression as a monitor of fear of the CS in the course of avoidance training. *Journal of Comparative and Physiological Psychology,* 1963, *56,* 497–501.

Kamin, L. J., and Schaub, R. E. Effects of conditioned stimulus intensity on the conditioned emotional response. *Journal of Comparative and Physiological Psychology,* 1963, *56,* 502–507.

Kamman, R., and Melton, A. W. Absolute recovery of first-list responses from unlearning during 26 minutes filled with easy or difficult information processing task. *Proceedings from the 75th Annual Convention of the*

American Psychological Convention, 1967, *2,* 63–64.

Kappauf, W. E., and Schlosberg, H. Conditioned responses in the white rat. III. Conditioning as a function of the length of the period of delay. *Journal of Genetic Psychology,* 1937, *50,* 27–45.

Kaufman, I. C., and Rosenblum, L. A. Effects of separation from mother on the emotional behavior of infant monkeys. *Annals of the New York Academy of Science,* 1969, *159,* 689–695.

Kaufman, L. W. Foraging strategies: Laboratory simulations. Unpublished doctoral dissertation, Rutgers University, 1979.

Kaye, H., and Pearce, J. M. The strength of the orienting response during Pavlovian conditioning. *Journal of Experimental Psychology: Animal Behavior Processes,* 1984, *10,* 90–109.

Kazdin, A. E. *The token economy: A review and evaluation.* New York: Plenum Press, 1977.

Kazdin, A. E. *History of behavior modification.* Baltimore: University Park Press, 1978.

Keesey, R. Intracranial reward delay and the acquisition rate of a brightness discrimination. *Science,* 1964, *143,* 702.

Kehoe, E. J. Overshadowing and summation in compound stimulus conditioning of the rabbit's nictitating membrane response. *Journal of Experimental Psychology: Animal Behavior Processes,* 1982, *8,* 313–328.

Kehoe, E. J., Poulos, C. X., and Gormezano, I. Appetitive differential conditioning of the rabbit's jaw movement response. *The Pavlovian Journal of Biological Science,* 1985, *20,* 29–38.

Kelleher, R. T. Intermittent reinforcement in chimpanzees. *Science,* 1956, *124,* 679–680.

Kelleher, R. T. Conditioned reinforcement in chimpanzees. *Journal of Comparative and Physiological Psychology,* 1957, *49,* 571–575.

Kelleher, R. T. Fixed-ratio schedules of conditioned reinforcement with chimpanzees. *Journal of the Experimental Analysis of Behavior,* 1958, *1,* 281–289.

Keller, F., and Schoenfeld, W. N. *Principles of psychology.* New York: Appleton-Century-Crofts, 1950.

Kellog, W. N., Pronko, N. H., and Deese, J. Spinal conditioning in dogs. *Science,* 1946, *103,* 49–50.

Keppel, G., and Underwood, B. J. Proactive inhibition in short-term retention of a single item. *Journal of Verbal Learning and Verbal Behavior,* 1962, *1,* 153–161.

Kesner, R. P., and Baker, T. B. A two-process model of opiate tolerance. In J. L. Martinez, Jr., R. A. Jensen, B. Messing, H. Rigter, and J. L. McGaugh (Eds.), *Endogenous peptides and learning and memory processes.* New York: Academic Press, 1981.

Kimble, G. A. Shock intensity and avoidance learning. *Journal of Comparative and Physiological Psychology,* 1955, *48,* 341–348.

Kimble, G. A. *Hilgard and Marquis' conditioning and learning.* New York: Appleton-Century-Crofts, 1961.

Kimble, G. A., and Dufort, R. H. Meaningfulness and isolation as factors in verbal learning. *Journal of Experimental Psychology,* 1955, *50,* 361–368.

Kimble, G. A., and Dufort, R. H. The associative factor in eyelid conditioning. *Journal of Experimental Psychology,* 1956, *52,* 386–391.

Kimmel, E., and Kimmel, H. D. A replication of operant conditioning of the GSR. *Journal of Experimental Psychology,* 1963, *65,* 212–213.

Kimmel, H. D. Instrumental conditioning of autonomically mediated responses in human beings. *American Psychologist,* 1974, *29,* 325–335.

Kinnaman, A. J. Mental life of two Rhesus monkeys in captivity. *American Journal of Psychology,* 1902, *2,* 233–235.

Kintsch, W. Recognition and free recall of organized lists. *Journal of Experimental Psychology,* 1968, *78,* 481–487.

Kintsch, W. *Memory and cognition.* New York: Wiley, 1977.

Klatzky, R. L. Armchair theorists have more fun. *Behavioral and Brain Sciences,* 1984, *7,* 244.

Klein, S. B., Mikulka, P. J., and Lucci, K. Influence of lithium chloride intensity on unconditioned stimulus-alone interference in a flavor aversion paradigm. *Learning and Motivation,* 1986, *17,* 76–90.

Klein, S. B., and Spear, N. E. Reactivation of avoidance-learning memory in the rat after intermediate retention intervals. *Journal of Comparative and Physiological Psychology,* 1970, *72,* 498–504.

Kling, J. W. Generalization of extinction of an instrumental response to stimuli varying in size dimension. *Journal of Experimental Psychology,* 1952, *44,* 339–346.

Kling, J. W. Learning: Introductory survey. In J. W. Kling and L. A. Riggs (Eds.), *Woodworth & Schlosberg's experimental psychology.* New York: Holt, Rinehart and Winston, 1971.

Klosterhalfen, W., and Klosterhalfen, S. Pavlovian

conditioning of immunosuppression modifies adjunctive arthritis in rats. *Behavioral Neuroscience,* 1983, *97,* 663–666.

Knapp, C. G., and Dixon, W. R. Learning to juggle: II. A study of whole and part methods. *Research Quarterly,* 1952, *23,* 398–401.

Knapp, T. J., and Shodahl, S. A. Ben Franklin as a behavior modifier: A note. *Behavior Therapy,* 1974, *5,* 656–660.

Knouse, S. B., and Campbell, P. E. Partially delayed reward in the rat: A parametric study of delay duration. *Journal of Comparative and Physiological Psychology,* 1971, *75,* 116–119.

Kochevar, J. W., and Fox, P. W. Retrieval variables in the measurement of memory. *American Journal of Psychology,* 1980, *93,* 355–366.

Köhler, W. Simple structural functions in the chimpanzee and in the chicken. In W. D. Ellis (Ed.), *A source book of Gestalt psychology.* New York: Harcourt, Brace, 1939.

Kolers, P. A. Remembering operations. *Memory & Cognition,* 1973, *1,* 347–355.

Konorski, J., and Szwejkowska, G. Reciprocal transformations of heterogeneous conditioned reflexes. *Acta Biologiae Experimentalis,* 1956, *17,* 141–165.

Koppenaal, R. J. Time changes in the strength of A-B, A-C lists: Spontaneous recovery? *Journal of Verbal Learning and Verbal Behavior,* 1963, *2,* 310–319.

Korman, A. K. *The psychology of motivation.* Englewood Cliffs, N.J.: Prentice-Hall, 1974.

Kraeling, D. Analysis of amount of reward as a variable in learning. *Journal of Comparative and Physiological Psychology,* 1961, *54,* 560–565.

Krechevsky, I. Antagonistic visual discrimination habits in the white rat. *Journal of Comparative and Physiological Psychology,* 1932a, *14,* 263–277.

Krechevsky, I. "Hypotheses" versus "chance" in the pre-solution period in sensory discrimination learning. *University of California Publications in Psychology,* 1932b, *6,* 27–44.

Krechevsky, I. A study of the continuity of the problem-solving process. *Psychological Review,* 1938, *45,* 107–133.

Kroger, W. S., and Douce, R. G. Hypnosis in criminal investigation. *International Journal of Clinical and Experimental Hypnosis,* 1979, *27,* 358–374.

Krueger, W. C. F. The effect of overlearning on

retention. *Journal of Experimental Psychology,* 1929, *12,* 71–78.

Kucera, H., and Francis, W. N. *Computational analysis of present-day American English.* Providence, R.I.: Brown University Press, 1967.

Lachman, R. The influence of thirst and schedules of reinforcement-nonreinforcement ratios upon brightness discrimination. *Journal of Experimental Psychology,* 1961, *62,* 80–87.

Landers, D. M. Observational learning of a motor skill: Temporal spacing of demonstrations and audience presence. *Journal of Motor Behavior,* 1975, *7,* 281–287.

Landers, D. M., and Landers, D. M. Teacher versus peer models: Effects of model's presence and performance level on motor behavior. *Journal of Motor Behavior,* 1973, *5,* 129–139.

Lang, P. J., and Melamed, B. G. Avoidance conditioning of an infant with chronic ruminative vomiting. *Journal of Abnormal Psychology,* 1969, *74,* 1–8.

Lashley, K. S. The accuracy of movement in the absence of excitation from the moving organ. *American Journal of Physiology,* 1917, *43,* 169–194.

Lashley, K. S. Learning: I. Nervous-mechanisms of learning. In C. Murchison (Ed.), *The foundations of experimental psychology.* Worcester, Mass.: Clark University Press, 1929.

Lashley, K. S. The problem of serial order in behavior. In L. A. Jeffress (Ed.), *Cerebral mechanisms in behavior.* New York: Wiley, 1951.

Lashley, K. S., and Wade, M. The Pavlovian theory of generalization. *Psychological Review,* 1946, *53,* 72–87.

Laszlo, J. I. The performance of a simple motor task with kinesthetic sense loss. *Quarterly Journal of Experimental Psychology,* 1966, *18,* 1–8.

Laszlo, J. I. Training of fast tapping with reduction of kinesthetic, tactile, visual and auditory sensations. *Quarterly Journal of Experimental Psychology,* 1967, *19,* 344–349.

Laszlo, J. I., and Bairstow, P. J. Accuracy of movement, peripheral feedback and efferent copy. *Journal of Motor Behavior,* 1971, *3,* 241–252.

Laszlo, J. I., Shamoon, J. S., and Sanson-Fisher, R. W. Reacquisition and transfer of motor skills with sensory feedback reduction. *Journal of Motor Behavior,* 1969, *1,* 195–209.

Lavery, J. J. Retention of simple motor skills as a function of type of knowledge of results.

Canadian Journal of Psychology, 1962, *16*, 300–311.

Lavery, J. J., and Suddon, F. H. Retention of simple motor skills as a function of the number of trials by which KR is delayed. *Perceptual and Motor Skills*, 1962, *15*, 231–237.

Lawrence, D. H., and DeRivera, J. Evidence of relational transposition. *Journal of Comparative and Physiological Psychology*, 1954, *47*, 465–471.

Lea, S. E. In what sense do pigeons learn concepts? In H. L. Roitblat, T. G. Bever, and H. S. Terrace (Eds.), *Animal cognition*. Hillsdale, N.J.: Erlbaum, 1984.

Lea, S. E. and Harrison, S. N. Discrimination of polymorphous stimulus sets by pigeons. *Quarterly Journal of Experimental Psychology*, 1978, *30*, 521–537.

Leaf, R. C. Avoidance response evocation as a function of prior discriminative fear conditioning under curare. *Journal of Comparative and Physiological Psychology*, 1964, *58*, 446–449.

Leary, R. W. Homogeneous and heterogeneous reward of monkeys. *Journal of Comparative and Physiological Psychology*, 1958, *51*, 706–710.

Lee, B. S. Effects of delayed speech feedback. *Journal of Acoustical Society of America*, 1950, *22*, 824–836.

Lee, B. S. Artificial stutter. *Journal of Speech and Hearing Disorders*, 1951, *16*, 53–55.

Lenneberg, E. H. *Biological foundations of language*. New York: Wiley, 1967.

Leonard, D. W., Fishbein, L. C., and Monteau, J. E. The effects of interpolated US alone (USa) presentations on classical membrane conditioning in rabbit (Oryctolagus cuniculus). *Conditional Reflex*, 1972, *7*, 107–114.

Lett, B. T. Delayed reward learning: Disproof of the traditional theory. *Learning and Motivation*, 1973, *4*, 237–246.

Lett, B. T. Visual discrimination learning with a 1-minute delay of reward. *Learning and Motivation*, 1974, *5*, 174–181.

Lett, B. T. Long delay learning in the T-maze. *Learning and Motivation*, 1975, *6*, 80–90.

Lewis, D. J. Partial reinforcement: A selective review of the literature since 1950. *Psychological Bulletin*, 1960, *57*, 1–28.

Lewis, D. J. Psychobiology of active and inactive memory. *Psychological Bulletin*, 1979, *86*, 1054–1083.

Lewis, D. J., and Duncan, C. P. Effect of different percentages of money reward on extinction of a lever pulling response. *Journal of Experimental Psychology*, 1956, *52*, 23–27.

Lewis, D., and Shephard, A. H. Devices for studying associative interference in psychomotor performance: I. The modified Mashburn apparatus. *Journal of Psychology*, 1950, *29*, 35–46.

Ley, R., and Long, K. A distractor-free test of recognition and false recognition. *Bulletin of the Psychonomic Society*, 1987, *25*, 411–414.

Lichko, A. E. Conditioned reflex hypoglycemia in man. *Pavlovian Journal of Higher Nervous Activity*, 1959, *9*, 731–737.

Lichtenstein, P. I. Studies in anxiety: I. The production of a feeding inhibition in dogs. *Journal of Comparative and Physiological Psychology*, 1950, *43*, 16–29.

Lieberman, D. A., Davidson, F. H., and Thomas, G. V. Marking in pigeons: The role of memory in delayed reinforcement. *Journal of Experimental Psychology: Animal Behavior Processes*, 1985, *11*, 611–624.

Lieberman, D. A., McIntosh, D. C., and Thomas, G. V. Learning when reward is delayed: A marking hypothesis. *Journal of Experimental Psychology: Animal Behavior Processes*, 1979, *5*, 224–242

Light, J. S., and Gantt, W. H. Essential part of reflex arc for establishment of conditioned reflex. Formation of conditioned reflex after exclusion of motor peripheral end. *Journal of Comparative Psychology*, 1936, *21*, 19–36.

Lippman, L. G., and Lippman, M. Z. Isolation and similarity effects in a serial reconstruction task. *American Journal of Psychology*, 1978, *91*, 35–50.

Little, L. M., and Curran, J. P. Covert sensitization: A clinical procedure in need of some explanations. *Psychological Bulletin*, 1978, *85*, 513–531.

Lockhart, R. S., Craik, F. I. M., and Jacoby, L. L. Depth of processing, recognition, and recall. In J. Brown (Ed.), *Recognition and recall*. New York: Wiley, 1976.

Loftus, E. F. Leading questions and the eyewitness report. *Cognitive Psychology*, 1975, *7*, 560–572.

Loftus, E. F., Miller, D. G., and Burns, H. J. Semantic integration of verbal information into visual memory. *Journal of Experimental Psychology: Human Learning and Memory*, 1978, *4*, 19–31.

Logan, F. A., and Ferraro, D. P. *Systematic anal-*

ysis of learning and motivation. New York: Wiley, 1978.

Logue, A. W. Taste aversion and the generality of the laws of learning. *Psychological Bulletin,* 1979, *86,* 276–296.

Lorayne, H., and Lucas, J. *The memory book.* New York: Ballantine Books, 1974.

Lorenz, K. Der kumpan in der umwelt des vogels. *Journal für Ornithologie,* 1935, *83,* 127–213.

Lorenz, K. The comparative method in studying innate behavior patterns. *Society for Experimental Biology, Symposia,* 1950, *4,* 221–268.

Lorenz, K. The evolution of behavior. *Scientific American,* 1958, *199,* 67–78.

Lorge, I., and Thorndike, E. L. The influence of decay in the after-effect of a connection. *Journal of Experimental Psychology,* 1935, *18,* 186–194.

Lovatt, D. J., and Warr, P. B. Recall after sleep. *American Journal of Psychology,* 1968, *81,* 253–257.

Lovejoy, E. *Attention in discrimination learning.* San Francisco: Holden-Day, 1968.

Lowe, C. F. Determinants of human operant behaviour. In M. D. Zeiler and P. Harzem (Eds.), *Advances in analysis of behavior (Vol. 1). Reinforcement and the organization of behavior.* New York: Wiley, 1979.

Lowe, C. F., Harzem, P., and Hughes, S. Determinants of operant behavior in humans: Some differences in animals. *Quarterly Journal of Experimental Psychology,* 1978, *30,* 373–386.

Lubow, R. E. Latent inhibition: Effects of frequency of non-reinforced preexposure to the CS. *Journal of Comparative and Physiological Psychology,* 1965, *60,* 454–455.

Lubow, R. E. Latent inhibition. *Psychological Bulletin,* 1973, *79,* 398–407.

Lubow, R. E., Markham, R. E., and Allen, J. Latent inhibition and classical conditioning of the rabbit pinna response. *Journal of Comparative and Physiological Psychology,* 1968, *66,* 688–694.

Lubow, R. E., and Moore, A. U. Latent inhibition: The effect of nonreinforced pre-exposure to the conditioned stimulus. *Journal of Comparative and Physiological Psychology,* 1959, *52,* 415, 419.

Luh, C. W. The conditions of retention. *Psychological Monographs,* 1922, *31.*

Lukowiak, K., and Sahley, C. The in vitro classical conditioning of the gill withdrawal reflex of *Aplysia californica. Science,* 1981, *212,* 1516–1518.

Luparello, T., Lyons, H. A., Blecker, E. D., Jr., and McFadden, E. R. Influences of suggestion on airway reactivity in asthmatic subjects. *Psychosomatic Medicine,* 1968, *30,* 819–824.

Luria, A. R. *The mind of a mnemonist.* New York: Basic Books, 1968.

Lutz, K., and Lutz, R. J. Effects of interactive imagery on learning: Application to advertising. *Journal of Applied Psychology,* 1977, *62,* 493–498.

MacArthur, R. H., and Pianka, E. R. On the optimum use of a patchy environment. *The American Naturalist,* 1966, *100,* 603–610.

Mackintosh, N. J. *The psychology of animal learning.* New York: Academic Press, 1974.

Mackintosh. N. J. Blocking of conditioned suppression: Role of the first compound trial. *Journal of Experimental Psychology: Animal Behavior Processes,* 1975, *1,* 335–345.

Mackintosh, N. J. Overshadowing and stimulus intensity. *Animal Learning & Behavior,* 1976, *4,* 186–192.

Mackintosh, N. J. *Conditioning and associative learning.* New York: Oxford University Press, 1983.

Mackintosh, N. J., Dickinson, A., and Cotton, M. M. Surprise and blocking: Effects of the number of compound trials. *Animal Learning & Behavior,* 1980, *8,* 387–391.

MacLeod, C. M. Learning a list for free recall: Selective reminding versus the standard procedure. *Memory & Cognition,* 1985, *13,* 233–240.

Magill, R. A. Knowledge of results and skill acquisition. In L. D. Zaichkowsky and C. Z. Fuchs (Eds.), *The psychology of motor behavior: Development, control, learning, and performance.* Ithaca, N.Y.: Movement Publications, 1986.

Mahl, G. F., Rothenberg, A., Delgado, J. M. R., and Hamlin, H. Psychological responses in the human to intercerebral electrical stimulation. *Psychosomatic Medicine,* 1964, *26,* 337–365.

Mahoney, W. J., and Ayres, J. J. B. One-trial simultaneous and backward fear conditioning as reflected in conditioned suppression of licking in rats. *Animal Learning & Behavior,* 1976, *4,* 357–362.

Maier, S. F., and Seligman, M. E. P. Learned helplessness: Theory and evidence. *Journal of Experimental Psychology: General,* 1976, *105,* 3–46.

Maki, R. H., and Schuler, J. Effects of rehearsal

duration and level of processing on memory for words. *Journal of Verbal Learning and Verbal Behavior,* 1980, *19,* 36–45.

Maleske, R. T., and Frey, P. W. Blocking in eyelid conditioning: Effect of changing CS-US interval and introducing an intertial stimulus. *Animal Learning & Behavior,* 1979, *7,* 452–456.

Malmo, R. B. Heart rate reactions and locus of stimulation within the septal area of the rat. *Science,* 1964, *144,* 1029–1030.

Malmo, R. B. Classical and instrumental conditioning with septal stimulation as reinforcement. *Journal of Comparative and Physiological Psychology,* 1965, *60,* 1–8.

Mandler, J. M., and Goodman, M. S. On the psychological validity of storage structure. *Journal of Verbal Learning and Verbal Behavior,* 1982, *21,* 507–523.

Manning, A. A., Schneiderman, N., and Lordahl, D. S. Delay versus trace heart-rate classical discrimination conditioning in rabbits as a function of interstimulus interval. *Journal of Experimental Psychology,* 1969, *80,* 225–230.

Marchant, H. G., III, and Moore, J. W. Blocking of the rabbit's conditioned nictitating membrane response in Kamin's two-stage paradigm. *Journal of Experimental Psychology,* 1973, *101,* 155–158.

Marks, I. Flooding (implosion) and allied treatment. In W. S. Agris (Ed.), *Behavior modification: Principles and clinical applications.* Boston: Little, Brown, 1972.

Marks, I. Behavioral treatments of phobic and obsessive-compulsive disorders: A critical appraisal. In M. Hersen, R. M. Eisler, and P. M. Miller (Eds.), *Progress in behavior modification.* New York: Academic Press, 1975.

Marschark, M. Imagery and organization in the recall of prose. *Journal of Memory and Language,* 1985, *24,* 734–745.

Marschark, M., and Paivio, A. Integrative processing of concrete and abstract sentences. *Journal of Verbal Learning and Verbal Behavior,* 1977, *16,* 217–231.

Martens, R., Burwitz, L., and Zuckerman, M. Modeling effects on motor performance. *Research Quarterly,* 1976, *47,* 277–291.

Marx, M. H. Interaction of drive and reward as a determiner of resistance to extinction. *Journal of Comparative and Physiological Psychology,* 1967, *64,* 488–489.

Mason, J. R., Stevens, D. A., Wixon, D. R., and Owens, M. P. Assessment of the relative importance of S+ and S− in rats using differential training on intercurrent discrimination. *Learning and Motivation,* 1980, *11,* 49–60.

Masserman, J. H. *Behavior and neurosis.* Chicago: University of Chicago Press, 1943.

Mathews, R. Recall as a function of the number of classificatory categories. *Journal of Experimental Psychology,* 1954, *47,* 241–247.

Matthews, B. A., Shimoff, E., Catania, A. C., and Sagvolden, T. Uninstructed human responding: Sensitivity to ratio and interval contingencies. *Journal of the Experimental Analysis of Behavior,* 1977, *27,* 453–467.

Mayer, G. R., Butterworth, T., Nafpaktitus, M., and Sulzer-Azaroff, B. Preventing school vandalism and improving discipline: A three-year study. *Journal of Applied Behavior Analysis,* 1983, *16,* 355–369.

McAllister, W. R. Conditioning as a function of CS-US interval. *Journal of Experimental Psychology,* 1954, *45,* 417–422.

McAllister, W. R., and McAllister, D. E. Increase over time in the stimulus generalization of acquired fear. *Journal of Experimental Psychology,* 1963, *65,* 576–582.

McAllister, W. R., and McAllister, D. E. Behavioral measurement of conditioned fear. In F. R. Brush (Ed.), *Aversive conditioning and learning.* New York: Academic Press, 1971.

McAllister, W. R., McAllister, D. E., and Douglas, W. K. The inverse relationship between shock intensity and shuttle-box avoidance learning in rats. *Journal of Comparative and Physiological Psychology,* 1971, *74,* 426–433.

McCain, G. Partial reinforcement effects following a small number of acquisition trials. *Psychonomic Monograph Supplement,* 1966, *1,* 251–270.

McCain, G. The partial reinforcement effect after minimal acquisition: Single pellet reward. *Psychonomic Science,* 1968, *13,* 151–152.

McCloskey, M., and Santee, J. Are semantic memory and episodic memory distinct systems? *Journal of Experimental Psychology: Human Learning and Memory,* 1981, *7,* 66–71.

McCrary, J. W., and Hunter, W. S. Serial position curves in verbal learning. *Science,* 1953, *117,* 131–134.

McDaniel, M. A. Syntactic complexity and elaborative processing. *Memory & Cognition,* 1981, *9,* 487–495.

McDaniel, M. A. The role of elaborative and schema processes in story memory. *Memory & Cognition,* 1984, *12,* 46–51.

McDaniel, M. A., and Kearney, E. M. Optimal learning strategies and their spontaneous use: The importance of task-appropriate processing. *Memory & Cognition,* 1984, *12,* 361–373.

McElroy, L. A. The generation effect with homographs: Evidence for postgeneration processing. *Memory & Cognition,* 1987, *15,* 148–155.

McElroy, L. A., and Slamecka, N. J. Memorial consequences of generating nonwords: Implications for semantic-memory interpretations of the generation effect. *Journal of Verbal Learning and Verbal Behavior,* 1982, *21,* 249–259.

McGeoch, J. A. Forgetting and the law of disuse. *Psychological Review,* 1932, *39,* 352–370.

McGeoch, J. A. *The psychology of human learning.* New York: Longmans Green, 1946.

McGeoch, J. A., and Irion, A. L. *The psychology of human learning.* New York: Longmans Green, 1952.

McGeoch, J. A., and McKinney, F. The susceptibility of prose to retroactive inhibition. *American Journal of Psychology,* 1934, *46,* 429–436.

McGuigan, F. J. W. Horsley Gantt, multiple response measures, cybernetic circuits, and cognitive processes. In F. J. McGuigan and T. A. Ban (Eds.), *Critical issues in psychology, psychiatry and physiology.* New York: Gordon Breach, 1987.

McNulty, J. A. An analysis of recall and recognition processes in verbal learning. *Journal of Verbal Learning and Verbal Behavior,* 1965, *4,* 430–436.

Medin, D. L., Reynolds, T. J., and Parkinson, J. K. Stimulus similarity and retroactive interference and facilitation in monkey short-term memory. *Journal of Experimental Psychology: Animal Behavior Processes,* 1980, *6,* 112–125.

Meehl, P. E. On the circularity of the law of effect. *Psychological Bulletin,* 1950, *47,* 52–75.

Mellgren, R. Positive and negative contrast effects using delayed reinforcement. *Learning and Motivation,* 1972, *3,* 185–193.

Melton, A. W. (Ed.). *Apparatus tests.* Washington, D.C.: U.S. Government Printing Office, 1947.

Melton, A. W. Implications of short-term memory for a general theory of memory. *Journal of Verbal Learning and Verbal Behavior,* 1963, *9,* 596–606.

Melton, A. W., and Irwin, J. M. The influence of degree of interpolated learning on retroactive inhibition and the overt transfer of specific responses. *American Journal of Psychology,* 1940, *53,* 173–203.

Menzel, E. W. Cognitive mapping in chimpanzees. In S. H. Hulse, H. Fowler, and W. K. Honig (Eds.), *Cognitive processes in animal behavior.* Hillsdale, N.J.: Erlbaum, 1978.

Meyer, B. J. F., and McConkie, G. W. What is recalled after hearing a passage? *Journal of Educational Psychology,* 1973, *65,* 109–117.

Meyer, D. R., Cho, C., and Wesemann, A. F. On problems of conditioning discriminated lever-press avoidance responses. *Psychological Review,* 1960, *67,* 224–228.

Miller, G. A. The magical number seven, plus or minus two: Some limits on our capacity for processing information. *Psychological Review,* 1956, *63,* 81–97.

Miller, G. A., Galanter, E., and Pribram, K. H. *Plans and the structure of behavior.* New York: Holt, 1960.

Miller, L. B., and Estes, B. W. Monetary reward and motivation in discrimination learning. *Journal of Experimental Psychology,* 1961, *61,* 501–504.

Miller, N. E. Learning resistance to pain and fear: Effects of overlearning, exposure and rewarded exposure in context. *Journal of Experimental Psychology,* 1960, 137–149.

Miller, N. E., and Banuazzi, A. Instrumental learning by curarized rats of a specific visceral response, intestinal or cardiac. *Journal of Comparative and Physiological Psychology,* 1968, *65,* 1–7.

Miller, N. E., and Carmona, A. Modification of a visceral response, salivation in thirsty dogs, by instrumental training with water reward. *Journal of Comparative and Physiological Psychology,* 1967, *63,* 1–6.

Miller, N. E., and DiCara, L. Instrumental learning of heart-rate changes in curarized rats: shaping, and specificity to discriminative stimulus. *Journal of Comparative and Physiological Psychology,* 1967, *63,* 12–19.

Miller, N. E., and DiCara, L. Instrumental learning of urine formation in rats; changes in renal blood flow. *American Journal of Physiology,* 1968, *215,* 677–683.

Miller, N. E., and Dworkin, B. R. Visceral learning: Recent difficulties with curarized rats and significant problems for human research. In P. A. Obrist, A. H. Black, J. Brener, and L. V. DiCara (Eds.), *Cardiovascular psychophysiology: Current issues in response mechanisms, biofeedback, and methodology.* Chicago: Aldine, 1974.

Milner, B. Effects of different brain lesions on card sorting. *Archives of Neurology,* 1963, *9,* 90–100.

Milner, B. Visually-guided maze learning in man: Effects of bilateral hippocampal, bilateral frontal, and unilateral cerebral lesions. *Neuropsychologia,* 1965, *3,* 317–338.

Milner, B. Neuropsychological evidence for differing memory processes. Abstract for the symposium on short-term and long-term memory. *Proceedings of the Eighteenth International Congress of Psychology, Moscow, 1966.* Amsterdam: North-Holland Publishers, 1968.

Milner, B., Corkin, S., and Teuber, H. L. Further analysis of the hippocampal-amnesia syndrome, 14 year follow-up of H. M. *Neuropsychologia,* 1968, *6,* 215–234.

Milner, B., and Teuber, H. L. Alternation of perception and memory in man: Reflections on methods. In L. Weiskrantz (Ed.), *Analysis of behavioral change.* New York: Harper and Row, 1968.

Mineka, S. The role of fear in theories of avoidance learning, flooding, and extinction. *Psychological Bulletin,* 1979, *86,* 985–1010.

Mineka, S., Cook, M., and Miller, S. Fear conditioned with escapable and inescapable shock: Effects of a feedback stimulus. *Journal of Experimental Psychology: Animal Behavior Processes,* 1984, *10,* 307–323.

Mis, R. W., and Moore, J. W. Effects of preacquisition UCS exposure on classical conditioning of the rabbit's nictitating membrane response. *Learning and Motivation,* 1973, *4,* 108–114.

Moltz, H., and Stettner, L. J. The influence of patterned-light deprivation on the critical period for imprinting. *Journal of Comparative and Physiological Psychology,* 1961, *54,* 279–283.

Mook, D. G. *Motivation: The organization of action.* New York: W. W. Norton, 1986.

Moore, B. R. The role of directed Pavlovian reaction in simple instrumental learning in the pigeon. In R. A. Hinde and J. Stevenson (Eds.), *Constraints on learning.* New York: Academic Press, 1973.

Moore, R., and Goldiamond, I. Errorless establishment of visual discrimination using fading procedures. *Journal of the Experimental Analysis of Behavior,* 1964, *7,* 269–272.

Morton, J., and Bekerian, D. A. The episodic/semantic distinction: Something worth arguing about. *Behavioral and Brain Sciences,* 1984, *7,* 247–248.

Mountjoy, P. P., and Malott, M. K. Wave-length generalization curves for chickens reared in restricted portions of the spectrum. *Psychological Record,* 1968, *18,* 575–583.

Mowrer, O. H. On the dual nature of learning—A reinterpretation of "conditioning" and "problem-solving." *Harvard Educational Review,* 1947, *17,* 102–148.

Mowrer, O. H. *Learning theory and behavior.* New York: Wiley, 1960.

Mowrer, O. H., and Jones, H. M. Habit strength as a function of the pattern of reinforcement. *Journal of Experimental Psychology,* 1945, *35,* 293–311.

Mowrer, O. H., and Mowrer, W. M. Enuresis: A method for its study and treatment. *American Journal of Orthopsychiatry,* 1938, *8,* 436–459.

Moyer, K. E., and Korn, J. H. Effect of UCS intensity on the acquisition and extinction of a one-way avoidance response. *Psychonomic Science,* 1966, *4,* 121–122.

Murdock, B. B. The serial position effect of free recall. *Journal of Experimental Psychology,* 1962, *64,* 482–488.

Murdock, B., and Metcalfe, J. Controlled rehearsal in single-trial free recall. *Journal of Verbal Learning and Verbal Behavior,* 1978, *17,* 309–324.

Murray, D. J. Overt versus covert rehearsal in short-term memory. *Psychonomic Science,* 1967, *7,* 363–364.

Nachmias, J., Gleitman, H., and McKenna, V. V. The effect of isolation of stimuli and responses in paired associates. *American Journal of Psychology,* 1961, *74,* 452–456.

Nairne, J. S., Pusen, C., and Widner, R. L. Representation in the mental lexicon: Implication for theories of the generation effect. *Memory & Cognition,* 1985, *13,* 183–191.

Nallan, G. B., Sanders, Jr., R., Dykeman, C., Hughes, M., Rauth, M., McCann, S., and Morrison-Nallan, K. Identity relation can serve as a distinguishing feature in feature-positive & feature-negative learning research. *American Journal of Psychology*, 1986, *99*.

Nation, J. R., and Cooney, J. B. The time course of extinction-induced aggressive behavior in humans: Evidence for a stage model of extinction. *Learning and Motivation*, 1982, *13*, 95–112.

Naveh-Benjamin, M., and Jonides, J. Cognitive load and maintenance rehearsal. *Journal of Verbal Learning and Verbal Behavior*, 1984a, *23*, 494–507.

Naveh-Benjamin, M., and Jonides, J. Maintenance rehearsal: A two-component analysis. *Journal of Experimental Psychology: Learning, Memory, and Cognition*, 1984b, *10*, 369–385.

Neimeyer, R. Part versus whole methods and massed versus distributed practice in the learning of selected large muscle activities. *Proceedings of the College of Physical Education Association for Men*, 1959, *62*, 122–125. Washington, D.C.: American Association for Health, Physical Education and Recreation.

Neisser, U. *Cognitive psychology.* New York: Appleton, 1967.

Neisser, U. Interpreting Harry Bahrick's discovery: What confers immunity against forgetting? *Journal of Experimental Psychology: General*, 1984, *113*, 32–35.

Nelson, M. N., and Ross, L. E. Effects of masking tasks on differential eyelid conditioning: A distinction between knowledge of stimulus contingencies and attentional or cognitive activities involving them. *Journal of Experimental Psychology*, 1974, *102*, 1–9.

Nelson, T. O. Savings and forgetting from long-term memory. *Journal of Verbal Learning and Verbal Behavior*, 1971, *10*, 568–576.

Nelson, T. O. Repetition and depth of processing. *Journal of Verbal Learning and Verbal Behavior*, 1977, *16*, 151–171.

Nelson, T. O. Detecting small amounts of information in memory: Savings for nonrecognized items. *Journal of Experimental Psychology: Human Learning and Memory*, 1978, *4*, 453–468.

Nelson, T. O., Fehling, M. R., and Moore-Glascock, J. The nature of semantic savings for items forgotten from long-term memory. *Journal of Experimental Psychology: General*, 1979, *108*, 225–250.

Nelson, T. O., and Rothbart, R. Acoustic savings for items forgotten from long-term memory.

Journal of Experimental Psychology, 1972, *93*, 357–360.

Nevin, J. A. The maintenance of behavior. In J. A. Nevin (Ed.), *The study of behavior.* Glenview, Ill.: Scott, Foresman, 1973.

Newell, K. M. Knowledge of results and motor learning. *Journal of Motor Behavior*, 1974, *6*, 235–244.

Newell, K. M. Knowledge of results and motor learning. *Exercise and Sports Sciences Reviews*, 1977, *4*, 195–228.

Newell, K. M. Skill learning. In D. H. Holding (Ed.), *Human skills.* New York: John Wiley, 1981.

Newell, K. M., Morris, L. R., and Scully, D. M. Augmented information and acquisition of skill in physical activity. In R. L. Terjung (Ed.), *Exercise and sport sciences review.* New York: Macmillan, 1985.

Newell, K. M., Quinn, J. T., Jr., Sparrow, W. A., and Walter, C. B. Kinematic information feedback for learning a rapid arm movement. *Human Movement Science*, 1983, *2*, 255–269.

Newman, E. B. Forgetting of meaningful material during sleep and waking. *American Journal of Psychology*, 1939, *52*, 65–71.

Newman, J., Wolff, W. T., and Hearst, E. The feature-positive effect in adult human subjects. *Journal of Experimental Psychology: Human Learning and Memory*, 1980, *6*, 630–650.

Newman, S. E. Paired-associate learning as a function of stimulus term and response term isolation. Paper read at Psychonomic meeting, St. Louis, August 30, 1962.

Newman, S. E., and Saltz, E. Isolation effects: Stimulus and response generalization as explanatory concepts. *Journal of Experimental Psychology*, 1958, *55*, 467–472.

Newton, J. M., and Wickens, D. D. Retroactive inhibition as a function of the temporal position of the interpolated learning. *Journal of Experimental Psychology*, 1956, *51*, 149–154.

Nicholls, M. F., and Kimble, G. A. Effect of instructions upon eyelid conditioning. *Journal of Experimental Psychology*, 1964, *67*, 400–402.

Noble, C. E. The role of stimulus meaning (m) in serial verbal learning. *Journal of Experimental Psychology*, 1952a, *43*, 437–446.

Noble, C. E. The analysis of meaning. *Psychological Review*, 1952b, *59*, 421–430.

Noble, C. E. The meaning-familiarity relationship. *Psychological Review*, 1953, *60*, 89–98.

Noble, C. E. Measurements of association value (a), rated associations (a'), and scaled meaningfulness (m') for the 2100 CVC combinations of the English alphabet. *Psychological Reports*, 1961, *8*, 487–521.

Noble, C. E., and McNeely, D. A. The role of meaningfulness (m) in paired-associate verbal learning. *Journal of Experimental Psychology*, 1957, *53*, 16–22.

Noble, M., and Adams, C. K. Conditioning in pigs as a function of the interval between CS and US. *Journal of Comparative and Physiological Psychology*, 1963, *56*, 215–219.

Noble, M., Gruender, A., and Meyer, D. R. Conditioning in fish (Molienisia Sp.) as a function of the interval between CS and US. *Journal of Comparative and Physiological Psychology*, 1959, *52*, 236–239.

North, A. J., and Stimmel, D. T. Extinction of an instrumental response following a large number of reinforcements. *Psychological Reports*, 1960, *6*, 227–234.

Notterman, J. M., Schoenfeld, W. N., and Bersh, P. J. Conditioned heart rate responses in human beings during experimental anxiety. *Journal of Comparative and Physiological Psychology*, 1952, *45*, 1–8.

Oakley, D. A. The varieties of memory: A phylogenetic approach. In A. Mayes (Ed.), *Memory in animals and humans.* Wokingham, England: Van Nostrand Reinhold, 1983.

Odling-Smee, F. J. The role of background stimuli during Pavlovian conditioning. *Quarterly Journal of Experimental Psychology*, 1975, *27*, 201–209.

Öhman, A. Orienting reactions, expectancy learning, and conditioned responses in electrodermal conditioning with different interstimulus intervals. *Biological Psychology*, 1974, *1*, 189–200.

Öhman, A. The orienting response, attention, and learning: An information-processing perspective. In H. D. Kimmel, E. H. van Olst, and J. F. Orlebeke (Eds.), *The orienting reflex in humans.* Hillsdale, N.J.: Erlbaum, 1979.

Öhman, A. The orienting response during Pavlovian conditioning. In D. Siddle (Ed.), *Orienting and habituation: Perspectives in human research.* New York: Wiley, 1983.

Olds, J. Runway and maze behavior controlled by basomedial fore-brain stimulation in the rat. *Journal of Comparative and Physiological Psychology*, 1956, *49*, 507–512.

Olds, J., and Milner, P. Positive reinforcement produced by electrical stimulation of septal area and other regions of the rat brain. *Journal of Comparative and Physiological Psychology*, 1954, *47*, 419–427.

Olton, D. S., and Samuelson, R. J. Remembrance of places passed: Spatial memory in rats. *Journal of Experimental Psychology: Animal Behavior Processes*, 1976, *2*, 97–116.

Orlebeke, J. F., and Van Olst, E. H. Learning and performance as a function of CS intensity in a delayed GSR conditioning situation. *Journal of Experimental Psychology*, 1968, *77*, 483–487.

Ost, J. W. P., and Lauer, D. W. Some investigations of classical salivary conditioning in the dog. In W. F. Prokasy (Ed.), *Classical conditioning: A symposium.* New York: Appleton-Century-Crofts, 1965.

Ottenberg, P., Stein, M., Lewis, J., and Hamilton, C. Learned asthma in the guinea pig. *Psychosomatic Medicine*, 1958, *20*, 395–400.

Overmier, J. B., and Seligman, M. E. P. Effects of inescapable shock upon subsequent escape and avoidance learning. *Journal of Comparative and Physiological Psychology*, 1967, *63*, 28–33.

Owens, J., Bower, G. H., and Black, J. B. The "soap opera" effect in story recall. *Memory & Cognition*, 1979, *7*, 185–191.

Page, H. A., and Hall, J. F. Experimental extinction as a function of the prevention of the response. *Journal of Comparative and Physiological Psychology*, 1953, *46*, 33–34.

Paivio, A. Abstractness, imagery, and meaningfulness in paired-associate learning. *Journal of Verbal Learning and Verbal Behavior*, 1965, *4*, 32–38.

Paivio, A., Yuille, J. C., and Madigan, S. A. Concreteness, imagery and meaningfulness values for 925 nouns. *Journal of Experimental Psychology, Monograph Supplement*, 1968, *76*, 1–25.

Palmerino, C. C., Rusiniak, K. W., and Garcia, J. Flavor-illness aversions: The peculiar roles of odor and taste in memory for poison. *Science*, 1980, *208*, 753–755.

Patrick, J. R. Studies in rational behavior and emotional excitement. II. The effect of emotional excitement on rational behavior in human subjects. *Journal of Comparative Psychology*, 1934, *18*, 153–195.

Patten, R. L., and Rudy, J. W. The Sheffield omission of training procedure applied to the conditioning of the licking response in rats. *Psychonomic Science*, 1967, *8*, 463–464.

Patterson, M. M. Effects of forward and backward classical conditioning procedures on a spinal cat hind-limb flexor nerve response. *Physiological Psychology*, 1975, *3*, 86–91.

Patterson, M. M., Cegavski, C. F., and Thompson, R. F. Effects of a classical conditioning paradigm on hind-limb flexor nerve response in immobilized spinal cats. *Journal of Comparative and Physiological Psychology*, 1973, *84*, 88–97.

Paul, G. L. Outcome of systematic desensitization. I. Background, procedures and uncontrolled reports of individual treatment. II. Controlled investigations of individual treatment, technique variations, and current status. In C. M. Franks (Ed.), *Behavior therapy: Appraisal and status*. New York: McGraw-Hill, 1969.

Pavlik, W. B., and Carlton, P. L. A reversed partial reinforcement effect. *Journal of Experimental Psychology*, 1965, *70*, 417–423.

Pavlik, W. B., Carlton, P. L., Lehr, R., and Hendrickson, C. A reversed PRE. *Journal of Experimental Psychology*, 1967, *75*, 274–276.

Pavlov, I. P. *Conditioned reflexes* (translated by G. V. Anrep). New York: Dover Publications, 1927.

Payne, D. G. Hypermnesia and reminiscence in recall: A historical and empirical review. *Psychological Bulletin*, 1987, *101*, 5–27.

Pearce, J. M., and Kaye, H. Strength of the orienting response during inhibitory conditioning. *Journal of Experimental Psychology: Animal Behavior Processes*, 1985, *11*, 405–420.

Penfield, W. The permanent record of the stream of consciousness. *Proceedings of the Fourteenth International Congress of Psychology, Montreal, June 1954*. Amsterdam: North-Holland Publishing Co., 1955.

Perin, C. T. Behavior potentiality as a joint function of the amount of training and the degree of hunger at the time of extinction. *Journal of Experimental Psychology*, 1942, *30*, 93–113.

Perin, C. T. A quantitative investigation of the delay of reinforcement gradient. *Journal of Experimental Psychology*, 1943, *32*, 37–51.

Perkins, C. C., Jr., and Weyant, R. G. The interval between training and test trials as a determiner of the slope of generalization gradients. *Journal of Comparative and Physiological Psychology*, 1958, *51*, 596–600.

Perry, S. L., and Moore, J. W. The partial-reinforcement effect sustained through blocks of continuous reinforcement in classical eyelid conditioning. *Journal of Experimental Psychology*, 1965, *69*, 158–161.

Peterson, L. R., and Peterson, M. J. Short-term retention of individual items. *Journal of Experimental Psychology*, 1959, *58*, 193–198.

Peterson, N. Effect of monochomatic rearing on the control of responding by wavelength. *Science*, 1962, *136*, 774–775.

Pew, R. W. Acquisition of a hierarchical control over the temporal organization of a skill. *Journal of Experimental Psychology*, 1966, *71*, 764–771.

Pierce, W. D., and Epling, W. F. Choice, matching, and human behavior: A review of the literature. *The Behavior Analyst*, 1983, *6*, 57–76.

Pinto, T., and Bromiley, R. G. A search for "spinal conditioning" and for evidence that it can become a reflex. *Journal of Experimental Psychology*, 1950, *40*, 121–130.

Plotkin, R. C., and Oakley, P. A. Backward conditioning in the rabbit (Oryctolagus cuniculus). *Journal of Comparative and Physiological Psychology*, 1975, *88*, 586–590.

Pompi, K. F., and Lachman, R. Surrogate processes in the short-term retention of connected discourse. *Journal of Experimental Psychology*, 1967, *75*, 143–150.

Postman, L. Retention as a function of degree of overlearning. *Science*, 1962, *135*, 666–667.

Postman, L. Studies of learning to learn. II. Changes in transfer as a function of practice. *Journal of Verbal Learning and Verbal Behavior*, 1964, *3*, 437–447.

Postman, L. Verbal learning and memory. In M. R. Rosenzweig and L. W. Porter (Eds.), *Annual review of psychology*. Palo Alto, Calif.: Annual Reviews, 1975.

Postman, L. Interference theory revisited. In J. Brown (Ed.), *Recall and recognition*. London: Wiley, 1976.

Postman, L., Adams, P. A., and Phillips, L. W. Studies in incidental learning: II. The effects of association value and the method of testing. *Journal of Experimental Psychology*, 1955, *49*, 1–10.

Postman, L., and Gray, W. D. Response recall and retroactive inhibition. *American Journal of Psychology*, 1978, *91*, 3–22.

Postman, L., and Rau, L. Retention as a function of the method of measurement. *University of*

California Publications in Psychology, 1957, *8,* 217–270.

Postman, L., Stark, K., and Fraser, J. Temporal changes in interference. *Journal of Verbal Learning and Verbal Behavior,* 1968, *7,* 672–694.

Postman, L., and Underwood, B. J. Critical issues in interference theory. *Memory & Cognition,* 1973, *1,* 19–40.

Powell, R. W., and Curley, M. Instinctive drift in nondomesticated rodents. *Bulletin of the Psychonomic Society,* 1976, *8,* 175–178.

Premack, D. Toward empirical behavioral laws: I. Positive reinforcement. *Psychological Review,* 1959, *66,* 219–233.

Premack, D. Reversibility of the reinforcement relation. *Science,* 1962, *136,* 255–257.

Pribram, K. H. Brain systems and cognitive learning processes. In H. L. Roitblat, T. G. Bever, and H. S. Terrace (Eds.), *Animal cognition.* Hillsdale, N.J.: Erlbaum, 1984.

Prokasy, W. F. Developments with the two-phase model applied to human eyelid conditioning. In A. H. Black and W. F. Prokasy (Eds.), *Classical conditioning II: Current research and theory.* New York: Appleton-Century-Crofts, 1972.

Prokasy, W. F. Classical eyelid conditioning: Experimenter operations, task demands, and response shaping. In W. F. Prokasy (Ed.), *Classical conditioning: A symposium.* New York: Appleton-Century-Crofts, 1965.

Prokasy, W. F. First interval skin conductance responses: Conditioned orienting responses? *Psychophysiology,* 1977, *14,* 360–367.

Prokasy, W. F. Acquisition of skeletal conditioned responses in Pavlovian conditioning. *Psychophysiology,* 1984, *21,* 1–13.

Prokasy, W. F. A perspective on the acquisition of skeletal responses employing the Pavlovian paradigm. In I. Gormezano, W. F. Prokasy, and R. F. Thompson (Eds.), *Classical conditioning.* Hillsdale, N.J.: Erlbaum, 1987.

Prokasy, W. F., and Ebel, H. C. Three components of the classically conditioned GSR in human subjects. *Journal of Experimental Psychology,* 1967, *73,* 247–256.

Prokasy, W. F., and Harsanyi, M. A. Two-phase model for human classical conditioning. *Journal of Experimental Psychology,* 1968, *78,* 359–368.

Purdy, B. J., and Stallard, M. L. Effect of two learning methods and two grips on the acquisition of power and accuracy in the golf swing of college women. *Research Quarterly,* 1967, *38,* 480–484.

Purtle, R. B. Peak shift: A review. *Psychological Bulletin,* 1973, *80,* 408–421.

Rabinowitz, J. C., Mandler, G., and Barsalou, L. W. Generation-recognition as an auxiliary retrieval strategy. *Journal of Verbal Learning and Verbal Behavior,* 1979, *18,* 57–72.

Rabinowitz, J. C., Mandler, G., and Patterson, K. E. Determinants of recognition and recall: Accessibility and generation. *Journal of Experimental Psychology: General,* 1977, *106,* 302–329.

Rachlin, H. C., and Green, L. Commitment, choice, and self-control. *Journal of the Experimental Analysis of Behavior,* 1972, *17,* 15–22.

Rachman, S. Systematic desensitization. *Psychological Bulletin,* 1967, *67,* 93–103.

Rachman, S., and Teasdale, J. *Aversion therapy and behavior disorders: An analysis.* Coral Gables, Fla.: University of Miami Press, 1969.

Randich, A., and LoLordo, V. M. Associative and nonassociative theories of the UCS preexposure phenomenon: Implications for Pavlovian conditioning. *Psychological Bulletin,* 1979a, *86,* 523–548.

Randich, A., and LoLordo, V. M. Preconditioning exposure to the unconditioned stimulus effects the acquisition of a conditioned emotional response. *Learning and Motivation,* 1979b, *10,* 245–277.

Rashotte, M. E., Griffin, R. W., and Sisk, C. L. Second order conditioning of the pigeon's keypeck. *Animal Learning & Behavior,* 1977, *5,* 25–38.

Razran, G. H. S. A quantitative study of meaning by a conditioned salivary technique (semantic conditioning). *Science,* 1939, *90,* 89–90.

Razran, G. H. S. Backward conditioning. *Psychological Bulletin,* 1956, *53,* 55–69.

Razran, G. H. S. The dominance-contingency theory of the acquisition of classical conditioning. *Psychological Bulletin,* 1957, *54,* 1–46.

Razran, G. H. S. *Mind in evolution.* Boston: Houghton Mifflin, 1971.

Reder, L. M., Anderson, J. R., and Bjork, R. A. A semantic interpretation of encoding specificity. *Journal of Experimental Psychology,* 1974, *102,* 648–656.

Renner, K. E. Delay of reinforcement: A historical review. *Psychological Bulletin,* 1964, *61,* 341–361.

Rescorla, R. A. Predictability and number of pairings in Pavlovian fear conditioning. *Psychonomic Science*, 1966, *4*, 383–385.

Rescorla, R. A. Pavlovian conditioning and its proper control procedures. *Psychological Review*, 1967, *74*, 71–80.

Rescorla, R. A. Probability of shock in the presence and absence of CS in fear conditioning. *Journal of Comparative and Physiological Psychology*, 1968, *66*, 1–5.

Rescorla, R. A. Some implications of a cognitive perspective in Pavlovian conditioning. In S. H. Hulse, H. Fowler, and W. K. Honig (Eds.), *Cognitive processes in animal behavior*. Hillsdale, N.J.: Erlbaum, 1978.

Rescorla, R. A. Effect of inflation of the unconditioned stimulus value following conditioning. *Journal of Comparative and Physiological Psychology*, 1974, *86*, 101–106.

Rescorla, R. A. Second order conditioning of Pavlovian conditioned inhibition. *Learning and Motivation*, 1976, *7*, 161–172.

Rescorla, R. A. Some implications of a cognitive perspective in Pavlovian conditioning. In S. H. Hulse, H. Fowler, and W. K. Honig (Eds.), *Cognitive processes in animal behavior*. Hillsdale, N.J.: Erlbaum, 1978.

Rescorla, R. A. *Pavlovian second order conditioning: Studies in associative learning*. Hillsdale, N.J.: Erlbaum, 1980.

Rescorla, R. A., and Wagner, A. R. A theory of Pavlovian conditioning: Variation in the effectiveness of reinforcement and nonreinforcement. In A. H. Black and W. F. Prokasy (Eds.), *Classical conditioning II: Current research and theory*. New York: Appleton-Century-Crofts, 1972.

Restorff, H. von. Uber die wirkung vin bereichbildungen im spurenfeld (analyse von vorgangen in spurenfeld). *Psychologie Forschung*, 1933, *18*, 299–342.

Revusky, S. The role of interference in association over a delay. In W. K. Honig and P. H. R. James (Eds.), *Animal memory*. New York: Academic Press, 1971.

Revusky, S. H., and Garcia, J. Learned associations over long delays. In G. H. Bower and J. T. Spence (Eds.), *The psychology of learning and motivation*. New York: Academic Press, 1970.

Reynolds, G. S. Attention in the pigeon. *Journal of the Experimental Analysis of Behavior*, 1961, *4*, 203–208.

Reynolds, J. H. Confirmation, contiguity, and response practice in paired-associate learning. *Journal of Experimental Psychology*, 1967, *73*, 394–400.

Reynolds, W. F., and Pavlik, W. B. Running speed as a function of deprivation period and reward magnitude. *Journal of Comparative and Physiological Psychology*, 1960, *53*, 615–618.

Riccio, D., Richardson, R., and Ebner, D. L. Memory retrieval deficits based upon altered contextual cues: A paradox. *Psychological Bulletin*, 1984, *96*, 152–165.

Riccio, D. C., Urda, M., and Thomas, D. R. Stimulus control in pigeons based on proprioceptive stimuli from floor inclination. *Science*, 1966, *153*, 434–436.

Richardson, W. K., and Massel, H. K. The feature-positive effect in adult humans: Within-group design. *American Journal of Psychology*, 1982, *95*, 125–138.

Richter, C. P. A behavioristic study of the rat. *Comparative Psychological Monographs*, 1922, *1*, No. 2.

Richter, C. P. Animal behavior and internal drives. *Quarterly Review of Biology*, 1927, *2*, 307–343.

Riley, D. A., and Lamb, M. R. Stimulus generalization. In A. D. Pick (Ed.), *Perception and its development: A tribute to E. J. Gibson*. Hillsdale, N.J.: Erlbaum, 1979.

Riley, D. A., and Leuin, T. C. Stimulus-generalization gradients in chickens reared in monochromatic light and tested with single wavelength value. *Journal of Comparative and Physiological Psychology*, 1971, *75*, 399–402.

Rilling, M. Stimulus control and inhibitory processes. In W. K. Honig and J. E. R. Staddon (Eds.), *Handbook of operant behavior*. Englewood Cliffs, N.J.: Prentice-Hall, 1977.

Rilling, M., and Caplan, H. J. Extinction-induced aggression during errorless discrimination learning. *Journal of the Experimental Analysis of Behavior*, 1973, *20*, 85–92.

Rilling, M., Caplan, H. J., Howard, R. C., and Brown, C. H. Inhibitory stimulus control following errorless discrimination learning. *Journal of the Experimental Analysis of Behavior*, 1975, *24*, 121–133.

Rilling, M., Richards, R. W., and Kramer, T. J. Aversive properties of the negative stimulus during learning with and without errors. *Learning and Motivation*, 1973, *4*, 1–10.

Rizley, R. C., and Rescorla, R. A. Associations in second-order conditioning and sensory preconditioning. *Journal of Comparative and Physiological Psychology*, 1972, *81*, 1–11.

Roberts, S. Properties and function of an internal clock. In R. L. Mellgren (Ed.), *Animal cognition and behavior*. New York: North Holland, 1983.

Roberts, W. A. A further test of the effect of isolation in serial learning. *American Journal of Psychology*, 1962, *75*, 134–139.

Roberts, W. A. Resistance to extinction following partial and consistent reinforcement with varying magnitudes of reward. *Journal of Comparative and Physiological Psychology*, 1969, *67*, 395–400.

Roberts. W. A., and Grant, D. S. An analysis of light-induced retroactive inhibition in pigeon short-term memory. *Journal of Experimental Psychology: Animal Behavior Processes*, 1978, *4*, 219–236.

Robinson, J. S. Light onset and termination as reinforcers for rats living under normal light conditions. *Psychological Reports*, 1959, *5*, 793–796.

Roediger, H. L., III, and Payne, D. G. Recall criterion does not affect recall level or hypermnesia: A puzzle for generate/recognize theories. *Memory & Cognition*, 1985, *13*, 1–7.

Rogers, C. A., Jr. Feedback precision and postfeedback interval duration. *Journal of Experimental Psychology*, 1974, *102*, 604–608.

Rogers, M. P., Reich, P., Strom, T. B., and Carpenter, C. B. Behaviorally conditioned immunosuppression: Replication of a recent study. *Psychosomatic Medicine*, 1976, *38*, 447–451.

Roitblat, H. L. The meaning of representation in animal memory. *Behavioral and Brain Science*, 1982, *5*, 353–406.

Rosellini, R. A., DeCola, J. P., Plonsky, M., Warren, D. A., and Stilman, A. J. Uncontrollable shock proactively increases sensitivity to response-reinforcer independence in rats. *Journal of Experimental Psychology: Animal Behavior Processes*, 1984, *10*, 346–359.

Rosellini, R. A., DeCola, J. P., and Shapiro, N. R. Cross-motivational effects of inescapable shock are associative in nature. *Journal of Experimental Psychology: Animal Behavior Processes*, 1982, *8*, 376–388.

Rosenzweig, W. A. Salivary conditioning before Pavlov. *American Journal of Psychology*, 1959, *72*, 628–633.

Ross, J., and Lawrence, K. A. Some observations on memory artifice. *Psychonomic Science*, 1968, *13*, 107–108.

Ross, S. M., Ross, L. E., and Werden, D. Trace and delay differential classical eyelid conditioning in human adults. *Bulletin of the Psychonomic Society*, 1974, *3*, 224–226.

Roth, S., and Bootzin, R. R. Effects of experimentally induced expectancies of external control: An investigation of learned helplessness. *Journal of Personality and Social Psychology*, 1974, *29*, 253–264.

Rothkopf, E. Z. Incidental memory for location of information in text. *Journal of Verbal Learning and Verbal Behavior*, 1971, *10*, 608–613.

Rothstein, A. L., and Arnold, R. K. Bridging the gap: Application of research on videotape feedback and bowling. *Motor Skills: Theory into Practice*, 1976, *1*, 35–62.

Rozin, P., and Kalat, J. W. Specific hungers and poison avoidance as adaptive specializations of learning. *Psychological Review*, 1971, *78*, 459–486.

Rubin, D. C. Very long term memory for prose and verse. *Journal of Verbal Learning and Verbal Behavior*, 1977, *16*, 611–621.

Rubin, D. C. 51 properties of 125 words: A unit analysis of verbal behavior. *Journal of Verbal Learning and Verbal Behavior*, 1980, *19*, 736–755.

Rubin, D. C. Associative asymmetry, availability, and retrieval. *Memory & Cognition*, 1983, *11*, 83–92.

Rubin, D. C. Memorability as a measure of processing: A unit analysis of prose and list learning. *Journal of Experimental Psychology: General*, 1985, *114*, 213–238.

Rubin, D. C., and Friendly, M. Predicting which words get recalled: Measures of free recall, availability, goodness, emotionality, and pronunciability for 925 nouns. *Memory & Cognition*, 1986, *14*, 79–94.

Rudolph, R. I., Honig, W. K., and Gerry, J. E. Effects of monochromatic rearing on the acquisition of stimulus control. *Journal of Comparative and Physiological Psychology*, 1969, *67*, 50–57.

Ruggiero, F. T., and Flagg, S. F. Do animals have memory? In D. L. Medin, W. A. Roberts, and R. T. Davis (Eds.), *Processes of animal memory*. Hillsdale, N.J.: Erlbaum, 1976.

Rumelhart, D. E. Schemata: The building blocks of cognition. In R. J. Spiro, B. C. Bruce, and

W. F. Brewer (Eds.), *Theoretical issues in reading comprehension*. Hillsdale, N.J.: Erlbaum, 1980.

Rumelhart, D. E., and Ortony, A. The representation of knowledge in memory. In R. C. Anderson, R. J. Spiro, and W. E. Montague (Eds.), *Schooling and the acquisition of knowledge*. Hillsdale, N.J.: Erlbaum, 1977.

Rundus, D. Analysis of rehearsal processes in free recall. *Journal of Experimental Psychology*, 1971, *89*, 63–77.

Rundus, D. Negative effects of using list items as recall cues. *Journal of Verbal Learning and Verbal Behavior*, 1973, *12*, 43–50.

Rundus, D. Maintenance rehearsal and single-level processing. *Journal of Verbal Learning and Verbal Behavior*, 1977, *16*, 665–681.

Rundus, D., and Atkinson, R. C. Rehearsal processes in free recall: A procedure for direct observation. *Journal of Verbal Learning and Verbal Behavior*, 1970, *9*, 99–105.

Rusiniak, K. W., Hankins, W. G., Garcia, J., and Brett, L. P. Flavor-illness aversions: Potentiation of odor by taste in rats. *Behavioral and Neural Biology*, 1979, *25*, 1–17.

Russell, M., Dark, K. A., Cummins, R. W., Ellman, G., Callaway, E., and Peeke, H. V. S. Learned histamine release. *Science*, 1984, *225*, 733–734.

Sachs, J. S. Recognition memory for syntactic and semantic aspects of connected discourse. *Perception and Psychophysics*, 1967, *2*, 437–442.

Sage, G. H. *Introduction to motor behavior: A neuropsychological approach*. Reading, Mass.: Addison-Wesley, 1977.

Sainsbury, R. S. The "feature positive effect" and simultaneous discrimination learning. *Journal of Experimental Child Psychology*, 1971, *11*, 347–356.

Sainsbury, R. S. Discrimination learning utilizing positive or negative cues. *Canadian Journal of Psychology*, 1973, *27*, 46–56.

Saladin, M. E., and Tait, R. US preexposures retard excitatory and facilitate inhibitory conditioning of the rabbit's nictitating membrane response. *Animal Learning & Behavior*, 1986, *14*, 121–132.

Salmoni, A. W., Schmidt, R. A., and Walters, C. B. Knowledge of results and motor learning: A review and critical reappraisal. *Psychological Bulletin*, 1984, *95*, 355–386.

Scavio, M. J., Jr., and Gormezano, I. CS intensity effects on rabbit nictitating membrane conditioning, extinction and generalization. *Pavlovian Journal of Biological Science*, 1974, *9*, 25–34.

Schafer, D. W., and Rubio, R. Hypnosis to aid the recall of witnesses. *The International Journal of Clinical and Experimental Hypnosis*, 1978, *26*, 81–91,

Schendel, J. D., and Hagman, J. D. On sustaining procedural skills over a prolonged retention interval. *Journal of Applied Psychology*, 1982, *67*, 605–610.

Schiffman, K., and Furedy, J. J. The effect of CS-US contingency variation of GSR and on subjective CS-US relational awareness. *Memory & Cognition*, 1977, *5*, 273–277.

Schmidt, R. A. *Motor skills*. New York: Harper and Row, 1975a.

Schmidt, R. A. A schema theory of discrete motor skill learning. *Psychological Review*, 1975b, *82*, 225–260.

Schmidt, R. A. *Motor control and learning*. Champaign, Ill.: Human Kinetics, 1982.

Schneiderman, N., Fuentes, I., and Gormezano, I. Acquisition and extinction of the classically conditioned eyelid response in the albino rabbit. *Science*, 1962, *136*, 650–652.

Schneiderman, N., and Gormezano, I. Conditioning of the nictitating membrane of the rabbit as a function of the CS-US interval. *Journal of Comparative and Physiological Psychology*, 1964, *57*, 188–195.

Schrier, A. M., and Harlow, H. F. Effect of amount of incentive on discrimination learning in monkeys. *Journal of Comparative and Physiological Psychology*, 1956, *49*, 117–125.

Schroeder, S. R., and Holland, J. G. Reinforcement of eye movement with concurrent schedules. *Journal of the Experimental Analysis of Behavior*, 1969, *12*, 897–903.

Schulman, J. L., Suran, B. G., Stevens, T. M., and Kupst, M. J. Instructions, feedback, and reinforcement in reducing activity levels in the classroom. *Journal of Applied Behavior Analysis*, 1979, *12*, 441–447.

Schusterman, R. J. Transfer effects of successive discrimination-reversal training in chimpanzees. *Science*, 1962, *137*, 422–423.

Schwartz, B. *The psychology of learning and behavior*. New York: W. W. Norton, 1984.

Scott-Kelso, J. A., and Stelmach, G. E. Behavioral and neurological parameters of the nerve compression block. *Journal of Motor Behavior*, 1974, *6*, 179–190.

Sears, R. J., Baker, J. S., and Frey, P. W. The eyeblink as a time-locked response: Implications for serial and second-order conditioning. *Journal of Experimental Psychology: Animal Behavior Processes*, 1979, *5*, 43–64.

Seligman, M. E. P. On the generality of laws of learning. *Psychological Review*, 1970, *77*, 406–418.

Seligman, M. E. P., and Campbell, B. A. The effect of intensity and duration of punishment on extinction of an avoidance response. *Journal of Comparative and Physiological Psychology*, 1965, *59*, 295–297.

Seligman, M. E. P., and Maier, S. F. Failure to escape traumatic shock. *Journal of Experimental Psychology*, 1967, *74*, 1–9.

Seligman, M. E. P., Rosellini, R. A., and Kozak, M. J. Learned helplessness in the rat: Time course, immunization and reversibility. *Journal of Comparative and Physiological Psychology*, 1975, *88*, 542–547.

Senkowski, P. C. Variables affecting the overtraining extinction effect in discrete-trial lever pressing. *Journal of Experimental Psychology: Animal Behavior Processes*, 1978, *4*, 131–143.

Senter, R. J., and Hoffman, R. R. Bizarreness as a nonessential variable in mnemonic imagery: A confirmation. *Bulletin of the Psychonomic Society*, 1976, *7*, 163–164.

Seybert, J. A., Mellgren, R. L., and Jobe, J. B. Sequential effects on resistance to extinction at widely spaced trials. *Journal of Experimental Psychology*, 1973, *101*, 151–154.

Seymour, W. D. Experiments on the acquisition of industrial skills. *Occupational Psychology*, 1954, *28*, 77–89.

Shanab, M. E., and Biller, J. D. Positive contrast in the runway obtained following a shift in both delay and magnitude of reward. *Learning and Motivation*, 1972, *3*, 179–184.

Shanab, M. E., and Spencer, R. E. Positive and negative contrast effects obtained following shifts in delayed water reward. *Bulletin of the Psychonomic Society*, 1978, *12*, 199–202.

Shapiro, D. C., and Schmidt, R. A. The schema theory: Recent evidence and development implications. In A. S. Kelso and J. F. Clark (Eds.), *The development of movement control and coordination.* New York: Wiley, 1982.

Shapiro, K. L., Jacobs, W. J., and LoLordo, V. M. Stimulus-reinforcer interactions in Pavlovian conditioning of pigeons: Implications for selective associations. *Animal Learning & Behavior*, 1980, *8*, 586–594.

Shay, C. Part versus whole methods of learning in gymnastics. *Research Quarterly*, 1934, *5*, 62–67.

Shea, J. B., and Upton, G. The effects on skill acquisition of an interpolated motor short-term memory task during the KR-delay interval. *Journal of Motor Behavior*, 1976, *8*, 277–281.

Sheafor, P. J. "Pseudoconditioned" jaw movements of the rabbit reflex associations conditioned to contextual background cues. *Journal of Experimental Psychology: Animal Behavior Processes*, 1975, *3*, 245–260.

Sheafor, P. J., and Gormezano, I. Conditioning the rabbit's jaw-movement response: US magnitude effects on URs, CRs, and pseudo CRs. *Journal of Comparative and Physiological Psychology*, 1972, *81*, 449–456.

Sheffield, F. D. Relation between classical conditioning and instrumental learning. In W. F. Prokasy (Ed.), *Classical conditioning.* New York: Appleton-Century-Crofts, 1965.

Sheffield, F. D., and Roby, T. B. Reward value of a non-nutritive sweet taste. *Journal of Comparative and Physiological Psychology*, 1950, *43*, 471–481.

Shepard, R. N. Recognition memory for words, sentences, and pictures. *Journal of Verbal Learning and Verbal Behavior*, 1967, *6*, 156–163.

Shull, R. L., and Pliskoff, S. S. Changeover delay and concurrent schedules: Some effects on relative performance measures. *Journal of the Experimental Analysis of Behavior*, 1967, *10*, 517–527.

Shurrager, P. S., and Culler, E. Phenomena allied to conditioning in the spinal dog. *American Journal of Physiology*, 1938, *123*, 186–187.

Shurrager, P. S., and Culler, E. Conditioning in the spinal dog. *Journal of Experimental Psychology*, 1940, *26*, 133–159.

Shurrager, P. S., and Shurrager, H. C. The rate of learning measured at a single synapse. *Journal of Experimental Psychology*, 1946, *36*, 347–354.

Shurtleff, D., and Ayres, J. J. B. One-trial backward excitatory fear conditioning in rats: Acquisition, retention, extinction, and spontaneous recovery. *Animal Learning & Behavior*, 1981, *9*, 65–74.

Sideroff, S., Schneiderman, N., and Powell, D. A.

Motivational properties of septal stimulation as the US in classical conditioning of heart rate in rabbits. *Journal of Comparative and Physiological Psychology,* 1971, *74,* 1–10.

Sidman, M. Avoidance conditioning with brief shock and no exteroceptive warning signal. *Science,* 1953a, *118,* 157–158.

Sidman, M. Two temporal parameters of the maintenance of avoidance behavior in the white rat. *Journal of Comparative and Physiological Psychology,* 1953b, *46,* 253–261.

Sidman, M., and Fletcher, F. G. A demonstration of auto-shaping with monkeys. *Journal of the Experimental Analysis of Behavior,* 1968, *11,* 307–309.

Siegel, S. Conditioning of insulin-induced glycemia. *Journal of Comparative and Physiological Psychology,* 1972, *78,* 233–241.

Siegel, S. Conditioning insulin effects. *Journal of Comparative and Physiological Psychology,* 1975a, *89,* 189–199.

Siegel, S. Evidence from rats that morphine tolerance is a learned response. *Journal of Comparative and Physiological Psychology,* 1975b, *89,* 498–506.

Siegel, S. Morphine analgesic tolerance: Its situation specificity supports a Pavlovian conditioning model. *Science,* 1976, *193,* 323–325.

Siegel, S. Morphine tolerance and acquisition as an associative process. *Journal of Experimental Psychology: Animal Behavior Processes,* 1977, *3,* 1–13.

Siegel, S. Tolerance to the hyperthermic effect in the rat is a learned response. *Journal of Comparative and Physiological Psychology,* 1978, *82,* 1137–1149.

Siegel, S., and Domjan, M. Backward conditioning as an inhibitory procedure. *Learning and Motivation,* 1971, *2,* 1–11.

Siegel, S., and Domjan, M. The inhibitory effect of backward conditioning as a function of the number of backward pairings. *Bulletin of the Psychonomic Society,* 1974, *4,* 122–124.

Siegel, S., Hinson, R. E., Krank, M. D., and McCully, J. Heroin "overdose" death: Contribution of drug-associated environmental cues. *Science,* 1982, *216,* 436–437.

Siegel, S., and Wagner, A. R. Extended acquisition training and resistance to extinction. *Journal of Experimental Psychology,* 1963, *66,* 308–310.

Silver, A. I. Recent developments in classical conditioning of the galvanic skin response. Im-plications for the acquisition of anxiety. *Journal of Behavior Therapy and Experimental Psychiatry,* 1977, *8,* 337–338.

Silver, C. A., and Meyer, D. R. Temporal factors in sensory preconditioning. *Journal of Comparative and Physiological Psychology,* 1954, *47,* 57–59.

Silverstein, A., and Dienstbier, R. A. Rated pleasantness and association value of 101 English nouns. *Journal of Verbal Learning and Verbal Behavior,* 1968, *7,* 81–86.

Sisson, L. A., and Dixon, M. J. Improving mealtime behaviors through token reinforcement. *Behavior Modification,* 1986, *10,* 333–354.

Skinner, B. F. *The behavior of organisms.* New York: Appleton-Century-Crofts, 1938.

Skinner, B. F. A case history in scientific method. In S. Koch (Ed.), *Psychology: A study of science.* New York: McGraw-Hill, 1959.

Skinner, B. F. Some thoughts about the future. *Journal of the Experimental Analysis of Behavior,* 1986, *45,* 229–235.

Skinner, B. F. Whatever happened to psychology as the science of behavior? *American Psychologist,* 1987, *42,* 780–786.

Slamecka, N. J. An examination of trace storage in free recall. *Journal of Experimental Psychology,* 1968, *76,* 504–513.

Slamecka, N. J., and Graf, P. The generation effect: Delineation of a phenomenon. *Journal of Experimental Psychology: Human Learning and Memory,* 1978, *4,* 592–604.

Sluckin, W., and Salzen, E. A. Imprinting and perceptual learning. *Quarterly Journal of Experimental Psychology,* 1961, *13,* 65–77.

Small, W. S. An experimental study on the mental processes of the rat. *American Journal of Psychology,* 1900, *11,* 133–165.

Smith, J. C., and Roll, D. L. Trace conditioning with x-rays as an aversive stimulus. *Psychonomic Science,* 1967, *9,* 11–12.

Smith, M. C. CS-US interval and US intensity in classical conditioning of the rabbit's nictitating membrane response. *Journal of Comparative and Physiological Psychology,* 1968, *66,* 679–687.

Smith, M. C. Hypnotic memory enhancement of witnesses. Does it work? *Psychological Bulletin,* 1983, *94,* 387–407.

Smith, M. C., Coleman, S. R., and Gormezano, I. Classical conditioning of the rabbit's nictitating membrane response at backward, simultaneous and forward CS-US intervals. *Journal of Comparative and Physiological Psychology,* 1969, *69,* 226–231.

Smith, S. M. Remembering in and out of context. *Journal of Experimental Psychology: Human Learning and Memory,* 1979, *5,* 460–471.

Smith, S. M., Glenberg, A., and Bjork, R. A. Environmental context and human memory. *Memory & Cognition,* 1978, *6,* 342–353.

Snowdon, C. T. Ethology, comparative psychology, and animal behavior. In M. R. Rosenzweig and L. W. Porter (Eds.), *Annual review of psychology.* Palo Alto, Calif.: Annual Reviews, Inc., 1983.

Snyder, C., and Noble, M. Operant conditioning of vasoconstriction. *Journal of Experimental Psychology,* 1968, *77,* 263–268.

Solomon, R. L., Kamin. L. J., and Wynne, L. C. Traumatic avoidance learning: The outcomes of several extinction procedures with dogs. *Journal of Abnormal and Social Psychology,* 1953, *48,* 281–302.

Solomon, R. L., and Turner, L. H. Discriminative classical conditioning in dogs paralyzed by curare can later control discriminative avoidance responses in the normal state. *Psychological Review,* 1962, *69,* 202–219.

Solomon, R. L., and Wynne, L. C. Traumatic avoidance learning: The principles of anxiety conservation and partial irreversibility. *Psychological Review,* 1954, *61,* 353–385.

Spalding, D. A. Instinct with original observation on young animals. *MacMillans Magazine,* 1873, *27,* 282–283. (Reprinted in *British Journal of Animal Behavior,* 1954, *2,* 1–11.)

Sparrow, W. A. The efficiency of skilled performance. *Journal of Motor Behavior,* 1983, *15,* 237–261.

Spear, N. Retrieval of memory in animals. *Psychological Review,* 1973, *80,* 163–194.

Spear, N. E. *The processing of memories: Forgetting and retention.* Hillsdale, N.J.: Erlbaum, 1978.

Spear, N. E., Klein, S. B., and Riley, E. P. The Kamin effect as "state dependent" learning: Memory retrieval failure in the rat. *Journal of Comparative and Physiological Psychology,* 1971, *74,* 416–425.

Spelt, D. K. Conditioned responses in the human fetus *in utero. Psychological Bulletin,* 1938, *35,* 712–713.

Spence, K. W. The nature of discrimination learning in animals. *Psychological Review,* 1936, *43,* 427–449.

Spence, K. W. Analysis of the formation of visual discrimination habits in chimpanzees. *Journal of Comparative Psychology,* 1937a, *23,* 77–100.

Spence, K. W. The differential response in animals to stimuli varying within a single dimension. *Psychological Review,* 1937b, *44,* 430–444.

Spence, K. W. *Behavior theory and conditioning.* New Haven: Yale University Press, 1956.

Spencer, H. *Principles of psychology.* London: Williams and Norgate, 1872.

Spetch, M. L., and Wilkie, D. M. Duration discrimination is better with food access as the signal than with light as the signal. *Learning and Motivation,* 1981, *12,* 40–64.

Spiro, R. J. Remembering information from text: Theoretical and empirical issues concerning the "state of schema" reconstruction hypothesis. In R. C. Anderson, R. J. Spiro, and W. E. Montague (Eds.), *Schooling and the acquisition of knowledge.* Hillsdale, N.J.: Erlbaum, 1977.

Spiro, R. J. Accommodative reconstruction in prose recall. *Journal of Verbal Learning and Verbal Behavior,* 1980a, *19,* 84–95.

Spiro, R. J. Constructive processes in prose comprehension and recall. In R. J. Spiro, B. C. Bruce, and W. F. Brewer (Eds.), *Theoretical issues in reading comprehension.* Hillsdale, N.J.: Erlbaum,1980b.

Spivey, S. E. Resistance to extinction as a function of number of NR transitions and percentage of reinforcement. *Journal of Experimental Psychology,* 1967, *75,* 43–48.

Spooner, A., and Kellogg, W. N. The backward conditioning curve. *American Journal of Psychology,* 1947, *60,* 321–334.

Squire, L. R., and Slater, P. C. Forgetting in very long-term memory as assessed by an improved questionnaire technique. *Journal of Experimental Psychology: Human Learning and Memory,* 1975, *1,* 50–54.

Standing, L. Learning 10,000 pictures. *Quarterly Journal of Experimental Psychology,* 1973, *25,* 207–222.

Standing, L., Conezio, J., and Haber, R. N. Perception and memory for pictures: Single-trial learning of 2560 visual stimuli. *Psychonomic Science,* 1970, *19,* 73–74.

Starr, M. D., and Minkea, S. Determinants of fear over the course of avoidance learning. *Learning and Motivation,* 1977, *8,* 332–350.

Steckle, L. C. Two additional attempts to condition the pupillary reflex. *Journal of General Psychology,* 1936, *15,* 369–377.

Steckle, L. C., and Renshaw, S. An investigation of the conditioned iridic reflex. *Journal of General Psychology,* 1934, *11,* 3–23.

Stelmach, G. E. Efficiency of motor learning as a function of intertrial rest. *Research Quarterly,* 1969, *40,* 198–202.

Stephens, T. A., and Burroughs, W. A. An application of operant conditioning to absenteeism in a hospital setting. *Journal of Applied Psychology,* 1978, *63,* 518–521.

Stern, J. A., and Walrath, L. C. Orienting responses and conditioning in electrodermal responses. *Psychophysiology,* 1977, *14,* 334–342.

Stevens, D. A., Mason, J. R., and Wixon, D. R. Assessment of the relative importance of S+ and S− in rats, using intercurrent simultaneous and successive discriminations. *Bulletin of the Psychonomic Society,* 1981, *17,* 200–202.

Stitzer, M. L., Rand, C. S., Bigelow, G. E., and Mead, A. M. Contingent payment procedures for smoking reduction and cessation. *Journal of Applied Behavior Analysis,* 1986, *19,* 197–202.

Storms, L. H., Boroczi, G., and Broen, W. E., Jr. Punishment inhibits an instrumental response in hooded rats. *Science,* 1962, *135,* 1133–1134.

Strong, T. N., Jr. Activity in the white rat as a function of apparatus and hunger. *Journal of Comparative and Physiological Psychology,* 1957, *50,* 596–600.

Stroop, J. R. Studies of interference in serial verbal reaction. *Journal of Experimental Psychology,* 1935, *18,* 643–662.

Suiter, R. D., and LoLordo, V. M. Blocking of inhibitory Pavlovian conditioning in the conditioned emotional response procedure. *Journal of Comparative and Physiological Psychology,* 1971, *76,* 137–144.

Sulin, R. A., and Dooling, D. J. Intrusion of a thematic idea in retention of prose. *Journal of Experimental Psychology,* 1974, *103,* 255–262.

Sutherland, N. S., and Mackintosh, N. J. *Mechanisms of animal discrimination learning.* New York: Academic Press, 1971.

Swenson, R. P., and Hill, F. A. Effects of instruction and interstimulus interval in human GSR conditioning. *Psychonomic Science,* 1970, *21,* 369–370.

Switzer, S. A. Backward conditioning of the lid reflex. *Journal of Experimental Psychology,* 1930, *13,* 76–97.

Szwejkowski, G., and Konorski, J. The influence of the primary inhibitory stimulus upon the salivary effect of excitatory conditioned stimulus. *Acta Biologiae Experimentalis,* 1959, *19,* 162–174.

Tarpy, R. M., and Koster, E. D. Stimulus facilitation of delayed-reward learning in the rat. *Journal of Comparative and Physiological Psychology,* 1970, *71,* 147–151.

Tennant, W., and Bitterman, M. E. Blocking and overshadowing in two species of fish. *Journal of Experimental Psychology: Animal Behavior Processes,* 1975, *1,* 22–29.

Terell, G., and Ware, R. Role of delay of reward in speed of size and form discrimination learning in childhood. *Child Development,* 1961, *32,* 409–415.

Terrace, H. S. Discrimination learning with and without "errors." *Journal of the Experimental Analysis of Behavior,* 1963a, *6,* 1–27.

Terrace, H. S. Errorless transfer of a discrimination across two continua. *Journal of the Experimental Analysis of Behavior,* 1963b, *6,* 223–232.

Terrace, H. S. By-products of discrimination learning. In G. H. Bower (Ed.), *The psychology of learning and motivation.* New York: Academic Press, 1972.

Theios, J. The partial reinforcement effect sustained through blocks of continuous reinforcement. *Journal of Experimental Psychology,* 1962, *64,* 1–6.

Theios, J., Lynch, A. D., and Lowe, W. F., Jr. Differential effects of shock intensity on one-way and shuttle avoidance conditioning. *Journal of Experimental Psychology,* 1966, *72,* 294–299.

Thomas, D. R., and DeCapito, A. Role of stimulus labeling in stimulus generalization. *Journal of Experimental Psychology,* 1966, *71,* 913–915.

Thomas, D. R., and Jones, C. G. Stimulus generalization as a function of the frame of reference. *Journal of Experimental Psychology,* 1962, *64,* 77–80.

Thomas, D. R., and Lopez, L. J. The effects of delayed testing on generalization slope. *Journal of Comparative and Physiological Psychology,* 1962, *55,* 541–544.

Thomas, D. R., and Mitchell, K. The role of instructions and stimulus categorizing in a measure of stimulus generalization. *Journal of the Experimental Analysis of Behavior,* 1962, *5,* 375–381.

Thomas, D. R., and Williams, J. L. A further study of stimulus generalization following three-stimulus training. *Journal of the Experimental Analysis of Behavior*, 1963, 6, 171–176.

Thomas, G. V., Lieberman, D. A., McIntosh, D. C., and Ronaldson, P. The role of marking when reward is delayed. *Journal of Experimental Psychology: Animal Behavior Processes*, 1983, 9, 401–411.

Thompson, R. F. The neural basis of stimulus generalization. In D. I. Mostofsky (Ed.), *Stimulus generalization*. Stanford, Calif.: Stanford University Press, 1965.

Thompson, R. F. Sensory preconditioning. In R. F. Thompson and J. F. Voss (Eds.), *Topics in learning and performance*, New York: Academic Press, 1972.

Thomson, R. F. The neurobiology of learning and memory. *Science*, 1986, 233, 941–947.

Thompson, R. F., Berger, T. W., Cegavske, C. F., Patterson, M. M., Rosemer, R. A., Teyler, T. J., and Young, R. A. The search for the engram. *American Psychologist*, 1976, 31, 209–227.

Thompson, R., and McConnell, J. Classical conditioning in the planarian, *dugesia dorotecephala. Journal of Comparative and Physiological Psychology*, 1955, 48, 65–68.

Thorndike, E. L. Animal intelligence. *Psychological Review Monograph Supplement*, 1898, 2, No. 4.

Thorndike, E. L. *Animal intelligence*. New York: Macmillan, 1911.

Thorndike, E. L. *The psychology of learning*. New York: Teacher's College, 1913.

Thorndike, E. L. The law of effect. *American Journal of Psychology*, 1927, 39, 212–222.

Thorndike, E. L. Reward and punishment in animal learning. *Comparative Psychology Monographs*, 1932, 8.

Thorndike, E. L., and Lorge, I. *The teacher's word book of 30,000 words*. New York: Columbia University Press, 1944.

Till, R. E., and Jenkins, J. J. The effects of cued orienting tasks on free recall of words. *Journal of Verbal Learning and Verbal Behavior*, 1973, 12, 489–498.

Timberlake, W. A molar equilibrium theory of learned performance. In G. H. Bower (Ed.), *The psychology of learning and motivation*. New York: Academic Press, 1980.

Timberlake, W. Behavior regulation and learned performance: Some misapprehension and disagreements. *Journal of the Experimental Analysis of Behavior*, 1984, 41, 355–375.

Timberlake, W., and Allison, J. Response deprivation: An empirical approach to instrumental performance. *Psychological Review*, 1974, 81, 146–164.

Timberlake, W., and Wozny, M. Reversibility of reinforcement between eating and running by schedule changes: A comparison of hypotheses and models. *Animal Learning & Behavior*, 1979, 7, 461–469.

Tinbergen, N. *The study of instinct*. Oxford: Clarendon Press, 1951.

Tinklepaugh, O. L. An experimental study of representative factors in monkeys. *Journal of Comparative Psychology*, 1928, 8, 197–236.

Toglia, M. P., and Battig, W. F. *Handbook of semantic word norms*. Hillsdale, N.J.: Erlbaum, 1978.

Tolman, E. C. *Purposive behavior in animals and men*. New York: Appleton-Century-Crofts, 1932.

Tombaugh, T. N. Resistance to extinction as a function of the interaction between training and extinction delays. *Psychological Reports*, 1966, 19, 791–798.

Tombaugh, T. N. A comparison of the effects of immediate reinforcement, constant delay of reinforcement and partial delay of reinforcement on performance. *Canadian Journal of Psychology*, 1970, 24, 276–288.

Topping, J. S., and Parker, B. K. Constant and variable delay of reinforcement effects on probability learning by pigeons. *Journal of Comparative and Physiological Psychology*, 1970, 141–147.

Tracy, W. K. Wave length generalization and preference in monochromatically reared ducklings. *Journal of the Experimental Analysis of Behavior*, 1970, 13, 163–178.

Tranel, D., and Damasio, A. R. Knowledge without awareness: An autonomic index of facial recognition by prosopagnosics. *Science*, 1985, 228, 154–156.

Trapold, M. A., and Fowler, H. Instrumental escape performance as a function of the intensity of noxious stimulation. *Journal of Experimental Psychology*, 1960, 323–326.

Treichler, F. R., and Hall, J. F. The relationship between deprivation weight loss and several measures of activity. *Journal of Comparative and Physiological Psychology*, 1962, 55, 346–349.

Trowbridge, M. H., and Cason, H. An experimental study of Thorndike's theory of learning. *Journal of General Psychology*, 1932, 7, 245–258.

Trowill, J. A. Instrumental conditioning of the heart rate in the curarized rat. *Journal of Comparative and Physiological Psychology,* 1967, *63,* 7–11.

Tulving, E. Subjective organization in free recall of "unrelated" words. *Psychological Review,* 1962, *69,* 344–354.

Tulving, E. Episodic and semantic memory. In E. Tulving and W. Donaldson (Eds.), *Organization of memory.* New York: Academic Press, 1972.

Tulving, E. *Elements of episodic memory.* Oxford: Clarendon Press, 1983.

Tulving, E. Précis of elements of episodic memory. *Behavioral and Brain Sciences,* 1984, *7,* 223–268.

Tulving, E. How many memory systems are there? *American Psychologist,* 1985, *40,* 385–398.

Tulving, E., and Madigan, S. A. Memory and verbal learning. In P. H. Mussen and M. R. Rosenzweig (Eds.), *Annual review of psychology.* Palo Alto, Calif.: Annual Reviews, 1970.

Tulving, E., McNulty, J. A., and Ozier, M. Vividness of words and learning to learn in free-recall learning. *Canadian Journal of Psychology,* 1965, *19,* 242–252.

Tulving, E., and Osler, S. Effectiveness of retrieval cues in memory for words. *Journal of Experimental Psychology,* 1968, *77,* 593–601.

Tulving, E., and Pearlstone, Z. Availability versus accessibility of information in memory for words. *Journal of Verbal Learning and Verbal Behavior,* 1966, *5,* 381–391.

Tulving, E., and Thompson, D. M. Encoding specificity and retrieval processes in episodic memory. *Psychological Review,* 1973, *80,* 352–373.

Tulving, E., and Watkins, M. J. Continuity between recall and recognition. *American Journal of Psychology,* 1973, *86,* 739–748.

Turnbull, S. D., and Dickinson, J. Maximizing variability of practice: A test of schema theory and contextual interference theory. *Journal of Human Movement Studies,* 1986, *12,* 201–213.

Twitmyer, E. B. A study of the knee jerk. Ph.D. dissertation, University of Pennsylvania, 1902. Reprinted in the *Journal of Experimental Psychology,* 1974, *103,* 1047–1066.

Tyler, D. W., Wort, E. C., and Bitterman, M. E. The effect of random and alternating partial reinforcement on resistance to extinction in the rat. *American Journal of Psychology,* 1953, *66,* 57–65.

Uhl, C. N., and Young, A. G. Resistance to extinction as a function of incentive, percentage of reinforcement, and number of nonreinforced trials. *Journal of Experimental Psychology,* 1967, *73,* 556–564.

Underwood, B. J. Retroactive and proactive inhibition after five and forty-eight hours. *Journal of Experimental Psychology,* 1948a, *38,* 29–38.

Underwood, B. J. "Spontaneous recovery" of verbal associations. *Journal of Experimental Psychology,* 1948b, *38,* 429–439.

Underwood, B. J. Studies of distributed practice: XII. Retention following varying degrees of original learning. *Journal of Experimental Psychology,* 1954, *47,* 294–300.

Underwood, B. J. Interference and forgetting. *Psychological Review,* 1957, *64,* 49–60.

Underwood, B. J. Stimulus selection in verbal learning. In C. N. Cofer and B. S. Musgrave (Eds.), *Verbal behavior and learning.* New York: McGraw-Hill, 1963.

Underwood, B. J. False recognition produced by implicit verbal responses. *Journal of Experimental Psychology,* 1965, *70,* 122–129.

Underwood, B. J. Attributes of memory. *Psychological Review,* 1969, *76,* 559–573.

Underwood, B. J. *Attributes of memory.* Palo Alto, Calif.: Scott-Foresman, 1983.

Underwood, B. J., Boruch, R. F., and Malmi, R. A. Composition of episodic memory. *Journal of Experimental Psychology: General,* 1978, *107,* 393–419.

Underwood, B. J., and Ekstrand, B. R. An analysis of some shortcomings in the interference theory of forgetting. *Psychological Review,* 1966, *73,* 540–549.

Underwood, B. J., and Ekstrand, B. R. Linguistic associations and retention. *Journal of Verbal Learning and Verbal Behavior,* 1968, *7,* 126–171.

Underwood, B. J., Ham, M., and Ekstrand, B. R. Cue selection in paired-associate learning. *Journal of Experimental Psychology,* 1962, *64,* 405–409.

Underwood, B. J., and Postman, L. Extraexperimental sources of interference in forgetting. *Psychological Review,* 1960, *67,* 73–95.

Underwood, B. J., and Schulz, R. W. *Meaningfulness and verbal learning.* Philadelphia: Lippincott, 1960.

Urcuioli, P. J., and Zentall, T. R. Retrospective coding in pigeon's delayed matching-to-sample. *Journal of Experimental Psychology: Animal Behavior Processes,* 1986, *12,* 69–77.

Vandercar, D. H., and Schneiderman, N. Inter-stimulus interval functions in different response systems during classical discrimination conditioning of rabbits. *Psychonomic Science*, 1967, *9*, 9–10.

Van Ormer, E. B. Sleep and retention. *Psychological Bulletin*, 1932, *30*, 415–439.

Van Willigen, F., Emmet, J., Cote, D., and Ayres, J. J. B. CS modality effects in one-trial backward and forward excitatory conditioning as assessed by conditioned suppression of licking in rats. *Animal Learning & Behavior*, 1987, *15*, 210–211.

Vinogradova, O. S. On the dynamics of the OR in the course of closure of a conditioned connection. In L. G. Voronin, A. N. Leontiev, A. R. Luria, E. N. Sokolov, and O. S. Vinogradova (Eds.), *Orienting reflex and exploratory behavior*. Washington, D.C.: American Institute of Biological Sciences, 1965.

Visintainer, M. A., Volpicelli, J. R., and Seligman, M. E. P. Tumor rejection in rats after inescapable or escapable shock. *Science*, 1982, *216*, 437–439.

Wagner, A. R. The role of reinforcement and nonreinforcement in an "apparent frustration effect." *Journal of Experimental Psychology*, 1959, *57*, 130–136.

Wagner, A. R. Effects of amount and percentage of reinforcement and number of acquisition trials on conditioning and extinction. *Journal of Experimental Psychology*, 1961, *62*, 234–242.

Wagner, A. R. Conditioned frustration as a learned drive. *Journal of Experimental Psychology*, 1963, *64*, 142–148.

Wagner, A. R. Stimulus selection and a "modified continuity theory." In G. H. Bower and T. J. Spence (Eds.), *The psychology of learning and motivation advances in research and theory*. New York: Academic Press, 1969a.

Wagner, A. R. Stimulus validity and stimulus selection in associative learning. In N. J. Mackintosh and W. K. Honig (Eds.), *Fundamental issues in associative learning*. Halifax: Dalhousie University Press, 1969b.

Wagner, A. R., and Rescorla, R. A. Inhibition in Pavlovian conditioning: Application of a theory. In R. A. Boakes and M. S. Halliday (Eds.), *Inhibition and learning*. London: Academic Press, 1972.

Wagner, A. R., Siegel, L. S., and Fein, G. G. Extinction of conditioned fear as a function of percentage of reinforcement. *Journal of Comparative and Physiological Psychology*, 1967, *63*, 160–164.

Wagner, A. R., Siegel, S., Thomas, E., and Ellison, G. D. Reinforcement history and the extinction of a conditioned salivary response. *Journal of Comparative and Physiological Psychology*, 1964, *58*, 354–358.

Wahlsten, D. L., and Cole, M. Classical and avoidance training of leg flexion in the dog. In A. H. Black and W. F. Prokasy (Eds.), *Classical conditioning II: Current research and theory*. New York: Appleton-Century-Crofts, 1972.

Waldrop, M. M. The workings of working memory. *Science*, 1987, *237*, 1564–1567.

Walker, E. Eyelid conditioning as a function of intensity of conditioned and unconditioned stimuli. *Journal of Experimental Psychology*, 1960, *59*, 303–311.

Wallace, W. P. Review of historical, empirical and theoretical status of the von Restorff phenomenon. *Psychological Bulletin*, 1965, *63*, 410–424.

Wallace, W. P. Recognition failure of recallable words and recognizable words. *Journal of Experimental Psychology: Human Learning and Memory*, 1978, *4*, 441–452.

Wallace, W. P. On the use of distractors for testing recognition memory. *Psychological Bulletin*, 1980, *88*, 696–704.

Wallace, W. P., Sawyer, T. J., and Robertson, L. C. Distractors in recall, distractor-free recognition, and the word-frequency effect. *American Journal of Psychology*, 1978, *9*, 295–304.

Walsh, D. A., and Jenkins, J. J. Effects of orienting tasks on free recall in incidental learning: "Difficulty," "effort," and "process" explanations. *Journal of Verbal Learning and Verbal Behavior*, 1973, *12*, 481–488.

Walters, E. T., Carew, J. J., and Kandel, E. R. Associative learning in Aplysia: Evidence for conditioned fear in an invertebrate. *Science*, 1981, *211*, 504–506.

Walters, M. A., and Rogers, J. U. Aversive stimulation of the rat: Long term effects on subsequent behavior. *Science*, 1963, *142*, 70–71.

Warden, C. L., and Jackson, T. A. Imitative behavior in the Rhesus monkey. *Journal of Genetic Psychology*, 1935, *46*, 103–125.

Warren, J. M. Evolution, behavior and the prefrontal cortex. *Acta Neurobiologiae Experimentalis*, 1972, *32*, 581–593.

Warren, J. M., and Kolb, B. Generalizations in neuropsychology. In S. Finger (Ed.), *Brain damage*. New York: Plenum, 1978.

Warrington, E. K., and Ackroyd, C. The effect of orienting tasks on recognition memory. *Memory & Cognition*, 1975, *3*, 140–142.

Wasserman, E. A., Deich, J. D., Hunter, N. B., and Nagamatsu, L. S. Analyzing the random control procedures: Effects of paired and unpaired CSs and USs on autoshaping and chick's key peck with heat reinforcement. *Learning and Motivation*, 1977, *8*, 467–487.

Wasserman, E. A., Hunter, N. B., Gutowski, K. A., and Bader, S. A. Autoshaping chicks with heat reinforcement: The role of stimulus-reinforcer and response-reinforcer relations. *Journal of Experimental Psychology: Animal Behavior Processes*, 1975, *104*, 158–169.

Watkins, M. J. When is recall spectacularly higher than recognition? *Journal of Experimental Psychology*, 1974, *102*, 161–163.

Watkins, M. J., and Tulving, E. Episodic memory: When recognition fails. *Journal of Experimental Psychology: General*, 1975, *104*, 5–29.

Watson, J. B. Imitation in monkeys. *Psychological Bulletin*, 1908, *5*, 169–178.

Watson, J. B. *Behavior: An introduction to comparative psychology*. New York: Holt, 1914.

Watson, J. B. The place of the conditioned reflex in psychology. *Psychological Review*, 1916, *23*, 89–117.

Watson, J. B. The effect of delayed feeding upon learning. *Psychobiology*, 1917, *1*, 51–60.

Watson, J. B. *Psychology from the standpoint of a behaviorist*. Philadelphia: Lippincott, 1919.

Watson, J. B. *Behaviorism*. New York: Norton, 1924.

Watson, J. B., and Rayner, R. Conditioned emotional reactions. *Journal of Experimental Psychology*, 1920, *3*, 1–14.

Wattenmaker, W. D., and Shoben, E. J. Context and the recallability of concrete and abstract sentences. *Journal of Experimental Psychology: Learning, Memory, and Cognition*, 1987, *13*, 140–150.

Wayner, E. A., Flannery, G. R., and Singer, G. The effects of taste aversion conditioning on the primary antibody response to sheep red blood cells and Brucella abortus in the albino rat. *Physiology and Behavior*, 1978, *21*, 995–1000.

Wayner, M. J., and Carey, R. J. Basic drives. In P. H. Mussen and M. R. Rosenzweig (Eds.), *Annual review of psychology*. Palo Alto, Calif.: Annual Reviews, Inc., 1973.

Webber, S. M., and Marshall, P. H. Bizarreness effects in imagery as a function of processing level and delay. *Journal of Mental Imagery*, 1978, *2*, 291–300.

Weiner, H. Controlling human fixed-interval performance. *Journal of the Experimental Analysis of Behavior*, 1969, *12*, 349–373.

Weingartner, H., Adefris, W., Eich, J. E., and Murphy, D. L. Encoding-imagery specificity in alcohol state-dependent learning. *Journal of Experimental Psychology: Human Learning and Memory*, 1976, *2*, 83–87.

Weinstock, S. Acquisition and extinction of a partially reinforced running response at a 24-hour intertrial interval. *Journal of Experimental Psychology*, 1958, *56*, 151–158.

Weiskrantz, L., and Warrington, E. K. Conditioning in amnesic patients. *Neuropsychologica*, 1979, *17*, 187–194.

Welker, R. L., and McAuley, K. Reductions in resistance to extinction and spontaneous recovery as a function of changes in transportational and contextual stimuli. *Animal Learning & Behavior*, 1978, *6*, 451–457.

Wendt, G. R. An interpretation of inhibition of conditioned reflexes as competition between reaction systems. *Psychological Review*, 1936, *43*, 258–281.

Whitley, J. D. Effects of practice distribution on learning fine motor tasks. *Research Quarterly*, 1970, *41*, 576–583.

Whitten, W. B., II, and Bjork, R. A. Learning from tests: Effects of spacing. *Journal of Verbal Learning and Verbal Behavior*, 1977, *16*, 465–478.

Wickelgren, W. A. Acoustic similarity and intrusion errors in short-term memory. *Journal of Experimental Psychology*, 1965, *70*, 102–108.

Wickelgren, W. A. *Cognitive psychology*. Englewood Cliffs, N.J.: Prentice-Hall, 1979.

Wickens, D. D. Characteristics of word encoding. In A. W. Melton and E. Martin (Eds.), *Coding processes in human memory*. Washington, D.C.: V. H. Winston and Sons, 1972.

Wickens, D. D., Born, D. G., and Allen, C. K. Proactive inhibition and item similarity in short-term memory. *Journal of Verbal Learning and Verbal Behavior,* 1963, *2,* 440–445.

Wickens, D. D., and Briggs, G. E. Mediated stimulus generalization as a factor in sensory preconditioning. *Journal of Experimental Psychology,* 1951, *42,* 197–200.

Wickstrom, R. L. Comparative study of methodologies for teaching gymnastics and tumbling. *Research Quarterly,* 1958, *29,* 109–115.

Wike, E. L., and Chen, J. S. Runway performance and reward magnitude. *Psychonomic Science,* 1971, *21,* 139–140.

Wike, E. L., and McWilliams, J. Duration of delay, delay-box confinement, and runway performance. *Psychological Reports,* 1967, *21,* 865–870.

Wickler, A. Conditioning factors in opiate addiction and relapse. In D. M. Wilner and G. G. Kassebaum (Eds.), *Narcotics.* New York: McGraw-Hill, 1965.

Wickler, A. Some implications of conditioning theory for problems of drug abuse. In P. H. Blackly (Ed.), *Abuse data and debate.* Springfield, Ill.: Charles C. Thomas, 1970.

Wilcoxin, H. C., Dragoin, W. B., and Kral, P. A. Illness-induced aversions in rat and quail: Relative salience of visual and gustatory cues. *Science,* 1971, *171,* 826–828.

Wilkie, D. M., and Summers, R. J. Pigeon's spatial memory: Factors affecting delayed matching of key location. *Journal of Experimental Analysis of Behavior,* 1982, *37,* 45–56.

Williams, C. D. The elimination of tantrum behavior by extinction procedures. *Journal of Abnormal and Social Psychology,* 1959, *59,* 269.

Williams, D. R., and Williams, H. Auto-maintenance in the pigeon: Sustained pecking despite contingent non-reinforcement. *Journal of the Experimental Analysis of Behavior,* 1969, *12,* 511–520.

Williams, O. A study of the phenomenon of reminiscence. *Journal of Experimental Psychology,* 1926, *9,* 368–387.

Williams, S. Resistance to extinction as a function of the number of reinforcements. *Journal of Experimental Psychology,* 1938, *23,* 506–522.

Wilson, D. M. The central nervous control of flight in a locust. *Journal of Experimental Biology,* 1961, *48,* 471–490.

Wilson, M. P. Periodic reinforcement interval and number of periodic reinforcements as parameters of response strength. *Journal of Comparative and Physiological Psychology,* 1954, *47,* 51–56.

Windholz, G. A comparative analysis of the conditional reflex discoveries of Pavlov and Twitmyer, and the birth of a paradigm. *The Pavlovian Journal of Biological Science,* 1986, *21,* 141–147.

Wolfe, D. A., Mendes, M. G., and Factor, D. A parent-administered program to reduce children's television viewing. *Journal of Applied Behavior Analysis,* 1984, *17,* 267–272.

Wolfe, J. B. Effectiveness of token rewards for chimpanzees. *Comparative Psychology Monographs,* 1936, *12.*

Wolfle, H. M. Time factors in conditioning finger-withdrawal. *Journal of General Psychology,* 1930, *4,* 372–378.

Wolfle, H. M. Conditioning as a function of the interval between the conditioned and the original stimulus. *Journal of General Psychology,* 1932, *7,* 80–103.

Wollen, K. A., Weber, A., and Lowry, D. H. Bizarreness versus interaction of mental images as determinants of learning. *Cognitive Psychology,* 1972, *3,* 518–523.

Wolpe, J. Experimental neurosis as a learned behavior. *British Journal of Psychology,* 1952, *43,* 243–268.

Wolpe, J. *Psychotherapy by reciprocal inhibition.* Stanford, Calif.: Stanford University Press, 1958.

Wolpe, J. The systematic desensitization treatment of neurosis. *Journal of Nervous and Mental Disease,* 1961, *132,* 189–203.

Wolters, G. Memory: Two systems or one system with many subsystems? *Behavioral and Brain Sciences,* 1984, *7,* 256–257.

Wong, P. T. P. A behavior field approach to instrumental learning in the rat: II. Training parameters and a stage model of extinction. *Animal Learning & Behavior,* 1978, *6,* 82–93.

Wood, G., and Bolt, M. Mediation and mediation time in paired associate learning. *Journal of Experimental Psychology,* 1968, *78,* 15–20.

Woods, P. J. A taxonomy of instrumental conditioning. *American Psychologist,* 1974, *29,* 584–596.

Woods, S. C., and Burchfield, S. R. Conditioned endocrine responses. In J. M. Ferguson and C. B. Taylor (Eds.), *The comprehensive handbook of behavioral medicine, Vol. 1: Systems intervention.* New York: SP Medical and Scientific Books, 1980.

Woods, S. C., Makous, W., and Hutton, R. A. A new technique for conditioned hypoglycemia. *Psychonomic Science,* 1968, *10,* 389–390.

Woods, S. C., Makous, W., and Hutton, R. A. Temporal parameters of conditioned hypoglycemia. *Journal of Comparative and Physiological Psychology*, 1969, *69*, 301–307.

Woodward, W. T. Classical respiratory conditioning in the fish: CS intensity. *American Journal of Psychology*, 1971, *84*, 549–554.

Woodworth, R. S., and Schlosberg, H. *Experimental psychology*. New York: Holt, 1954.

Worsham, R. Temporal discrimination factors in the delayed matching-to-sample tasks in monkeys. *Animal Learning and Behavior*, 1975, *3*, 93–97.

Yarmey, A. D. *The psychology of eyewitness testimony*. New York: The Free Press, 1979.

Yarmey, A. D., and Paivio, A. Further evidence on the effects of word abstractness and meaningfulness in paired-associate learning. *Psychonomic Science*, 1965, *2*, 307–308.

Yaroush, R., Sullivan, M. J., and Ekstrand, B. R. Effect of sleep on memory. II. Differential effect of the first and second half of the night. *Journal of Experimental Psychology*, 1971, *88*, 361–366.

Yarmey, A. D., and Paivio, A. Further evidence on the effects of word abstractness and meaningfulness in paired-associate learning. *Psychonomic Science*, 1965, *2*, 307–308.

Yates, A. J. Delayed auditory feedback. *Psychological Bulletin*, 1963, *60*, 213–232.

Yates, F. A. *The art of memory*. Chicago: University of Chicago Press, 1966.

Yehle, A. L. Divergencies among rabbit response systems during three-tone classical discrimination conditioning. *Journal of Experimental Psychology*, 1968, *77*, 468–473.

Yelen, D. Magnitude of the frustration effect and number of training trials. *Psychonomic Science*, 1969, *15*, 137–138.

Yerkes, R. M., and Dodson, J. D. The relation of strength of stimulus to rapidity of habit-formation. *Journal of Comparative Neurology and Psychology*, 1908, *18*, 459–482.

Young, F. A. An attempt to obtain pupillary conditioning with infrared photography. *Journal of Experimental Psychology*, 1954, *48*, 62–68.

Young. R. K. A comparison of two methods of learning serial associations. *American Journal of Psychology*, 1959, *72*, 554–559.

Young, R. K. Tests of three hypotheses about the effective stimulus in serial learning. *Journal of Experimental Psychology*, 1962, *63*, 307–313.

Yuille, J. C., and Paivio, A. Abstractness and recall of connected discourse. *Journal of Experimental Psychology*, 1969, *82*, 467–471.

Zangwill, O. L. Remembering revisited. *Quarterly Journal of Experimental Psychology*, 1972, *24*, 123–138.

Zeaman, D. Response latency as a function of the amount of reinforcement. *Journal of Experimental Psychology*, 1949, *39*, 466–483.

Zechmeister, E. B., and McKillip, J. Recall of place on the page. *Journal of Educational Psychology*, 1972, *63*, 446–453.

Zelaznik, H. N. Transfer in rapid timing tasks: An examination of the role of variability in practice. In R. W. Christina and D. M. Landers (Eds.), *Psychology of motor behavior and sport—1976*. Champaign, Ill.: Human Kinetics, 1977.

Zener, K. The significance of behavior accompanying conditioned salivary secretion for theories of the conditioned response. *American Journal of Psychology*, 1937, *50*, 384–403.

Zentall, T. R., and Hogan, D. E. Short-term proactive inhibition in the pigeon. *Learning and Motivation*, 1977, *8*, 367–386.

Zoladek, L., and Roberts, W. A. The sensory basis of spatial memory in the rat. *Animal Learning & Behavior*, 1978, *6*, 77–81.

Author Index

Subject Index